Ravenna in Late Antiquity

Ravenna was one of the most important cities of late antique Europe. Between AD 400 and 751, it was the residence of western Roman emperors, Ostrogothic kings, and Byzantine governors of Italy, while its bishops and archbishops ranked second only to the popes. During this 350-year period, the city was progressively enlarged and enriched by remarkable works of art and architecture, many of which still survive today. Thus, Ravenna and its monuments are of critical importance to historians and art historians of the late ancient world. This book provides a comprehensive survey of Ravenna's history and monuments in late antiquity, including discussions of scholarly controversies, archaeological discoveries, and new interpretations of art works. As a synthesis of the voluminous literature on this topic, this volume provides an English-language entry point for the study of this fascinating city.

Deborah Mauskopf Deliyannis is assistant professor of history at Indiana University. She is the editor and translator of Agnellus of Ravenna's *Liber pontificalis ecclesiae Ravennatis*, and she is the executive editor of *The Medieval Review*.

RAVENNA IN LATE ANTIQUITY

Deborah Mauskopf Deliyannis

Indiana University

CAMBRIDGE UNIVERSITY PRESS
Cambridge, New York, Melbourne, Madrid, Cape Town, Singapore,
São Paulo, Delhi, Dubai, Tokyo, Mexico City

Cambridge University Press
32 Avenue of the Americas, New York, NY 10013-2473, USA

www.cambridge.org
Information on this title: www.cambridge.org/9780521836722

First published 2010
Reprinted 2010

Printed in the United States of America

A catalog record for this publication is available from the British Library.

Library of Congress Cataloging in Publication Data

Deliyannis, Deborah Mauskopf, 1966–
Ravenna in late antiquity / Deborah Deliyannis.
    p.   cm.
Includes bibliographical references and index.
ISBN 978-0-521-83672-2 (hardback)
1. Ravenna (Italy) – Civilization. 2. Ravenna (Italy) – History. 3. Ravenna (Italy) –
Antiquities. 4. Art – Italy – Ravenna. 5. Architecture – Italy – Ravenna.
6. Ravenna (Italy) – Buildings, structures, etc. I. Title.
DG975.R25D45   2010
945'.47101 – dc22   2009012175

ISBN 978-0-521-83672-2 Hardback

Published with the assistance of the Getty Foundation.

To Con

CONTENTS

LIST OF ILLUSTRATIONS

Plates

Plates follow page 204.

Figures

LIST OF TABLES

PREFACE

I was first introduced to the study of Ravenna in Cecil L. Striker's graduate seminar at the University of Pennsylvania. Lee oversaw my dissertation on Agnellus of Ravenna, and was the motivating force behind this book. I am enormously grateful to him for his encouragement, for his comments on the various parts of the text, and for generously providing me with photographs. My colleages Ann Carmichael and Diane Reilly have been constant sounding boards for my ideas, and I am indebted to them for their advice and support, especially to Ann for her insistence that I find a way to work plague into the book, and to Diane for her reassurance that I could write for art historians. Others who have helped on specific questions include Jonathan J. Arnold, Thomas Brown, Paul Dutton, Andrew Gillett, Nicole Lopez-Jantzen, Lawrence Nees, James J. O'Donnell, Glenn Peers, Leah Shopkow, Eugene Vance, Dorothy Verkerk, and Edward Watts. I am also very grateful to Kate Copenhaver, Seymour Mauskopf, Scott McDonough, Urs Peschlow, Mary Ann Sullivan, and Eugene Vance for their magnificent photographs; the Internet truly is a marvelous way of connecting people with similar interests. Invaluable help was provided by Rhonda Long of Document Delivery Services at the Herman B. Wells Library and Mary Buechley of the Fine Arts Library at Indiana University, and Paola Pilandri of the Soprintendenza per i Beni Architettonici e Paesaggistici di Ravenna. Financial support, especially through a pretenure leave, has been provided by Indiana University. I would especially like to thank Beatrice Rehl of Cambridge University Press for her kind advice and encouragement as this book took shape, and especially for her patience with my delays as the manuscript was completed.

When I signed the contract for this book, I had two children; when the manuscript was completed, I had three – it has been a very busy three years! Spending time with my sons, Alex, Harry, and Simon, has meant that I have not traveled, especially to Italy, as much as I might have. The boys may not quite understand their mother's interest in the late antique world, but one day we will all go to Ravenna and they will understand my enthusiasm. My husband, Constantine, has seen and understood; he has supported my career from its beginning with love, patience, and practicality, and I dedicate this book to him.

ABBREVIATIONS

CARB   Corso di cultura sull'arte Ravennate e Bizantine
HL   Paul the Deacon, Historia Langobardorum
LP   Liber pontificalis
LPR   Agnellus, Liber pontificalis ecclesiae Ravennatis
MGH   Monumenta germaniae historica
PL   Patrologia Latina
RIS   Rerum Italicarum Scriptores

CHAPTER ONE

INTRODUCTION

Ravenna Capital?

The city of Ravenna in northeastern Italy contains some of the most spectacular works of art and architecture to have survived from late antiquity. These monuments were created between AD 400 and 600, at a time when Ravenna was one of the most important cities in the Mediterranean world. After 600 Ravenna experienced both economic and political downturns, but the artistic and architectural monuments remained as a testament to the splendor of the Christian Roman Empire in its early centuries, and as an inspiration both to later generations of the city's inhabitants and to visitors. In the absence of an extensive body of written sources for the late antique city, the art and architecture have become the main source for our understanding of Ravenna's role in Italy and the Mediterranean.

Since the ninth century, Ravenna has been considered the "capital of the late antique west." This is what Ravenna's own ninth-century historian Agnellus called it; it is the title of the four-volume history of the city by F. W. Deichmann, *Ravenna, Hauptstadt des spätantiken Abendlandes* (1969–89), and it was the title of a conference held in 2004 in Spoleto, subsequently published as *Ravenna: da capitale imperiale a capitale esarcale*. The word "capital" (*Hauptstadt*, *capitale*) refers to the city's political function as the residence of the western Roman emperors after 400, of the Ostrogothic kings from 493–540, and of the rulers of the Byzantine province of central Italy from 540–751. These rulers, along with the bishops of Ravenna, made a determined effort to create a city that would provide a worthy setting for the rituals that demonstrated their authority. But did late antique rulers want the city to be regarded as a capital, and if so, did they successfully convince their contemporaries?

In order to address this question, we must first define what a capital was in the fifth and sixth centuries. The word as it is used today, defined as a city serving as a seat of government, has no exact correlate in late antique Latin or Greek. E. Chrysos has recently noted that in late antique sources the word *caput* is used only for Rome and Constantinople, and carries symbolic connotations, whereas the term *sedes imperialis*, referring to the location of the emperor and administration, really corresponds better to what we would consider a capital city.[1] This ambiguity – the fact that Rome could be a *caput* without housing a central government – was the result of the political circumstances of the Roman Empire in the fourth and fifth centuries. For 300 years the city of Rome had been the center of imperial administration and the showplace of the empire's glory. However, Rome's location was not particularly convenient for administering the affairs of an empire that extended east to Persia and north to Scotland. The military emperors of the third century spent less and less of their time in Rome, and other cities rose to prominence as places where an emperor (or a would-be emperor) might reside.[2] After a century of political disarray, the emperor Diocletian (284–305) took the momentous step of dividing the empire into western and eastern halves ruled by coemperors (*augusti*), each of whom had a junior colleague (*caesar*). These four rulers and their administrations were based in different cities: initially these were Nicomedia and Milan (for the *augusti*) and Thessalonike and Trier (for the *caesares*). After 324 Constantinople, founded by the emperor Constantine, replaced Nicomedia as the eastern imperial capital. Rome was conspicuously omitted from the list of new capitals, probably largely for strategic reasons, but it is also possible that Diocletian hoped to break away from Roman traditions that he felt had been deleterious to the empire in the previous century, and in particular that he wished to minimize the threat of revolt by powerful military units stationed in Rome.[3]

Although most of these cities had been important administrative centers in the Roman period (with the exception of Constantinople), none of them had permanent structures for housing the imperial court. After Diocletian designated them imperial seats of government, each city began to build facilities that would accommodate the imperial ceremonial and the administration that would now be situated there.[4] All of these new capitals looked to Rome for inspiration, while at the same time reflecting the new political, administrative, and eventually religious circumstances of the empire.[5] As we will see in Chapter 3, the central feature was the palace, around which were arrayed hippodromes, colonnaded streets, fora, baths, and churches.

A new capital city that is intended to "... break away from, in particular, developed elite or bureaucratic institutions..." is known to anthropologists as a disembedded capital. A. H. Joffe's study of ancient disembedded capitals notes that they are very expensive, because they have to be built from scratch on a grandiose scale, and highly unstable, especially in a situation of political variability.[6] The Roman Empire in the fourth to sixth centuries was extremely unstable, and while Constantinople achieved lasting success, most of the other new capitals enjoyed relatively brief building booms.[7] Ravenna, on the other hand, had a tenuous existence in its first century as a capital, but managed to hold on to its role as a political center for a second century and beyond. This enabled it to have not just one but several phases of commemorative monuments, cumulatively reinforcing the sense that Ravenna was a traditional seat of government.

Rivalry with Rome is a persistent theme in the political and ecclesiastical history of Ravenna. Emperors had not lived in Rome since 284, but the city remained the showplace of the Roman republic and empire, the repository of its history, and the home of the Senate, the group of powerful Italian landowners whose authority waxed and waned in the course of Rome's imperial history. Rome was the *caput orbis*, the "head of the world," even when political power was no longer centered in it.[8] Milan had been viewed as a rival to Rome in the fourth century, and this rivalry was inherited by Ravenna when it was chosen to be the imperial residence after 402. We will discuss in detail the reasons for the choice of Ravenna in Chapter 3; certainly ease of communication with Constantinople was a major factor in its enduring political success, but it also seems clear that the "disembedded" nature of the city was important to the emperor Honorius and his advisers, as well as their successors. Most of the rulers who established themselves in Ravenna did so deliberately in order to counter the power of the Roman Senate and later of the popes: we will see this in the case of the Honorian emperors, of Odoacer, of Theoderic the Ostrogoth, and eventually of the Byzantine exarchs. Ravenna's monumentalization was thus an important and successful component of a propaganda contest about authority in Italy.

Another factor that came to play a significant role in Ravenna's history was the rise of its bishop. In addition to its secular importance, Rome was also the city of the pope, whose status as the head of the entire Church might be contested, but whose authority in Italy and the west was not doubted. The bishops of Milan rose to preeminence when the emperors resided in that city, and once the court moved to Ravenna, its bishops likewise rose in the hierarchy of the Italian church, eventually holding the rank of archbishop, ranking second after the pope and making periodic bids for autocephaly, or independence from the papal see. In a society in which the authority of bishops rivaled, or even exceeded, that of secular rulers, Ravenna's bishops and archbishops used the city's topography and monuments to stake their own claims both alongside the secular rulers of the city and against the popes.

All these rivalries produced a situation in which Ravenna's history of urban development ran directly counter to the experience of most other western cities in the period from 400 to 600. Ravenna's period of prosperity coincides with a time in which cities throughout the Roman world were undergoing dramatic transformations.[9] The city of the Roman Empire had been a center of secular administration, with a dense urban fabric that included public amenities such as theaters and baths, aqueducts and sewers, elaborate Roman-style houses for the elite, and evidence of long-distance trade. By the year 600 many of those features had disappeared from western Europe, replaced by towns centered on the church, with the bishop as the main authority figure, a much lower density of buildings, meaner and less architecturally integrated houses, no secular elite residents, fewer urban amenities (except for churches), and a dramatic reduction in items obtained from trade; the "ruralization of the city" is a term often used.[10] Progressive invasions, sacks (Rome was sacked in 410 and 455, Milan in 539), plague, and economic problems led to dramatic depopulation, a slowdown in new construction, and decay of the old urban fabric. The same processes eventually occurred in Ravenna, but at a different pace. Ravenna was not, as far as we know, sacked in any of the invasions or wars that beset the Italian peninsula, perhaps testimony to its perceived invulnerability provided by the swamps of the Adriatic coast. Ravenna had a resident secular governmental administration until the eighth century, which led to different political dynamics in the city than were found elsewhere.[11] In Ravenna, construction of magnificent new buildings continued until the end of the sixth century; indeed, the middle years of the sixth century produced some of the most dramatic and spectacular works of art and architecture anywhere. After 600 Ravenna suffered from the cumulative effects of the economic downturn and the political events of the previous fifty years, but the extra time had allowed the city to build up a collection of monuments that few other cities could rival.

Ravenna may have been beautiful and prosperous, but the literary texts show us a contemporary *mentalité* in which Rome reigned supreme. Because of its political importance, Ravenna is briefly mentioned in many texts, from letters to histories to poems, from the Roman and early medieval periods. Few of these offer praise of the new political center. Roman authors through the fifth century scorned Ravenna's marshy landscape, and sneered at its flies, bad water, and frogs.[12] Emperors might live at Ravenna, but they came to Rome for the important ceremonial events that were praised in panegyrics. Byzantine authors mentioned Ravenna's defensibility, but thought of the west in terms of Rome. Even the Romans who worked for the Ostrogothic king Theoderic praised Rome's monumental past far more than Ravenna's glittering present.

For strategic and economic reasons, then, Ravenna maintained its political role through several changes of regime, but its monuments do not seem to have convinced contemporaries of glory or prestige. The process of creating a convincing capital city took 200 years, and the monumentalization that we admire was completed just in time for the economic and political decline that was to spell the end of Ravenna's dominance. It was not until the ninth century that viewers could admire Ravenna as a glorious capital: Ravenna was not commemorated in literary sources until Agnellus wrote a history of the episcopal see in the 830s, a century after the city had ceased to be a seat of anything but local and episcopal government. Only in the context of the Carolingian renaissance, as Italians began to develop a renewed sense of urban consciousness that included pride in their Roman and late antique heritage,[13] could Ravenna's status as a former capital of the west be fully appreciated. When we talk about Ravenna as a capital, then, we must remember that we are doing so in historical hindsight.

History of Scholarship on Ravenna

Through the centuries, Ravenna's history has attracted the attention of a variety of authors and scholars. Starting with Agnellus in the ninth century, medieval authors wrote saints' lives, sermons, and chronicles that document specific moments in the city's history. From the fifteenth century, local historians and antiquarians produced ever-more-learned historical texts, as well as publishing the primary sources on which these histories were based. With the development of the disciplines of archaeology and art history in the nineteenth century, Ravenna began to occupy an ever-larger place in the historical consciousness not just of its own inhabitants, but also of outsiders. And with the recent growth of interest in late antiquity as a historical period, scholarly interest in Ravenna has exploded. Before we begin to examine Ravenna's history and monuments, it is useful to understand the way that these have been described and modified over the centuries, because early historians and artists provide us with crucial information, particularly about monuments, inscriptions, documents, and other sources that no longer survive.

Premodern Historiography

The historiography of Ravenna begins with Agnellus. The way he presented his city and its history has heavily influenced our understanding of Ravenna down to the present. Historians' preoccupation with Ravenna's rivalry with Rome, as described above, originates with Agnellus. Indeed, it is hardly possible to consider any aspect of late antique Ravenna without reference to what he had to say on the subject. Certainly he is the person who constructed a past for the city on the basis of its splendid monuments. Agnellus is our source of chronological information for many of the surviving buildings as well as our only source for the many buildings that no longer survive. Moreover, his presentation of figures such as Galla Placidia, Theoderic, and Archbishop Maximian has influenced all subsequent ideas about them. Although his text was not widely known outside of Ravenna until the nineteenth century, we can trace its influence from the tenth century on in texts written by Ravennate authors, or by authors who came to Ravenna and consulted its archive.[14]

There is no external evidence for Agnellus's existence; everything we know about him comes from the passages in his *Book of Pontiffs of the Church of Ravenna* (*Liber pontificalis ecclesiae Ravennatis, LPR*) in which he tells us something about himself. Agnellus was born circa 800 into one of the leading families of the city. He became a high-ranking priest in the Ravennate church, and seems to have been actively involved in construction and maintenance of antiquities and monuments in the see. Agnellus wrote the *LPR* in the 830s and 840s.[15] The work consists of a biography of each bishop of Ravenna from the time of the conversion to Christianity to Agnellus's own day. Depending on the sources available to him, Agnellus tells us about the historical background, artistic and architectural patronage, political and/or ecclesiastical controversies, and other notable events for each bishop. The text was directly modeled on the *Liber pontificalis* of Rome, a history of the papacy that by the early ninth century was widely known throughout Europe. One of Agnellus's main preoccupations was the rivalry between the sees of Ravenna and Rome, and he deliberately structured his text as a response to the Roman version of Italian history.[16] Agnellus was also preoccupied with the rights of the clergy in the face of oppression by bishops. Both of these themes color his accounts of individual bishops and of the history and monuments associated with them.

One of the issues that must be addressed when using the *LPR* for studying Ravenna's past is that it was written several centuries after the most exciting events. Agnellus was well aware of the impact of Ravenna's material remains; indeed, he exploited it throughout his text as evidence that Ravenna's history was equal to that of Rome. What he tells us, however, is not so much what actually took place in Ravenna in the fifth through eighth centuries, as how these things were perceived in the ninth century, and this distinction is not often appreciated by modern readers of the text.

Despite more than two centuries of archaeological, historical, and art historical investigation, it is remarkable how little we know about late antique Ravenna, and how much our ideas are shaped by Agnellus's account of this period. It is Agnellus who tells us that Ravenna was made the capital of Italy;

that Bishop Ursus built the cathedral; that Galla Placidia, Theoderic, and Archbishop Maximian monumentalized the city; and that the struggle with the popes consumed the seventh and eighth centuries. Since Agnellus's statements match the remains of churches and walls, they continue to provide the basic outline for Ravenna's history. Agnellus himself used as sources a chronicle or annal attributed to Archbishop Maximian, the sermons of Bishop Peter Chrysologus, and a few documents; he otherwise looked at buildings and inscriptions (many of which are now lost), and relied on hearsay current in the ninth century. Although today we have information from archaeology and better access to more historical texts, we do not know much more than Agnellus did.

After Agnellus, little else was written about the city of Ravenna until the thirteenth century.[17] Biographies of some individual bishops and saints were produced starting in the tenth century, often taken more or less exactly from the *LPR*; there was an increase in production of these biographies in the thirteenth century.[18] In addition to hagiography, there were several other texts produced in this period that are interrelated, and probably related to the manuscript of the *LPR* that remained in the archive. In the first half of the thirteenth century, the list of bishops in the *LPR* was brought up to date, with short entries written for each bishop, based on the *LPR*. In the 1260s, two works were written about Ravenna's history. One, the *Aedificatio ciuitatis Rauennae*, is a short text describing the foundation of Ravenna at the time of Noah and its subsequent construction history and geography through late antiquity, largely based on Agnellus. The other, the *Chronica de ciuitate Rauennatis*, was based on the earlier texts. Shortly after this, around 1296, the episcopal list was codified as the *Reuerendi Patres* by an anonymous author, possibly Riccobaldo da Ferrara.[19] The *Chronica* was subsequently continued and brought up to date, ending in 1346. This upsurge in historiographical interest in the city is linked to the political situation at the time: the rise of the commune, the wars between the Guelfs and the Ghibellines, struggles for independence from the Papal States, and the eventual dominance of the ravennate da Polenta family from 1275 to 1440. As in the ninth century, the autonomy of Ravenna was in question throughout the twelfth and thirteenth centuries, and hagiographers and historians were producing new works, often based on the highly proautonomous *LPR*, to bolster Ravenna's status.[20]

In these texts, the late antique period of Ravenna's history is again given prominence, as are the buildings. The main focus of both the *Chronica* and the *Aedificatio* is the built environment of the city. The *Aedificatio* attributes many buildings to the Babylonians and then to the Romans, but for the fifth century on, both texts depend on the *LPR* as their main source of information; indeed, the *Chronica* contains only four entries for the entire period between 810 and 1205. After 1205, the entries become more frequent, but are concerned now with the secular political history of the city, although some major building activities are described, such as the reconstruction of the nave of the Ursiana cathedral in 1314. It is thus not possible to reconstruct from the *Chronica* much information about the condition of the city in this period, as could be done for the ninth century.

From the fifteenth century on, antiquarian historians of Italy began to include information about Ravenna in their works. About 1413 the *LPR* was copied, along with most of the other historical texts, into one volume, which today is housed in the Biblioteca Estense in Modena; all earlier manuscripts of the texts were subsequently lost.[21] The *Codex Estensis*, as it is known, was consulted by several non-Ravennate historians, including Flavio Biondo, who described Ravenna's churches in his *Historiarum ab inclinatione Romanorum imperio Decades III* written in the first half of the fifteenth century, while Ambrogio Traversari likewise praised San Vitale and Sant'Apollinare in Classe in letters written at about the same time.[22] The influence of these texts in Ravenna, on the other hand, seems to have declined: Desiderio Spreti wrote *De amplitudine, de uastatione et de instauratione urbis Rauennae* in 1489, while Ravenna was under Venetian rule (1440–1509), but cites Agnellus only once, although he knew Biondo's text.[23]

The *LPR* was rediscovered by Gian Pietro Ferretti, a native of Ravenna who became Bishop of Lavello (d. 1557) and who wrote a history of the church of Ravenna that survives in manuscript form.[24] Part of Ferretti's copy of the *LPR* survives as our second manuscript witness to the text; sometime before 1589 the original manuscript in Ravenna disappeared.[25] The most notable Renaissance historian of Ravenna was Girolamo Rossi (also cited frequently by his Latinized name, Hieronymus Rubeus), whose *Ten Books of Histories of Ravenna* (*Historiarum Rauennatium libri decem*) first appeared in 1572, with a revised edition published in 1589. Rossi depended heavily on the *LPR* as a source for late antique Ravenna, and was influenced by Agnellus's presentation to use buildings, works of art, and inscriptions as historical sources. He provides invaluable information about monuments that survived in the sixteenth century but are now lost.

The eighteenth century saw a new burst of interest in Ravenna and its sources and monuments.[26] In 1708 Benedetto Bacchini, the librarian of the Duke of Modena, published the first edition of the *LPR*, based on the *Codex Estensis* manuscript that he had found in his library. His colleague and successor at the library, L. A. Muratori, who initiated the series *Rerum Italicarum Scriptores*, published Bacchini's edition along with most of the other texts from the *Codex Estensis* in two volumes of his new series. A new interest in late antique works of art also now became evident. G. G. Ciampini's *Vetera monimenta* of 1690–9 included drawings of many of

Ravenna's mosaics, invaluable evidence of their pre restoration state. Antonio Zirardini, a Ravennate lawyer and historian, published a work entitled *Degli antichi edifizii profani di Ravenna* in 1762; he also wrote a companion volume, *De antiquis sacris Ravennae aedificiis*, which was published only in 1908. The papyrus documents surviving in Ravenna's archive were first published in 1805 by G. Marini, in an edition that is still used as a reference today, although it was largely superseded by H. O. Tjäder's edition of the 1950s. Count Marco Fantuzzi, also of Ravenna and a student and colleague of Zirardini and Marini, published his six-volume work *Monumenti ravennati de' secoli di mezzo per la maggior parte inediti*, containing the texts of medieval documents in the archepiscopal archive, during the period 1801–4. Finally, the eighteenth century saw attempts at restoration in several of the city's surviving monuments, most notably at San Vitale and Sant'Apollinare in Classe.

Modern Historiography of Ravenna

Despite the increasing scholarly interest in Ravenna's monuments, by the early nineteenth century many of them were completely destroyed or in a very fragile state. Under Napoleon the city became part of the Italian Republic (1796–1814), and many of its monasteries were dissolved; some churches were deconsecrated, others were simply abandoned. At the same time, the increasing interest in antiquities, and the new discipline of archaeology, led to the first attempts to uncover Ravenna's lost past through excavation.[27] As far back as the late eighteenth century, local antiquarians were investigating underground remains, and this activity continued into the nineteenth century; construction of the railroad started in 1881, revealing many ancient remains, especially in Classe.[28] The religious monuments and mosaics also received attention. Filippo Lanciani and Alessandro Ranuzzi, engineers employed by the state department of civil engineering, conducted excavations and restorations of some of the buildings between 1859 and 1897. From the 1850s to the 1870s a Roman artist named Felice Kibel was commissioned by the municipal government of Ravenna to restore the surviving mosaics; he worked in the "mausoleum of Galla Placidia," the Orthodox Baptistery, Sant'Apollinare Nuovo, Sant'Apollinare in Classe, and San Vitale, and his work was highly controversial, both for the techniques he used and for the iconographical details that he restored.[29] Mosaic restoration work by the Ravennate mosaicists Carlo Novelli and Giuseppe Zampiga continued into the 1890s. The Museo Nazionale of Ravenna was established in 1885, with its original collection representing that of the Camaldolensian monastery of Sant'Apollinare in Classe, housed in the buildings formerly belonging to the Benedictine monastery of San Vitale.

In 1897 the Italian government established the Soprintendenza ai Monumenti di Ravenna, the first such bureau in Italy, under the direction of Corrado Ricci, a native of Ravenna who went on to become the national Director General of Arts and Antiquities in 1906.[30] Ricci's vision was to restore Ravenna's ancient monuments to their original condition, which meant that archaeological investigation had to determine what the original state was, and later accretions and decorations had to be removed.[31] He immediately initiated work on the "mausoleum of Galla Placidia" and San Vitale, and under his leadership, and with the assistance of Giuseppe Zampiga, Alessandro Azzaroni, and his eventual successor Giuseppe Gerola, many more monuments were excavated and restored. Gerola oversaw publication of the results of many of these projects during the period from about 1910 until the 1930s, and Ricci himself oversaw the publication of the eight-volume *Monumenti: tavole storiche dei mosaici di Ravenna* (1930–7), which contain drawings made before and during the restorations by Zampiga and Azzaroni. Since 1897 Ravenna's Soprintendenza has been modified, divided, and recombined with a confusing number of names. The current configuration, created in 1975, consists of the Soprintendenza per i Beni Archeologici dell'Emilia Romagna (Archaeology) and the Soprintendenza per i Beni Architettonici e per il Paesaggio di Ravenna (Monuments and Environment).[32]

Ricci and Gerola played an active role in stimulating other historical work in the city. The journal *Felix Ravenna* was founded in 1911 to publish scholarly research on the city and its monuments; it continued publication until 2000.[33] Under Ricci's and Gerola's auspices, a major excavation of the site of the "Palace of Theoderic" southeast of Sant'Apollinare Nuovo took place between 1908 and 1914.[34] In 1924 the first two fascicles of a new edition of the *LPR*, edited by Alessandro Testi-Rasponi, appeared in the new series of the *Rerum Italicarum Scriptores*. This edition was never completed, but has remained influential; it contains extensive notes, very inadequately referenced, which have been used uncritically by many scholars who have subsequently made use of the *LPR*.

During World War II Ravenna was bombed by the Allies, which resulted in major damage to the church of San Giovanni Evangelista and minor damage to other buildings. The destruction resulted in an intense campaign of excavation and restoration after the war. These efforts were headed by new groups of researchers, some local and some from elsewhere. In particular, faculty and students of the Università di Bologna began to play a prominent role in Ravenna scholarship. In the 1950s Giuseppe Bovini, professor of Christian archaeology, began to convene an annual conference, the *Corso di Cultura sull'Arte Ravennate e Bizantina* (*CARB*), which brought together archaeologists, art historians, and historians from Italy and abroad. The proceedings of each conference were published in volumes of the same name; the last conference took place in 1998 (vol. 44). Bovini founded and was the director of the Istituto di Antichità Ravennati e Bizantine, associated with the university but housed in the Casa Traversari in Ravenna, which continues to serve as a center for researchers studying Ravenna.

Felix Ravenna and *CARB* published numerous important studies of Ravenna's history and monuments, but there were no syntheses of the material, except in books aimed at tourists and popular audiences. The task of producing a scholarly history of late antique Ravenna was undertaken by Friedrich Wilhelm Deichmann, a German scholar based at the Deutsches Archäologisches Institut in Rome. In 1958 he published a collection of photographs of art, architecture, and sculpture that he called *Frühchristliche Bauten und Mosaiken von Ravenna*. The accompanying book, *Ravenna, Hauptstadt des spätantiken Abendlandes, Geschichte und Monumente* (1969), contained a narrative of the history of Ravenna as well as a section for each surviving monument, largely without any bibliographical references. In 1974 and 1976 two more volumes (2.1 and 2.2) appeared, devoted to detailed studies of the individual monuments, this time with full consideration of all previous scholarship (although the reference system is very haphazard). Finally, in 1989 Deichmann published volume 2, part 3, *Geschichte, Topographie, Kunst und Kultur*, which largely repeats volume 1 in a more dense and comprehensive fashion, this time including references but often summarizing arguments from the earlier volumes. Deichmann's volumes are fundamental resources for all students of Ravenna, as will be obvious from the footnotes in this book, although the appearance of comprehensiveness disguises the fact that some topics receive much more detailed treatment than do others. Moreover, it is sad to say that the massive amount of German text has been off-putting for non-German-speaking students of late antiquity.

Scholarly work on Ravenna did not stop after Deichmann; indeed, at least 600 scholarly publications that address Ravenna have appeared since 1989. In the 1990s, a series of edited collections in Italian began to meet the need for syntheses in languages other than German. The series *Storia di Ravenna* (1990–6), produced under the general direction of Domenico Berardi and Gian Carlo Susini, comprises six large volumes containing articles that cover the entire history of Ravenna from the Roman period to the modern age, written by the foremost archaeologists, art historians, and historians. Two of these volumes are devoted to the late antique period. Several exhibition catalogs and excavation reports with detailed scholarly discussions have appeared in the last decade, as have lavishly illustrated

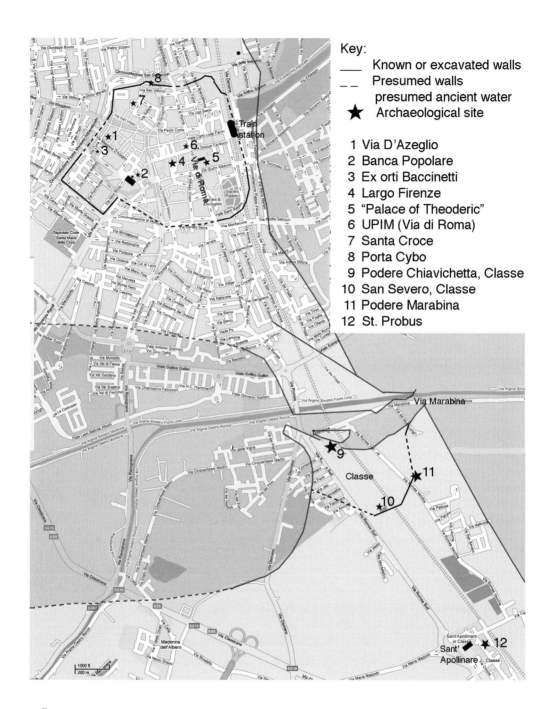

Key:

_____ Known or excavated walls

_ _ _ Presumed walls
      presumed ancient water

★ Archaeological site

1 Via D'Azeglio
2 Banca Popolare
3 Ex orti Baccinetti
4 Largo Firenze
5 "Palace of Theoderic"
6 UPIM (Via di Roma)
7 Santa Croce
8 Porta Cybo
9 Podere Chiavichetta, Classe
10 San Severo, Classe
11 Podere Marabina
12 St. Probus

1. Current street plan of Ravenna, overlaid with the late antique walls and waterways, with major archaeological sites

collaborative studies on the "mausoleum of Galla Placidia" (1996), San Vitale (1997), and San Michele *in Africisco* (2007). Finally, the Fondazione Centro Italiano di Studi sull'Alto Medioevo at Spoleto held a conference on late antique Ravenna in 2004, whose proceedings were published in two volumes as *Ravenna: da capitale imperiale a capitale esarcale*. There has as yet been no sustained scholarly treatment of Ravenna in English, and this book is intended to address that void.

Archaeological and restoration work continues apace in Ravenna, and given the number of questions about the late antique city that are still unanswered, new information will no doubt necessitate revision of the historical profile of Ravenna in the decades to come.

Some Archaeological Considerations

Given the shortage of contemporary written sources for late antique Ravenna, archaeology provides crucially important information about the city's topography, economics, and population. Before World War II, most excavation was directed toward Ravenna's churches, and to large structures that could be linked to buildings mentioned in the *LPR*; indeed, association of archaeological sites with Agnellus's text continues down to today. But, especially in the latter part of the twentieth century, other sites, representing private houses, manufacturing and warehouse facilities, and walls, harbors, and other man-made features have come to the fore, allowing us to gain a much more complete picture of life in the late antique city (for a map showing major sites, see Fig. 1). Because many of these sites will be mentioned in the chapters that follow, it is useful for us to understand some of the factors that have contributed to Ravenna's archaeological profile.[35]

Ravenna's ground level has been sinking for centuries, and this has raised challenges for those interested in digging up the past. The land surrounding Ravenna is subject to two geomorphological processes. First, Ravenna is located in an alluvial basin; the rivers and streams that flow into it bring sediment with them. Over time, except in periods in which it has been deliberately prevented, this sedimentation has filled in swamps, marshes, and lagoons, eventually creating new solid ground along the shores of the sea. This is why Ravenna, founded as a coastal port in the Roman period, today sits 9 km from the Adriatic coastline. The sedimentation along the shore also contributes to the second major process that has affected Ravenna, namely the subsidence, or progressive lowering, of the ground level, which has been calculated at approximately 16–23 cm per century.[36]

These two processes, along with the continuous occupation, destruction, spoliation, and rebuilding of the city, have produced a stratigraphy in which material from the Roman republican period is found 4–8 m below the current ground level, Roman imperial material is 3–6 m below current ground level, and fifth- to sixth-century material is 2–4 m below current ground level, with great variability from place to place within the city.[37] Moreover, Ravenna has always had a watery environment. Although the swamps of the Roman period are no longer much in evidence, the level of groundwater is relatively high. Even Agnellus noted cases in which things buried in previous eras were covered in water, and today most features that lie more than a few meters below the ground surface are enveloped in groundwater.[38] As a result, pre-Roman and Roman remains are sparse in the archaeological record and hard to excavate, and some sites, especially those excavated more than fifty years ago, are missing material from their lower levels.[39]

A final impediment to archaeological discovery in Ravenna, as in any city that has been continuously occupied since antiquity, is the presence of later structures, most of which postdate the medieval period. Some topographical problems remain insoluble, while many important archaeological discoveries of the twentieth century have taken place during or in advance of the construction of new buildings, roads, railroads, and sewers.

People have been digging up Ravenna's remains since the sixth-century. Archbishop Maximian moved the bodies of several of his predecessors into basilicas that he constructed for their veneration. Agnellus described his own investigations into Ravenna's hidden past, some at the instigation of his archbishop and some on his own initiative. Documented examples of deliberate excavation begins in the fifteenth century; the history of archaeological investigations in Ravenna from the fifteenth to the nineteenth century has been cataloged by Paola Novara, who shows that they were haphazard, and even more haphazardly published.[40] Early excavations were carried out by local antiquarians, who often had close connections to the church.

In the late nineteenth and early twentieth centuries, Corrado Ricci and Giuseppe Gerola sponsored systematic excavations in many of the churches that they were restoring. From 1908 to 1915 Gherardo Ghirardini oversaw the excavation of a large area to the south of Sant'Apollinare Nuovo, the site known as the "Palace of Theoderic."[41] Throughout the century, the Soprintendenza per i Beni Archeologici dell'Emilia-Romagna has sponsored and published many excavation projects in Ravenna and Classe, most notably since the 1960s under the direction of Giovanna Bermond Montanari and Maria Grazia Maioli. Sites excavated extensively include Podere Marabina, Via Marabina, Podere Chiavichetta, and the basilica of San Severo in Classe, the sites of the Banca Popolare and Via D'Azeglio in the heart of Ravenna, and the site known as Palazzolo to the north of the city. Members of the Università di Bologna's Istituto di Antichità Ravennati e Bizantine have also been actively involved in excavations, and after 1996, the Istituto was reorganized as part of the Dipartimento di Archeologia, with a specific unit based at Ravenna, the Facoltà di Conservazione dei Beni culturali (Sede di Ravenna). Its director, Andrea Augenti, has initiated a new series of excavations in collaboration with the Soprintendenza.[42]

A series of residents of Ravenna with historical and archaeological expertise have worked alongside, and often in collaboration with, the Soprintendenza and the University. In particular, many of the excavations of Ravenna's churches have been conducted by these scholars. Mario Mazzotti, a Ravennate priest, became involved with archaeological excavation in the late 1930s. He obtained a degree in Christian Archaeology, and served as the director of the archiepiscopal archive and museum in Ravenna from the 1950s until his death in 1983. Mazzotti excavated and published extensively on Ravenna's history and monuments, most notably Sant'Apollinare in Classe, the Arian Baptistery, and San Francesco. In the 1960s and 1970s Giuseppe Cortesi (head of the Biblioteca Classense) and Arnaldo Roncuzzi carried out a campaign of test-pit sampling and excavation in Ravenna and Classe, which revealed the locations of several late antique sites including the basilica of San Severo and the one known as the Ca'Bianca, which have been variously published; Cortesi also oversaw excavations at Santa Croce.[43]

More than two centuries of archaeological investigation have produced a bewildering variety of finds; these data are now being collected and synthesized. Valentina Manzelli has recently published a valuable catalog of the sites on which Roman material has been found, and has analyzed the results to produce a comprehensive survey of Roman Ravenna.[44] Enrico Cirelli, of the Università di Bologna, is directing a project to create GIS maps that represent all archaeological interventions resulting in Roman and medieval materials, which will be an extraordinarily useful resource.[45]

Ravenna and the Historiography of Late Antique Art and Architecture

Imagery from Ravenna is central to our conceptions of late antiquity; it is not surprising, for example, that mosaics from San Vitale are featured on the cover of the encyclopedic *Late Antiquity: A Guide to the Postclassical World*.[46] Ravenna's monuments have always been fundamental to studies of late antique art and architecture, both because they resulted from patronage at the highest levels of society and because they are remarkably well preserved. Ravenna's surviving mosaics from the fifth and sixth centuries outnumber those of any other city, while Ravenna's political and cultural links with Constantinople and the east meant that artists and architects were influenced by a very wide range of styles. Ravenna thus occupies an important place in every chronological narrative of medieval and Byzantine art, and Ravenna's monuments are cited in analyses of style, technique, iconography, viewer reception, color theory, and many other subjects of art historical interest. Questions raised by the study of the art and architecture – about construction techniques; building layout; architectural, sculptural, and artistic style; and iconography – also shed light on late antique economics, communication, theology, ecclesiastical organization, liturgy, and power politics. We can use them to enlarge our picture of life in late antique Ravenna.

In this book, the surviving monuments will be treated individually in the context of the historical development of Ravenna. In order to provide an overview of the art historical concerns that will be presented in the individual sections, I would like to introduce some of the scholarly discussions in which they have been featured.

One art historical methodology that has often been, and continues to be, applied to Ravenna's monuments is known as formalism. Stylistic features that do not seem typical of their time and place are compared to possible analogues and models from other places. Once comparative material has been identified, the atypical features are attributed to the arrival of foreign designers and workmen, the promotion of a particular theological or liturgical innovation, the making of a political statement, or to the taste or wealth of a patron. Depending on the sophistication of the analysis, these interpretations can relate the art and architectural meaning to wider contexts and cultural exchanges of the period.

Many of the features found in Ravenna's buildings and works of art do not correspond to any one tradition of art and architecture, and in particular are different from those used elsewhere in Italy. Because of Ravenna's specific status as a focus of contact between Italy and the eastern Mediterranean in late antiquity, the question of whether Ravennate art and architecture was influenced primarily from the eastern Mediterranean or from Italy and the west has engaged scholars for more than a century. This debate came out of the wider discussion of the origins of Christian art initiated by Josef Strzygowski,[47] but the question was applied particularly to Ravenna by Giuseppe Galassi. Galassi's *Roma o Bisanzio, I Musaici di Ravenna e le Origini dell'Arte Italiana* (1930), was written as a response to Strzygowski, and asserted, based on the examples from Ravenna, that the crucial point of departure was not in the fourth century but in the sixth century, when "Roman" and "Byzantine," which had emerged from the same Romano-Hellenistic Mediterranean milieu, diverged. For Galassi and many other scholars, the monuments of Ravenna represented a distinct "Ravennate

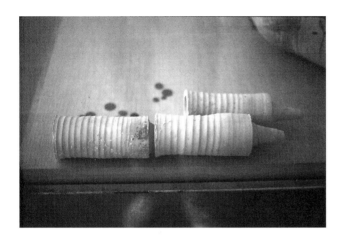

2. *Tubi fittili*, Museo Nazionale, Ravenna (courtesy Soprintendenza per i Beni Architettonici e Paesaggistici di Ravenna [MiBAC-ITALIA])

school," which borrowed from a variety of traditions and remained influential for centuries.[48] Nevertheless, the contrast between East and West has continued to play a role in art historical discussion of Ravenna down to the present: Deichmann was more inclined to emphasize Eastern models with "Western" modifications, while Eugenio Russo has argued in favor of a greater recognition of western models, but insists that the major Justinianic buildings are the product of a master builder from Constantinople.[49]

The conclusions drawn from this type of formal analysis can be problematic. There is a long tradition in Western scholarship of depicting the East as degenerate, which was Strzygowski's point; Italian and other scholars elevated the *romanitas* of Christian art for nationalistic reasons.[50] But, as Jas Elsner has pointed out, if those grand narratives are removed, formal analysis appears to lose much of its force.[51] Models and borrowings must then be understood in their specific historical contexts, either as symbolic of the aspirations of patrons and designers, or as evidence of trade and artistic practice of the past. In any given case, answers are proposed, but given the complete absence of documentation for this subject, such explanations must remain hypothetical.

Let us examine some architectural examples. Most of the churches in Ravenna from the fifth century and beyond make use of impost blocks (*pulvini*), or truncated pyramidal stone blocks placed between each capital and the springing of the arcade (see Figs. 12, 49, 81, and 92). The use of impost blocks was an architectural innovation that became widely used, particularly in Greece and the eastern Mediterranean, during the fifth century. Ravenna's buildings are often cited as the earliest examples of using impost blocks in the west, and while early fifth-century examples are also known from Naples and Rome, only at Ravenna were impost blocks used so consistently in later centuries.[52] Likewise, most of Ravenna's churches had apses that were polygonal on the exterior and semicircular on the interior, another feature known from Constantinople and the eastern Mediterranean in the fifth century, but rare in Italy. On the other hand, most of the domes and half domes in Ravenna's churches were constructed using *tubi fittili*, or hollow ceramic tubes approximately 0.20 m long that were interlinked and arranged in concentric rings, held together with cement (Fig. 2). This technique was widely used in Roman architecture of Italy and the west, but did not spread to the eastern Mediterranean.[53]

Taken together, these three features are seen as typically Ravennate. But what does this combination of features mean? Clearly, a variety of architectural ideas were being combined in new ways. This could mean that eastern architects and/or craftsmen were brought to Ravenna to build the great churches of the new imperial capital, either because such craftsmen did not exist in Ravenna, or to lend Constantinopolitan luster to the Ravennate structures. These masters then would have adopted some local techniques. Or were the impost blocks and polygonal apses foreign techniques adapted by local masters, and if so, why? In the case of marble sculpture, it can be shown not only that sculptural techniques and styles were derived from Constantinople, but that the marble itself originated in the eastern Mediterranean, which proves that there was an interest in Ravenna in high-status art from the east.[54] Archaeological evidence shows that Ravenna's ports carried on a busy trade in wine, oil, and other goods with both North Africa and the eastern Mediterranean, so clearly the city was fairly cosmopolitan. At the same time, links with Rome, Aquileia, and especially Milan were strong, and there are many similarities of architectural form and dedication between these cities also. Would these features have impressed people as being typically eastern or western? Did people notice that decorative motifs were more similar to Rome than to the Aegean? *Tubi fittili*, for example, are invisible once a vault is decorated. Did impost blocks impress people as a radically different element in a basilica? Given that these features were used for two centuries, they must have acquired meaning at some point, but we can only speculate about the reasons for their use.

The use of *spolia*, or reused building materials, is another feature of late antique architecture whose meaning has been fiercely debated.[55] From the time of Constantine, religious and secular architectural monuments frequently incorporated reused marble into building elements and sculpture, especially columns and capitals, as parts of their structure. As we will see, in Ravenna most of the churches of the fifth century followed this trend and included sculptural elements taken from earlier Roman structures;

moreover, Ravenna's walls and churches were usually built of reused brick. Scholars disagree over whether the use of these *spolia* was symbolic (triumph over Roman paganism, for example) or whether their use simply had to do with the availability and expense of materials. In other words, was their use meaningful, or practical, or both? Did it demonstrate the power of the emperors to control construction of preexisting buildings, or the power of the church to demolish them? Or, by the time Ravenna's buildings were constructed, were Roman *spolia* simply considered *de rigueur* for impressive public buildings?

The beauty and complexity of Ravenna's sculpture and mosaics have led scholars to attempt to elucidate the meaning of the images presented there, a study known as iconography. Frequently, studies of individual monuments have argued for one "real" iconographic meaning, presumably the meaning that was intended by its creators or patrons. More recently, scholars have recognized that in late antique art, images may not have been intended to mean just one thing, but may have been intended to evoke multiple meanings and associations. As Henry Maguire has pointed out, early Christian exegesis was based on the concept that any given Biblical passage might be interpreted in several different ways. If Christian exegetes understood the Word of God to have more than one meaning, surely they would also have expected religious images to be polyvalent, that is, to have more than one way of being "read." Moreover, the idea that a viewer might meditate on a set of images and draw further associations from them is one that was probably understood and even expected by designers of religious decorative programs.[56] In this book, therefore, no attempt has been made to present an account of every interpretation ever offered about a particular image, although certainly there are references to summaries, particularly those given by Deichmann, that do provide such references. Nor, in most cases, has one interpretation been singled out as the "true" one; in many cases several alternative suggestions are presented that seem to work in the context of the images' creation and location, and in some cases it is suggested that multiple meanings may be operating at the same time. Presenting these multiple frames of reference is most useful for exploring how early Christian imagery worked in the context of early Christian Ravenna.

Finally, it should be said that this book does not attempt to trace a complete history of the art and architecture of Ravenna; rather, it is conceived as a history of the city of Ravenna in late antiquity, a city that is largely understood through surviving works of art and architecture. Individual monuments are presented in considerable detail because such surveys are not available, for the most part, in English, but comprehensive summaries of all of the scholarship on them was not practical, given the scale and focus of this book. Rather, the monuments are presented as tangible sources of information about the city in which they were created, whose history they both reflect and helped to shape. Through their beauty and complexity we can still today experience Ravenna, if only in fragments, as did its inhabitants 1,500 years ago.

CHAPTER TWO

ROMAN RAVENNA

The Origins of Ravenna

The main feature that determined the history of Ravenna in antiquity was its changing hydrological situation.[1] Today Ravenna lies 9 km inland from the sea, but in the prehistoric and Roman periods it was located directly on the Adriatic coast, at the southern edge of the delta of the Po river. The Po (in Latin, *Padus*) is the longest river in Italy, flowing west to east through a river basin that contains many of northern Italy's most important cities. The watercourses of the Po network have changed dramatically in the past 2,500 years, sometimes naturally and sometimes because of human intervention. In the Ravenna area, sedimentation and subsidence have concealed the earliest courses of the river and its branches; reconstructions of the network before the era of modern maps is hypothetical, based on descriptions by ancient and medieval authors and examination of settlements, bridges, canals, and other evidence of human interaction in the past.[2]

Ancient authors include Ravenna in the riverine network of the Po, and most of them speak of Ravenna's environment as marshy; it seems clear that, from its earliest days, the site of Ravenna was a patch of dry land in a mostly watery landscape.[3] According to Pliny the Elder, in the first century AD the southernmost branch of the Po entered the Adriatic at the city of Spina, which is approximately 25 km to the north of Ravenna.[4] To the north of Spina were marshes and lagoons, known to Pliny as the "seven seas" (*septem Maria*), and other river branches extended to the south in the direction of Ravenna.[5] A large lagoon, separated from the sea by large, sandy dunes, existed to the south and west of Ravenna's site. Several rivers and canals emptied into the lagoon, including the *Lamone* from the west, perhaps the Vatrenus from the northwest, and certainly the Bidente, the Ronco, and the Montone from the southwest. The exact configurations of the rivers, lagoons, marshes, and canals are controversial,[6] but all scholars agree that

21

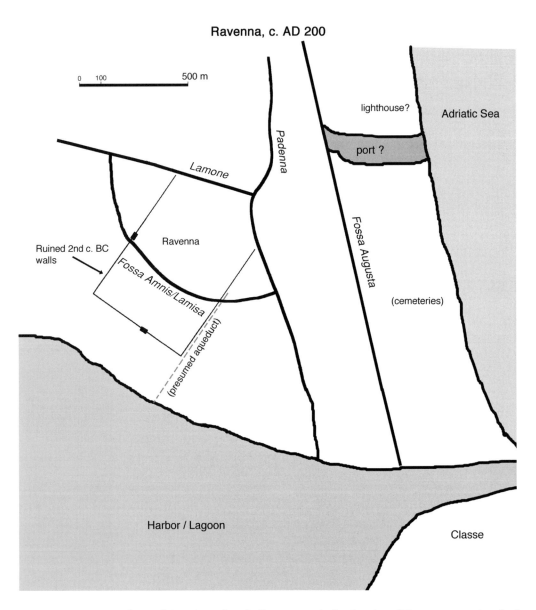

Ravenna, c. AD 200

0   100   500 m

lighthouse?

Adriatic Sea

Padenna

port ?

Lamone

Fossa Augusta

Ravenna

Ruined 2nd c. BC
walls

Fossa Amnis/Lamisa

(cemeteries)

(presumed aqueduct)

Harbor / Lagoon

Classe

3. Map show-
ing Ravenna
in the Roman
imperial period,
ca. AD 200

in the prehistoric and early Roman periods, the site of Ravenna consisted of
larger and smaller pieces of land surrounded by water, and separated from
the seacoast by a line of large, sandy, coastal dunes.

Small groups of people undoubtedly inhabited this region far back
into prehistory, but pre-Roman archaeological evidence is very fragmentary.[7] Bits and pieces of Etruscan objects dating back perhaps to the sixth or
fifth century BC have been discovered in Ravenna, as well as pottery from
Greece and from neighboring parts of Italy dating between the fifth and

the third centuries BC.[8] From the fifth century BC on, there were probably settlements among the rivers and canals of the area, perhaps even by peoples of different ethnic origins.[9]

What we know about the early history of northeast Italy comes from scattered references to the region by Greek and Roman authors, and from archaeology.[10] As far back as the mid–2nd millennium BC, inhabitants of Greece began trading with those of the Adriatic coast in Italy. Classical authors gave a variety of rather nonspecific names to these Italian peoples, who do not emerge from historical obscurity until the sixth century BC, when the Etruscans, Venetians, and Umbrians developed into ordered political and cultural units that were recognizable to Greek authors. Celts from north of the Alps also began to settle in Italy north of the Po in the late fifth century BC, leading the Romans to label the region Cisalpine Gaul ("Gaul on this side of the Alps").

The origins of Ravenna were a mystery even to the Greeks and Romans, and our earliest textual sources for the city date only to the first century BC.[11] Classical authors disagreed about Ravenna's origins: according to the first century AD historian Strabo, who was using Greek ethnographic sources, it was founded by the Thessalians (Θετταλῶν κτίσμα) and then inhabited by Umbrians.[12] Pliny the Elder called it a town (*oppidum*) of the Sabines,[13] while Ptolemy in the second century AD identified it as a city of the Celtic Boii.[14] These attributions probably do not correspond to any underlying "reality," but rather reflect the manner in which each author was conceptualizing the entire region within his larger historical program.[15] Modern scholars have attempted to explain the place-name "Ravenna" as derived from a river, *Rave*, with a suffix -*na* that might be Pelasgian or Tyrrhenian,[16] or from a word referring to gravel, with the Etruscan suffix -*enna*,[17] but in fact we don't even know how old the place-name is, since we first encounter the word *Ravenna* in the first century BC.

Whoever originally lived here, the earliest archaeological evidence for a permanent settlement at Ravenna dates to the Roman occupation of the region in the late third century BC. The Romans had first become involved in northeast Italy a century earlier; in the wake of the Gallic invasion of Italy in 390 BC, Rome had formed alliances with various Italian city-states, and throughout the fourth century BC fought a series of wars with Italian peoples who resented Roman dominance of the peninsula. After the second Samnite War (326–304 BC) the Romans began developing a network of allied cities in the direction of the Adriatic coast. In 295 BC they defeated an army made up of Samnites, Gauls, Etruscans, and Umbrians at the Battle of Sentinum, after which they established colonies such as Rimini (founded in 268 BC) on the border of their new territory. The Carthaginian invasion in 218 BC, conducted by the general Hannibal, also influenced Roman ideas about the defense of Italy, and after the Romans finally defeated the Carthaginians, they extended their hegemony all the way along the Adriatic coastline, founding the city of Aquileia in 181 BC.

At the same time, the economic network along the Adriatic coast was also changing. Spina had been founded by Greeks in the later sixth century BC and since then it had served as the major Adriatic port for the Po river basin.[18] Difficult political circumstances, first in Greece in the fourth century BC and then in Italy, partially disrupted Spina's trading networks, but it was probably the silting up of its harbor in the mid–third century BC that led to Spina's ultimate decline.[19] Ravenna in the third century had riverine access to the Po, a large natural harbor on the Adriatic, and dry land on which to build a city. These were the right conditions for a commercial port, and they led to the construction of the first fortified settlement at Ravenna.[20]

The Republican City

Ravenna's late antique walls follow an irregular plan, but the southwest corner incorporates three sides of a rectangle. Scholars have long assumed that the rectangular corner reproduced the outline of the original Roman city (Fig. 3), since a rectangular plan such as this, with a street grid aligned with two main roads intersecting in the center, was commonly used in newly founded Roman colonies and cities.[21] The city, usually referred to as the *oppidum* or as *Ravenna quadrata*, until recently was thought to have been founded in the first century BC by the emperor Augustus.[22]

In 1980, archaeologists working at the construction site of the Banca Popolare (see Fig. 1), along the eastern line of the rectangle, revealed the remains of a city wall that was much earlier than anyone had thought, with pottery dating to the second half of the third century BC.[23] The wall's remains were found 7.50–4.75 meters below the current ground level, and consisted of a stretch of wall 24 meters long and 2.6 meters high, with a rectangular tower measuring 3.80 × 6 meters.[24] Both wall and tower were constructed of square bricks of dimensions similar to those found in Greece and southern Italy, and, unusually, each brick was stamped with a letter or pair of letters, perhaps indicating which local producer had made each brick.[25] The early date of this wall would make Ravenna the oldest Roman fortification, after Rimini, north of the Apennines.[26]

There is evidence that the lower courses of the south and west walls of the rectangle also date to the same period as the Banca Popolare wall.[27] We can therefore suppose walls for three sides of a rectangle; there is no archaeological evidence for the northern stretch of wall, and so it is not clear whether the Padenna and the *flumisellum Lamone* formed the boundary on this side, or whether there was a wall on one or other side of the watercourses.[28] These two waterways played an important role in the definition of the site, and by the first century BC they were supplemented by a new canal, the *fossa Lamisa*, which entered the *oppidum* from the west and also flowed into the Padenna.[29]

Why was this city wall built, and by whom? Unfortunately, in the absence of any textual sources, we can only hypothesize about what was going on in the area at this time. Ravenna seems to have lain just outside the *ager Gallicus* conquered by Rome in 295; in 266 the Umbrians of Sarsina allied themselves with Rome, and it has been suggested that the settlement of Ravenna became at this point an allied city (*civitas foederata*).[30] Another suggestion is that the settlement was fortified in the context of Hannibal's invasion of Italy in 218 BC.[31] V. Manzelli notes that it is likely by this time that Ravenna was becoming an important commercial center that needed to be protected from pirates.[32] F. Rebecchi reads Strabo's statement that "Rimini, like Ravenna, is an ancient colony of the Umbri, but both of them have received also Roman colonies," to mean that Ravenna was founded by colonists from Rimini.[33] Rimini, which had been founded in 268 BC, was linked directly to Rome by the construction of the *Via Flaminia*, and in the 180s BC Rimini was linked to other Roman colonies of Piacenza and Cremona by the *Via Aemilia*. Ravenna was not directly on any of the main roads, although there was a roadway that connected the city to the *Via Aemilia*. It was not until 132 BC that the Romans built the *Via Popilia*, which linked Ravenna directly with Rimini to the south and Adria to the north, perhaps a sign of the Ravenna's increasing importance.[34] The *Via Popilia* must have run somewhere near the town, but it is not known whether it would have gone through the *oppidum* or to the east along the line of the dunes.[35] In sum, the wall shows that a permanent community had formed at Ravenna by the late second century BC, but it is nevertheless strange that the city was not mentioned in any witten sources until a hundred years later.

Republican Ravenna had more than just walls. Material from the Via D'Azeglio excavation with third-century BC pottery includes a drainage system on wooden piles, indicating a planned Roman settlement,[36] and bricks identical to those found in the early wall were found at the base of the sewer system found in the neighboring Via Morigia excavation.[37] The only building that can definitely be dated to the republican period, specifically to the second century BC, is the atrium house found in the Via D'Azeglio excavation, with its polychrome mosaics representing the myth of the battle between the Argonauts Pollux and Amicus.[38] These fragments show that the *oppidum* of Ravenna had a street grid, a sewer system, and some relatively elaborate houses. Other structures in the republican city seem to have been constructed out of local materials, often perishable, like reeds and wood, which have left few traces, but also out of locally available stone.[39] Other fragmentary objects from the Roman republican period have been found to the east of the *oppidum*, in the area of the later "Palace of Theoderic," suggesting that buildings, perhaps even a temple, were also constructed in this sector nearer the sea.[40] It has not been possible to determine whether an eastern settlement existed earlier than the construction of the *oppidum*, or contemporary with it.[41]

Ravenna first appears in Roman historical sources in the context of the Social and Civil wars of the first century BC.[42] Plutarch mentions that a marble statue of Gaius Marius still existed in the first century AD in Ravenna.[43] The Roman orator Cicero in 56 BC described one Publius Caesius as having been, before the end of the Social War in 90 BC, "...a Ravennate from the federated people."[44] The implication is that Ravenna was an allied city before 90 BC, and that even in Cicero's day Ravenna held federate status, although the city would be raised to the rank of a Roman *municipium* sometime after 49 BC.[45] Julius Caesar famously stayed at Ravenna the night before he took his army across the Rubicon to start the Civil War in 49 BC.[46] Suetonius reports that during the course of that day, Caesar had gone to the theater and inspected the site of a proposed gladiatorial school.[47] Those references represent the extent of written information that we have about Ravenna in the republican period: a city that stood on the fringes of the Roman world, integrated culturally and politically into the Roman sphere of influence.

Classe: The Roman Imperial Harbor and Fleet

Roman authors tell us that Octavian, later known as Augustus, decided to establish a permanent navy for the Roman state. Two bases for this new navy were chosen, one for the western Mediterranean at Misenum on the Bay of Naples, and the other, for the east, at Ravenna.[48] The reasons for this decision seem clear: Octavian had been involved in two major military campaigns that involved naval action, one against the pirate-fleet of Sextus Pompey, which culminated in the Battle of Naulochus in 36 BC, and one against Mark Anthony that concluded with the Battle of Actium in 31 BC. Scholars debate the date of the fleet's foundation, but it happened sometime between 35 and 12 BC.[49] For the next 300 years Ravenna would house one of Rome's main naval bases, which would have important consequences for the city.

First and most important, Ravenna's harbor had to be developed into a facility that could hold, repair, and provision the ships of the fleet. Ravenna's harbor facilities must have been developed already in the republican period; the historian Appian says that in 39 BC Octavian "brought war-ships from Ravenna and an army from Gaul" and "ordered the building of new triremes at Rome and Ravenna," implying that Ravenna was already a naval station.[50] Octavian recognized that Ravenna was ideally situated to control piracy in the Adriatic, which was a threat to Octavian's imperial peace, and that the lagoon could be developed into a facility capable of holding the entire Adriatic fleet.[51] Thus, under Octavian, the harbor was enlarged and stabilized. Pliny the Elder in the first century AD describes the large canal, known as the *fossa Augusta*, which joined the Po river to the harbor:[52]

> There is no river [the Po] known to receive a larger increase than this in so short a space; so much so indeed that it is impelled onwards by this vast body of water, and, invading the land, forms deep channels in its course: hence it is that, although a portion of its stream is drawn off by rivers and canals between Ravenna and Altinum, for a space of 120 miles, still, at the spot where it discharges the vast body of its waters, it is said to form seven seas. By the Augustan Canal [*Augusta fossa*] the Po is carried to Ravenna, at which place it is called the Padusa, having formerly borne the name of Messanicus. The nearest mouth to this spot forms the extensive port known as that of Vatrenus, where Claudius Caesar, on his triumph over the Britons, entered the Adriatic in a vessel that deserved rather the name of a vast palace than a ship. This mouth, which was formerly called by some the Eridanian, has been by others styled the Spinetic mouth, from the city of Spina, a very powerful place which formerly stood in the vicinity, if we may form a conclusion from the amount of its treasure deposited at Delphi; it was founded by Diomedes. At this spot the river Vatrenus, which flows from the territory of Forum Cornelii [Imola], swells the waters of the Po.

The main branch of the Po in this period was the branch that ran through Spina;[53] what Pliny called the Padusa is probably the same as what was later called the Padenna, a southern branch of the Po that was regularized under Augustus to create the canal.[54] The *fossa Augusta* formed part of a system of navigable waterways that linked Ravenna with cities all along the Adriatic coast as far as Aquileia, as well as with the interior of Italy, a system that was used both for commerce and for official government business at least into the sixth century.[55]

What happened to this watercourse when it reached Ravenna is not clear because of a lack of secure archaeological evidence. Some scholars have proposed that part of the water was diverted into a new canal 350 m to the east of the Padenna, to improve circulation in the harbor's mouth by having water flow directly into the channel, while the Padusa/Padenna continued to flow directly to the east of the *oppidum* (see Fig. 3).[56] However, E. Cirelli has recently proposed that the Padenna *was* the *fossa Augusta*, strengthened by massive cement and masonry embankments;[57] adjacent to the *oppidum* the Padenna was 50–65 m wide. A paved road 9 m wide, identified by the excavators as the *via Popilia*, ran along the western bank of this canal to the north of the city.[58] At a point along the eastern side of the *fossa Augusta*, now occupied by the Venetian fortress called the Rocca Brancaleone, a second port was developed, open to the sea and fed by the canal, which remained in use until the fifth century AD or later.[59] Pliny the Elder notes that Ravenna had a famous lighthouse, similar to that of Alexandria in Egypt, which is thought to have been located to the northeast of the *oppidum*, since Agnellus in the ninth century refers to this location as "at the lighthouse." In that case the lighthouse would have functioned as a beacon for the northeastern harbor rather than the southern one.[60]

The main harbor of Ravenna was located just to the south and the west of the *oppidum*, perhaps as little as 200 m south of the *oppidum*'s southern wall.[61] Very little is known of its dimensions, or of the many buildings that must have been erected all around it,[62] but a fair amount is known about the structures built at the mouth of the port. A channel led from the Adriatic into the harbor; the channel was 80 m long, and it widened on the interior, flowing around at least two small islands.[63] The channel's banks were strengthened with quays and with piles of building rubble. The mouth leading to the sea was fortified with very strong moles, made of cement, extending to the south and presumably to the north. To the north the coastline on either side was then provided with cement barrier walls, 4.5–5 m wide and 40 m long, to prevent erosion. This canal led into the harbor where the *fossa Augusta* entered from the north, with the Padenna's mouth slightly farther to the west. One section of the harbor extended to the west, south of the city of Ravenna, while another stretched to the south. Portions of the quays have been found in the excavations on Via S. Alberto in Classe: the earliest constructions of the Augustan port were made of large oak beams, strengthened in the first century AD by large numbers of ceramic fragments, and then finally replaced with brick in the second century.[64]

We have only one piece of evidence for the size of Ravenna's imperial fleet: Jordanes in the sixth century quotes a text by the early third-century historian Cassius Dio, now lost, that says there were 250 ships.[65] Because the Roman navy is much less well documented than the army, even for the imperial period, the main sources of information are funerary inscriptions that mention the deceased's ship, which have provided names and types of some vessels based at Ravenna (Fig. 4).[66] The commander of the Ravenna fleet held the title *praefectus classis*, and was subordinate to the *praefectus* of the fleet at Misenum.[67] The fourth-century *Notitia Dignitatum* mentions the "prefect of the Ravennate fleet, with responsibility for that city of

4. Funerary stele of Publius Longidienus, a ship builder (*faber navalis*) of Classe, first century BC/AD, Museo Nazionale, Ravenna (courtesy Soprintendenza per i Beni Architettonici e Paesaggistici di Ravenna [MiBAC-ITALIA] Cl. 28.13.10/95–1 R2)

Ravenna"; this has been interpreted as meaning that the prefect of the fleet was the civilian head of government in Ravenna, although such an interpretation is controversial, because we do not know how much earlier this situation may have applied.[68] Fragments of inscriptions from the first and second centuries, found both in Ravenna and elsewhere in Italy, seem rather to indicate that Ravenna in the imperial period had a regular town council with magistrates.[69]

Ravenna's fleet sent its ships throughout the Mediterranean, as funerary inscriptions for its sailors (*classiari ravennati*) have been found in the eastern Mediterranean, the Aegean, and the Black Seas and on the Danube.[70] Inscriptions from Ravenna and abroad name at least 590 people who were attached to the Ravennate fleet.[71] At least in the first century AD, a large percentage of the navy was made up of Dalmatians and

Pannonians, who received Roman citizenship upon their discharge after twenty-six years of service.[72] One single inscription from the second or third century lists 100 individual members of the fleet, in apparently descending order of rank: carpenters (*fabri*), upper-level soldiers (*beneficiarii*), flag bearers (*vexillarii*), players of various kinds of horns (*cornicines, tubicines, bucinatores*), lower-level officers (*suboptiones*), and on-duty soldiers (*munifices*). It is interesting that on this inscription, all the names are Latin, indicating perhaps a shift in the makeup of the navy.[73] Other inscriptions mention additional occupations associated with the navy, including soldiers (*milites*) and their officers (*centuriones* and *optiones*), pilots (*gubernatores*), underpilots (*proretae*), men who called out the rhythm to the rowers (*pausari*), masters of weapons (*armicustodes*), repair personnel (*nauphylaces*), ax makers (*dolabrari*), flag bearers (*vexilliferi*), doctors (*medici*), and scribes (*scribae*) of various sorts.[74] Some of these inscriptions give the person's cognomen as *Classicus*, or "member of the fleet."[75]

The sailors of the fleet were sometimes married (although they were not legally allowed to be while enlisted), and were associated also with slaves and freedmen, but the ships do not seem to have been crewed by slaves. We know that the sons and brothers of sailors also went into the navy. Scholars estimate that there may have been as many as 10,000 men attached to the fleet, although they were not all resident at one time; and if even one third of them had female companions of some sort that would be a very large population that had to live somewhere. It is likely that many of them lived to the southeast of the main harbor, in the area that eventually became the city of Classe.[76]

The port city of Classe to the south of the harbor channel developed slowly after the establishment of the fleet. In the Augustan period, the area was largely occupied by cemeteries.[77] Only in the second century does evidence of habitation emerge. An imposing structure excavated under the church of San Severo, dating to the early second century, contained several rooms with elaborate mosaic pavements, glass windows, and other indications of high status, and has been interpreted as a public bath complex.[78] A street and sewer system developed, and evidence of lower-class habitations and manufacturing facilities have been identified dating to between the second and the fourth centuries.[79]

The large military installation had a dramatic effect not just on Ravenna's population, but also on the surrounding countryside. In order to provision the fleet, Ravenna's hinterland was mobilized to produce necessary products; one example of such a site, where a large Roman villa has been excavated, is at Russi, 14 km west of Ravenna along a stream that fed the harbor. While originally a simple rustic villa that produced grain, in the late first or early second century AD it was transformed into a much larger-scale operation, producing grain and wine, with facilities for storage and large-scale production, presumably for sale to the navy.[80]

The City of Ravenna in the Roman Empire

In the first century AD, Ravenna as a city finally begins to appear in written sources.[81] In historical works by authors such as Tacitus and Suetonius, Ravenna is the base of the fleet and its commander, and is occasionally used as a place of exile or refuge.[82] The satirist Martial and others complain about the flies, frogs, bad water, and other unpleasant features of the city, while others commend the vegetables, especially asparagus, grown in the area.[83] Finally, some authors comment on the nature of the city itself, and record its reputation in the Roman world.

The most notable feature of Ravenna for Roman authors was its watery location.[84] The early first-century AD author Strabo, in his *Geography*, devotes a considerable amount of space to the city, which he describes as follows:[85]

> Situated in the marshes is the great [city of] Ravenna, built entirely on piles, and traversed by canals, which you cross by bridges or ferry-boats. At the full tides it is washed by a considerable quantity of sea-water, as well as by the river, and thus the sewage is carried off, and the air purified; in fact, the district is considered so salubrious that the [Roman] governors have selected it as a spot to bring up and exercise the gladiators in. It is a remarkable peculiarity of this place, that, though situated in the midst of a marsh, the air is perfectly innocuous. . . . Another remarkable peculiarity is that of its vines, which, though growing in the marshes, make very quickly and yield a large amount of fruit, but perish in four or five years.

The phrase translated here as "built entirely on piles" is, in the original Greek, ξυλοπαγὴς ὅλη; it has also been translated "built entirely of wood."

Vitruvius, too, after noting that towns built in marshes are generally not healthy, observes that:[86]

> If the walled town is built among the marshes themselves, provided they are by the sea, with a northern or northeastern exposure, and are above the level of the seashore, the site will be reasonable enough. For ditches can be dug to let out the water to the shore, and also in times of storms the sea swells and comes backing up into the marshes, where its bitter blend prevents the reproductions of the usual marsh creatures . . . an instance of this may be found in the Gallic marshes surrounding Altinum, Ravenna, Aquileia, and other towns in places of the kind, close by marshes. They are marvelously healthy, for the reasons I have given.

In describing different kinds of timber to be used for construction, Vitruvius speaks of piles of alderwood used as the substructure of buildings in marshy areas: "One can see this at its best in Ravenna; for there all the buildings, both public and private, have piles of this sort beneath their foundations."[87] Excavations and soundings, for example at Via Guerrini to the east of the cathedral and at Via C. Morigia in the center of the *oppidum*, have shown that wooden piles were indeed used at the base of Roman structures in Ravenna.[88] These wooden supports would not have been stakes lifting the buildings up above the water/street level, but rather packing to create a stable foundation, as found in other excavated sites such as Spina.[89] Although Strabo and Vitruvius present Ravenna as a city surrounded by swamps, the archaeological evidence shows that while there were lagoons and marshes to the south in the Roman period, no evidence of a wet environment could be identified to the north of the city.[90]

Ravenna in the first century AD was an important and interesting city but we still know relatively little about its features. By the first century AD the republican city walls were at least partially in ruins; at the Banca Popolare site a house was built on top of them.[91] Defensible city walls were abandoned throughout Italy in the early imperial period, taken to be a sign of peace within the empire.[92] Traces of Ravenna's walls must still have been visible, as in AD 42 a large gate was built or rebuilt as a triumphal arch in honor of the emperor Claudius (Fig. 5).[93] The Porta Aurea ("Golden Gate"), as it was later known, was on the short south side of the *oppidum*, a monumental double-arched portal that bore an inscription commemorating its construction.[94] It was not a gate that could be closed for defense, but rather a monumental arch leading from the port to the center of the town, as are also known from cities such as Ancona and perhaps Pozzuoli; it is possible that an existing gate was modified to give it monumental form.[95] The arch was destroyed by the French in 1582, but is known from Renaissance drawings to have been a double archway clad in marble, whose architrave, surmounted by two triangular pediments, was held up by six engaged Corinthian columns; flanking the openings were aediculae surmounted by clipei decorated with vegetation (one of which survives), and flanking the aediculae and the gateways were more decorated colonettes.[96]

The Porta Aurea's location at the center of the south wall of the *oppidum* has led to the conclusion that this region must have remained at the heart of the Roman imperial city. It is hypothesized that the *cardo* or the *decumanus* of the Roman town led from the Porta Aurea northeast across the city, eventually crossing the *flumisellum* to the northeast by means of the *pons Augusti*, which was excavated in 1983.[97] Excavations at the site of Via D'Azeglio uncovered a paved roadway, with a maximum width of 6 m, that led from

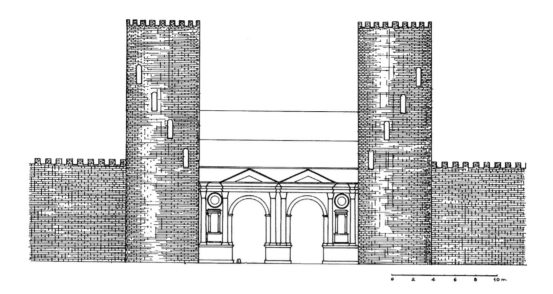

5. Reconstruction of the Porta Aurea embedded within the late antique walls (after Mansuelli, 1967, fig. 7)

the Porta Aurea to the northeast. This street had been repaved several times starting in the republican period, first in brick and then in stone.[98] Beneath the street ran a sewer system dating to the second century AD, which probably replaced an earlier sewer already in place, into which the drains from the houses flanking the street discharged.[99]

It is assumed that, like other Roman cities, imperial Ravenna would have had a forum, a *capitolium*, a praetorium, and other public buildings such as temples and places of entertainment, but we know little about where these were located.[100] Archaeological soundings have revealed a large public piazza or forum at the junction of the Padenna and the *fossa Lamisa* and outside the *oppidum* wall. Assuming that the original forum was inside the *oppidum*, this must have been a second monumental piazza, perhaps a market area, as it was associated with a large quay along the waterway and with many fragments of late republican and early imperial amphorae.[101] Elsewhere in the city, fragments of column capitals bear witness to monumental sculpture, probably associated with public buildings, temples, and possibly even houses built starting in the first century AD. A piece of an architrave with the inscription "[di]vi Iuli p(atris) p(atriae)" was probably part of a *Caesareum*, a temple to the deified Julius Caesar, built at the end of the reign of Augustus.[102] Numerous pieces of architectural sculpture dating to the first and second centuries are supplemented by others that date to the third and fourth centuries; many of them survive because they were reused in Ravenna's Christian churches in the fifth and sixth centuries.[103] Beyond these fragments, however, we cannot say anything about Ravenna's public spaces in the imperial period.

Ravenna's increasing importance and its associated population expansion in the second century led to the further development of its infrastructure, and particularly its supply of fresh water.[104] An aqueduct was built, reportedly by the emperor Trajan (98–117 AD), to bring in water from the southwest.[105] Remains of the course of the aqueduct have been observed and excavated, and its route is fairly certain; it began at Meldola, 35 km to the southwest, and followed the course of the river Ronco toward Ravenna and Classe.[106] How it crossed the harbor is not clear, but once on the northern side it ran along the eastern wall of the *oppidum*. A tower that is currently part of the sixth-century archiepiscopal palace, known as the *Torre Salustra*, perhaps originally part of a gate in the republican walls, also served as the *castellum aquae*, the water distribution tower for the aqueduct.[107]

While the *oppidum* seems to have remained the focus of imperial Ravenna, the city's population increased dramatically in the first and second centuries AD, and construction and habitations spread outside of the original *oppidum* on all sides. Several large houses throughout the city have been excavated, most notably at the sites of Via D'Azeglio, the Banca Popolare, Santa Croce, and the "Palace of Theoderic." Many of these houses show evidence of modification over time, generally keeping within the existing street layout until the late fifth century. The houses of the republican and early imperial periods follow the trends and layouts found throughout the Roman Empire in this period. They are centered on an atrium or peristyle, and surrounded by dining rooms (*triclinia*), studies (*tablina*), and other rooms, with walls of masonry or wood, and decorated with fresco and with mosaic or *opus sectile* floors.[108] In the second century many of these houses were newly decorated and upgraded, sometimes with the addition of hypocausts and central heating.[109] At the Banca Popolare site, the so-called House of the Triclinium was first built in the first century AD on top of the *oppidum* wall, then substantially modified in the late second century with the addition of a central-heating system and new mosaic floors and paint, and then similarly modified again in the third century to include a fountain.[110] The elaborate floor mosaics as well as remains of furnishings, such as bronze furniture fittings dating to the second century, indicate a high standard of living.[111]

With a large and busy port, trade also increased dramatically in Ravenna and Classe. We hear from Vitruvius that the river Po was used to transport timber from inland to the cities on the Adriatic coast,[112] and it is likely that Ravenna gradually developed a mercantile identity.[113] To the southwest of the *oppidum* excavations have revealed evidence of ceramic production from the first century BC through the first century AD, particularly of *terra sigillata* cups and beakers.[114] Ceramics produced in other locations in central Italy were also brought to Ravenna to be filled with wine from the region, which was then exported to places throughout the Mediterranean in the first to third centuries AD.[115] From the second century, Ravennate workshops were producing marble sarcophagi and other sculpted works.[116]

Ravenna also imported a variety of products from throughout the Mediterranean, particularly from the east. Remains of vessels containing products such as wine from the Dalmatian coast and Rhodes, along with some evidence for olive oil from Spain, have been found at Ravenna,[117] as has a mid–second century tombstone with an inscription in Greek commemorating "Titus Julius Nicostratus the Rhodian," perhaps a wine merchant.[118] In the mid–second–century marble from the island of Proconnesus near Constantinople began to be imported into Ravenna, to be made into sarcophagi and public monuments.[119] As mentioned above, the provisioning of the fleet must have led to an enormous increase in the amount of trade between Ravenna and its terrestrial and maritime neighbors, and the creation and maintenance of one or more large ports fostered the development of the city as a commercial center.

Most houses, public, and commercial buildings were located to the west of the presumed *fossa Augusta*. The region between the canal and the coastline was the city's cemetery zone, extending the length of the inhabited area and then all the way down to Classe, where very large cemeteries contained the tombs of members of the fleet. The oldest cemetery that has been found, dating from the first century AD and continuing in use until the fourth or fifth century, was located on the east side of the *fossa* near the northern port;[120] the *fossa*, constructed just prior to this, is not known to have had bridges connecting its two sides, and seems to have become the delimiting feature between the living and the dead.[121]

Roman tombstones provide us with more information about the inhabitants of the city than we will have for later periods. The 1,302 people who either lived in Ravenna or came from Ravenna are known from the Roman period, mainly from inscriptions.[122] Based on ages recorded on tombstones, A. Donati has calculated that men in Ravenna lived to an average age of 23.40 years, while members of the fleet specifically (58 of the 85 known male epitaphs) had an average age of death of 40.86 years. Women (on the basis of 29 epitaphs) lived an average of 20.55 years. These data are similar to those calculated for other areas of the Roman Empire.[123]

A Third- and Fourth-Century Crisis?

The third century was a period of crisis in the Roman Empire. In addition to a demographic crisis caused by epidemic disease (probably smallpox)

and internal political instability, Italy was beset by external enemies; the
Alamanni invaded in 254 and again in 258–60, and the Jutungi raided in
270–1.[124] From texts we hear little about Ravenna in the third and fourth
centuries. In 238, Maximus Pupienus set up a military base in Ravenna to
deal with his rival Maximinus Thrax, who was besieging Aquileia.[125] The
fourth-century historian Eutropius reports that in 254 "the Germans came
as far as Ravenna," and Jerome also says that rampaging Germans and Alans
came as far as Ravenna in 264.[126] The next historical event recorded for
Ravenna occurred in 304 when Diocletian assumed his ninth consulship
in Ravenna rather than Rome.[127] According to several authors, during the
succession dispute of 306–7 the western *augustus* Severus fled to Ravenna,
where he was captured or killed by Maximian.[128] This scanty evidence shows
that Ravenna at the end of the third century and into the fourth retained
a role in Roman provincial government. We also know that sometime in
the third century Ravenna became the provincial capital of *Flaminia et
Umbria*,[129] and under Diocletian after 297 the province was enlarged to
become *Flaminia et Picenum*, in the diocese of *Italia Annonaria* under the
authority of the *vicarius Italiae* in Milan.[130] However, after Diocletian's
reign and for the rest of the fourth century, there is almost no recorded
evidence of imperial or any other activity in Ravenna.[131]

Ravenna's importance undoubtedly decreased because the Roman navy
suffered in the political and military instability of the third century.[132] Sep-
timius Severus seized the Ravenna fleet on his way to Rome in 193,[133] and
it seems to have been used for various purposes in the early third century,
from transporting troops to battling pirates, but in the later part of the
century it collapsed, or, at least, there is no mention of any fleet from Italy
being involved in any of the invasions, raids, or fighting that was happening
all over the empire in these years. Significantly, inscriptions with names of
members of the navy disappear from Ravenna's cemeteries after the mid–
third century.[134] The Italian fleet did not entirely disappear, and seems
to have been part of the military reorganization undertaken by Diocletian
at the end of the century, but references to Ravenna disappear from both
texts and inscriptions. Scholars debate the reasons for this, whether it was
because of Constantine's establishment of the new capital in Constantinople or attributable to the general provincialization of the army, but in any
case the size and importance of Ravenna's fleet, and thus Ravenna's role
in government, seem to have been sharply reduced by the early fourth
century.[135] Direct evidence for an imperial fleet based at Ravenna comes
only from the *Notitia Dignitatum* of the late fourth or early fifth century,
which names the prefect of the fleet of Ravenna as one of the three naval
commanders of Italy (along with Aquileia and Misenum).[136]

The decline of the fleet had an impact on Ravenna's watercourses also. It is likely that in the third century, either because of the decline of the fleet or as a cause of it, the water systems in Ravenna's surrounding area had not been properly maintained. Given three centuries of subsidence and sedimentation, the result was that the lagoon and the harbor had been drying out and filling with silt. Some evidence of layers of alluvial deposits over the Roman-era structures implies a period of excessive flooding in the areas to the east of the *oppidum* in the later fourth century; at this time habitation ceased at other cities such as Butrium to the north, perhaps because of hydrological changes.[137] By the end of the fourth century, however, the *fossa Augusta* east of the Padenna had gone out of use.[138]

Many Italian cities were in decline in the third and fourth centuries, and Ravenna was no exception; the archaeological material shows a progressive depopulation of the city after the mid–third century, probably as a result of the invasions.[139] A majority of the excavated cemeteries contain burials from before the third century or after the fifth, but not in between.[140] Almost all of the houses excavated both in the *oppidum* and in the areas to the east and north were abandoned in this period, many of them after destruction by fire.[141] Only three sites contain evidence of activity in the later third or fourth century. At Via D'Azeglio in the northwest corner of the *oppidum*, the "House of the Floral Threshold" was burned in the third century but then partially reused in the fourth by an elaborate private bath complex with Christian floor mosaics. The UPIM site east of the *oppidum* along the presumed *fossa Augusta* had mosaics dating to the late third or early fourth century.[142] Finally, the "Palace of Theoderic" provided evidence implying continuous use and a rebuilding of the villa in either the fourth or the early fifth century; if the former date is upheld by further excavation, the building would probably represent the residence of the provincial governor or military commander.[143] Thus, while some activity continued, V. Manzelli goes so far as to say that by the later fourth century Ravenna was a city made up almost entirely of ruins.[144]

Habitation seems to have shifted to the suburban areas, especially around Classe, which shows a measure of prosperity in the third and fourth centuries.[145] As the western part of the lagoon progressively dried up, the focus shifted to its more southern branch, and to the area immediately south of the harbor mouth.[146] Houses excavated there, while smaller than the earlier mansions in and around Ravenna, were still being built and maintained,[147] and in the late fourth century a wall encircled a new urban center. Building material from the former urban core of Ravenna was brought to Classe to be used in this new construction,[148] and, as we will discuss later, the new city became a focus of the earliest Christian community. While trading patterns changed in Ravenna in the third and fourth centuries, trade did not come to a halt. Connections with the Aegean remained important, and the ceramic evidence shows a dramatic increase in imports from North Africa.[149]

Thus, in the fourth century there was still some life in the Ravenna area, and perhaps even a certain level of administrative and commercial wealth, but the city was a shell of what it had been at its height in the second century. The Gallic author Ausonius, writing around 385, does not mention Ravenna in his "List of noble cities," although Rome, Milan, Aquileia, and Capua are described. No one could have foreseen what was to happen in the years after 400.

Ravenna's Christian Origins

In Ravenna as in most cities of the Roman world, Christianity was introduced in the imperial period. Agnellus tells us that the first bishop of Ravenna, Apollinaris, was a disciple of St. Peter and was martyred at the time of the emperor Vespasian (69–79). Agnellus took his information from a text that we know as the *Passio sancti Apollinaris*, which was probably written in the sixth or seventh century.[150] Both the *Passio* and Agnellus tell us that Apollinaris was sent by the apostle St. Peter to Ravenna, began to convert people and perform miracles, was brought before a Roman judge, tortured, and ended his life as a martyr.

Certainly by the mid–sixth century the story of Apollinaris as the first bishop was established in its basic outlines, because at that time a church was built in his honor outside Classe, presumably over his tomb (as noted in Chapter 6). Modern scholars, however, have expressed skepticism about the apostolic origins of Ravenna's Christian community. Archaeological evidence from the cemeteries of Classe shows an identifiable Christian presence only after the late second century. The first bishop of Ravenna to be mentioned in any written text is Severus, who attended the Council of Sardica in 343.[151] Coins found around the tomb in which Apollinaris is thought to have been originally buried date to no earlier than the late second century, and certainly to the mid–third century; the site is generally accepted as the original tomb of the founder-bishop.[152] The tombs of other early bishops that were later endowed with churches were also built outside Classe, indicating the port city's role as the focus of urban life in the third and fourth centuries.[153] It was claimed by F. Lanzoni and A. Testi-Rasponi, on the basis of these churches and Agnellus's statement that "in the basilica of blessed Euphemia which is called *ad Arietem* he [Apollinaris] first performed baptism," that originally the bishop of Ravenna was based in Classe rather than in the city of Ravenna itself.[154] This often-repeated hypothesis cannot be sustained on the basis of Agnellus's statements, especially since there were two churches dedicated to St. Euphemia, and the one called *ad Arietem* was in the *oppidum* itself. A Christian focus in Classe is certainly possible, however, given the state of Ravenna and Classe in the third and fourth centuries.[155] Attempts to establish dates for the eleven bishops who, according to Agnellus, preceded Severus are speculative; it is likely that some of the bishops in the series listed by Agnellus were invented, perhaps in the sixth century when the episcopal chronology was being established, or perhaps by Agnellus himself.[156]

While we are told by Agnellus (almost our only source) that Christians were living in Ravenna in the Roman period, he does not describe any church construction there until the early fifth century. The first structure that he mentions is the chapel of St. Pulio, "not far from the gate which is called the *porta Nova*," built about the year 400.[157] The large house excavated at the north side of the Via D'Azeglio site, richly redecorated in the third and fourth centuries with mosaics that could contain Christian symbolism, lies just to the south of the location of the church of St. Euphemia, perhaps the one identified by Agnellus as *ad Arietem* and said to be the location of Apollinaris's first baptisms in Ravenna. J. Baldini Lippolis notes that there might be some kernel of truth to the idea that an early Christian place of worship in the city was located here.[158] But other than Severus, we know nothing about the bishops or other personalities of the church of Ravenna before the arrival of the imperial court in 402.

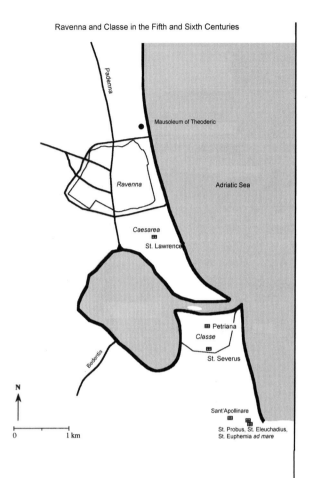
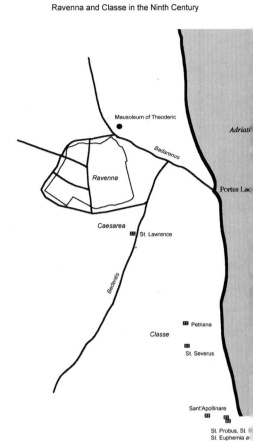

Ravenna and Classe in the Fifth and Sixth Centuries

Padenna

Mausoleum of Theoderic

Ravenna

Adriatic Sea

Caesarea

St. Lawrence

Bedentis

N

0   1 km

Petriana

Classe

St. Severus

Sant'Apollinare

St. Probus, St. Eleuchadius,
St. Euphemia *ad mare*

Ravenna and Classe in the Ninth Century

Mausoleum of Theoderic

Badarenus

Adriati

Ravenna

Portus Lac

Caesarea

St. Lawrence

Bedentis

Petriana

Classe

St. Severus

Sant'Apollinare

St. Probus, St.
St. Euphemia a

6. Map showing
Ravenna, Classe,
and the Adriatic
coastline in the
fifth, sixth, and
ninth centuries

CHAPTER THREE

RAVENNA AND THE WESTERN EMPERORS, AD 400–489

Shortly after the year 400, the western Roman emperors moved their base of operations from Milan to Ravenna. An imperial residence was established there, new walls were built to surround an essentially new city, a mint was established, and infrastructure and institutions were created in order to make them commensurate with the city's new status. The bishop of Ravenna was made a metropolitan with authority over fourteen churches in the region, a dramatic promotion in the Church hierarchy, and the prestige of the ecclesiastical see was enhanced by the episcopacy of the famous Peter Chrysologus. The first half of the fifth century saw a building boom in Ravenna; the structures that have survived are primarily churches, but residential, commercial, military, and other structures were also built in the region surrounded by the new walls. No other Italian city saw growth on this scale in the fifth century; Ravenna stands out as an anomaly, a true disembedded capital.

The Last Century of the Western Roman Empire

The emperor Diocletian (284–305) reformed the administration of the Roman state at the end of the third century; among his many innovations, his decision to divide the empire into eastern and western halves, and to divide its administration among several capital cities, would have lasting consequences for Ravenna. In 324 Constantine reunited the two halves of the empire and established his capital in the new eastern city of Constantinople. Milan remained the west's main administrative center, and after Constantine's death the empire was divided again and his western successors ruled from Milan. Rome remained the seat of the Roman Senate and the symbolic heart of the empire, but lacked the permanent presence of the emperors.

41

Ravenna, c. AD 480

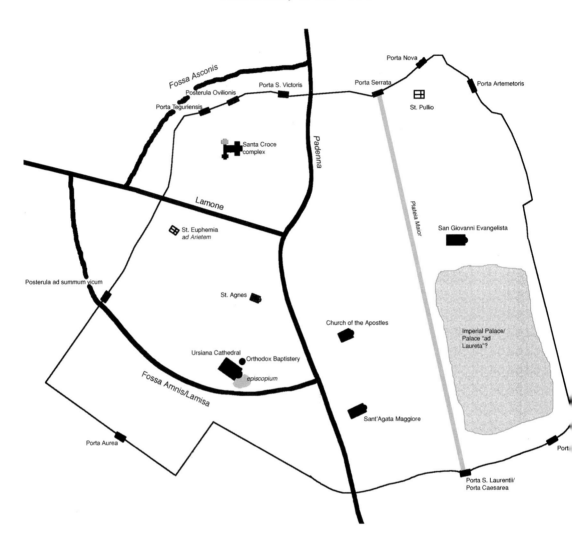

Fossa Asconis

Porta Nova

Porta S. Victoris

Porta Serrata

Porta Artemetoris

Posterula Ovilionis

St. Pullio

Porta Teguriensis

Padenna

Santa Croce complex

Lamone

San Giovanni Evangelista

St. Euphemia ad Arietem

Platela Maior

Posterula ad summum vicum

St. Agnes

Church of the Apostles

Imperial Palace/ Palace "ad Laureta"?

Ursiana Cathedral

Orthodox Baptistery

episcopium

Sant'Agata Maggiore

Porta Aurea

Fossa Amnis/Lamisa

Port

Porta S. Laurentii/ Porta Caesarea

7. Map of
Ravenna,
ca. AD 480

BZC.1948.17.932

8. Gold solidus of Galla Placidia, obverse and reverse, AD 426–30 (courtesy Dumbarton Oaks, Byzantine Collection, Washington, DC)

In 394 the emperor Theodosius I, who had reunited the empire under his sole command, established his son Honorius as emperor in Milan, and his older son Arcadius in Constantinople. Theodosius died in 395, leaving Honorius, age eight, under the guidance of Theodosius's military commander (*magister militum*) and trusted friend Stilicho. The following years were difficult ones for the western empire; the Visigoths, an immigrant group who had been settled in the Balkans in the 370s, were dissatisfied by their treatment while serving as imperial troops and were caught up in the rivalry between leaders at the eastern and western courts. In 402, the Visigoths entered Italy and raided for a year before Stilicho chased them back to Illyria. To do so, he had to pull troops from the borders along the Rhine River, which were breached in 406, and various groups began raiding deeper and deeper into imperial territory. In response, a general named Constantine proclaimed himself emperor in Britain in 407; he moved imperial troops to the continent to defend Gaul from the invaders, and the empire essentially abandoned Britain. Stilicho, in addition to facing the disasters to the north, was also deeply enmeshed in Constantinopolitan politics, and as a result of complex intrigues, in 408 Honorius had him arrested and killed. Subsequently the Visigoths reappeared in Italy, and after attempting to supplant Honorius with a senator named Attalus, in 410 they sacked Rome and then proceeded to Gaul, where they were eventually settled by treaty in the southwestern province of Aquitaine. Other groups, most notably Alans, Sueves, and Vandals, entered Spain in 409, where they began to establish themselves. Constantine and other usurpers continued to challenge central authority until order was restored by Honorius's general Constantius in 413. Italy was left relatively quiet for the last ten years of Honorius's reign; however, imperial authority had been reduced in that short space of time to Italy, North Africa, and part of Gaul.

Honorius is usually portrayed as weak, indecisive, unsuccessful at negotiating with barbarians, and influenced by court favorites. Moreover, he fought with his sister Galla Placidia, one of the most extraordinary women

of her day, subject of both ancient and modern romantic legend. The outlines of her life come from fifth-century chroniclers[1] who also offer intrigu-
ing glimpses into the personality of Galla, although these probably tell us
more about their authors than about the empress herself.[2]

Aelia Galla Placidia was born sometime between 388 and 393, the daughter of Theodosius I and his second wife Galla; she was thus the half sister of
Honorius and Arcadius.[3] She seems to have spent her youth in Italy under
the care of Serena, her cousin and the wife of Stilicho. When Stilicho was
murdered in 408, Serena and Galla Placidia were living in Rome; when the
Visigoths first attacked the city in 409, Serena was accused of conspiring
with the enemy and was executed with Galla Placidia's consent, according to
one source.[4] When the Visigoths sacked Rome in 410, the twenty-year-old
Galla Placidia was taken into custody and carried along with the Visigothic
army into Gaul. As part of a Visigothic pact with Honorius, Galla was married to the Visigothic leader Athaulph in 414 and went with him into Spain,
where she bore him a son who was given the hopeful name Theodosius,
but the child died shortly afterward. Athaulph was assassinated in 416 and
Galla returned to the court of Honorius in Italy, where she was married
(against her will, one source says) to the Roman general Constantius in
417.[5] She bore him two children: Iusta Grata Honoria (b. 417 or 418) and
Valentinian (b. 419). Constantius was made *augustus* in 421, and Galla was
named *augusta*; however, these titles were not recognized by her nephew
the emperor Theodosius II in Constantinople.

Constantius died later in 421, and Galla quarreled with Honorius; in 423
she took her children to Constantinople to seek refuge with Theodosius II.
Honorius died in the same year, leaving no children, and the throne was
seized by a government official, the *primicerius notariorum* John, who had
the support of the Senate and of powerful generals including the Roman
Aetius. The eastern court decided that Galla's son Valentinian was the
rightful emperor, and the youth was betrothed to Theodosius's daughter,
Licinia Eudoxia. Theodosius sent an army headed by the eastern *magister
militum* Ardabur to remove John and place Valentinian on the throne.[6]
Aetius was brought over to Valentinian's side, and Galla took the reins as
regent for her son in 425.

From 425 to 437, Galla was at the forefront of Roman politics, which
remained extremely volatile. Galla was suspicious of, and often opposed to,
the policies of Aetius, and was said to have attempted his assassination; a
conflict among the three main generals of the empire lasted from 426 to
433. Although Aetius eventually triumphed over his rivals, he had to spend
the next twenty years fighting against one revolt or invasion after another.
North Africa was lost to the Vandals between 429 and 439, largely as a
result of this infighting in Italy. Valentinian's marriage to Licinia Eudoxia

was celebrated first at Constantinople and then at Rome in 437, after which he took control of the empire in his own right. After 437 Galla fades from written sources, although it is assumed that she was still influential until her death in 450.

By the late 440s, the Huns had emerged as a new threat to the empire. The Huns had occupied the Hungarian plain in central Europe since the late fourth century, and had been actively involved in imperial politics. Aetius, for example, made extensive use of them as soldiers in the western Roman army, and the eastern empire had alternately fought them and paid them subsidies to prevent them from attacking. In 450, the new eastern emperor Marcian ended the subsidies to the Huns, and their leader Attila turned his army against the western empire. According to several sources, his pretext was a scandal in the imperial family. Iusta Grata Honoria, who had never married, had an affair with her estate manager; when they were discovered, her paramour was executed and she was imprisoned. She wrote to Attila and told him that if he invaded the western empire, she would marry him and he would have half of the empire as her dowry. The entire story is fantastic, but the fact that so many historians repeated it tells us something about late antique attitudes to imperial women and politics.[7] Whatever his motivation, in 451 Attila and his armies invaded Gaul. Aetius formed a coalition that included the Visigoths, and blocked Attila's advance at Chalons. Attila withdrew eastward, but in the following year he took his army directly into Italy. The Huns captured several cities, most notably Aquileia and Milan, but for various reasons Attila was eventually persuaded to withdraw.[8] What Attila might have done next we do not know, but he died unexpectedly in 453 and his federation collapsed, ending the Hunnic threat.

After Galla died in 450, conditions in the empire went from bad to worse.[9] Valentinian, perhaps feeling that he no longer needed his greatest general to defend the empire from the Huns, murdered Aetius in 454. Then he was assassinated in Rome in 455. Valentinian had two daughters, Eudocia and Placidia, who were married, respectively, to the Vandal royal heir Huneric and the Roman senator Olybrius, neither of whom was a serious contender for the imperial throne in 455. (Olybrius finally got his chance in 472, but died shortly after his accession). The Vandals, who had established a kingdom in North Africa, raided Italy and sacked Rome in 455 taking the imperial women back with them upon their return to Africa. The Visigoths aggressively attacked the remaining Roman possessions in Gaul. The imperial throne was occupied by a series of senators and Roman generals, while the eastern emperors sent their own candidates selected from the eastern aristocracy.[10] None reigned for more than four years, as real power was wielded by other generals of less Roman background such as

Ricimer, Gundobad, Orestes, and Odoacer. In the meantime, no one could pay much attention to the Vandals or the Visigoths, nor to the population of Italy, which was all that was left of the empire. After a complex series of events in 474–6, the general Odoacer took control of Italy, but, rather than choosing a Roman to be emperor, he returned the imperial regalia to the emperor Zeno. He proclaimed himself king and *patricius* of the west, and Zeno tacitly accepted his claim. Odoacer set about stabilizing the regions around Italy; he reconquered Sicily from the Vandals by 477, took Dalmatia in 480, defeated the Rugians of Noricum in 487, and allied himself with the Visigoths and Franks. With his borders secure, Odoacer was able to restore some semblance of Roman law and order to Italy, governing (or at least minting coins) in the name of Zeno. He ruled Italy for thirteen years, until Zeno sent the Ostrogoths against him.

Moving the Capital to Ravenna

At the time of the Visigothic invasion of 402, Honorius and his advisers seem to have felt that Milan was too hard to defend, and so the emperor moved to Ravenna; the first imperial decree to have been issued at Ravenna is dated December 6, 402.[11] The year 402 appears in almost every modern account as a pivotal date in Ravenna's history, even though no contemporary authors mention such a transfer in that year.[12] We do know that many of the important events in fifth-century imperial history took place in Ravenna, and some of the emperors spent much of their time there.

    Why Ravenna? The usual answer is that Ravenna's marshy hinterlands made it difficult to attack by land, and as a result armies like the Visigothic army that sacked Rome in 410 left Ravenna alone.[13] Socrates Scholasticus, writing in Constantinople in the late 430s, describes the establishment of Valentinian III on the throne at Ravenna:[14]

> Then again at this crisis the prayer of the pious emperor prevailed. For an angel of God, under the appearance of a shepherd, undertook the guidance of Aspar and the troops which were with him, and led him through the marshy lake [λίμνη] near Ravenna – for in that city the usurper [John] was then residing – and there detained the military chief. Now, no one had ever been known to have forded that lake before; but God then rendered that passable which had hitherto been impassable. Having therefore crossed the lake, as if going over dry ground, they found the gates of the city open, and overpowered the usurper.

According to Socrates it was Ravenna's λίμνη, or marshy lake, that gave it an almost impregnable defense.[15] The defensible nature of Ravenna was mentioned in writings by the sixth-century historians Jordanes and Procopius. Jordanes, describing the fact that Alaric the Visigoth did not attack Ravenna in 408, says, "This city lies amid the streams of the Po between marshes (*paludes*) and the sea, and is accessible only on one side.... But on the west it has marshes through which a sort of door has been left by a very narrow entrance (*uno angustissimo introitu ut porta*)."[16] Procopius, in the *Gothic War*, repeats this description, with a military analysis that has colored all subsequent interpretations:[17]

> This city of Ravenna lies in a level plain at the extremity of the Ionian Gulf, lacking 2 stades [= ca. 380 m] of being on the sea, and it is so situated as not to be easily approached either by ships or by a land army. Ships cannot possibly put into shore there because the sea itself prevents them by forming shoals for not less than 30 stades; consequently the beach at Ravenna, although to the eye of mariners it is very near at hand, is in reality very far away by reason of the great extent of the shoal water. And a land army cannot approach it at all; for the river Po, also called the Eridanus, which flows past Ravenna ... and other navigable rivers together with some marshes (λίμναις), encircle it on all sides and so cause the city to be surrounded by water.

Certainly Ravenna was perceived to be a defensible location, although this may not have actually been the case; in fact Ravenna was repeatedly captured by armies in the fifth and sixth centuries, probably because the marshes were not as defensible as they were perceived to be.[18]

Several scholars have argued that Ravenna was chosen for reasons more complex than a dubious strategic advantage. F. W. Deichmann observed that the development of Ravenna after 402 came soon after the establishment of Constantinople as the permanent residence of the eastern emperors under Theodosius I and Arcadius, rendering sea contact between Italy and the eastern Mediterranean more desirable.[19] Imperial couriers traveling from Rome to Constantinople via Brindisi could make the journey in twenty days, but to be able to depart directly from Ravenna would have reduced the journey time.[20] Communication with the east was particularly important during the reigns of Honorius and Valentinian III, whereas after 455 the emperors were instead dependent on the support of the western army and Rome's Senate, and communication with the east became less significant. Ravenna offered the additional advantage of being easily provisioned, because it was an important part of the maritime network.[21] Alternately, V. Neri has noted that while Milan and Aquileia had been strategically important in the second and third centuries, by the late fourth century the rivalry between Rome and Milan had increased, and Ravenna may have been chosen to promote Rome at the expense of Milan, while Aquileia was rejected as too exposed to attacks from the north and east.[22]

A final reason for the choice of Ravenna may have been the state of the city in the year 402. As noted in the previous chapter, archaeology has shown that by the third century the city seems to have been mostly abandoned in favor of the port city of Classe to the south. V. Manzelli has called what was left a "palimsest" on which the imperial administrators could build an entirely new imperial city, full of relevant public buildings including churches.[23] In this, perhaps, Ravenna may have been rather like Byzantium before Constantine transformed it. Under Theodosius I, Christianity was strongly promoted as the official religion of the empire, and public pagan religious practices were banned. It has been argued that at Constantinople, Constantine constructed a specifically Christian capital city, with a cathedral and palace in close proximity at the city's core.[24] Honorius may have seen Ravenna in the same way, strategically useful and without a strong pagan core, a blank slate on which a new Christian capital could be built. We have no evidence for pagan temples at Ravenna, except for a story that St. Apollinaris destroyed one by his prayers, and that is a *topos* of hagiography rather than necessarily a memory of a historical event.[25] But we do know that in the new imperial Ravenna, the cathedral and the palace formed the two foci of the city.[26]

Ravenna as a Capital

The idea that Ravenna became the capital of the western Roman Empire really only begins with Agnellus, who says that Valentinian III (425–55) "...ordered and decreed that Ravenna should be the head of Italy (*caput Italiae*) in place of Rome."[27] Agnellus's accounts of the building activities of Honorius, Galla Placidia, and Valentinian III promoted a legend that has affected views of Ravenna down to the present. Recently, A. Gillett has presented a detailed analysis of the known residence of emperors in the early fifth century in order to show that despite imperial activity in Ravenna, it was Rome that was viewed by almost everyone as the true center of the empire. The panegyrist Claudian extols Rome as the emperor's "true" home, but no contemporary author ever praises Ravenna in this way.[28] Celebrations of imperial accessions, consulates, and other significant milestones at Rome, Honorius's construction of his mausoleum in Rome, and Valentinian's ultimate transfer of the court to Rome in 450, are for Gillett signs that, even for Honorius, Rome was the symbolic center of the western empire.

And yet, clearly Ravenna did have a special status in the fifth century. While Rome retained its symbolic value as *caput orbis*, Ravenna nevertheless became a *sedes imperii* ("imperial residence") perceived as a place where emperors might live and govern. Indeed, at the end of the century Pope Gelasius, addressing the question of whether the bishop of a *regia civitas* ("regal city") should have a special status, lists Milan, Trier, Ravenna, and Sirmium as imperial residences whose bishops are not otherwise privileged.[29] In the power struggles between Stilicho, the Theodosian dynasty, Ricimer, and different factions of the Roman Senate, the residence of the emperor and court was very significant. Stilicho, Honorius, and Galla Placidia, among others, preferred to keep their distance from Rome and to govern from Ravenna;[30] others, including the adult Valentinian III and various emperors of the Roman senatorial class, preferred to emphasize their connections with Rome. Ravenna was thus deliberately used as an alternative to Rome, and seen as a viable alternative, so the city's physical makeup both reflected and contributed to political rhetoric.[31] Ravenna may not have inspired an Ausonius or a Claudian to extol its merits, but for more than thirty years it served as a main imperial residence and seat of ceremonial, and it is this half century that saw the city's dramatic growth from a ruined town into something with much greater pretensions.

Ravenna as a *sedes imperii*

What was a *sedes imperii* in the Roman world, and how does Ravenna fit the definition?[32] After the third century, the Roman Empire developed a bureaucratic administration that was centralized around the person of the emperor. We know that the imperial bureaucracy in the early fifth century was extensive; just how extensive can be seen from the *Notitia Dignitatum*, a list of civil and military government officials for the eastern and western empires that is thought to have been compiled between 395 and the 420s,[33] exactly at the time that the emperors were resident in Ravenna.[34] Government officials of the central administration include the Praetorian Prefect of Italy, the Masters of Foot and Horse in the Presence, the Praepositus of the Sacred Bedchamber, the Master of the Offices, the Quaestor, the Counts of the Sacred Bounties (taxes and provisioning) and Private Domains, the Counts of the Household Horse and Foot, the Primicerius of the Sacred Bedchamber, the Chief of the Notaries, the *Castrensis* of the Sacred Palace, the Masters of the Bureaus of Memorials, Correspondence, and Requests, and perhaps the Vicar of Italy. Each of the officials had his own staff consisting of accountants, custodians, chiefs of staff, assistants, registrars, secretaries, clerks and subclerks, and notaries. Scholars estimate that the number of government officials who would have been part of the central administration was well over 1,500, not including military personnel.[35]

There is no clear consensus about where all these people lived and worked in the fifth century. It is sometimes stated that the entire administration traveled with the emperor in this period.[36] On the other hand, it seems clear that at least after 395, or even after Constantine, the eastern administration settled down in the palace at Constantinople,[37] and it is sometimes assumed that a similar establishment of administration in the West took place at Ravenna, although on a less grandiose scale.[38] You can't put a 1,500-person bureaucracy in a place that does not have buildings to accommodate them; and since, in the case of Ravenna, this accommodation had to be built up from scratch, the emperors must have intended to live there for a good part of the time. It is likewise often assumed that all government officials served in Ravenna, yet the only secure evidence for this are a few imperial rescripts addressed to officials there. C. Pietri and J. Matthews have shown that officials who held the highest offices, who often came from the great Roman senatorial families, lived in Ravenna only during their terms of office.[39] However, these studies consider only a handful of men for whom we have information; in this period there is no evidence from inscriptions or documents that can tell us about lower level functionaries. Pietri concludes that while cultivated aristocrats spent some time in Ravenna, they did not make it into an intellectual center, although they did stimulate the production of luxury goods such as marble sarcophagi and carved ivory in this period.[40] Aristocratic houses such as the one found at the site at Via D'Azeglio, show that the city had a population of wealthy and important people,[41] and estimates of its population range from 5,000 to 10,000, a reasonable size, although only a fraction of the population of Rome.[42] As we can see by looking at any modern capital in which some government officials come and go based on their terms of office, a fairly large base of career bureaucrats and people involved in services creates a lively urban community, as we can see from Sidonius Apollinaris's satirical description of Ravenna:[43]

> ...the sick promenade while the doctors lie abed, the baths freeze while the houses burn, the living are thirsty while the buried swim, thieves are vigilant while the authorities sleep, the clergy lend money while the Syrian merchants sing psalms, businessmen fight while soldiers do business, the elderly apply themselves to ballgames, the youths to dice, the eunuchs to weapons, the federate troops to letters...

For now we can only surmise that this is what existed in fifth-century Ravenna.[44]

We may know relatively little about the people who lived and worked in Ravenna, but we know more about its physical topography, which can be compared with the layout of other similarly ranked cities of the late third and fourth centuries, most notably Constantinople and Milan.[45] In Constantine's new capital, the main governmental buildings were constructed adjacent to the cathedral and the imperial palace, which was also flanked by a large circus, the Hippodrome. Colonnaded streets connected this core area with the rest of the city, punctuated by fora, baths, and monuments.[46] Protected on three sides by water, the city's land limit was walled by Constantine, and new walls enclosing a much larger area were built during the reign of Theodosius II. Milan had a similar layout: originally a provincial capital and prosperous trading center, with the arrival of the imperial court new walls, palaces, and other structures were built. The late fourth-century poet Ausonius, who compiled a series of poems in honor of the great cities of the empire, lists for Milan walls, a circus, a theater, temples, a palace, a mint, baths, porticoes, and statues.[47] Churches, although not mentioned by Ausonius, were a major component of both Milan's and Constantinople's topography. These features were found in various combinations also in other imperial cities of the period.

Inside Ravenna's new walls, at least some of these facilities must have been constructed in the first half of the fifth century. The transformation did not happen overnight, and its chronology is unclear. Many survivals are fragmentary and without context, for example a sculpted torso made of porphyry, part of a statue of an emperor imported from Constantinople, whose original location is unknown.[48] Agnellus implies that most of the work was carried out under Valentinian III and perhaps especially during the regency of Galla Placidia,[49] and this information is repeated in most current histories of imperial Ravenna. This does not really make sense, given that Honorius is said to have lived in the city for almost twenty years; certainly some, even much, of the construction that turned Ravenna into an imperial city must have been begun during his reign.[50] The main elements for which we have textual, archaeological, and architectural evidence are the city walls, the palace(s), the mint, and churches, and we will consider each of these in turn.

It is often observed that in Ravenna the emperors were particularly inspired by the city of Constantinople. We will examine individual pieces of evidence for this, but here it should be pointed out that almost all of our written evidence dates to after 550. Constantinople remained a model for Ravenna's leaders for two centuries, and we cannot say precisely when most of the Constantinopolitan epithets were applied.[51] Moreover, although many features in Ravenna are assumed to imitate lost Constantinopolitan originals, we must also recognize that Ravenna was not simply a pale imitation of the eastern capital, but a place in which new ideas and elements were introduced into the imperial repertoire.

The City Walls of Ravenna

The urban topography of Ravenna from the late antique period to the present has been defined by a set of walls that were built sometime in the fourth or fifth century (Fig. 7).[52] The republican walls of Ravenna had enclosed a rectangular space of approximately 33 hectares, although in the first and second centuries AD habitation had spread beyond these limits and the walls themselves were ruined, at least in places.[53] The new walls, many parts of which are still preserved today, form a circuit 4.5 km long and enclose an area of 166 hectares.[54] The construction of this wall was an extraordinary event for this period in northern Italy. In every other case that we know, cities were shrinking; Ravenna is the only city in which a new wall circuit enclosed a much larger area than its predecessor.[55] Agnellus tells us of Valentinian III:[56]

> ... here and there on each side he adorned the streets of the city with great walls, and he ordered iron bars to be enclosed in the bowels of the wall. And so great was his care that the iron bars not only appeared ornamental, but also if at some time some other people should want to threaten this city, and if not as many weapons could be found as were needed, from these bars arrows and lances and even swords could be made; or, as we said, the walls would supply the iron for some other purpose. He added much to this wall of the city [*civitas*], where formerly it had been girded as merely a town [*oppidum*]. And this emperor made great what was smaller in former times, and he ordered and decreed that Ravenna should be the head of Italy in place of Rome. ...

Agnellus's account has been the basis of the interpretation of the topographical development of Ravenna; however, there has been, and continues to be, considerable controversy about the date(s) of construction of this wall circuit.

A. Testi-Rasponi, as part of his 1924 edition of Agnellus's text, proposed that an original Roman core, *Ravenna quadrata*, which corresponds to what we have been calling the republican *oppidum*, was supplemented several times, once during the reign of Valentinian III, and once by Odoacer in the later fifth century.[57] Testi-Rasponi's map is still sometimes reproduced in studies of the city. It is only in the past two decades that scholars have seriously questioned this view, and only very recently that the question of the wall's purpose and its relationship to Ravenna's expansion in the early fifth century has been explored.

N. Christie and S. Gibson's study of the masonry of the surviving parts of the walls indicated that the expanded wall circuit was built at one time, not in several stages as proposed by Testi-Rasponi.[58] This proposal has been accepted by many subsequent scholars.[59] Christie concludes that Ravenna's imperial defenses stood 9 meter high and were approximately 2.2 meter thick, which would make them lower than the walls of Verona, Milan, and Rome at this time. The circuit included several towers, fourteen main gates, and more than thirty posterns including openings for waterways, all built as part of the original plan.[60] In the course of this new work, Claudius's arch was flanked by round towers and incorporated into the wall system, and was subsequently known as the Porta Aurea, or "Golden Gate."[61] The walls were made mostly of reused bricks,[62] not surprising given that the city's landscape was littered with ruins.[63]

What remains a mystery is exactly when these walls were built: were they built because the court had moved there, or did the court move there because the walls were already built? Christie accepts Agnellus's attribution of the walls to the reign of Valentinian III (425–55). One reason he gives for this dating is the similarity of the bricks in the wall to those used to construct San Giovanni Evangelista and the Santa Croce complex, but Christie admits that the similarities are not secure enough for precise dating, and Gelichi states instead that the bricks are in fact rather different; moreover, in all three cases, most of the bricks were reused from earlier Roman structures.[64] Christie argues that in the years after 402, many new buildings had been built and needed to be defended; he suggests that the Vandal threat of 439 might have been the catalyst.[65] This seems very strange. Surely 402 was a very dangerous time in Italy; how could Honorius build a palace, mint, military barracks, and other sensitive structures in an unwalled area? Only recently have some scholars noted the contradiction that although the reason given for the court's move from Milan to Ravenna is security, the city is not thought to have had functioning walls until 30 years afterward. P. Fabbri is one of the few to have suggested that the expanded wall circuit was built earlier, in the fourth or even the third century, and that its presence was the reason that the court moved to Ravenna in 402,[66] while S. Gelichi says that large walls were built anticipating the need for many government buildings after the transfer of the imperial capital.[67]

All of these hypothetical suggestions are put forward because of the relative lack of either textual or archaeological evidence for Ravenna's walls. Fabbri cites, as evidence that Ravenna already had walls under Honorius, Claudian's panegyric on Honorius's sixth consulship, delivered in 404, in which Honorius "...spoke, and moved his standards from the walls of ancient Ravenna...."[68] In addition, the fifth-century historians Zosimus and Sozomen mention the manning of the "walls of Ravenna" by troops from the east in the context of a proposed siege of the city by Attalus and Alaric in 410,[69] while Socrates Scholasticus mentions the city's gates being open when Ardabur's troops took the city in 425. Are "walls" and "gates" simply poetical forms (synecdoche) meaning "city," or do they refer to actual walls? At the least, we can say that these eastern authors were visualizing a city surrounded by walls when describing these strategically important events, and I would argue that the scattered bits of textual evidence do suggest that the "imperial" walls existed by the very early fifth century.[70]

When we turn to archaeology, we encounter further contradictions and differences of interpretation. V. Manzelli shows that archaeology reveals little activity outside of the *oppidum* in the fourth century,[71] although Classe was being developed in this period, and was enclosed by a wall at this time.[72] Why would the inhabitants of Ravenna in the fourth century create a grand circuit wall to enclose ruins? On the other hand, E. Russo and A. Augenti argue that the second construction phase on the site known as the "Palace of Theoderic" should be dated, on the basis of comparison with other villas, to the fourth century. We will discuss the palace in the next section; but if that date is substantiated by further investigation, it would indicate a major public building project sometime in the fourth century, in the heart of what was to become the imperial city. Augenti notes that this must have been an extramural villa because the walls were not built until the mid–fifth century,[73] but in fact the existence of this structure would beg the question of whether walls might have been built to surround it. In the fourth century Ravenna continued to serve as a provincial and perhaps even a military center, and we know nothing of what this might have involved. S. Gelichi notes there is relatively little archaeological evidence for activity within the walls of Ravenna even in the fifth century; he concludes therefore that the walls were built primarily to enclose public buildings rather than to contain inhabited areas.[74]

The date of the walls cannot be determined without additional archaeological investigation. Taken all together, however, the evidence suggests that the walls were not built by Valentinian III, but that Ravenna was fortified shortly before or after 402.

The Watercourses

Ravenna's new topography did not only involve the laying out of a new wall circuit; the hydrology of the site was adapted to the new urban confines. As we have seen, the watery nature of Ravenna was its distinguishing characteristic in ancient literature, and this was to continue for writers of the late Roman Empire.[75] Sidonius Apollinaris, a Gallo-Roman aristocrat who visited Ravenna in 467 on his way to Rome, describes the city in two letters.[76] In the first, which narrates the story of his journey through Italy, he discusses the water supply in various places; he describes the watercourses through Ravenna, in order to complain that none of it was fit to drink. In the second letter, Sidonius describes Ravenna's flies and frogs, a city where "the walls fall, the waters stand, the towers sink, the ships sit....a place that more easily has a territory [*territorium*] than solid ground [*terram*]," in other words, a city of hydraulic instability.[77]

The complex hydrological system of Ravenna, which had contributed to the city's importance as a naval and mercantile center, deteriorated in the fourth and fifth centuries.[78] The subsidence of the ground, to which Ravenna was always subject, was supplemented by the neglect of the water system, particularly the *fossa Augusta*; the separate canal to the east of the Padenna went out of use in this period. It is likely that the *via Popilia*, which had followed the course of the canal, continued in use, becoming the main road through the eastern part of the new city; this road was known as the *platea maior* and is now the Via di Roma (Figs. 1, 7).[79] The water that had once flowed through this canal was diverted elsewhere in the city. In his first letter, Sidonius says of Ravenna:

> ...Above, the two-fold branches of the Po wash around and through the town [*oppidum*]; led away from its main bed by public dykes, through them by diverted channels it divides, diminished, with divided flow, so that part surrounds the walls providing protection, part flows within and provides trade, as convenient an arrangement for commerce as epecially for bringing in provisions...[80]

We have seen that in the Roman period, the Padenna and the Lamone flowed along the north and east sides of the *oppidum*, and the *fossa Lamisa* or *Amnis* passed through the *oppidum* from east to west. Sidonius's description implies that new canals were dug to create a branch of the Padenna flowing around the northwest corner of the new city into the Lamone to provide additional defenses.[81] It is reasonable to assume that this happened at the same time as the walls were built (this channel was later known as the *fossa Asconis*). Ravenna thus would have become a city largely surrounded by water.

The Palace(s)

There was certainly an imperial residence in Ravenna, and whether or not it was called a *palatium* or "palace" at the time, it became known by this name in later periods.[82] The centralization of the government bureaucracy in the fourth century meant that the palace had to house a large staff of officials, and it was the setting for the elaborate ceremonies in which the centrality of the emperor and his government were demonstrated to his subjects.[83] Emperors had sporadically stayed at Ravenna in the third and fourth centuries,[84] so a residence suitable for temporarily housing the court must have existed. The permanent residence of Honorius and then Valentinian III, however, required a more significant set of buildings. There are faint hints in literary texts of the splendor of this structure: two poems written around 443 by Flavius Merobaudes describe depictions of Valentinian III and his family on the walls and ceiling of a palace, perhaps one in Ravenna.[85]

Our only textual evidence for imperial palaces in Ravenna comes from Agnellus, who tells us:

1. Honorius wanted to build a palace in Caesarea, the area between Ravenna and Classe, but his official Lauricius built instead a church dedicated to St. Lawrence (ch. 35); later Agnellus refers to the "Laurentian palace" near the Caesarean gate (*quae est uicina portae Caesarea, relicto Laurenti palatio*), so perhaps a palace was built there too? (ch. 132)

2. Theoderic killed Odoacer in the palace At the Laurel (*in palatio in Lauro*) (ch. 39) – it is also mentioned in two sixth-century chronicles that Odoacer was killed "in Laureto."[86]

3. Valentinian III built a royal hall at the place called At the Laurel (*in loco qui dicitur ad Laureta*). (ch. 40)

These passages tell us that by the sixth century, the palace that was considered to be imperial had the name At the Laurel. This designation probably imitates the name of the palace of Daphné/Δάφνη ("Laurel") in Constantinople, built, according to tradition, by Constantine.[87] In chapter 132 Agnellus distinguishes between the *palatium Laurenti* and the *palatium Theodoricanum* later used by the exarch, implying that they were two distinct structures;[88] however, it is not clear whether the *palatium Laurenti* is the same as the *palatium in Lauro/ad Laureta*, although the similarity of the words has led to modern confusion.

The location of this palace, or of any imperial palace (if indeed Honorius would have inhabited a different one), is entirely conjectural. It has been suggested that the imperial palace must have been located near San Giovanni Evangelista, a church known to have been built by Galla Placidia; it has been suggested that the palace quarter as described by Agnellus must have covered the entire southeastern sector of the city. And it was even suggested, although now discredited, that there was a palace in the northwestern quarter of the city, also built by Galla Placidia.[89] As described in the previous chapter, the only part of the eastern sector of the city to have been subjected to extensive archaeological excavation is the site known as the "Palace of Theoderic," so identified because Theoderic's church, now

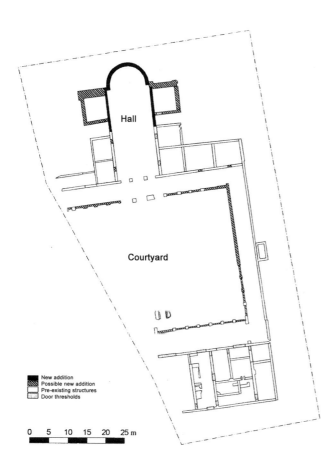

Hall

Courtyard

New addition
Possible new addition
Pre-existing structures
Door thresholds

0   5   10   15   20   25 m

9. Plan of the palace, as known from excavations, ca. AD 450 (after Augenti, "Archeologia e topografia," 2005, fig. 6)

called Sant'Apollinare Nuovo, was attached to it. It is often assumed, based on Agnellus, that this building must have been different from the palace of Valentinian III, and perhaps also of Honorius, which would have been farther to the south. N. Duval goes so far as to argue that the remains found at this site are merely those of an aristocratic house, not an imperial palace.[90] But it is hard to understand why Theoderic and later the exarchs would have preferred to inhabit an old aristocratic house rather than the former imperial palace. Recent studies have shown that on the foundations of a Roman villa there was a major rebuilding in the fourth century, presumably to create the residence of the provincial governor or military commander, followed by another elaboration in the early fifth century (Fig. 9).[91] Another piece of evidence in favor of this interpretation is that the western entrance to the palace is called by Agnellus and other sources "ad Calchi," which probably imitates the Chalke/Χαλκή gate of the Great Palace in Constantinople, built by Constantine. While the date at which this name was applied is uncertain, an attribution to the fifth century is not unlikely.[92]

The excavated area was just part of what must have been a much larger administrative and residential complex, extending presumably to the east, north, and south, and flanked on its western side by the *platea maior*, or main road. The structures that were built or adapted for imperial use on this site in the early fifth century were typical of luxurious villas in the late antique world. A large colonnaded courtyard was flanked by suites of rooms on at least the north and south sides. On the north side the focal point was a large apsed hall, which was increased in size at some point in the fifth century to 27 × 11 m and was paved with a notable *opus sectile* pavement of imported marble. Around and to the south of the courtyard, the corridors and smaller rooms were decorated and redecorated with mosaic pavements; the rooms to the south were eventually turned into a bath complex complete with a hypocaust system.[93] These elements of high-status living probably formed only a part of the palace complex. Since we do not know the full extent of the palace at any period in Ravenna's history, we cannot reach any conclusions about how Ravenna's palace may have compared to those in other imperial capitals.

Other Public Buildings

One of the mysteries of Ravenna in the late imperial period is how much other construction took place within the new city walls. As J. Ortalli has noted, "Popular opinion has it that the transfer of the capital revitalized the city with new buildings and a higher urbanistic level. In reality there is no memory of such a direct initiative by Honorius; when it happened it probably didn't integrate the court functionaries into the local urban network. It guaranteed to the city a good public appearance and maintenance of a certain technological vitality."[94] It is inconceivable that the transfer of administrative functions to Ravenna could *not* have meant an increase in population, but there is almost no archaeological evidence of widespread construction activities in the city. Is this attributable to the nature of archaeological evidence, and of the failure of earlier archaeologists to recognize fifth-century materials? Or did most of the population continue to live in Classe at this time, with only a few imposing public buildings standing in a landscape of ruins? The latter seems impossible to imagine – and yet, that is all the evidence we have.

One of most important structures to be built soon after 402 was the mint. In the Roman Empire, coins could only be minted in specific locations authorized by the emperors; most imperial capitals had a mint (Rome, Trier, Milan, Constantinople, Thessalonike, Nicomedia), as did other major cities such as Aquileia. A mint was opened in Ravenna in 402, an important indication of the city's sudden elevation in rank.[95] Ravenna's mint produced a complete range of gold and silver coins from 402–55, and continued, with some interruptions, straight through to the end of the century and beyond, an indication of importance of Ravenna even after the death of Valentinian III.[96] A mint that produced gold and silver coins required protection. This leads to questions about its location. Agnellus refers twice to a location "at the mint" (*ad monetam*) in the northwest sector of the city.[97] Documents, one from the year 572 and several from the eleventh century and later, name a region of the "golden mint" (*moneta aurea*) as near the palace in the eastern sector of the city.[98] F. W. Deichmann suggested that there must have been two mints in the city, perhaps one (the *moneta aurea*) for gold and silver coins and the other, founded in the late Ostrogothic or Byzantine period, for copper and bronze issues.[99]

In 1969, excavations at the UPIM site at the corner of Via di Roma (the *platea maior*) and Via Mariani, near the presumed entrance to the palace (see Fig. 1) revealed the southeast corner of a large rectangular structure. Very thick exterior walls surrounded a corridor and then an interior core of small rooms that in turn surrounded a courtyard. At least two building phases were identifiable, the latter of which dated to the sixth century. This building has been plausibly identified as the *moneta aurea*, because of its proximity to the palace, and because the thick walls and small interior rooms meet the defensive and production requirements of a mint. In addition, no other large public building is identified from the written sources as having been located in this area.[100]

In other imperial cities such as Rome and Constantinople, an important part of the palace complex inside the city walls was the public racecourse or *circus*.[101] Was a circus built in the city of Ravenna? Evidence for a circus in the imperial period is almost nonexistent. A poem written by Sidonius Apollinaris in the 460s, which describes the emperor's appearance at a circus, almost certainly refers to Rome.[102] The earliest real reference to a circus in Ravenna is found in the Roman *Liber pontificalis* for the 640s, which tells that the head of Maurice, the *cartularius*, was "placed on a pole in the circus at Ravenna as an example to many."[103] Agnellus mentions a *stadium tabulae* outside the city walls to the north, and Deichmann has suggested that this was the location of the city's racetrack.[104] The fact that Agnellus does not mention a circus within the walls is significant, as most monuments and topographical references can be traced back to his text. Beginning in the tenth century, a few documents refer to a *circulum* near the *platea publica* in topographical references for the southeast corner of the city,[105] but none of these later references provide evidence for the date of origin of such an entertainment facility. Perhaps most significant, the Gallic author Salvian, writing in the 440s, contrasts "Roman plebs in the circus, and the people of Ravenna in the theater...."[106] Finally, given what we know of the location of gates, waterways, streets, and churches in fifth- and sixth-century Ravenna, it is difficult to know where a large circus could have been located. All of the circuses built in imperial capitals in the fourth and fifth centuries were over 440 meter long, and most were oriented north–south.[107] M. Johnson's suggestion that a circus was oriented east–west just to the south of the church of Sant'Agata[108] raises the problem that the distance between the Padenna and the *platea maior* at this point was only 350 m; if a circus had been squeezed in here, it would have been an impossibly small one. E. Cirelli, on the other hand, proposes a circus oriented north–south on the west side of the *platea maior*, which could have been 450 m in length.[109] However, all of these proposals are completely hypothetical; in the absence of any archaeological evidence, it is hard to make the case that Ravenna had a circus attached to the imperial palace.

We have even less evidence for other public facilities. With the arrival of the court and the ever-increasing population of the town, another problem was the provisioning of the city and its inhabitants.[110] Sidonius Apollinaris's letter written around 467, after describing the canals around Ravenna, goes on to say, "But the drawback is that, with water all about us, we could not quench our thirst; there was neither intact aqueduct nor filterable cistern, nor gushing spring, nor unclouded well. On the one side, the salt tides assail the gates; on the other, the movement of vessels stirs the filthy sediment in the canals, or the sluggish flow is fouled by the bargemen's poles, piercing the bottom slime."[111] Sidonius seems to be saying that Trajan's aqueduct no longer functioned;[112] whether this was the situation earlier in the century when the emperors still resided in Ravenna, or whether this is a result of the semiabandonment of the city after 450, we have no way of knowing.

Churches

Churches are the one set of buildings for which we have much more sound evidence, since some of them still survive today. In the post-Constantinian era it was expected that Christian emperors would build churches, especially in important cities, and in this one aspect, at least, Ravenna provides plenty of suitable evidence. Major parts of at least five structures from the fifth century still stand and relatively detailed information about others comes to us from texts. Together these structures form an important part of the corpus of early Christian art and architecture, and thus have been extensively studied by art historians for the last 200 years.

One striking feature common to all of these buildings is that, like the city walls, they were made of bricks that had been reused from earlier Roman structures. In addition, they incorporate columns, capitals, and other pieces of architectural sculpture that were likewise taken from earlier monuments. This use of *spolia* is evidence for the ruined state of Ravenna, and for the large amounts of reusable building materials available in 400. Scholars today still debate whether this was simply a question of practicality, or whether the reuse of *spolia* had symbolic meaning, especially of the reappropriation of the Roman past, but most of these discussions are about the Constantinian period.[113] By 400 when Ravenna's churches began to appear, both might have been true: By this time it was expected that a noble church would be built of *spolia*, and in the case of Ravenna, where speed was of the essence and a ruined city lay all around, the use of *spolia* solved several problems at once.

Churches in the Honorian Period

There must have been some churches in Ravenna before the arrival of the imperial court, but of those we have only vague references. However, for the period after 400, we have ever more certain evidence for the construction of churches sponsored by the emperors and by others, most notably the bishops. The cathedral and baptistery complex, begun soon after 400, will be considered in detail below. It should be noted here that while there is no evidence of imperial patronage of the cathedral, it is not unlikely that Honorius and his family materially assisted the construction and decoration of these buildings, as they are known to have done in Rome.

The only church specifically attributed to the reign of Honorius was dedicated to St. Lawrence, the deacon of the Church of Rome who, according to tradition, was martyred in 258. Lawrence became the object of widespread devotion in the late fourth and fifth centuries,[114] and was particularly promoted by the Theodosian dynasty.[115] The early date of this church is confirmed by a reference to it in a sermon by Augustine of Hippo delivered about 425.[116] As usual, Agnellus is our main source for the existence of this church in Ravenna. He tells us that Honorius wanted to build a palace to the south of Ravenna, and he commissioned his *maior cubiculi* Lauricius to supervise it, but the pious Lauricius took the money and built instead a church dedicated to St. Lawrence. Honorius was angry that his orders had been disobeyed, but a vision of St. Lawrence induced him to overlook this misappropriation of funds.[117] The extramural church, built in an existing cemetery, was a martyrial basilica that was used for funerary purposes, thus it functioned like the fourth-century basilica of St. Lawrence outside

Rome.[118] Lauricius himself was eventually buried in a chapel dedicated to Sts. Stephen, Gervase, and Protase, martyrs whose veneration was particularly promoted in the years around 400.[119] Agnellus quotes the dedicatory inscription of the chapel that says that "Lauricius dedicated this on September 29, in the 15th year of Theodosius [II] and Placidus Valentinian [III]," thus in the year 435.[120] Agnellus also tells us of another inscription commemorating one Opilio,[121] who generously supported the church and was buried in the south aisle. The church of St. Lawrence was demolished in 1553 and its building components were taken to various other churches; from the little surviving documentary evidence it seems to have been a basilica with a nave and aisles separated by rows of twelve or fifteen columns, but beyond that we know nothing about its exact location or appearance.[122]

Galla Placidia's Churches

Galla Placidia's chief claim to fame in Ravenna was her support of the Church and her patronage of churches. An active promoter of religious orthodoxy, along with Theodosius II and his sister Pulcheria in the east, she supported the Church at a time when heresies about the nature of Christ were flourishing, and she wrote to Theodosius II and Pulcheria in support of Pope Leo I's position at the Second Council of Ephesus in 449.[123] She was closely connected with various popes; she had been actively involved in a schism involving the papacy in 418–19,[124] and it is possible that she gave her palace in Constantinople to the popes, since in the seventh and eighth centuries their residence in Constantinople is called the "house of Placidia."[125] She contributed to decoration and renovation at the basilica of St. Paul Outside the Walls and Santa Croce in Gerusalemme in Rome.[126] Galla's piety is also highlighted in the biography of St. Germanus of Auxerre, an ascetic bishop from France who visited the imperial court on business and died while in Ravenna in the 430s or 440s.[127] Her coins, minted first in Constantinople and then in Ravenna, Aquileia, and Rome, depict her in imperial costume, with the monogram of Christ prominently embroidered on her shoulder, and, in some cases, the Hand of God holding a crown over her head, while on the reverse a personification of Victory holds a jeweled cross (Fig. 8). These motifs were derived from the coinage of the eastern emperors, first used for Theodosius II and his sister Pulcheria shortly after 420.[128]

Agnellus makes Galla the star of his section on imperial Ravenna, chiefly because of her patronage of the Church. She is credited with the construction of the major churches of Santa Croce and San Giovanni Evangelista in

Ravenna, and Agnellus says that her niece also built a chapel dedicated to St. Zacharias. Galla also gave precious objects to the church of Ravenna, such as a large lamp with her image on it and a chalice.[129] Her portrait, along with images of her children, could still be found in San Giovanni Evangelista in the ninth century. She was a major supporter of one of Ravenna's most notable bishops, Peter Chrysologus (ca. 431–50), and Agnellus erroneously credits a church dedicated to Sts. John the Baptist and Barbatian to Galla's and Chrysologus's joint patronage.[130] As we have seen, Agnellus attributes the construction of the walls and palaces of Ravenna to Valentinian III, which would also have been sponsored by Galla.

Some of the churches built by Galla Placidia still survive, and are thus extremely important for an understanding of the development of art and architecture in Ravenna at this time. As we will see, the form and decoration of these structures expressed new iconographies developed to link Christianity and imperial rule. The use of imperial portraits in church decoration was something new, reminding the community of God's protection of imperial dynasty and empire. This iconography would be repeated in other churches in Ravenna, literally creating a Christian capital through the images found on its churches.

SAN GIOVANNI EVANGELISTA

During a sea voyage the ship carrying Galla Placidia and her two children was beset by a storm.[131] The empress cried out to St. John the Evangelist for protection, vowing to build him a church in Ravenna if the ship was spared. Upon her return to Ravenna, she built this church, near to the small harbor in the northeast corner of the city, and arranged to have it decorated with mosaics that told the story of her preservation and glorified the imperial dynasty of which she and her children were a part.[132] We do not know exactly when the church was built, but it was probably shortly after Galla and her children had taken triumphant control of Ravenna in 425.

San Giovanni Evangelista still stands, in large part rebuilt after it was accidentally bombed by Allied forces in World War II (who were aiming at the nearby train station), and, like all the churches of Ravenna, it was redecorated and rebuilt several times in its history: the floor was raised and repaved in 1213,[133] and the nave arcade and walls were raised in the fifteenth century.[134] The church was the object of extensive restorations from 1919–21, and after the bombing during World War II, further investigation was carried out as part of the reconstruction. The original wall decoration had been removed in 1568, but written descriptions have allowed scholars to reconstruct something of what it might have looked like, and we can therefore see how it fits with Galla's general aims and intentions as empress.

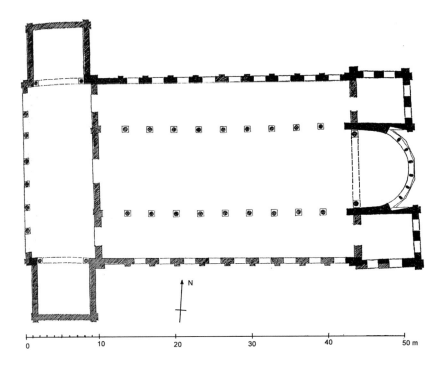

N

10. San
Giovanni Evan-
gelista, plan of
the early fifth-
century phase
(after Gross-
mann, 1964,
fig. 2)

San Giovanni Evangelista is a basilica made almost entirely of reused
Roman materials: brick for the walls, and first- to fourth-century columns
and their bases and Corinthian capitals to separate the nave from the
aisles.[135] The original building (Fig. 10) had an interior colonnade of nine
columns on each side; newly carved impost blocks (truncated pyramidal stone blocks) were placed between each capital and the springing of
the arcade. The upper parts of the walls are later construction, but they
originally contained windows both on the exterior aisle walls and on the
clerestory walls above the nave arcade, resulting in an unusually brightly lit
interior.[136] When first built, the church was entered through a narthex that
was 9 meters deep; north and south of the narthex were small chambers,
approximately 7 × 6.5 meters, entered from the narthex through arches supported by columns. Rooms like this are well known from Greek churches
built at the same time.[137] Their location is similar to the chapels/mausolea
at the ends of the narthex of Santa Croce, and Agnellus mentions someone who was buried in the eighth century "in the corner of the entrance-
way" of San Giovanni Evangelista, which might refer to a side chamber.[138]
The narthex opened to the exterior through a colonnade composed of six
columns, and probably contained three doorways into the church, one for
the nave and one for each of the aisles.

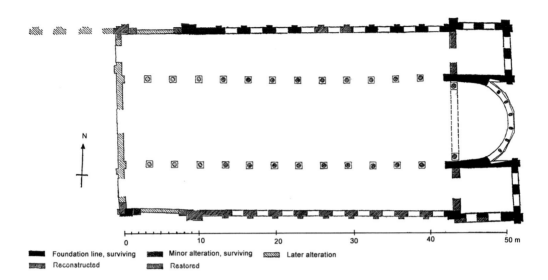

Foundation line, surviving **Minor alteration, surviving** **Later alteration**
Reconstructed **Restored**

At some point the narthex was absorbed into the nave, which was elongated to its present dimensions with twelve columns on each side; at this time an atrium was added and the side chambers were removed (Fig. 11).[139] No distinction can be made between the original eighteen columns and the six that were added; all twenty-four impost blocks were made at one time in the fifth century. The impost blocks (and the columns and capitals) of the westernmost three bays of the nave must therefore have been part of the original church, and Grossmann has suggested that they were used originally in the narthex.[140] The date of this modification is the subject of controversy. It has been suggested that the plan was changed shortly after its original construction, or that it was modified when new mosaics were installed around 600.[141] However, R. Farioli points out that Agnellus refers in the ninth century to the narthex of this church, and thus it is most likely that the changes should be dated to the tenth or eleventh century, at the time of the construction of the campanile to the southeast of the narthex.[142]

The eastern end of the nave terminated in an apse of the same width, circular on the interior and polygonal (seven-sided) on the exterior, as was to become traditional for Ravenna's churches. Inside the apse, a bench for the clergy, with a throne for the bishop at the center, was attached to the interior wall, terminated at each end by columns that upheld the triumphal arch over the apse.[143] The apse was vaulted with a semidome made of *tubi fittili*, interlinked hollow clay tubes, but the layout of the windows below the vault is also the subject of debate.[144] The current apse,

11. San Giovanni Evangelista, plan of the modified church, seventh–tenth centuries (after Grossmann, 1964, fig. 3)

rebuilt in the 1940s (Fig. 12), contains seven windows that are 2.75 meters high, immediately below the level of the springing of the dome; these windows are separated by double-colonnettes, flooding the apse with light. The colonnettes date stylistically to the fifth century and came from the Proconnesian workshops of Constantinople, which implies that this feature was original to the building, although it has also been proposed that the seven-arch feature had been a loggetta that articulated the wall surface only on the exterior of the building.[145] Below these windows the outlines of three smaller windows, now filled in, can be seen along the back wall of the apse; either these were a lower row of windows–or they were the original windows, with the upper zone added later. Since no other surviving apse from Ravenna has a feature like the seven-arched opening, neither windows nor loggetta, and since in all other cases the apse windows are taller than the lower triple array, we can only conclude that the original arrangement in San Giovanni was unique, whichever form it took.

The apse was flanked by two rectangular chambers that were entered from the aisles; they measure 5 × 6 meters, and each of their external walls contains two arched windows approximately 1.5 meters wide and 2 meters high. Below the level of the windows, the interior northern, eastern, and southern walls each contain two niches 1 × 1.25 meters and 0.56 meters deep. These rooms are often called *pastophorie*, a term that refers to spaces with particular liturgical functions during the Eucharistic service, but these rooms cannot have had this function, since they did not communicate directly with the apse. J. Smith has presented evidence that the northern chamber, at least, had a hypocaust, or wall-heating, system in it, and suggests that these spaces were used as libraries. As she notes, such side chambers flanking the apse were known from many churches in Ravenna, but in each case the function or functions were different.[146]

St. John is the only evangelist who frequently had churches dedicated to him in late antiquity. Revered as the author of the Gospel of John and the Book of Revelation, biographies of him began to circulate in the early fifth century, and included references to his connection with sea travel and storms. John's burial site at Ephesus in Asia Minor was marked by a fourth-century church, and another church in his honor existed by the time of Theodosius I in the suburb of Constantinople known as the Hebdomon, near a harbor and an imperial palace.[147] Deichmann asserts, on the basis of a few later topographical references, that San Giovanni Evangelista was built near the imperial palace in Ravenna.[148] But, while the eastern zone of the city certainly contained buildings that were part of the administrative complex, there is no evidence that San Giovanni Evangelista was in any way a "palace church," as it is often called.[149]

12. San Giovanni Evangelista, interior view

One reason for its attribution as a palace church is the apse mosaics, in which portraits of Christian emperors featured prominently. The mosaics no longer survive, but descriptions of them are found in Agnellus, in two sermons from the fourteenth century written on the occasion of the rededication of the church, and in Rossi's *Historiarum Ravennatum*.[150] The two reconstructions most often reproduced are those of C. Ricci and G. Bovini, which differ mainly in their ideas about the original window arrangement; Ricci's inclusion of a seven-arched opening has been followed here (Fig. 13).[151] The wall above the arch featured a depiction of Christ giving a book (probably the Book of Revelation) to John the Evangelist, surrounded by the glassy sea and the seven candlesticks mentioned in Revelation, and flanked by palm trees.[152] Connected with this image was the inscription, "For the love of Christ the noble St. John, son of thunder, saw mysteries."[153] On either side of this image, or perhaps below it, appeared ships sailing on the sea, perhaps with Galla Placidia and her family in at least one of them, being saved by St. John, with the inscription, "Galla Placidia fulfils her vow on behalf of herself and all of these."[154]

Associated with the triumphal arch were images of ten emperors, perhaps busts in medallions. Rossi's and Bovini's drawings place them on the facade of the triumphal arch, but the textual descriptions do not support this interpretation. Surviving sixth-century examples of such series of medallions, including several in Ravenna, are found on the soffit of the arch, and that is where they have been placed in this reconstruction.[155] Rossi lists them: on the right, Constantinus, Theodosius, Arcadius, Honorius, and Theodosius *nep.*; on the left, Valentinianus [I], Gratianus, Constantius [III ?], Gratianus *nep.*, and Johannes *nep.* These figures link imperial rule, and Galla's family members in particular, to orthodoxy; notably, emperors whose orthodoxy was questionable, such as Valens, Valentinian II, and Constantius II, were not depicted.[156] The epithet *nep.* is probably Rossi's misreading of *NP*, the abbreviation for *nobilissimus puer*, a title bestowed upon imperial children; these boys may have been deceased sons of Theodosius I,[157] or perhaps Theodosius *nep.* was the son of Galla Placidia by Athaulph.[158] Deichmann supposes that Rossi may have gotten some of the names wrong, either because of his source or because they were degraded with time.[159] In any case, the main male rulers of the Christian empire are obviously the focus of this series.

In the apse itself, the semidome contained a large image of Christ seated on a throne holding an open book in his hand that contained a quote from Matthew 5:7, "Blessed are the merciful, for God will show mercy to them."[160] Christ was surrounded by twelve books representing the apostles; this is an extraordinary concept that is not known from any other apse image, although Gospel books in bookshelves do appear in the St. Lawrence mosaic in the "mausoleum of Galla Placidia," dating to exactly the same period. Below the dome, probably just above the window level around the interior of the apse, was the main dedicatory inscription:[161]

> The empress Galla Placidia with her son Emperor Placidus Valentinian and her daughter Empress [Iusta] Grata Honoria fulfil their vow to the holy and most blessed apostle John the Evangelist for their deliverance from danger at sea.

Symbols of the evangelists may have flanked the windows. Below the windows ran another inscription from Psalm 67(68):29–30: "Confirm, O God, that which you have wrought for us; from your temple in Jerusalem, kings shall offer you gifts."[162] Below this, on the wall above the clergy's bench, were shown on the right Theodosius II and his wife Eudocia, and on the left Arcadius and his wife Eudoxia. The depiction of these eastern rulers in such a prominent position underscored the western court's relationship with the east. Given the inscription above their heads, it is possible that they were shown in the act of presenting something to Christ or to the central figure on this wall, Bishop Peter I Chrysologus, who was depicted celebrating mass in the presence of an angel.[163]

As far as we know, San Giovanni Evangelista is the first church anywhere to contain imperial portraits as part of its decoration.[164] San Giovanni Evangelista's entire decorative program emphasizes the piety of the

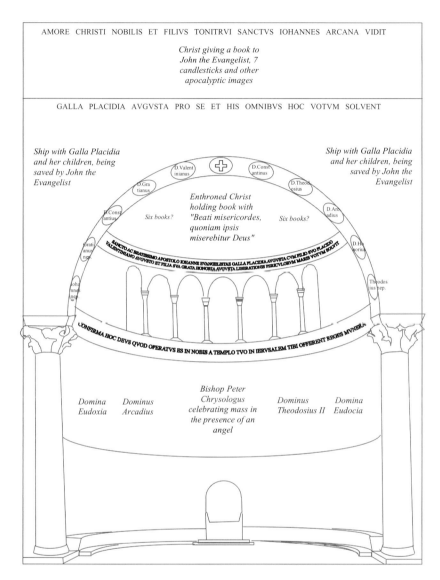

AMORE CHRISTI NOBILIS ET FILIVS TONITRVI SANCTVS IOHANNES ARCANA VIDIT

Christ giving a book to
John the Evangelist, 7
candlesticks and other
apocalyptic images

GALLA PLACIDIA AVGVSTA PRO SE ET HIS OMNIBVS HOC VOTVM SOLVENT

Ship with Galla Placidia
and her children, being
saved by John the
Evangelist

Ship with Galla Placidia
and her children, being
saved by John the
Evangelist

D.Valent inianus

D.Const antius

D.Gra tianus

D.Theod osius

Enthroned Christ
holding book with
"Beati misericordes,
quoniam ipsis
miserebitur Deus"

D.Const antius

Six books?

Six books?

D.Arc adius

grati anus nep.

SANCTO AC BEATISSIMO APOSTOLO IOHANNE EVANGELISTAE GALLA PLACIDIA AVGVSTA CVM FILIO SVO PLACIDO VALENTINIANO AVGVSTO ET FILIA SVA GRATA HONORIA AVGVSTA LIBERATIONIS PERICVLORVM MARIS VOTVM SOLVIT

D.Ho norius

Ioha nnes nep.

Theodos ius nep.

CONFIRMA HOC DEVS QVOD OPERATVS ES IN NOBIS A TEMPLO TVO IN IERVSALEM TIBI OFFERENT REGES MVNERA

Bishop Peter
Chrysologus
celebrating mass in
the presence of an
angel

Domina
Eudoxia

Dominus
Arcadius

Dominus
Theodosius II

Domina
Eudocia

13. San Gio-
vanni Evange-
lista, reconstruc-
tion diagram of
the mosaics of the
triumphal arch
and apse

imperial dynasty and its connections to God and the Orthodox Church. All
of the inscriptions emphasize the role of kings in the divine plan; even the
book held by the enthroned Christ in the apse quotes the Beatitude of particular relevance to rulers, emphasizing compassion and charity by those
in positions of power. The very depiction of Christ on a throne underscores the parallelism between the earthly and heavenly rulers. Bishop Peter
Chrysologus, as we will see, was closely connected with the imperial court,
and he specifically praises Galla Placidia for her mercy (*misericordia*) in his
Sermon 130.[165]

The construction of a church in commemoration of the salvation of Galla and her children underscored God's protection of the dynasty, represented by the portraits of its members. At this particular moment, Galla's triumph over the usurper John, she reminded the members of the Roman elite establishment of her divine claims to power and of the support of the rulers in the eastern empire.[166]

SANTA CROCE

In addition to San Giovanni Evangelista, Agnellus tells us that Galla Placidia built a church dedicated to the Holy Cross, and he notes a tradition that she prayed there at night, prostrate on the porphyry pavement, by the light of candles.[167] The church was built in the northwest part of the new city, on top of Roman houses that had been in ruins since the third century AD.[168] It retained its original form until the later Middle Ages; in the late fouteenth century the north–south arms and the chancel were removed, in the late sixteenth century the narthex was destroyed, and in 1602, 7 meters of the western end of the nave was destroyed to make way for a street now named Via Galla Placidia.[169] Parts of the church are still visible; it was extensively excavated in the early twentieth century, in 1967–80 and in the 1980s–90s, and so the history of the site and its construction stages are well understood.[170]

The church dedicated to the Cross was built of reused Roman bricks; the exterior of the walls were articulated with pilasters and perhaps blind arcades, as have survived for the southern chapel. Unique in Ravenna, the church has a ground plan in the form of a Latin cross, with a single aisleless nave (11.20 m wide), wide transepts to the north and south, and a rectangular chancel (Fig. 14).[171] The individual parts of the church do not follow a strict rectilinear design; the angles of various parts of the walls are quite skewed, especially ends of the crossarms. In plan, the building is very similar to other cross-shaped churches built in capital cities, especially the *Basilica Apostolorum* and the *Basilica Virginum* (now San Simpliciano) in Milan, both built by Ambrose in the late fourth century on the model of Constantine's Church of the Apostles in Constantinople.[172] We know that the cross-ground plan was symbolically important; Ambrose wrote a poem about the *Basilica Apostolorum* in Milan that says, "The temple has the form of a cross, the temple stands for Christ's victory, the triumphal, sacred image marks the place."[173] The churches in Milan and Constantinople were, however, dedicated to the Apostles;[174] the adoption of this form for a church dedicated to the Holy Cross was a new and creative idea, and, as we will see, the iconography of the cross was given a variety of expressions in the Santa Croce complex.

Excavations have shown that the rectangular chancel was raised 0.26 meters above the floor level of the rest of the church, creating a platform

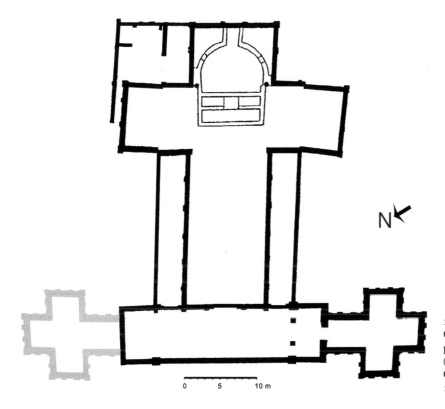

N

0   5   10 m

14. The Santa
Croce com-
plex, ca. AD 450
(adapted from
Gelichi/Novara,
1995, fig. 3a)

(*bema*),[175] that there was a semicircular bench (*synthronon*) around the interior of the rectangular chancel,[176] as well as a raised pathway (*solea*) along
the nave leading to the pulpit (*ambo*). All of these features show the influence of Constantinopolitan architectural/liturgical trends.[177] The chancel was surrounded by additional rooms, some of which may have been
open courtyards, directly connected to either the chancel or aisles. J. Smith
has suggested that the entire complex was intended as an imitation of the
Holy Sepulchre complex in Jerusalem, with a large open courtyard, a small
shrine off that courtyard analagous to the shrine of Golgotha, and other
rooms to facilitate the passage of clergy and congregants during the Easter
ceremonies.[178] An unusual feature is the presence, on the north and south
sides of the nave, of external colonnaded porches or porticoes, 4 meters
wide, which extended from the narthex to the cross-arms. Such external
porches are not known from any of the other basilicas in Ravenna, although
San Simpliciano in Milan had a closed passage along its nave walls. Santa
Croce's porches were used for burial starting at least in the sixth century,[179]
although we do not know whether they were built for this purpose. The
porches had figured mosaic floors with geometric and vegetal motifs which
were subsequently cut into by the burials.[180]

At its western end, the church was fronted by a narthex that was 6 meters deep and extended 4 m wider than the nave, at least on the southern side, where its presence has been determined. The southern end of this narthex was connected to a small cross-shaped chapel that is now known as the "mausoleum of Galla Placidia." Excavations in the mid–nineteenth and early twentieth centuries showed that the chapel was entered through a triple archway leading to a vestibule that was raised up a step from the level of the narthex; two further steps led from the vesibule into the chapel.[181] The triple archway was sustained by two columns set on bases of red Verona marble, with colonnettes on the sidewalls on inlaid marble bases.[182] The floor level of the "mausoleum" was 11 centimeter higher than the narthex, and the type of bricks and mortar are different in the chapel from those of the main church, which has led to the conclusion that it was built slightly later than the narthex.[183]

It has been proposed that originally there was a corresponding chapel at the north end of the narthex, which is now relatively inaccessible to excavation,[184] and that this northern chapel might be the one described by Agnellus as built by Galla's "niece" Singledia near Santa Croce and dedicated to St. Zacharias.[185] G. Pavan's description of the mosaics found in excavations identifies the ones found by Di Pietro in 1925–6 as dating to the Roman period, and they thus do not provide information about a northern chapel.[186] Gelichi and Novara, on the basis of the most recent excavations, indicate the existence of a vestibule on the north end of the narthex, but do not show a chapel.[187] In the fifth century this part of the city contained several small chapels; one, for example, lay on the site of the sixth-century church of San Vitale.[188] Thus, it is not necessary to presume that Singledia's chapel was at the northern end of Santa Croce's narthex. On the other hand, San Giovanni Evangelista had chapels flanking both ends of its narthex, so it is certainly possible that the same layout was found here.

The richness of Santa Croce's decoration is indicated by the surviving mosaics in the "mausoleum." From archaeology we know that the church was paved in large panels of geometric *opus sectile* and contained elaborate wall revement, all made of black, white, and polychrome marble.[189] Agnellus tells us that Galla used to lie on porphyry roundels on the floor; these have now disappeared, but their use is well known both in Ravenna and elsewhere in this period.[190] What we know about the imagery in the main church also comes from Agnellus, who tells us:

The Empress Galla built the church of the Holy Cross, constructed of most precious stones and with carved stucco;[191] and in the roundness of the arches there are metrical verses reading thus:

"John washes Christ at the font in the seat of paradise; where he gives a happy life, he points the way to martyrdom."

On the facade of that temple, entering the main doors, above the depicted Four Rivers of Paradise, if you read the verses in hexameter and pentameter, you will find:

"O Christ, Word of the Father, concord of all the world, you who know no end, so also no beginning.[192] The winged witnesses, whom your right hand rules, stand around you saying 'holy' and 'amen.' In your presence the rivers run, flowing through the ages, the Tigris and Euphrates, Fison and Geon. With you conquering, savage crimes are silenced by true death, trodden for eternity under your feet."

The first verse, about John the Baptist and Christ, implies baptismal imagery of the sort found in the Orthodox Baptistery, although there is no evidence that Santa Croce was used for baptism.[193] It is not clear whether the pictures on the facade were in the narthex over the main doors or on the inner western wall of the church.[194] Agnellus says that the Four Rivers of Paradise were depicted, and they are also mentioned in the poem, which suggests that other elements found in the poem, namely the winged witnesses and the enemies trampled under Christ's feet, were also depicted in mosaic.[195] In that case, the image would have been an apocalyptic vision of Christ either standing or enthroned, treading on a lion and a serpent or basilisk, surrounded by the four symbolic beasts and/or the elders of Revelation 4:4–8, with the Rivers of Paradise at the base.[196] Various combinations of all of these elements are found in other surviving mosaics from the fifth and sixth centuries; for example, Christ seated over the Rivers of Paradise and surrounded by the symbolic beasts survives in the apse of Hosios David in Thessalonike.

The image of Christ trampling beasts derives from Psalm 90(91):13, and can be seen in various other works of art still existing from fifth-century Ravenna, namely in stucco in the Orthodox Baptistery, on the side of the fifth-century Pignatta Sarcophagus now in the Quadrarco di Braccioforte next to San Francesco, and in the mosaic in the narthex of the *capella arcivescovile*. A depiction of Christ trampling enemies was also found on the vestibule of the imperial palace in Constantinople, and it has been argued that its representation in Santa Croce forms a kind of imperial iconographical reference.[197] However, its popularity in other contexts, for example, as a motif on clay lamps,[198] and the fact that two of its other uses in Ravenna were episcopal rather than imperial imply that the image had many resonances in the fifth century.

Why this church? There is still discussion about exactly when it was built; some scholars have proposed that it was built between 417 and 421, when Galla lived in Ravenna with Constantius,[199] while others have suggested that it was built after 425.[200] Bodies were buried both in the porches and around the church after it was first built, probably after the end of the fifth century, and perhaps subsequent to the construction of the southern narthex chapel. It has been suggested that Santa Croce was intended as a cemeterial church,[201] although since the burials date later than the first phase of the church, it does not seem that a funerary purpose was originally meant.[202]

The construction of this church dedicated to the Holy Cross by an empress, was most likely intended as a reminiscence of the most powerful and pious Christian empress, Helena, the mother of Constantine, who was by this time famous for her discovery of the True Cross in Jerusalem. Helena had built a church dedicated to the Cross in Rome, a fact of which Galla Placidia was well aware, since she and her children sponsored a mosaic in that church also.[203] The Theodosian dynasty used the motif of the cross on its coins as a symbol of victory (Fig. 8),[204] and Galla Placidia may have felt that the imperial family should sponsor the veneration of the Cross; perhaps she had acquired a relic of the True Cross, which was to be housed in this church,[205] or perhaps she felt that a church of this sort would provide a suitable focus for an imperial mausoleum.

THE "MAUSOLEUM OF GALLA PLACIDIA"

When Galla Placidia died in Rome, she was probably buried in the imperial mausoleum at St. Peter's;[206] but by the ninth century the legend had grown up that she was buried in a side chapel in San Vitale in Ravenna, and by the thirteenth century this legend had become confused and her burial was attributed to the structure that is still known as the "mausoleum of Galla Placidia."[207] This small cross-shaped structure, which now stands detached from any other building, was originally attached to the southern end of the narthex of Santa Croce.[208] It is therefore correct to attribute the construction of this chapel to Galla's patronage, and to see it as one small part of what must have been a magnificent complex. This chapel is one of only three late antique structures in Ravenna that retain their complete decorative programs. It thus provides a small sample of the richness of interior decoration found in imperially sponsored buildings at this time. We will return to the question of whether it was intended as Galla Placidia's mausoleum.

The "mausoleum" is a small cross-shaped structure built mainly of reused Roman brick,[209] which may originally have been covered with plaster (Figs. 15, 16).[210] The east–west branch measures 3.4 × 10.2 meters (interior), while the north–south branch is 3.4 × 11.9 meters, longer because it originally connected the structure to the vestibule and narthex. Interestingly, the angles of the corners are not precisely 90 degrees, but are slightly skewed so that each component of the plan is not a rectangle but a

15. "Mau-
soleum of Galla
Placidia," exte-
rior view from
the southwest
(photo E. Vance)

parallellogram. Originally the ground level was approximately 1.5 m lower
than it is today, and thus the building would have had a higher profile.
Each of the external walls is articulated with a blind arcade, whose pilasters
rest on a plinth now partially below ground.[211] The entrance wall, with

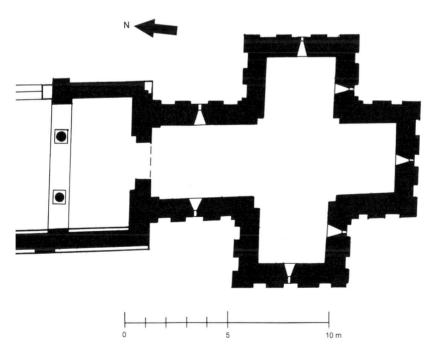

16. "Mau-
soleum of Galla
Placidia," plan
at ground level
(after Deichmann,
1976, pl. 8)

the door that led to the vestibule, has no arcade, but was covered with marble revetment;[212] the doorway's lintel is a reused marble cornice with a first-century AD Bacchic frieze.[213] Around the building, a brick cornice complete with dentils on the underside marks the roofline; behind the cornice, wooden beams were inserted in the interior of the wall, presumably for stability. Over the central core of the building a square tower rises 11 m, topped by a brick cornice identical to the one on the lower level. At the summit of the central tower is a marble pinecone.[214]

The chapel's walls are pierced by windows at three levels. Each of the walls of the central tower has a rectangular window just about the roofline. The ends of the east, south, and west arms have a window in the rectangular pediment (which corresponds to the lunette formed by the barrel vault on the interior). And at the level of the exterior blind arcade, narrow slits are found on seven of the wall surfaces (as shown in Fig. 16).[215] The windows now are covered with thin slabs of alabaster, a gift from King Victor Emmanuel III in 1908–11,[216] but it is more likely that they were originally coated with glass.

Inside the building, the space repeats what is demarcated by the architecture of the exterior. Each crossarm is surmounted by a barrel vault that rises 6.3 meters above the original floor level, and the central space is covered by a domical vault (a vault in which the dome continues down through pendentives) to a height of 10.7 meters. All of the vaulting is done in brick; for the dome, the bricks are laid in concentric circles. In both barrel vaults and dome, clay amphorae were laid on top of the bricks of the vaults, beneath the roof, for support.[217]

The floor in the building today, made of marble *opus sectile*, was laid in 1540 when the floor level was raised 1.43 meters above the original level. The lower part of the walls on the inside are sheathed in marble revetment; the yellowish Siena marble is mostly a restoration done in 1898–1901, but was based on fragments of *giallo antico* that were presumed to have been part of the original decoration.[218] A marble stringcourse with a bead-and-reel pattern articulates the flat revetment; a plain stucco cornice separates the revetment from the zone of glass-tesserae mosaic that covers the upper parts of the walls and the vaults (Pl.Ia).

The brilliance of the colors of the mosaic, the lavish use of gold, the richness and variety of the abstract decorative motifs, and the clarity of the figural images are overpowering; a term often used to describe the effect in this small space is "jewel box." The fact that the mosaic program has been preserved in its entirety has invited scholars to identify meanings uniting the different parts, based on the presumed origin and function of the building. Other studies have examined the iconographic and stylistic models for the imagery, and still others have considered the origin and number of artists,

17. "Mausoleum of Galla Placidia," west arm with a lunette of deer drinking (photo Institut für Kunstgeschichte der Johannes Gutenberg Universität Mainz, Bilddatenbank)

based on style and technique.[219] We will first see what is depicted in the mosaics, and will then discuss the meaning of the architecture and the iconography considered as a whole.

The barrel vaults of the arms are covered with abstract patterns. On the north and south arms, the vaults contain a regular pattern on a dark blue ground consisting of larger and smaller rosettes, worked primarily in red, light blue, gold, and white, which has been compared to Eastern textiles (Pl. Ia).[220] In the east and west arms, the vault contains against a dark blue ground a gold grapevine that springs from an acanthus plant to fill the space. At the center of each side, standing on a sort of candelabrum springing from the acanthus plant, stands a small gold male figure wearing a tunic (*dalmatica*) and mantle (*pallium*) and holding a scroll (Fig. 17); these have been interpreted as four apostles, as the evangelists, or as prophets.[221] The vine was a popular decorative motif in Roman art, adopted by Christians as a visual reference to John 15:1: "I am the true vine, and my Father is the vinegrower." At the apex of each barrel vault the Chi–Rho monogram of Christ with alpha and omega (Rev. 22:13: "I am the Alpha and the Omega . . .") is surrounded by a red and blue wreath.

At the center of the chapel, the arches that support the central tower are marked out by abstract borders in completely different color schemes from the vaults. The eastern arch contains a richly colored, three-dimensional meander pattern,[222] while the western arm is marked by a leafy, fruit-filled garland rising from baskets and culminating in a gold cross in a blue medallion, all set against a white background.[223] The arches on both north and south are marked by a lozenge or scale pattern in shades of green and turquoise.

The mosaics of the lunettes at the ends of the arms are brilliantly conceived to accommodate a semicircular space with a window in the middle. The lunettes in the east and west arms are filled with acanthus scrolls worked in green and gold, against a dark blue background. On a narrow groundline, two deer, entwined in the acanthus, face each other across a pool of water, which fits below the window (Fig. 17). This image visualizes Psalm 41(42):2: "As a hart longs for springs of water, so my soul longs for thee, O God"; the use of deer as symbols of devotion and of baptism is common in the fifth century.[224]

The lunette on the south arm is the first one visible to someone who enters from the door on the north side. The vivid depiction consists of three elements resting on a shallow green ground, set against a background gradated in shades of blue (Fig. 18). To the left of the window is a cupboard, or *armarium*, that contains four codex books labeled as the four Gospels: from the top left, they are Mark, Luke, Matthew, and John. In the center of the lunette, beneath the window, is a metal grill on wheels over a roaring fire. To the right of the window, a haloed and bearded man dressed in a striped *dalmatica* and white *pallium* runs toward the grill. Over his right shoulder he bears a large processional cross and in his left hand he displays an open book whose pages seem to depict writing, although no real letters are shown.

The particularity of the elements of the scene, and its prominence on the wall facing the entrance, imply that it had particular meaning in this chapel, and yet the identity of this figure is controversial.[225] While some have suggested that the figure is Christ,[226] it is generally agreed that because the person is dressed as a deacon, carrying the objects borne by deacons in the mass, he must be a deacon and martyr who was grilled alive. The most widely venerated saint who fits this description is St. Lawrence, who, as we have seen, was the object of particular veneration by the Theodosian dynasty. In this interpretation, the presence of the cupboard with the Gospels is seen as a symbol of that for which Lawrence was martyred. Although in early Christian art Lawrence is often shown being roasted on the grill, there are also representations of him as a deacon carrying a processional cross,[227] and the artist here has brilliantly found a way to use the space defined by the lunette and the window to best advantage.[228] It has also been argued by G. Mackie that this image instead depicts St. Vincent of Saragossa, Spain, another deacon who was tortured on a gridiron. Vincent's cult spread widely

18. "Mausoleum of Galla Placidia," St. Lawrence, south lunette mosaic (photo E. Vance)

in the Mediterranean (including Ravenna) in the fifth century, and may have been known to Galla Placidia from her time in Spain. Mackie points out that Prudentius's poem on St. Vincent specifically mentions books, which are depicted in this image, and also says that Vincent hastened toward his torture.[229] No early sources from Ravenna name this chapel,[230] and in the absence of any definite evidence one way or the other, we can only say that in either case, the saint would have had special meaning for Galla Placidia. Here, because it seems the most likely solution, I will continue to refer to the figure as St. Lawrence.

Over the entrance, facing the St. Lawrence panel, is a representation of Christ as the Good Shepherd of John 10:11–21 and 21:15–17 (Pl. Ib).[231] Christ as shepherd is a common motif in early Christian art, but this rendering of the subject is striking in a number of ways.[232] Christ is depicted as a beardless youth, with his hair flowing softly over his shoulders and his head surrounded by a halo. He is dressed in a gold tunic with purple stripes, and has a purple pallium draped across one shoulder and lap; he is thus not a simple shepherd, as he is usually shown, but a divine or imperial figure.[233] With one hand he holds a tall golden cross, and with the other he reaches across his body to feed one of six sheep that surround him in a rocky pastoral landscape. The pose of Christ in a landscape owes something to late Roman depictions of Orpheus, especially those that show him in a gold tunic and purple mantle, as, for example, a mosaic found at Adana in Turkey from the third or fourth century in which Orpheus, seated on a rock in a landscape, wears a gold tunic and sits in an almost identical pose to our

Good Shepherd.[234] Among the plants growing in the scene, palm fronds in the background are also highlighted in gold, perhaps emphasizing their role in Christ's narrative. Here as in the St. Lawrence panel, the background is light blue, and shadows of the cross, Christ's feet and halo, and some of the sheep are rendered against the background. A pattern of three-dimensional rocks defines the edge of the foreground. Once again, the image has been designed to fit the space it occupies: The northern lunette does not contain a window (since it would have been connected to the narthex), but the head of Christ, surrounded by a gold halo, falls in the spot in which the windows are found in the other lunettes, emphasizing Christ's role as "light of the world." Moreover, the location of the image of Christ above the doorway to the chapel echoes John 10:7–10: "I am the gateway of the sheep...if anyone enters by me, he will be saved, and will go in and out and find pasture."[235]

The upper lunettes of the central tower also each contain a window at the center, surrounded by a dark blue field. We find the same composition on all four sides. Flanking these windows, standing on greenish blocks, are male figures wearing white striped tunics and pallia, with their right arms upheld in a gesture of acclamation (Pl. Ia).[236] Each of these figures has a different physiognomy; some are beardless, some are bearded, and they are assumed to represent apostles, since the two on the eastern lunette can be identified as Peter and Paul. Paul is the only figure who gestures across his body to the left instead of to the right; he and Peter face each other across the eastern window, directing the viewer's attention to the east. Peter, likewise, is the only figure to hold something in his covered left hand, apparently a key. Beneath each window, a pair of doves either faces a small fountain (north and south) or perches on the edge of a basin of water, from which one of them drinks (east and west), representing the souls of the dead drinking the water of eternal life, the "living water" of John 4:10–14 and Revelation 21:6.[237] The top of each lunette contains a representation of a scallop shell semidome in gold and white; beneath the feet of the apostles is another grapevine on a dark blue background, and surrounding the lunette is a ribbon pattern on a red background, which unites the lower and upper zones of the mosaic decoration.[238]

We finally reach the dome over the central space (Fig. 19). Against a dark blue background, 567 gold eight-pointed stars swirl in concentric circles; at the apex of the dome is a gold cross whose long arm points toward the east side of the structure. Amid the arms of the cross are seven stars, three each in the spaces below the crossarm, and one in the upper left space. These seven stars have been interpreted as the seven stars of the apocalypse, or the seven planets, or their number may be simply attributable to chance.[239] In

19. "Mausoleum of Galla Placidia," mosaics of the central vault (photo E. Vance)

the corners of the dome, rising from striped clouds of red and light blue, we see the gold winged figures of the four living creatures of the apocalypse: counterclockwise from the southeast (the bottom right as you view the cross) they are the Lion, the Ox, the Man, and the Eagle, which is the order that the living creatures around the throne of God are listed in Revelation 4:7. Already by the early third century Christian scholars associated these creatures with the four evangelists, and they appear frequently in fourth- and fifth-century art.[240] Many scholars have argued that in this chapel the figures are only apocalyptic symbols, as they are not holding books,[241] but it is surely significant that in the *armarium* in the south lunette, the Gospel books are arranged in the order Mark, Luke, Matthew, John (Fig. 18), thus in the same order as the creatures in the vault.[242]

The nighttime effect of this ceiling is extraordinary, but the overall meaning of the dome's imagery has been hotly debated by scholars. Certainly the four living creatures are apocalyptic, as could be seven stars, but a nighttime sky covered with stars, with a cross at the center, is not part of the vision of Revelation; there the creatures surround a throne. A blue dome covered with stars was a well-known decorative feature in Roman art, but here its meaning, with the inclusion of the cross, is not clear. Scholars have

interpreted the cross as a reference to the Second Coming of Christ from
the east, the vision of the cross at Jerusalem in 351; the heavenly cross;
the city of heaven; Christ himself; Christ as creator of the world; or simply as a symbol of redemption. It seems most reasonable to assume that
in this particular context, the vault mosaic may not have had only one
meaning.[243]

Can this collection of images help us to understand the chapel's original
function? Many scholars have wanted to call it *either* a memorial chapel for
a saint *or* a mausoleum; the second interpretation is the most common, with
the mosaics interpreted as expressing Christian ideas about death and the
afterlife. However, the binary opposition between a memorial chapel and a
mausoleum has been overdrawn; in fact, memorial chapels were frequently
used for burial, while burial chapels were commonly dedicated to a saint
or saints, as we have seen in Ravenna itself.[244] The form and decoration of
our structure easily allow for both functions to coexist, and the meanings
of the decoration are most understandable in this context.

It certainly appears that one of the functions of this space was for the burial
of important people. When one enters the structure, the first impression is
of darkness, and the chamber has been compared to other Roman mausolea
that were also dimly lit.[245] The funerary motif is reinforced by the large
marble sarcophagi that are today located in three of the crossarms, where
they fit perfectly. These sarcophagi date to the mid–fifth century;[246] we
do not know when they were placed in the structure or who their occu-
pants were, but by the thirteenth century they were believed to contain
the bodies of various late Roman emperors.[247] The images found on the
sarcophagi correspond to, or enhance, the mosaics in the vaults, which
implies that they were made specifically for this space, although it should
be noted that such motifs are common on sarcophagi of this period.[248] The
funerary character of the building is also demonstrated by the pinecone
on the summit of the roof, which symbolized immortality in Roman and
early Christian art.[249] Many of the images can be interpreted as carrying
particular meaning related to death and the afterlife; for example, the doves
and the deer drink the water of salvation,[250] the landscape of the Good
Shepherd represents paradise,[251] and the elements in the dome refer to the
Last Judgment.[252]

The depiction of St. Lawrence is the only image that does not fit easily
into funerary interpretations of the iconography. Attempts to interpret this
scene to conform with an overall theological program (for example, that
the martyrdom of Lawrence represents the allegorical sense of salvation)
seem forced.[253] Lawrence is clearly a central focus of the chamber since he
appears in the lunette directly facing the entrance. It is likely that the chapel
was dedicated to him, with an altar in the eastern arm that would explain the

overall orientation of the imagery (especially the apostles and the cross in the central tower) toward the east.[254] Lawrence's reputation certainly made him a suitable saint for a chapel or a mausoleum in an imperially sponsored church. His prominence is enhanced by the way that this image fits into the general decorative program of the chapel. Lawrence is the only moving figure in the whole space; everything else represents ordered calm – the Good Shepherd, the books in the cabinet, the deer, the apostles, and the stars in their courses. Except for Lawrence, everything is outside of time and space; and the heavenly peace contrasts with the torments of the earth represented by the martyr. Lawrence literally and visually "leaps out" at the viewer, crossing the boundary between the living worshipers and the mosaic stasis of eternity.

Another important iconographic motif, found both in the architecture and the iconography of this chapel, is the cross.[255] In this cross-shaped chapel, attached to the cross-shaped church dedicated to the Holy Cross, the cross is held by both St. Lawrence and the Good Shepherd, and appears also in the vaults and at the center of the dome. In each case it is a multivalent symbol. St. Lawrence's cross is both a sign of his function as a deacon and a symbol of his martyrdom in imitation of Christ; the Good Shepherd's cross is both symbol of the flock that he leads and symbol of his passion. The cross in the vault likewise may represent the Second Coming of Christ, awaited by those buried in the tomb, but also the symbol of salvation for which Lawrence died, and perhaps a relic of the True Cross venerated in the main church. As we have noted, the cross was used as a symbol of victory by the Theodosian dynasty, and personifications of Victory holding a long-handled jeweled cross appear on coins of the dynasty, for example, for Theodosius II, his sister Pulcheria, Honorius, Iusta Grata Honoria, and for Galla Placidia herself (see Fig. 8).[256] The long-handled crosses held by St. Lawrence and Christ echo this imagery very clearly, and thus the chapel, and the entire complex, reflect the imperial iconography.

Did Galla Placidia intend this chapel to be her mausoleum, even though she was eventually buried elsewhere? Ultimately we cannot know the answer to this question. Certainly the richness of decoration and the themes of the images would have been suitable for such a use; it has also been suggested that it was planned as a burial space for her infant son Theodosius, who died in Spain.[257] Either St. Lawrence or St. Vincent would have been a suitable dedicatory saint for this Theodosian empress. Agnellus's account of a cross-shaped building near Santa Croce that contained the tomb of Singledia, whom he identifies as a niece of Galla, indicates that in this area there were mausolea of important people. All we can say is that in fifth-century Ravenna, the elite were constructing elaborate shrines and mausolea that they decorated to reflect their beliefs and aspirations about their faith.

The Rise of the Church of Ravenna

The other structures that date to the early years of imperial rule in Ravenna are the cathedral, known as the Ursiana, and its associated baptistery, whose development is connected to the rise of Ravenna's church in the imperial period. Under the western emperors, Ambrose of Milan had made the church of Milan second only to Rome in the Italian ecclesiastical hierarchy. Ravenna had a bishop, as we have seen, at least from the mid–fourth century, but none distinguished themselves before the arrival of the imperial court. However, when the city's political importance increased in the early fifth century, the status of the bishops of Ravenna rose dramatically.

At some point in this period, the bishop of Ravenna was given metropolitan status, that is, authority over bishops in the surrounding area.[258] The Diploma of Valentinian III, which bestows on the bishop of Ravenna the *pallium* and metropolitan jurisdiction, lists fourteen subordinate bishops and names a Bishop John; however, this document was shown in the eighteenth century to be a late sixth- or early seventh-century forgery, and the name of John is probably an error.[259] It seems likely that both the emperor and the pope granted this status to a bishop of Ravenna, despite opposition from the bishop of Milan.[260] The first evidence of a bishop acting as a metropolitan by consecrating other bishops comes from sermons delivered by Peter I,[261] one of Ravenna's great bishops, who, after the time of Agnellus, was known as Chrysologus, or "golden word."[262]

Peter Chrysologus is Ravenna's most notable bishop; his main claims to fame are his sermons, which were collected and published by his eighth-century successor Felix.[263] Agnellus wrote the earliest biography of Chrysologus, based on local tradition and on his sermons, in which we learn that he was a native of Imola, appointed as bishop by a pope in about 430.[264] The involvement of the pope in his selection is an indication of the dramatic rise in status of Ravenna's church;[265] and Chrysologus became for Ravenna what Ambrose had been for the see of Milan sixty years earlier. Galla Placidia may have had something to do with Chrysologus's elevation, and in his Sermon 130, perhaps delivered just after his consecration, he praises her specifically:[266]

> Also present is the mother of the Christian, eternal, and faithful Empire herself, who, by following and imitating the blessed Church in her faith, her works

of mercy, her holiness, and in her reverence for the Trinity, has been found worthy of parenting, marrying, and possessing an imperial trinity.

Elsewhere Chrysologus preaches in glowing terms about the cooperation of rulers and the church;[267] he was obviously immensely proud of having the imperial family as his congregants, and as we will see, he worked actively with Galla Placidia on the construction and furnishing of churches in Ravenna. Chrysologus was also active in church politics, and in particular was involved in the condemnation of Eutyches as a heretic at the Council of Chalcedon of 451; a letter survives that he wrote to Eutyches before the council, at the request of the pope.[268]

After the emperors moved to Rome in the 450s, and with the disunity and eventual demise of the imperial office, the bishop emerged as one of the major authority figures in Ravenna. Bishop Neon (ca. 450–73) undertook several major building programs in and around the city, which were continued by his successor Exuperantius (473–7). We know very little about the status of Ravenna under Odoacer, other than the fact that he used it once again as his capital; but upon the arrival of the Ostrogoths in Ravenna, it is Bishop John (477–94) who is said to have negotiated a peace deal between Odoacer and the Ostrogothic leader Theoderic that led to the former's surrender of the city in 493.[269]

THE CATHEDRAL

The relationship between Galla and Chrysologus highlights one of the features of Ravenna that is often pointed out as characteristic of late antique capital cities, namely the linkage between the palace and the ecclesiastical center. Ravenna's cathedral,[270] with a rather unusual dedication to the Anastasis (the Resurrection of Christ), became the central focus of a group of buildings directly controlled by the bishop.[271] The cathedral's location, at the eastern edge of the former *oppidum*, provided the city with two poles of authority: the emperor to the east, and the bishop to the west.[272] Evidence for the linking of these two areas by a colonnaded street, as attested in tenth-century and later documents, has very recently been found through excavation;[273] the centrality of both foci represents the confident incorporation of Christianity as part of imperial ideology in the mid–fifth century.[274]

There is controversy over the date that the cathedral was constructed, a crucial point of chronological information that has broad implications for the development of the city. Agnellus tells us that the cathedral was built by Bishop Ursus (hence it was known throughout the Middle Ages as the Ursiana), and that it was dedicated to the Anastasis on Easter Sunday.[275] The problem is that there is no agreement on the date of Ursus's reign; scholars place it either from ca. 370–96 or from ca. 405–31. This issue has important ramifications: if Ursus was bishop before 402, then the very grand cathedral would have been built before the arrival of the emperors, indicating a high status for Ravenna that might have been an inducement for the emperors to move the capital there.[276] If, on the other hand, the later dates for Ursus are accepted, then the construction of the cathedral was a consequence of the events of 402.[277] The dating depends on the interpretation of a complex variety of texts, and on the question of whether there was a bishop named John between Ursus and Peter I. My own interpretation, based on a close examination of Agnellus's sources and research methods, is that Ursus reigned from ca. 405–31, followed by Peter Chrysologus,[278] and thus that the grand cathedral was a product of Ravenna's new imperial importance.

Ravenna's current cathedral, designed by Gian Francesco Buonamici and begun shortly after 1734, was built on the site of the earlier building that was largely demolished at that time.[279] Bishop Matteo Farsetti, who initiated the work, insisted that the new structure should follow the outline of the earlier building and include some parts, including the tenth-century campanile and two sixteenth-century side chapels. The floor of the current building is made up of reused marble from various sources, some clearly taken from the older building, and some apparently brought from the former church of Santa Euphemia; several large slabs that had originally been *transennae* were moved to the Museo Arcivescovile in the 1890s.[280]

What we know about the late antique cathedral comes from records and drawings of investigations made between the eighteenth and twentieth centuries and analyzed in detail by P. Novara. While we cannot know precise details of either the plan or chronology, we do know that the original structure consisted of a nave flanked by two aisles on each side, with an apse to the east, of the same width as the nave (Fig. 20). The apse had a semicircular interior and a polygonal exterior (in effect, half of an octagon), and was crowned with a half dome made of *tubi fittili*, both features that we have already seen at San Giovanni Evangelista. The basilica with double aisles was a type widely known in the fourth- and fifth-century Mediterranean; certainly found in imperial cities such as Rome and Milan, this type of building could also be found in other, nonimperial cities.[281] Ravenna's cathedral measured approximately 60 × 35 meters (nave and aisles). It was therefore smaller than the Lateran in Rome (75 × 55 m) and Ambrose's cathedral in Milan (82 × 45 m), but was comparable in scale to the new basilica built at Aquileia just before 400 (ca. 72 × 31 m), although that structure had only single aisles. Certainly Ravenna's new cathedral was an imposing building, up-to-date with the main architectural developments of the late fourth and fifth centuries.

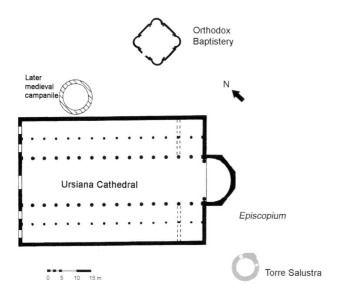

Later medieval campanile

Orthodox Baptistery

N

Ursiana Cathedral

Episcopium

0 5 10 15 m

Torre Salustra

20. Plan of Ravenna's cathedral complex, including the Ursiana Cathedral (ca. 405), the Orthodox Baptistery (420s–50s), and the *Torre Salustra* (second century AD) (adapted from Novara, "La cattedrale," 1997)

Other information about Ravenna's original cathedral comes from much later sources, the most important of which are drawings made by Buonamici at the time of the eighteenth-century rebuilding.[282] According to these pictures, corroborated to some extent by written descriptions, the cathedral's aisles were separated from each other by rows of fourteen columns each, for a total of fifty-six columns, which ran uninterrupted right up to the eastern wall. Two additional columns flanked the entrance to the apse, again as at San Giovanni Evangelista. Buonamici's drawing of the nave of the cathedral before its demolition shows that the columns were surmounted by capitals topped by impost blocks. Novara cautions that the nave arcade of the Ursiana was probably completely rebuilt at least three times, in the tenth, the fourteenth, and the sixteenth centuries, and thus the impost blocks shown by Buonamici may not have been part of the original structure.[283] However, we have seen that impost blocks were one of the characteristic features of fifth-century churches in Ravenna, and were used in the contemporary Orthodox Baptistery, so it is not farfetched to presume that they were also used in the Ursiana.[284]

Agnellus's ninth-century description remains our main source of information about the decoration of the cathedral:[285]

He lined the walls with most precious stones; he arranged diverse figures in multi-coloured mosaics over the vault of the whole temple.... Euserius and Paul decorated one wall surface, on the north side, next to the altar of St. Anastasia, which Agatho made. That is the wall where columns are placed in a row up to the wall of the main door. Satius and Stephen decorated the other wall on the south side, up to the above-mentioned door, and here and there they had carved in stucco different allegorical images of men and animals and quadrupeds, and they arranged them with greatest skill. . . . And he [Ursus] was buried, as some assert, in the aforementioned Ursiana church . . . in front of the altar under a porphyry stone, where the bishop stands when he sings the mass.

It is impossible to know when all this decoration may have been inserted; Euserius, Paul, Agatho, Satius, and Stephen were probably not artists, but rather the patrons of the decoration, whose generosity was commemorated by inscriptions.[286] The original floor was 3.55 m below the current level, and eighteenth-century drawings indicate that it may have been covered with mosaic; traces found in the apse indicate the presence of marble wall revetment.[287] Elsewhere Agnellus refers to a portrait of the late fifth-century Bishop John I in the Ursiana, although what its context was is not known.[288] If the decoration of the baptistery is anything to go by, Ravenna's cathedral must have been a splendid building, corresponding to the ambitions of its bishops.

THE ORTHODOX BAPTISTERY

Baptism is the sacrament that marks a person's entry into the Christian community. In the early fifth century, Christianity had only recently been established as the sole publicly celebrated religion in the Roman Empire, and ideas about baptism and conversion were in a process of flux. Through the fourth century, it was common for adults to be baptized, often only toward the ends of their lives, and most liturgical texts that describe baptism through the fifth century assume that those being baptized are adults. The bishop was required to preside over the ceremony of baptism in his episcopal city, and was the only person who could confer the Holy Spirit by anointing and laying on of hands, which in this period were part of the same ceremony.[289] Thus, about the year 400 the bishop of Ravenna would have been the gatekeeper, as it were, of the city's Christian community, the prime actor in a semipublic ritual enacted every year on the eve of Easter Sunday.[290]

Special spaces set aside within religious complexes for baptism are known as early as the third century,[291] and when Christian buildings began to take on monumental form in the early fourth century, religious authorities in Rome and elsewhere decided that it would be appropriate to have a separate space for baptism attached or close to the cathedral.[292] Most of the structures built for this purpose were relatively small, with a centralized ground plan (round, polygonal, or square) and a large font in the center.[293] The Lateran Cathedral in Rome, built at the time of Constantine, apparently had a separate baptistery as part of its original conception, a centralized space with an octagonal ground plan.[294]

Numerous explanations have been proposed for the choice of octagonal structures for baptisteries.[295] It was not a new architectural form; the Romans built octagons as part of elaborate villas, bath complexes, and tombs. The theological suitability of the octagon for baptism was most famously expressed by Ambrose of Milan, who, in addition to building a new octagonal baptistery next to the cathedral of Milan in the 370s, wrote extensively on the meaning of baptism. A poem in Milan's baptistery that is attributed to Ambrose said, "eight corners has its font, worthy of that number, it was suitable to build this hall for sacred baptism with this number . . . ," identifying the number 8 as symbolic of baptism, because it corresponds to the Resurrection of Christ that took place on the eighth day.[296] There were additional layers of meaning: Both bathing complexes and baptisteries are associated with water, and similarities with Roman mausolea associated baptism with the death of the catachumen and the beginning of his new life as a Christian.[297] Finally, a freestanding octagonal building is a striking addition to a city's landscape, and baptism and the bishop's role in the Christian community thereby became visually accentuated.[298] On the model of Rome and Milan the idea of an octagonal, or at least a centrally planned, baptistery spread through Italy in the fifth and sixth centuries.[299]

It is perhaps particularly significant that octagonal baptisteries appear in the cities described above that were rivals for power and imperial presence in the late fourth and early fifth centuries. In addition to Milan and Rome, Aquileia also acquired an octagonal baptistery, to replace (or supplement) earlier less notable structures, in the late fourth century.[300] Ravenna's is also one of the earliest attested; it was initially built at the same time as the cathedral, in the early years of the fifth century. Is it a coincidence that in the 430s Pope Sixtus III redecorated the Lateran Baptistery, and that in the 450s Bishop Neon redecorated Ravenna's? There may have been religious rivalry between the two sees even in the fifth century.[301] It should also be noted that this was not to be Ravenna's only baptistery; Agnellus tells us of one next to the Petriana church in Classe, one associated with the Arian cathedral, one attached to the Arian church we call Sant'Apollinare Nuovo, and another, known only from excavation, was built south of Classe at the site called Ca'Bianca.[302] Of these, the only one that still survives is the Arian Baptistery, which we will examine in Chapter 5.

Ravenna's Orthodox Baptistery was built 15 meters to the north of the cathedral, and on exactly the same alignment (see Fig. 20); both the Ursiana and the baptistery were oriented to the southeast).[303] It was built of reused Roman bricks, as an octagonal prism with four projecting apsidioles at the

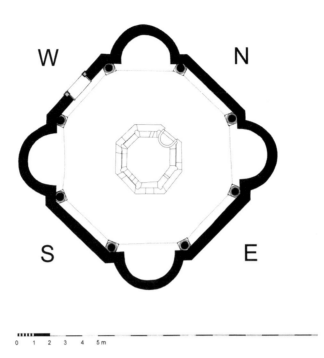

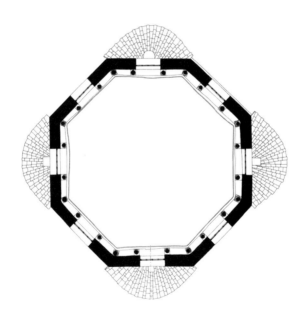

21. Ortho-dox Baptistery, reconstructed plan at ground level, with curent door and font, and plan at window level (after Deichmann, 1976, pls. 4 and 2)

22. Ortho-
dox Baptistery,
view of the exte-
rior from the
southeast

ground level (originally the ground level was approximately 3 meters below today's level).[304] Today the building has the footprint of a square with rounded corners, but it is likely that originally the absidioles did not extend all the way to the corners of the octagon (Fig. 21).[305]

Viewed from the exterior, the tall octagonal structure creates a striking silhouette (Fig. 22). It has been proposed that the top portion of the walls, which are ornamented with a blind frieze consisting of two double-arched panels on each side, were a later addition to the walls built at some time in the tenth century or later to raise the structure's profile at a time when the city's subsidence may have buried the lower parts of the building;[306] but other scholars argue that the rebuilding could have taken place in a second

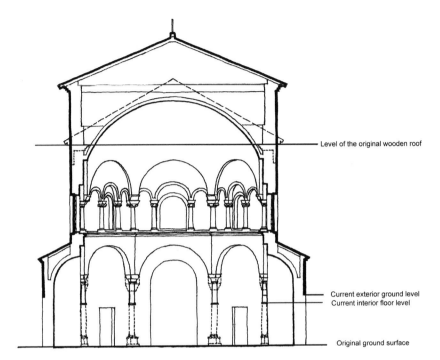

Level of the original wooden roof

Current exterior ground level
Current interior floor level

Original ground surface

23. Ortho-
dox Baptistery,
reconstructed
cross section
showing the
original and sub-
sequent floor and
roof levels (after
Kostof, 1965)

fifth-century phase, when the dome was added.[307] The sides of the octagon
are 5.0–5.3 meters long externally and 4.5 meters long internally.

The original baptistery built by Ursus had a wooden roof approximately
11 m above the floor;[308] under Bishop Neon (ca. 450–73) there was an
extensive rebuilding and redecorating program, resulting in the structure
that survives today (Fig. 23).[309] A shallow dome, 9.60 meters wide at its
springing point and rising to a peak of 14.60 meters above the original
floor, was constructed of a double thickness of *tubi fittili*; at the summit of the
dome, blocks of light pumice replaced the *tubi*, presumably to create an even
lighter structure.[310] The exterior walls of the building are only 0.60 meters
thick, which explains the concern for the weight of the dome; moreover,
the masonry of the dome and its supporting arches is not bonded to the
outer shell of brick, but forms an inner skin, as it were, to the structure,
held up by the interior arches and columns.[311] The dome is pierced by
eight small holes made of *tubi* placed perpendicular to the rings of the
dome, directly above the eight windows; these were probably for ropes to
suspend lamps in the interior, since the baptismal ceremonies took place
at night.[312] Two smaller windows on the west and southeast sides of the

24. Orthodox Baptistery, view of the interior facing southeast

building give access to the space between the extrados of the dome and the roof.[313]

A. Wharton has reconstructed elements of the baptismal ritual based on the writings of Ambrose of Milan and explains how they would be performed in this structure.[314] On the evening of Holy Saturday, the baptistery would be exorcised by the bishop and clergy, and the bishop took his place in or in front of the southeast absidiole.[315] The baptisands entered from one of the two original doors on the north and west sides (the door on the west side is the only one that is still open today)[316] and were "opened" by having their ears and noses touched. They faced west and rejected the Devil, then faced east and confirmed their allegiance to Christ. They were then immersed three times in the font at the center of the floor. The font that can be seen today, composed of marble and porphyry slabs and columns 3.45 meters wide and 0.84 meters deep, with a semicircular pulpit on the east side, was built sometime in the later Middle Ages when the floor level was raised. However, it stands on the foundations of the original font, which, according to nineteenth-century excavations, was circular on the inside and 3.10 m across.[317] Such a font, like those in Milan and Rome, provided a vessel for the bodily immersion of adult initiates who still formed the majority of candidates around the year 400.[318] After the immersion, the bishop anointed the new initiates with oil and washed their feet. They were dressed in white garments and proceeded, with their sponsors and the clergy, into the cathedral for the Easter Eucharist.

The beauty and mystery of this ceremony were enhanced by the decoration of the space in which these rituals took place. Agnellus says of Bishop Neon:

"He decorated the baptisteries of the Ursiana church most beautifully: he set up in mosaic and gold tesserae the images of the apostles and their names in the vault, he girded the side-walls with different types of stones. His name is written in stone letters:

Yield, old name, yield, age, to newness!
Behold the glory of the renewed font shines more beautifully.
For Neon, highest priest, has generously adorned it,
arranging all things in beautiful refinement.[319]

The Orthodox Baptistery is the only late antique baptistery whose interior decoration survives almost intact, and thus its decoration is extremely important for understanding the rituals and theology of baptism in this period. We can here get a sense of the complexity of the artistic program and the splendor of its effects in a way that can be only imagined for most of the other buildings in the late antique world.

The baptistery is decorated with mosaic, marble, stucco, and paint. This is a relatively small space, 12 m across and 14.6 m high, and one's natural impulse upon entering it is to look up, into the ever-rotating heavenly realm of the dome.[320] But as the eye travels back down, it encounters an ever-more-real and tangible space. From the glittery flatness of the glass mosaics in the vault, we pass through a mosaic zone that depicts a three-dimensional range of architecture using both glass and marble tesserae.[321] Below this is an architectural zone worked in shallow stucco relief, consisting of colonnettes and pediments framing windows and figures; and below this, at ground level, a real series of arches defines absidioles and embrasures, the frames for the real flesh-and-blood participants in the drama of baptism.[322] As Wharton has noted, the figures of the newly baptized, in their white robes, would have been reflected by the stucco figures and the mosaic apostles above them, all clad in white and gold, in a progressively more dematerialized world that finally reaches heaven.[323]

At ground level, the interior is surrounded by an arcade supported by eight reused Roman columns and third-century Corinthian capitals that do not match one another. These are surmounted by impost blocks that date to the fourth or fifth century, and are among the oldest surviving examples of this architectural feature in late antique Italy.[324] The floor level and this arcade have been raised several times, so the original proportions are no longer visible.[325] The arcade frames absidioles recessed into four sides of the octagon, alternating with flat wall surfaces that are today covered with an elaborate marble wall revetment, created at the turn of the twentieth century on the presumed basis of an earlier decoration.[326] The vision of Christ at the apex of the dome is correctly oriented if the viewer is facing the absidiole on the southeast side that presumably contained the altar or throne.

In lunettes above the absidioles are mosaic inscriptions that were first recorded in the late seventeenth century, and were renewed in the late nineteenth. They paraphrase or quote biblical verses that relate to baptism, as follows:

> southwest (heavily restored): "Jesus walking on the sea takes the hand of the sinking Peter, and with the lord commanding the wind ceased." (paraphrase of Matt. 14:29)
>
> southeast: "Blessed are those whose iniquities are forgiven, and whose sins are covered. Blessed is the man to whom the Lord has not imputed sin." (Psalm 31[32]:1–2)
>
> northeast: "Where Jesus laid aside his clothing and put water in a basin and washed the feet of his disciples." (paraphrase of John 13:4–5)
>
> northwest: "He makes me lie down in green pastures; he leads me by still waters." (Psalm 22[23]:2)

Each of these quotes can be specifically related to the meaning of baptism, and it is certainly significant that the southeast inscription, the one directly in alignment with the baptismal scene in the dome, speaks directly to the concept of baptism's removing sin. The quote on the northeast side seems to be evidence that the feet of the initiates were washed as part of the ceremony, which Ambrose tells us was a general practice in much of the west, although not in Rome.[327] It has been suggested that the texts might refer to images originally decorating the absidioles, but there is no evidence either way for this.[328] The spandrels above the arcade are covered with mosaic decoration depicting a gold acanthus scroll on a dark blue ground. At each of the eight corners the scroll forms a medallion with a gold background that encloses a male tunic- and pallium-clad figure holding a book or a scroll; these figures are interpreted as prophets.[329] The soffits of the arches are covered with elaborate decorative mosaic bands.

Above a marble cornice, the second zone, at the level of the windows, is defined by eight broad arches corresponding to the ones below, which support the dome (Pl. IIa). Within these arches is an arcade created by twenty-four colonnettes, again reused and not all matching (although they were originally stuccoed and painted to hide this fact). These colonnettes are surmounted by matching Ionic capitals and plain impost blocks and atop the impost blocks at each of the eight corners are additional stone brackets carved with crosses on which rest the arches of the dome. The central unit of each wall takes up about 40 percent of the width, and is flanked by two slightly narrower units.[330] The windows are 2.4 meters high and 1.4 meters wide, rather large, especially for a space that was used primarily at night.[331] An elaborate decoration in stucco relief fills the spaces that flank the windows, one of very few examples of stucco relief decoration to have survived from late antiquity, although we know that there were other contemporary examples in Ravenna.[332] Each interstice of the arcade contains an additional stucco architectural frame composed of fluted pilasters and alternating triangular or semicircular pediments sorrounding half-scallop shells. In these frames are standing beardless male figures clad in tunics and pallia, holding books or scrolls that are either open or closed; some of the standing figures seem to step out of their frames, creating the illusion of a gallery.[333] These figures, who are usually interpreted as the sixteen prophets, were created by two different artists and were originally brightly painted with the tunics probably white like the mosaic figures below.[334]

The awkward spaces between the pediments and the arcade also hold stucco figures. Twelve of the spaces contain birds or animals facing a vase or plant between them (Pl. IIa).[335] However, on the north and northwest sides, four of these spaces contain instead narrative representations as follows, clockwise from the northwest side: Daniel between two lions, Christ dressed as a philosopher giving the law to Peter in the presence of Paul, Christ dressed as a warrior trampling the lion and a serpent, and Jonah between two whales. These are all motifs that are found on carved stone sarcophagi and in other media throughout Ravenna.[336] These particular scenes had significance for the baptismal ceremonies, as they represent triumph over danger and evil: both Daniel and Jonah are Old Testament types of salvation and of Christ's resurrection, while the other two images present the triumph of Christ over the old law and over evil. According to Ambrose's liturgy for baptism, the catachumens would be facing the northwest wall and looking at these images precisely at the point in the ceremony in which they were renouncing the Devil.[337]

Above the arcade, eight large arches define the octagonal base of the dome. The intervening spaces and soffits of the arches are filled with more vegetal and abstract mosaic and painted decoration. A new ground-line, intersected by the arches of the dome, underlies a three-dimensional architectural zone rendered in mosaic. Each side of the octagon corresponds to a tripartite architectural unit consisting of a recessed niche in the center, flanked by square compartments with coffered ceilings (Pl. IIa; Fig. 25).[338] On the southeast, southwest, northeast, and northwest sides the central niche contains an empty jeweled throne with a purple and gold garment in the seat, surmounted by a cross in a medallion, and the side compartments

25. Orthodox Baptistery, throne in fantastic architectural scene, mosaics of the middle zone

contain topiary and other garden imagery. On the north, south, east, and west sides the central niche contains an altar with an open Gospel book on top, and the side compartments contain chairs beneath conch-shaped semidomes. The books contain inscriptions identifying them as the four Gospels, but the meaning of the four empty thrones is not explained, and has been the subject of intensive scholarly discussion. Such thrones are a common motif in church mosaics of this period,[339] and here they have been interpreted as *etimasia* (ἑτοιμασία, literally, "preparation of the throne") referring to the Second Coming of Christ,[340] as symbols of the sovereignty of Christ,[341] as episcopal thrones, and in various other ways.[342] The overall program of this register, depicting a lavish and fantastical setting far removed from everyday life, may represent the heavenly kingdom attained by those being baptized.

Above the architectural register, separated by a red and blue border, is the dome itself, around which march the twelve apostles to whom Jesus assigned the mission of baptizing believers (Pl. IIb).[343] The apostles hold jeweled crowns and are dressed in tunics with broad stripes covered with mantles; these costumes are alternately white tunic with gold mantle and gold covered by white. The apostles are processing toward a point beneath the baptismal scene at the apex of the dome and each is labeled by name.

Peter leads the right side of the procession, followed by Andrew, James, son of Zebedee, John, Philip, and Bartholemew; Paul leads the left side, followed by Thomas, Matthew, James son of Alphaeus, Simon the Canaanite, and Jude the Zealot.[344] The faces are individualized: some are shown as young beardless men, some as older men with beards of brown or gray. Peter's and Paul's faces correspond to the portrait types for these apostles already established by the fifth century, but the facial features of the others do not exactly match those of other surviving depictions.[345] The apostles are walking on a narrow green ground space that displays the shadows cast by their feet, and stand in front of a dark blue background. They are separated from each other by what S. Kostof calls a "plant-candelabra," and above and behind their heads a drapery swag encircles the central medallion; the central drape effectively creates the illusion of a halo behind each head.[346]

It is not clear to whom or to what the apostles are offering their crowns.[347] It is likely that they are offering them to Christ who is depicted in the central medallion.[348] Nordström's interpretation of the scene as reflecting the ceremony of *aurum coronarium*, in which senators offer gold wreaths to the emperor upon his coronation, resonates with the imperial ceremonial that pervaded Ravenna at this time.[349] However, given that it was the apostles and their successors, the bishops, who were charged by Christ with the task of baptizing believers, A. Wharton's suggestion that the crowns are being offered to the newly baptized congregants is equally convincing.[350] It is likely that all of these associations were either intended by the mosaic's creators or experienced by its audience in the mid–fifth century.

We finally reach the central medallion of the dome (Fig. 26). The scene was heavily and controversially restored in the 1850s by Felice Kibel and perhaps also earlier, but enough of the original survives to show that it depicted the baptism of Christ. On the left, John the Baptist stands on a rocky prominence holding a tall jeweled staff (which has been restored as a cross, but may have been a shepherd's staff or crook). In the center a nude Christ stands in the river, while on the right the upper torso of a bearded nude man holding a green mantle and a reed is labeled as a personification of the river Jordan. The central axis of the depiction is the space between John and Christ, highlighting their relationship in the context of baptism. The heads of John and Christ, John's hand, the top of John's staff, and the dove are all later restorations, and we do not know what was originally there. For example, we do not know whether Christ and John had halos, and it is unlikely that Christ was originally bearded. It is equally unlikely that John held a paten in his hand, and much more probable that in the original composition he placed his hand on Christ's head, as was almost universal in fifth-century depictions of this scene.[351]

26. Orthodox Baptistery, central medallion of the dome, depicting the baptism of Christ (photo S. Mauskopf)

The central scene is set off from the apostle register by the mosaic representation of a circular marble cornice with egg-and-dart molding, which creates the effect that one is looking through a hole in the center of the dome straight up into heaven. The action takes place against a gold background, which further removes it from the natural world and places it in a separate, divine space.[352] The scene as a whole depicts the baptism of Christ as reported in Mark 1:9–11 and Matthew 3:13–17, both of which mention John the Baptist, the river Jordan, and the dove of the Holy Spirit. Obviously this scene represents the prototype for Christian baptism. It also serves as a model for the ceremonies held in the baptistery itself, with the baptisand identifying himself with Christ, John the Baptist with the bishop, and the river Jordan with the deacon who assisted with the immersion and the clothing of the baptisand afterward.[353]

Many modern viewers find the figure of the river Jordan confusing, but it would not have seemed unusual in the fifth century. Personifications of rivers as gods and goddesses were common in Greek and Roman art, and were quite commonly adapted for use in early Christian art, for example, for the Four Rivers of Paradise.[354] The river-god Jordan appears fairly frequently in early Christian depictions of Christ's baptism and in other scenes, such as the ascension of Elijah.[355] The river Jordan is personified in Psalm 113 and the importance of the Jordan as part of Jesus's baptism was stressed in fifth-century exegesis. For example, Ravenna's own Peter Chrysologus preached a sermon for Epiphany (the date of Christ's baptism) in which he notes, referring to Psalm 113 and also to Joshua 3:14–17, that the river Jordan did not flee from the presence of the Trinity at the baptism, which shows that the pious need not fear God. In this image the personified Jordan faces the baptism scene, reinforcing this point.[356]

As the setting for the religious pageant of baptism, the interior of the Orthodox Baptistery overwhelms the viewer with color, texture, and imagery, creating, as Kostof noted, a visionary realm removed from ordinary space and time.[357]

THE EPISCOPAL PALACE

An important part of the cathedral complex was the residence of the bishop, known as the *episcopium*. As the public role of the bishop was enlarged in the late antique empire, his residence became a public space in which he could give audiences, judge legal cases, hold assemblies of clergy, and entertain guests. Evidence of *episcopia* from the fourth and fifth centuries is sparse. In places such as Milan, Rome, Geneva, Naples, Grado, Parenzo, and Aquileia, we know that one component was a large audience hall, in some cases richly decorated,[358] but beyond this there does not seem to be any standard layout or type for a bishop's residence.[359]

Ravenna's episcopal palace is unusually well documented, thanks to Agnellus and to its partial survival, which has allowed M. Miller to trace its history and significance within the broader context of episcopal residences in northern Italy.[360] One of the defining characteristics of Ravenna's *episcopium* was that, according to Agnellus, it was an agglomeration of buildings that had been built by different bishops, making it an articulation of the history of the episcopal see.[361] We will trace these additions throughout the course of this book, noting the significance of each addition in its historical context.[362]

Nothing is known of the earliest *episcopium*, but Agnellus assumed that one existed near the cathedral.[363] It developed around a tower that was later known as the *Torre Salustra*, which, as we have seen in the previous chapter, served as the water distribution tower for the aqueduct. The first distinct building identified by Agnellus was the "house which is called *quinque accubita*," built by Bishop Neon. *Quinque accubita* means "five dining couches," and refers to a type of high-status *triclinium*, or dining hall, that contains a niche for a number of semicircular dining couches. Agnellus describes the dining hall as follows:

> On each side of the dining hall he built wondrous windows, and he ordered the pavement of the dining hall to be decorated with different types of stones. The story of the psalm which we sing daily, that is "Praise ye the Lord from the heavens," together with the Flood, he ordered to be painted on the side-wall flanking the church; and on the other side-wall, which is located over the

stream, he had it adorned in colors with the story of our Lord Jesus Christ, when, as we read, he fed so many thousands of men from five loaves and two fishes. On one side of the interior facade of the dining hall he set out the creation of the world.... And on the other facade was depicted the story of the apostle Peter....

Each of these scenes was accompanied by a poem in hexameter, which Agnellus quotes; the whole decorative effect was luxurious, and at the same time presented religious scenes with messages about the sanctity of food and the role of bishops as the heirs of Peter.[364] This dining hall was apparently built immediately behind the cathedral, adjacent to the *fossa Amnis*.[365] Dining halls of this type were typical of aristocratic residences and palaces; Neon's *triclinium*, built at a time in which the imperial palace at Ravenna was largely unused, emulated and perhaps competed with the imperial palace,[366] at a time in which the bishop was becoming the main authority figure in the city.[367]

OTHER EPISCOPAL CHURCH FOUNDATIONS

We know less about other churches built in Ravenna in the fifth century, although it seems that much more building activity was taking place. Evidence for other constructions is very scanty, and, as usual, comes mostly from Agnellus, in some cases supplemented by surviving remains or archaeological evidence.

One of the most notable churches built in the first half of the fifth century was a large basilica founded in Classe by Peter Chrysologus, apparently dedicated to Christ and named after its founder as the Petriana; it was completed by Peter's successor Neon.[368] Agnellus, who is our sole source for this church, tells us that it collapsed in an earthquake in the mid–eighth century and had not been rebuilt; he tells us:[369]

No church like it in construction was larger, either in length or in height; and it was greatly adorned with precious stones and decorated with multi-colored mosaics and greatly endowed with gold and silver and with holy vessels, which he [Peter] ordered to be made. They say that there an image of the Saviour was depicted over the main door, the like of which no man could see in pictures; it was so very beautiful and lifelike that the Son of God himself in the flesh would not have disliked it, when he preached to the nations....

Agnellus goes on to relate a legend about the image of Christ, from which we learn specifically that the image was above the main doors in the narthex. It is difficult to know whether this story provides evidence of an actual image, given that the church had been destroyed for about a century before Agnellus's day,[370] but it is not implausible, given that images of Christ are often found over doors in the churches of Ravenna. At the end of the fifth century a baptistery was built next to the Petriana. This circumstance, and the grandeur described by Agnellus, have led to the suggestion that the Petriana was founded to be a cathedral for the city of Classe, but there is no evidence for a separate see, and thus the Petriana must simply have been intended to serve the large Christian population of Classe.[371]

The location of the Petriana is today controversial; a site within the city walls of Classe was identified in 1875, 350 meters to the northeast of the church of San Severo, and remains of mosaic and *opus sectile* pavements were found. Some archaeological sondages and limited excavation were done in the 1960s; G. Cortesi reconstructed a basilica, 78 × 43.56 m, with the nave double the width of the aisles, preceded by an atrium that had rooms flanking it to the north and west.[372] This would have been the largest basilica in Ravenna or Classe, bigger than the Ursiana cathedral. Recently A. Augenti has cast doubt on the data and the proposed reconstruction, noting that aerial photography does not show an apse, but simply a large space surrounded by smaller rooms, which might or might not have been a church. The identification of the Petriana awaits further investigation; excavations begun in 2008 will provide essential information.[373]

Since Agnellus is our main source of information about churches that no longer survive, it should come as no surprise that most of the structures that he mentions are connected to one of Ravenna's bishops. In many cases these structures contained the burial of one or more bishops, but this need not mean that the church was built by that bishop, or even necessarily before his reign, since Agnellus also tells us that the bodies of bishops were sometimes reburied.[374] Of the fifth-century bishops, Liberius III was buried in a chapel dedicated to St. Pullio, built just outside the city gate known as the *porta Nova*.[375] Ursus was buried in the cathedral, Peter Chrysologus in Imola, Neon in the Church of the Apostles, Exuperantius in St. Agnes, and John I in Sant'Agata Maggiore. Most of these churches lay within the fifth-century city walls, as did Santa Croce and San Giovanni Evangelista, which also contained burials.[376]

One major basilica in the center of Ravenna was the church identified by Agnellus as the Church of the Apostles (*basilica Apostolorum*), probably originally dedicated to Sts. Peter and Paul.[377] Agnellus implies that this church was built before or during the reign of Bishop Neon who was buried there.[378] The original church was completely rebuilt in the tenth or eleventh century; it was given to the Franciscan order in 1261 and still survives as San Francesco. The present church's twenty-four columns, capitals, and impost blocks date to the mid–to late-fifth century and thus were probably used in the original church; the marble was imported from the island of Proconnesus near Constantinople, the first example of this useage that would become a regular feature of sixth-century churches.[379] The crypt

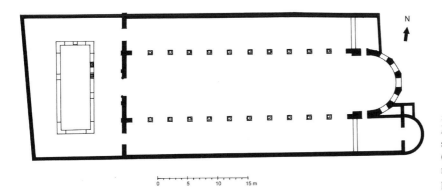

27. Sant'Agata Maggiore, reconstructed plan (after Deichmann, 1976, pl. 52)

of the tenth-century church was excavated at various times in the twentieth century, and a rectangular mosaic floor with inscriptions and burials, dating perhaps to the sixth century, was uncovered. It is not known exactly what form the church took, whether a basilica or a cruciform structure; the rectangular mosaic floor found in the crypt has led some to hypothesize that, like Santa Croce, this church had a square chancel.[380] The dedication to the apostles, or to Peter and Paul in particular, imitates churches in both Rome and Constantinople.

Agnellus says that the subdeacon Gemellus built a church dedicated to St. Agnes during the reign of Bishop Exuperantius (473–7), who was buried there. Agnellus himself lived near this church, and says that it was located in the center of the old *oppidum*.[381] The entire site was destroyed in 1936, but parts of the church were still visible in the early twentieth century, showing that it had been a basilica made of spoliated brick with a nine-column colonnade that included impost blocks.[382]

Sant'Agata Maggiore, according to Agnellus, is where John I (477–94) was both buried and depicted on the wall of the apse.[383] Sant'Agata lies in the eastern part of the city, to the south of the Church of the Apostles. A church still exists on the site and contains elements from the original structure, although it was damaged by several earthquakes and radically rebuilt in the fifteenth and eighteenth centuries.[384] Nevertheless, we know that Sant'Agata was a basilica (today 49.5 × 25 meters, Fig. 27) very similar in design to San Giovanni Evangelista. It had an apse that was polygonal on the exterior, pierced by five windows; more windows in the upper walls of the nave and the aisle walls; and small chambers flanking the apse on either side, entered from the aisles.[385] The nave was separated from the aisles by an arcade of ten columns; the columns, bases, capitals, and impost blocks vary widely and range in date from the first to the sixth centuries, indicating that spolia were used in the original construction, but the original set was probably supplemented with additional material in the fifteenth century.[386]

Parts of the church were rebuilt in the mid–sixth century, namely the apse vault (using *tubi fittili* that were filled with mortar) and a colonnaded atrium.

Agnellus's attributions are sometimes wrong; for example, he says, "In the time of the Empress Galla Placidia, as we have found written, the same Peter Chrysologus with the above-mentioned empress preserved the body of blessed Barbatian with aromatics and buried him with great honor not far from the Ovilian gate. And he consecrated the church of Sts. John and Barbatian, which Baduarius built."[387] A Baduarius was the commander of the Byzantine armies of Italy in 575–7; a church built by him would have been dedicated by Bishop Peter III (570–8).[388] The legend of St. Barbatian as the confessor of Galla Placidia is entirely derivative; it was developing in Agnellus's time, but the full version was composed sometime between the ninth and eleventh centuries.[389] The church itself, in the area around San Vitale, disappeared in the course of the sixteenth century, and thus any information about its date is entirely speculative.[390]

Enough secure evidence testifies to a continual process of Christian monumentalization in fifth-century Ravenna. If at the beginning of the century most of the construction was attributed to emperors, after the 450s the bishops took the lead in developing an ecclesiastical topography for their city.

The End of Imperial Ravenna

Valentinian III moved the court to Rome in the 440s, and is not attested at Ravenna after 450. In the chaotic years after his assassination and the sack of Rome by the Vandals in 455, the short-lived emperors are attested alternately at Rome or Ravenna. It is notable that those emperors with strong connections to the Senate and/or the eastern empire were proclaimed emperor and ruled in Rome (Petronius Maximus, Avitus, Anthemius, Olybrius, Nepos), while those who were generals, or heavily supported by generals (Majorian, Libius Severus, Glycerius, Romulus Augustulus), took many of their significant actions in Ravenna.[391] Apparently by the later fifth century, Ravenna and Rome were viewed as the seats of the military and the senatorial establishments respectively. Each party viewed its own city as a place that could legitimize imperial action, but as events proved, this division was disastrous for the empire, since no emperor proved to be the master of both factions at once.

After 450, then, Ravenna's status as a capital was rather tenuous. The parallels between the development of Ravenna and Constantinople in the early fifth century are striking,[392] yet Ravenna did not attain the heights of the eastern capital.[393] Constantinople, as a "new Rome," could adopt many of the significant features, including a senate, that made it a Roman capital. Ravenna could not be a "new Rome" because the old Rome, with its Senate and monuments, was still there; Ravenna therefore filled only some of the functions of an imperial capital.[394] However, this ambiguity would be partially resolved in Italy's next political configuration.

CHAPTER FOUR

RAVENNA, THE CAPITAL OF THE OSTROGOTHIC KINGDOM

The sixth century was a pivotal time for Ravenna in terms of the direction that its history as an urban entity would take. The increased size and importance of Ravenna was recognized and maintained even after the decline of the imperial office in Italy. Odoacer, the general who deposed the last emperor and assumed the title of King of Italy, was living in Ravenna when he was defeated and murdered by the Ostrogothic ruler Theoderic in 493, and Theoderic in turn made the city his main residence. Under Theoderic, Ravenna truly became a capital city. Ostrogoths added to the ethnic mix of the city, and government offices attracted officials from Rome and other centers. Theoderic is credited in written sources both with repairing existing structures and building new ones; from archaeology we know that Classe too received new life at this time. Churches were built for the Arian Christians in the city; Theoderic also worked well with Ravenna's Orthodox bishops, who undertook interesting new building initiatives. Symbolically, on coins and mosaics, Ravenna was compared to the capitals of Rome and Constantinople, and it served as the symbolic and functional power base of the Amal dynasty until the last member of the line, Theoderic's granddaughter Matasuintha, was captured there and taken to Constantinople in 540.

Ostrogothic Italy has been the subject of intense study during the past century, largely because of the comparatively abundant contemporary textual sources. Most of these texts were written by learned Romans who liked and worked with Theoderic. Ennodius, eventually bishop of Pavia, wrote letters, poems, and a panegyric to Theoderic delivered in 507. Cassiodorus Senator worked at the highest levels of Ostrogothic government in 506–12, 523–7, and 533–8, and served as consul in 514; about 537 he published a set of letters written by him on behalf of the various rulers he served. Known as the *Variae*, these 468 documents are written in an elaborately rhetorical style and cover everything from legal cases to official government

Ravenna, c. AD 530

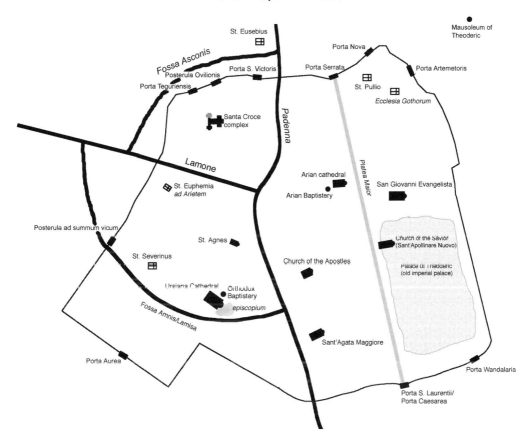

appointments to correspondence with foreign rulers; they are read by scholars for information on everything to do with Ostrogothic Italy. In addition to his government work, Cassiodorus wrote history: a chronicle, the *Chronica*, and a history of the Goths that is now lost (but is thought to have been an important source for much of Jordanes's *Getica*, a history of the Goths written in the 550s). An anonymous author, probably in the 540s, wrote a history of Theoderic's reign that is known today as the *Anonymus Valesianus pars posterior*. Procopius of Caesarea, who was a staff officer in Justinian's army of the reconquest of Italy, provides historical background and then describes in minute detail the war between the Byzantines and the Goths in his *De bello gothico*. And finally Agnellus's *LPR* offers certain very useful information about this period of Ravenna's history. It is significant that no texts survive that reflect an Ostrogothic perspective;[1] as we will see, this considerably slants our views of the period. The literary texts are

28. Map of Ravenna, ca. AD 530

29. Gold triple solidus of Theoderic (the Senigallia Medallion), gold, 3.3 cm diam., Museo Nazionale, Rome (courtesy Ministero per i Beni e le Attività Culturali – Soprintendenza Speciale per i Beni Archeologici di Roma)

supplemented by a few surviving documents in the archives of Ravenna, and by fragments of manuscripts written in Gothic; archaeology and numismatics, likewise, have added to our understanding of the Ostrogothic kingdom.

As we interpret what these sources tell us about Ostrogothic Ravenna, and as we examine the tangible remains from this period of the city's history, we will see that the city and its monuments both reflect and provide us with important information about Theoderic's ideology, Arian Christian belief, Gothic identity, and Roman and Orthodox reaction to the new regime.

Theoderic and Italy

The people who would become the Ostrogoths were relative latecomers to the "barbarian scene"; a number of small tribes living in the Balkans from the 380s to the 480s, some of which were undoubtedly connected to the Visigothic community, were gradually consolidated over the course of that century into one large group.[2] Theoderic's family, known after an eponymous ancestor as the Amals, had come to prominence under the Huns, and after the death of Attila they and their followers were officially settled in Pannonia by the emperor Marcian in 455. The settlement was uneasy, and at various times the Amal-led Goths rebelled against the empire or fought with other groups in the same region.

In 461,[3] Theoderic was sent as a hostage to Constantinople after a revolt. This was standard diplomatic procedure. Theoderic, age seven, was to be the guarantor of good behavior on the part of his father, Thiudimir. We know almost nothing about Theoderic's life in the capital; as a noble hostage, he would have been well housed, treated as a foreign guest of the palace, and possibly educated in Greek and Latin.[4] In 470 or 471 Theoderic, who was by now eighteen years old, was returned to his people, and upon his father's death in 474 he became its leader. He and his troops spent the next years fighting in various wars, sometimes against the empire, sometimes against other Gothic factions, and sometimes as part of the imperial army in Asia Minor. Theoderic built a reputation both among his people and in the empire: in 476 he was raised to the rank of *patricius* and named *magister militum praesentalis*, and in 484 he served as the consul of the eastern empire.

In 488, Theoderic led his group of Ostrogoths, now the dominant military force in the Balkans, into Italy.[5] Some sources say that this was on his initiative, and some that it was at the command of the emperor Zeno.[6] The target was Odoacer, who had begun to attack the western Balkans. Procopius tells us that the Ostrogothic migration into Italy was an entire tribe, men, women, and children; estimates of the number of people range from 20,000 to 100,000.[7] The war for Italy lasted from 489 to 493. Theoderic had taken control of most of Italy by 490, whereupon Odoacer retreated to Ravenna, which was, in theory, attackable only by sea.[8] Theoderic besieged the city for three years; in 492 he was finally able to assemble a fleet of ships to create a blockade, and in February 493, Bishop John served as a mediator to negotiate a treaty for shared rule, which called for Theoderic and Odoacer to occupy Ravenna jointly. Ten days after Theoderic entered Ravenna Odoacer was dead, apparently killed by Theoderic's own hand at a banquet.[9]

Theoderic rounded out his kingdom by reconquering Sicily (an important grain-producing region) from the Vandals in the early 490s, and taking over the Balkan provinces of Dalmatia and Savia after 504. He set about building not just a kingdom in Italy, but also a network of allies covering the former Roman territories in the west, by forging alliances through marriage with several of the other Germanic royal families.[10] The first marriages were made in the early to mid–490s: his daughter Ostrogotho Areagni married Sigismund, son of the king of the Burgundians; another daughter Theodegotha married Alaric II, king of the Visigoths, perhaps shortly afterward,[11] and Theoderic himself married Audofleda, sister of Clovis, king of the Franks, in or shortly after 493. In or after 500 Theoderic's widowed sister Amalafrida married Thrasamund, king of the Vandals in North Africa, and her daughter Amalaberga married Herminifrid, king of the Thuringians. These marriage alliances did not, however, produce peace throughout Europe. Theoderic's co-rulers continued to pursue their own policies despite Theoderic's exhortations, and his most notable failure came when Alaric II was killed in battle fighting against Clovis's Franks in 507.[12] Thrasamund supported Alaric's illegitimate son Gesalic as Visigothic king against Theoderic's legitimate young grandson Amalaric, but after Gesalic's death in 511 Theoderic ruled Visigothic Spain as regent for his grandson.[13]

Despite his extensive territories and his attempts to position himself as the leader of the western rulers, Theoderic did not call himself emperor, but ruled as *rex* (king), the title that had also been used by Odoacer.[14] He deliberately minted gold coins only in the name of the emperors of Constantinople (the Senigallia medallion [Fig. 29], which bears the only known portrait of him, was a special commemorative issue, and on it he is called *rex* and *princeps*).[15] In 490, Theoderic had sent an embassy to Zeno requesting imperial recognition of his title as *rex* in Italy. Zeno seems to have ignored the request and died in 491; the matter was only settled in 497 when, according to the *Anonymus Valesianus*, the emperor Anastasius returned to Theoderic the insignia (*ornamenta palatii*) that Odoacer had sent to Constantinople.[16] In 500 Theoderic finally visited Rome, was welcomed by the Senate and the pope, and was officially recognized as the ruler of Italy.[17] At the time he was celebrating his *tricennalia*, the thirty year anniversary of his rule as king. Interestingly, this assumes that he became "king" of the Ostrogoths in 470 around the time of his release from Constantinople, although his father did not die until 474.[18] Procopius notes that despite the title *rex*, Theoderic acted like, and presented himself as, an emperor: "in fact he was as truly an emperor as any who have distinguished themselves in this office from the beginning."[19]

In Italy, Theoderic established himself at Ravenna and set about developing an administration with which he could govern his kingdom. The Ostrogoths, augmented by the remains of Odoacer's followers and others, were a very small minority in Italy, perhaps only about 5 to 10 percent of the total population. Theoderic does not seem to have wanted to disperse his followers throughout Italy; that would not have been good for military readiness or group cohesion and loyalty.[20] Archaeological evidence from cemeteries and snippets of textual information imply that Ostrogoths settled mainly in northern and eastern Italy, especially in Liguria west of Pavia, along the Adriatic coast and at strategic places in the Alps, in Picenum (slightly northeast of Rome, on the east coast), and, of course, in Ravenna.[21] The exact mechanism by which the Ostrogoths were settled on Roman territory has been the matter of intense debate in recent decades. In some fashion, Theoderic, like Odoacer before him, used the Roman system of *hospitalitas*, by which the barbarian troops were assigned a third of something, either actual property or the land tax assessment, as well as having provision made for their billeting.[22]

Theoderic was well aware that he could not rule Italy without the support of the powerful Roman landowners of Italy. Members of the Senate had quarreled with the fifth-century emperors and supported Odoacer's rule. The position of senators in the later fifth and early sixth centuries was the strongest it had been since the time of Augustus and represented the culmination of a development fostered by the absence of imperial residence in Rome since the late third century.[23] Theoderic cultivated Roman senators and the Senate as an institution, he appeared with senators in ceremonies such as his anniversary at Rome in 500, he wrote many letters to the Senate in which he commended some action or appointment, and he employed many of them in his government. They reciprocated by supporting his aspirations and creating a Roman rhetorical structure that praised them. The concept of *civilitas*, repeatedly mentioned in the *Variae* of Cassiodorus and the writings of Ennodius, underpinned Theoderic's program as a ruler, at least in the first two decades of his reign.[24] *Civilitas* in these texts means a society that is run according to the Roman legal system and ordered by the norms of Roman city-based government.[25] The government Theoderic created was based on the old imperial bureaucracy, and many Romans served on its staff. He also used Gothic leaders as advisers, military heads, and local administrators. Theoderic's kingdom became famous for the way in which Romans and Goths worked together.[26] We will examine his religious policies, which display a similar tolerance, below. Procopius notes that Theoderic "was exceedingly careful to observe justice, he preserved the laws on a sure basis, he protected the land and kept it safe from the barbarians dwelling round about, and attained the highest possible degree of wisdom and manliness. And he himself committed scarcely a single act of injustice against his subjects, nor would he brook such conduct on the part of anyone else who attempted it . . . and love for him among both Goths and Italians grew to be great. . . ."[27]

For the first three decades of Theoderic's reign, Italy prospered. Theoderic actively promoted economic and commercial activity, regulating trade and prices where necessary.[28] He maintained the Roman tax system and was able to accumulate a surplus. The peace that he was able to enforce, coupled with his economic policies and a stable legal system, meant that both newcomers and Romans were able to settle down and get on with life;[29] at least, that is how it seemed in the hindsight of the Gothic war. As a result, Italy enjoyed a cultural renaissance; one of Theoderic's initiatives, as described in many letters in the *Variae*, was the revival and restoration of Roman culture.[30] Theoderic patronized Roman scholars such as Cassiodorus, Arator, Jordanes, Boethius, Ennodius, and Helpidius, who produced medical and religious treatises, poems, panegyrics, and histories, many of which were dedicated to him.[31] Greek texts were imported, translated, and commented on both by noted scholars such as Boethius and Cassiodorus, and lesser-known doctors, geographers, and others.[32]

Patronage of public buildings and infrastructure was an important aspect of *civilitas*, a highly visible reminder of good government.[33] Theoderic promoted himself as a rebuilder of the infrastructure of Roman Italy in the tradition of Roman leaders of the past; he also encouraged wealthy Romans to fund these works themselves.[34] Cassiodorus in his *Chronica* says that "in his happy reign many cities were renovated, strong forts were founded, marvellous palaces rose up, and ancient miracles were surpassed by his great works."[35] In many letters in which he requests renovations of buildings, Cassiodorus has Theoderic state the desire to revive the glory of the past.[36] C. La Rocca has very usefully pointed out that Theoderic's rhetoric about revival and restoration of *antiquitas* was propaganda that, among other things, contrasted him with immediately preceding rulers who had let the cities decay.[37] The portrayal of Theoderic as a builder was a convincing indicator of his greatness for later historians; the *Anonymus Valesianus* calls him "a lover of construction and restorer of cities," while Fredegar, a Frankish chronicler writing in the seventh century, recalls of Theoderic that "all the cities that he ruled he restored and fortified most ingeniously with wonderful works."[38] G. Brogiolo, however, warns that despite Theoderic's reputation as a great patron, and the classical Roman rhetoric about cities that appears in writings from his reign, in fact he contributed relatively little to most of the cities of Italy which had declined greatly by this period.[39]

Certainly Theoderic was particularly attentive to Rome and Ravenna.[40] Of Rome, Cassiodorus has him say, "what is worthier than to maintain the repairs of that place which clearly preserves the glory of my state?"[41] At Rome Theoderic ordered numerous repairs to the walls, sewers, palace, Curia, Theater of Pompey, aqueducts, and granaries.[42] In one letter, he grants a senator named Faustus leave to be absent from Rome for four months, but requires him to return, lest Rome, "the most glorious place on earth," be depopulated.[43] But Theoderic's interest in monuments of Roman civic life such as walls, baths, theaters, amphitheaters, porticoes, palaces, and aqueducts also extended beyond Rome to other cities, such as Arles, Abano, Catania, Spoleto, Parma, Pavia, and Verona.[44] It is interesting to note that the categories of structures patronized by Theoderic divide almost equally between monumental and functionally useful; and B. Saitta has noted that even works that seem purely commemorative contributed nevertheless to the development of industries that benefited the infrastructure of his kingdom.[45] It is also interesting that most of the items named in contemporary sources are secular constructions; Theoderic's church patronage is not listed, although this is perhaps not surprising given that they were built for Arian worship and all of our authors were Orthodox.[46]

We are much less well-informed about Theoderic's attitudes toward Ostrogothic culture; most of our information that there even was such a thing as non-Roman culture comes from the period after Theoderic's death. P. Amory traces a decline in *civilitas* rhetoric after 520, and the gradual predominance of a different strain, one that had always been present, in which the Goths' military prowess was presented as the key to the success of the Amal dynasty.[47] Cyprian, a Roman aristocrat, is commended in the *Variae* for knowing and teaching his sons the Gothic language.[48] Procopius describes antagonism on the part of certain Goths to Amalasuintha's determined program of Roman *civilitas*, centering on the education of her son Athalaric as not sufficiently militaristic, but his account uses stereotypes of Goths and Romans to justify Justinian's invasion of Italy.[49] Thus, while there apparently was a Gothic reaction to *civilitas*, even under Theoderic, it is difficult to pin down exactly what was at stake.

Most written sources (with the exception of Cassiodorus) note that toward the end of Theoderic's life there was a marked falling-off in his tolerance. The texts, which were written by Orthodox Christian writers, usually attribute this to Theoderic's Arianism (and, of course, the just judgment of God). In fact, in the last years of Theoderic's life a very complex set of political and religious circumstances were in rapid flux. In 518 the eastern emperor Anastasius, who had been a supporter of Theoderic, died and was succeeded by his guard captain Justin. One of the things that had contributed to the Romans' willingness to work with Theoderic was the fact that since 484 the popes had been in schism with the church in Constantinople over the emperor Zeno's attempt to reconcile Christological doctrine, and specifically over the status of Acacius as patriarch of Constantinople. The Acacian Schism, as it is known, was resolved by Justin in 519, and although in 520 a new theological controversy (theopaschism) arose, that too was resolved by 523, and the popes and Orthodox Romans began a new era of rapprochement with Constantinople. The leadership of the Italian church was also changing. Peter II, who had reigned as bishop of Ravenna for almost all of Theoderic's reign, died in 520; his successor Aurelian lived only one year, and Ecclesius was then seated as bishop in 522. Then in 523 Pope Hormisdas, with whom Theoderic had good relations, died and the new pope, John I, did not sympathize with the aging Arian ruler of Italy. At this time, Justin apparently began to persecute Arian Christians in his reach, which inflamed Theoderic, who considered himself the senior Arian king of the west. And, of course, anti-Gothic factions in Italy took advantage of these events to urge reunion with the empire.

At the same time, Theoderic's plan for the royal succession was falling apart. One of Theoderic's main political problems was that he did not have a son to succeed him. In 515 he had married his daughter Amalasuintha to Eutharic, a Goth from Spain who was supposedly of the Amal line. Eutharic was named consul jointly with the emperor Justin in 519, and was adopted as son-at-arms by Justin, a clear sign that the imperial court recognized him as Theoderic's successor. However, there are hints that Eutharic did not intend to rule as tolerantly as Theoderic had, and his elevation may have exacerbated anti-Ostrogothic elements among the Roman elite. Amalasuintha and Eutharic had two children, Athalaric and Matasuintha, but Eutharic died in 522, when Athalaric was only four or five years old.

In these circumstances, the sources say that in his last years Theoderic became paranoid, seeing plots everywhere and striking out at those who had formerly supported him, including, most famously, the patricians Symmachus and Boethius, who were executed on Theoderic's orders in 524 and/or 525. The turnaround was all the more striking as Boethius's two sons (who were Symmachus's grandsons) had shared the consulship at Rome in 522, a mark of high distinction.[50] Pope John was sent on a mission to Constantinople with various other bishops (including Ecclesius of Ravenna) to persuade the emperor to stop persecuting and forcibly converting Arians; the mission apparently failed, and John died in Ravenna upon his return in 526. The death of Theoderic a few days later on August 30, was, at least later, viewed by the Orthodox as a sign of God's disfavor.[51] Nevertheless, for the next several years Italy remained relatively peaceful.

Theoderic's Ravenna

If the imperial status of Ravenna had been somewhat ambivalent, Theoderic made the city indubitably the capital of his kingdom, the *urbs regia*.[52] Although he could have settled his court in Rome, he chose to develop a form of government in which the Roman Senate was respected as a rather independent component, and he left Rome to the senators.[53] Rather remarkably, after defeating Odoacer, Theoderic never again took personal command of an army, but settled down in Ravenna, and to a lesser extent Verona and Pavia, where he built palaces.[54] He is known to have visited Rome only once, in 500, and he seems mostly to have stayed in Ravenna and its environs. As we will see, at least two palaces were built in the countryside around the city. Goths, Romans, ambassadors, envoys, and anyone else who wanted to see the king made the journey to Ravenna.[55]

30. Bronze decanummium, obverse with bust of Ravenna and the legend "Felix Ravenna," reverse with a monogram of Ravenna sur- rounded by a wreath (courtesy Princeton Uni- versity Numis- matic Collection)

Theoderic, like Odoacer and the early fifth-century emperors, spent time and money establishing Ravenna as a suitable center for his govern- ment, constructing both sacred and secular buildings there in imitation of Constantinople and Rome.[56] As in the imperial era, Ravenna's prestige was actively rivaled by that of Rome.[57] Theoderic seems to have recognized the symbolic significance of this pair of cities: according to Agnellus, a mosaic prominently displayed in the palace depicted "an image of Theoderic, won- derfully executed in mosaic, holding a lance in his right hand, a shield in his left, wearing a breastplate. Facing the shield stood Rome, executed in mosaic with spear and helmet; and there holding a spear was Ravenna, fig- ured in mosaic, with right foot on the sea, left on land hastening toward the king."[58] Since the founding of Constantinople it had been traditional to depict the two imperial capital cities as paired female personifications, and it was also common to depict an emperor on horseback between female personifications.[59] If Agnellus's description is accurate, the importance of Ravenna as a port city, "with right foot on the sea," was stressed in this image, as indeed it would also be in the depictions of Ravenna and Classe in Theoderic's palace church (see Chapter 5). Thus, Theoderic introduced the new pairing Ravenna–Rome in his political iconography, and the concept was later reflected on Ostrogothic bronze coins minted respec- tively with the legends *Invicta Roma* and *Felix Ravenna* (Fig. 30).[60] Finally, although Theoderic's thirty year anniversary celebrations took place in Rome, the festivities associated with Eutharic's consulship in 519 were apparently celebrated in both cities.[61]

We have already seen that most of what we know about Theoderic's political and ideological programs come from Roman authors; and these men do not seem to have been impressed with Ravenna. Under Theoderic Ravenna became a center of education and literary culture, housing authors who worked for his government and who produced poems and philosoph- ical, historical, medical, and geographical texts.[62] Yet, as in the imperial period, although members of the upper Roman aristocracy lived in Ravenna while occupying government posts, and up-and-coming members of new families carved out exalted careers there, most returned to Rome or to their estates when their terms of office were completed.[63] Theoderic may have kept the royal court in Ravenna because of its port, but the Roman senatorial aristocracy does not seem to have liked it; none of the various poets and authors retained by Theoderic praise his capital city. Ennodius, in his panegyric to Theoderic, praises his building activities in a general way but does not mention Ravenna;[64] even Cassiodorus, who spent many years in Ravenna, reserves praise for Rome.[65] This complete absence of praise for a capital city in the context of a lively literary culture is surprising; imperial Milan, for example, had been the subject of a laudatory poem by Ausonius. One is forced to take one of two choices. Either Theoderic's attempts to create an imperial capital completely failed to convince the Roman aristocracy; or Theoderic's audience was really the Goths and nonaristocratic Italians, who seem to have had no role in Rome, little incentive to take up seats in the Senate to which they were entitled, and whose focus was on Ravenna.[66] Ravenna's central role in Ostrogothic policy can be seen in the issuing of donatives to Gothic soldiers: grants of money given to all Gothic soldiers had to be picked up, in person, in Ravenna.[67] Clearly this was a way of reinforcing military and/or group loyalty in a situation in which the Goths were dispersed throughout Italy. It reinforced their personal connection with the king, but it also brought all Gothic soldiers to his capital city, where they could see the splendor of his kingdom.

We know relatively little about how Ravenna was laid out in Theoderic's time (Fig. 28). One often-repeated idea is that there was a Gothic zone, a particular area of the city where Goths lived and worshiped, in the northeastern part of Ravenna.[68] This has been argued primarily on the basis of maps showing the distribution of churches identified by Agnellus as Arian (on these churches, see Chapter 5). The Arian episcopal complex was to the southwest of this area. A church dedicated to St. Eusebius was outside the northern *porta S. Victoris*, and Theoderic's mausoleum was outside the northeastern corner of the wall. However, it should be noted that a church dedicated to Severinus, a saint beloved by Arians, was found in the center of the old *oppidum*.[69] There were Arian churches in Classe and Caesarea, and Theoderic made the former imperial palace his own and added to it a large basilica dedicated to the Savior. Moreover, documents show some Goths living side by side with Romans.[70] Thus evidence is too scanty and inconclusive to propose a concentration of Goths in one part of the city.

Under Theoderic the population of Ravenna swelled to its largest size, perhaps as large as 10,000.[71] The city probably retained a large number of government functionaries from previous administrations, since as far as we know Odoacer had continued the administrative practices of his imperial predecessors. Information about Theoderic's administrative system comes largely from Cassiodorus's *Variae* and indicates that the chief officials of the central government were based in Ravenna.[72] High government officials under Theoderic held office for longer periods of time than in the imperial period and thus the society of the court must have been somewhat more stable in this period. In addition to the government and palace officials, both aristocratic and bureaucratic, a municipal elite served as the magistrates and members of the local *curia*, or town council. The few documents that survive from the Ostrogothic period indicate that these officials consisted of notaries and *tabelliones*, bankers and businessmen, doctors and lawyers.[73] The names of both Jews and people from the eastern Mediterranean are found in inscriptions and in the *Variae*, although it is interesting that of the artisans and businessmen, none have recognizably "Gothic" names except for Wiliarit the scribe, whom we will meet again.[74]

The members of Ravennate society under Theoderic lived in an urban center that was being changed and modified to suit them, as has been demonstrated by archaeological evidence found at the Via D'Azeglio excavation in the northeastern part of the old *oppidum*. Since the second century BC two houses had faced each other across a 5-m-wide street, but now in the late fifth or early sixth century the street was blocked off by a room that served as a monumental entrance to a new, grander house built to the north of the street, with a second, equally grand house built to the south, perhaps both opening on to a street to the west. The main rooms on both the north and south sides were covered with elaborate mosaic and *opus sectile* floors.[75] These buildings must have housed members of Theoderic's court or the Ravennate upper classes; and the modification of the imperial-era street network indicates new urban priorities at work.

Major works were also undertaken at Classe's port, although it was no longer the naval station that it had been in the early imperial period. Part of the Augustan harbor was now completely dried up, according to Jordanes, who says, "that which was once a harbor now displays itself like a spacious garden full of trees; but from them hang not sails but apples."[76] Nevertheless, Classe continued to function as an important commercial port throughout the Ostrogothic period, actively encouraged by Theoderic. Excavations at the site of Podere Chiavichetta have revealed a section of the port city that flanked the canal leading to the harbor. The island in the center of the canal contained paved roads, shops, and food vendors, and was linked by a bridge to the city to the south. On the south bank, at the time of Theoderic, a major street was repaved and buildings in this area were modified, rebuilt, and systematized with continuous porticoes. A row of large warehouses and public buildings faced the canal through one such portico and to the street on their other side through another; on the other side of the street were production facilities such as a ceramics kiln and a glass furnace.[77] From the many thousands of ceramics fragments found on these sites, we can identify imports, especially from North Africa, but also from Palestine and Syria, the Aegean and Asia Minor, Egypt, Lusitania, and Sicily (mainly wine, but also oil and honey).[78] The imported ceramics are significant because in much of inland Italy they had almost entirely disappeared by this time, demonstrating the anomalous status of Ravenna.[79]

It was clearly in the royal interest to support commerce and trade in Ravenna, both for the purposes of catering to the members of the community, and for provisioning the troops who were stationed there.[80] The archaeological evidence is borne out by various letters in the *Variae* that specifically deal with economic matters in Ravenna. Military provisions were most important, especially wine and oil; in two letters Cassiodorus refers to the *mansio* at Ravenna, which must mean the military encampment. One of these letters commands that supplies be sent to Ravenna from Istria, and in another Cassiodorus notes that Istria is "the store-room of the royal city (*urbis regiae cella penaria*). . . . Istria clearly refreshes our hard-working court (*comitatenses excubias*), it supplies the *imperium* of Italy; it feeds the nobles on its luxuries, lesser men on its output of foodstuffs, and almost its entire produce is enjoyed by the royal city."[81] Cassiodorus goes on to note that these supplies are to be brought to Ravenna by ship, either directly across the sea, or via the network of canals that linked the entire Adriatic coastline.[82] That Ravenna was the storehouse of the royal administration can also be seen by a letter written when Theoderic was at Pavia, commanding that grain stored at Ravenna be loaded onto ships and brought to the royal court.[83] The *urbs regia*, like the other major Roman capital cities, also distributed grain to its citizens to prevent civil unrest.[84] Procopius mentions grain warehouses within the city of Ravenna.[85] The importance of ships is underscored in a series of letters written in 525–6, commissioning a fleet to be based at Ravenna, "which might convey the public grain supplies and, if necessary, oppose enemy ships."[86] Classe, its harbor, and its warehouses thus formed a vital part of the royal administration.

Quantities of building materials and possibly workmen were imported from the eastern Mediterranean under Theoderic; at the same time, there were also workshops for luxury items in Ravenna that may have continued to exist from the previous century. Large numbers of stone sarcophagi from the early sixth century still survive in Ravenna, and their sculptural style and iconography show influences derived both from Constantinople and from earlier local practices.[87] Impressive manuscripts were made in Ravenna: A Bible copied from one made in Ravenna in the early sixth century names Bishop Ecclesius as the original sponsor, and an Orosius manuscript bears the name of one "Viliaric magister antiquarius," who may be the same as the Wiliarit *spodeus* (scribe) named on a Ravennate document written in 551.[88] A letter in the *Variae* from Theoderic to a marble-worker named Daniel gives the latter a monopoly on the furnishing of sarcophagi to the inhabitants of Ravenna, but abjures him not to overcharge grieving family members for his products.[89] Other than these fragments, there is little other tangible evidence of manufacturing or crafts in Ravenna, although it is generally assumed that notable ivory-carving, gold-working, and manuscript workshops were located here, largely on the basis of stylistic and iconographical similarities between these portable works of art and the mosaics and sculpture found in Ravenna's buildings.[90]

Theoderic's Palaces

The palace was the preeminent symbol of royal authority, as was recognized by Theoderic and his propagandists. Cassiodorus's *Variae* famously refer twice to the importance of the palace: "it is truly worthy of a king to decorate his palaces [*palatia*] with buildings," and at greater length, as part of the formula for the appointment of the palace architect:[91]

> These [halls/*aulae*] are the delights of our power, the worthy face of our rule, the public witness of our kingdoms: they are shown to admiring ambassadors, and at first sight one believes that as is the house so is its lord. And moreover it is the great delight of a most prudent mind [i.e., of the king] to rejoice perpetually in a most beautiful habitation and to refresh his spirit, worn out by public cares, in the pleasure of the architecture.

Other accounts also mention Theoderic's construction of palaces. Cassiodorus in his *Chronica* refers to Theoderic's *admiranda palatia*, and Ennodius in his panegyric says, "I see an unhoped-for beauty rise from the ashes of cities and the palatine roofs gleam everywhere under the plenitude of *civilitas*."[92] Cassiodorus uses the *palatium* at Ravenna as a synonym for the court and royal government. We have already seen in the previous chapter that a site to the east of Sant'Apollinare Nuovo has been identified as the "palace of Theoderic." The time has finally come to discuss this palace in the context of Theoderic himself!

The *Anonymus Valesianus* says that at Ravenna Theoderic "completed the palace, but did not dedicate it; he completed porticoes around the palace."[93] This indicates that he was working on a palace whose construction was already underway. As we have seen, the archaeological site in question shows evidence of palatial construction going back into the fourth century, with extensive renovations and additions in the early sixth century, including the construction of Sant'Apollinare Nuovo, attributed by Agnellus to

Theoderic. A. Augenti's recent study of the different phases of construction concludes that some significant rebuilding took place during the early sixth century (Fig. 31). A large triconch triclinium to the east of the great apsed hall and its adjoining rooms was built, measuring almost 15 meters east–west.[94] This space was paved with a multicolored marble mosaic floor whose central figural panel depicted the mythological story of Bellerophon and the Chimera, surrounded by personifications of the Four Seasons with accompanying inscriptions in hexameter, all of which were images with imperial connotations.[95] A semicircular apse was also added to one of the rooms to the east of the great hall, and both this room and the hall were newly paved with mosaic, as were the floors of the corridors around the courtyard. Other modifications were made to the rooms at the southern side of the courtyard, including new mosaic pavements in some of the rooms, and this construction work also extended farther south. Finally, pilasters were added to the external walls of the complex, whether for decoration or to reinforce the wall is not clear.[96] The magnificence of the decorative program is echoed in a fragment of an oration delivered in praise of Witigis and Matasuintha around 536, in which Cassiodorus praises a palace's decoration: "The marble surface shines with the same color as gems, the scattered gold gleams..., the gifts of mosaic work delineate the circling rows of stones; and the whole is adorned with marble hues, where the waxen pictures are displayed."[97] In other words, the existing palace was utilized and refurbished in the latest decorative modes, which both emphasized continuity with the past and added to the visual splendor of Theoderic's court.

It seems clear from evidence provided by Agnellus and to some extent by later topographical references that this was Theoderic's main palace, and moreover that the entrance to the palace was just south of Sant'Apollinare Nuovo, opening onto a ceremonial plaza. In front of this entrance Theoderic erected a bronze equestrian statue of himself, probably imitating the statue of Marcus Aurelius in Rome, which at this time may have stood in the courtyard of the Lateran palace, and similar equestrian statues in the Augusteion in Constantinople.[98] The statue was not the only way in which Theoderic placed his imprint on the palace in Ravenna. The image of Theoderic between Rome and Ravenna, described above, is said by Agnellus to have been located "in the palace which he built in this city [Ravenna], in the apse of the dining hall which is called By the Sea, above the gate, and in the facade of the main door which is called Ad Calchi, where the main gate of the palace was, in the place which is called Sicrestum, where the church of the Savior is seen to be. In the pinnacle of this place was an image of Theoderic...."[99] The word *sicrestum* is thought to be a degeneration of a word like σέκρετον, σεκρετάριον, or in Latin, *sacristia, secretarium*; the words imply some sort of official government function.[100] The whole

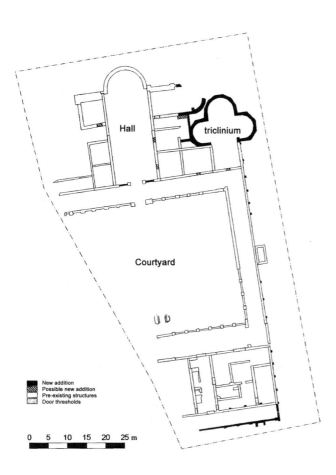

Hall

triclinium

Courtyard

New addition
Possible new addition
Pre-existing structures
Door thresholds

0   5   10   15   20   25 m

31. Plan of the palace, as known from excavations, ca. 526 (after Augenti, "Archeologia e topografia," 2005, fig. 8)

passage is very difficult to understand; many scholars have interpreted it to mean that the image of Theoderic was in the pinnacle over the main gate of the palace.[101] A closer reading of the text indicates that it was the *dining hall* that was over the main gate and that the image was in its apse.[102] We must remember that Agnellus would not have seen the original mosaic to which he refers in the past tense as though it was no longer there. In any case, it is clear from the account of this image that the main gate of the palace was located between Sant'Apollinare Nuovo and the ruin that is often erroneously called the "Palace of the Exarchs," but which was in fact an eighth-century church dedicated to the Savior. The entire entrance complex was intended to recall Constantinople, and thus to impress both friends and foes with the legitimacy and power of Theoderic's rule.

As noted, Theoderic spent almost his entire reign at Ravenna in the imperial palace and perhaps in several other residences around Ravenna. Excavations have revealed three grand sixth-century villa-type structures, containing apsed halls, baths, elaborate mosaics, and other indications of wealth and interpreted as hunting lodges or rural palaces: these existed at Meldola, 35 km southwest of Ravenna along the course of the Bidente-Ronco River and the aqueduct; at Galeata, 50 km southwest of Ravenna; and at the interestingly named Palazzolo, 8 km to the north of the city.[103] There is no contemporary evidence to link any of these structures directly with Theoderic, and indeed they merely indicate that a wealthy class residing in Ravenna was building country houses in the surrounding area. The structure at Palazzolo, measuring ca. 44 × 55 m and taking the form of a forti-fied villa with associated bath structures, is often identified as the *palatium modicum* that Agnellus says Theoderic built on an island, not far from the sea, in a bath, six miles from Ravenna, during his three-year siege of the city.[104]

Theoderic's Other Secular Constructions

Various pieces of evidence exist for Theoderic's other building works in Ravenna. The best documented of these is his repair of the aqueduct. We have already seen that, according to the report of Sidonius Apolli-naris, Ravenna's Roman aqueduct was no longer functioning in the 460s. Theoderic's restoration of this aqueduct was seen as a major feat: The *Anonymus Valesianus* says that "He [Theoderic] restored the aqueduct of Ravenna, which the ruler Trajan had built, and after much time he intro-duced water," and Cassiodorus in his *Chronica* also specifically mentions the restoration of the aqueduct.[105] The reconstruction of the aqueduct was confirmed in 1938 by the discovery in Ravenna of lead *fistulae*, or water pipes, with the inscription *D[ominus] N[oster] Rex Theodericus Civitati red-didit*.[106] Moreover, in a letter, Theoderic declares to the landowners around Ravenna that he has a particular concern for aqueducts and charges them to clean out all the bushes and saplings that have grown in the channel so that "we will have a fit maintenance of the baths, then the pools will swell with glass-like waves, then the water will cleanse, not stain, and it will not be always necessary to rewash things . . . if sweet water for drinking shall flow in, all that is used in our food will be better, since no food seems pleasing to human life where clear sweet water is lacking."[107] It is worth noting in this context that aqueducts in major Roman cities still seem to have functioned in the sixth century, and new ones were still being built, for example, as reported by Procopius. Rome's aqueducts still functioned in the early sixth century, since they are said to have been cut by Witigis during the course of the Gothic War in mid–century; Constantinople's aqueduct was cut dur-ing the Avar siege of 626.[108] From these examples we can see that one of the actions taken by a besieging army was to cut the aqueduct, and we can

32. Marble panel depicting Hercules and the Stag of Cerineia, early sixth century, Museo Nazionale, Ravenna (courtesy Soprintendenza per i Beni Architettonici e Paesaggistici di Ravenna [MiBAC-ITALIA])

speculate whether Theoderic himself had contributed to Ravenna's water decline during his three-year siege of Odoacer.

Three letters from the *Variae* order individuals or groups to send fine building materials to Theoderic's capital: From Aestuna, from the Pincian Hill in Rome, and from Faenza he requests old marble and columns that are lying around, "so that our desire for the adornment of that city may be gratified."[109] Some of this material must have been intended for the palace, but in *Variae* I.6 Theoderic asks Agapitus, the Praetorian Prefect of Rome, to send marble workers and mosaicists from Rome for the construction of a *basilica Herculis*.[110] There is no other definite information, textual or archaeological, for this structure, although a sixth-century marble relief plaque depicting Hercules and the Stag of Ceryneia, now in the Museo Nazionale in Ravenna, may have been executed as part of a series of the Labors of Hercules to decorate this basilica (Fig. 32).[111] The location and nature of the building are controversial, since the only evidence for it comes from this letter. In the pre-Christian Latin tradition, a *basilica* was, as Vitruvius says, a sheltered public hall off the forum;[112] however, by the sixth century the word *basilica* was a word used almost exclusively for churches.[113] Cassiodorus does not use the word elsewhere in the *Variae*, where large royal halls are called *aulae*; the structure and its dedication to Hercules imply that some classical tradition was consciously being revived for Ravenna. Agnellus twice refers to a *regio Herculana*, which he says was the location of the cathedral and not far from St. Andrew Major,[114] thus in the center of the old *oppidum* and possibly near the forum. Somewhere in this location stood a 5-meters-tall statue of Hercules holding a sundial on his shoulders, which was supposedly erected by the emperor Tiberius and survived until 1591. Some scholars have thus proposed that Theoderic's basilica was probably associated with this region, and must have been a secular civic building in the heart of the old *oppidum*.[115] On the other hand, Cassiodorus's letter begins by saying, "it is indeed worthy for a king to adorn [*decorare*] his palaces with buildings." Another group of scholars has therefore seen this building as part of the palace, of which, as we have seen, we know very little.[116] The fact that *basilicae* were not normally part of palaces remains problematic, and thus the question remains open.

The Mausoleum of Theoderic

From his own day to the present, the extraordinary structure in which Theoderic was buried has been considered one of his most remarkable achievements.[117] The *Anonymus Valesianus* points out the features that are still considered worthy of notice today: "while still alive he made himself a monument (*monumentum*) of blocks of stone, a work of marvellous size, and he sought out a huge rock to place on the top."[118] This description reflects Jerome's account of the tomb of the ancient ruler Mausolus of Halicarnassus, which was extant in Theoderic's day and was widely known to ancient and medieval authors; Cassiodorus lists it as one of the Seven Wonders of the World.[119] In many respects Theoderic's mausoleum is unique, and he probably intended it to echo the famous tombs of rulers such as Mausolus and various Roman emperors, while at the same time testifying to his own unique greatness. The fact that it today appears incomplete, and that it is unlike any other known structure, has made it the subject of much speculative interpretation. Some have wanted to see it as a "Roman" monument, whereas others have read it as something strange and therefore "Gothic"; it is possible that this ambiguity, which was so much a part of Theoderic's political ideology, was intentional.

33. Mausoleum of Theoderic, view from the west (photo S. Mauskopf)

Located just outside the northeast corner of the city wall at the time it was constructed, the mausoleum would have been close to the small harbor and coastline. The site lay within Ravenna's cemetery zone, and graves excavated to the southeast in the mid–nineteenth century contained jewelry identified by archaeologists as "Gothic."[120] Agnellus refers to its location as "at the lighthouse" (*ad farum*); as we have seen, Ravenna had a famous lighthouse in the Roman period, mentioned by Pliny the Elder, which may have given its name to this area.[121]

The first thing to note is that, unlike any other building in Ravenna, Theoderic's mausoleum was built not of brick but of limestone that came from Istria, across the Adriatic Sea from Ravenna.[122] The wall surfaces present beautiful squared ashlar blocks, shaped to fit together perfectly using the technique of *anathyrosis*, in which the inner surfaces of the ashlar blocks are made slightly concave, so that a perfect fit has only to be attained around the edge of each block. Some of the blocks were carved in situ to create the interior wall surfaces; for example, on the interior of the lower chamber, the corner angles are not made of joins between blocks, but instead large blocks have been shaped in place with the corner angles cut out of them (Fig. 34). The arches and lintels are made using "joggled voussoirs," blocks cut with a zig-zag that links with the next block (Fig. 35); this technique, while used throughout the Roman Empire in the imperial period, by the sixth century is known to have been used only in the eastern Mediterranean,

34. Mauseoleum of Theoderic, view of the interior of the lower level

which has led to the suggestion that Theoderic imported architects from Syria or Asia Minor to construct his tomb.[123] Beneath the finely crafted surfaces, the interior core of the walls consists of irregular blocks of stone, smaller fragments, and mortar.[124] The entire weighty structure rests on a platform of brick and mortar that is at least 1.5 m deep and rests on the natural sand, which extends in a circle 7.9 m beyond the corners of the mausoleum.[125] Originally a fence, composed of metal grilles supported by thirty carved marble piers, 2.29 m high, surrounded the building at a distance of 4.8 m.[126] The care taken with the design and engineering of the building demonstrates craftsmanship of the highest level.

The mausoleum itself is a centrally planned building with two stories; each story is visually articulated on the exterior and has a vaulted chamber on the interior. Centrally planned structures are typical of Roman elite mausolea, and it is often noted that Theoderic's mausoleum imitates Roman imperial mausolea known from Rome, Spalato, Milan, Thessalonike, and Constantinople.[127] Although most of these structures were made of brick, there is evidence that some, such as the mausoleum of Augustus in Rome, were plastered and painted on the exterior to look like stone.[128] Despite obvious similarities, Theoderic's mausoleum also contained some significant differences from contemporary imperial mausolea. One difference is the fact that while some pre-Christian Roman mausolea had an upper and a lower chamber, after the fourth century imperial mausolea generally had only one level, and were usually attached to adjacent churches.[129] Theoderic's tomb was a freestanding monument, and although

35. Mausoleum of Theoderic, entrance, lower level

it has been argued that one of the chambers took on the functions of a chapel, this layout is found in no other contemporary royal tomb. Some fourth-century pre-Christian imperial examples from the Balkans, such as the mausoleum of Diocletian at Spalato and two funerary structures found at Gamzigrad, with which Theoderic would certainly have been familiar, were not attached to churches and had two stories and were moreover made of ashlar masonry making them better models for our monument.[130] We will return to this question.

Another difference is that imperial mausolea generally had circular or octagonal ground plans, whereas Theoderic's building had ten sides at ground level (Fig. 36). Explanations of this feature usually center on the writings of Boethius, who wrote a treatise on mathematics in which number

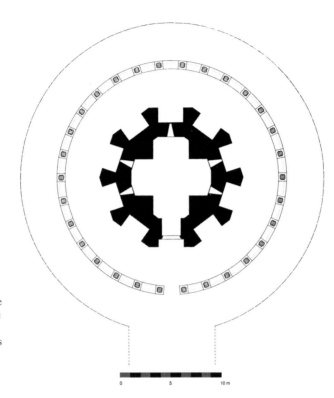

36. Mausoleum of Theoderic, plan at ground level showing the structure and the original location of the fence posts (after Heidenreich/Johannes, 1971, fig. 137)

symbolism and Pythagorean ideas were explicitly discussed, and whose knowledge was specifically praised by Cassiodorus. Ten was considered by Boethius to be a perfect number, symbolic of heaven, and by this reasoning would be a very appropriate layout for a tomb.[131] If Boethian mathematical theory influenced the construction of Theoderic's tomb,[132] Theoderic was aiming for originality rather than conformity with established imperial tradition.

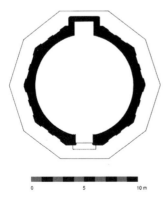

37. Mausoleum of Theoderic, plan of the upper level (after Heidenreich/Johannes, 1971, fig. 11)

Let us examine the building level by level. The exterior outline of the lower level has ten sides, with the entrance on the west side. On each of the other nine sides, a niche with a rectangular plan and an arched top (2.44–46 meters wide, 1.42 meters deep, and 6.50 meters high) takes up a majority of the wall surface and creates an undulating effect. A cornice runs continuously around the exterior at the level of the springing of the arches of these niches; a drawing made ca. 1500 by Giuliano da Sangallo shows another cornice at the top of the lower story, but no trace of such a detail survives.[133] The geometries of the lower level are subtle and brilliantly worked out. The interior room on the lower level is cruciform; the ends of the cross arms are not flat, but each have three facets which are angled so that they are parallel to the exterior walls and niches of the decagon. In the east and west arms, the angled facets are carved in the upper corners with seashells, a funerary symbol. Two small slit windows, one above the other, pierce the center of the wall on the east side, while in the north and south arms of the cross two similar windows pierce the side facets of each end wall. A simple cornice runs around the entire interior space at the level of the springing of the barrel vaults, which are made of long ashlars (Fig. 34). There is no evidence of any other interior decoration on the walls or vaults.

The upper level has a smaller diameter than the lower, and a platform 1.30 m wide runs around the exterior; the upper door is directly above the lower, although there is no evidence of a staircase giving access to this level (Fig. 37). The structure here is decagonal up to the level of the cornice above the door, but then becomes circular. Nine sides of the decagon (excluding the wall with the door) are articulated with shallowly carved rectangular niches topped by projecting lunettes and separated by pilasters, with triangular brackets projecting at the upper level on the corners, flanked by additional slots (Fig. 38). This wall articulation is part of some more complex decorative plan for this level; it is not clear whether the decoration was originally completed and was subsequently completely dismantled or whether it was never completed.[134] The statement in the *Anonymus Valesianus* rather implies that the structure was completed, but only because it does not say that it was left unfinished. Also, since seven years elapsed between Theoderic's death and the start of the Gothic War, it seems likely that it would have been completed after 526 even if not before, although, of course, the original design might then have been modified.

There has been a great deal of debate about what the original decoration of the upper exterior story was (or was intended to be). One suggestion, made most forcefully by Heidenreich and Johannes after detailed examination of the architecture, is that only a flat wall articulation was originally intended, decorated with relatively shallow relief, as well as statues of

38. Mausoleum of Theoderic, monolithic capstone (photo C. L. Striker)

winged victories set on the corner brackets (Fig. 39).[135] While their statues are somewhat fanciful, this reconstruction corresponds to some of the imperial mausolea in the Balkans, which, unlike those in Milan, had a plain upper exterior drum set back from a lower colonnade. On the other hand, several scholars have proposed that there was originally meant to be an arcaded loggia or gallery surrounding this level, composed of short barrel vaults perpendicular to the walls of the decagon and supported by the lunettes and slots in the walls (Fig. 40).[136] Such reconstructions are based on the proposal that Theoderic's mausoleum imitated imperial mausolea in Milan, in particular the now-lost chapel of San Gregorio at San Vittore al Corpo, the burial place perhaps of Maximian or Valentinian II, and the chapel of San Aquilino attached to San Lorenzo, each of which had an exterior loggia or "dwarf gallery" at the upper level.[137] San Aquilino, at least, had only one interior chamber, and moreover the loggia was set above the window zone, thus did not flank a door; on the other hand, both Mausoleum 2 at Gamzigrad and the Tomb of Mausolus at Halicarnassus had a colonnade at the upper level, and some depictions of the Holy Sepulchre show a similar arrangement.[138] Since ultimately we cannot know what was intended or what was built, we can only conclude that given the variety of models available to Theoderic and his architects, any one of the proposed reconstructions would have carried connotations of classical monumental tombs.

The upper chamber is circular on the interior, 9.20 meters in diameter, with a small square niche (1.8 meters wide, 1.28 meters deep, 1.90 meters

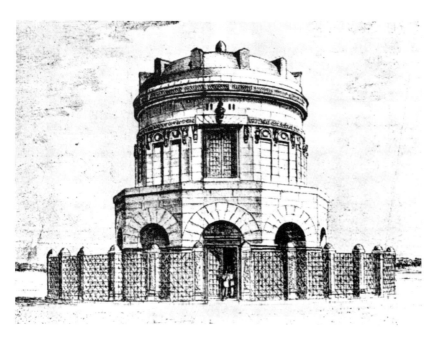

39. Reconstruction of the Mausoleum of Theoderic (by Heidenreich/Johannes, 1971)

40. Reconstruction of the Mausoleum of Theoderic (by De Angelis d'Ossat, 1960)

41. Mausoleum of Theoderic, porphyry bathtub now in the upper room

high) set into the east wall directly opposite the entrance.[139] The walls are articulated by a cornice at the level of the lintel over the door. Above this cornice is a window zone: four small windows are inserted above the door. Small windows face directly north and south, slightly larger windows face northeast, southeast, northwest, and southwest,[140] and a window facing directly to the east takes the form of an equal-armed cross. Above the niche in the eastern wall, below this window, another cross is carved in high relief on the keystone of the arch. Above the window zone is another plain cornice and surmounting the whole is the monolithic dome. In the center of the dome can be seen the outline of a circle, shallowly carved and embossed as though it originally held plaster for a fresco or mosaic (the painted cross that appears today is medieval or later).[141] Sixteenth- and seventeenth-century descriptions mention a figural mosaic floor in this level, although we do not know if this was original or from a later date. The floor of the upper level was remade in 1903, at which time a drawing was made of the vaulting of the lower chamber.[142]

Where in this structure was Theoderic buried? Agnellus says, "But it seems to me that he has been cast out of his tomb, and that very marvelous vessel lying there, made of porphyry stone, was placed before the entrance of that *monasterium*."[143] Since 1913 a late antique porphyry bathtub has stood in the upper chamber of the mausoleum, which is presumed to be the object that Agnellus describes (Fig. 41). It is impossible to determine whether Theoderic was really buried in this vessel. Certainly the bathtub had imperial connotations, as only emperors were allowed to own objects

42. Mausoleum of Theoderic, "Zangenfries" relief ornament at the base of the capstone (photo C. L. Striker)

made of porphyry, and it was the right size for burial.[144] But in which chamber would it have been placed? It seems most likely that Theoderic's body was in the upper story, to avoid the flooding that besets Ravenna, and in order to be directly under the dome. As there is no evidence for stairs to the upper story, the tomb chamber would have been inaccessible after Theoderic's burial, whereas the lower chamber would be used as a memorial chapel.[145] On the other hand, in earlier imperial mausolea, including those in the Balkans, the lower space was used for the tombs and the upper chamber for a shrine. The cruciform layout of the lower chamber is similar to chapels such as the "mausoleum of Galla Placidia," which, as we have seen, may not have been an imperial mausoleum but certainly was similar to a type of late antique mausoleum-chapel. Thus, some scholars have proposed that the upper chamber was the intended memorial chapel, while the lower space would have contained the tombs of Theoderic and his family.[146] We do not know when Theoderic's body would have been removed from the tomb, as our *terminus ante quem* is Agnellus in the ninth century, nor do we know whether other members of Theoderic's family were originally intended to be buried there. There is no record, for example, of the burial place of his grandson Athalaric. Once again, therefore, we are left only with speculation.

We finally come to the uppermost level of the structure and its amazing roof. Above a flat zone into which the windows are set, a band decorated in relief with a curious "tongs" (*Zangenfries*) pattern marks the transition to the monolithic dome (Fig. 42). The mausoleum is capped, as the

43. Mausoleum
of Theoderic,
spur on the
capstone with
the inscription
"S(an)c(tu)s
Petrus" (photo
C. L. Striker)

Anonymus remarks, by a single huge slab of stone (Fig. 38). With a diameter
of 10.76 meters, it is 3.09 meters high and estimated to weigh over 300 tons;
its summit rises 15.41 meters above the original ground level. At the top
of the dome the rock has been carved to form a shallow ring 3.75 meters
across, at the center of which is a raised rectangular platform (0.76 × 0.52
meters).[147] At the edge of the roof, carved out of the same block of stone,
are twelve evenly spaced spurs, pierced on their undersides, and inscribed
with the names of apostles on their outer edges (Fig. 43).[148]

The placement of the monolith was an impressive technical feat; indeed,
it may have been too difficult for the builders. A large crack on the south side
of the monolith is thought to have developed at the time it was placed on the
mausoleum.[149] Since the spurs are not symmetrically disposed relative to the
doors and other features of the building, it is thought that when the cracking
began, the architects simply left it where it was. The spurs themselves may
have been used to help move the monolith; it has been proposed that a
massive earth ramp was constructed, up which the monolith was drawn,
and that the spurs were used to attach ropes to lift it into place.[150]

And yet, the spurs cannot have been only functional, because in that
case they would have been removed after the dome was in place; they must
have served some decorative or symbolic purpose. Some have seen them
as imitations of the spurs that were used to load the edges of domes constructed of brick or cement, such as can be seen on the (much later) dome
of Hagia Sophia in Constantinople;[151] or, completely different, as imitations of a large tent, or to look like a mural crown, or simply to render the

monolith visually less heavy.[152] But why were there twelve of them? Indeed, ten would have been a choice more consistent with the decagonal ground plan. That the spurs also had a symbolic purpose is seen from the fact that they are inscribed with the following names clockwise from the south, each preceded by the abbreviation SCS [sanctus]: Petrus, Simeon, Thomas, Lucas, Marcus, Matthias, Martholom(aeu)s [for Bartholomaeus], Felippus, Iohannis, Iacopus, Andreas, Paulus.[153] This is not the standard list of apostles known in the west, for example, as named in the Orthodox Baptistery, San Vitale, and the capella arcivescovile, since here the evangelists Luke and Mark are included instead of Judas Zelotes and one of the James. Because this list of names is similar to those found in the eastern Mediterranean in the sixth century, including perhaps in the church of the Holy Apostles in Constantinople, some scholars have concluded that Theoderic wished to be buried in the symbolic presence of the apostles, like the emperors in Constantinople.[154] While it is curious that Theoderic's tomb would contain a Constantinopolitan list of apostles while the Orthodox churches built at the same time do not, the eastern origins of the workmen, and Theoderic's own experiences in Constantinople, make it a plausible suggestion.

As already noted, many scholars have read Theoderic's tomb as symbolic of the ideology of his reign, and in particular it has been seen as a sign of his rule as both a Roman and as an Ostrogoth. The differences between this monument and Roman examples are therefore sometimes taken as evidence of "Gothicness." It has been proposed, for example, that the lower level is "Roman" while the upper level instead contains "anticlassicizing" features, because that is where Theoderic's body was to lie.[155] F. W. Deichmann has traced the history of this idea from the seventeenth century through twentieth-century German Nazi ideology, showing that it has more to do with romantic ideas of "Germanic" aesthetics than actual historical evidence.[156] Nevertheless, the monolith, for example, has been interpreted as a holdover from Theoderic's "Gothic" past, as a reminiscence of the large rocks placed on prehistoric tombs, even though such tombs are not known from any of the regions in which Theoderic lived or visited.[157] Since, as we have seen, the monolith was viewed as something unique and different about Theoderic's tomb, it is certainly possible that he intended it as a monument to his own unique power, without necessarily having any "Gothic" connotations.[158]

The one feature that most scholars agree is not a Roman decorative motif is the relief band just below the bottom edge of the roof slab (Fig. 42). Called a *Zangenfries* ("frieze of tongs") by Heidenreich and Johannes, it has been linked to decorative motifs on "Germanic" jewelry, and is often identified as the distinctive feature that keeps the mausoleum from being wholly Roman in inspiration. Only one of Heidenreich and Johannes's examples has an Ostrogothic context: the gold cuirass or harness fitting excavated near the mausoleum in 1854 and now lost.[159] Otherwise, the motif compares most closely with one used as a border on early sixth-century brooches made in southern Denmark.[160] Thus, while the *Zangen-fries* is an abstract ornamental design of a sort that might have been found on jewelry made in the sixth century, we cannot assume that such a motif would have been read as typically "Ostrogothic" or even "Germanic" in this context. Once again, it appears to be a sign of difference or uniqueness of the sort that we have seen in other elements on this monument.

As a memorial to Theoderic's reign, the mausoleum has been eminently successful. The mysteries of its meaning that amaze and bemuse modern viewers were intended to do just that; Theoderic and his advisers were constructing a monument that might strike different chords with the different constituencies within his kingdom, Romans, Goths, and others, a durable testament to his power and his claims to greatness that would keep his name alive down through the centuries.

The Ostrogothic Kingdom after Theoderic to 540

In the kingdom created by Theoderic, the king was the linchpin between competing factions of Romans, Goths, and external forces. Theoderic was successful because his vision and his abilities inspired respect or fear from all sides. For a variety of reasons his successors did not have the abilities or the favorable political circumstances to enable them to maintain the balance. Most of our information about this period comes from the history of the Gothic War written by Procopius, who was a member of the staff of the Byzantine army that reconquered the peninsula. While, as we have seen, Procopius admired Theoderic, he was hardly an impartial observer, and his constructs of "Roman" and "barbarian" identity, for example, are stereotypical in the extreme.[161] Our other major source for this period is Cassiodorus, who continued to serve the Ostrogothic rulers, notably as praetorian prefect from 533 until 537 or 538, and more than 160 of the letters in the *Variae* were written after Theoderic's death. These letters continue to be about routine administrative matters; Cassiodorus seems intent on stressing the peacefulness and normality of the kingdom.[162]

However, the kingdom was anything but peaceful and normal. After Theoderic's death in 526, his eight-year-old grandson Athalaric was proclaimed king under a regency headed by his mother Amala-suintha.[163] Amalasuintha had been given a Roman education and could speak several languages; Procopius says that she "administered the government and proved to be endowed with wisdom and regard for justice in the highest degree, displaying to a great extent the masculine temper."[164]

Perhaps with Theoderic's support, she attempted to educate her son in the Roman manner. As we have already seen, this does not seem to have endeared her to a powerful faction of Gothic warriors of the court who felt that his martial abilities would thus be compromised. Procopius tells us that these men removed the young prince from his mother's care, and resolved to bring him up "more barbarically" (βαρβαρικώτερον), which apparently involved drunkenness and debauchery, so that Athalaric died in 534 from a wasting disease. Amalasuintha proclaimed herself queen in association with her cousin Theodahad, the son of Theoderic's sister Amalafrida. Theodahad was noted for his love of Greco-Roman learning and of other people's property, for which he had been called to account by Amalasuintha. She had thus apparently alienated enough of the Gothic nobility that Theodahad was able to imprison her on the island of Volsena, where she was murdered in 535.[165]

Amalasuintha's murder presented the eastern emperor Justinian with a political opportunity that was impossible to resist, since she had appealed to him for support. In 533, Justinian had begun a quest to reconquer the western empire; he had sent an army, led by his general Belisarius, against the Vandal kingdom in North Africa, and had won a remarkably quick victory. Amalasuintha had written to Justinian, asking for his support of her rule when she became queen (in the same way that Theoderic and Athalaric had obtained imperial support for their rule). Her death provided Justinian with a pretext for war,[166] and even a cause in the person of her daughter Matasuintha, who was now Theoderic's only legitimate heir. In 535, Belisarius took a small army to Sicily and conquered it for Justinian; Theodahad was first conciliatory and then defiant, and Belisarius brought his army to the Italian mainland. Naples was captured in late 536, and then Belisarius entered Rome; Theodahad was deposed and murdered, replaced by a Gothic leader named Witigis, who married Matasuintha. Witigis besieged Belisarius in Rome from 537 to 538, but the imperial army was reinforced, and Witigis had to fall back to Ravenna. A new imperial general, Narses, appeared on the scene, confusing the Roman military command, and Witigis scored some victories, including the recapture and sack of Milan in 539. After Narses was recalled to Constantinople, Belisarius decided that the quick way to resolve the war was to capture Ravenna. A fleet cut the city off by sea and armies besieged the land and river approaches. The desperate Goths finally surrendered the city to Belisarius in March of 540;[167] the army entered peacefully, and Witigis, Matasuintha, and other Gothic notables were sent to Constantinople. This ended the first phase of the war.

Procopius's account reveals the meaning of Ravenna for the Goths and particularly for the Amal dynasty. Amalasuintha ruled from Ravenna, where she resided after putting down a plot against her.[168] As a letter by

Cassiodorus implies, she was very aware of her predecessor Galla Placidia, also a regent for a young son, whose works were so evident in the city.[169] Agnellus reports a story that Amalasuintha built a house where there was in his day a chapel dedicated to St. Peter at the Orphanage; this was in the western part of the old *oppidum*, and thus far away from the main palace.[170] Theodahad exiled her from Ravenna so that he could rule there. The first thing that Witigis did when he was chosen as king was to consolidate control of Ravenna, and it was there that he married Matasuintha, who was presumably living in the palace.[171] The approach of the imperial army against Ravenna was viewed by Goths as something to be avoided at all costs.[172] Perhaps because of Ravenna's reputation as being impregnable, the Byzantine generals did not start what might be a lengthy siege until they could be assured that they would not be attacked from the rear.[173] Ravenna was therefore left in peace until 540, unlike other major cities such as Naples, Rome, and Milan. No construction works in Ravenna are credited to Athalaric, Theodahad, Witigis, or Matasuintha, although, as we have seen, it is perfectly possible that projects begun under Theoderic were completed by his successors. It is notable that, as at other times in the city's history, Ravenna was spared a sack in this war, which allowed the city to continue as a governmental center.

The surrender of Ravenna did not mean the end of the Gothic kingdom; other kings ruled from other cities until 554. However, the capture of Ravenna meant the capture of Matasuintha and the royal treasury and marked the end of any pretense that a Gothic king could be the heir of Theoderic.

CHAPTER FIVE

RELIGION IN OSTROGOTHIC RAVENNA

Arianism and the Goths

The proposition that Christ was a creation of God the Father, and hence a subordinate being, is attributed to Arius, a priest of Alexandria (d. 336). While many church leaders accepted Arius's formulation, others vehemently opposed it, and the debate over the nature of the Trinity energized the Christian world at a critical time. The emperor Constantine, who publicly supported Christianity after 312, called an assembly of representatives from the entire Church at Nicaea in 325. Arianism was condemned, the first heresy to be so defined by an ecumenical council, and the term *homoousios*, "of the same substance," was used in the new creed to emphasize the equality of Father and Son. Despite its condemnation, Arius's theology retained numerous supporters, and was developed in different directions in the following decades. Supporters of Nicene belief often labeled as Arians all those who opposed the homoousian formula "Glory to the Father and the Son and the Holy Spirit," using instead the phrase "Glory to the Father through (*per*) the Son in (*in*) the Holy Spirit."[1] While all "Arian" groups believed that Christ was not equal in status to God the Father, and that the Holy Spirit was a being created by Christ and/or the Father, their exact beliefs about the Trinity varied: Some believed that Father and Son were "like" (*homoios*) but not the same as each other, while others, like Eunomius and his followers, thought that the two were completely different (*anhomoios*).[2]

Several of Constantine's key advisers and Constantine himself had Arian sympathies; his son Constantius II, who ruled the empire from 337–61, was an Arian (of the *homoios* variety), as was the eastern emperor Valens (364–78). Although Arianism was condemned a second time at the ecumenical Council of Constantinople of 381 at the urging of the emperor Theodosius I, and no subsequent emperors supported it, Arians continued to exist in parts of the empire, especially the Balkans and Italy.[3] "Barbarians" who were Arian served in the imperial armies in Constantinople, and thus there was an Arian presence in that city also until the time of Justinian.[4]

Some Goths and/or their slaves were apparently already Christian in the 340s, before they entered the Roman Empire. In 341, Ulfilas (sometimes called Wulfila), a Goth, was consecrated in Constantinople as the bishop for these Christians; at that time the ecclesiastical hierarchy in the eastern capital city was Arian, and fourth-century historians attribute the Arianism of the Goths to Ulfilas.[5] Ulfilas produced a translation of the Bible into Gothic, copies of which survive and are our primary evidence for the Gothic language.[6] Ulfilas, according to a letter written by his pupil Auxentius, emphatically believed in a Christ created by the uncreated Father, which put him somewhere to the radical side of the *homoios* party, but not as far as the *anhomoios* side, and he may have changed his theology between 341 and 383.[7] Gothic Christians were persecuted by some pagan Visigothic leaders, but as a result of various negotiations and treaties with Valens in the 370s, the Visigoths, or at least their leaders, who settled in the empire in 376 had committed to Ulfilas's version of Arian Christianity.[8] However, the Goths in the fourth and fifth centuries were not a religiously unified group, and some Goths followed more moderate forms of Arianism,[9] some were Orthodox, and some remained non-Christian.[10]

The Ostrogoths do not appear as a distinct group until the 450s; it is said that they had converted to Arian Christianity by the time they entered Pannonia in 455. We do not know how or when this happened; there seems to have been influence from the Visigoths, as the Ostrogoths in Italy used the Gothic Bible produced by Ulfilas, which would have been a more radical version.[11] On the other hand, B. Luiselli convincingly argues that Theoderic in particular, and the Ostrogoths in general, are likely to have been influenced by a more moderate form of Arianism followed by Visigoths who remained in and around Constantinople in the mid–fifth century.[12]

The importance of Arianism for the Ostrogoths in Italy is a hotly debated topic; the sources are too scanty to tell us anything about personal belief, and we have nothing written by an Arian. Some scholars believe that Theoderic used Arianism as a way to keep the Ostrogoths unified and distinct from their Roman neighbors.[13] Others note that there were both Roman and Gothic Arians,[14] and that the theological differences probably didn't matter much to anyone outside the church hierarchy,[15] or indeed that Theoderic's moderate Arianism could be accommodated by the Orthodox.[16] In fact it seems likely that all these facts were true: At times Arianism was used as political and theological justification for uniting people,

44. Arian Baptistery, head of an apostle

either in favor of or against it, while at the same time the creed of individuals was fluid and mutable and did not need to correspond to any ethnic identification.[17] Theoderic's attitude toward Arianism was almost certainly colored by his experience in Constantinople. When he arrived in 461 the Gothic-Alan generals Aspar and Ardabur controlled the imperial army and their Arianism was tacitly tolerated, but anti-Arian riots and persecution were part of their overthrow in 471.[18]

The chief ecclesiological issue of the early sixth century was the debate between Nestorians, Eutychians (monophysites), miaphysites, and those in between. Nestorius had said that Christ had two separate persons, one human and one divine; this was condemned at the Council of Ephesus of 431. In response, Eutyches had proposed that Christ had only one divine nature, which had completely subsumed his human nature (monophysitism). Eutyches was condemned at the Council of Chalcedon in 451, at which it was stated that Christ had two natures contained in one person. The Chalcedonian position was accepted by the churches of Rome and Constantinople. However, some theologians, especially in Egypt, rejected Nestorius, Eutyches, *and* Chalcedon, and instead proposed that Christ had one nature that was both fully human and fully divine (miaphysitism). All sides, unlike the Arians, accepted the equality of the three persons of the Trinity. Both Nestorian and miaphysite positions had many supporters, and attempts to find a compromise between the different parties consumed much of the sixth century. In this context, Arianism seems to have been almost ignored, at least in eastern theological circles. In the west, however, the presence of Arian rulers produced a different theological climate.

Odoacer had ruled Italy as an Arian for thirteen years before the arrival of the Ostrogoths, apparently without ecclesiastical conflict. For much of Theoderic's reign, the popes were in dispute with the Constantinopolitan church over the emperor Zeno's attempt to reabsorb the miaphysites into the imperial Church and over the election of Acacius (484–519) as the patriarch of Constantinople. Acacius was regarded as not quite Chalcedonian in his conception of the natures of Christ, but this had nothing to do with Arianism. In addition, from 498–506 the Roman clergy could not agree on one legitimate pope. Amory notes that the popes seem to have regarded both Odoacer and Theoderic as *magistri militum* and not emperors, and thus their personal beliefs were not a matter of major concern.[19] The *Anonymus Valesianus* praises Odoacer as someone who "was of good will and followed the Arian doctrine...," and says of Theoderic, "he so governed the two peoples, Romans and Goths, together that although he himself was of the Arian doctrine, he nevertheless did nothing against the catholic religion...."[20] Indeed, his tolerance of Jews was equally well known and disapproved of by his Orthodox critics; in a letter to the Jews of Genoa is found this famous statement: "I cannot command your faith, for no one is forced to believe against his will."[21] Luiselli argues that this tolerance was a result of Theoderic's moderate Arian theology, unlike the more radical and intolerant Arianism of the Visigoths and Vandals.[22]

It was only after the accession of the eastern emperor Justin I in 518 and the subsequent resolution of the Acacian Schism in 519, that Arianism came once more to the fore, perhaps because of increasing pressure from the Byzantines, who were now supported by the popes.[23] We hear from the *Anonymus Valesianus* of three-way religious conflict in Ravenna: some Orthodox Christians burned a synagogue, and when the Jews, supported by various Arians, appealed to Theoderic, the Orthodox were punished. This, according to the author of the text, shows that Eutharic, the son-in-law of Theoderic who had been raised in Visigothic Spain and was consul in 519, was an enemy of the faith.[24] Moreover, in the early 520s Boethius wrote two short works on the Trinity, which are specifically directed against Arianism, and are concerned to show that the Son was consubstantial with the Father. While Boethius's critique is fairly mild, the fact that the treatises were written show that he and his party were gathering arguments against the Arians.[25] The treatises are dedicated to a deacon John, who has been assumed to be the man who in 523 became Pope John I.[26] The *Anonymus* depicts Theoderic acting more and more anti-Orthodox, including his imprisonment of the pope, and finally, immediately before Theoderic's death, "...the Jewish Symmachus *scholasticus*, at the order of a tyrant rather than a king, issued an edict on Wednesday, the 26th of August, in the fourth indiction, in the consulship of Olybrius, that on the following Sunday the Arians would take possession of the Catholic churches."[27] This was presumably a retaliation in response to Justinian's similar actions against the Arian churches of Constantinople.[28] By the judgment of God, according to the author, Theoderic died before this could be carried out. Arianism had thus become an issue in Theoderic's last years, with political, ethnic, and theological issues intertwined, but overall it seems that the political aspects were more significant than the theological ones.[29]

As the capital of Theoderic's kingdom, Ravenna became a center of Arian Christianity in the sixth century. There must have been Arians in Ravenna throughout the fifth century, perhaps among soldiers of the imperial army and certainly under Odoacer.[30] There is only very scanty information about Arian church organization in the west. It seems that in general it was much less centrally organized than the contemporary Orthodox Church, with one senior cleric or bishop associated with the royal court and a network of *sacerdotes* for other areas, rather than a centralized authority such as the pope.[31] Theoderic's church was based in Ravenna and Ravenna's documents and monuments provide us with most of what we know about Ostrogothic Arianism.

Evidence for Arian church buildings comes almost entirely from Ravenna. On the basis of slight documentary references, churches in Rome and other cities have been proposed as of Arian foundation or use, mainly because of their associations with known imperial, Ostrogothic, or Lombard Arians, but the data are too scanty to inform us of whether these churches were continuously Arian in the whole period. In any case, little of their architecture or art survives.[32] Our most detailed evidence for Arian churches in Ravenna comes from Agnellus, who links them with Theoderic. Agnellus describes the rededication of former Arian churches to Orthodox worship under Archbishop Agnellus, sometime between 566 and 570:[33]

> Therefore this most blessed one [Archbishop Agnellus] reconciled all the churches of the Goths, which were built in the times of the Goths or of King Theoderic, which were held by Arian falsehood and the sect, doctrine and credulity of the heretics. He reconciled the church of St. Eusebius priest and martyr, which is located not far from the Coriandrian field outside the city, on November 13, which Bishop Unimundus built from its foundations in the twenty-fourth year of King Theoderic. And likewise he reconciled the church of St. George in the time of Basilius the younger, as is told in its apse. He reconciled the church of St. Sergius, which is located in the city of Classe next to the *viridiarium*, and that of St. Zeno in Caesarea. Indeed in the city of Ravenna the church of St. Theodore, not far from the house of Drocdon, which house together with a bath and a monasterium to St. Apollinaris, which was built in the upper story of the house, was the episcopal palace of that [Arian] church. And where now there is a *monasterium* to the holy and always inviolate virgin Mary, there was the baptistery of the church of the said martyr.... Therefore the most blessed Bishop Agnellus reconciled the church of St. Martin the confessor in this city, which King Theoderic founded, which is called the Golden Heaven....

Agnellus based his account on the imperial decree that gave Ravenna's archbishop all the property of the Gothic churches and on inscriptions that he found in the churches, namely those in St. Eusebius, St. George, and St. Martin. He refers later in his text to *episcopia* built by the Arian bishop Unimundus at St. Eusebius and St. George.[34] Finally, he mentions an *ecclesia Gothorum* in the northeast part of the city, which does not seem to be one of the buildings reconciled by Archbishop Agnellus.[35] There were thus several churches in and around Ravenna that were used for Arian worship by the mid–sixth century. Some of these are linked by inscriptions to the reign of Theoderic, but others might have been older, although there is no direct evidence for this.[36] The dedicatee-saints cited in the document are probably rededications after their reconciliation; Sts. George, Sergius, Martin, and Theodore are all soldier-saints, which could be interpreted as the heavenly army acting against the Arians, or perhaps as a preference of Archbishop Agnellus, a former soldier.[37] St. Eusebius of Vercelli was a notable anti-Arian fourth-century bishop, as was St. Zeno of Verona, and by the 550s St. Martin was also viewed in this way. On the other hand, there were many holy men named Eusebius in the fourth century, including

Eusebius of Nicomedia, who was venerated by Arians, as was George bishop of Alexandria.[38]

One other piece of evidence for Arian churches in Ravenna comes from a papyrus in which the clergy of an *ecclesia legis Gothorum Sce Anastasie* sell some property. The document is dated to 551,[39] thus after the Byzantine reconquest of Ravenna but before the reconciliation of the churches under Archbishop Agnellus. The clergy listed on the document (those who signed it in Gothic indicated by italics) are the following:[40]

(ll. 82–85)…universus clerus, idest Optarit et Vitalianus praesb(yteri), Suniefridus diac(onus), Petrus subdiac(onus), Wiliarit et Paulus clerici nec non et Minnulus et Danihel, Theudila, Mirica et Sindila spodei, Costila, Gudelivus, Guderit, Hosbut et Benenatus ustiarii, Wiliarit et Amalatheus idem spodei.…

(signatures, ll. 88–136):

† *Ik Ufitahari papa ufm<el>ida handau meinai* …
ꝺignum † Vitaliani praeꝺb(yteri), ꝺ(upra)ꝺ(crip)ti venditoris, qui f[acien]te invecillitate oculorum suscribere non potuit, signum f[ecit].
Ik Sunjaifriþas diakon handau meinai ufmelida …
ego Petrus, subdiac(onus) aclisie gotice sancte Anastasie …
signum † Wiliarit clerici, s(upra)s(crip)ti venditoris, qui facien[te] invecillitate oculorum suscribere non potuit ideoque signum f[ecit]
ego Paulus, clericus eclesie legis Gothorum s(a)nc(t)ae Anastasie …
ego Willienant [Minnulus] …
ego Igila [Danihel] …
ego Theudila clericus eclesiae s(upra)s(criptae) legis Gothorum s(an)c(t)e Anastasie …
Ik Merila bokareis handau meinai ufmelida …
signum † Sinthilianis spodei s(upra)s(crip)tae basilicae Gothorum
signum † Costilanis ustiarii s(upra)s(crip)tae basilicae Gothorum
signum † Gudelivi ustiarii s(upra)s(crip)tae basilicae Gothorum
signum † Guderit ustiarii s(upra)s(crip)tae basilicae Gothorum
signum † Hosbut ustiarii s(upra)s(criptae) basilicae Gothorum
signum † Benenati ustiarii s(upra)s(criptae) basilice Gothorum
Ik Wiljariþ bokareis handau meinai ufmelida …

Although most of the names are Gothic, there is no indication in the document that these clerics were necessarily Arian, or for that matter even Gothic. Amory notes that the fact that only a minority signed the document in Gothic implies that the majority of the Arian clergy did not use the Gothic language, but only Latin, and that it is not possible to identify people as either necessarily Arians or Goths on the basis of their names.[41]

The fact that in the 550s the Arian church of Ravenna, in the absence of a bishop, was selling property to the Orthodox is perhaps an indication of both political and financial straits. It is perhaps surprising that the complete suppression of Arianism did not happen until after 565;[42] T. Brown attributes the previous lack of interference to a wish to absorb the Goths peacefully within the Byzantine regime.[43] It is significant that anti-Arian polemic was something developed by Justinian's government in order to justify the conquests of Africa, Italy, and Spain.[44] In the 560s, the Byzantines were faced with the increasing threat of yet another non-Orthodox group of barbarians, the Lombards, who, it was felt, might become Arians, and this might have induced them to take a stronger action against the Arian churches under their authority.[45] In any case, the document of 551 is the last witness to an Arian presence in Ravenna, but the memory of heretical origins would become part of the mystique of Ostrogothic rule associated with the glory of Theoderic.

Sant'Apollinare Nuovo

The church most closely associated with Theoderic is the one that he built next to his palace, known since the later ninth century as Sant'Apollinare Nuovo.[46] Agnellus the historian describes this church as "the church of St. Martin the confessor in this city, which King Theoderic founded, which is called the Golden Heaven.... Indeed in the apse, if you look closely, you will find the following written above the windows in stone letters: 'King Theoderic made this church from its foundations in the name of our Lord Jesus Christ.'"[47] Based on this inscription, it is assumed that Theoderic dedicated the church to Christ, and that it was rededicated to St. Martin at the time of its conversion to Orthodoxy.[48] This transformation was apparently accompanied by a radical renovation of the mosaic decoration along the nave walls, which we will discuss in detail.

Agnellus provides further information about this church:

And he [Archbishop Agnellus] reconciled [to Orthodoxy] the baptistery of the church of St. Martin and decorated it with mosaic; but the apse of that church, greatly shaken by an earthquake, fell in ruins in the reign of Archbishop John V the younger [r. 726–44]. Afterwards he adorned the buildings of the vault with colors. (*LPR* ch. 89)

In his [Archbishop Theodore's, r. 677–91] reign the *monasterium* of St. Theodore the deacon was built by the *patricius* Theodore, not far from the place which is called *ad Chalchi*, next to the church of St. Martin the confessor which is called the Golden Heaven, which King Theoderic built, but restored under the power of that bishop. (*LPR* ch. 119)

45. Sant'-Apollinare Nuovo, mosaic of the south wall, Christ flanked by angels (photo E. Vance)

Thus the church, according to Agnellus, also had a baptistery and later a chapel dedicated to St. Theodore, but no evidence of these survives.[49] The main church, except for the apse, is one of Ravenna's better-preserved basilicas, and the only one for which the decoration of the nave walls has survived.

The church lay immediately to the northwest of the "palace of Theoderic," and was apparently closely connected to this building. In most of the scholarly literature, it is called the "palace chapel" of Theoderic, although in truth we know neither that this is what it was nor what such a designation would mean in the early sixth century.[50] Presumably it was the place where Theoderic ordinarily worshiped and in which certain royal ceremonies took place, but we do not know exactly what these would have been.[51] As we will see, interpretations of the mosaic imagery, both that which survives and that which is now lost, often focus on the close connections between this church and the royal court.

Architecture. The original church built by Theoderic had been modified even by the time of Agnellus because the apse collapsed in an earthquake in the early eighth century; the upper part of the west facade is thought to have fallen at the same time.[52] Bomb damage in World War I and World War II allowed excavation and investigation of various parts of the building. In 1950 the foundations of the original apse were excavated; the baroque apse, which had been constructed in the sixteenth century, was shut off from the church by a reconstruction of the original apse made on the basis of comparison with the apse of Santo Spirito; many recent photographs of the church show this reconstructed apse. This reconstruction in turn was removed in 1990–6 and the baroque apse has now been reopened to the church.

Theoderic's church, like most of the other religious structures in Ravenna, was built of reused brick as a basilica with a nave, single aisles that were half as wide as the nave, and an apse directly connected to the nave that was five sided on the exterior and semicircular on the interior (Fig. 46).[53] We know nothing about the elevation of the apse, but fragments of *tubi fittili* found in excavations show that it was vaulted in Ravenna's customary manner.[54] Both the layout and the dimensions are very similar to those of San Giovanni Evangelista, founded by Galla Placidia and ostentatiously imperial in its decoration;[55] Theoderic no doubt intended to evoke the earlier rulers of Ravenna in his new building.

The original floor level was 1.25–1.50 m below that of today; the entire colonnade was raised in the sixteenth century together with its arches, without modifying the mosaics on the walls above (no mean technical feat!). Originally, then, there must have been another horizontal zone between the arcade and the current lowest mosaic zone. This may have been decorated with gilded stucco, as Agnellus describes, and was set off from the upper mosaic zones by a marble cornice with a palmette and egg-and-dart pattern.[56] Agnellus reports a story that the elaborate marble floor of the basilica was miraculously damaged to prevent a *rex Vandalorum* from stealing the materials. From his use of the term *lastra* ("slab"), and from excavation, it seems that the floor was made of deluxe polychrome *opus sectile*.[57] Originally there may have been a narthex or atrium of some sort at the western end of the building, with three doors leading into the nave and aisles.[58] It is possible that another room, perhaps even the baptistery mentioned by Agnellus, was found at the northern end of the narthex.[59] Another door on the wall of the south aisle, below the middle window, led directly into the palace.[60]

The nave colonnade, of twelve columns on each side, had bases, capitals, and impost blocks fashioned from marble from the island of Proconnesus near Constantinople, all dating to the early sixth century (Figs. 47, 48). They must have been made and exported as a set, the earliest such example

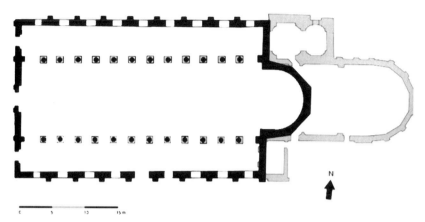

46. Sant'-Apollinare Nuovo, recon-structed plan (black) with still-existing baroque apse and chapels in gray (north wall reconstructed to match the surviving south wall)

from Ravenna.[61] The Corinthian capitals, variations of a type known as *a lira*, are decorated with rather flat acanthus leaves, and the impost blocks contain only a cross on the side that faces the nave (Figs. 48, 49). Both columns and capitals have incised in them Greek letters that refer to the workshops in which they were made; the same marks are found on marble in churches in Constantinople and Ephesus.[62]

On the walls above the nave arcade open eleven windows, corresponding to the arches of the arcade except at the eastern and western ends (Fig. 47).

47. Sant'-Apollinare Nuovo, view of the north nave wall (photo C. L. Striker)

The aisles were also lit by windows on their outer walls, nine on each side (only the windows on the southern side survive) (Fig. 48). The exterior wall surfaces of the building are enlivened by engaged arcades of pilasters that surround the windows. Because the spacing of the windows of the nave is different from those of the aisles, this external articulation visually produces different rhythms.[63] The ceiling was apparently made of gilded beams and coffers; we do not know if the one described by Agnellus went back to Theoderic's time, but we do know that the building was called *coelum aureum* in many later sources.

Liturgical furnishings gave additional articulation to the interior of the church.[64] The apse was raised above the level of the nave by a step. More-over, marble *transennae*, or openwork screen panels, enclosed a space in the nave that extended west to the third pair of columns, and an *ambo* was placed farther west. All of this material was also made of Proconnesian marble, produced in the East. All that survives of the ambo is its central section, decorated with geometric motifs and crosses very similar to other examples made in Constantinople in the early sixth century (Fig. 48).[65] The chancel screen in the church today consists of a *pluteum*, or solid flat panel, that is carved on the one side with a Chi–Rho monogram over a vase, flanked by peacocks and a grapevine and on the other side a man (Daniel) between two lions, also surrounded by acanthus, grape, and other vines. This panel also seems to date to the early to mid–sixth century. Three *transennae*, two almost square and one rectangular, also make up part of the modern chancel screen; they too are decorated with geometric figures, crosses, birds, vases, and vines, and have an equally vague date. Differences in style between these *transennae* and those known to have been installed in the Byzantine period have led scholars to posit a workshop operating in Ravenna, influenced by the Constantinopolitan styles, that may have cre-ated some of these. In the apse of the church today is an altar of marble inlaid with green serpentine, which was designed to hold relics. It is sur-rounded by four porphyry columns with reused Roman capitals and bases of white marble, which form the bottom part of a *ciborium*, or canopy over the altar, although originally the pieces may have come from Theoderic's palace.[66] All of these furnishings date to the early to mid–sixth century, and it is not clear which of them were provided in the Ostrogothic period and which at the time of the church's rededication to Orthodoxy.[67] Since worked marble in large quantities was imported from Constantinople throughout the sixth century, resolving this question is significant with regard to the question of whether there were local workshops operating in Ravenna as early as the Theoderican period.

48. Sant'-Apollinare Nuovo, south colonnade with the ambo (photo Mary Ann Sullivan, Bluffton University)

49. Sant'-Apollinare Nuovo, column capital (photo C. L. Striker)

Mosaics

Sant'Apollinare Nuovo is one of only two churches (the other being Santa Maria Maggiore in Rome) that preserves the decoration of its nave walls, and these mosaics are spectacular and complex enough to have provided material for generations of scholarly analysis. The collapse of the apse in the eighth century was a major loss for our knowledge of the overall icono-graphic program of decoration of Theoderic's church. The apse was the main focus of any basilica, and its imagery was the centerpiece of the entire building. Agnellus, as above, tells us that Archbishop Agnellus decorated the apse and side walls with processional images; however, Agnellus could not have seen the original apse, and thus we cannot interpret his statement to tell us anything about the apse's decoration.

The mosaics of the nave walls are divided into three horizontal registers. The lowest zone, 3 meters high, contains imagery in one long strip that runs from west to east. At the west end, we find depictions of the cities of Classe (north wall [Fig. 50]) and Ravenna (south wall [Pl. IVa]). Out of these cities march processions of saints offering crowns; on the north wall, virgin saints are led by the Three Magi (Figs. 47, 50, and 56) to the Virgin and Child (Pl. IIIa), while on the south wall twenty-six male martyrs (Pl. IIIb) offer their crowns to the enthroned Christ (Fig. 45).

The middle zone, also 3 meters high, is at the level of the windows. Rectangular frames fill the spaces between the eleven windows on each side, each occupied by a standing male figure. At the eastern and western ends, in the absence of a window three frames are placed in a row, for a total of sixteen figures on each side of the church. The spandrels above each window are filled with birds facing a vase.

Finally, the uppermost zone, approximately 1.1 m high, contains alter-nating rectangles. The spaces over the male figures of the middle zone have a striking dark blue background against which is set a colorful shell cupola, edged with pearls and with a jeweled crown suspended in the middle, capped by a pair of doves facing a gold cross. The intervening rectangles, which measure 1.37 × 1.15 m, present twenty-six scenes from the life of Christ: thirteen scenes of the ministry of Christ on the north wall and thirteen scenes of the Passion on the south.

One other small fragment of mosaic now found on the western entrance wall, a head of a ruler that is labeled Justinianus, may also date from this period.

Close analysis, both of the style and technique of the mosaics and of the mortar in which the tesserae are embedded, has shown that these mosaics were not all set up at one time, but rather in two phases. Since Agnellus tells

50. Sant'-Apollinare Nuovo, mosaic of the north wall, the city and port of Classe (photo C. Copenhaver)

us that the church was built by Theoderic and decorated at the time of its rededication to Orthodoxy under Archbishop Agnellus, it is assumed that the two phases of the mosaic decoration correspond to these events. In part because of their excellent preservation, in part because of their sensational (even sinister) erasure, the mosaics have excited lively scholarly debate in the last century. The most extensive arguments have concerned the meaning of the structure identified as the "palatium," and the meaning of the cycle of Christ's life and passion found in the top register, and whether it can be linked to Arian theology. Other points of the decoration have also been the subject of debate and each of these will be discussed in the context of its connection to the overall program.

The Christological Cycle. The Christological cycle consists of panels in which a few figures (ranging from two to fourteen) are presented against a gold background, each representing a scene from the life of Christ.[68] In most cases the figures stand on a narrow green ground; in some scenes furniture, architecture, or more complex landscape is presented. The images are small and in each case the minimal elements allow the viewer clearly to interpret exactly which scene is depicted.[69] In order from west (entrance door) to east (apse), the scenes depicted on the upper register of the nave walls are the following:

North Wall	South Wall
Jesus heals the paralytic of Bethesda	Jesus appears to Thomas and apostles
Jesus sends demons into swine	Jesus appears on the road to Emmaus
Jesus heals the paralytic of Capernaum	Two Marys and the angel at the tomb
Parable of the sheep and the goats	Jesus is led to the crucifixion
Parable of the poor widow's mite	Jesus before Pilate
Parable of the Pharisee and Publican	Judas's repentance
Jesus raises Lazarus	Peter's denial
Jesus and the Samaritan woman	Jesus prophesies Peter's denial
Jesus with the hemorrhaging or Canaanite woman[70]	Jesus before Caiaphas
Jesus heals the two blind men	Jesus taken prisoner
Jesus calls Peter and Andrew (Fig. 51)	The betrayal by Judas
Jesus multiplies bread and fishes	Jesus prays in the Garden of Gethsemane
The wedding at Cana[71]	The Last Supper (Fig. 52)

Because of differences between these cycles and others known from the same period, and because of discordances within the cycle and the rest of the decoration in the church, many scholars have expended much ink attempting to understand what the artists and the creators of this program were doing. A few obvious points can be noted:

- The scenes from the ministry (miracles, parables, and historical events) do not occur in the order that they are found in the New Testament, although Jesus's first miracle, the wedding at Cana, is found at the east end. The Passion cycle begins at the east end and moves back chronologically through the church to the west. Note that the window zone has no direction, but the procession of the lowest zone moves from west to east. J. Elsner has noted that the denial of one directional reference point deliberately creates disorientation on the part of the viewer, emphasizing the transcendent reality of the depictions.[72]

- The two scenes that immediately flank the apse, namely the miracle at the wedding at Cana and the Last Supper (Fig. 52), both are directly connected to the meaning of the Eucharist that takes place at that end of the church; likewise the next two scenes, the Bread and Fishes and the Prayer at Gethsemane, also relate liturgically to the altar.[73] Otherwise, while some themes can be found in corresponding north and south pairs of images, for the most part the two cycles seem to be independent of each other.[74]

- On the north wall Christ is shown as a beardless youth; in the Passion scenes he is a mature bearded man. No other known narrative cycle uses two different pictorial types of Christ. Did this have some meaning?

51. Sant'-Apollinare Nuovo, mosaic of the north wall, upper zone, Christ calling Sts. Peter and Andrew

- In the Passion cycle there is no depiction of the Crucifixion itself, although this is not unusual in the context of late antique art.[75] The focus is instead on the Resurrection.

By the early sixth century there existed a well-developed iconographical repertoire of scenes from the life of Christ, although no surviving group

52. Sant'-Apollinare Nuovo, mosaic of the south wall, upper zone, Christ and the apostles at the Last Supper

of images is as extensive as the cycle in Sant'Apollinare Nuovo. Collections of scenes are found, for example, on late antique stone sarcophagi, on catacomb paintings, on pilgrim flasks from the Holy Land, on the cypress-wood doors of the church of Santa Sabina in Rome, on carved ivories such as the Brescia Casket, the British Museum box, and the bookcovers in the Treasury of the Cathedral of Milan and the Bibliothèque Nationale,[76] and in manuscripts such as the St. Augustine, Rossano, Rabbula, and Sinope Gospels. These few remains from a vast corpus of images created in the fourth to seventh centuries demonstrate that the iconographical elements of certain popular scenes had become fairly standardized by this period, and the choice of which elements to include on any given work was very variable. Parallels with many of these other images have been noted for the Sant'Apollinare Nuovo cycle,[77] some close enough to indicate common currents, but although some scholars have wanted to interpret this as evidence of direct influence from Syria or Rome,[78] it is better to understand our mosaics as part of a Mediterranean-wide visual tradition.

Detailed studies of the style, technique, and indeed the types of tesserae used on the north and south sides indicate that two different workshops were responsible for creating each side. Most notably, on the north side marble tesserae are used for the faces, hands, and feet of the figures, but glass tesserae for most of the rest of the compositions, whereas on the south side (except for the Last Supper and Garden scenes) the mosaics are all made of glass tesserae.[79] P. J. Nordhagen says that the former technique is typically Byzantine, whereas the latter is Italian;[80] some have tried to argue that the different facial types are the result of the preferences of these workshops. However, R. Jensen notes that the costume and halo of Christ are identical on both sides, implying that if there were two workshops, they were using the same visual vocabulary, and thus the distinction was deliberate.[81]

This distinction between the beardless and bearded faces of Christ on the two sides of the nave is one of the most striking aspects of the Christological scenes.[82] Could this represent some aspect of doctrine? One of the problems with attempts to interpret them in this way is the fact that many doctrines existed in the early sixth century. The main theological issue debated with Arians was the equal status of Christ in the Trinity. We do not know, however, what side Arians took on the fifth- and sixth-century question of the dual nature of Christ, although later they were accused of denying his human nature.[83] O. von Simson argued that at Sant'Apollinare Nuovo the beardless Christ represents Christ's divine nature and the bearded one his human nature, and that Theoderic approved this quasi-Nestorian, Roman response to miaphysitism; but this seems unlikely.[84] R. Jensen argues that the two faces in Sant'Apollinare Nuovo indicate the transformation of Christ from miracle-working Son of Man to a glorified Son of God, a transformation that took place at the Last Supper, when Jesus tells the disciples "Now the Son of Man has been glorified, and God has been glorified in him" (John 13:31), which she identifies as an otherwise unknown Arian theological belief.[85] While this is plausible, and would certainly fit with the portrayal of Christ as *rex Gloriae* on the lower level, Jensen offers no textual evidence to back up her contention. In fact, the distinction between the two types of face cannot have been unique to Arianism for two reasons. First, these mosaics were not altered when the church was converted to Orthodoxy; and second, both a bearded and a beardless Christ are depicted in different places among the mosaics in both San Michele *in Africisco* and San Vitale, Orthodox churches that were executed later in the century. Thus, while the different physiognomies undoubtedly were significant, their meaning must have been applicable to Orthodox belief also.[86]

Some scholars have attempted to read elements of Arian theology into the choice of scenes or the way that the scenes are depicted. For example, R. Sörries and R. Zanotto propose that the mosaics illustrate passages that Arians interpreted as proof of the subordination of the Son to the Father.[87] Sörries further argues that the images themselves, in keeping with Arian theology that emphasized Christians as followers of Christ, prominently feature the followers of Christ by including disciples in every scene and by illustrating miracle scenes that turn witnesses into followers.[88] Unusual elements in individual scenes are also examined for Arian meaning.[89]

One problem with all of these interpretations, as A. Grabar pointed out, is that we do not really know enough to be able to reconstruct sixth-century Arian theology or liturgy.[90] Moreover, all of the scenes come from the Gospels, which were accepted by all theological factions; and as such, all were subject to interpretation by every faction. For example, Arian commentators argued that Christ's statement at the Resurrection of Lazarus indicated his subordination to the Father,[91] but Orthodox theologians argued the opposite. An image such as this, therefore, could serve either theology, as indeed could any passage from the Gospels. This explains why they were not altered or removed when the church was rededicated to Orthodoxy; as Gospel scenes, they were by definition acceptable to any sect.

Other scholars have taken a more functional approach to the choice of scenes by attempting to link them with the liturgy that would have been enacted in the church. C. O. Nordström rightly criticized A. Baumstark's proposal that the images reflected a liturgy from Syria, but Nordström's own proposal that the scenes followed Italian liturgical readings more closely is likewise valid only for some of the images.[92] It is possible that the liturgy used in the Arian church at the time of Theoderic, for which we have no evidence, did incorporate all of these particular Gospel passages and perhaps the same was done by their Orthodox successors.[93] A problem with the liturgical explanation is the absence of an image of the crucifixion. Scholars usually explain this by noting that depictions of the crucifixion were very rare in late antique art,[94] but the crucifixion certainly was the central feature of the Easter liturgy. Thus, if the images were to correspond to a liturgical cycle, it surely would have been depicted. Another general objection to any didactic function for these scenes is that the images are so small and high up that they would barely have been visible to congregants directed to look at them.[95] It thus seems better to conclude that liturgies and artistic representations of Christ's life, both of which reflected ideas about what was important in the Christian message, developed side by side and mutually influenced each other.

The Male Figures in the Window Zone. At the level of the windows we see thirty-two full-size male figures (there may originally have been thirty-four), each of whom wears a white tunic with *clavi* and a white mantle with *gammadia*, holds a red codex book or a scroll, and has his head surrounded by a silver halo. Eleven have books, twenty-one have scrolls (Fig. 53). Note that the two figures in the northeast corner are restorations. The figures stand on small green squares against a solid gold background. They have different facial characteristics; some are bearded and some beardless. They are very similar to figures we have already seen, for example those in the lower levels of the Orthodox Baptistery, and like the others, are assumed to be prophets, evangelists, and/or patriarchs.[96] Since, unlike the saints, they are not labeled, they seem to represent "biblical authors" in a generic sort of way, reinforcing the primacy of the written Word of God. Many late antique texts describe the various ranks of the glittering heavenly court, and M. J. Roberts convincingly argues that the figures of the second tier form part of the heavenly court that surrounds the enthroned Christ and Virgin, which will be discussed further in the following section.[97]

Christ and the Virgin. On the nave wall immediately to the right of the apse, Christ appears seated on a lyre-backed, gem-studded throne,[98] dressed in imperial purple and gold; the cross in his halo is likewise gemmed (Fig. 45). The right side of the mosaic is a restoration and we do not know exactly what was being held in Christ's left hand (the pointed scepter dates to the mid–nineteenth century); a sixteenth-century description says that he held an open book with the words "Ego sum rex gloriae."[99] The figure has been a central part of art historical interpretations of the image of Christ

53. Sant'-Apollinare Nuovo, mosaic of the north wall, window zone (far left side), two male figures holding a scroll and a codex (photo E. Vance)

as emperor. Indeed, with his purple robes and throne he does incorporate many symbols that viewers would have recognized as shared with emperors, a suitable image in the chapel of the king.[100] The Virgin, too, is seated on a jeweled throne, but she is dressed not like an empress, but simply in a purple tunic with gold clavi and a purple *maphorion*, or overmantle, part of which forms her headdress, a depiction that had become standard in the eastern Mediterranean by this time (Pl. IIIa).[101] She sits on a red cushion with gold stars and holds her right hand up in a gesture of blessing. The Christ child wears a white tunic with gold *clavi* and a white mantle like the flanking angels. He holds his hand apparently in a gesture of acclamation, but of whom? This image deserves as much serious examination as has been devoted to Christ on the opposite wall.

The pairing of an enthroned, bearded Christ with the Virgin and Child is found elsewhere in early Christian art, for example on ivory panels,[102] where they are not read as expressing any particular Christological doctrine. When we note that the enthroned Christ is reflected in the bearded Christ in the passion panels above, and the Christ child mirrors the beardless Christ in the miracle scenes, this parallelism seems to be the best explanation of why Christ is depicted differently in the Christological scenes of the upper zone. An interesting question is, since these two images are found on the nave walls, what was originally depicted in the apse? Would there have been a third image of Christ there, and, if so, what form could it have taken?

The angels who flank the thrones are dressed in white robes with gold clavi and their heads are surrounded by pale blue halos (the two to the right of Christ are restorations). Beneath their feet, flowering plants hint at a landscape. In their covered left hands the angels hold long wands, of the sort that would be held by the *hostiarii* or *silentarii*, court officials who flanked the emperor in imperial ceremonial. The angels who stand between the three Magi and the Virgin present the procession to her with gestures of their hands; perhaps their counterparts originally did the same on the south side.[103]

***The* palatium *and Classe*.** At the western ends of the nave walls are renderings of architectural forms that are labeled as the cities of Ravenna (Pl. IVa) and Classe (Fig. 50). These depictions were created in the Ostrogothic period and originally included male figures, subsequently removed, whose existence is witnessed by mosaic shadows and fragments. Obviously the interpretation of the structure depends on what was removed as well as what survives; we will therefore discuss the erasures in the context of the buildings, whose meaning has been the subject of extensive conjecture.

On the southern wall, we see at the center of the structure a large triple-arched opening surmounted by a pediment; the central arch is the widest, and its background is gold. On the cornice above the central arch is the label PALATIVM; in the pediment above this there was once an image that was subsequently replaced with a plain gold field. On either side of this central structure extends an arcade of three smaller arches, with a windowed upper story and roof above. Winged victory figures fill the spandrels above the colonnade.[104] The openings of the colonnade, like the two arches flanking the central one, are filled with a dark purple background. On the right side of this architectural unit is a large stone gateway, labeled CIVITAS RAVENN(AS), with round towers flanking a single entrance and three small figures depicted in the tympanum over the opening. Finally, within or behind this complex can be seen other structures; to the left and right of the central pediment we can see what look like basilicas and rotundas or other centrally planned structures, with a wall behind them.

The image of the *civitas Ravennas* corresponds to the image labeled CLASSIS or CIVITAS CLASSIS on the opposite wall.[105] Most of the upper-right part of the Classe mosaic is a nineteenth-century restoration by Felice Kibel, but what survives shows us the port of Classe, with three ships in it,[106] flanked by towers that represent the entrance to the harbor. Even if this mosaic had been made before Theoderic ordered his great fleet of warships to be constructed in 525, it underscores the importance of ships and the port to the capital and the kingdom. To the right, the city of Classe is presented as a solid wall, with a white tower midway along and a gateway at the right side. Buildings were depicted within these walls, in the same way as in the Ravenna mosaic, but the ones visible today are mostly Kibel's inventions; the only original one is the round building at the far left, perhaps an amphitheater.

As we have seen, the *palatium* of Ravenna represented the heart of Theoderic's realm, and this image with its label must have been an important representation of this royal ideology. For over half a century, scholars have debated whether the *palatium* image represents a real or imaginary residence, and in either case, what it means symbolically. At face value, the image depicts a facade composed of colonnades flanking a projecting central pedimented entrance. Such a facade could have been found either on the exterior of the palace or as one side of a colonnaded courtyard within a palace, perhaps leading to the throne room.[107] This simple explanation is perfectly satisfying.[108]

However, some scholars have noted that in late antique art, building facades are infrequently represented and that often the front and sides of a three-dimensional building are laid out side by side, as, for example, can be seen in the basilicas depicted behind this very image. E. Dyggve therefore proposed that this image represents the pedimented end and colonnaded sides of an open courtyard used for imperial ceremonial, of a type used, for example, in the peristyle of the early fourth-century palace of the emperor Diocletian in Spalato.[109] The pediment surmounting an arch, according to Dyggve, created a frame for the emperor on ceremonial occasions, as seen in representations such as the image of Theodosius I on his late fourth-century silver dish, or *missorium*.[110] N. Duval, noting that the idea of an open-air audience hall is not supported by other examples, interpreted the image as representing both the exterior and the interior of an apsed basilical audience hall, similar to depiction of basilicas in the ninth-century Utrecht Psalter.[111] These theses turn on two questions: How did images of architecture relate to actual structures, and how was architecture used to present and/or represent authority? Both Dyggve and Duval assume that in late antiquity, three-dimensional buildings such as basilicas or peristyle courtyards were depicted in a way that, to the twenty-first-century realist viewer, looks like a flattening out of the component elements into a two-dimensional line, or even, according to Duval, representing the interior and exterior of a building in the same image. Following this reasoning, both scholars reconstruct narrow buildings with facing colonnades whose short end provided a visual focus in which the ruler appeared, that is, some sort of basilica.

For many reasons the three-dimensional thesis is unconvincing.[112] The comparative material consists of only the Spalato peristyle, some early fifth-century mosaics from North Africa, and the Utrecht Psalter, all completely different in time and place from sixth-century Ravenna. F. W. Deichmann and N. de Francovich argue that the Spalato peristyle was not a ceremonial area, and that the arcuated lintel or pediment was found on many images and buildings with no imperial connections.[113] The pediment of the *palatium*, unlike the Spalato peristyle and the *missorium*, surmounts not one but three arches. The artists of the Christological cycle in the upper zone do not seem to have had difficulty distinguishing between the interior and the exterior of buildings. And most significant, although ignored in most studies of the *palatium* mosaic, is the fact that behind the roofed arcade are buildings that symbolize the city of Ravenna;[114] the arcade fronting them is thus much more likely to represent a flat wall than a three-dimensional interior space. There are many depictions from late antiquity in which an assembly gathers in front of an arcade: Constantine addressing the citizens of Rome on the Arch of Constantine; various sarcophagi such as the "Sarcophagus of Stilicho" in Milan or the two sarcophagi now in San Francesco in Ravenna;[115] the Trier Ivory, which depicts some part of the imperial palace in Constantinople;[116] or, even more closely, the apse mosaic of Santa Pudenziana in Rome, which dates to the 430s, and which also shows a roofed arcade with elaborate buildings behind it. The Santa Pudenziana mosaic is usually understood as depicting a heavenly Jerusalem, and C. Frugoni has suggested that here a reference to Jerusalem is intended also.[117]

A related question is whether this mosaic is intended to be an accurate representation of Theoderic's palace in Ravenna or simply portrays an idealized image of a palace.[118] The palace in Ravenna is known from several written sources to have included porticoes, as we saw when discussing the imperial mint in the previous chapter.[119] Moreover, the excavations of the palace next to Sant'Apollinare Nuovo have revealed a colonnaded courtyard with a main entrance into the audience hall on the widest side, not the narrow end.[120] The main gate of the palace probably fronted a plaza to the south of the church. It is likely, therefore, that the *palatium* entrance depicted here is one of the facades of Ravenna's palace, although it may contain elements that are more symbolic of authority rather than were necessarily found in any precise location.[121]

The doorway at the right side is interesting in its own right (note that it is often omitted from reproductions of the mosaic).[122] Three small figures in the arch over the doorway represent in the center a male figure in a tunic and mantle, holding a cross over one shoulder and a book in his other hand and trampling a serpent; he is flanked by two other male figures.

We have already seen in the previous chapter that the figure of Christ trampling the basilisk and serpent was quite popular in Ravenna even in the early fifth century, and it is therefore usually asserted that this figure represents Christ between two apostles,[123] although elsewhere in Ravenna Christ is always dressed in purple.[124] On the Chalke Gate in of the Great Palace in Constantinople, Constantine and his sons were depicted treading on serpents, and this image may also be recalled here, although again the figures are not wearing imperial purple or military costumes.[125] D. Longhi proposes that the central figure represents St. Lawrence, who, as we have already seen, is depicted in this pose in the "mausoleum of Galla Placidia," although Longhi does not explain who the other figures are. This gate would therefore be the *porta San Lorenzo* mentioned in several early sources, the gate at the southern end of the *platea maior* that led out of the city to the church of St. Lawrence and to Classe.[126] C. Frugoni sees this image as a pendant to the lost image in the pediment of the *palatium*,[127] but that is only speculation; at the least we can say that this image was not controversial to Orthodox redecorators, whereas the first image was.

What buildings are depicted behind the palatium facade? We see, on the left and the right, a basilica and a centrally planned building. Interpretations have ranged widely, from those who identify particular buildings in Ravenna, to those who feel that this representation presents Ravenna as a type of the heavenly Jerusalem.[128] The pairs look very much like the combination of church and baptistery that we have already encountered at the Orthodox cathedral. A. Testi-Rasponi proposed that one of the pairs represented the Arian cathedral with its baptistery, built, as we will see, on the Orthodox model.[129] M. G. Breschi, building on this, suggested that one pair was the Orthodox and the other the Arian cathedral and baptistery, and that this mosaic was a symbol of Theoderic's famous religious tolerance.[130] M. Johnson thought that they were the Arian cathedral and baptistery and Sant'Apollinare Nuovo itself with its baptistery, along with S. Andrea dei Goti, thus all structures built by Theoderic.[131] All interpretations must remain hypothetical in the absence of any labels.

The pairing of Ravenna, the city of the palace, and Classe, the city of the fleet, indicates the value of this region to the king; and indeed, this meaning would have been just as acceptable to the Byzantine rulers who later used this as their palace church.[132] There was a well-developed tradition of depicting pairs of cities on two sides of a church, especially Jerusalem and Bethlehem, which can be seen, for example, on the triumphal arch at Sant'Apollinare in Classe and on the arch above the apse in San Vitale. While C. Frugoni argues that here Ravenna plays the role of Jerusalem and Classe that of Bethlehem,[133] I would suggest instead that probably the two Holy Cities were depicted on the triumphal arch of this church also, directly associated with the Virgin (Bethlehem) and Christ (Jerusalem), and that the depictions of Ravenna and Classe at the west end were pendants to those depictions. The nave images would thus represent mediation between the real world of Classe and Ravenna, as experienced by one entering the church at the west end, and the divine realm represented by the Holy Cities and the Heavenly Kingdom at the eastern end.[134]

Modifications to the **palatium** *and Classe.* In the Ravenna gateway and in the intercolumniations of the *palatium* facade, except for the central arch with the gold background,[135] stood figures who were purged in the Orthodox rededication of the church (Fig. 55). The figure in the Ravenna gateway at the right may have been seated,[136] but in the intercolumniations, figures stood with their hands raised in a gesture of acclamation. On the first, third, fifth, and eleventh columns, respectively, from the left we can see the remains of hands belonging to these figures (Fig. 54). They must have looked very like the figures of the Publican and the Pharisee depicted in the north wall's upper zone. The figures between the columns were carefully excised, tessera by tessera, and replaced with the curtains seen today. In the pediment of the central arch of the *palatium* a figure or figural group was also purged. Most scholars want to see it as a depiction of Theoderic, because, as we have seen, Agnellus describes this sort of image very precisely in relation to the main gate of the palace. However, R. Farioli has shown that the shape of the section excised could not accommodate a depiction of Theoderic on horseback between two standing figures, so that at most this might have been an abbreviated version of that image.[137] Finally, Classe also had figures standing in front of the walls which were subsequently erased: five standing figures can be identified, apparently male, as the outlines of their ankles and feet can be made out (Fig. 55).

It is curious that the hands of these figures were allowed to remain. W. Urbano notes that in any *damnatio memoriae* the point is not to completely erase a figure from memory, but to remind the viewer that the figure has been erased; Urbano interprets the hands as such a signal, making the viewer "remember to forget."[138] It is likely all these figures somehow defined the depictions of Ravenna and Classe as belonging to Theoderic; the architecture was thus, as de Francovich and others have called it, an "architecture of power," and even when stripped of inhabitants, it still underlined the importance of Ravenna's palace and its port to the administration of authority in sixth-century Italy.

The Processions of Saints. When Theoderic's palace church was converted to Orthodox Christian worship by Archbishop Agnellus in the 560s, it was

54. Sant'-Apollinare Nuovo, mosaic of the south wall, detail of the left side of the "palatium" (photo Mary Ann Sullivan, Bluffton University)

rededicated and redecorated. Originally dedicated to Christ, it was now renamed in honor of St. Martin, a late fourth-century ascetic, monk, and bishop of the city of Tours in Francia. Veneration of St. Martin had been growing in popularity in early sixth-century Italy, and from the 550s onward

55. Sant'-Apollinare Nuovo, diagram of the images of Classe and the Ravenna "palatium" with the areas replaced in the 560s shaded (after Penni Iacco, 2004)

he was being viewed as a particularly effective intercessor against Arian enemies.[139] The choice of St. Martin as a dedicatee of this church was thus both an anti-Arian statement and also a political statement invoking the alliance of the Byzantines and the Franks in the face of the Lombard threat; the fact that the exarchs continued to use Theoderic's palace emphasizes the political nature of the dedication.[140]

Agnellus the historian attributes some of the church's decoration to Archbishop Agnellus:[141]

> ...he [Agnellus] decorated the apse and both side-walls with images in mosaic of processions of martyrs and virgins; indeed he laid over this stucco covered with gold, he stuck multi-colored stones to the side-walls and composed a pavement of wonderful cut marble pieces. If you look on its facade on the inside you will find the image of Emperor Justinian and Bishop Agnellus decorated with gold mosaics. No church or house is similar to this one in beams and coffers of its ceiling.

We do not know how Agnellus knew which decoration his namesake sponsored, but research on the fabric of the nave mosaics has largely borne out his attributions. Specifically, when the church was rededicated, whatever was originally depicted between the *palatium* and Christ, and between Classe and the Virgin, was replaced by processions of holy figures:[142]

> From Ravenna the martyrs lead forth, on the men's [south] side, going to Christ; from Classe the virgins proceed, proceeding to the holy Virgin of virgins, and the Magi going before them, offering gifts.

It has been demonstrated by analysis of the mortar beds beneath the tesserae that the martyrs, virgins, and Magi were made later than the rest of the images on the wall, at the same time that the *palatium* and Classe mosaics were modified.[143] This modification was rather crudely done, as it can be clearly seen that the ground line changes between the first of the three Magi and the angel in front of him (Pl. IIIa; see also Fig. 55). It should also be noted that parts of these processions are modern restorations undertaken in the mid–nineteenth century, specifically most of St. Martin and the parts above the waist of the three Magi, although in each case part of the original mosaic survives.[144] All that remains of St. Martin is part of his shoulder and back (Pl. IIIb), enough to determine that he is wearing a purple rather than a white mantle, but not enough to say whether he too is offering a crown (Martin, unlike all the others, was not a martyr). In addition, one fifteenth-century source describes the procession as led by St. Stephen, the first martyr, and scholars disagree about whether another figure would have fit between Martin and Christ in the original remodeling, or whether St. Stephen might have been added subsequently.[145]

The twenty-two female martyrs (plus three Magi) and the twenty-six male saints are separated from one another by palm trees, date-bearing on the women's side (and in a few cases on the men's). The saints include the following, from east (the front of the procession) to west:[146]

Female Martyrs	Origin	Male Saints	Origin
Caspar	*magus*	[Ma]rtinus	Tours
Melchior	*magus*	Clemi[n]s	pope
Balthasar	*magus*	Systus	pope
Eufi[mia]	Chalcedon	Laurentius	Roman deacon
Pelagia	Antioch	Yppolitus	pope
Agatha	Rome	Cornelius	pope
Agnes	Rome	Ciprianus	Carthage
Eulalia	Spain	Cassianus	Imola
Caecilia	Rome	Iohannis	Rome
Lucia	Rome	Paulus	Rome
Crispina	Africa	Vitalis	Milan/Ravenna
Valeria	Milan/Ravenna	[Gerv]asius	Milan/Ravenna
Vincentia[147]	Africa?	Protasius	Milan/Ravenna
Perpetua[148]	Africa	Ursicinus	Milan/Ravenna
Felicitas	Africa	Namor [Nabor]	Milan
Justina	Padua	Felix	Milan
Anastasia	Sirmium	Apollinaris	Ravenna
Daria	Rome	Sebastianus	Milan
Emerentian(a)	Rome	Demiter	Thessalonike
Paulina	Rome	Policarpus	Smyrna/Antioch
Victoria	Sabina	Vincentius	Saragossa, Spain
Anatolia	Sabina	Pancratus	Rome
Cristina	Tyre	Crisogonus	Rome
Savina	Rome	Protus	Rome
Eugenia	Rome	Iac[in]tus	Rome
		Sabin[us]	Spoleto

One of the striking visual features about these saints is the uniformity of their poses, expressions, and dress; indeed, comparison of these scenes with a more naturalistic Roman procession scene such as that found on the Ara Pacis of Rome is a standard examination question for undergraduates. The female saints, in particular, have the same hairstyle (with different hair color), the same costume (except for details of ornament), the same tilt of the head, and the same expression; the only difference among them is that some have their right hand covered and some do not. The male martyrs, like every other group of male saints that we have seen, have varying hair color and facial hair, different *gammadia* on the mantles, and differently ornamented crowns. They tilt their heads at slightly different angles to one another, and also vary as to whether their left hands are covered, but the overall impression is of sameness.[149]

Only three saints are visually singled out: Martin by his purple mantle, the fourth male martyr Lawrence by his gold tunic (Pl. IIIb),[150] and the fourth female martyr Agnes (Fig. 56), who has a lamb at her feet (a pun on her name, Agnes = *agnus*). Martin was the Orthodox dedicatee of the church, and was not a martyr; the latter circumstance might explain his purple cloak.[151] There is clearly some significance to the fourth place in the procession, the position shared by Lawrence and Agnes.[152] The leader of the female saints, St. Euphemia of Chalcedon, is not visually distinguished, but her position here is certainly a reference to the anti-Arian Council of Chalcedon of 451.[153]

The specific saints in the processions are those who are known to have been venerated in early church litanies, specifically litanies of Italy. O. von Simson tabulated litanies for Ravenna, Rome, and Milan, and showed that many of our saints appear in more than one of these, especially the lengthy Canon of the Mass of Milan.[154] However, as none of the Canons list more than twelve female saints, clearly the creators of the mosaics, intent on producing parallel male and female processions, had to step outside the confines of the liturgy to come up with additional female martyrs.[155] As can be seen from the table, a majority of the saints were Italian, with several from North Africa and Spain; only Euphemia, Pelagia, Anastasia, Christina, Demetrius, and Polycarp were from the eastern Mediterranean. The order of the saints in the procession does not follow any of the known litanies; attempts to make sense of it, to explain Apollinaris's relatively late place as a "courtesy" to foreign martyrs, for example, are not convincing. Many saints whose veneration is documented in Ravenna are missing here.[156]

While the connection of these saints with liturgical practice offers insight into their meaning, it should be noted that lists of martyrs are not found only in litanies and other liturgical sources. Historical texts such as Eusebius's *Historia ecclesiastica* are virtual catalogs of martyrs. Eusebius wrote a separate work called *The Martyrs of Palestine*, and Gregory of Tours wrote *Glory of the Martyrs*, which includes many of our saints. Poems by authors such as Venantius Fortunatus, for example, his *De virginitate*, contain lists of saints and martyrs. While these influenced and were influenced by litanies, they illustrate a general interest in compiling lists of notable Christians for particular purposes, and I would argue that the saints in the processions in Sant'Apollinare Nuovo represent a similar compilation, whose choice was based upon conditions that we can no longer reconstruct.

56. Sant'-Apollinare Nuovo, mosaic of the north wall, Sts. Caecilia, Eulalia, Agnes (with the lamb), Agatha, and Pelagia (photo Mary Ann Sullivan, Bluffton University)

As for the three Magi (Pl. IIIa), they represent, among other things, the men who would have led a procession of women into the church.[157] But the Magi also have several other significant meanings in this context. Many depictions of imperial court scenes include representations of foreign peoples paying tribute to the enthroned ruler, and the Magi, always depicted as eastern foreigners, here provide another visual link to this concept.[158] More significantly, while the Trinity is almost never depicted in late antique art, representations of three figures, such as the three Magi, can represent the concept of the Trinity.[159] Thus, the placement of the three Magi at the head of the procession of virgins was almost certainly an anti-Arian statement. That these Magi were, at least later, interpreted in this manner can be seen in an exegetical passage included by Agnellus as part of his description of this image:[160]

> But why are they depicted in different clothing and not all wearing the same garment? Because the artist followed divine Scripture. For Caspar offered gold in a reddish garment [*vestimentum*], and in this garment signifies marriage. Balthasar offered frankincense in a yellow garment, and in this garment signifies virginity. Melchior offered myrrh in a multi-colored costume [*vestitum*], and in this costume signifies penitence. He who went first, wearing a purple mantle [*sagum*], through it signifies the King who was born and suffered. He who offered his gift to the Newborn in a multi-colored mantle signifies

through this that Christ cares for all the weary, and was whipped by the various injuries and diverse blows of the Jews. Of him it is written, "He hath
borne our infirmities and carried our sorrows: and we have thought him as it
were a leper," etc., and then, "he was wounded for our iniquities, he was cru-
cified for our sins." He who offered his gift in white signifies that He exists
in divine clarity after the resurrection. For likewise the three precious gifts
contain divine mysteries in them, that is, by gold is meant regal wealth, by
frankincense the figure of the priest, by myrrh death, thus through all these
things they show him to be the one who undertook the iniquities of men, that
is Christ.... Why did not four, not six, or not two, but only these three come
from the east? So that they might entirely signify the perfect plenitude of the
Trinity.

This exegesis of the three Magi seems to have been culled from an unknown
sermon that no longer exists, perhaps one written by a past bishop of
Ravenna.[161] The fact that visual references are found in a sermon indicates
the way in which sermon and image might work together in the course of
the liturgy. In particular, this sermon emphasizes the divine and human
natures of Christ and the consubstantial Trinity, both concepts that were
particularly anti-Arian.

It is often remarked that, except for the Magi in the procession, scenes
from Christ's infancy are absent from the church. It should first be noted
that much of the original mosaic decoration is missing, and in particular the
mosaics of the triumphal arch. In the church of Santa Maria Maggiore in
Rome, this is precisely where scenes from the Infancy are depicted, while
the nave walls contain other sorts of typological narrative scenes. Thus,
it is perfectly possible that originally such scenes were present.[162] Several
scholars have interpreted their absence as evidence that Arians were uncom-
fortable with anything indicating the Incarnation,[163] although the depiction of the Virgin and Child, even without the Magi, would tend to refute
this.

What do these processions represent? Agnellus himself draws attention
to the fact that traditionally the southern side of a church (the right as one
faces the apse) was where the men stood, while the northern side (the less
prestigious left side) was allocated to the women.[164] Thus, the processions
of saints and virgins correspond in gender to the congregants below them.
Processions of saints bearing crowns were found in several other religious
buildings in Ravenna, most notably the Orthodox and Arian Baptisteries. In
Sant'Apollinare Nuovo, because all the saints except Martin were martyrs,
it is usually assumed that they are offering the crowns of their martyrdom to
Christ and the Virgin, an association made particularly strong by the offerings of the three Magi to the Virgin at the head of the procession of virgins.

The congregants, who would offer the bread and wine of the Eucharist in the course of the ceremony, would thus imitate and be associated with the martyrs and the Magi; indeed, von Simson notes that the bread offered in such ceremonies was called *coronae* and was made in the form of a crown.[165] The congregants, mirrored by the saints, are themselves meant to imitate the sacrifice of the martyrs.[166]

Another explanation that works in parallel, already noted, is that the virgins and martyrs, and the male figures above them, represent the heavenly court, which continually venerates the enthroned Christ and the Virgin. In this interpretation, like the apostles of the Orthodox Baptistery but in an even more vivid way, the pose of the saints offering crowns to the ruler reflects the Roman imperial ceremony of *aurum coronarium*:[167] lords and ladies of heaven, dressed in rich, gleaming robes, crowns, and jewels, pay tribute to the emperor and empress of heaven. Such a depiction would be evocative of the earthly court of Theoderic's palace whose place of worship this was.[168] Descriptions of such a heavenly court, whose members present gifts as they represent their cities, are found among the writings of Venantius Fortunatus, a poet who was educated in Ravenna in the 550s. Such a court should also be considered to include the male figures of the middle zone.[169] And one final possibility: saints are often depicted receiving crowns from Christ; a nearby example is seen in the apse mosaic of San Vitale. The saints in Sant'Apollinare Nuovo might also be read as receiving their crowns in these images, in much the same way that A. Wharton has interpreted the apostles in the Orthodox Baptistery.[170]

What Was Originally There to Be Replaced? Close analysis of the tesserae and mortar showed that the bottom row of green and a top row of gold were part of Theoderic's original mosaic. It is thus very likely that a similar field of figures walking on a green ground against a gold background was originally depicted along the walls. It is usually asserted that the original procession must have been of Theoderic and members of his court, setting out from Ravenna and Classe, since that scene would have had to be replaced in a political and theological rededication of the church.[171] While we may never know for certain what was originally there, there are various problems with this proposal.[172] It is based on two weak assumptions: (1) since both San Giovanni Evangelista[173] and San Vitale contain imperial images, it is likely that Theoderic also had political imagery in his church; and (2) since Theoderic tried never to upset his Orthodox subjects, he would not have had anything too overtly Arian depicted here.

On the first point, if Theoderic's church were similar to the others with imperial imagery, it is more likely that he would have had himself depicted in the apse. While it is true that we know relatively little about what was depicted on nave walls, there is no other example of such a court procession known from any other late antique church.[174] The closest example, the walls flanking the altar in San Vitale, which von Simson proposed were inspired by the original mosaics in Sant'Apollinare Nuovo,[175] are located in the presbytery of the church, which is not a basilica with a longitudinal nave.[176] In Santa Maria Maggiore in Rome the nave walls are decorated with biblical scenes. According to textual descriptions, much the same sort of depictions were found in the church of St. Sergius at Gaza, St. Martin at Tours, and St. Felix at Nola; St. Nilus of Sinai recommends this decoration for the nave walls of a church.[177] Many surviving mosaics depict saints on the walls of churches, for example, at St. Catherine's church in Sinai, at Porec, and in Ravenna's *capella arcivescovile* (see Fig. 68), although none of these examples includes nave decoration. But there are no textual references, copies, imitations, or any other evidence for a court procession that covered the walls of a basilica's nave.[178] If this were indeed what was originally found in Sant'Apollinare Nuovo, it would have been a dramatic new iconographical form, linking earthly secular power with that of heaven.

The assumption that Theoderic would not have had overtly Arian imagery in this church is based on a circular argument, since if there had been something overtly Arian here, then all our assumptions about Theoderic's religious attitudes would have to be revised. Surviving texts, including a fragment of a calendar from sixth-century Ravenna, indicate that a whole host of saints and martyrs were venerated by the Goths – some Arian, some Gothic, some just generically Christian, and both male and female[179] – more than enough to have populated the walls of this church with figures who were incompatible with Orthodox Byzantine ideology. Such a procession would provide the most obvious model for its own replacement, and would have equally well have presented the court of heaven, as we have seen a very common metaphor in late antique literature.

Regardless of what was originally there, W. Urbano is surely correct that the partial erasure of figures in Sant'Apollinare Nuovo, which retained the hands and dedicatory inscription, were a way of reminding people of the condemnation, emphasizing the disgrace rather than erasing all memory of the Arian past.[180] The very fact that we are still wondering about it indicates how successful this strategy was!

The Head of Justinian? One final fragment of a mosaic survives from the late antique church, the bust of a man dressed as an emperor, and labeled

57. Sant'-
Apollinare
Nuovo, mosaic
fragment
from the west
wall, head of
Justinian (photo
C. Copenhaver)

Justinian (Fig. 57).[181] Agnellus tells us that pictures of Archbishop Agnellus and the emperor Justinian were found on the interior entrance wall of
the church, decorated with gold mosaic.[182] In the sixteenth century several
authors mention portraits of Justinian, Theodora, and a third person who is
variously identified. Girolamo Rossi identified Justinian on the south side of
the main door, and Archbishop Agnellus on the north, although a century
later only Justinian survived. The surviving fragment was restored by Felice
Kibel in 1863, and the label IUSTINIAN, which is currently part of the
fragment, is attributable to Kibel. Despite Agnellus's and later attestations
that the figure was Justinian, some scholars have suggested that it originally
depicted Theoderic. The fact that the face of the figure does not look like
the portrait of Justinian in San Vitale has led to the supposition that this
ruler had been relabeled, and perhaps even reclothed, as Justinian after the
Orthodox rededication.[183] This attribution is often repeated in scholarly literature and has played a role in debates about Theoderic's self-presentation

as an emperor, although even if the face itself were Theoderic's, there is no indication of how he would have originally been dressed.

I. Baldini Lippolis notes that most of the scholarly debate concerns questions of imperial and royal portraiture in the sixth century. There is only one surviving portrait of Theoderic, on the Senigallia medallion (Fig. 29), although we know from Agnellus that several other depictions of this ruler existed in Ravenna and elsewhere. The face on the mosaic does not look like that of the Senigallia medallion, but it is very probable that official portraits could have different appearances in different contexts. However, by the same reasoning there is no reason that it could not have originally depicted Justinian. Baldini Lippolis notes that the mosaic has been damaged, removed, and restored so many times that it is no longer possible to say whether it was all made at one time, but concludes that most likely the entire mosaic portrait was Justinian right from the start, created as a pendant to a portrait of Archbishop Agnellus to indicate their joint reintegration of this church into the Orthodox empire.[184]

Santo Spirito (the Arian Cathedral)

The church that since the fifteenth century has been known as Santo Spirito[185] was built originally as the cathedral for the Arian bishop of Ravenna; at least, this is implied by Agnellus, who says that there was an *episcopium* and a baptistery there. In Agnellus's day the church was dedicated to St. Theodore, presumed to originate with its rededication to Orthodox worship.[186] The document from 551, cited above, mentions a Gothic bishop and refers to an *ecclesia legis Gothorum sanctae Anastasie*, which has been interpreted as the Arian cathedral, originally dedicated, like its Orthodox counterpart, to the Anastasis. As we have seen in the previous chapter, by the sixth century there was a confusion between dedications to the Anastasis and to St. Anastasia. Notably, in the 380s Gregory Nazianzus built a church in Constantinople called the Anastasia, in reference to Gregory's *anastasis* or resurrection of Nicene Christianity under the threat of Arianism. This church was rebuilt in the 460s and dedicated to St. Anastasia of Sirmium, precisely when Theoderic was living in Constantinople. It was endowed with vessels by the Arian generals Aspar and his son Ardabur, in thanks for which it was decreed that the Gospels were to be read in this church in Gothic.[187] The history of that church was known in sixth-century Italy, as Cassiodorus reports it in his *Historia ecclesiastica tripartita*, in a section derived from Sozomen's history.[188] A Gothic church in Ravenna dedicated to St. Anastasia thus makes sense, and it seems likely that this was in fact

58 Santo Spir-
ito, view of the
interior (photo
Institut für
Kunstgeschichte
der Johannes
Gutenberg Uni-
versität Mainz,
Bilddatenbank)

the Arian cathedral, perhaps with an intentional ambiguity of dedication to
Anastasia/Anastasis.[189]

By the eighth century a monastic community is known to have been
established in this church, which took its name from the dedication of the
baptistery to Santa Maria in Cosmedin. After the tenth century modifications were made to both buildings, including the amplification of the nave
colonnade with pointed arches, perhaps in the thirteenth century. The raising of the nave colonnade by 1.82 m, the addition of the current porch and
of several chapels at the ends of the aisles and on the sides of the church
occurred in the sixteenth century. In the 1930s and 1940s, especially after
the northern chapels were destroyed by bombing in 1943, a campaign to
restore the basilica to its "original" form was undertaken, resulting in the
structure visible today (Fig. 58).[190]

The Arian cathedral is a basilica with single aisles and seven-column
colonnades; at 28.3 × 18.5 meters it is noticeably smaller than the Ursiana

(Fig. 59).[191] The relative width of the church compared to its length give it a boxier ground plan than is usual in Ravenna's basilicas. Its length relative to width is 1.24, whereas the usual ratio is 1.5. G. De Angelis d'Ossat linked these proportions with those of the church of Sant'Agata dei Goti in Rome, built by Ricimer, and argued that they somehow reflect Arian ideology.[192] But Deichmann correctly noted that some churches in Constantinople, as well as others in Rome and Ravenna, also have these proportions, which therefore probably have nothing to do with doctrinal or ethnic difference.[193] These proportions give the church a more vertical feel than is usually found in a longitudinal church; and given that the floor level was originally 1.82 m lower, this verticality would have seemed even more pronounced than it does today. Originally the church had neither narthex nor atrium, and later construction on the west side of the building has obscured how it was linked to its baptistery (Fig. 59).[194]

The church was made of a combination of reused Roman bricks and new bricks of the type that are also found in later sixth-century buildings in Ravenna.[195] At the eastern end, a fairly deep apse was a five-sided polygon on the exterior and semicircular on the interior, with three large windows on the three central sides; the semidome of the apse was vaulted with bricks rather than with *tubi fittili*.[196] On the facade wall three doors led into the nave and aisles; above the central door, at the level of the clerestory windows, are three windows which give additional light to the nave. On the walls above the nave arcades, six large windows (now mostly filled in) are clustered toward the center of the wall surface and do not correspond to the arcade below. On the north and south aisle walls, seven windows did correspond to the columns of the colonnade; on the south side these windows opened onto a covered corridor parallel to the aisle, with a door in place of the central window.[197] The windows were outlined on the exterior with pilasters and arcades of brick, again similar to other Ravennate churches.

The nave colonnade consists of bases, columns, capitals, and impost blocks of different sizes and types of marble.[198] Workshop marks on some of the columns do not correspond to any known from Ravenna or from Constantinople. Two different types of capitals are attributable, according to Deichmann, to a north Italian workshop (not from Ravenna or Constantinople), perhaps of the late fifth or early sixth century. Part of an ambo that dates to the early sixth century is still found in the building, made of Istrian limestone (like the Mausoleum of Theoderic) and beautifully carved with abstract ornament. The decoration is similar to that of the ambo in Sant'Apollinare Nuovo, which is known to have come from Constantinople; it is presumed that the cathedral ambo was made locally, imitating the other.[199] No trace of the original wall decoration survives, although fragments of mosaic of uncertain date have been found in excavations.[200]

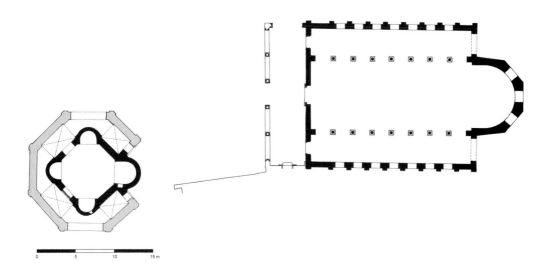

59. The Arian
Cathedral (today
Santo Spirito)
and Baptistery,
reconstructed
plan showing
octagon and
now-lost sur-
rounding spaces
(shaded) (after
Deichmann,
1976, Fig. 15)

Of the *episcopium* of the Arians we know nothing beyond what Agnellus tells us, namely, "…the house of Drocton [*domo Drocdonis*], which house together with a bath and a *monasterium* to St. Apollinaris, which was built in the upper story of the house, was the *episcopium* of that church."[201] An *episcopium* for Agnellus was the residence of an *episcopus*, or bishop; it is curious that Agnellus also says that Arian *episcopia* were found at the churches of St. George and St. Eusebius, outside the walls of the city.[202] This implies that the Arian bishops had three residences, which is nowhere said of the Orthodox bishops. The Orthodox *episcopium*, as we will see, had a chapel on an upper story constructed in the early sixth century, and a bath refurbished in the 540s, and the *episcopium* at St. Theodore would seem to have had the same facilities. *Drocdonis* in Agnellus may refer to Droctulfus, identified by Paul the Deacon as Drocton, a Sueve who fought under the Lombards but then fled to Ravenna and joined the imperial army, serving in Thrace and Africa. He was eventually buried in San Vitale in Ravenna sometime after 606.[203] A still-visible wall between Santo Spirito and the Arian Baptistery, often called the "Casa di Drogdone," contains tenth- to twelfth-century decoration on its upper level, but its date of construction is put anywhere from the seventh to the twelfth century. It certainly seems to have some relationship with the two religious structures, but we cannot be sure what it was or when it was built.[204]

The Arian Baptistery

The Arian Baptistery[205] stands 43 m to the southwest of the facade of its cathedral.[206] It is not as well preserved as its Orthodox counterpart, but

enough survives to enable us to see that it was in part inspired by the earlier building but included significant differences.[207] No historical sources
mention the construction of the Arian Baptistery. Our first information
comes from Agnellus, who tells us only that in his day it was a *monasterium*
to the Virgin Mary *in Cosmedin*, and at that time it contained an altar to
St. Nicholas.[208] The mosaics in the baptistery's dome are well preserved;
like the mosaics of Sant'Apollinare Nuovo, they have come under scrutiny
for evidence of Arian theology and iconography. As we will see, like all
images in Ravenna these can be interpreted in a variety of ways, none
entirely satisfactory. Nevertheless, it is clear that there was an attempt to
differentiate these mosaics from those of the Orthodox Baptistery, and to
make them meaningful to the Ostrogoths and Romans who might have
been baptized here.

The meaning of baptism was a topic of intense discussion in the early
Church, both because of the centrality of the rite in civic and daily life,
and because of its relationship to Christological controversies. The core
text for the ritual is Matthew 28:19, where Christ says to the apostles, "Go
therefore and make disciples of all the nations, baptizing them in the name
of the Father and the Son and the Holy Spirit." Since the Trinity is invoked
in this Gospel passage, it became one of the most important pieces of evidence in discussions about the nature of Christ and the Holy Spirit. There
is evidence that potential differences between Arian and Orthodox baptism
were an issue for church leaders in the fourth through sixth centuries in
the east and in Spain. In the fourth century the extreme Arian followers of
Eunomius drew attention for their unusual baptismal practices: they used
one immersion instead of three, baptized in the name of the death of Christ
or in the names of an unequal Trinity, and rebaptized all those previously
baptized in any other tradition. All of these things were counter to Orthodox practice. Rebaptism in particular was something that was condemned
by Orthodox theologians, except in cases (such as Eunomianism) in which
a person had not been baptized in the name of the Trinity. However, there
is no evidence of Eunomians in Italy and other Arians do not seem to have
had distinctive baptismal rituals.[209] Indeed, in the *De trinitate* attributed to
the late fourth-century bishop Eusebius of Vercelli, the author calls Arians
hypocrites for baptizing in the name of a Trinity whose consubstantiality
they do not admit.[210] More relevant for Ostrogothic Italy, the lack of differences in baptismal rites between Arians and Orthodox were of major concern to Spanish theologians in the Visigothic era. Some Orthodox priests in
Spain instituted baptism by single immersion in order to differentiate themselves from the Arians who practiced triple immersion. Single immersion
was opposed by leading bishops as well as by Pope Vigilius (537–55), who
argued that the Orthodox must baptize using triple immersion.[211] In his

60. Arian Baptistery, exterior view

letter to Bishop Profuturus of Braga, Vigilius also condemns rebaptism of Arians, which surely would also have been an issue in Italy. Bishop Martin of Braga, writing about the triple immersion question in the late sixth century, specifically notes that Arian and Orthodox ritual and liturgy were extremely similar, and only their belief in the Trinity distinguished them.[212] We therefore have no evidence of any difference in Arian baptismal rituals from those of the Orthodox in Italy.[213]

The Arian Baptistery appears today as an octagonal prism with four absidioles projecting on the north, south, east, and west sides, which looks very like the Orthodox Baptistery (Fig. 60). Originally the Arian building's profile was rather different, as the octagonal core was surrounded on seven of its sides by a covered or enclosed ambulatory 1.90 m wide, leaving only the larger eastern apse exposed (Fig. 59). The entrances to the ambulatory

flanked the eastern apse (thus facing the cathedral),[214] while the entrances
to the octagonal core were on the northwest and southwest walls, thus at
the opposite side (today only the entrance on the northwest wall is open).[215]
Parts of the exterior wall have been excavated, and the evidence, coupled
with projecting elements from the surviving building, especially at the corners of the octagon, show that the ambulatory consisted of a series of rectangular rooms and irregular passageways around the absidioles, each separated
by an arched opening and vaulted with brick. Access to the ambulatory may
also have been gained on the north and south sides facing the absidioles,
but there would have been no unobstructed view from the outside into
the octagonal core.[216] As S. Cummins shows, polygonal ambulatories surrounding octagonal baptisteries are known for the pre-Eufrasian baptistery
at Porec, San Giovanni in Canosa, and apparently at the Ca'Bianca south of
Classe; and ambulatories with other layouts are known from several other
baptisteries. They may have provided waiting or disrobing areas, spaces for
particular parts of the liturgy, or storage rooms.[217] Some have suggested
that concealing the interior mysteries from the casual observer may have
been a reason for the arrangement of the doors.[218] But, as this is the only
baptistery securely known to have been used by Arians, and since other baptisteries hypothesized as Arian in Salona, Grado, and Milan do not show
differences from the Orthodox buildings in those cities, it is impossible to
know whether this had anything to do with the Arian ritual.[219]

The Arian Baptistery was built of very varied reused Roman brick,[220]
perhaps an indication that by the sixth century the supply of imperial-era
bricks was running low. As is usual in Ravenna, the original floor level
lay 2.31 m below the present ground level; because of ground water, the
current reconstructed floor is only 1.04 m below ground level.[221] The floor
was raised at least four times in the structure's history; this is fortunate, as
the remains of the original walls can only be traced in places below the level
of the first repaving. The baptistery has an overall width of ca. 9 meters,
an interior diameter of 6.75–6.85 m, an exterior wall length of 3.40 m, and
an interior wall length of ca. 2.86 m; from the original ground level to
the top of the exterior walls the building measures 8.5 m, and the walls of
the octagon are 0.75 m thick.[222] A window was inserted into each wall just
above the level of the external ambulatory, which is marked today by a brick
cornice; the windows are 1.70 m high. The vault springs from a point 9.35 m
above the original floor level; the apex of the dome rises 11.07 m above the
original floor level. The transition from the octagon to the circular base
of the dome is made with small pendentives. The dome, like that of the
Arian cathedral and the "mausoleum of Galla Placidia" but unlike others
in Ravenna, was made of brick, and the roof is supported by a fill made

of amphorae and mortar. Some have seen this as a sign that workers were brought in from Constantinople for these buildings.[223] Overall, the Arian Baptistery's diameter is 56 percent of that of the Orthodox Baptistery, and the dome's height is 76 percent of the height of the Orthodox Baptistery.[224] It is generally assumed that the smaller size is because of the minority status of Arian Christianity in Ravenna, although we should not forget that a second baptistery existed just down the street at Sant'Apollinare Nuovo, perhaps dating back to the Ostrogothic period.

The apsidiole on the east side is wider and deeper (2.80 meters wide, 2.75 meters deep) than the others (2.10 m wide, 1.73 m deep), and its floor level was apparently raised a step above the rest of the space, perhaps separated by a railing. Each of the absidioles had at least one small niche cut into the lower part of the wall (the only part that is preserved), perhaps to hold liturgical implements. These niches are not original, but stem from some later period of use. The remains of small brick altars, not from the original phase of building but installed at a later point, were found in the south and west absidioles; perhaps one was the altar of St. Nicholas mentioned by Agnellus.[225] The font, which was removed at some point, possibly when the building was reconsecrated, was not in the exact center of the building, but was oriented slightly to the east of center.[226] The purpose of the deeper eastern apse is not known. Many late antique baptisteries have one prominent apse, and it may have contained the throne of the bishop.[227]

Interestingly, six graves have been excavated within the octagon; they broke through the original pavement and must have been installed before the first repaving.[228] The use of a baptistery as a funerary chapel is somewhat unusual. M. Mazzotti proposed that the burials occurred when the building was rededicated from Arian worship as a way of marking the fact that it was no longer a baptistery.[229] On the other hand, we know that burial in baptisteries was not unknown in late antiquity, since laws against it were passed by church councils.[230]

On the interior, excavations of 1916–19 and also of 1969 revealed large amounts of mosaic and stucco fragments, and bits of painted imitation marble were found at the lower edges of the south and east absidioles.[231] The only decorations that have been preserved are the mosaics of the dome (Pl. IVb). These were restored in the seventeenth century and again in the mid–nineteenth century, but these repairs consisted mostly of small patches, except for the lower halves of the fourth and fifth apostles who follow St. Peter; thus, the original iconography is intact. Based on differences in workmanship and materials, it seems clear that the work was done in different phases or by different artists.[232] Deichmann, following G. Gerola,

61. Arian Baptistery, central medallion depicting the baptism of Christ

proposed that the mosaics were made in two phases: the first, contemporary with construction, would consist of the central medallion, throne, Peter, Paul, and the apostle behind Paul. The remainder of the mosaics would have been set in the mid–sixth century.[233] C. O. Nordström instead proposed three periods of composition: the first consisting of the central medallion; the second the throne and Sts. Peter, St. Paul, and his follower; and the third the rest of the figures, but Nordström does not suppose a large chronological break between the phases.[234] It should be remembered that the building, begun perhaps as early as 500, would not have been turned over to the Orthodox Church until 561 or later; thus, all of the decoration was probably made during the building's Arian period.

The mosaics of the dome consist of two zones. In a central medallion, set off from the outer circle by a decorative wreath, is a depiction of the baptism of Christ by John the Baptist (Fig. 61). John stands on a rocky prominence in the right of the circle, his right hand on the head of Christ. John is dressed in a spotted tunic and carrying a shepherd's crook; he is bearded, and has no halo. In the center, the nude Christ stands in the waters of the river Jordan, which reach almost to his waist; he is beardless with

62. Arian Baptistery, Sts. Peter and Paul flanking a throne (photo Institut für Kunstgeschichte der Johannes Gutenberg Universität Mainz, Bilddatenbank)

flowing brown hair down to his shoulders and a halo around his head. His navel is literally the center of the dome.[235] Above Christ's head hovers the dove of the Holy Spirit, shown in top view, with an effusion of something that looks like water or light flowing from his beak to Christ's head and John's hand.[236] On the left we see a personification of the river Jordan as a reclining white-haired and bearded man with orange horns coming out of this head; he is nude to the waist, and his legs are covered with a green mantle of the same color and shading as the rock on which John stands. His left hand is raised in acclamation, with his right he holds a reed as a scepter, and behind him is an upside-down amphora out of which flow the waters of the river. The figures are set against a background of gold tesserae. The scene is oriented so that it is properly viewed when the viewer is facing west.

Surrounding the central medallion, we find a procession of the twelve apostles raising objects toward a jeweled throne upon which sits a jeweled cross with a purple pallium draped over its arms (Fig. 62). The apostles are dressed in white tunics with *clavi* and mantles; the latter cover their hands, which emphasizes the four different types of *gammadia* on them.[237] Peter's head is surrounded by a white halo, Paul's and his successor's by a blue halo, and the other nine apostles have beige halos. Peter holds his keys, Paul holds the scrolls of the law, and the other ten apostles hold crowns. They walk on a narrow green ground line and are separated from each other by stylized palm trees; they, like the baptism scene, are set against a flat gold background. The most unusual aspect of this procession is that it is oriented in the opposite direction from the baptismal scene; that is, it is properly viewed when the viewer faces the east, so that the enthroned cross is exactly in line with Christ's head and the dove, but upside down from it (Fig. 62).

Comparing these mosaics with those of the Orthodox Baptistery (Pl. IIb and Fig. 26) reveals both striking similarities and differences. While the similarities imply that the Arian artists were modeling their imagery on that found in the earlier building, it is the differences that have caught the attention of scholars who hope to identify in them some hints of Arian theology or religious practice. As we will see, the search for *Arian* meaning has obscured the even more radical *ethnic* meaning that is found in the imagery in the baptistery.

First let us examine the similarities: the scene of Christ's baptism with John the Baptist, a nude Christ, the river Jordan, the dove, the water of the Jordan, surrounded by a procession of apostles, repeats the Orthodox design. Enthroned crosses likewise are found in the third zone of the Orthodox Baptistery. The differences can be listed as follows (excluding matters relating to the heads, dove, and hands of John the Baptist in the Orthodox Baptistery, which, as we have already discussed, are a reconstruction):[238]

Orthodox Baptistery	Arian Baptistery
John the Baptist on the viewer's left	John the Baptist on the viewer's right
Jordan only top half, smaller	Jordan full-figure, as large as other figures
Apostles and baptism same orientation	Apostles and baptism opposite orientation
Apostles offer crowns to nothing	Apostles offer crowns to enthroned cross
Blue background for apostles	Gold background for apostles
All apostles offer crowns	Peter and Paul offer keys and law
Apostles not haloed	Apostles haloed with different colors
Apostles labeled by name	Apostles not named

These differences have been interpreted as the result of the skill of the artists or as evidence of functional, aesthetic, and/or theological intention. It was surely a combination of factors that resulted in the images that we

see, and, as with any religious image from late antiquity, the depictions may
have been intended to carry different messages to different viewers. Let us
start with the center and work outward.

The reversal of the baptismal scene and the importance of the river Jordan here, are striking compositional differences from the earlier depiction.
Much has been written about the clumsiness of the figures in the baptismal
scene and Deichmann attributes deviations from the Orthodox imagery to
artistic inadequacy.[239] Those who prefer to see it as a result of some intention offer different explanations. It has been suggested that the image in the
Arian Baptistery mirrors the act at the font where the bishop would be on
the baptisand's right side.[240] Some have argued that the image was reversed
deliberately to be different from the Orthodox rendering – something that
is impossible to prove. The larger size of the river Jordan has been explained
as an aesthetic choice, to better balance the composition.[241] Finally, the
bearded, aggressively male figures of the river Jordan and John have been
seen as a deliberate contrast to the youthful, even hermaphroditic, figure
of Christ, although no specifically Arian message is implied.[242]

The different orientations of the baptism scene and the apostolic procession are troubling to the viewer; it is impossible to determine how an
observer should stand to see it all properly. Some scholars have argued
that the mosaicists simply got it wrong, perhaps because of a break in time
between the central composition and the procession, and having started
work, they then had to complete it.[243] Others have related the two view-
points to the ritual. The bishop in the east could see the baptism scene from
the start, whereas the baptisand begins by viewing the procession and the
throne (associated with the bishop), and only sees the baptism of Christ
at the moment in which he turns in the font to face the west.[244] Visually,
the separation of the two zones means that the apostolic procession is not
related to Christ's baptism.[245] R. Sörries suggests that the Arians did not
want the apostles to seem to offer their crowns to Jesus at the moment
when he was being pronounced the Son of God as they do in the Orthodox
Baptistery.[246] Since the baptism of Christ is the moment in which the Trinity is foregrounded in the Gospels, and since Matthew 28:19, in which the
apostles are charged to baptize in the name of the Trinity, is the key text
for the form of baptism of believers, the change in orientation becomes a
subtly anti Trinitarian statement. Finally, as I show in the section to follow,
it can also be argued that the figures one sees when one is facing west are
not intended to be identified as apostles at that moment, but as generic
followers of Christ, an emphasis in Arian ideology, as we have already seen
for Sant'Apollinare Nuovo.[247]

Many of the arguments about the procession are connected to the presence of the throne as the focus of the apostolic procession. The functionalist

argument states that the procession zone in the Arian Baptistery conflates two zones of the Orthodox Baptistery's dome, thus the throne has simply been transposed up into the procession image.[248] Others have found the "simplification" theory troubling and assume that the throne at this level must have had some specific meaning. Sörries suggests that the apostles offer their crowns to the eternal presence of Christ, as symbolized by the cross on the throne, rather than to the baptized Son of God.[249] The throne is aligned with the dove of the Holy Spirit and with Christ in the baptism scene, linking the three, and some have seen it as representing God the Father.[250] Others have seen the throne as symbolic of the bishop who performed the ceremony or as emphasizing the similarities between God and king.[251] Finally, crowns being offered to a throne also evoke the image of the twenty-four elders of the Book of Revelation, and thus the empty throne becomes an *etimasia*, also a reference to the Second Coming of Christ.[252] One interesting question here, as we have already seen in the Orthodox Baptistery, is whether the apostles are in fact offering things to the throne or receiving things from it. In this depiction, Peter and Paul are holding keys and scroll, objects that they usually receive from Christ; thus, as we have already seen in the Orthodox Baptistery, the apostles here may be receiving their crowns from God/Christ, just as the baptisands do.[253]

One final unusual aspect of the procession is that the apostles are not labeled by name. Peter, Paul, and Andrew can be identified by their now-standard facial features and attributes,[254] but the other apostles are not readily distinguishable. This is only unusual if one remembers that the apostles *are* labeled in the Orthodox Baptistery, the *capella arcivescovile*, San Vitale, and other sixth-century churches in which they are represented as a group.[255] Since some of the other buildings had limited available space, one cannot argue that there was no room in the Arian Baptistery to put the names; the omission must have been deliberate. Each apostle's physiognomy is different: some are bearded, some beardless, some with gray hair, some with brown. The apostles who are identified in the Orthodox building as Simon, James Alfaeus, Matthew, Thomas, Paul, Peter, and Andrew all have analogous positions and facial features in the Arian Baptistery, but the remainder do not correspond.[256] As we saw, the names of the apostles on the Mausoleum of Theoderic are not the same as those in the Orthodox buildings of Ravenna, and this series may have been intended to differ also. But it is also possible that these figures are not only intended both to represent the apostles, when seen from the west, but also to represent generic followers of Christ when viewed from the east in the same orientation as the central medallion.[257]

The generic nature of these figures is also related to their audience. Remarkably, the apostle who walks fourth behind Peter is depicted with a mustache that connects to sideburns, but with no beard – in other words, what we would call a muttonchop (Fig. 44). No studies of the mosaics have suggested that this is a nineteenth-century restoration and thus this extremely unusual facial hair must be original.[258] As P. Dutton has shown, mustaches without beards are an extremely unusual type of facial hair in late antiquity and the only examples known from the pre-Carolingian era are the one sported by Theoderic on the Senigallia medallion (Fig. 29) and those found on some bronze coins of Odoacer, Theodahad, and Totila,[259] although none of these are connected to sideburns. Dutton concludes that Theoderic was depicted in this way to distinguish him from Romans;[260] at the least, these coin portraits show that the mustache was a type of facial hair known at the Ostrogothic court. Ennodius pokes fun at his friend Jovinian's *barba gothica* and *barbarica facies*, implying that a distinctive type of facial hair was worn by Goths and those who wanted to look like them.[261] I would argue that this mustachioed apostle was intended visually to make the point that Goths were part of the Christian community. When facing west and looking up at the baptism scene, one does not see the easily recognizable Peter, Paul, and Andrew, but their more generic followers. Thus, the Gothic baptisand, in addition to associating himself with Christ, also could associate himself with the followers of Christ. Indeed, the very lack of labels allows this ambiguity, as it then becomes possible to understand these figures as both apostles and Christians of associated ages and backgrounds receiving their baptismal crowns.

Ultimately, the only features that can be clearly identified as "Arian" about these mosaics is the fact that they are different from those in the Orthodox Baptistery. As S. Cummins notes, the fact that these mosaics were not changed or destroyed upon the Orthodox rededication means that they were not offensive to the Orthodox and did not ostentatiously represent Arian doctrine.[262] At the most, as we have seen for the Christological cycle in Sant'Apollinare Nuovo, a viewer could come up with an Arian interpretation of certain features, but equally likely could provide an Orthodox explanation. However, while the images may be theologically neutral, the Arian Baptistery's iconography accommodates the inhabitants of Ostrogothic Ravenna in what was certainly an Arian context, but with an ethnic spin.

The Orthodox Church in Ostrogothic Ravenna

While Ravenna was under Ostrogothic rule, its Orthodox bishops, John I (477–94), Peter II (494–520), Aurelian (521), Ecclesius (522–32), Ursicinus (533–6), and Victor (538–45), had to share episcopal authority with

the Arian bishops installed by Theoderic and the exalted position that they
had established under the emperors may have slipped somewhat. Nevertheless, for most of the period the Orthodox bishops seem to have been
supported by the Ostrogothic rulers. A letter in the *Variae* indicates that
Theoderic had treated Ravenna's Orthodox Church with favor, since the
church of Milan asks for similar privileges, while in another, Theodahad
asks Justinian to favor the business affairs "of the Ravennate Church."[263]
As we have seen, there were religious tensions in Ravenna during the latter part of Theoderic's reign, and these may well have included opposition
between Arians and the Orthodox Church.[264] There also seem to have
been tensions within Ravenna's Orthodox Church, which might reflect the
strains imposed by Ostrogothic rule. What is clear is that when Ravenna
emerged from the chaos of the Gothic Wars, the bishop had become one
of the dominant figures in the city.

Our understanding of the role of the long-serving Peter II is compromised by the fact that his biography is confused by Agnellus with that of
Peter I Chrysologus. As we have seen, he sided with Theoderic in the controversy over the Jewish synagogue of 519 and he seems to have worked
well with Theoderic. His name appears in various synodal documents and
letters, indicating that he was considered to be fourth in rank among the
clergy of Italy, behind the pope and the bishops of Milan and Aquileia.[265]
In Ravenna Peter II undertook three building projects: a chapel (the *capella
arcivescovile*) and a house called *Tricollis* in the *episcopium*, and a baptistery
in Classe at the Petriana basilica.[266] The fact that at the same time the
Arians were building large churches in the center of the city underscores
the marginality, or one might say the liminality, of Peter's constructions.
Within the episcopium Peter was presumably free to do as he pleased,
and a baptistery in Classe was likewise not in the ceremonial center of
Theoderic's capital.

The Capella Arcivescovile

Under Peter II, the *episcopium* of Ravenna began to be enlarged and beau-
tified, no doubt a reflection of the aspirations of the Orthodox bishops
of the city (Fig. 63). Agnellus tells us that Peter "...founded a house
inside the episcopal palace of the Ravennate see, which is called *Tricollis*, because it contains three *colla*, which building is constructed inside with
great ingenuity. And not far from that house he built the *monasterium* of St.
Andrew the apostle...."[267] The *Tricollis* took a long time to build; Agnellus
later reports the dedicatory inscription of the building, which names all of

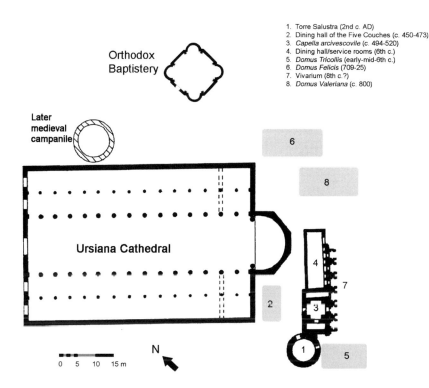

Orthodox
Baptistery

1. Torre Salustra (2nd c. AD)
2. Dining hall of the Five Couches (c. 450-473)
3. *Capella arcivescovile* (c. 494-520)
4. Dining hall/service rooms (6th c.)
5. *Domus Tricollis* (early-mid-6th c.)
6. *Domus Felicis* (709-25)
7. Vivarium (8th c.?)
8. *Domus Valeriana* (c. 800)

Later medieval campanile

6

8

Ursiana Cathedral

4

7

2

3

1

5

N

0   5   10   15 m

63. Plan of Ravenna's episcopal complex, including the cathedral, baptistery, and various buildings of the *episcopium*

Peter's successors up to Maximian as patrons of the structure.[268] The meaning of the word *colla* is not known, and explanations have ranged from a building with three stories to one with three rooms to a triconch dining hall.[269] Since nothing survives of this building (unless it is the one with three stories), we can say nothing further, except to note that either the cost or the ingeniousness of the construction must be the cause of its lengthy construction time.

A rare example of a late antique chapel whose function is known, and whose decoration survives almost intact, the *capella arcivescovile* illuminates many sixth-century ecclesiastical, political, theological, and iconographical issues.[270] Since it is found in the heart of the *episcopium*, it is assumed to have served as a private chapel for the archbishops. It is the least studied of Ravenna's surviving monuments, although it clearly is connected with all of the others in various ways. By Agnellus's time it was dedicated to St. Andrew, although since Andrew is not mentioned in the dedication inscription cited by Agnellus or featured in the surviving mosaics, Deichmann thought that relics of the saint must have been introduced later.[271] However, it is possible that an image of Andrew was, in fact, depicted over the

64. *Capella arcivescovile*, southeast exterior wall with the remains of the eighth-century *vivarium* (?)

doors of the chapel; Agnellus says "...he [Peter II] built the *monasterium* of St. Andrew the apostle, and his image is depicted in mosaic inside this *monasterium*, over the doors."[272] "His image" is usually interpreted as referring to a portrait of Peter II, but it is equally, if not more likely that the portrait was of St. Andrew, much as an image of St. Lawrence was found in a lunette in the mausoleum of Galla Placidia. Andrew was one of the patron saints of Constantinople, a fact that Agnellus emphasizes,[273] and this dedication would reinforce the connections of Ravenna's bishops with the imperial capital.

The chapel, today located within the Museo Arcivescovile, was found on the top floor of a three-story structure built by Bishop Peter II as an addition to the episcopal palace, adjacent to a tower known as the *Torre*

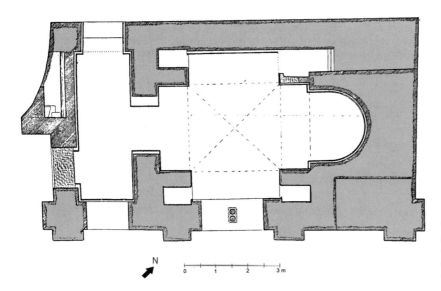

65. *Capella arcivescovile*, plan of the narthex and chapel (after Gerola, 1932)

Salustra, which may originally have been a water distribution tower of the aqueduct,[274] and which was now used as a stairwell for the new building (Fig. 64). The three-story building is built of reused brick; the first and second floors each contain three vaulted rooms that correspond to the layout of the top floor with the chapel. The second floor had three vaulted chambers; the one below the chapel's narthex was accessible only through a trapdoor in its ceiling, and Gerola proposed that it served as a crypt containing the episcopal treasury.[275] We do not know what these other chambers were used for, although it is usually assumed that they did not have a sacral function.[276] Parts of this building were modified in the sixteenth and seventeenth centuries, and in particular the apse of the chapel was completely removed and rebuilt during the extensive reconstructions that were executed between 1911 and 1930, but much of the building survives in its original form.[277] The decoration of the chapel has been heavily restored everywhere, based on the careful analysis of surviving traces of the original as described in detail by G. Gerola.

The chapel is preceded by a narthex, or entry hall, whose doors opened on the southwest to a triangular space adjacent to the tower (walled up in the Byzantine period), on the northwest to the hallway of the building, and on the northeast, through a thick wall into the chapel (Fig. 65). The floor was originally covered with an *opus sectile* pavement made of marble from Proconnesus and elsewhere, whose pattern was recovered from surviving traces of mortar.[278] The lower parts of the walls were originally covered by a revetment of large slabs of marble, again now entirely restored with Proconnesian marble, as described by Agnellus.[279] The brick barrel vault is covered with a mosaic of an abstract pattern of lilies, discs, and birds against a gold background (Fig. 66). Much of the southeastern wall is taken up with a large window (much altered and now completely restored); the mosaics above the window are not original. Over the northwestern door is a mosaic depicting a youthful Christ dressed as warrior-emperor, trampling on a lion and a serpent in a rocky landscape with a gold background; the lower part of this image is entirely restored.[280] Christ holds a long-handled cross in his right hand and an open book in his left, which displays the words "Ego sum via, veritas et, vita" (John 14:6). Agnellus quotes the lengthy inscription, which he says was found in the narthex.[281] The restorers found small fragments identifiable as the ends of some of the lines, indicating that this was a mosaic inscription covering the upper part of the long walls of the narthex and they recreated it accordingly.[282] The first part of the inscription is notable for its emphasis on light and the metaphor of its radiance in a small chapel:

> Either light was born here, or captured here it reigns free; it is the law, from which source the current glory of heaven excels. The roofs, deprived [of light], have produced gleaming day, and the enclosed radiance gleams forth as if from secluded Olympus. See, the marble flourishes with bright rays, and all the stones struck in starry purple shine in value, the gifts of the founder Peter. To him honor and merit are granted, thus to beautify small things, so that although confined in space, they surpass the large. Nothing is small to Christ; He, whose temples exist within the human heart, well occupies confining buildings.

Given the brilliance of the gold mosaics in the chapel, this poem offers a remarkable insight into its meaning as intended by the patron, Bishop Peter.[283]

The chapel itself is cruciform, with shallow (0.90–0.97 meter) arms covered by barrel vaults (Fig. 65). Its orientation is rather curious, being perpendicular to the cathedral. Since the cathedral's apse actually faces southeast, the apse of the chapel faces northeast. The current apse is a complete restoration of the original deep (1.75 meter) semicircular apse covered by a semidome made of *tubi fittili*.[284] The wall to the right of the apse includes two large windows separated by a column, capped by a simple impost block.[285] Hollowed out of three of the corner masonry blocks were small rectangular niches (0.5 × 0.9 meter), which Gerola suggests were intended to hold relics; in the northwest corner of the chapel a narrow

66. *Capella arcivescovile*, view of the narthex facing northwest, Christ trampling the beasts (photo S. Mauskopf)

passageway led to the hallway outside.[286] The *opus sectile* floor in the chapel is largely original, as is the revetment of a dado surmounted by large slabs of Proconnesian marble, with an upper border of reddish pavonazzetto marble from Dokimeion in Asia Minor, that covers the lower 2.75 meter of the wall surfaces. This wall covering is set off from the mosaics by a mostly restored cornice of stucco.

The decoration of the lunettes in the arms does not survive; again, Agnellus says that a portrait originally existed over the door, and the restorers painted an inscription testifying to this in the lunette above the door on the west wall. The mosaics of the vaults do survive almost in their entirety

(Pl. V; Figs. 67, 68). The barrel vaults over the arms of the cross are wide enough for one row of medallions containing the heads of various holy people, as follows (from left to right):

Northeast (Apostles)	Southeast (Male Martyrs)	Southwest (Apostles)	Northwest (Female Martyrs)
Iohannis	Chrysanthus	Simon Cananeus	Caecilia
Iacobus	Chrisoconus	Taddaeus	Eugenia
Paulus	Cassianus	Iacobus	Eufimia
Beardless Christ	Chrismon A/Ω	Beardless Christ	Chrismon A/Ω
Petrus	[Polyca]rpus*	Thomas	Daria
Andreas	[Cos]mas*	Mattheus	Perpetua
Filippus	Damianus*	Bartholomeus	Felicitas

*Restored

The heads of the saints, without halos, are set against blue backgrounds; the medallions are bordered by a multicolored ring and set against the gold background on which the names of the saints are written. Such series of portraits are known to have existed at Santa Sabina in Rome from the 420s and are often presumed to have been found in San Giovanni Evangelista in Ravenna; they became very popular in the sixth century and we will see them again in San Vitale.[287]

The twelve martyrs depicted here are an oddly assorted bunch and no one has attempted to explain their selection other than to suggest that their relics were found in the chapel. As in Sant'Apollinare Nuovo, the male saints are on the right and the female on the left as one faces the apse. Certainly Euphemia of Chalcedon, as we have seen in Sant'Apollinare Nuovo, represents Chalcedonian Orthodoxy. Chrysogonus, Perpetua, Felicitas, and Caecilia were among the most popular of the martyrs, appearing in early Canons of the Mass from Milan and Rome.[288] Cassian was the patron saint of Ravenna's subordinate see of Imola. Eugenia, Daria, and her husband Chrysanthus were venerated at Rome. Polycarp of Smyrna, like several of the others, would later be depicted in the martyr procession in Sant'Apollinare Nuovo, indicating a certain familiarity with him in Ravenna. The cult of Cosmas and Damian was known in Constantinople in the early fifth century, and was brought to Rome by Pope Symmachus (498–514); their church next to the Roman forum was built by Theoderic's appointee Pope Felix IV (526–30).[289] Thus, as a whole these saints can be said to have been popular in the early sixth century, but the reasons for their selection are obscure.

The central space of the chapel is covered by a groin vault made of brick (Pl. V). Shallow slivers of lunettes above the barrel vaults contain rinceaux,

67. *Capella arcivescovile*, northeast arch of chapel, Christ and the apostles (photo S. Mauskopf)

68. *Capella arcivescovile*, northwest arch of chapel, female saints (photo S. Mauskopf)

lambs, and the monogram of Bishop Peter, and are set off by abstract borders from the other elements. At the apex of the vault is a gold *chrismon* against a blue background set within a medallion. It is held up by four angels, haloed, winged, and dressed in white tunics and *pallia* and standing on green spits of ground at the four corners. Between the angels, the four beasts of the Apocalypse, here holding books and thus symbolizing the four evangelists, float as winged figures in multicolored clouds. Finally, the restorers found many dark blue and silver tesserae in the area of the apse, which led them to reconstruct it (on the model of the mausoleum of Galla Placidia) as gold and silver stars surround a gold Latin cross against a dark blue sky.

The chapel and its decoration make clear references to earlier structures in Ravenna. Many, of course, have since disappeared, but we can recognize adaptations from the Santa Croce complex in the ground plan,[290] the evangelist symbols of the vault, and in the trampling Christ of the narthex, which, as we saw, also appeared in the Orthodox Baptistery. Unlike the fifth-century monuments, however, here the taste for gold mosaic as a background completely changes the visual experience from one of mournful contemplation to one of brightness and splendor. As we have seen, gold backgrounds were used in the Arian churches built at this time, and stylistically these mosaics are similar to those both in the Arian Baptistery and in Sant'Apollinare Nuovo.[291]

Built by Bishop Peter II (494–520), at the height of Theoderic's reign, the chapel has always attracted attention for the anti-Arian elements of its decoration. One of the key biblical passages used by Orthodox theologians against Arianism was John 14 and the selection depicted on the book held by Christ in the narthex was a key expression of trinitarian doctrine.[292] As we have noted, St. Euphemia was a symbol of Chalcedonian Orthodoxy and her appearance in this context cannot be accidental. With this chapel, Peter reminded his clergy that even though they could accommodate an Arian ruler they were the guardians of Orthodox belief.

The Early Sixth-Century Churches of Classe

As we have already seen, early sixth-century Classe was a thriving center of trade and military activity. To accommodate these populations, new ecclesiastical structures were built in the area. The elaborate complex that Agnellus calls the Petriana, built first by Peter I and added to by Peter II and Victor, has completely disappeared; and yet archaeologists in the 1960s discovered an apparently different and elaborate complex to the south of the city at a site known as Ca'Bianca whose identity remains a mystery.

In the previous chapter we discussed the Petriana church, built in the mid-fifth century and destroyed by the ninth. Agnellus says that the Petriana had a baptistery, built by Bishop Peter II, that "was wonderful in size, with doubled walls and high walls built with mathematical art," although it is not known what this means. Later Agnellus says, "[Victor] decorated the tetragonal baptistery, which most blessed Peter Chrysologus built in the city of Classe next to the Petriana church, and in the middle of the vault, on the men's side, under the arch there is a small medallion, which even today contains the following, 'by our holy lord,' and facing on the other side, the women's, there is found another little medallion, as above, with gold letters in turn on its side, reading thus, 'father Victor.'"[293] Thus the Petriana baptistery seems to have been a basilica or some other square shape (perhaps even like the *capella arcivescovile*?) rather than an octagon. Agnellus reports that it had *monasteria*, or side chapels, attached to it, dedicated to Sts. Matthew and James, and even reports having investigated a tomb in one of these.[294]

Why was this baptistery built at this time? Some scholars have seen the Petriana complex as a sign that Classe had its own church organization separate from that of Ravenna. The fact that in Sant'Apollinare Nuovo Classe is depicted equal in status to Ravenna is interpreted as indicating a separate civic identity for Classe by the early sixth century.[295] Since we have no evidence ever for a bishop of Classe, this seems unlikely. But by this time baptism was becoming more decentralized and there was probably a perceived need for a second baptistery in Classe in which a priest would administer baptism.[296] Other new baptisteries start to appear at this time, as we will see, and *pievi*, or rural churches equipped for baptism, began to be built in surrounding towns such as Padovetere and Argenta.[297] These examples show that the office of baptism was expanding beyond the episcopal church. In the case of the Petriana baptistery, though, we might wonder whether Bishop Peter II intended it as an alternative for the Orthodox clergy in case of an Arian takeover of the cathedral in Ravenna. As we have seen, according to Agnellus the Petriana was magnificently built and decorated, and Peter II may have felt that, as it was not in the center of Theoderic's capital city, it had a better chance of maintaining its status as an Orthodox church.

The Ca'Bianca basilica, excavated through sondages in 1965 and not scientifically surveyed, remains a mystery (Fig. 69).[298] It lay 2 kilometers south of Sant'Apollinare in Classe, and 800 meters to the east of the *via Popilia*, south of a river that ran to the nearby coastline, and is assumed to have been built for the use of an unknown *vicus* to its south.[299] At least two phases of construction have been identified. The earlier, dated to the late fifth or early sixth century, includes a large basilica (nave + aisles 37.50 x 22.50 m including the walls), with an apse polygonal on the exterior and circular on the interior, a colonnade of twelve columns, an atrium wider than the narthex, and an adjacent octagonal building (inner core 9.20 m across), interpreted as a baptistery, to the north. The later phase includes small chambers flanking the apse to the north and south, some of which may have been used as mausolea,[300] and the porches along the aisles, and is assumed to date to the later sixth century.[301] The buildings were built of reused Roman brick and were paved with marble and with mosaic, the latter datable to the middle of the sixth century. A raised rectangular *bema* occupied the first of the bays of the nave in front of the apse.

It is not known when this church was abandoned; there is no record of it in any textual sources, unless it is one of the churches mentioned by Agnellus that is now lost.[302] The basilica is of almost the same dimensions as Sant'Apollinare Nuovo, which led De Angelis d'Ossat to propose that it must date to the Ostrogothic period and perhaps even be Arian;[303] the baptistery has the same layout and dimensions as the Arian Baptistery. Why would magnificent buildings, on the same scale as those being built in the heart of the new Arian capital, be erected to serve a suburban *vicus*? It has been suggested that perhaps the church excavated at the Ca'Bianca was Agnellus's Petriana basilica, but most scholars reject this interpretation, as the dating is wrong and Agnellus several times says that the Petriana was in the city of Classe (*in civitate Classis*).[304] Without further excavation, the Ca'Bianca complex remains a sign of the wealth and power of Ravenna's elite in the early sixth century, even if we do not know to which elite to attribute it.

The Orthodox Church after Theoderic

Our knowledge of church affairs becomes more extensive for the period after the death of Theoderic, when it seems that the Orthodox Church quickly began to recoup its authority. As described mainly by Agnellus, in Bishop Ecclesius we see a man who played a role both within Ravenna and in the broader world. Ecclesius was one of the clerics whom Theoderic sent with Pope John I to Constantinople in 525 to protest the emperor Justin I's treatment of the Arians.[305] Unlike John, Ecclesius did not attract Theoderic's ire upon their return, but kept his throne in what must have been difficult circumstances. His actions during this period, however, made him enemies. Sometime between 526 and 530, some of Ecclesius's clergy

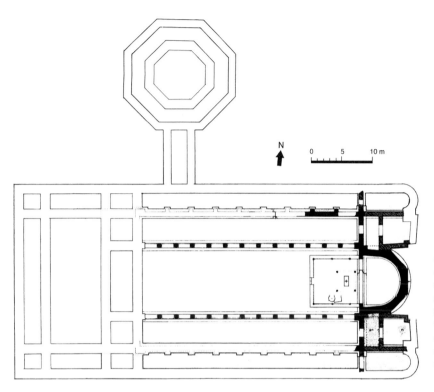

69. Ground plan of the basilica and octagonal structure found at the site of Ca'Bianca, with excavated areas in black and gray (after Cortesi, 1965)

protested about him to Pope Felix IV, who issued a document of reconcil-iation that is quoted in full by Agnellus.[306] Felix issues the following rather severe rebuke in the introduction: "From envy, the priests of the church of Ravenna have done things which are known to have saddened the souls of all catholics: altercations, seditions, depravities, which strive to disrupt all ecclesiastical discipline."[307] The document goes on to proscribe simony, political intrigue, and clerics' appearances at public entertainments and to set out arrangements for episcopal finances to prevent corruption. The ori-gin of this dispute is not known; it seems an odd time for a quarrel among Ravenna's Orthodox clergy and one wonders which of the offenses listed in the document was the main stimulus.[308] The document is signed serially by the members of each faction; the leader of the opposition to Ecclesius was a priest named Victor, who may be the same man who became bishop in 538. Could they have been on opposite sides politically, one in favor of Ostrogothic rule and the other supporting the Byzantines and Pope John?

After 526, the Orthodox Church was emboldened to embark upon an extremely ambitious program of church construction in both Ravenna and Classe. We will consider the actual buildings in the following chapter, but here it is important to note that the construction activity began in the

Ostrogothic period. Agnellus says that after Ecclesius returned from the east (thus presumably between 526 and 532), he began construction of the church of Santa Maria Maggiore and then of San Vitale, both sponsored by the banker (*argentarius*) Julian.[309] Ecclesius's successor Ursicinus (533–6), again with the help of Julian the banker, began construction of the church of Sant'Apollinare in Classe.[310] Finally, Agnellus says that the church of San Michele *in Africisco* was built by Julian and his son-in-law Bacauda; although we do not know when it was begun, it was dedicated in 545.[311] This construction activity has been interpreted as evidence of a Machiavellian conspiracy by Justinian, abetted by his secret agent Julian, to prepare the way for the eventual reconquest of Italy by the empire.[312] This interpretation, however, is not supported by any evidence,[313] and it is better to see Julian *argentarius* simply as an extremely wealthy private individual whose piety and political sympathies matched those of the Orthodox bishops of Ravenna. Most of these constructions were begun during the reign of Amalasuintha, and it is possible that her encouragement of the pretensions of the Orthodox Church was one of the things that alienated the opposing faction of Ostrogoths. Victor (538–45), who was bishop at the height of the Gothic War and the reconquest of Ravenna by the Byzantines, is not mentioned by Procopius, and thus probably maintained a low profile during the war. After the Byzantine army retook the city in 540, however, he successfully cultivated the eastern emperors, as did his successors, who were now ready to claim an important place in the city's new governing hierarchy.

CHAPTER SIX

RAVENNA'S EARLY BYZANTINE PERIOD, AD 540–600

The mid–sixth century was a bad time for much of Italy. After the death of Theoderic, Justinian's army fought a long and debilitating war against the Ostrogoths, which was interrupted by the plague and followed by the invasion of the Lombards, who conquered much of the peninsula from the Byzantines. Despite the debilitating effects of these events on cities such as Rome, Ravenna seems to have been spared and became the capital of the Byzantine territory, remaining the seat of the Byzantine exarchs and their administration until the early eighth century. A city council, or *curia*, composed of members of families who were socially distinct from the members of the court, existed at least until the early seventh century. The aqueduct was repaired in the early seventh century. New public baths were built by the bishop in the sixth century and continued to be used until the ninth century. Justinian gave the bishop of Ravenna the title of archbishop and from this time a series of monumental additions were made to the episcopal palace. Ravenna's prosperity seems to have been minimally affected by the demographic crisis of the mid–sixth century. Contact with Constantinople and the East was made stable again, and large amounts of imported materials continued to be brought to Ravenna. There was a building boom that resulted in some of the most famous surviving monuments, including San Vitale and Sant'Apollinare in Classe: architectural styles, building materials, and imagery ostentatiously underscored the close relations with Constantinople.

In other words, in the later sixth century, when the other cities of Italy were reeling from the effects of plague, war, and other natural disasters, the city of Ravenna continued to develop in the same directions it had taken since the early fifth century. Ravenna's "decline" was to be delayed until the seventh century or later; and even when economic decline set in, the presence of the exarchs and the connection with Constantinople ensured

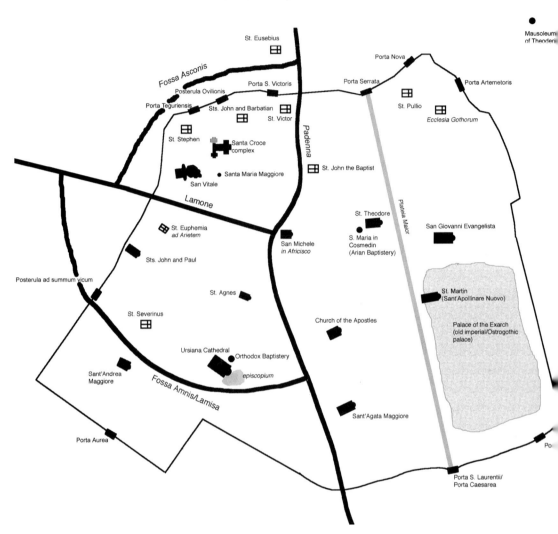

Ravenna, c. AD 600

70. Map of
Ravenna, ca.
AD 600

what we might call a certain late antique mindset that carried over into the
next two centuries.

When we leave the era of Cassiodorus and Procopius, we enter a period
that is much more poorly documented. Historical texts written in Italy
between 540 and the mid–seventh century do not survive; even the Roman
Liber pontificalis was set aside after its first redaction and only taken up again
in the 640s. Papal letters and the writings of Pope Gregory I form the
largest part of our contemporary textual information for this period, and,
as we will see, the popes did not have very high opinion of Ravenna. For

the period 540–600 there are only a handful of surviving documents, some of which we have already discussed in the previous chapter.

Our knowledge of this period thus comes largely from later histories. Paul the Deacon, a monk of Lombard descent who became associated with the court of Charlemagne, wrote in the 760s a chronicle known as the *Historia Romana*, and then in the later 780s and '90s a history of the Lombards up to the year 744, the *Historia Langobardorum*. For the sixth century Paul relied on the Roman *Liber pontificalis*, on a short seventh-century work known as the *Origo gentis Langobardorum*, and on a lost history by the early seventh-century historian Secundus of Trent. Since the Lombards did not control Ravenna until the 750s, Paul's works do not contain a lot of information directly pertinent to the city, although they are extremely important for Italian history in this period. The *LPR* therefore stands out as our major source for the period. Agnellus's interest in episcopal history and church construction caused him to report a large number of inscriptions from this period, and they, together with the surviving monuments, have shaped our concept of the period and what was accomplished in it.

The Environment and Italian Urbanism

The sixth century is often viewed as an era in which climatic, epidemiological, and aquatic events disrupted previously established economic patterns, and even led to the end of the late antique world.[1] There is evidence from Cassiodorus, Procopius, and other authors from as far away as China of a climatic event in 536 or 537: sources report dim skies and darkening of the sun that lasted more than a year. Scientists speculate that it may have been caused by a massive volcanic eruption or a comet; in any case, it was said to have affected crops.[2] This event seems to have been viewed at the time as a temporary misfortune, but evidence from tree rings shows that the earth's climate became significantly cooler for the next ten years, possibly a result of this event.[3] Gregory the Great records severe flooding in Rome and Verona in 589; this is presumed to have been caused by excessive rain.[4] Taken together, many scholars propose that the sixth century marked the beginning of a cooler and wetter period, known as the Vandal Minimum, that lasted until around about 850.[5] At the same time, the urban and rural populations of Italy were devastated by the bubonic plague which hit Italy beginning in 543 and returned in successive waves until the 740s. Mortality rates are almost impossible to deduce, but some scholars think that it must have been similar to the Black Death, killing 30 percent or more of the population, at least in urban areas. Outbreaks of the disease are documented in Ravenna for the 560s, 591–2, and 600–2.[6]

In Italy, cities were devastated both by these natural events and by debilitating wars, first between the Ostrogoths and the Byzantines, and then the Byzantines and the Lombards. Milan was sacked and destroyed in 539. Rome changed hands four times in the course of the Gothic War, which, combined with the plague, led to dramatic depopulation, the disappearance of the Senate, and a complete reorganization of the city's social order.[7] In other places the changes may have been less dramatic, although certainly many cities experienced a continuation of a decline that had been marked since the third or fourth century. Authors from Procopius to Gregory the Great describe landscapes denuded of men; whether these are rhetorical exaggerations or indicate a demographic crisis in the countryside is not yet resolved.[8]

Some of these disasters must have had an impact on Ravenna, yet we will see in this chapter that trade and building activity continued apace, and indeed reached their height, until after the end of the sixth century. A. Guillou has suggested that in Ravenna the demographic crisis of the sixth century was ameliorated to some extent by the flight of people to the city from the territory taken over by the Lombards.[9] Conversely, there may simply have been continual immigration from the countryside to meet the city's needs. The changes in water levels must have had some effect in a marine city such as Ravenna, and we know that, perhaps because of the wetter climate, in the sixth century the courses of the Po river's branches shifted, initially toward Ravenna.[10] More water flowing from inland to the coast would have meant massive amounts of silt deposited in the marshes and harbors around Ravenna, with the result that the coastline moved farther to the east and the immediate surroundings of the city became ever more landlocked. Scholars still debate whether these changes were attributable to climate change or human intervention.[11] As we will see, long-term changes would become significant for Ravenna in the seventh and eighth centuries. However, no changes to Ravenna's internal waterways can be documented in the sixth century. The aqueduct, which had been restored by Theoderic, received further restoration by the exarch Smaragdus around 600, as witnessed by a surviving inscription.[12] We know that the aqueduct was used, since Agnellus tells us that Bishop Victor (538–45) restored a bath complex near the cathedral. Thus, in spite of a changing landscape, Ravenna's leaders and population continued to function much as they had for the previous century and a half.

The Byzantine Reconquest and the Lombards

The war for the reconquest of Italy was far from over when the Byzantine army under Belisarius took Ravenna in 540. Some sections of the Gothic

Ia and Ib. "Mausoleum of Galla Placidia,": interior view looking toward the south (above), Christ as the Good Shepherd, north lunette mosaic (below) (photo S. Mauskopf)

IIa. Orthodox Baptistery, stucco decoration at the window zone (photo C. Copenhaver)

IIb. Orthodox Baptistery, mosaics of the dome (photo S. J. McDonough)

IIIa. Sant'Apollinare Nuovo, mosaic of the north wall, the Virgin and Child flanked by angels, and the three Magi (photo C. Copenhaver)

IIIb. Sant'Apollinare Nuovo, mosaic of the south wall, detail of St. Martin leading the procession of male saints

IVa. Sant'Apollinare Nuovo, mosaic of the south wall, Ravenna and its "palatium"

IVb. Arian Baptistery, mosaics of the dome (photo S. J. McDonough)

V. *Capella arcivescovile*, view of the chapel's vaults (photo Institut für Kunstgeschichte der Johannes Gutenberg Universität Mainz, Bilddatenbank)

VIa. San Vitale, the presbitery and apse (photo S. J. McDonough)

VIb. San Vitale, mosaic of the south presbitery wall, Melchisedek and Abel (photo S. J. McDonough)

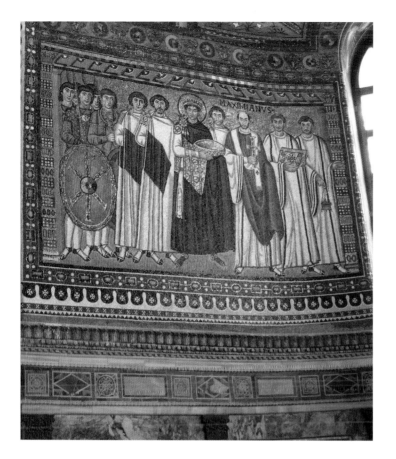

VIIa. San Vitale, mosaic of the north apse wall, Justinian and his court (photo S. J. McDonough)

VIIb. San Vitale, mosaic of the south apse wall, Theodora and her court (photo S. J. McDonough)

VIIIa. Sant'Apollinare in Classe, view of the interior (photo S. J. McDonough)

VIIIb. Sant'Apollinare in Classe, mosaics of the apse vault

army held out at Pavia and Verona. There were no more members of the Amal family, but various generals were raised to the kingship, the last being Totila, a relative of Theudis, king of the Visigoths. Under Totila's leadership the war continued from 541 until 552 and the Ostrogoths once more enjoyed some success, taking Rome back in 546 and in 550. Justinian's army was plagued by instability at the top ranks, especially the struggle for power between various generals, including Belisarius. In 552 the seventy-four-year-old eunuch Narses was sent to take command. Totila was finally killed in battle, and although other leaders continued the struggle for two more years, the Byzantines prevailed and the Ostrogoths disappeared from Italian history.[13]

However, the military problems were not over; indeed, the Gothic War initiated a period of conflict between the Byzantines and external forces that would last for centuries. Byzantine control over plague-ravaged Italy was tenuous to begin with and an ecclesiastical conflict known as the Three Chapters Controversy hindered unification, as we will see. In this unstable situation, peoples over the borders saw Italy as an attainable prize. The Franks had long been involved in the Gothic War, sometimes on one side and sometimes on the other. In 553 and 554 an expedition of Franks and Alamanni devastated northern Italy and were repulsed by Narses only with difficulty. A serious revolt broke out among the Herul imperial garrisons in the Alps in 566.[14]

There was therefore no real unity in Italy when yet another group of barbarians, the Lombards, appeared at the Alpine passes in 568.[15] The Lombards (*Langobardi*, "long-beards") had coalesced as a group in the Balkans in the late fifth century and moved into Pannonia after the death of Theoderic, where they were settled as *foederati* by Justinian. Their ambitious King Alboin married Chlodosinda, daughter of the Frankish king Lothar I. Alboin annihilated another group, the Gepids, in 567 and after Chlodosinda's death he married the Gepid princess Rosamunda, a move that was, as Paul the Deacon says, "to his own injury, as afterward appeared."[16] The group that Alboin led into Italy was made up of people from a variety of "ethnic" backgrounds, and may have numbered anywhere from 80,000 warriors to 400,000 total people, representing 5 to 8 percent of the population of the areas in which they settled.[17] In three years Alboin's Lombard armies had captured most of Italy north of the Po river as well as the central section of Italy, largely without opposition. Justinian had died in 565, and Paul the Deacon says that the Italians had been weakened by a bout of the plague in 566. By 575 the Byzantines were left only with the following: Naples and its hinterland, Calabria; Sicily; the coast north of Genoa; Ravenna and its surrounding territories (later known as the Pentapolis after the five cities of Rimini, Pesaro, Fano, Senigallia, and Ancona); Rome; and a strip of land between Rome and Ravenna along the *via Flaminia*.

This political configuration would remain roughly the same for the next 200 years.

That any territory at all was left to the Byzantines was the result of the instability of the Lombard kingdom. In 572 Alboin was murdered by one of his followers, who was apparently in league with Alboin's Gepid wife Rosamunda. The couple are said to have fled to Ravenna, where they gave the Lombard treasure to the exarch Longinus and were subsequently murdered/executed.[18] Alboin's successor Cleph was also murdered in 574, and for the next ten years the Lombards did not have a king. Individual leaders who held the title *dux*, and who had been placed in key cities by Alboin, consolidated their own authority and fought among themselves. Some of the dukes as well as individual Lombards allied themselves with the Byzantines, further complicating the picture. The Byzantines dug in and attempted to fight back. Agnellus cryptically reports that the Prefect Longinus about 570 built a "fence in the form of a wall" to protect Caesarea, the region between Ravenna and Classe. This may have been a stake and ditch palisade, a type of fortification known elsewhere in Italy at the time, and is assumed to have been made in response to Lombard aggression.[19] A Bzyantine army under the command of Justin II's son-in-law Baduarius was sent to Italy in 575, but it was defeated. This emboldened the Lombards to attack the Byzantine capital; Faroald, Duke of Spoleto, plundered Classe around 579, and the port city was only recovered by Drocdulf, a Sueve who fought for the Byzantines.[20]

In 584, assailed by both the Franks and the Byzantines, the Lombard dukes came together and chose Cleph's son Authari (r. 584–90) as their king. Authari achieved success against a combined Frankish-Byzantine attack in 590, and negotiated a deal by which he paid tribute to the Franks, but he died the same year. In 589 he had married Theodelinda, daughter of the Duke of Bavaria, who was one of the remarkable women of her day: A correspondent of Pope Gregory I, upon her husband's death she was granted the right to choose the next king, and she ruled alongside her second husband Agilulf until his death in 616, after which she ruled with her son Adaloald until his death in 626. Agilulf himself, freed of the Frankish threat, went on the offensive against the Byzantines, threatening Rome from 593 to 594, and counterthreatened by the prefect Romanus about 595, with short-term truces negotiated several times before his death.[21] The situation thus remained precarious at the turn of the seventh century.

The Establishment of a Byzantine Administration

Beginning with Narses, Ravenna was established by the Byzantines as the seat of their authority and the home base of their administration and army.

Their choice was dictated, as earlier, by logistics and ease of transport to Constantinople, by security, by prestige, and by the fact that if there were still any bureaucratic institutions surviving, they would have been found in Ravenna. Rome remained an important center, and, as previously, the rulers of Italy preferred to keep some distance between themselves and Rome's rulers, now increasingly the popes in place of the defunct Senate. Ravenna, as the home of the army and the civil administration, remained important both practically and ideologically, and retained a stronger economy longer than most other contemporary urban centers.

The long war with the Byzantines had destroyed the Ostrogothic kingdom – not just the warriors, but the entire governmental system created by Theoderic. The tax system broke down under the impact of the wars and of the demographic crises. Order had to be restored, and in 554 Justinian issued an imperial edict known as the Pragmatic Sanction, which details how this was to be achieved.[22] It is notable that Justinian claims to have issued the decree at the request of Pope Vigilius and that it is addressed to the military commander Narses and the Praetorian Prefect Antiochus.

The Pragmatic Sanction is a curious document, attempting to portray the new social and political order as the reimposition of the best elements of the prewar era. Laws promulgated by Amalasuintha, Athalaric, and Theodahad were to be respected, but not those of Totila; property that had changed hands during the war was to be restored to its original owners. Payments to *grammatici*, orators, doctors, and lawyers were to be continued so that knowledge and education would continue to flourish![23] Senators were recognized as important political figures, but the edict includes a number of notable political changes: The right to elect provincial governors (*iudices*) was now granted to bishops as well as local magnates, and the same two groups were made responsible for military requisitions, a recognition that the authority of bishops was now an important element in local politics.

Conditions changed so rapidly in the decades after 540, especially after the Lombard conquest, that the new conditions do not seem to have been well received by Justinian's Italian subjects or even to have applied at all.[24] The Roman Senate is last mentioned as a functioning body in 580; personal names with links to senatorial families disappear by the early seventh century. The senators had been appointed by the emperors and then by the Ostrogothic kings; the removal of central authority out of Italy after the Gothic War meant that senators too had to remove to Constantinople in order to maintain access to court appointments and some are known to have done so.[25] Their place was taken by a new hierarchy of officials whose authority derived from their military role, as has been described by T. Brown.[26]

Byzantine rule in Italy was marked by almost continuous military activity. When the Byzantine army first appeared in Italy, its commanders assumed

complete authority over the territory that was regained from the Ostrogoths. Indeed, in a war situation, what else could have happened? Narses,
in particular, set about the task of restoring order in Italy, until he was
relieved in 566; in later accounts he was accused of enriching himself
with the property of Italians.[27] By then, the army had been fighting for
thirty years, and the authority of military commanders in civil affairs had
become entrenched. When in 565 a civilian Praetorian Prefect, Longinus,
was appointed to have an equivalent measure of authority, he was almost
immediately required to assume a significant military role in the aftermath
of the Lombard invasion.[28] After that, the continuous Lombard military
threat meant that army officers rose to the top of the hierarchy in Byzantine Italy.

By the year 600, the leader of Byzantine administration was a figure
called the exarch. This office seems to have developed sometime after the
Pragmatic Sanction; the term *exarchus* first appears in Italy in 584, but not
as an official title, and subsequently it often appears in conjunction with
patricius.[29] Other people with varying degrees of authority, most notably
the civilian prefects, also appear in the years before 600.[30] It seems clear,
however, that from the time the title *exarchus* first appeared, exarchs exercised both military and civil authority.[31] The exarchs were always sent from
Constantinople, but we do not know the criteria by which such officials
were chosen, or how long they might have expected their official tenure
to last. Whenever one died or was murdered, a new one was sent out, and
occasionally there are references to changes upon the accession of a new
emperor. Several exercised authority twice, others for more than ten years
at a stretch (see the list in Table 4).

Below the exarch, the government that was centered on Ravenna was
composed of both local and foreign officials who performed a variety of
functions. Individuals with military titles such as *magister militum*, *dux*, and
tribunus also exercised civil functions in the late sixth century.[32] Before 600,
at least, these authority figures were sent to Ravenna from Constantinople and came with contingents of troops, sometimes recruited from among
the barbarian populations of the Balkans and sometimes brought directly
from the east.[33] Some of these officials and soldiers bought land and settled
down in Italy, a trend that would accelerate in the following decades.[34] On
the other hand, most of the clerks, tax collectors, and other bureaucrats
seem to have been drawn from the local population. And in addition to
the representatives of imperial government, Ravenna also retained its city
council, or *curia*, as late as 625, which functioned as the body that certified
and preserved legal documents and collected taxes.[35]

Thus, thanks to its status as a political center, Ravenna remained a cosmopolitan city with an ethnically diverse population whose statuses and

roles were in flux in this period. Analyses of papyrus documents show that people with Gothic-looking names continued to exist in Ravenna up to the end of the sixth century, alongside individuals with Greek or eastern names. Scholars are divided over the question of how many Greek-speakers there were in Ravenna at any time; we know that a notable medical school, with an emphasis on Greek medical texts, existed at Ravenna in this period,[36] and some documents are signed in Greek or in Latin using Greek characters, but Latin remained the common and official language.[37] Bankers, silk merchants, doctors, and notaries are all attested in the documents and bear witness to a still-thriving economy.

Indeed, the new administration made every attempt to stress that affairs were continuing as usual in the capital city of Italy. Immediately after 540, Ravenna's mint began producing gold coins on the imperial model and continued right through the Byzantine period to produce coins in gold, silver, and bronze.[38] The exarchs moved into Theoderic's palace,[39] which, as early as 572, was referred to as the *sacrum palatium*, a deliberate imitation of the designation of the imperial palace in Constantinople.[40] Other topographical designations in and around the palace that also evoke Constantinople, if they had not come into use already, were probably imported at this time.[41] Although politically motivated modifications were made to the iconography in the church of Sant'Apollinare Nuovo, images and statues of Theoderic in and around the palace remained in situ until the ninth century, and the palace itself was not much modified despite the change to the regime it housed.[42]

Although Ravenna in 567 was still the *caput Italiae*, after 570 the city was no longer the capital of an empire or a kingdom, but only of a rapidly shrinking province. The exarch may have had vice-regal powers, but he was only a representative, and a relatively minor one, of a ruler who lived elsewhere. It is interesting that, as far as we can tell from the surviving images, no "exarchal" iconography developed in this period or later. Instead, it was the bishops who developed an identity – iconographically, historiographically, and politically – as the heirs to the earlier secular rulers of Ravenna.

The Archbishops of Ravenna

After the Byzantine reconquest of Italy, the bishops of Ravenna increased even more in power and prestige; indeed, the see was arguably the main beneficiary of the ecclesiastical and political turmoil of the mid–sixth century. Victor (538–45), who was bishop at the height of the Gothic War and the reconquest of Ravenna by the Byzantines, cultivated good relationships with the Eastern emperors, and was rewarded by a grant of tax remissions, which he used to erect a large silver canopy (*ciborium*) over the altar of the Ursiana cathedral. The dedicatory poem states that this was done in fulfillment of a vow, and mentions that Victor "increased faith among the people with love"; is this a reference to the overthrow of Ostrogothic/Arian authority in the city?[43]

Clearly the archbishopric of Ravenna was viewed as an important post, since both the emperors and the popes appointed non-Ravennate individuals to hold it. Maximian (546–57), a deacon from the city of Pola in Istria, was elevated to the see by Justinian after a vacancy of a year and a half.[44] Maximian's successor Agnellus (557–70),[45] a former soldier who had entered the Ravennate church before the Byzantine reconquest, also worked closely with Justinian's government, as did Peter III (570–8), who, like Agnellus, seems to have been a local appointment. Peter's two successors, John II (578–95) and Marinian (595–606), however, were from Rome, the former a friend of Pope Gregory I the Great and the latter actually appointed by the pope after a controversy in which he rejected the candidates favored by the exarch.[46] Gregory himself played an active role in the politics of Italy, dealing with exarchs, emperors, and Lombard rulers; he recognized and encouraged the influence of the archbishops of Ravenna on exarchal administration, and accepted his colleagues as subordinate partners in both political and ecclesiastical affairs.[47] Since the mid–fifth century, Ravenna's bishops had exercised jurisdiction over several other sees in northern Italy; in 592 Gregory I assigned a number of sees now in Lombard territory to Ravenna's care.[48]

The elevation of Ravenna's see, and the new authority exercised by its leaders, was marked by new titles and symbols that were assiduously exploited by the holders of the see. Sometime before 553 Justinian gave Maximian the title *archiepiscopus* (archbishop). This elevation was part of a general policy of raising church leaders in rank to match the secular status of their cities; through this act, Justinian distinguished Ravenna as a major provincial capital.[49] It is often stated that along with the title, Justinian granted Ravenna's archbishops the right to wear the *pallium*, or stole, a symbol of metropolitan authority. This assumption is based on Agnellus's statement that the *pallium* was given to Maximian upon his consecration;[50] however, Agnellus had earlier directly linked the wearing of the *pallium* to the metropolitan status that was achieved in the fifth century, and throughout his text the *pallium* is a metaphor for the appointment or confirmation of a bishop by an outside authority, either the pope or by the emperor.[51] In the Justinianic mosaics in Ravenna, as we will see, bishops are all prominently depicted wearing the *pallium*, but some of these mosaics were made before the time of Maximian. Thus, use of the *pallium* must not have been linked to the new title, but simply to the new ambitions of the post-Theoderican bishops.[52] After Maximian's accession the bishops took to displaying this symbol of authority more frequently, and eventually it became a political issue between them and the popes.[53] Gregory I reprimanded Archbishop John II for wearing his *pallium* more often than custom required and accused his friend of being corrupted by secular influence; Gregory wrote similarly to Marinian.[54] The archbishops cannot simply have been using the *pallium* as a symbol of authority within Ravenna because then there would be no reason for papal opposition. They were expressing wider aspirations, and indeed Gregory also reprimanded the bishop of Milan for mentioning John of Ravenna's name during the mass, as would be done for a patriarch.[55]

The reasons for Ravenna's ecclesiastical importance went beyond the status of the city as a provincial capital and are directly related to the theological struggle known as the Three Chapters Controversy.[56] Although monophysitism had been condemned at the Council of Chalcedon in 451, the miaphysites who rejected the Chalcedonian formula, found especially in Egypt and Syria, were causing political problems for Justinian. In 543 or 544, Justinian's theological advisers came up with a plan to reconcile the opposing factions. Justinian issued an imperial edict that condemned as heretical works by Theodore of Mopsuestia, Theodore of Cyrrhus, and Ibas of Edessa: known as the Three Chapters, these texts had previously been accepted as Orthodox. Supporters of Justinian's edict included the patriarchs of Constantinople, Alexandria, Antioch, and Jerusalem. However, the western bishops refused to accept the condemnation. The pope, who was the fifth patriarch, was thus a key player, and in 544 he also was a controversial figure.

In 536, Pope Agapitus had died in Constantinople while on an embassy to Justinian from Theodahad. Theodahad forcibly had one Silverius, son of Pope Hormisdas, ordained in Rome, but Theodahad was killed a few months later, after which Belisarius took Rome. Silverius's politics and theology were declared suspect; the *Liber pontificalis* claims that the empress Theodora's monophysite/miaphysite leanings led her to accuse Silverius of heresy, while Belisarius's wife Antonina, Theodora's friend, accused him of being allied with the Goths. The papal ambassador in Constantinople at the time was Vigilius the archdeacon. He was sent back to Rome with instructions that Belisarius was to depose Silverius and make Vigilius pope, and this was done in 537.[57] It was Vigilius who was pope when the Three Chapters Controversy broke out, but despite being Justinian's appointee, Vigilius vacillated on this crucial question. He was forcibly brought to Constantinople in 546 and persuaded to agree to the condemnation in 553, dying upon his return journey in 555. In the meantime, the metropolitan bishops of Milan and Aquileia had broken with the pope and emperor over the Three Chapters and were in active schism. In this set of circumstances the bishop of Ravenna, the only metropolitan of northern Italy not in schism, was an important agent of imperial church policy in Italy, which probably prompted Justinian to elevate his supporter Maximian to the vacant see in 546.[58]

In the years after 554, the popes and the archbishops of Ravenna continued to be staunch supporters of Justinian's condemnation of the Three Chapters. As we have seen, it was under Archbishop Agnellus that the Arian churches and their property were officially transferred to the Orthodox Church of Ravenna, perhaps as a reward for loyalty, since the document praises "the holy mother church of Ravenna, the true mother, truly orthodox, for many other churches crossed over to false doctrine because of the fear and terror of princes, but this one held the true and unique holy catholic faith, it never changed, it endured the fluctuations of the times, though tossed by the storm it remained unmovable."[59] Ravenna's archbishops ordained clergy and bishops for the schismatic sees and they attempted to coerce the rebel bishops; in this they were aided by Narses and his successors. The controversy also became political, especially after Milan and Aquileia, as well as most of the other schismatic cities in Istria, were conquered by the Lombards, removing them from Byzantine political pressure. Gradually the schismatic bishops were reconciled with Rome and the mainstream: Milan in 581, but Aquileia, the last holdout, only in 698, and there were always elements within the churches of Byzantine Italy that opposed the policy.[60]

By 600, therefore, the archbishops of Ravenna had made a place for themselves near the top of the episcopal hierarchy of Italy. Maximian, in particular, shaped, or even created, an image of Ravenna's episcopal see that has dominated later discourse, particularly as reported by the historian Agnellus, who credits Maximian with many lasting contributions. Maximian had two Bibles carefully emended and written according to Jerome's translation, one of the earliest indications of the use of the Vulgate translation in Italy. He also produced a missal that Agnellus knew, and it is possible that Agnellus attributes to him the spread of the Justinianic legal code into Italy.[61] More significant in our context, Maximian appears to have been the first to produce a history of the episcopal see of Ravenna. Agnellus tells us that he wrote a chronicle, which seems to have been a typical secular world chronicle.[62] But we also learn that Maximian was responsible for several commemorative pieces on which sequences of Ravenna's bishops were depicted: an altar cloth with pictures of all his predecessors; an inscription on the *Tricollis* listing all bishops who had helped on the building; the images of some early bishops in Sant'Apollinare in Classe; and depictions of early bishops on the facade of the church of St. Probus. Episcopal lists were first compiled for many Italian cities in the early sixth century (this is when the Roman *Liber pontificalis* was begun), and it is probable that Maximian's was the earliest such list for Ravenna.[63]

In addition to establishing a historical basis for the see's importance, Maximian also worked hard visually to define the prominence of Ravenna's archbishop. He completed, decorated, and/or dedicated the *Domus Tricollis* in the *episcopium* and the churches of San Vitale, Sant'Apollinare in Classe, San Michele *in Africisco*, St. Andrew, St. Probus, and St. Euphemia; he founded in Ravenna a church dedicated to St. Stephen.[64] In many of these buildings, as we will see, Maximian oversaw decoration that prominently featured bishops. The altar cloth and images of bishops mentioned above are examples of this; and it is no accident that the most famous mosaic in Ravenna, in San Vitale, depicts Maximian next to Justinian. In many of the buildings that enjoyed Maximian's patronage, his monograph is prominently displayed either in mosaic or carved into marble. Prior to this period, Ravenna had not had any major churches dedicated to local saints or martyrs, so it is particularly significant that early Christian martyrs and episcopal saints were claimed for Ravenna at the same time that the archbishops were claiming new status and privileges for themselves.

Veneration of Ravenna's early bishops, sponsored by Maximian, was continued by his successors. Archbishop Agnellus rebuilt the apse of Sant'Agata, and decorated it with a portrait of John I, who was buried there.[65] Peter III founded a church in Classe in honor of St. Severus, which was completed by John II.[66] Severus is the earliest attested bishop of Ravenna, documented as present at the Council of Sardica of 343. Nothing else is known about him, and even Agnellus tells us that nothing was known about him in the ninth century; nevertheless, by the mid–sixth century he was being venerated as a saint. His church was located in Classe, near Sant'Apollinare and St. Probus; together, as we will see, they formed a group of churches in honor of Ravenna's early bishops.

The Cathedral and the Episcopal Throne

The Ursiana cathedral was given a new gloss in the wake of the Byzantine reconquest.[67] Agnellus the historian says that Bishop Victor provided it with an altar cloth of gold and silk and with a silver *ciborium* (canopy) over the altar (destroyed by invading French troops in 1512), paid for by the taxes of Italy that were granted to Victor by Justinian for one year.[68] This set of furnishings may also have included a new set of intricately carved *transennae*, some of which were later reused in the pavement of the current cathedral and are now found in the Museo Arcivescovile.[69] Made of Proconnesian marble, they were probably imported directly from Constantinople. Archbishop Agnellus gave the cathedral a new ambo (Fig. 71),

71. Ambo of
Agnellus, now in
the cathedral

of a type that was common in the eastern Mediterranean and had already
been brought to Ravenna's Arian churches under Theoderic.[70] Agnellus's
ambo, made of Proconnesian marble, was also probably imported from
Constantinople. Its central section survives, with the dedicatory inscription
"*Servus Xr(ist)i Agnellus epis(copus) hunc pyrgum fecit*";[71] its sides contain a
grid of squares, in each of which a bird or animal is carved in flat relief.
Archbishop Agnellus also made a large (1.22 m wide) cross of wood coated
with embossed silver for the Ursiana cathedral, which still survives (with
later additions and restorations) in the Museo Arcivescovile; its arms are
decorated on each side with 20 medallions with images of saints, surrounding larger roundels of Christ and the Virgin at the center.[72]

In terms of episcopal imagery, the most significant object to have survived from Byzantine Ravenna is the throne of the archbishops of Ravenna,
which bears Maximian's monogram (Fig. 72).[73] The throne's form is typical of late antique chairs, with a curved back and straight arms.[74] Panels
of ivory, each 9–12 centimeters wide (side panels 17–19 centimeters wide),
were attached to a wooden frame.[75] Thirty-nine panels were carved with

72. Throne of Maximian, front view, ivory on a wooden frame, 540s–50s (courtesy Opera di Religione della Diocesi di Ravenna)

scenes or figures from the Old and New Testaments (twelve are now missing, although the subjects of some of them are known from earlier drawings); the figurated panels are surrounded on all sides of the throne by borders of vine scrolls inhabited by peacocks, birds, dogs, deer, cows, and other animals.[76] As a whole, it is one of the most remarkable ivory objects to have survived from late antiquity.

On the front of the throne below the seat we see five figures standing beneath niches of conch shell: John the Baptist in the center, flanked by the four evangelists, who are not individually identified but who are presented as men in tunics and mantles, holding codices. The other figurated panels depict the following:

Location	Images	Survives?
Inner seat back, upper row		
left	? [Shepherds and animals?]	
center-left	Nativity	yes
center-right	Virgin and Child, angel, Joseph, star	yes
right	[Three Magi]	
Inner seat back, lower row		
left	Dream of Joseph, Flight to Egypt	yes
center-left	[Visitation]	
center-right	Test of the bitter waters	yes
right	Annunciation (Fig. 73)	yes
Left side of throne		
top	Joseph: Benjamin before Joseph	yes
upper-middle	Joseph: Joseph gives brothers grain	yes
middle	Joseph: Joseph interprets pharaoh's dreams	yes
lower-middle	Joseph: Joseph greets Jacob	yes
bottom	Joseph: Pharaoh's dream	yes
Right side of throne		
top	Joseph: grief of Jacob (Fig. 74)	yes
upper-middle	Joseph: Joseph put in well	yes
middle	Joseph: Joseph sold to Ishmaelites	yes
lower-middle	Joseph: Joseph sold to Potiphar	yes
bottom	Joseph: Potiphar's wife	yes
Back: top row		
left	? [Flight into Egypt? Escape of Elizabeth and Baptist? Massacre of Innocents?]	
center-left	Baptism of Christ	yes
center-right	Entry into Jerusalem	yes
right	?	
Back: 2nd row		
left	Distribution of loaves and fishes	yes
center-left	Christ divides loaves and fishes	yes
center-right	[Miracle of Cana, part]	
right	Miracle of Cana	yes
Back: 3rd row		
left	?	
center-left	?	
center-right	Christ heals blind and lame	yes
right	Christ and the Samaritan woman	yes
Back: bottom row		
left	?	
center-left	?	
center-right	?	
right	?	

73. Throne of
Maximian, panel
depicting the
Annunciation
(courtesy Opera
di Religione
della Diocesi di
Ravenna)

74. Throne of
Maximian, detail
from side, Jacob
mourning Joseph
(courtesy Opera
di Religione
della Diocesi di
Ravenna)

The style of carving on the throne has many similarities with ivories from Constantinople and the eastern Mediterranean, and scholars therefore usually assume either that it was made in the capital (perhaps ordered by Justinian), or in Egypt, or that it was made in a Ravennate atelier by workmen from the east.[77] Most of the imagery is very conventional for the sixth century; we have already discussed examples of cycles of the life of Christ in the context of the mosaics of Sant'Apollinare Nuovo. What is striking is the prominence of the story of Joseph from the Old Testament. C. Rizzardi notes that the juxtaposition of Old and New Testament imagery is a hallmark of the post-Theoderican art of Ravenna, as we will see also in San Vitale; she argues that the difference in artistic styles between the Old and New Testament scenes are deliberate, to draw attention to their difference.[78]

But why did the story of Joseph feature so prominently on a bishop's throne? Since the Joseph story was very popular in late antique Egypt and since Maximian is known to have visited Alexandria, many scholars have proposed an Egyptian workshop or workmen for the throne.[79] But as M. Schapiro has demonstrated, there was more to the iconography than that. In early Christian exegesis, Joseph was seen as a type of Christ, and also as a type of John the Baptist, and in fact many of the Joseph scenes on the throne are typologically linked to the image of the Baptist and the New Testament scenes on the throne.[80] Joseph was also seen as a model of good stewardship: In particular, Ambrose of Milan, in his writings on the roles of priest and bishop, praises Joseph for his chastity, charity, and generosity, and holds him up as an ideal counselor to a secular ruler.[81] Joseph is thus a model of a good bishop who can feed and protect his people, serve as an intermediary between God and men, and be an adviser to the secular ruler. Indeed, in many of the images on the throne, Joseph is shown seated on a throne himself, emphasizing the connection.

Finally, Schapiro notes a more personal reason that Joseph may have figured on a throne connected with Maximian. Joseph was a slave who was raised to a position of power by the pharaoh. According to Agnellus, Maximian was not from Ravenna, but from Pola; he rose from humble origins through the favor of the emperor (and through judicious bribes) to become archbishop. Agnellus quotes inscriptions on two altar cloths in which Maximian notes that the Lord "has raised me from the dung."[82] Agnellus's story of Maximian's rise may be embroidered but Maximian obviously cultivated the idea that he was a nobody, elevated by the favor of Justinian, and this can also be seen in the mosaic in San Vitale. Joseph was thus a suitable model for this particular bishop and for the particular political and ecclesiastical situation in sixth-century Ravenna.

Church Building

Between 540 and 600, Ravenna and Classe were lavishly provided with new churches (see Fig. 70), heavily subsidized by the donations of the mysterious banker Julian, but also sponsored by the bishops and archbishops (interestingly, none of the exarchs or prefects are credited, at least by Agnellus, with any architectural patronage in this period). Bishop Ecclesius inaugurated the building boom after his return from Constantinople in 525, and we may suppose that he had been inspired by the buildings, both old and new, that he saw there. While Ecclesius and Ursicinus founded major churches, it is likely that much of the construction activity took place only after the Byzantine reconquest of 540. In addition to his *ciborium*, Victor (538–45) managed to complete decoration of the Petriana baptistery, to build a luxurious bath complex near the *episcopium*, and to donate an altar cloth to the Ursiana. Agnellus says that the bath complex was decorated with fine marbles and gold mosaics; excavation at the Banca Popolare site has revealed the remains of these baths, built over a house that was destroyed in the fourth century. It still operated in Agnellus's day, and indeed the excavated remains show that the baths continued in use until the tenth or twelfth century.[83] As we will see, it is also likely that much of the construction work for San Vitale and Sant'Apollinare in Classe took place under Victor's authority.

Building materials poured into the city's ports from Constantinople and the east, along with innovative ideas in both architecture and mosaic artistry.[84] In particular, marble from the island of Proconnesus, located in the Sea of Marmara about seventy-five miles east of Constantinople, was ostentatiously used in this period. Marble from Proconnesus had been used in buildings in Ravenna from as early as the mid–fifth century – the apse of San Giovanni Evangelista, the *basilica apostolorum*, Sant'Apollinare Nuovo, and the *capella arcivescovile* – but the importation of such materials reached its height in the later sixth century. The quarries, which were actively exploited from the first century AD to the end of the sixth century, were under imperial control. Because they were near the sea, it was easy to ship their marble throughout the Mediterranean, and the color, white with bluish gray veins, was highly prized (Fig. 75).[85] The craftsmen who manufactured objects from this marble used the veins to create different effects; on columns, for example, stripes could run vertically or horizontally, while on large slabs used for wall revetment, slices could be laid side by side to produce spectacular bilaterally symmetrical effects. We know from excavated shipwrecks that materials were exported from Proconnesus as complete sets, either completely or partially carved; this implies that someone building a church would have to know the design to be able to order the materials, which might then be custom made or furnished from stock available in the quarry's stockyards. If the designs were delicate, it is possible that rough blocks were shipped, with instructions, drawings, or actual sculptors, so that they could be completed at the construction site.[86] We know that stone-carving workshops and other local manufacturers thrived during this period in Ravenna, whether or not they routinely finished material that was sent in roughed-out form from Proconnesus.[87] In any case, the presence of marble church furnishings from Proconnesus shows that the island's workshops must have been a point of diffusion both for sculptural motifs and for architectural ideas.

The building boom also gave rise to a new local industry, the manufacture of bricks. Already in the Ostrogothic period the supply of Roman materials available for reuse had started to run out. Unlike the earlier buildings in Ravenna, many of the later sixth-century structures, notably San Vitale, Sant'Apollinare in Classe, San Michele *in Africisco*, Sant'Agata, and the building excavated at the Via di Roma identified as the *Moneta Aurea*, were built of new (rather than reused) bricks that were flatter and broader than those usually scavenged from Roman buildings. Modern scholars often refer to these as Julian bricks (named after Julian the banker).[88] N. Lombardini argues that their adoption was deliberate to create aesthetic effects for the exteriors of these buildings that would be markedly different from those of earlier eras, much as new mosaic and sculptural styles did also.[89]

Most of our information about churches in this period comes from Agnellus. Because he was writing a history of the bishops of Ravenna, he emphasized their contributions to the Church and the city, and clearly they were the central figures in the building boom of this era. Sometimes they spent their own personal money on these buildings, but in many cases they directed other people's money toward projects that the Church sponsored. We have already seen that the banker Julian was the primary financial sponsor of these constructions, but there are hints from a few surviving inscriptions of patronage by other secular figures. For example, in 596 an Adeodatus *primus strator praefecturae* (the first groom of the prefecture) paid for an ambo for the church of Sts. John and Paul, which was directly modeled on the one in the Ursiana but probably made by local artisans.[90] Thus, while the bishops used their function as dedicator of churches to actively promote an aggressively episcopal agenda, they did so with the active cooperation of the citizens of Ravenna, who sometimes were pursuing their own aims. The result by the year 600 was a region packed with large, impressive churches celebrating both local and international saints demonstrating a long history of imperial authority combined with episcopal oversight.

75. Sant'-Apollinare in Classe, columns of Proconnesian marble, seen from the north aisle

Church Building in the City of Ravenna

Six major churches and several smaller ones were built in and around Ravenna and Classe between 540 and 600; in addition, some of Ravenna's older churches were modified. Most of the new structures were built in the northwestern sector of the city around the existing church of Santa Croce (Fig. 70), or to the south of the city of Classe. Ecclesius owned property in the former area, which may have been the initial stimulus for the concentration of activity there. Classe, as we have seen, had been a focus of building activity since the construction of the Petriana complex, and its continued activity indicates that it was viewed as an important part of Ravenna's Christian topography.

SANTA MARIA MAGGIORE

Bishop Ecclesius, "on his own legal property built the church of the holy and always inviolate Virgin Mary . . . of wonderful size, the vault of the apse and the façade decorated with gold, and in this vault of the apse the image of the holy Mother of God."[91] The church was located in the northwest corner of the city, just to the south of Santa Croce and to the east of San Vitale, which, as we will see, was also founded by Ecclesius. What is known about the original church comes from sixteenth- and seventeenth-century descriptions of it (in ruined state), and from analysis of the apse, whose structure survives in the present building.[92] An inscription reported by G. Rossi in the sixteenth century reports work on the church at the time of Archbishop Felix, in the early eighth century; another surviving inscription from the time of Peter III might also refer to this church. Rossi tells us that the apse mosaic, by then in a ruinous condition, depicted the Virgin and Child with Ecclesius offering them the church, perhaps similar to the depiction of the bishop in San Vitale's apse.[93] The mosaics were destroyed in 1550, and in 1671 Santa Maria Maggiore was largely rebuilt in the baroque style.

Santa Maria Maggiore is one of the least-studied churches in Ravenna. In the seventeenth century, before its rebuilding, the church was described as a cruciform basilica with a nave and aisles separated by arcades of eight columns. One report describes the triumphal arch as being held up by two columns, presumably flanking the entrance to the apse. The current polygonal apse appears to have been originally a dodecagon, 10 meters in diameter (thus about the same size as the Orthodox Baptistery), connecting to the nave of a church through an 8-meters-wide triumphal arch (Fig. 76). It has therefore been suggested that the church built by Ecclesius was a freestanding dodecagon and that a basilica with a transept was attached later (perhaps in the later sixth century, perhaps in the eighth, certainly by the ninth century), connected by an arch and perhaps also by a presbitery. Twelve columns and Corinthian capitals of Proconnesian marble were reused in the baroque building, but they are smaller than would be expected for a nave colonnade, and thus they may have originally been found in a narthex or gallery.[94] Obviously, further study is required to determine the original form of the building.

If Ecclesius's church of the Virgin had originally been a twelve-sided polygon, it would have followed earlier prototypes such as the Church of the Nativity in Bethlehem,[95] the church of the Virgin in Jerusalem, and the shrine of the Virgin at Blachernae in Constantinople, the latter two examples built in the early to mid–sixth century.[96] Perhaps Ecclesius's trip to

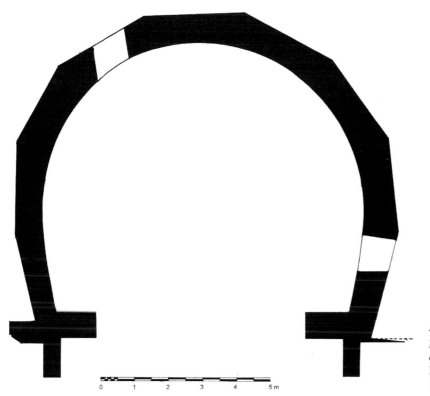

76. Santa Maria Maggiore, plan of the apse (after Deichmann, 1976, pl. 53)

the capital inspired him to build some of the new, domed shrines in Ravenna; certainly we can see this influence in his other foundation, San Vitale.

SAN VITALE

The church of San Vitale is unquestionably a building "like no other in Italy."[97] Built according to a design that reflected the most up-to-date architectural ideas from Constantinople, it has impressed visitors since the time it was founded, both because of its unusual and impressive layout and because of the beauty and splendor of the mosaics that are still preserved in its presbitery and apse. Founded by Bishop Ecclesius during the reign of Amalasuintha, it reflects a multitude of ideologies and concepts in its design and decoration.

The construction of this church established St. Vitalis as Ravenna's chief martyr. The origins of this cult and its connections to Ravenna are obscure, but it is somehow connected to the rivalry between the sees of Milan and Ravenna. St. Ambrose of Milan famously discovered the relics of Sts. Gervase and Protase in Milan in 386, and housed them in a great basilica;[98] Ambrose also found the relics of St. Nazarius in Milan, and in Bologna the relics of St. Agricola and his slave St. Vitalis, which he transferred to churches in Milan and Florence.[99] All were martyrs, but nothing more is told about them in the Ambrosian literature, and no connection of any kind is made with Ravenna.

At some unknown point, probably in early sixth-century Ravenna, a letter attributed to Ambrose was composed that contained a narrative about some of these figures; it is known as the *Passio sanctorum martyrum Gervasii et Protasii*.[100] In the story, Gervase and Protase are the children of Vitalis and Valeria; Vitalis, a *miles consularis* ("soldier of consular rank," and thus different from the slave Vitalis), is martyred in Ravenna after he gives encouragement to a doctor named Ursicinus when the latter is being tortured for his adherence to Christianity. Valeria is also martyred after this, as are Gervase and Protase. According to the text, "Saint Vitalis, the glorious martyr of Christ, next to the city of Ravenna grants benefits (*beneficia*) through prayers and intercessions for all believers of Jesus Christ up to the present day."[101] By making Vitalis the father of Gervase and Protase, the author demonstrates the superiority of Ravenna over Milan.

Archaeological investigations in 1911 and 1925 revealed, 70 centimeters below the original floor of the church, a small rectangular chapel (5.40 × 8.48 meters) with remains of an altar surrounded by mosaic floors, which is thought to be the remains of an earlier structure consecrated to St. Vitalis, dating perhaps to the fifth century.[102] In the late 520s, Bishop Ecclesius decided to turn this chapel into an architectural showplace. Agnellus provides three pieces of information about the construction of San Vitale. He paraphrases the epitaph (*elogium*) of Julian which says that the banker spent 26,000 gold *solidi* on the construction.[103] He quotes a poetic dedication made of silver tesserae in the atrium of the church, as follows:[104]

> The lofty temples rise to the venerable rooftop, sanctified to God in the name of Vitalis. And Gervase and Protase also hold this stronghold, whom family and faith and church join together. The father fleeing the contagions of the world was to these sons an example of faith and martyrdom.

> Ecclesius first gave this stronghold to Julian, who wonderfully completed the work commissioned to him. He also ordered it to be maintained by perpetual law that in these places no one's body is permitted to be placed. But because tombs of earlier bishops are established here, it is allowed to place this one, or one like it.

The discussion of tombs refers to the fact that Bishops Ecclesius, Ursicinus, and Victor are all buried in the chapel of St. Nazarius, a round chapel

77. San Vitale,
view of the exte-
rior from the
north

to the south of the apse.[105] Finally, Agnellus also quotes the inscription
commemorating the dedication by Maximian:[106]

> Julian the banker built the basilica of the blessed martyr Vitalis from the foun-
> dations, authorized (*mandante*) by the most blessed Bishop Ecclesius, and dec-
> orated and dedicated (*dedicavit*) it, with the most reverend Bishop Maximian
> consecrating (*consecrante*) it on 19 April, in the tenth indiction, in the sixth year
> after the consulship of Basilius. [the year 547]

F. W. Deichmann exhaustively analyzed these inscriptions, and proposed
that the various terms *mandare*, *dedicare*, and *consecrare* describe specific
legal and/or ritual procedures for constructing a church in the sixth century.[107] He concluded that Ecclesius's role was limited to authorizing Julian
to construct the church. If this were the case, why would Ecclesius be
depicted in the apse offering the church to Christ? It seems clear that Ecclesius was viewed as a donor; since Agnellus tells us that, directly to the east
of San Vitale, he built Santa Maria Maggiore on his own property, perhaps
the small chapel of St. Vitalis had been built by his family, and he donated
this property, too, to the church.[108]

The date of the foundation and original construction of San Vitale matters because of what it implies about the relationship of this building to
others being constructed in Constantinople at about the same time, in particular, the church of Sts. Sergius and Bacchus, which was built between

527 and 536. Ecclesius left Constantinople before 526, therefore he cannot have seen Sts. Sergius and Bacchus. Deichmann therefore argued that the design and construction of San Vitale only began after 540, under Bishop Victor, whose monograms are found on the impost blocks.[109] Deichmann argued that it was unlikely to have taken fifteen years – that is, between a foundation before 532 and a dedication in 547 – to build the church. However, given that these years correspond to the Gothic War, the plague, and long gaps between bishops who constantly traveled back and forth to Constantinople, a long building period is instead rather likely.[110] Scenarios can easily be imagined by which the initial design was created under Ecclesius but, perhaps because of the war, the marble pieces were not completed and shipped until after 540. Likewise, it is possible that sculptors from Proconnesus were sent to Ravenna to carve the unfinished pieces *in situ*, and that by the time they completed the impost blocks, Victor was bishop. We should conclude that both Ecclesius and Victor had substantial roles in the construction of the church.

San Vitale has survived remarkably well through the centuries.[111] It became part of a Benedictine monastery some time before the mid–tenth century, and remained its primary church until the monastery was dissolved in 1860. The major structural changes were the vaulting of the ambulatory and gallery and the construction of exterior buttresses to carry the extra weight, perhaps the late twelfth century, as well as the transformation of the southern stair tower into a campanile.[112] The church was apparently in a ruinous condition by 1495; beginning in the 1540s a major restoration was undertaken that resulted in the removal of most of the marble incrustation from the walls and its replacement with much of the wall, vault, and floor decoration that survives today. The campanile collapsed in 1688, and many more changes were made in the eighteenth century, including the addition of several chapels and other rooms around the building. Modern restorations began in the mid–nineteenth century, starting with Felice Kibel's work on the mosaics; in 1899 the building came under the authority of the newly constituted Soprintendenza, and Corrado Ricci initiated an extensive program of work. The original building began to be isolated, excavated, and reconstructed in its presumed original form. The apse wall incrustation of *opus sectile* was remade in 1900 and 1904, and the alabaster windows now in the church were also installed at that time. Excavations were carried out by Giuseppe Gerola in the 1910s and additional restoration was undertaken in the 1930s, including the lowering of the pavements in the core to the original level and the reconstitution of the narthex. Excavations in the ambulatory and exedrae of the core from 1975–83 resulted in the reconstitution of those floor levels also. F. W. Deichmann, in his 1976 study of the building, provides an extremely detailed analysis of which parts

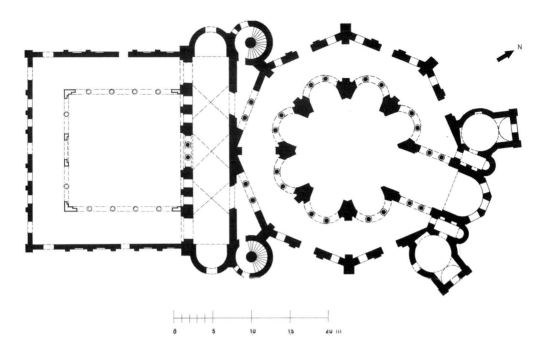

of the structure are original and which restored; only his conclusions can be summarized here.

Architecture. The architecture of San Vitale is unique in Ravenna. While there were several other domed, polygonal structures, namely the several baptisteries and possibly Santa Maria Maggiore, none was as large as San Vitale and none had such a complex layout. San Vitale is a double-shell octagon, that is, a building with a domed octagonal core surrounded by a passageway (Fig. 78). At San Vitale, the central core (33 meters in diameter) is surrounded on seven sides by an ambulatory with a second-story gallery above it (40 meters in diameter total); the eighth side, to the east, opens into a high vaulted presbitery and an apse, polygonal on the exterior and circular on the interior, that projects beyond the exterior octagon (Fig. 79). The apse is flanked to the north and south by round chambers with rectangular *arcosolia* on the eastern and western sides. Access to them is provided from the ambulatory via small rectangular chambers that fill the space between these chapels and the apse.

Remarkably, there were doors on all seven exterior walls of the church, five of which led directly to the outside. There was also a door from the southern round chapel to the exterior. The main entrance of the church, though, faced southwest. A colonnaded atrium, much of which was excavated in 1902, extended 25 m to the west of the narthex facade.[113] The

78. San Vitale, reconstructed original ground plan (after Deichmann, 1976, pl. 37)

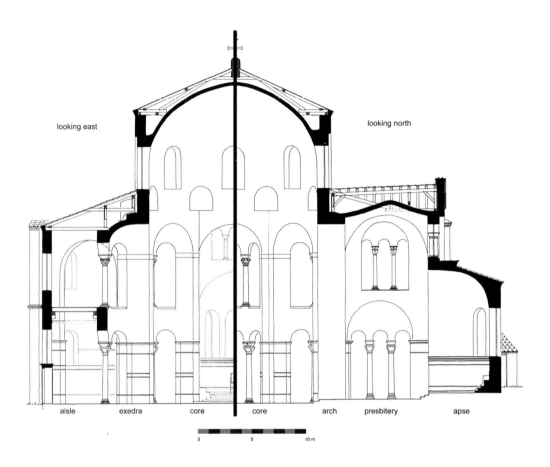

looking east

looking north

aisle   exedra   core   core   arch   presbitery   apse

0   5   10 m

79. San Vitale, section drawings, two views – looking east and looking north (after Deichmann, 1976, pl. 38)

narthex, apsed at its ends, provides the entrance to the building.[114] The narthex is set at an angle to the south-southwest corner of the octagon, and triangular chambers that include the entrances to the stair towers mediate the awkward spaces between the narthex and the church. The narthex is thus on a different alignment from the apse. Two doors lead from the narthex into the church; the one on the left is on the western wall of the octagon, directly opposite the apse, but the one on the right leads only to one side of the ambulatory. This curious asymmetry has been explained in a number of ways. Basilicas often had three entrances, one leading into the nave and the others into the aisles, which were used at different points in the liturgy, and it was likely that here too multiple entrances from the narthex were required. It is possible that a preexisting street or building prevented construction on the axis. Finally, Deichmann follows G. Jonescu in pointing out the exterior corners of the octagon were all heavily buttressed to provide support for the dome, and that the off-axis narthex helped to

80. San Vitale, central octagon facing south (photo C. L. Striker)

support three of the exterior corners of the octagon, whereas if it had been aligned on the west face it would only have supported two corners.[115]

The central core consists of eight multilobed piers, between each of which is a two-story, triple-arched semicircular exedra vaulted by a brick half dome; the octagon thus undulates as it opens on all sides to the outer corridors (Fig. 80). The columns at the gallery level are slightly shorter than those of the ground level (3.7 meters vs. 4.1 meters), which accentuates the sense of verticality.[116] On the east side, an arch that is the same height as those of the exedrae leads into the presbitery. The ambulatory and gallery terminate here, and communicate with the presbitery through triple-arched openings. Above the exedrae and the presbitery arch rises an octagonal drum 9 meters high, pierced by eight large windows, that resolves by means of shallow niches into the circular base of the dome of *tubi fittili*, whose apex rises 28.7 meters above the floor.[117] The ambulatory and the galleries, although now covered by later-medieval groin vaults, originally were roofed at both levels with wood, supported by cornices and brackets.[118] The presbitery space is vaulted by a brick groin vault that rises 17.7 meters above the floor, while the eastern apse is vaulted by a brick half dome whose apex is 11.7 meters high.

The architects paid careful attention to light, which enters the building from all directions. Eight windows in the drum of the dome provide light directly to the core, while the apse has three broad windows at ground level and three windows in the tympanum above the springing of the apse. The six walls of the ambulatory that are open to the exterior each have two or three windows, and equivalent windows are found directly above them in the galleries. The light from all these sources passes through the open arcades into the core and the presbitery, creating brilliant effects of light and shadow throughout the building. It should be noted that the alabaster windowpanes currently in the windows were installed in 1904, and it is likely that originally the windows would have been covered with glass.[119]

The chambers flanking the apse are all vaulted with brick barrel vaults, domes, and half domes. The round domed chapels have rectangular *arcosolia* to the east, with niches on either side and a window; they were used as mausolea and also as chapels with altars and screens.[120] The small rectangular chambers between the apse and the mausolea have three stories; the lowest-level rooms served as vestibules for the mausolea with access from the ambulatory, while doors led from the galleries into the top level, and wooden stairs led down into the intermediate space. The rooms on the ground floor have niches embedded in the walls, and small windows in their apses; they are interpreted by Deichmann as sacristies, or rooms for storing liturgical vessels, but J. Smith notes that, given the particular nature of the niches, they may have been used for books, especially liturgical books.[121]

From the exterior, the building appears as a complex collection of juxtaposed volumes rising to the central dome (Fig. 77). Together with the cruciform volumes of the Santa Croce complex and the centrally planned structure of Santa Maria Maggiore, the ensemble must have struck the viewer as a remarkable accumulation of exotic building types.[122]

It has long been recognized that the building with the closest formal and structural similarities to San Vitale is the church of Sts. Sergius and Bacchus in Constantinople, built by Justinian between 527 and 536. Not only is Sts. Sergius and Bacchus a double-shelled building with an octagonal core, but the superposition of triple arcades in the four exedrae and three flat walls of the core, and the two-story presbitery and apse to the east, also create the same effect as at San Vitale. Since this church was begun at about the same time as San Vitale, presumably after Ecclesius had returned from his trip to Constantinople, it cannot have served as a direct model, although it is certainly possible that people in Constantinople were talking about such buildings in the 520s.[123] Another church with many similarities to San Vitale is San Lorenzo in Milan, a double-shelled tetraconch (the central core has four exedrae) built in the late fourth century, which has five-column arcades only on its four exedrae and no open east side. Since St. Vitalis was a Milanese saint, it is likely that the designers of San Vitale took from Milan the idea to construct a central-plan church; whether this was because a centrally planned church was regarded as particularly suitable form for a *martyrium*,[124] or simply to enhance the splendor of Ravenna, is not known. Both Sts. Sergius and Bacchus and San Lorenzo were related to other examples from the east such as Constantine's cathedral at Antioch, which was also a double-shell octagon with a gallery.[125]

The churches in Antioch, Milan, and Constantinople were imperially sponsored and attached to palaces,[126] and in the eighth century Charlemagne was to imitate San Vitale when he built the chapel for his palace in Aachen. These connections have given rise to the idea that there was some special symbolism that made octagonal double-shell buildings a suitable form for palace-churches.[127] San Vitale, with its imperial portraits, is viewed a pivotal component of this argument. However, since there is absolutely no evidence of any connection between San Vitale and a palace in Ravenna, this thesis, at least as regards San Vitale, must be rejected.[128]

Sculpture, Marble Wall Coverings, Stucco, and Floor. Not only was the architectural design of San Vitale intended to recall the splendid buildings of other imperial capitals, but, like many other sixth-century churches in Ravenna, the marble structural elements were imported directly from the East, and were moreover carved in the latest Constantinopolitan styles. The original columns, capitals, and impost blocks are still in place, but most of the wall and floor coverings in the church today are modern reconstructions, approximating what we know (or Ricci thought) the original forms were like.[129]

Proconnesian marble for ordinary basilicas was mass-produced in the sixth century and could be furnished from pre-made stock in the quarry warehouses,[130] but San Vitale was a different case. San Vitale's builders required four columns for the narthex, fourteen columns for the triple arcades at the ground level, fourteen slightly smaller columns for the upper level, eight columns in two sizes for the triple arcades leading to the presbitery, two colonnettes for the window arcade above the apse, and, of course, bases, capitals, and impost blocks for all of them, not to mention wall revetment and cornices for the peculiarly shaped piers and the wall surfaces of the ambulatory. We can only speculate about the procedure that was followed for the design of the building: Did an architect in Ravenna create the design and send the specifications to Proconnesus or Constantinople, or, as seems more likely, did Ecclesius and Julian send their representatives to the mine with instructions to obtain a design and materials for a double-shell building?[131] In either case, by 530 the mining officials would at the same time have been assembling the materials for Sts. Sergius and Bacchus and would have been very familiar with the architectural requirements of such buildings. Whether the architect was western or eastern,[132] he probably finalized the design at Constantinople.[133]

The columns are almost all monoliths, except for two in the gallery that were apparently broken in transport and reassembled at the time of construction. Most of them have more or less vertical veining, but the ones used in the presbitery instead display almost horizontal stripes, more rare and thus an indication of prestige.[134] The use of impost blocks follows Ravennate tradition; most of the pyramidally shaped blocks have something carved in flat relief at least on the main sides, including, in the case of the ground floor arcade, the monogram of *Victor episcopus* in a medallion, and on two imposts at the gallery level, the monogram of Julian the banker.[135] The imposts in the presbitery are deeply carved on all four sides, with pairs of lambs flanking a cross on the sides facing the altar and vases between doves on the back side. Columns, capitals, and bases have masons' marks inscribed on them in Greek letters which provide additional evidence that they were quarried and shaped in Proconnesus.[136]

The capitals atop the columns, carved in the new style that had developed in Constantinople in the first part of the sixth century, must have looked radically innovative to the inhabitants of Ravenna and W. Betsch has suggested that the change in style was developed to mark distinctively the buildings of the new imperial dynasty.[137] The capitals are of two basic shapes: twenty are paneled impost capitals (Fig. 81), so called because their profile is like that of impost blocks, only taller, and sixteen are mask acanthus capitals (Fig. 85).[138] Two exceptions, the capitals on the north side of the presbytery gallery are fold capitals (Fig. 86), of the type found in Sts. Sergius and Bacchus. The impost capitals have patterned flat surfaces that are undercut by deep drilling (the *à jour* technique); on each surface, a patterned border surrounds a trapezoidal panel. The ground level, central-core arcade capitals have basket patterns surrounding stylized lotus palmettes (Fig. 81), while in the presbitery we find acanthus borders surrounding scrolls of a different type of acanthus as well as some geometric motifs. The capitals and impost blocks would originally all have been painted; restored examples can now be seen in the presbitery (Pl. VIb).

Scholars debate where these capitals were made: Deichmann says that the impost and fold capitals, at least, must have been made in Constantinople

81. San Vitale, column capital from the ground level of the octagonal core

although the composite capitals may have been made in Ravenna, but Betsch argues that *à jour* carving was very prone to damage during transport and these capitals were probably carved in Ravenna.[139] Related to this question is the issue of the monograms of Victor: Despite Deichmann's claim that they must have been cut in Proconnesus, it again seems more likely that they were finished in Ravenna, perhaps by workmen from Constantinople. R. Krautheimer notes that although the sculptural styles were new to Ravenna, the capital types used in San Vitale were slightly old-fashioned when compared to strictly contemporary examples from Constantinople.[140] On the other hand, nearly identical capitals together with impost blocks were used at the Basilica Eufrasiana at Poreč, built in the 550s, and may even have been exported there from Ravenna.[141] Regardless of where they were made, the new and different style helps to make the point that this building is linked to the capital city of the empire.

Elaborate cornices run around the walls and piers of most parts of the building; they mark changes in decorative material or changes in architectural space. Some are extremely ornate, especially the one just below the mosaics in the apse, and all seem to be closely related to similar examples from the east, leading to the conclusion that they, too, were imported. Additional material sent from the East, although probably shaped and finished at Ravenna, included the slabs of marble that were used as wall revetment. Marble revetment covered the lower portion of the walls, up to the level of the springing of the arches of the lower central arcade, the narthex, the ambulatory, and the central piers, and was also used in the chapels flanking the apse. The revetment that we see in the church today is mostly restored, but enough of the original survives to show that two types of marble were used: Proconnesian marble, which is white with gray veins, and marble from Iasos in Caria on the west coast of Asia Minor (*cipollino rosso*), which is a magnificent deep red color with white veins.[142] Spectacular effects were created by setting two panels sliced from the same block side by side so that the veining patterns appear mirrored (Fig. 82). Such panels were then surrounded by frames of "plain" Proconnesian marble. The nineteenth-century restorations on the piers in the central core have obliterated traces of how the original was laid out, but in the outer ambulatory walls enough remains to show that the revetment was laid in two zones with a horizontal cornice between them just below the level of the windows (see Deichmann's reconstruction, Fig. 82).[143]

In the apse, the wall below the zone of the mosaics was covered with an elaborate veneer made of *opus sectile*. This was entirely removed in the 1540s, but some of the elements were in good enough condition that they were moved to different parts of the church. Descriptions written before the removal enabled Ricci to recognize these fragments for what they were, and he used them to reconstruct the incrustation that now appears on the wall (Pl. VIIa). The central features are large roundels of porphyry, enclosed in rectangular panels made up of smaller marble pieces and mother of pearl; these were surrounded probably by a plain marble field (today a pink marble has been used), and the rectangular panels were separated by pilasters of green serpentine marble carved with fluted pilasters and Corinthian capitals.[144] We do not know what was above these panels; today an *opus sectile* frieze sets the lower zone off from the elaborate cornice above. Below the *opus sectile* panels ran the *synthronon*, or bench for the clergy, with the episcopal throne at the center; these also are today restored in Proconnesian marble to approximate their presumed original state.

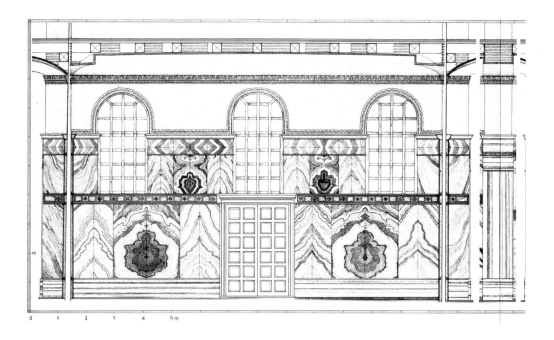

82. San Vitale, reconstruction of the original marble revetment on the outer walls of the ambulatory (Deichmann, 1976, pl. 47; courtesy Franz Steiner Verlag, Stuttgart, Germany)

Little is known about the materials that covered parts of the walls that did not carry marble or mosaic, but in a few arcades (Pl. VIb) and window arches, and in the southern triangular vestibule of the narthex, stucco work of very high quality has survived.[145] We have already seen, especially in the Orthodox Baptistery, that stucco on walls was used for everything from abstract patterns to architectural and figural motifs. Since it is more fragile than marble or mosaic, and since it leaves fewer traces, we can say much less about it. Stucco, unlike marble, must be worked in situ, and from the elaborate geometric and vegetal patterns that survive we can see the high quality of stucco workshops in Ravenna at this time. In the absence of other evidence, stucco or plaster decoration has also been proposed for all of the wall surfaces about which we have no other information, but there is no evidence about what forms this decoration might have taken, whether flat or three-dimensional, or whether and how it would have been painted.[146]

Finally, the floors, like the rest of the church, were richly decorated with mosaic. The layout of the octagonal core consisted of eight triangular slices, divided by marble strips, radiating out from a central medallion. Six of these segments were remade between 1539–45 in an *opus sectile* pattern that reproduced the layout of the earlier floor and utilized fragments of older mosaics (some dating to the twelfth century) as part of the design; the remaining two segments were made in 1702. The excavations of 1931 revealed two segments of the original mosaic, 80 cm below the later floor; the entire level was then lowered to the original level, and the eighteenth-century segments were replaced by the original (restored) mosaic. The floor currently in the presbitery and apse was created between 1911–36.[147]

Overall, it is clear that the sculptural and decorative elements help to define a hierarchy of space in the church. The most elaborate elements – columns, capitals, impost blocks, and *opus sectile* – are used in the presbitery, while the least original are used in the gallery arcade of the central core.[148] Finally, we should note that San Vitale, like other churches in Ravenna, had a full complement of liturgical furnishings, including an altar, delicately carved transennae (now in the Museo Nazionale), and a *ciborium*, all made of Proconnesian marble. One can easily see how important Julian's 26,000 gold *solidi* were to this project!

Mosaics. The brilliance of the mosaics in the presbitery and apse of San Vitale is overwhelming, and no reproduction can do justice to the subtle colors and to the ever-changing effects of light. The arch leading into the presbitery, the walls on either side, and the vaults and apse are covered with some of Ravenna's finest mosaic work, which, although many times restored, still display the effects and the iconography created in the sixth century. Color, predominantly green and gold, is used to achieve subtle effects;[149] the faces of many of the figures are worked with a marvelous attention to physiognomic detail.[150] A range of imagery is displayed, including depictions of the imperial court, scenes from the Old Testament, Old and New Testament holy figures, abstract but symbolic ornament, and the central figure of Christ flanked by Vitalis and Ecclesius. Much of the imagery is related to the celebration of the Eucharist that took place in this space, but there is plenty of other symbolic meaning as well. These images have provided material for generations of scholarly interpretation, as we will see.

One interesting question is whether there were originally more mosaics that have now been lost. There were almost certainly mosaics in the narthex and in the domes of the round chapels flanking the apse.[151] We have no idea what material decorated in the semidomes and the main dome of the core. Mosaic workmen were not lacking in Ravenna in this period, and it seems almost inconceivable that the dome should not also have been covered with mosaics. As we have seen in the baptisteries, Ravenna's mosaicists were perfectly capable of creating a mosaic design for a dome. However, no traces of mosaic have ever been found in or around these areas, which have been many times restored; the earliest description of the dome, from the early sixteenth century, reports figures made of *graecanicum opus*, but this could refer to fresco as well as mosaic.[152] The question thus remains open.

Scholars have identified at least two different sixth-century styles for San Vitale's mosaics. In addition to technical differences of mosaic artistry, the first style uses gold for scenic backgrounds and glass tesserae for all parts of human figures, including their skin, while the second style uses green for scenic backgrounds and stone tesserae for the skin of human figures.[153] The first style is used in the apse mosaics, the vault of the presbitery, and the top of the arch that leads from the presbitery into the core, whereas the second style is used on the walls of the presbitery, the lower parts of the presbitery arch, and for the heads of Maximian and the man who stands between him and Justinian. Some scholars have interpreted the two styles as deliberately different modes of representation, with the more naturalistic backgrounds and figures suitable for Old Testament subjects and the more hieratic, formal poses with gold backgrounds for the Christian images in the apse.[154] While it is possible that this might have been in the minds of the workshop responsible for the Old Testament scenes, it is more likely, as pointed out by I. Andreescu-Treadgold and W. Treadgold, that these phases simply correspond to two periods of work, the first dated to before 545 and the second to between 546 and 549.[155] Given that the war and the plague intervened between these two building periods, breaks and even changes in the workshops do not seem unlikely.

The mosaics in San Vitale today are not entirely original.[156] As we have already seen, the building went through periods in which it was damaged and not well maintained, and others in which it was restored: in the twelfth to fourteenth centuries; the sixteenth century; the late eighteenth century; and then the more or less scientific programs of restorations in the 1850s, 1890s, 1930s, 1960s, and then from 1988 to the present. By comparing today's mosaics with drawings and paintings made at various times, and also by conducting a close analysis of the mosaics themselves, the tesserae, mortar, and other features, scholars have learned much about their history. In the periods for which we have documentation, it is clear that parts of the mosaics were continually falling off the walls. It is therefore assumed that in most cases the medieval and Renaissance modifications were replacements for damaged sections. Such interventions, made for unknown reasons at various times, will be noted in the descriptions below, as it is essential to understand, when we look at mosaics, what is original and what is not.[157]

The Apse.   The half dome of the apse features at its center a beardless Christ seated on a blue globe (Fig. 83). He wears a purple, gold-bordered tunic and mantle with a prominent *clavus* Z, and a halo inscribed with a gemmed cross surrounds his head. In his left hand Christ holds a scroll closed with the seven seals of the Apocalypse; his right hand extends a crown toward the martyr St. Vitalis. Red and blue clouds float in the gold background above

Christ's head, and beneath the globe the Four Rivers of Paradise flow out from the rocks. Christ is flanked by two winged angels dressed in white who hold staffs in the crooks of their arms. Both angels face away from Christ and gesture toward the outermost figures on whose shoulders they lay their hands. On our left, (Christ's right), we see St. Vitalis (labeled SCS VITALIS), who holds out both his covered hands to receive the crown offered by Christ. He is portrayed as a gray-haired man with a halo, dressed in Byzantine court costume, with a *segmentum* on his shoulder, a white tunic, and a patterned *chlamys* clasped by a fibula (the part of his body below the waist was entirely remade about 1100; originally, he was probably dressed like the officials next to Justinian, with a slightly more elaborate mantle).[158] On our right, we see a bishop labeled as ECLESIVS EPIS, dressed in purple chasuble (the lower part of his costume is likewise a medieval replacement) and prominently wearing the *pallium* over his shoulders. He is shown as a round-faced man with graying hair (his tonsure is also a medieval modification).[159] He holds a model of a centrally planned building, obviously San Vitale itself, which he offers to Christ with both covered hands. This is one of the earliest examples of the depiction of a patron offering a church and indicates the perceived importance of Ecclesius's role in founding San Vitale.[160] All of the figures stand on a rocky landscape of several levels in which lilies and roses bloom. The apse is bordered by a broad arch, decorated with a pattern of intersecting cornucopia, with a gemmed Chi–Rho monogram in a medallion upheld by eagles at the apex.[161] The entire composition is then surrounded by another border of medallions and leaves against a green background, with yet another border of blue and green gems and pearls against a red background.

The three large windows of the apse are below this scene; on the strips between them are represented in mosaic gold columns encrusted with gems and mother of pearl. Columns of the same type are used to frame the panels on the left and right walls of the apse that depict the processions of the imperial court. Above the heads of the figures in the north panel is a coffered ceiling, while the top of the right panel is bordered by a false cornice depicted in mosaic.

In the left (north) panel, we see at the center the emperor Justinian (Pl. VIIa). He is dressed in a white tunic and a purple *chlamys*, which is embellished with a large gold-embroidered and gemmed *tablion*, and which is clasped at his shoulder with a brooch featuring a large red stone surrounded by pearls. On his feet we can see the famous red and purple shoes, worn only by emperors, which indeed stand out among the feet in this image. On his head the emperor wears a heavy crown set with red and blue gems and pearls (the top of which is a twelfth-century modification),[162] with pairs of pearl *pendilia* dangling on either side, and his head is surrounded

by a gold halo outlined in red. In his hands Justinian holds a large gold paten, which he offers in the direction of Christ. The face of this emperor is very distinctive, as indeed are all the faces in this panel. The ruddy, jowly, clean-shaven face with short dark hair is assumed to be Justinian because he was the only emperor who reigned during the period in which the church was constructed and the images made, but since it does not resemble other portraits of him, we do not know the source of this physiognomy. Justinian, like the other figures in this panel, is not turned toward Christ, but instead faces outward, and is thus venerating Christ and being presented to viewers at the same time.[163]

On the emperor's left (our right) is a bishop labeled MAXIMIANUS. The heads of both Maximian and the man between him and Justinian, along with the name, were inserted at a slightly later date than the original production of the mosaic, which can be discerned because the faces are made of stone rather than glass tesserae (Fig. 84). Andreescu-Treadgold and Treadgold argue that the mosaic originally depicted Bishop Victor, and was made after the Byzantine reconquest of Ravenna in 540, specifically after Belisarius's return to Ravenna in 544.[164] The archbishop wears a white tunic with a gold chasuble over it, and, like Ecclesius in the apse, the *pallium* prominently draped over his shoulders. He holds in his right hand a gemmed gold cross. His physiognomy is perhaps the most distinctive of the

83. San Vitale, mosaics of the vault of the apse (photo C. Copenhaver)

group: he appears as a balding figure with blazing blue eyes and a slight beard on his lean, intense face.

The perspective in this composition is very ambiguous, which is probably deliberate; from the position of the feet, Maximian seems to lead the entire procession, closely followed by two deacons, dressed alike in white, who hold a jewel-encrusted Gospel book and a censer burning incense (the tonsure of the deacon on the left is a twelfth-century modification).[165] Justinian is the first secular figure in the procession, and he is followed by members of his court, first three aristocratic officials and then five or six soldiers (altogether there are twelve or thirteen figures in this scene, surely a number chosen to represent the apostles).[166] On Justinian's left, between him and Maximian, we see the head of a heavy-faced man with gray hair, wearing a *chlamys* clasped by a gold fibula, presumably similar in rank to the two younger-looking men on Justinian's right, whose white *chlamides* with purple *tablia* and embroidered *segmenta* on their shoulders mark them as officials of the court. The five or six soldiers are found in a much more undifferentiated cluster behind shields bearing the Chi–Rho monogram; they wear short, brightly hued tunics and have gold torcs around their necks, indicating perhaps their barbarian origin;[167] over their shoulders they bear long spears. These are the soldiers who have recently conquered Ravenna, and their presence here at the shrine of the city's martyr integrates them into the Ravennate community.

The facing panel depicts an empress and her court, presumed to be Justinian's wife, Theodora (Pl. VIIb). This image has more complex composition than the facing panel. At the eastern edge, the jeweled column flanks an entryway screened by a curtain, with a marble fountain in front of it. A beardless man of high rank, possibly a eunuch, wearing a white tunic and gold chlamys with purple *tablion*, raises one arm to open the curtain as he turns toward the empress. A second man, dressed in a white tunic and *chlamys* with purple *tablion*, with embroidered *segmenta* at his shoulder and knee, stands immediately next to the empress; the pair and a female attendant are framed by a marble niche with a shell-shaped conch, the apex of which is directly above Theodora's head.[168] The empress herself wears a white underdress with a jeweled hem, jeweled shoes, and a purple *chlamys* with the images of the three Magi offering gifts to Christ depicted at the hem; the *chlamys* is a male court costume that was also worn by empresses.[169] Theodora's shoulders are covered by an elaborate jeweled collar. She also wears a narrower emerald necklace with dangling earrings of emerald, pearl, and sapphire, and on her head she wears a high jeweled crown with long pearl *pendilia*.[170] Her face is rather narrow and she too has a halo outlined in red. She holds a gold chalice encrusted with gems which she extends in offering to the east. On Theodora's left stand seven women;

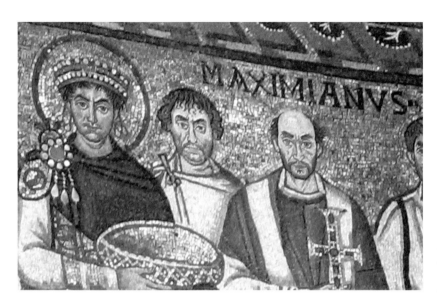

84. San Vitale, mosaic of the north apse wall, detail, head of Maximian

the first two are allotted more space than the others, who crowd together on the right-hand side, perhaps to echo the arrangement of the men opposite. The faces of these women are less differentiated than those of their male counterparts, but their clothing is much more splendid, displaying a range of textile patterns, colors, and designs; interestingly, some of them have embroidered *segmenta* on their mantles or tunics. The six women at our right have walked through another entryway, which has a short curtain of red, white, and blue stripes above it.

Who are all these people, and what are they doing? First, it is clear that what we see is an idealized presentation of an emperor, empress, and their courts at an ecclesiastical ceremony, rather than a depiction of a specific event. Justinian and Theodora never visited Ravenna, but neither had the emperors and empresses depicted as offering gifts in the apse of San Giovanni Evangelista. By now the depiction of imperial or royal couples, along with their bishops, in the apses of churches had become quite common in Ravenna, and perhaps the new regime wanted to follow the lead of Galla Placidia in this respect.[171] The halos around the heads of the imperial couple are not unusual; in this period they referred to imperial power that was eternal and derived from God.[172] The inclusion of a bishop is certainly intended to emphasize the connection between Ravenna's archbishops and their imperial sponsors, especially important at the time of the Three Chapters Controversy. Maximian, who, according to Agnellus, was initially unpopular in Ravenna, perhaps had good reason to modify the mosaic and depict himself to emphasize his connection with Justinian and his officers.

As for the other figures, their individualistic facial features have led many scholars to propose that they too had specific identities that would have been recognizable to their contemporaries. As A. McClanan notes, scholars who attempt these identifications simply look in the sources for individuals of the right ages to correspond to the figures in the mosaics.[173] Given the number of important Byzantine leaders who are known to have lived or passed through Ravenna in the 540s, it is perfectly possible that the men next to Justinian might have been Belisarius and the general John, and that the woman next to Theodora might have been Belisarius's wife Antonina, but there is no way of knowing for certain.[174] McClanan has also noted that individualized faces serve to create a hierarchy among the figures in the same way that the costumes do, without necessarily being "real" portraits; in other words, the more important the figure, the more individualized a face he has.[175] We can note that St. Vitalis also has an arresting countenance, and certainly his was not intended as an actual portrait (although the artist might have modeled it on a real person). When it comes down to it, we really cannot know who these people are, but we, and sixth-century viewers, conclude that they are important.

What event these scenes commemorate has likewise been the topic of heated discussion, although, as S. MacCormack and J. Deckers have pointed out, the images are capable of bearing several meanings at once.[176] Deichmann proposed that the imperial couple is offering vessels on the occasion of the dedication of the church, while, at the other extreme, Deckers notes that the act of offering is a generic illustration of imperial piety.[177] Other scholars, noting the strongly liturgical appearance of the bishop and deacons at the head of the procession, have read the panels as depicting a church ceremony,[178] and the leading candidate, as proposed by T. Mathews, is the First Entrance of the liturgy, the procession before the celebration of the Eucharist. The order of the procession (derived from tenth-century texts but thought to be based on earlier ceremonial) includes the bishop preceded by the Gospels and incense, together with the emperor, and followed by his guard and court.[179] Justinian would be proceeding to his seat adjacent to the altar, while Theodora and her ladies, who are not, strictly speaking, supposed to be in the sanctuary at all, are shown in the act of leaving this space, perhaps in the atrium or narthex about to enter the stairwell that will take them up to their places in the gallery.[180] There are, however, several problems with this interpretation, the chief one being that the Constantinopolitan liturgy does not mention any role for the empress.[181] Stricevic's suggestion that the imperial figures are presenting the bread and wine for the Eucharist makes more sense, but not, as he proposed, necessarily corresponding to the Great Entrance at Constantinople, but simply in accordance with the ordinary Eucharistic liturgy, in which men and women offer these items in order of their rank.[182] The emperor and empress (unlabeled, and thus also able to be interpreted as generic symbols for imperial rule) eternally offer the holy gifts to Christ and to St. Vitalis,[183] while the prominence of Maximian underlines the role of the bishop as intermediary between God and ruler.[184]

We should also note the interesting fact that, contrary to most liturgical information that we have, and contrary to the mosaics in Sant'Apollinare Nuovo, the male procession is on the left (north) side and the women are on the right (south). In general, the south side was considered the more highly favored, which is why it was known as "the men's side" in liturgical texts; however, here the designers seem to have taken their lead from the depiction of Christ and the fact that St. Vitalis is on Christ's right side (the north). The male procession is thus led by the upper-class male military figure of Vitalis in the apse, on Christ's right, while the female procession corresponds to Bishop Ecclesius. We do not know whether in this church the men and women of the congregation would, contrary to the usual liturgical practice, have stood on the sides that correspond to the imperial panels, or whether, standing on their usual places, they would have been able to look across the apse to see the imperial panel corresponding to their gender.[185]

The Presbitery. The presbitery is a soaring space whose vault rises above the level of the apse, but not as high as the dome (compare Fig. 79). It communicates with the central core through a high arched opening, with the ambulatory and galleries through triple-arcaded openings surmounted by lunettes, and with the apse through a lower arch that is topped by a tympanum that also contains a triple-arched set of windows. All of the surfaces above the level of the columns are sheathed with glittering mosaics, depicting a variety of subjects. Most of them are organized symmetrically around an east–west axis, and in some cases also a north–south axis.[186] The mosaics of this space emphasize Old Testament typology, which was a feature of Justinianic art in other contexts also, as we have seen on the Throne of Maximian.[187] Here the typology is derived from the examples used in Paul's Epistle to the Hebrews. From the Old Testament scenes in the bottom zones to the depiction of paradise in the vault, apostles, evangelists, and Christ and Christians completely surround their Old Testament predecessors, visually making the point that the Old Law was a precursor for, and overtaken by, the New.

On the north and south walls of the presbitery, the lunettes above the arcades contain depictions of scenes from the Old Testament that were viewed as precursors of the Eucharist. On the north wall (Fig. 86) the lunette contains two scenes from the life of Abraham: his feeding of the three strangers at Mambre (Gen. 18:1–15) and the Sacrifice of Isaac (Gen. 22:1–13). The first scene takes up the majority of the lunette; at the center, the three strangers, dressed in white and with gold halos, are seated at a table on which are three loaves of bread inscribed with crosses. Two of the strangers raise their hands in blessing, the third gestures to the bread. A tree to the left spreads its branches over them; beyond the tree Abraham, with white hair and beard, dressed in a short brown tunic with what looks like a *pallium* tied around his waist, offers a cooked calf to the visitors, while his wife Sarah (dressed in the same costume as Theodora's companions) stands laughing with one hand to her face in a small thatched hut (the *tabernaculum*). The right side of the lunette depicts Abraham, now dressed in white mantle and tunic, in the act of raising his sword to sacrifice his son Isaac, who wears a short brown tunic and is kneeling, bound, on the altar. From a cluster of red and blue clouds in the sky, the Hand of God appears telling Abraham to sacrifice instead the white ram that can be seen at his feet. All of the actions in the lunette take place in one green landscape whose parts are variously defined by changes in the groundline, by bushes and clusters of rocks, and in which lilies and roses bloom, as in the apse.

The lunette of the south wall likewise depicts two scenes from the Old Testament, united by a common altar in the center (Pl. VIb). The altar itself is made of four colonnettes upholding a rectangular slab, and is covered with a purple undercloth and a white-fringed altar cloth with an eight-sided embroidered appliqué on the front. On the altar are set an elaborate chalice and two round loaves of Eucharistic bread; above it, amid clouds of red and blue, the Hand of God descends with thumb and first and fourth fingers extended. On the left side stands Abel, labeled by name, dressed in skins with a scarlet cloak over his shoulder; he raises a lamb in offering (Gen. 4:4). Behind him is a tree and a hut that is almost identical to the one in which Sarah stands on the opposite wall. On the right, Melchisedek the Priest-King (Gen. 14:18–20), haloed and dressed in an eastern-looking garment,[188] holds up a third round loaf of bread. Behind him is a representation of a temple, an elaborate building with fluted columns flanking a door and upholding a pediment, with what looks like the superstructure of a basilica behind it. Again, lilies and roses bloom at the feet of the actors.

Above these lunettes are a series of portraits of figures from the Old and New Testaments, the juxtaposition of which emphasize the role that typology plays in the application of Old Testament examples to Christian thought. On the north wall, flanking the lunette on the left (west) side is IEREMIA [Jeremiah], white haired and bearded, who stands reading an open scroll next to a sort of tower on which rests a crown; opposite him on

the south wall is ISAIAS [Isaiah], like Jeremiah but with a closed scroll. On the east sides of the lunettes we find three scenes from the life of Moses, who is depicted as a beardless young man (labeled MOSE on each side). On the north wall Moses, standing in a rocky landscape, receives the law from the Hand of God that issues from the divine clouds, while looking back to the scene of sacrifice. Below his feet, a crowd of men represent the Israelites at the foot of Mt. Sinai. On the opposite wall we again find Moses, here depicted twice: in the upper scene his body faces the lunette as he ties his sandal, but he turns his head to look over his shoulder at the Hand of God again emerging from clouds; on either side are burning bushes. Below this scene is another depiction of Moses with three sheep, one of which he feeds while holding a scroll with his other hand. The triple depiction of Moses contains clear comparisons to Christ and also perhaps to the emperor.[189] We should also note that Moses, the prophets, Abraham, Abel, and Melchisedek all appear as types of the priesthood of Christ in the Epistle to the Hebrews.

In the upper zone, flanking the windows that open into the gallery, are the four evangelists (Fig. 86). On the north wall we see on the left John, white headed and bearded, his eagle above his head, seated in a landscape reading a codex with the words SECUNDU[M] IOHANNEM, his writing desk in front of him. On the right is Luke, his ox above him, seated in the same landscape next to an open tub, or *capsa*, of scrolls, displaying an open codex with the words SECUNDUM LUCA. On the south wall on the left is Matthew, who, like Luke, sits in a landscape next to his desk and a *capsa* of scrolls writing in a codex, in an illegible script that may be intended to be Hebrew,[190] looking at his symbol, a winged man, who gestures toward the evangelist's head; and finally on the right, Mark, seated with his writing utensils on his desk, displaying an open codex with the words SECUNDUM MARCUM and gesturing to his symbol, the lion, above him, with his other hand.

All of these biblical male figures wear white tunics and mantles and are haloed; all except Moses are depicted as older men with white hair and beards. It has been suggested that the portraits of the evangelists were derived from an illustrated Gospel book; such a manuscript does not survive from the sixth century, but Carolingian manuscripts that include such portraits may have been derived from late antique exemplars.[191] All the evangelists either look up to or gesture toward their symbolic beasts which seem to communicate with them (the lion roars, the man reaches out). Overall, as B. Brenk has pointed out, the depictions of the evangelists correspond very closely to Jerome's prologue to the Gospels. They are seated in landscapes, and the beasts themselves, derived from Ezekiel 1:5–13 and then Revelation 4:6–7, are Old Testament symbols that were taken to prefigure the four Gospels.[192] Moreover, in the foreground of each evangelist's landscape there runs a river which may represent the Four Rivers of Paradise that also flow from the feet of Christ in the apse and which were viewed as a symbol of the Gospel teachings spreading through the world.[193] That the Old Testament figures are forerunners of the new is obvious and helps to integrate the rest of the Old Testament imagery into the Christian meaning of the church.

On the soffit of the arch that leads from the presbitery into the central core of the church, between elaborate borders we find medallions with the busts of the apostles (Fig. 87).[194] At the summit of the arch is Christ (almost entirely restored), shown here as bearded, holding a book, wearing purple, and set against a gold background, with a cross-inscribed halo. The image is correctly viewed when looking east, that is, by a viewer standing beneath the dome, from where it can be perceived as aligned with the lamb in the apex of the vault and Christ in the apse, a complete set of the three different ways that Christ could be represented. The apostles, on the other hand, are depicted with their heads toward the vault, so that they can be viewed from either side; the borders of their medallions alternate white and gold, and their heads, surrounded by gold halos, are set against a bright turquoise background. Their names are written in white on either side of their heads. In addition to the apostles, the brother-saints Gervase and Protase are also depicted at the bottom of the series, as follows:

South	North
Petrus	Paulus
Andreas	Iacobus
Iohannis	Philippus
Bartolome[us]	Thomas
Mattheus	Iacobus Al[phaeus]
Thaddeus	Simon Chan[aneus]
Gerbaius	Protasius

As we have discussed in the previous chapter, the representation of the apostles here is similar to earlier examples found in Ravenna – some are old, some young, some bearded, some beardless. The only consistent types are Sts. Peter, Paul, and Andrew. Gervase and Protase, as befits their status as sons of Vitalis, are shown as beardless youths. Andreescu-Treadgold has shown that two teams of mosaicists were at work here, presumably working from the same scaffolding, one on the north side and one on the south; as a result, the border elements do not line up exactly.[195]

On the eastern tympanum, above the apse arch, abstract ornament surrounds the windows. On the haunches of the arch of the apse, Jerusalem and Bethlehem are depicted as walled, gem- and pearl-encrusted cities above date palms (Fig. 87). Surrounding the triple-arched windows are grapevines that emerge from large baskets at the bottom, and acanthus vines springing from chalices above the capitals of the window colonnettes, all set against a dark blue background. Much the same motif (heavily restored) is found on the lunettes above the triple-arched openings to the gallery to the north and south, where the scroll is an inhabited grapevine. Directly beneath the triple-arched openings on all three walls, a pair of winged angels, floating horizontally, hold up at the center a medallion; on the east wall this contains a rayed eight-arm cross, while on the north and south the medallions contain gemmed crosses with A and Ω dangling from the arms.

We finally reach the vault of the presbitery, which is divided into four sections by decorative bands that follow the groins of the vault, and that contain peacocks and flower- and fruit-filled plant motifs (Fig. 87). The four triangular panels have alternating green and gold backgrounds and are filled with brightly colored acanthus scrolls inhabited by a variety of birds in the gold-ground fields and animals in the green-ground ones.[196] In the center of each field, a winged angel stands on a blue globe[197] with arms upraised to support the central medallion in which is found the Lamb of God with a gold halo against a dark blue background, surrounded by twenty-six gold and silver stars. The lamb is aligned to be viewed by someone facing east. Altogether, the images illustrate Revelation 5:13: "And every creature, which is in heaven, and on the earth, and under the earth, and such as are in the sea, and all that are in them: I heard all saying: To him that sitteth on the throne, and to the Lamb, benediction, and honour, and glory, and power, for ever and ever."[198]

The Overall Mosaic Program. The imagery in San Vitale's presbitery and apse, when considered together, has a coherent program that reflects both mid–sixth-century political and theological currents and the liturgical meaning of the Eucharist. While individual studies of the decoration have tended to emphasize one aspect of the program at the expense of the others, the fact that all the ideas work together enables the decoration to be both timely and timeless.

The changes made to the decoration by Maximian emphasize the significance of the political program for the building's patrons. Justinian and Theodora, Maximian and Ecclesius, and the other contemporary people are linked to the biblical figures. Moses has been interpreted as a reference to leadership, and thus a model for Justinian.[199] God speaks directly to Moses, Isaiah, Jeremiah, and the apostles – and perhaps also to Justinian and Maximian? The parallels draw attention to the priestly role played by

87. San Vitale, arch and vault of the pres- bitery (photo C. Copenhaver)

the emperor and empress, which was perhaps useful given Justinian's desire to resolve long-standing Christological debates.

    Some symbols seem pointedly to emphasize Orthodox, anti-Arian doctrine, significant in a church that was built when Arians were still an active presence in Ravenna.[200] The many repetitions of the number 3 – the Magi on Theodora's *chlamys*, the strangers at Mambre who, in Genesis, represent God alternately as three and as one figure,[201] the loaves of bread on both altars, the different depictions of Christ – emphasize the Trinity and its consubstantiality. The Chi–Rho monogram, the cross with the alpha and omega (indicating that Christ is co-eternal with God the Father), and especially the rayed eight-sided cross, may also have had anti-Arian associations.[202] Sts. Vitalis, Gervase, and Protase were associated with Ambrose of Milan, who was famous for his controversies with Arian rulers.[203] Most convincing is the fact that the mosaics in the presbitery can all be connected to the Epistle to the Hebrews, a text that was rejected by some Arians because it seems to say that the Son is of one substance with the Father.[204]

The overarching theme that links all the mosaic images from the floor to the vault is Offerings to God.[205] The scenes depicted were viewed as types, or foreshadowings, of the Eucharistic offering; the relevant biblical texts are invoked in the Canons of the Roman and Milanese mass,[206] and are specifically identified as such in the Epistle to the Hebrews. The offering metaphor was in fact fully multidimensional, since the offering of the Eucharist was enacted at the church's main altar just below the mosaics; the liturgical drama both enhanced and was enhanced by the imagery above it. In the vault, all creation offers praise; in the apse, Ecclesius offers the church, Justinian and Theodora offer the chalice and paten, and the three Magi on Theodora's robe offer their gifts. In the lunettes of the presbitery, Abel's is the offering acceptable to God, Melchisedek offers bread and wine, Abraham feeds the three strangers with three loaves of bread, and offers up his son on an altar. In these conflated scenes, the central element is the table or altar, above which the Hand of God receives the offerings, while in the background are the tabernacle and the temple. Thus Old and New Testament narratives are linked to the real-life world of the court, the bishop, and the Eucharistic celebrant, which themselves become part of universal Christian history, existing outside of time and space.[207] Mosaics and participants are united by the Lamb in the vault of the presbitery and by Christ in the apse, to whom all the gifts are ultimately presented.

SAN MICHELE IN AFRICISCO

Another small church sponsored privately by Julian the banker and a man named Bacauda was dedicated to the archangel Michael.[208] In medieval documents it is called San Michele *in Africisco*; Agnellus says that the church was in the region known as *Ad Frigiselo*. This curious term is probably a reference to the famous shrines of St. Michael in Phrygia.[209] The church was located just east of the junction of the Padenna and the Flumisellum, and thus immediately to the west of the Arian episcopal complex; its west facade probably opened onto the street that ran alongside the Padenna.[210] It continued in use until sometime before the early nineteenth century when it was sold to a fishmonger. A sketch made in 1842 shows the surviving apse mosaics and part of the nave; in 1844 the mosaics were sold to King Friedrich Wilhelm IV of Germany, taken down and removed to Venice, where a

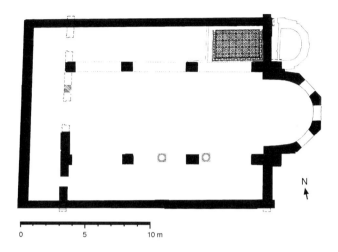

88. San Michele *in Africisco*, plan of original layout (after Brenk, 2007)

reconstruction was made and sent to Berlin; most of the originals are now lost.[211] After this the building slowly deteriorated and had almost entirely disappeared by 1904; today only the lower parts of the apse are visible, along with parts of the east and north walls (the site is now occupied by a clothing shop in whose walls these fragments can be seen). P. Grossmann performed a detailed architectural survey of the surviving building, allowing him to reconstruct its original form.[212]

The church was a basilica with a narthex, nave, and single aisles (Fig. 88). The nave was separated from the aisles by a triple arcade formed not of columns, but of masonry piers (in the fifteenth century, when the campanile was built, the south arcade was replaced with columns; at the same time or slightly later, the floor level was raised).[213] The fact that there were only two freestanding piers meant that the intercolumniations were wider (average 4.0 meter) than was usual for a colonnade. This is the only example in Italy of a basilica with piers; comparisons have been proposed with several larger churches erected in Syria at this time,[214] but B. Brenk more plausibly suggests that the piers simply represent an ad hoc solution for a quickly built church, also seen in the lack of perfect right angles and precise measurements.[215] The proportions of the building, with a greater width–length ratio than is usual for a Ravennate basilica, are similar to those found in the Arian cathedral.[216] The apse had five sides externally and was pierced by three windows, as was usual for Ravennate basilicas. The church was built of the so-called Julian bricks.[217] Part of the original mosaic floor, from the eastern corner of the north aisle, was excavated in 1930; covered with a simple geometric pattern and made of terra cotta, marble, and limestone, it has affinities with contemporary floor mosaics in Ravenna, Pesaro, and elsewhere.[218]

Agnellus reports the dedicatory inscription in the vault of the apse:

Having received benefits (*beneficia*) of the archangel Michael, Bacauda and Julian have made from the foundations and dedicated [this church] on 7 May, the fourth year after the consulship of Basilius the younger *vir clarissimus* consul, in the 8th indiction [the year 545].

Agnellus claims that Bacauda was the son-in-law of Julian and that he was buried in a nearby tower, but in fact we know nothing about him, although two men with this name are known to have been political appointees of Theoderic.[219] Nor do we know why he and Julian together might have sponsored this church, although it came about because they both attributed some act of beneficence to St. Michael. The inscription is curious because no bishop is mentioned as having consecrated the church; and indeed there was no bishop of Ravenna in May of 545.[220] As already noted, this church was hastily built and seems to have been hastily dedicated. What might have been the need for such haste? I would suggest that the hazard from which Michael preserved these two men was the plague, which struck Ravenna in 543 or shortly afterward.[221]

St. Michael the archangel was known by the mid–sixth century as a healing saint and his shrines in Phrygia were famous for their healing miracles.[222] Since the time of Constantine many churches and shrines had been dedicated to Michael in and around Constantinople and Justinian rebuilt and enlarged three of them.[223] Veneration of Michael appears in Italy in the late fifth century: Pope Symmachus (498–514) enlarged a church dedicated to St. Michael in Rome, and other churches dedicated to the archangel existed by the late sixth century in Perugia, Naples, and Monte Gargano (the latter, according to later legend, existed from 492).[224] Our church in Ravenna belongs in this same period. Although the story that St. Michael saved Rome from the plague of 590 seems to date only to the thirteenth century,[225] Justinian's reconstructions are suggestive of one reason for the archangel's popularity in the mid–sixth century. As we will see, the mosaic imagery in San Michele indicates that it was indeed a church dedicated in the wake of the plague of 543.[226]

The mosaics of San Michele have a remarkable history. Upon their removal in 1844, they were taken to Venice, where the mosaic restorer Giovanni Moro made a reproduction based on drawings and some original fragments. In 1904 this restoration was installed in the Kaiser-Friedrich-Museum in Berlin (now called the Bode Museum),[227] where it remains to-day (Fig. 89). The only surviving original fragments from this church are the heads of two angels now in the Museo Provinciale in Torcello and the head of a beardless Christ in the Victoria and Albert Museum in London.[228] The mosaics in Berlin were, for most of the twentieth century, considered to be

89. San Michele *in Africisco*, reconstructed mosaic of the apse and triumphal arch, now in the Skulpturensammlung und Museum für Byzantinische Kunst, Staatliche Museen zu Berlin, Berlin, Germany (courtesy Bildarchiv Preussischer Kulturbesitz / Art Resource, NY)

the restored originals, and only a study by I. Andreescu-Treadgold in 1988 revealed that the entire work in Berlin was a reproduction.[229] Nevertheless, this reproduction was based on drawings made as early as Ciampini's *Vetera Monimenta* of 1699, as well as drawings made in situ before the removal.[230] We can thus say a few things about the iconography found in the church, even if details should not be considered reliable.[231]

The surviving mosaics covered the vault of the apse and the upper part of the triumphal arch (Fig. 89). In the apse, a beardless Christ, dressed in a purple tunic and mantle with a halo inscribed with a jeweled cross,[232] held in his right hand a processional cross and in his left an open book that bore the inscription, "Whoever has seen me has seen the Father: I and the Father are one" (a conflation of John 14:9 and 10:30).[233] Flanking Christ and facing him stood the archangels Michael (left, but Christ's right) and Gabriel, labeled by name; each was dressed in a white tunic and mantle with *clavi*, was winged, and held in his left hand a staff, with his right hand raised in a gesture of blessing or acclamation. All three figures stood on a narrow grassy landscape strewn with flowers, against a solid gold background. The apse was bordered by a band of acanthus leaves and doves with the Lamb of God in a medallion in the center; the sections of the triumphal arch were surrounded by bands of blue and white gems against a red field. On the haunches of the triumphal arch that flank the apse stood Sts. Cosmas (left) and Damian (right); above the apse vault, in the center, was a bearded Christ seated on a throne and holding a book, flanked again by two archangels and then on either side by three and four angelic figures blowing long trumpets, all standing with their feet partly hidden by red and blue clouds.

Many aspects of these mosaics are similar to other contemporary examples from Ravenna. A triumphal Christ holding a book and processional cross is also seen in the narthex of the *capella arcivescovile*.[234] The angels flanking Christ are similar to those found in Sant'Apollinare Nuovo from the Ostrogothic period, and also from the apse of San Vitale, where in both cases they form part of a heavenly court. The presence of a beardless Christ, a lamb, and a bearded Christ likewise reflects imagery in those two churches, especially in San Vitale, and may, as proposed by C. Rizzardi, reflect two concepts of Christ found in the Book of Revelation.[235] The landscape in the apse, representing paradise, is very similar to those in San Vitale and Sant'Apollinare in Classe. Sts. Cosmas and Damian, whose cult had recently been introduced into Italy, are also found in the mosaics of the *capella arcivescovile*. The archangels Gabriel and Michael are found in Sant'Apollinare in Classe. There are also many similarities between this mosaic and those in the Basilica Eufrasiana in Poreč, both in the layout and in the figures of archangels flanking the throne.[236]

Interpretations of the meaning of these mosaics usually focus on their anti-Arian, Trinitarian content.[237] The inscription in the book held by Christ conflates two passages from John that were used by Orthodox theologians to argue for the consubstantiality of the Son and the Father.[238] The juxtaposed images of Christ, with two facial types but dressed the same way, emphasize his divinity and his identity with the Father, as does the apocalyptic imagery of the triumphal arch.[239]

While anti-Arian imagery is *de rigueur* in Justinianic buildings in Ravenna, it is likely that these images were also closely related to the reason for the church's foundation. As already noted, St. Michael was venerated as a healer in the sixth century, and Sts. Cosmas and Damian, depicted on the triumphal arch, were also medical saints.[240] This cluster of healing saints must surely be related to the danger through which Julian and Bacauda had passed. In Revelation 12:7 the archangel Michael and his armies battle the dragon, a creature that in the sixth century had become a metaphor for plague.[241] Moreover, the angels with trumpets must be the ones described in the Book of Revelation (see chs. 8–10),[242] in which the trumpet of the sixth angel releases afflictions (*plagae*) that kill a third of the earth's people, and is to be followed by the seventh trumpet announcing the Last Judgment. Thus, imagery derived from the Book of Revelation is certainly suitable for a church erected after the epidemic of 543–4, dedicated in thanksgiving to the archangel Michael.

ST. STEPHEN

Maximian is famous today for the churches he completed and dedicated; but Agnellus praises him especially for the church that he built entirely himself, dedicated to St. Stephen.[243] We learn that this church was large and splendidly decorated, and it is all the more remarkable, then, that we know absolutely nothing about it outside of Agnellus's text.[244] It seems to have been in excellent repair in the ninth century, but no later documents mention it or its location. No fragments of marble or other materials are assigned to this church; no location has been identified for it; no excavations have revealed any part of it. As we see what Agnellus says, we will see how remarkable this is.

The church of St. Stephen was located "not far from the *posterula Ovilionis*," thus in the northwest corner of the city, somewhere around Santa Croce. It thus formed part of the large ecclesiastical complex that had been growing up in this area since the time of Ecclesius. Agnellus gives the dedication inscription for the church:

> In honor of holy and most blessed first martyr Stephen, Bishop Maximian, servant of Christ, by God's grace built this church from the foundations and dedicated it on 11 Dec. in the fourteenth indiction, in the ninth year after the consulship of Basilius the younger [the year 550].

In the dedicatory poem found around the border of the triumphal arch, we learn that "when the gleaming moon was new for the eleventh time, the church which had been begun shines established in beautiful completion"; in other words, the whole church was completed in eleven months. Agnellus goes on to tell a story of how the workmen couldn't build the church until Maximian gave them materials; this may have been invented by Agnellus to explain the inscription. In any case, these eleven months would include the time after the completion and dedication of Sant'Apollinare in Classe. We assume that this church was a basilica because of Agnellus's mention of a *cameris tribuna* (his term for "apse") and of columns. Maximian attached smaller chapels (*monasteria*) to the north and south sides of the church (one is specifically described as *parte virorum*, thus on the south).

As for the decoration, Agnellus tells us that Maximian "furnished it most beautifully, and in the vault of the apse his image is fixed in multi-colored mosaic, and is surrounded by wonderful glass-work." We must thus imagine an image of Maximian, perhaps presenting the church to Christ, like the image of Ecclesius in San Vitale. The chapels "all appear marvelously with new gold mosaics and various other stones fixed in plaster," obviously another splendid presentation. Maximian's monograms appear on the capitals, again like the monograms of Victor in San Vitale. One gets the feeling that after completing San Vitale, Maximian wanted to have a church with his stamp all over it!

Finally, Agnellus says that Maximian gathered together the relics of the following twenty saints and martyrs and placed them in the church: Peter, Paul, Andrew, Zacharias, John the Baptist, John the Evangelist, James, Thomas, Matthew, Stephen, Vincent, Lawrence, Quirinus, Florian, Emilian, Apollinaris, Agatha, Euphemia, Agnes, and Eugenia. This list is so precise that it must come from a source in the church, and while it could have been a list or inscription, it is tempting to think that these saints may have been pictured (perhaps in medallions? perhaps in procession along the walls of the nave?) in the church.

OTHER CHURCHES

Several other churches in and around Ravenna are said by Agnellus to have been restored in this period and some others are mentioned by him under circumstances that make it likely they were built in the later sixth century. At some point prior to 560 a church was built in honor of Sts. John and Paul in the northwestern part of the *oppidum*. In this church the poet Venantius Fortunatus, praying in front of an image of St. Martin, was cured of an eye affliction, as he records in his poem about the life of that saint.[245] The existence of the church is also confirmed by an inscription on its ambo which dates to 596, now in the Museo Arcivescovile; the church on the site today is medieval.[246] Another church built at this time is mentioned in a papyrus document dating to the year 546, which lists the donation of property to a *basilica sancti Victoris Rav(ennae)*; Agnellus mentions the "porta sancti Victoris" in the Life of Maximian as located near the northern wall of the city, just east of the Padenna.[247] Remains of a medieval church with this dedication existed in this location until World War II.

Archbishop Maximian restored a church of St. Andrew which was located in the *regio Herculana*, thus in the old *oppidum* south of the *fossa Amnis*, not far from the cathedral.[248] According to Agnellus, "having removed the old wooden columns made of nut trees, he [Maximian] filled the church with columns of Proconnesian marble."[249] The church was completely rebuilt around the year 1000; studies in the 1820s showed that an earlier church had been built on top of older Roman buildings dating from the first to the fifth century, but there is no evidence for the original date of the church.[250] It was a basilica with, oddly, its apse oriented to the north; it is possible that it was originally a Roman building that was reused.[251] The eleventh-century basilica was 40 meters long and 20 meters wide, with a triumphal arch supported on columns like San Giovanni Evangelista, and a colonnade of nine columns per side. Ten of the columns were of Proconnesian marble and two of *cipollino rosso* from Iasos (as in San Vitale); the impost capitals featured *à jour* carving, and other marble fragments indicate that the impost blocks had the monogram of Maximian on them.[252] There is no evidence in Italy for churches with columns of wood,[253] but it seems likely that Maximian set up the columns. Perhaps a predecessor started the church and he had to finish it.

We should not forget that in these years, Archbishop Agnellus sponsored major modifications to the mosaics of Sant'Apollinare Nuovo. Agnellus also rebuilt parts of Sant'Agata, which dated originally the late fifth century, where he had served as deacon and where he was later buried.[254] A colonnaded atrium was added, the apse and vault were completely rebuilt using Julian bricks and *tubi fittili* filled with mortar, as in San Michele *in Africisco*, and chambers flanking the apse were added, accessed from the aisles.[255] The apse later fell in an earthquake in 1688; fragments of polychrome stucco and *opus sectile* have been found in excavations.[256] A drawing made a few years before the earthquake, when the mosaic was already in ruins, depicts a bearded Christ seated on a throne with a cross-halo, holding a closed book in his left hand and gesturing with his right, flanked by angels, against a gold background, with a landscape along the bottom.[257] The image was thus similar to the Christs on the nave wall of Sant'Apollinare Nuovo and in the apse of San Michele *in Africisco*.[258] Bishop John I had been buried in Sant'Agata in the late fifth century, and he was now depicted in the lower part of the apse, in the act of saying mass; thus the reconstruction by Agnellus was part of the general trend of valorizing earlier bishops of Ravenna.[259] An ambo and other fragments of carved marble dating to the sixth century also survive from in Sant'Agata.

Church Building in Classe

Classe continued to thrive in the late sixth century, at least as far as we can tell from the evidence of church building there. Construction continued at the Petriana complex: Archbishop Agnellus oversaw the mosaic decoration of two *monasteria*, or small chapels, attached to the Petriana baptistery and dedicated to St. Matthew and St. James. The inscription attributes the decoration to servants of God "who were lost and found again with the aid of God," perhaps a reference to the war or the reconversion of Arians to Orthodoxy.[260] Peter III, Agnellus's successor, was buried in the chapel of St. James in a Proconnesian marble sarcophagus.[261] Work also continued on the church at the Ca'Bianca; the second building phase consisted of external porticoes along the aisles and apsed chambers and their eastern ends.[262] A monastery dedicated to Sts. John and Stephen was the subject of a jurisdictional dispute at the time of Pope Gregory I and is mentioned in two of his letters; Agnellus says that it was "located across Caesarea in the former city of Classe."[263]

In addition to these structures, a number of large, richly decorated basilicas were built in and around Classe to honor Ravenna's earliest bishops. While Apollinaris had been venerated at least since the time of Peter Chrysologus, we hear nothing about the sanctity of Eleuchadius, Probus, and Severus until their churches were constructed, although in some cases we learn that smaller chapels existed on the site. San Severo was built within the walls of Classe, but the others formed a group 1 kilometers south of that city's walls on the site of former Roman cemeteries. Visitors to Ravenna would have passed this imposing complex on their way north along the *via Popilia* and their first impression of the city would be the antiquity and importance of Ravenna's bishops.

ST. PROBUS, ST. ELEUCHADIUS, AND ST. EUPHEMIA AD MARE

Several of the Ravenna's earliest bishops are said by Agnellus to have been buried in basilicas to the south of Classe.[264] Six early bishops were buried in a basilica dedicated to St. Probus, the seventh bishop in Agnellus's list; St. Eleuchadius, the fourth bishop, along with two of his successors, was buried in a basilica that bore his name, which later documents imply was located next to the basilica of St. Probus.[265] Both of these churches disappeared after the thirteenth century, although a ninth-century *ciborium* from St. Eleuchadius still survives in Sant'Apollinare in Classe (Fig. 104).[266] The earliest *vitae* of these saints date to the late tenth century when the relics were translated to the Ursiana and are based on the *LPR*;[267] it is impossible to know why these particular saints were deemed worthy of basilicas in the sixth century or whether their veneration began earlier than this.

Agnellus says that the church of St. Probus was next to the narthex of St. Euphemia *ad mare*, which was demolished in his day, and one stade (approximately 180 m) south of Sant'Apollinare in Classe.[268] Maximian is said to have decorated St. Euphemia with mosaic and to have "preserved the body of blessed Probus with the other bodies of the holy bishops with aromatics and placed them fittingly, and on the facade of that church he decorated the images of blessed Probus and Eleuchadius and Calocerus with various mosaics, and under their feet you will find . . ." (the inscription is unfortunately lost from the manuscript of the *LPR*).[269] The fact that Probus and Eleuchadius were depicted on the same church is confusing, unless the bishops were buried in separate chapels attached to a larger basilica. The relationship of St. Euphemia is also confusing, although it was obviously a different structure.

In the 1950s, from 1964–7, and again in the early 1970s, a site 180 m southeast of Sant'Apollinare in Classe was investigated by various types of excavation (Fig. 1). G. Cortesi, who conducted the twentieth-century excavations, reconstructed the plan of a very large building, 70×32 m, which is larger than any of the known basilicas in the area. An apsed chapel extended to the south, apparently added in a second stage of construction, while additional small rooms were clustered to the west of the atrium. No dates beyond very general ones in the fifth and sixth century were obtained.[270] Cortesi subsequently proposed that the building had not been a basilica church but a large U-shaped building of a type known in Rome as a *coemeterium*, or funerary basilica.[271] Both proposals seem very unlikely, and, in fact, Cortesi excavated only a very small part of the complex. Until further excavations can be carried out, all that can be said is that the structure was large and elaborate.[272]

Finally, Agnellus adds the odd statement about the church of St. Probus: "And in no churches inside the city of Ravenna or Classe is the mass celebrated over the people except in this one alone."[273] The mention of the *missa super populum* suggests that an older liturgical practice was maintained only in this basilica, but it is not clear what the phrase means. A. Testi-Rasponi suggested that it refers to a prayer said by the bishop over the people, the *oratio super populum* known from liturgical manuscripts, while G. Gerola noted that elsewhere Agnellus says the bishop stands "before the altar" (*ante altare*) during the mass, hence with his back to the congregation, and explains the *missa super populum* as meaning that the bishop faced the congregation only in St. Probus.[274] However, theories derived from this suggesting that St. Probus was the "first cathedral" of Ravenna are entirely unfounded.[275]

SANT'APOLLINARE IN CLASSE

The centerpiece of Christian worship in the Classe region, both geographically and symbolically, was the church dedicated to the first bishop of Ravenna, St. Apollinaris.[276] Peter Chrysologus devoted a sermon to his saintly predecessor,[277] and there may already have been a shrine to him at the site when Bishop Ursicinus (533–6) decided to build a large basilica in his honor.[278] The site was the location of one of Classe's many Roman-era cemeteries, and so it is entirely possible that, sometime in the second century, Ravenna's first bishop had been buried there.[279] The early sixth century was a time in which many episcopal sees contructed histories in which the legend of the founding bishop was a key part of claims to antiquity. Ursicinus's foundation took place in this atmosphere during the reign of Amalasuintha and thus before Ravenna's see was elevated to archiepiscopal status. Certainly Maximian enthusiastically continued and expanded Ursicinus's original concept to create an imposing shrine to the memory of Ravenna's episcopal leaders.[280]

In the mid–sixth century Apollinaris was revered as Ravenna's founding bishop, and it was only later that he acquired the status of a martyr. This may have resulted from a misinterpretation of Peter Chrysologus's sermon, which first says that Apollinaris is Ravenna's only martyr, but then says that he deserves the title of martyr even though he did not die of wounds inflicted on him; in other words, he was *not* a martyr.[281] The inscription on his tomb, set up at the time of Maximian, calls him "priest (*sacerdos*) and confessor," and in the apse of the church, as we will see, he is not depicted receiving a crown, as would have been usual for a martyr.[282] By the ninth century, however, Apollinaris was considered a martyr. Agnellus took his version of the story of the saint from a text known as the *Passio S. Apollinaris*, in which the saint's martyrdom is narrated. There has been considerable scholarly discussion about the date of the *Passio*, but since some of its details differ from those commemorated by Maximian in other contexts, it seems most likely that it was written in the seventh century during the autocephaly controversy.[283]

As one of the most important churches of Ravenna, Sant'Apollinare in Classe has a history of almost constant additions, modifications, and restorations; at the same time, its location far to the south of the city of Ravenna has meant that it was notably subject to depradation and neglect, especially after the decline of the city of Classe in the eighth century. The very fact that it survived at all, when none of the other churches in or outside of Classe did, is an indication of its unique importance.[284]

Archbishops from the late sixth century onward were buried in Apollinaris's church, and Archbishop John II (578–95) and the exarch Smaragdus built and decorated with mosaics a chapel dedicated to Sts. Mark, Marcellus, and Felicula, Roman saints whose relics, according to the poem on its facade, were donated by Pope Gregory I. This is thought to have been a chamber at the southern end of the narthex that was completely destroyed in the nineteenth century.[285] In the late seventh century, Archbishop Maurus translated the body of the saint from the narthex to the center of the church (*in medio templi*), and his successor Reparatus made important modifications to the apse and its mosaics.[286] Archbishop Damian (692–708) donated an episcopal throne that stood at the back of the apse. A ring crypt was constructed in the apse at an unknown date, perhaps under Maurus or perhaps in the Carolingian period.[287] The roof and narthex were renovated between 810–16 under the sponsorship of Pope Leo III.[288]

Muslim raiders sacked Classe in the mid–ninth century, and Sant'-Apollinare in Classe must have been a primary target, since subsequently Apollinaris's relics are said to have been moved to Sant'Apollinare Nuovo inside Ravenna's walls. The church was not abandoned, however, since a campanile was built perhaps in the tenth century on the north side of the nave. About 1000 a Ravennate noble named Romuald entered the reformed

Benedictine monastery at Sant'Apollinare in Classe, although he later left and eventually founded a new order of Benedictine monks, the Camaldolesians. Sant'Apollinare in Classe became one of the main churches of Romuald's order in 1138, and a major series of alterations are documented in 1173–4, when the relics of the saint were supposedly rediscovered under the altar in Classe.[289] At some point the floor level was raised by approximately 44 cm.

Despite the presence of a monastic community, by 1258 the church's fabric was reported to be in bad condition, and around 1450 much of the marble from the basilica, including the wall revetment, *opus sectile* from wall and floors, and furnishings were carried to Rimini by Sigismondo Malatesta, where they can still be seen as part of the Tempio Malatestiano. During the Battle of Ravenna of 1512 the abbot was killed while defending his monastery, which was subsequently plundered again, after which the monks abandoned the site for the safety of Ravenna. They took the relics with them, and they were only returned in 1654. A new wave of renovations lasted most of the eighteenth century and included the current wall revetment in the apse and the plaster and painted medallions with the portraits of Ravenna's bishops in the nave and aisles. However, when Ravenna became part of Napoleon's empire, the monastery was dissolved in 1797 and affairs reached a low point, with grass growing in the nave, green mold on the marble, and windows either blocked up or exposed to the elements. Restoration activity began in 1870 and took off under the leadership of Corrado Ricci after 1897. The atrium was excavated, the narthex and parts of the nave walls rebuilt, but then the church suffered further damage in World War II. Excavations were undertaken as part of a second wave of restorations after 1949, the apse and narthex were excavated in the 1970s and 1980s, and work has continued on both the buildings and mosaics up to the present.[290]

Architecture and Sculpture. Sant'Apollinare in Classe is, as E. Russo has called it, "the Parthenon of wooden-roofed basilicas," the largest and grandest still surviving in the Ravenna area.[291] Located directly east of the *via Popilia*, which determined the orientation of the site, the basilica was originally preceded by a narthex that had rectangular towers to the north and south (today the southern one is gone and the current narthex and northern tower were completely reconstructed in 1908–9 (Fig. 90).[292] By the ninth century, at least, the road seems to have deviated from its original route and a colonnaded atrium (32 × 24.50 meters) had been built in front of the narthex.[293] A curious feature, known only in this basilica, is the presence of small semicircular niches at the western end of the aisles, just inside the entrance, whose purpose is unknown.

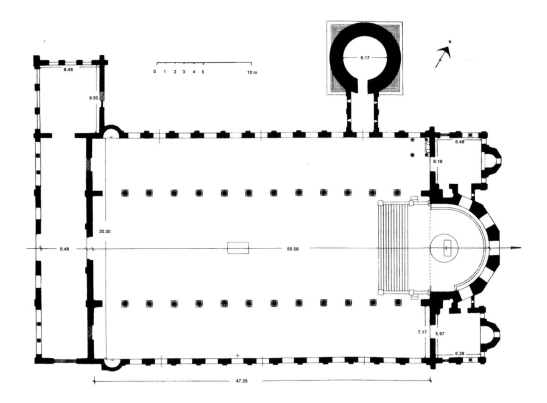

90. Sant'-Apollinare in Classe, plan, including the later campanile on the north side (after Mazzotti, 1954)

The church proper consists of a nave with single aisles separated by arcades of twelve columns. In addition to the three doors leading from the narthex into the nave and aisles, this church also had three doors each on the north and south exterior walls of the aisles.[294] At the eastern end of the church is the apse, polygonal externally and circular on the interior. Flanking the apse are square, apsed chambers, accessed both from the aisles and from the exterior of the church and provided with numerous windows. Two small rooms were squeezed in between each chamber and the apse, the western of which was two storied and not visible from inside or outside the church; these spaces, like the ones in the *capella arcivescovile*, may have been used for secreting church treasure.[295] The plan, a basilica with chambers flanking the narthex and the apse, is very similar to that of San Giovanni Evangelista, and it is likely that imitation of the earlier basilica was intentional.[296]

The church was built of Julian bricks, using masonry techniques that are almost identical to those used in San Vitale.[297] On the exterior, the surface of the walls was articulated by pilasters that formed an arcade surrounding the windows, as was usual in most Ravennate churches (Fig. 91). As in San Vitale, the apse was vaulted with brick rather than with *tubi fittili*.

91. Sant'-Apollinare in Classe, view of the exterior from the southeast (photo C. L. Striker)

Today the apse is raised over the crypt, approached by a large staircase that was built in 1723 (Pl. VIIIa). Originally, the floor level, as in other late antique basilicas, would have been at most a step or two above the level of the nave. Excavations have revealed a large bema, or platform, that originally extended from the apse almost 12 meters into the nave, which would have been surrounded by *transennae*. Three fragments of floor mosaic have been excavated inside the church. Those found in the nave were 35 centimeters higher than those in the aisles, although there is no evidence that they represent a repaving, so it is possible that originally the nave floor was higher than the aisles.[298] The mosaic fragment from the western part of the southern aisle includes a fragment of an inscription commemorating a donation by secular figures, and Agnellus reports that the epitaph of Maurus was likewise made of mosaic in the floor.[299]

As at San Vitale, Sant'Apollinare in Classe required shiploads of marble imported from the Sea of Marmara. Agnellus comments about Sant'-Apollinare in Classe: "No church in any part of Italy is similar to this one in precious stones, since they glow at night almost as much as they do during the day."[300] Indeed the nave arcade is made of some of the most spectacular Proconnesian marble columns to have survived anywhere (Fig. 75). The horizontal swirls of the veins are matched by the swirling nature of the composite windblown acanthus capitals, also of Proconnesian marble and carved with very delicate details. The fact that they show no signs of shipping damage indicates that they must have been carved on the site (Fig. 92).[301] The impost blocks are plain, decorated with crosses in shallow

92. Sant'-Apollinare in Classe, column capital of the composite wind-blown acanthus type (photo C. L. Striker)

relief, but the column bases, unlike others in Ravenna, are decorated on all four sides with geometric designs (Fig. 75). Originally the walls of the aisles, the apse, and the west wall were covered with Proconnesian marble wall revetment. Finally, the large marble sarcophagi that today line the walls of the aisles were moved here from the narthex, and most of them contained the bodies of Ravenna's archbishops (Fig. 102).[302]

The glow reported by Agnellus may also have been due to the ample light that flooded the basilica. The apse has five large windows; in addition, twelve large windows are found both at ground level and above the nave arcade on each side of the building. When they were being restored to their original form in 1899, wooden frames for rectangular glass panes were found in two of them, dating perhaps to the original building.[303] The basilica was thus full of light, which reflected off the polished marble and the sparkling glass tesserae of the mosaics, creating dazzling effects.

93. Sant'-Apollinare in Classe, view of the apse and triumphal arch

Mosaics. Although Sant'Apollinare in Classe almost certainly had mosaic decoration on its nave walls, today only the mosaics of the triumphal arch and apse have survived. Although these have been damaged and heavily restored (in the 1970s red mosaic lines were added to indicate which portions of the mosaic were original),[304] we have a good idea of their

94. Sinopie (underdrawing) from the lower apse wall of Sant'Apollinare in Classe, today in the Museo Nazionale, Ravenna (courtesy Soprintendenza per i Beni Architettonici e Paesaggistici di Ravenna [MiBAC-ITALIA])

original iconography and style. Moreover, during restorations undertaken in 1948–9 and 1970–3, some of the apse mosaics were removed, revealing the walls underneath, on which were sketched in red paint the outlines of a mosaic design (Fig. 94). A wooden peg sticking out at the center of the medallion served to mark the center of the vault during the mosaic's construction.[305] Remarkably, the sketch on the lower part of the apse did not correspond to the extant mosaic, indicating that at some point the design was changed. This *sinopie* represents the only evidence we have for workshop procedures from this period and for the aims and interests of mosaic designers, which heightens the importance of this church and its decorative program.

While the mosaic program in the apse vault dates to the mid–sixth century, other surviving mosaics in the church were made later (Fig. 93). The mosaics of the triumphal arch were largely made or remade between the seventh and the twelfth centuries, except for two panels that depict the archangels, which appear to belong to the original program. The upper levels, in particular, may date to the rebuilding of the roof in the ninth century or may belong to the seventh century.[306] The mosaics on the lower side-walls of the apse also date to the late seventh century or later and are heavily restored. What we do not know is what was originally on those surfaces. It is possible that when the mosaics were remade the designers were reproducing the original design, at least to some degree. In any case, the later mosaics reflect motifs and iconographical details found in Ravenna's great fifth- and sixth-century churches.

The Triumphal Arch. In the top zone in the center is a medallion with a bearded, haloed Christ dressed in purple, holding a book in his left hand and making a gesture of blessing with his right (Fig. 93). The medallion is set against a dark blue background that is filled with red and blue clouds, and floating in these clouds are the winged, haloed upper torsos of the four beasts that symbolize the evangelists, holding their books: from the left John's eagle, Matthew's man, Mark's lion, and Luke's ox. Below this zone, the arch of the apse has been cleverly utilized as a mountain, on the green flanks of which stand twelve sheep, proceeding from the walled cities of Jerusalem on the left and Bethlehem on the right. The gold sky above them is likewise filled with divine clouds. On the haunches of the arch are date palms (almost entirely restored in 1906–7), and on the sides of the vertical part of the apse are the archangels Michael and Gabriel holding banners on which are written (in Latin) the Greek words "agios agios agios" (Holy, Holy, Holy), a reference to the heavenly hosts of which they are the leaders.[307] The angels date to the mid-sixth century and are dressed not in white, as in all the other depictions of them in Ravenna, but in the imperial

95. Sant'-Apollinare in Classe, the Transfiguration mosaic in the apse vault: medallion flanked by Moses, Isaiah, the Hand of God (above), and three sheep representing apostles (photo S. H. Mauskopf)

costume of white tunic, purple *chlamys*, and red shoes.[308] Below them busts of the evangelists Matthew and Luke were made in the twelfth century. We have seen the four evangelist symbols appear in the mausoleum of Galla Placidia and the *capella arcivescovile*, the clouds in San Michele *in Africisco* and San Vitale, the sheep proceeding from the holy cities in San Vitale, and the archangels in several churches. We cannot say, therefore, whether the artists of later centuries were inspired by mosaics from other Ravennate churches or from the original concepts in this church.

Apse Vault. The vault of the apse contains a striking and completely original design (Pl. VIIIb). The central element is a medallion containing a jeweled gold cross with a tiny bearded bust of Christ at its center and the words ΙΧΘΥΣ above and SALVS MVNDI below it (Fig. 95). The cross is set against a light blue sky set with ninety-nine gold stars,[309] the alpha and omega, and is surrounded by a red and gold jeweled border. The whole medallion floats in a scene that is half gold sky and half green landscape. Above the cross, the Hand of God points down toward it, and divine clouds fill the gold background. Floating in this sky are two male figures depicted from the waist up, wearing tunics and mantles that float in the breeze: on the left, youthful and beardless, is Moses (labeled MOYSES) and on the right, with white hair and beard, is Elijah (labeled HbELYAS). Their right hands gesture toward the cross. Standing in the upper part of the landscape and gazing up at the cross are three sheep, one on the left and two on the right. The entire scene is a very curious depiction of the Transfiguration, the event described in the Gospels (Matt. 17:1–9, Mark 9:2–8, Luke 9:28–36). In the narrative, Jesus takes his disciples Peter, James, and John up Mt. Tabor, is transfigured (his face and his white garments radiate light), and speaks to Moses and Elijah, after which they are overshadowed by a bright cloud and spoken to by God the Father, who says, "This is my Son, whom I love; with him I am well pleased. Listen to him!" In this mosaic, the three disciple-witnesses are shown as sheep, and instead of a glowing Christ we have the cross in the medallion.

Gospel figures are not the only witnesses to this Transfiguration: below the medallion stands the titular saint of the church, Apollinaris, dressed as an archbishop in a gold chasuble, white robe, and *pallium*, with white tonsured hair and beard,[310] identified by name as SANCTVS APOLENARIS. He stands with both arms raised in a gesture of prayer, the pose adopted by the bishop at the beginning of the Eucharistic ceremony.[311] However, Apollinaris does not look up at the Transfiguration scene or the cross, but out into the church. He is flanked on the baseline of the vault by twelve more sheep, separated by clusters of white lilies with red roses under their feet; the number 12 implies the apostles, but since three of the apostles are also depicted above, these sheep may be intended to represent Apollinaris's congregation.[312] Peter Chrysologus, in his sermon on Apollinaris, says, "behold as a good shepherd he stands in the midst of his flock," and this seems to have been the effect intended by the mosaic's creators. The effectiveness of the image can be seen in a story told by Agnellus, in which Ravenna's clergy flee to Classe and implore their founder to save them from a rapacious bishop: "Holy Peter gave you to us as a shepherd. Therefore we are your sheep."[313] All the figures stand in a landscape that is filled with rocks, rather fantastic trees, and a variety of birds. Different shades of green also add variety and texture to the scene. The arch of the apse is filled with a pattern of geometric and floral elements and birds that was made in the seventh century.[314]

Restorations of the apse mosaics in 1948–9 and 1970–2 revealed the underdrawings, or *sinopie* that represent the original design of these mosaics, painted directly on the bricks (Fig. 94).[315] Today these drawings, carefully removed, can be viewed in the Museo Nazionale in Ravenna. On the upper part of the apse the dimensions of the medallion with the cross were lightly sketched, although when it was actually made in mosaic it was 10 cm larger than the drawing. No *sinopie* were found under the other elements of the Transfiguration scene, so we may wonder whether originally the meaning of the cross was something different. On the lower part of the wall, the sketches show that originally there was to be another cross in the center, flanked by peacocks, birds confronting vases, and plants, and a border above and below, all motifs known from other mosaic and sculpted images in Ravenna.[316]

It is likely that this lower decoration was never executed in mosaic, but that the plan was changed, perhaps by Victor or Maximian, both of whom recognized the potential for visually enhancing the episcopal ideology of this church.[317] We will return to this question in the next section.

Many of the iconographical elements, symbols, and themes in this mosaic can be compared to those from other contemporary monuments. The Transfiguration appears in other apse mosaics of this period; the only one that survives is the example in the church in the monastery of St. Catherine at Sinai in Egypt, sponsored by Justinian.[318] The Sinai mosaic, however, does not include any extra figures and features a conventional image of Christ at the center, as do almost all later images of the scene.[319] Two-zone compositions in which the figures in the lower zone look up at a divine event above are depicted on small *ampullae*, or flasks for holding holy liquids, from the Holy Land that date to the fifth and sixth centuries and may reflect large-scale works of art at the major pilgrimage sites there.[320] Jeweled crosses were a common motif in late antique art, and we have already seen several examples in Ravenna; a jeweled cross was also an actual object present in churches and used in liturgical processions.[321] Notwithstanding these similarities, no other representation offers this particular combination of elements which has led scholars to argue that there must be some particular theological meaning attached to it.[322]

Many scholars have attempted to explain the meaning of Sant'Apollinare in Classe's apse mosaic by emphasizing its eschatological, visionary, or liturgical dimensions, usually by referring to patristic exegesis.[323] Thus, for example, the substitution of the cross for Christ can be read as emphasizing the connections between the Transfiguration and the Crucifixion; as alluding, along with the paradisiacal landscape, to the Transfiguration as the prefiguration of the Second Coming; as representing Christ's overall history; and/or as reflecting the cross that stood on the altar during the performance of the liturgy.[324] In fact, just as in biblical exegesis, there are numerous possible interpretations, any and all of which may be viable. It may not be possible to know what the mosaic's creators intended when they designed it; and in fact, as we have seen, parts of the design were significantly modified during the course of the work. Based on the evidence from the *sinopie*, it seems that originally the designers had planned a central cross flanked by figures, perhaps Apollinaris and a founder-bishop, with an abstract design below. When the plan was changed to emphasize Apollinaris, someone came up with the clever idea of using the cross as the focal point of a Transfiguration scene, a subject that was gaining popularity in Justinian's empire. The result was a vertical axis (Apollinaris praying to the cross) and a horizontal axis (the Transfiguration), with the cross as the link between the two. Whichever theological meaning was intended initially, surely the designers would have welcomed the multitude of meanings generated by different viewers.

As with other mid–sixth-century Orthodox churches, some motifs in Sant'Apollinare's mosaics may represent a specifically anti-Arian theology, although here this theme seems more muted than in some of the other churches. While the Transfiguration can represent the moment of consubstantiality between the Father and the Son,[325] the Arians probably interpreted God's words on Mt. Tabor as depicting Christ's lesser status, since God has to tell the apostles to listen to him. There are certainly groups of threes: three hands gesturing to the cross in the apse, three sheep, three figures at the altar in the right panel (although these may not be original), but they do not seem overt. The archangels on the triumphal arch hold banners with the Trisagion prayer (Holy, Holy, Holy), also perhaps Trinitarian and representative of the eastern Liturgy.[326] As we have seen for San Vitale, the three Old Testament figures at the altar all relate to the Epistle to the Hebrews. Overall, however, anti-Arian theology does not seem to play a prominent role in this church.

Apse Window Zone. The mosaics of the window zone of this church highlight the various roles of the bishops of Ravenna, as befits a church dedicated to their founder.[327] Within the soffits and jambs of the window arches are mosaic columns and geometric borders, now remade on the basis of fragments found there. Between the five windows we find four notable bishops of Ravenna, labeled by name (Fig. 96): from left to right, these are Ecclesius, Sanctus Severus, Sanctus Ursus, and Ursicinus. Each is dressed like Apollinaris above and holds a jeweled book in his left hand, while his right is raised in blessing. Severus and Ursus, identified as "sanctus," stand in a niches flanked by jeweled columns, surmounted by gold conches, beneath which are suspended curtains and votive crowns; Ecclesius and Ursicinus have the same frames, but their columns are brown and their conches are green. Certainly the presence of four bishops holding books must be intended to evoke the four evangelists.[328] But why these four bishops? Maximian, who was well versed in the history of the see, must have selected them as his most notable predecessors; the presence of historical and contemporary bishops, along with the founder St. Apollinaris, all wearing the *pallium*, provides an abbreviated history of the see, linking the great bishops of the past to the present. Ursus was the founder of the cathedral, but not otherwise venerated, as far as we know; Severus's cult was obviously growing, as he would be honored with his own church at the end of the century. Ursicinus was the founder of the church, and his predecessor Ecclesius was clearly seen at this time as a major figure, although we have no information linking him directly with this church.[329] Why was Peter

96. Sant'-Apollinare in Classe, St. Apollinaris and (left to right) Bishops Ecclesius, St. Severus, St. Ursus, and Ursicinus

Chrysologus not represented? Perhaps in the sixth century he was not as famous locally as he would later become; his collection of sermons was only edited and published by Archbishop Felix in the early eighth century, and Agnellus wrote the first version of his biography in the ninth.

The two panels on the outmost walls of the apse were made, or remade, in the seventh century or later.[330] We do not know whether similar representations were here originally, but it seems that the later artists took their inspiration from the mosaics of San Vitale.[331] These mosaics have also been heavily restored.[332] On the left wall, we see a scene set between jeweled columns with an open curtain behind. In the center an archbishop stands next to an emperor; both are haloed (Fig. 97). The archbishop is dressed like all the other archbishops in this church; the emperor wears a purple chlamys with gold *tablion* over a white tunic. To the right of the archbishop we see first another archbishop, without a halo, who receives from the emperor a scroll with the word *privilegia* written on it; behind him stand a priest in a gold chasuble, then two deacons bearing censer and pyxis. On the left, two more heads seem also to represent emperors, since they are also haloed (their bodies, now dressed like the figures next to Justinian in San Vitale, are entirely restored). A final figure, holding what seems to be a *ciborium* on a purple-covered pillow, stands behind them (his body below the waist is likewise completely restored).

While the composition and formal elements clearly reflect the San Vitale panel, the scene depicts a specific historical moment, the granting of privileges to Ravenna's church by a Byzantine emperor or group of emperors.

97. Sant'-
Apollinare in
Classe, mosaic on
the north wall of
the apse depict-
ing emperors
with Archbishop
Reparatus

What event this was is the subject of debate. Agnellus reports that the
image depicts the granting of a set of privileges by Emperor Constantine IV
(668–85) and his brothers Heraclius and Tiberius to Archbishop Reparatus (671–7). Below this image was the inscription "This Reparatus, that
he might be a comrade to the saints, made new decorations for this hall,
to blaze through the ages," and above the heads it read, "Constantine the
senior emperor, Heraclius and Tiberius emperors."[333] The specificity of
the privileges listed by Agnellus suggests that he saw a document listing
them.[334] However, Deichmann argued that by Agnellus's day part of the
inscription was missing, and that instead the scene depicts the grant of autocephaly made to Bishop Maurus by the emperor Constans II, installed by
Reparatus to commemorate his own role as the ambassador who obtained
the privilege.[335] This was a significant event in Ravenna's history and will be
discussed at greater length in the following chapter. The most we can say is

98. Sant'-Apollinare in Classe, mosaic on the south wall of the apse depicting Abel, Melchisedek, and Abraham and Isaac (photo Institut für Kunstgeschichte der Johannes Gutenberg Universität Mainz, Bilddatenbank)

that Reparatus was active in a number of political events and commissioned the mosaic to commemorate them.

Facing this scene is a conflation of the lunette mosaics from San Vitale, again very heavily restored.[336] Between jeweled columns and backed by a curtain, we see an altar identically laid out to the one in San Vitale, with Abel to the left offering a lamb, Abraham and Isaac to the right, and Melchisedek (identified by name) in the center, with the Hand of God descending from clouds to the left (Fig. 98). Scholars do not agree whether this depiction originally goes back to the time of the church's construction, or whether it dates from the time of Reparatus's mosaic opposite. Given that the latter was so clearly inspired by the mosaics of San Vitale, it would not be out of place for both to date to the same period, but by the same token the offering mosaic's correspondence with those of San Vitale can also argue for a sixth-century date.[337] The offering figures emphasize the role of the bishop, the successor of Melchisedek,[338] presiding at the altar directly in front of the mosaic. As in San Vitale, they unite the actors in the liturgical drama with the figures depicted around them, giving additional meaning to both.

Over time, therefore, the mosaics of Sant'Apollinare in Classe came to represent the various functions of the archbishop, from his liturgical role to his political importance to his status as heir of Apollinaris and thus ultimately of Christ. The program brilliantly reinforced the status of the archbishops as they rose in importance, and would contain the seeds of their aspirations in the following centuries.

SAN SEVERO

The church dedicated to Ravenna's fourth-century bishop Severus was the last major construction undertaken in Classe in the sixth century.[339] Begun by Archbishop Peter III sometime after 570, it was completed by his successor John II and dedicated in 582.[340] The church was located 1 km to the north of the recently completed Sant'Apollinare, just inside the city walls of Classe.[341] The building remained in use through the eighteenth century (its monastery was used as a residence by the Ottonian emperors in the tenth century), was partially rebuilt in 1468 and again in 1754, but was entirely destroyed by 1820.[342] The site was excavated in 1964–7, in the 1970s, in 1981–91, and is now the subject of new investigations. These operations have revealed a complete ground plan (Fig. 99) and some of the mosaic floors of the sixth-century church, overlying an earlier chapel and before that a very large Roman bath complex.[343]

Agnellus says that John moved the body of the saint from the adjacent chapel of St. Rufillo, on the south side, into the church;[344] excavations have indeed revealed a suite of rooms to the south of the western end of the church, including a small rectangular cell measuring 6.6 × 5.9 m with a western apse, connected to the main church by another room and having an additional room or rooms farther to the south. These rooms were originally thought to date to the sixth century, but have recently been redated to the fifth.[345] In addition, a square room with mosaics from the fifth or early sixth centuries was found under the floor of the basilica and has been suggested as the earlier chapel dedicated to the saint, although it could also have been some other sort of building.[346]

The main church measured 64.7 × 27.3 meters (including the apse, narthex, and walls). The building had a nave flanked by single aisles, with a narthex and an apse that was polygonal externally, circular internally. The nave was 12.35 m wide, just over twice the width of the aisles and thus in perfect accord with the dimensions of most other Ravennate basilicas. The foundations, at least, were made of reused Roman brick, and no remains of Julian bricks have been associated with the site. Remains in the apse area

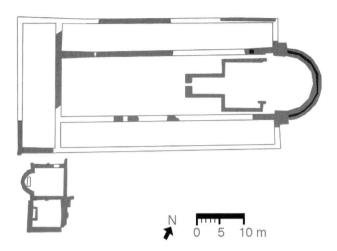

99. San Severo, Classe, ground plan of the late sixth-century basilica (including its *solea*) and the earlier chapels to the south, as revealed from excavations (after Maioli/Stoppioni, 1987 and Augenti, "Ravenna e Classe," 2006)

of both *tubi fittili* and glass tesserae in green, blue, red, gold, and silver indicate that the church was similar in this respect to others of its class. From the surviving remains, it is deduced that the nave colonnade included 12 columns.[347] Excavations also revealed that an unusually large *bema*, or platform, extended from the apse 7 m into the church, and from this a *solea*, or elevated walkway, led farther east to where an ambo would have been placed.[348] Almost half of the sixth-century mosaic pavements from the nave and aisles were uncovered during excavations; they consist of a series of rectangular polychrome *tappeti*, each of which had a different geometric pattern; several of them included birds, fish, and other animal motifs.[349]

As a whole, this structure was about the same size as its neighbor Sant'Apollinare; it represents the continuing ambitions and financial resources of Ravenna's church at the end of the sixth century, but it was to be the last large church built until the ninth century.

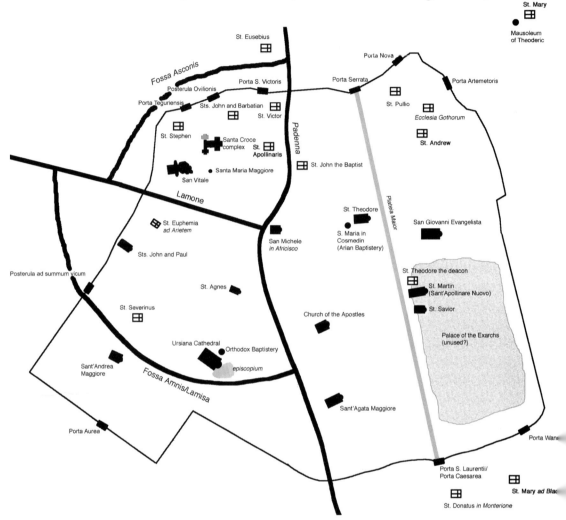

Ravenna, ca. AD 840 (at the time of Agnellus)

St. Mary

Mausoleum of Theoderic

St. Eusebius

Fossa Asconis

Porta Nova

Porta Serrata

Porta Artemetoris

Porta S. Victoris

Posterula Ovilionis

St. Pullio

Porta Teguriensis

Sts. John and Barbatian

Ecclesia Gothorum

St. Victor

St. Stephen

St. Andrew

Santa Croce complex

St. Apollinaris

Padenna

San Vitale

Santa Maria Maggiore

St. John the Baptist

Lamone

St. Theodore

San Giovanni Evangelista

Plateia Maior

St. Euphemia *ad Arietem*

S. Maria in Cosmedin (Arian Baptistery)

Sts. John and Paul

San Michele *in Africisco*

St. Theodore the deacon

Posterula ad summum vicum

St. Agnes

St. Martin (Sant'Apollinare Nuovo)

St. Severinus

St. Savior

Church of the Apostles

Palace of the Exarchs (unused?)

Ursiana Cathedral

Orthodox Baptistery

episcopium

Sant'Andrea Maggiore

Fossa Amnis/Lamisa

Sant'Agata Maggiore

Porta Wane

Porta Aurea

Porta S. Laurentii/ Porta Caesarea

St. Mary *ad Blac*

St. Donatus *in Monterione*

100. Map of Ravenna ca. AD 840 (at the time of Agnellus)

CHAPTER SEVEN

RAVENNA CAPITAL, AD 600–850

By the year 600, Ravenna had finally become a notable city. With a 200-year history as a capital, a leading member of the ecclesiastical hierarchy, and an international port, and containing splendid monuments commemorating its political and ecclesiastical history, the city had achieved elite status, especially at a time in which so many other formerly great cities, not least Rome, had drastically declined. Until this point, Ravenna's fortunes had gone in a completely opposite direction from those of the rest of western Europe. But alas, fate was finally to catch up with Ravenna, and if the buildings remained in relatively good condition for the next 150 years, the port, the population, and the infrastructure began a slow decline. The Frankish emperor Charlemagne viewed Ravenna, around 800, as an impressive capital, worthy of emulation; but the fact that he was able to remove precious building materials from the city for his own capital of Aachen shows that Ravenna was no longer a living, growing capital, but a museum of past glory.

There are a number of reasons why the early seventh century marks a crucial division in the fortunes of Ravenna.[1] Archaeologists point to this period as the time when imports and evidence of commerce, especially with the East, declines dramatically; this was linked to the silting up of the harbor of Classe, a process whose effects began to be felt at this time. Political events after 600 also reduced the empire's capacity to invest in the small imperial province in Italy, except for a short-lived revival under Constans II. Benign neglect can be a good thing; in Ravenna a status quo was maintained for more than a century, probably to the advantage of the city's inhabitants. It may only be historians looking at earlier evidence of greatness who see this period as a time of decline and stagnation. Certainly Agnellus, writing at the end of this period, displays little regret about the current status of his city. He depicts a community and its leaders still engaged with a large outside world, actively engaged in an ongoing historical process.

The closer we come to the ninth century, the more potentially useful Agnellus becomes as a source for Ravenna's history, although in many cases his stories are opaque. One of Agnellus's themes was the rivalry between the archbishops of Ravenna and the popes, which reached its height in the seventh and eighth centuries. Agnellus demonstrates Ravenna's long, proud history and uses it to justify the independence of his church from Rome. This rivalry also strongly influenced our other main source for the period, the Roman *Liber pontificalis*, which contains information that directly contradicts Agnellus's accounts. We cannot, however, simply reject Agnellus as an ahistorical partisan, since the Roman text was just as propagandistic on behalf of the popes.[2] Both texts together, along with Paul the Deacon's *Historia Langobardorum*, which narrates events up to the year 785, enable us to write a fairly comprehensive political history of this period. However, information about social, religious, and cultural activity in Ravenna in this period is much more restricted. A fire destroyed the episcopal archive around 700, and thus most of the 31 documents that survive for the period 600–800 date to the later eighth century.[3] Several of these are preserved because in the late tenth century they were copied into a register of deeds known as the *Codex Bavarus* or the *Breviarium ecclesiae Ravennatis*.[4] Recent archaeological investigations, especially at the Via D'Azeglio and Podere Chiavichetta sites, have revealed long sequences that include this period, and provide invaluable information about certain aspects of Ravenna's life, but they represent only two areas of a large inhabited region. Conclusions about the urban fabric and inhabitants of Ravenna in this period therefore remain hypothetical.

Ravenna, Capital of the Byzantine Exarchate

The years between 600 and 750 represent one of the most interesting periods of Ravenna's history, one that saw fundamental changes in the political alignment of central Italy.[5] In 600 the major players were the Byzantines and the Lombards; by the 750s it was the Franks and the popes who dominated Italy. Ravenna, as the seat of the Byzantine exarch, remained a political center, but in the course of the 150 years the Byzantine administration became increasingly irrelevant. By the time the Franks conquered Italy, it was once again Rome, not Ravenna, that was the center of political activity.

At the start of the seventh century, the Lombards and the Byzantines were reaching an equilibrium in Italy. Although the Lombard king Agilulf went on the offensive against the Byzantines, threatening Rome in 593–4, counterthreatened by the prefect Romanus in 595 with short-term truces negotiated several times before his death in 616, after 619 there was a twenty-year period of peace in which both sides consolidated their territories and established defenses.[6] The Byzantine administration fortified old centers and founded new towns along the border with the Lombard kingdom, notably at Ferrara, Comacchio, and Argenta; several of these were new establishments because, as we will see, the branches of the Po had shifted since the Roman period.[7] The Lombards under King Rothari resumed the attack in 641 and conquered Genoa and the region around it, defeating the exarch Isaac's army in 642, but Ravenna and the Pentapolis were spared.

In the early seventh century, the government in Constantinople had more serious things to worry about than the fate of its Italian colony. Invasions by Slavs, Avars, Bulgars, and Persians led to internal dissension, exacerbated by the financial crisis that had resulted from Justinian's combination of too many wars and depopulation because of the plague. The invasions cut the land routes between Constantinople and Italy and also reduced, over time, the number of ships that sailed in the Mediterranean; from now on, it would take much longer (three to six months) to make the journey.[8] The emperor Maurice (582–602) introduced fiscal and military reforms that were so vastly unpopular that he was finally murdered; his successor Phocas introduced a reign of terror that was only ended when Heraclius (610–41), son of the governor of Africa, captured Constantinople and had Phocas executed in turn. The Persian empire, resurgent under ambitious new rulers, had taken the opportunity in the meantime to capture Egypt, Syria, and much of Asia Minor, and, along with the Avars, besieged Constantinople in 626. Most of Heraclius's attention during his long reign was directed toward the defeat of the Persians and their northern allies, and then, finally, the new Arab armies. Moreover, from the 630s until 680 the Byzantine emperors supported the doctrine of monothelitism, a compromise between the miaphysite and the Chalcedonian positions on the nature of Christ that was not satisfactory to either side; this put the emperors theologically at odds with the popes and the western church. The Arab threat likewise preoccupied most Byzantine rulers until the mid-eighth century.

Italy was not exempt from the empire's troubles. Slavs and Avars attacked the northeast corner of the exarchate in the period 610–19 and within the territory there was a continual series of revolts against imperial authority. In 616, the exarch John and other officials were killed in an upheaval of unknown cause.[9] Heraclius sent as the new exarch Eleutherius, a eunuch who punished the rebels, put down a revolt in Naples,[10] and signed a treaty with Lombards by which the imperial government paid them massive tribute. Ravenna seems to have gone to Eleutherius's head; in 619, although a eunuch, he tried to make himself emperor, but he was killed on the way to Rome by some of his army.[11] The exarch Isaac held power for eighteen years (625–43), the longest of all the exarchs; his epitaph, in Greek and

Latin, still survives on an early fifth-century sarcophagus that he reused (Fig. 101), in San Vitale, which reads:[12]

> Here lies he who was leader of the army and who for 18 years kept Rome and the West safe for the serene sovereigns: Isaac, support of the emperors, great glory of all Armenia, descended as he was from glorious Armenian stock. After his glorious death his wise wife Susannah grieved without cease, like a pure dove, deprived of her husband who by his mighty deeds acquired fame in East and West, since from the West and the East he led his armies.

Isaac loyally supported the emperors, which caused him to be involved in the monothelite controversy against the popes. In 639, the *chartularius* Mauricius led his troops to sack the Lateran treasury, with the participation of Isaac; when in 643 Mauricius decided to side with the popes, Isaac led his army to Rome, captured and beheaded Mauricius, and displayed his head in the circus at Ravenna.[13] Olympius, another eunuch exarch, was sent to arrest Pope Martin I because he would not accept the imperial dogma. Olympius, however, changed sides, allying with the pope. He died in Sicily in 652, and in 653 the new exarch, Theodore Calliopas, arrested Pope Martin for complicity in the revolt and sent him to Constantinople, where he was condemned and died in exile.[14]

Constans II Pogonatus (641–68), the grandson of Heraclius, inherited at age eleven an empire at extreme risk of invasion from the Arabs and Slavs. The early years of his reign saw the loss of Egypt, parts of North Africa, and various Mediterranean islands to the Arabs. Although he managed to hold off the Slavs, his religious policies and his murder of his brother made him very unpopular in Constantinople. In the summer of 662 he came west, first to Greece and then in 663 into Italy, the first emperor to set foot on the peninsula since 476. Apparently he had decided to abandon Constantinople and transfer the imperial residence to Sicily. Naturally, this would have had many important repercussions for the government of Italy. Constans II fought and negotiated with the Lombards as he marched north from Taranto to Naples, and then to Rome, where he stayed only twelve days. He did not visit Ravenna, but he certainly took an interest in its bishop: in 666 he issued an edict conceding the right of autocephaly, or independence from the popes of Rome, which will be discussed further in the next section. After Rome Constans made his way to Sicily and established his court at Syracuse, where he was murdered in his bath in the summer of 668. Back in Constantinople, Byzantine military leaders established Constans's son as Constantine IV (668–85), and the Italian experiment was over.[15]

After 668, there was a shift in political alliances in Byzantine Italy.[16] Whereas earlier the popes and the exarchs had had independent relationships with the emperors, now these two parties were frequently aligned,

101. San Vitale, sarcophagus of the exarch Isaac (d. 643), early fifth-century sarcophagus with seventh century inscription (photo C. Copenhaver)

sometimes against imperial policy. Moreover, the local aristocracy in Italy, who controlled the army in Ravenna, exerted their own authority more and more, rendering the foreign exarchs essentially powerless. The most obvious examples of the change are the attempts to forcibly bring the pope to Constantinople. In 653 Theodore Calliopas had successfully apprehended Pope Martin. But in 693, when the emperor Justinian II sent his *protospatharius* (commander) Zacharias to bring Pope Sergius to Constantinople, the Ravennate army marched to Rome to defend the pope. Zacharias was forced to hide under the pope's bed, and he ultimately returned to the capital empty handed. In 701, in a similar situation, the army of Ravenna protected Pope John VI from the exarch Theophylact.[17]

The eighth century was a time of great confusion and upheaval in Italy, both for ecclesiastical and political reasons.[18] Justinian II was furious about Pope Sergius's defiance of his summons to his council, but he was also deeply unpopular at home, and in 695 he was deposed, his nose and tongue were slit, and he was sent into exile on the Black Sea coast.[19] Justinian escaped to the Khazars, and, aided by the Bulgars and Slavs, was returned to power in 705. He made peace with Pope Constantine, but he also inaugurated a bloodbath upon his enemies, and among the victims were certain Ravennate leaders, including Archbishop Felix, who were arrested, brought to Constantinople, and variously tortured.[20] Agnellus says that this event precipitated an uprising in Ravenna, led by one of his ancestors, a man named George whose father had been arrested and taken to the capital. The new exarch, John Rizocopus, landed not in Ravenna but in Naples, and only came to Ravenna after executing several officials in Rome, whereupon he died a nasty death (*turpissima morte occubuit*), possibly murdered by the rebels.[21] When Justinian was eventually murdered in 711, his head was brought to Italy and displayed in Ravenna and Rome, and his successor Philippicus gave rich gifts to Felix.[22]

The violence of the previous decades apparently made many Italians feel that they could do without the Byzantine empire, although it is interesting that very few seem to have wanted to become part of the Lombard kingdom. From 711 to 717 there was political turmoil in the East, but in 717 Leo III restored order and repelled an Arab siege of Constantinople. In order to pay for Byzantine administration in Italy, he imposed heavy taxes on the Italians; he also, starting in 726 or 727, began to promulgate Iconoclasm, an anti-image religious policy, which alienated much of the western Church including the prelates of Ravenna and Rome. The Lombards had begun to attack the exarchate starting in 717–18, when the Lombard Duke Faroald of Spoleto took Classe, but returned it to "the Romans" at the order of King Liutprand; Liutprand himself captured Classe slightly later.[23] The port was returned to the new exarch, Paul, but in 727, apparently in the context of an uprising against the imperial policy of Iconoclasm, or perhaps in resentment of greatly increased taxes, Paul was killed in Ravenna.[24]

After the death of Paul, the aggressive popes Gregory II, Gregory III, and Zacharias staked their claim to be the rulers of the former exarchate, as T. Noble has demonstrated.[25] Emperor Leo III sent another exarch, Eutychius, who made an alliance with Liutprand against the pope, then Liutprand made peace with the pope, then Eutychius allied with the pope against Liutprand. Local leaders were in charge in Ravenna and Eutychius was initially not accepted; in 732 Leo III sent a naval raid against Italy which must have been making for Ravenna when it foundered in the Adriatic.[26] The Lombards under Liutprand became more and more aggressive; Eutychius was eventually received in Ravenna, but the city was captured in 739 by a Lombard army, and the archbishop, exarch, and leading citizens had to flee to the Venetian swamps, whence, at the request of Pope Gregory III, they retook Ravenna with the fleet of the Duke of Venice.[27] Liutprand attacked Ravenna again in 743, and again Eutychius and Archbishop John V (at least according to the Roman *Liber pontificalis*) asked Gregory's successor Zacharias for help.[28] Upon Liutprand's death in 744, Ratchis signed a peace treaty for "all Italy" with the pope, but in 749 he abdicated in favor of his brother Aistulf, who aggressively attacked the Pentapolis. The Lombard army took Ferrara, Comacchio, and finally, in 751, Ravenna, whereupon

Byzantine rule in northern Italy ceased.[29] Aistulf was impressed by Ravenna and may have intended to make it his capital, issuing his first diploma "in palatio" on July 4, 751, but the popes had other ideas. In 755 Aistulf was compelled by the Frankish king Pepin to relinquish the city and it went not to the Byzantines but to the popes. Ravenna's days as a capital were over.

Archbishops and Popes: The Autocephaly Question

In the seventh and eighth centuries the popes became effectively secular as well as religious leaders in both Rome and their territory. Ravenna's archbishops, residing in a city in which the secular authority of the exarchs was constantly present, did not have the opportunity to assume the same kind of authority, but some of them clearly envied their papal rivals. The struggle over the status of Ravenna's archbishops that had begun in the late sixth century was taken up again in the mid–seventh, and eventually developed political as well as ecclesiastical dimensions.[30]

In 642 Ravenna acquired a new archbishop, Maurus, who seems to have had ambitions exceeding even those of his predecessors. Maurus initiated a historical project to demonstrate his see's importance: as we have already seen, the *Passio* of Apollinaris may well date to his reign, and so may the false Diploma of Valentinian III, which purports to be the document that conferred metropolitan status on Ravenna's bishop in the mid–fifth century.[31] Agnellus tells us that Maurus "went to Constantinople on many occasions, so that he might free his church from the yoke or domination of the Romans." We have no way of verifying these voyages, but we do know that in 666 Constans II, who had recently come to Italy, granted a privilege (*typus*) of autocephaly, or independence from Rome, to the see of Ravenna. The privilege stated that the archbishop of Ravenna would be consecrated by three of his suffragan bishops rather than by the pope and that he would not be subject to orders from the pope.[32] Presumably this change was intended to weaken the influence of the popes in the Italian church; not surprisingly, Pope Vitalian strongly objected to the decree and excommunicated Maurus, who in return removed the pope's name from the liturgy in Ravenna.[33]

Maurus's successor Reparatus continued his policies and received tax concessions from the emperors in Constantinople; Agnellus tells us that these privileges were commemorated in the mosaic in the apse of Sant'-Apollinare in Classe (Fig. 97).[34] The Roman *Liber pontificalis*, on the other hand, tells us instead that the church of Ravenna was reconciled with Pope Donus, after which Reparatus died.[35] Most scholars have tended to believe the Roman version, but there is no real reason to prefer it to Agnellus's account.[36] However, it is true that autocephaly did not last long: Maurus's second successor, Theodore, although consecrated in Ravenna, resubmitted Ravenna's church to Pope Agatho in 680, and returned the *typus* of autocephaly to Pope Leo II. By 682, the emperor Constantine IV had issued a decree formally revoking it.[37]

Several of the archbishops of the eighth century, notably Felix and Sergius, continued the struggle for autonomy with limited success. Upon his consecration at Rome in 708, Felix refused to sign a document guaranteeing that he would not disturb the unity of the church; in Justinian II's sweep of Ravennate leaders Felix was arrested and taken to Constantinople, where he was blinded. When Justinian was murdered in 711, Felix returned to Ravenna, where he reigned for another fourteen years. The Roman *Liber pontificalis* tells us that Felix had rebelled against the authority of the pope and portrays his capture and blinding as divine punishment. Agnellus makes Felix one of the saintly bishops of Ravenna; no mention is made of a quarrel or reconciliation with Rome, but the entire story is set in the frame of Ravennate–Byzantine politics. Since Agnellus's account is a reaction against the very anti-Ravennate bias of the Roman text, it is not clear what "really happened."[38] Felix's successor John V seems to have been of the pro-papal party; the Roman *Liber pontificalis* states that John and the exarch jointly appealed to Pope Zacharias to save the city and the Pentapolis from the Lombards. Zacharias arrived secretly in Ravenna, celebrated mass in Sant'Apollinare in Classe, and then proceeded to Pavia where he talked King Liutprand out of attacking.[39] T. Noble points out that this passage in the *Liber pontificalis* indicates that the popes thought of Ravenna and the exarchate as part of their "flock;" in other words, under the control of Rome.[40]

After the Exarchate

After 751, the struggle for control of the former exarchate involved the papacy, the archbishops of Ravenna, the Lombards, the Byzantines, and the Franks, in various combinations. After this point, it becomes difficult to discern exactly what Ravenna's archbishops were after; on the one hand, there had always been ecclesiastical autonomy, but after 751 that issue seems to have been superseded by the concept of outright rule in the exarchate. Occasionally the archbishops were allied with the popes, as over Iconoclasm. In 731, Pope Gregory III held a council at Rome that condemned Iconoclasm, attended by Archbishop John V, while in 769 Pope Stephen III convened a council at Rome to reject the Acts of the Iconoclastic Council of Hiereia, at which a deacon John represented the dying Archbishop Sergius.[41] But for the most part, antagonism to papal authority was the principle that guided Ravennate politics.[42]

Many of the political currents of the time can be seen in the events of the reign of Sergius (744–69), who was archbishop throughout this particularly complex period. Sergius was consecrated at Rome after a contested election, and when he returned to Ravenna the clergy refused to work with him. The political situation was extremely delicate, and Sergius seems to have supported the Lombard king Aistulf, who held Ravenna from 751–5.[43] Stephen II, consecrated as pope in 752, appealed to both Byzantines and Lombards for the "return" of Ravenna but made no headway. Stephen turned to Pepin, the new king of the Franks, who entered Italy with an army and forced Aistulf to give Ravenna and its territories "back" to the pope. It is significant that the Roman *Liber pontificalis* says outright that Pepin gave the exarchate to Stephen, along with keys and hostages.[44] Sergius, who must have opposed this outcome, was sent to Rome by the pro-papal faction of Ravennate citizens, where he remained for two years until the death of Stephen II in 757.[45] Sergius seems to have come to terms with the next pope, Paul, with whom he conspired to arrest another (or the same?) group of Ravennate officials, who were taken to Rome where Agnellus says that they died.[46] The end of Sergius's biography in the *LPR* is missing, as is most of that of his successor Leo. From the Roman *Liber pontificalis* we learn of yet another contested election in 769, this time involving the clergy, the Duke of Rimini, the Lombards, the pope, and the Carolingians. Leo, the successful candidate, was the choice of Charlemagne, and no friend to the popes.[47]

With the conquest of the Lombard kingdom by Charlemagne in 774, previous power relationships were changing again. Ravenna was caught between Charlemagne's kingdom in Italy and the emerging political entity that would later be known as the Papal States. T. Noble identifies the political situation of Ravenna at this time as a "double-dyarchy": "on the one hand pope and king shared rule, and on the other hand pope and archbishop divided authority."[48] Throughout this turbulent period, Ravenna's leaders maintained a policy of denying the pope's authority. Several letters from Pope Hadrian to Charlemagne complain that Archbishop Leo had sent an embassy to Francia to discuss Ravenna's autonomy and had even gone to Francia himself, after which he had refused to acknowledge papal authority.[49] After Leo's death, a group of Ravennate *iudices* (officials) likewise complained to Charlemagne in 783.[50] Something strange happened after the death of Archbishop Gratiosus in 789, perhaps a contested election or even two rival archbishops; Pope Hadrian writes that he has just intervened in the election of Gratiosus's successor (who is not named), and asks Charlemagne not to listen to "wicked and lying lips" speaking out against the pope.[51]

In the early ninth century, the bishops apparently curried favor with the popes and the Carolingian emperors in order to bolster their authority both within and beyond their local jurisdiction. Archbishop Martin (ca. 810–18) sent messages to Charlemagne, "and the emperor was pleased." Martin was summoned to Rome by Pope Leo III in 815–16, but feigned illness so that the Carolingian representative assigned to the case could not make him go; Pope Stephen IV, however, came to Ravenna and celebrated mass together with Martin in the Ursiana.[52] Petronax (ca. 818–37) pursued a pro-papal policy: he received a privilege from Pope Paschal I in 819, and later attended a council held in Rome in 826 by Pope Eugene II.[53] Petronax's successor George (ca. 837–46), on the other hand, represented the anti-papal party. He was the godfather of the emperor Lothar's daughter at her baptism, and went to Francia, against papal advice, apparently in order to gain influence with Lothar's brother Charles the Bald; at the Battle of Fontenoy of 841 he lost a large part of Ravenna's treasure and historic documents.[54] At this point Agnellus's text breaks off, but we know that later archbishops continued the struggle against the popes. Despite their best efforts, Ravenna's leaders were never able really to rival the popes, whose "papal state" was based on the foundations of the old exarchate.

Ravenna's Byzantine and Post-Byzantine Elite

From the summary presented above, and from the few other sources available to us, we are able to deduce some things about the people who inhabited and ruled Ravenna.[55] Whereas in Rome the disappearance of the Senate in the late sixth century presented an administrative power vacuum that was quickly filled by the popes, in Ravenna the secular administration was a continuing presence. Certainly the archbishops were acquiring ever more power and prestige; the episcopal palace, for example, continued to be enlarged in the seventh and eighth centuries even as construction elsewhere in the city had declined, which follows a pattern seen in other cities.[56] But in Ravenna the secular administration and the military continued to play an important role in regional government, and thus in the life of the city.[57] If the episcopal palace was one pole of the city, then the exarchal palace, probably in the same structures inherited from the Ostrogoths, was another.

The political/administrative/military system established for the exarchate by the early seventh century seems to have operated in much the same way throughout its history. The head of the Byzantine administration was the exarch, always sent from Constantinople, who might be a military official like Isaac, a eunuch bureaucrat like Eleutherius, Olympius, and Eutychius, or some other government functionary. Serving under the exarchs were dukes (*duces*) of provinces, based in major cities (Rome, Naples, Rimini, eventually Venice), and in smaller towns authority was exercised by tribunes (*tribuni*). Dukes and tribunes performed both military and civil duties, and they, along with the lower-level officers and troops, administrators, clerks, and tax collectors were drawn primarily from the local population, although on occasion one might be sent from Constantinople. T. Brown sees a deterioration in the sophistication of the bureaucracy in the seventh century and later, but even in these later periods, the scribes, clerks, *tabelliones*, notaries, and others remained laymen, indicating that education was available outside of the church.[58] Ravenna did not have a duke, but was governed directly by the exarchal administration. The *curia* disappears from view after the mid–seventh century,[59] but we do find in Ravenna men with the title *iudex*, which literally means "judge" but in the seventh and eighth centuries was used to designate any sort of government official, or indeed any member of the leading class of landowners.[60]

It was these landowners who made up the army, military service being expected as a condition of their status. As the authority of the exarchs declined, it was the dukes, in their local territories, who emerged as leading political players; indeed, the fact that Ravenna did not have its own duke eventually put the city at a disadvantage in post exarchate politics, and we see, for example, the duke of Rimini becoming deeply involved in Ravenna's episcopal elections. We know very little about the actual military organization; Agnellus provides much of the evidence which comes in the form of naming particular regions of the city as the home base of military units and occasionally mentioning barracks. The rebel leader George names eleven military *numeri*, or squadrons, that are to defend Ravenna at the time of revolt against Justinian II, and it is thought that these represent, if nothing else, ninth-century militia units within Ravenna that perhaps had their origin in the early eighth century.[61]

The relationship between the archbishops and the exarchs was close. It is possible that the exarch had some role in the choice of the archbishop, and certainly the two worked together in legal cases, foreign affairs, papal relations, and other similar sorts of situations.[62] Church and secular leaders were bound together through property relationships: church lands were frequently leased out to secular individuals as grants of *emphyteusis*, in which the recipient would manage the land and pay rent to the church. These could be large estates, granted for three generations, or small plots granted for twenty-nine years.[63] The Ravennate church was one of the largest landowners in Italy, with extensive property in Sicily and in Istria as well as in the Pentapolis, and their estates produced large incomes, which meant in turn that Ravenna's archbishops were among the most important taxpayers to the imperial government.[64] Agnellus relates a story about Archbishop Maurus and his delegate in Sicily in which he states that the Sicilian estates yielded 50,000 *modia* of wheat and 31,000 gold *solidi*, of which 15,000 *solidi* were sent to Constantinople.[65] This story, embroidered by Agnellus but perhaps based on a real document, has been overused by scholars who are eager to find any kind of numerical figure for the economics of Ravenna's church, but it probably contains a kernel of truth. T. Brown suggests that many of the church's lands were given to it by the imperial government, precisely because the church would be a responsible steward and taxpayer.[66] Finally, the church and the local secular leadership were bound together socially as well as economically because many families provided leaders to both; the fiercely political Archbishop Sergius, originally a lay military leader, is one example, and Agnellus the historian, whose family members were involved in many historical events, is another.[67]

The Environment and Urban Life

We can relatively easily trace a political and ecclesiastical history of Ravenna's elites in this period, and we can see that in the seventh and eighth centuries they were continually and actively involved in the extremely complex issues of the day. Archbishops plotted, armies marched back and forth to Rome or out against the Lombards, exarchs were murdered, and the city's leaders took and changed sides and fought continually among themselves. But what was the urban environment in which these events took place? And what effect did they have on the city of Ravenna?

The seventh century saw the beginning of a dramatic decline in Ravenna's economic fortunes, some of which was attributable to the state of the Mediterranean economy generally, and some of which had to do with the state of the city's harbors, ports, and coastlines (Fig. 6). In the seventh or early eighth century the hydrological network of the Po river basin underwent dramatic changes.[68] New branches, the *Padus Primarius* and the *Badarenus/Eridanus*, replaced the existing courses and now flowed through Ferrara, cutting off the flow of water to the Padenna and thus breaking Ravenna's direct connection to the riverine network. The Badarenus flowed into the Adriatic north and east of Ravenna, close to the mouth of the former Roman port in the northeast part of the city where a new harbor developed.[69] The Padenna did not completely disappear; it perhaps continued to be fed, on a smaller scale, by small streams to its north. The Lamone, which had flowed in from the west to the Padenna through the southern part of the *oppidum*, now became the main water source feeding the canals inside Ravenna, and sometime before the late ninth century the old *fossa Asconis* was extended to carry water from the Lamone to the Badarenus, with only a small branch feeding the canals within the city.[70]

We saw in the previous chapter that temporarily increased water flow, and thus sedimentation, along with a decline in the kind of centralized government system that could maintain artificial waterways, had resulted in the silting up of the harbor of Classe beginning in the mid–sixth century.

When direct influx of water from the Po (via the Padenna) ceased by the early eighth century, the harbor of Classe completely dried up.[71] Archaeological evidence shows that by the early eighth century the city of Classe had shrunk dramatically.[72] Classe was conquered by the Lombards in 717–18 and the 720s, and according to Paul the Deacon was destroyed.[73] During the reign of Archbishop John V (726–44) Ravenna suffered a serious earthquake; Agnellus mentions this disaster in the context of its destructive effects at two major churches, Sant'Apollinare Nuovo and the Petriana church in Classe. The former was rebuilt but the Petriana was not, despite the efforts of King Aistulf in the early 750s,[74] which underscores the demise of Classe in this period.

Economically, historians and archaeologists agree that Ravenna underwent a reduction in its trade, size, and construction history during the course of the seventh and eighth centuries,[75] which was part of a seventh-century economic and urban crisis that was empire wide in the eastern Mediterranean, and was caused by a number of factors, including the Persian and Arab invasions and the plague.[76] While Ravenna's mint produced Byzantine coins in gold, silver, and copper until the Lombard conquest, after the early seventh century foreign coins cease to appear in the exarchate, another indication that long-distance trade had been drastically reduced.[77] The archaeological evidence from sites such as the Podere Chiavichetta in Classe shows ceramic imports and a ceramics kiln in use until the end of the seventh century, after which activity ceases.[78]

Culturally, Ravenna also experienced a sharp downturn in production after the end of the sixth century. T. Brown has identified from the documentary sources a reduction in the numbers of merchants, craftsmen, bankers, guild members, notaries, and other people with specialized occupations, and notes that only in the ninth century did such people reappear in documents as individuals of significant rank.[79] From surviving monuments we know that in the seventh and eighth centuries Ravenna sustained an artisan class that was capable of imitating, in a crude way, the products of earlier centuries – for example, the mosaic panels in Sant'Apollinare in Classe, the sarcophagi of Archbishops Felix, John VII, and Gratiosus (Fig. 102), or the ambo presented to the church of St. Andrew at the time of Theodore.[80] However, when the family of the exarch Isaac wanted a grand sarcophagus for his burial, they reused one that had been made in the fifth century (Fig. 101).

There are traces of literary and scientific enterprises that continued into the ninth century. A school of medical studies that was active from the early sixth century into the seventh produced translations of and commentaries on the works of Hippocrates and Galen, especially by a certain Agnellus *iatrosofista* ("medical scholar," not the historian) who worked between 550 and 700.[81] A remarkable poetic epitaph was composed for Archbishop

Maurus, consisting of miscellaneous lines taken from poems by the fourth-to-fifth-century authors Prudentius and Ausonius.[82] An anonymous geographer in the early eighth century wrote a cosmography, or catalog of world geography, that includes regions, bodies of water, and an exhaustive list of cities from India to Britain. The geographer was proud of his home city of Ravenna: he calls it *nobilissima*, like Constantinople and Rome, while Antioch and Alexandria are *famosissima*, the only five cities to be so distinguished.[83] Archbishop Felix oversaw the compilation of the 176 sermons of Peter Chrysologus.[84] Finally, of course, Agnellus wrote his history in the ninth century.

The population of Ravenna in this period was probably ethnically fairly homogeneous, Latin-speaking, and local, although with a certain influx of officials and possibly soldiers from the east from time to time.[85] Agnellus provides a colorful description of urban factionalism, which may reflect underlying political tensions: on every Sunday and holiday, Ravenna's citizens form teams that go outside the city walls and fight each other. Eventually the violence gets out of control, people are killed, others are killed in revenge, and finally Archbishop Damian has to lead penitential processions to discover the truth so that the wrongdoers can be punished.[86]

A. Augenti proposes that in the seventh century Ravenna was less densely occupied, with wealthy houses side by side with poor, and burials and gardens found within the walls.[87] This would conform to the "ruralization" identified in other Italian towns in this period,[88] but the evidence from Ravenna is not sufficient to establish a more certain picture at this time. S. Cosentino proposes a population for Ravenna in the eighth and ninth centuries of around 7,000–7,500 people, which would represent only a slight decrease from his estimate of 9,000–10,000 in the imperial period.[89] On the other hand, perhaps Ravenna's walls had never been completely filled with dense occupation. This question awaits further archaeological study.

One type of change in the Italian urban habitat that has received a lot of scholarly attention is the layout of houses: there was a dramatic change in the layout and construction materials of wealthy residences between the third and the tenth centuries.[90] From archaeology we know quite a bit about the layout, construction materials, and decoration of Roman houses, namely that they usually contained a suite of rooms on one level enclosing a courtyard or courtyards, were built of stone or brick, and had mosaic or stone-tiled floors and frescoes on the walls. By the ninth and tenth centuries, as far as we can tell from descriptions of property in documents, wealthy houses instead consisted of multistory structures built in wood and/or stone, with several buildings arranged around a central court.[91] Archaeological evidence from Brescia and Luni shows several structures made of wood

102. Sant'-
Apollinare in
Classe, sarcoph-
agus of Arch-
bishop Gratiosus
(d. ca. AD 789)

adjacent to one another, on the site of the former Roman forum. However, there is little evidence, written or archaeological, to explain at what point in the period between the third and the tenth centuries these changes became significant. The Via D'Azeglio sixth-century house had an upper story with mosaics,[92] and some papyri from early seventh-century Ravenna describe two-story houses with interior courtyards and porticoes,[93] but the cases are so isolated that it is difficult to discern trends. S. Gelichi has noted that in Ravenna, Roman house types and building materials lasted "surprisingly late," that is, into the seventh century and perhaps beyond.[94] We have indications from Agnellus, at least, that houses were being built in the eighth and ninth centuries within Ravenna, often out of spolia from older buildings, but there is very little evidence about what these houses looked like. The large sixth-century mansion at the Via D'Azeglio site was leveled in the seventh century and replaced by a cemetery and a much smaller and simpler two-room house; a similar house has also been found at the Podere Chiavichetta site in Classe, built within an earlier warehouse.[95] The palace of Theoderic, used by the exarchs, went out of use sometime between the sixth and the tenth centuries, with tombs and postholes on top of the ruins.[96] Since no elite houses dating to this period have been identified archaeologically, we cannot be entirely sure of the meaning of this trend – surely small houses had likewise always existed in Ravenna. Perhaps the wealthy had simply moved to other parts of the city.

The changed economic and civic circumstances can be seen most clearly in drastic reduction in church construction during the seventh and eighth centuries. Unlike earlier secular rulers, the exarchs are not credited with sponsoring large-scale construction (indeed only Theodore, 678–87, has

103. So-called "Palace of the Exarchs," actually the facade of a church dedicated to the Savior, mid–eighth century (photo C. L. Striker)

any patronage attributed to him), and in the 250 years after the completion of St. Severus in Classe, only one large church was built in Ravenna.[97] This was a church dedicated to the Savior, just to the south of the entrance to the palace. The first reference to this church is by Agnellus, and archaeologically its remains date to the eighth or ninth century. While not as large as earlier basilicas, this structure had a monumental, two-story entrance that still survives in modified form (Fig. 103). It has been proposed that it was built by Aistulf as a new palace-church in the moment when he was planning to establish his court in Ravenna; and indeed there is no apparent reason that any later individual would build a church here.[98]

It could be argued that by the seventh century no more large churches were needed; Ravenna and Classe now had a large cathedral; several large basilicas in honor of a spectrum of saints, including a martyr and the founding bishop; three or four baptisteries; and many smaller churches and monasteries. Church construction activity does not entirely disappear, however. Agnellus mentions several structures in his narratives that we assume were built before the event he mentions. If this methodology is valid, we see a pattern of continuous, if small-scale, construction and/or decoration in Ravenna after 600. First, several *monasteria*, or small chapels, were built, many of them in Caesarea, implying that this region had become rather more important; today it is densely built up, and little archaeological investigation has been possible, so we do not know the nature of this occupation. Eleven *ecclesiae* or *monasteria* that are not attested before 600 are mentioned either by Agnellus or in a document, as follows:

Name	Date	Details	LPR
Oratorium of St. Polyeuktos	bef. 620	Listed in the *Martyrologium* attributed to Jerome as being in Caesarea in Ravenna.[99]	–
Monasterium of St. Mary, which is called *ad Blachernas*	630s–680s	Agnellus's church; Exarch Theodore (ca. 678–687) and his wife buried there, "not far from Wandalaria, outside the gate of St. Lawrence," thus in Caesarea.[100]	26, 119, 162, 167
Monasterium of St. Bartholemew	bef. 642	Archbishops Maurus and Felix were abbots here, as were Agnellus and his uncle Sergius.[101]	64, 110, 136, 149, 158
Ecclesia of St. Apollinaris *in veclo*	bef. 671	Archbishops Reparatus and Gratiosus were abbots here; "not far from the Ovilian *posterula* in the place which is called the Public Mint," namely in the northwest corner of the city.[102]	115, 164
Ecclesia of St. Paul the Apostle	679–687	Theodore the exarch with Archbishop Theodore built it; formerly it was a synagogue, near Wandalaria, in Caesarea.[103]	119
Monasterium of St. Theodore the deacon	679–687	Theodore the exarch built it next to Sant'Apollinare Nuovo, not known.[104]	119
Monasterium of St. Andrew the Apostle	bef. 691	Archdeacon Theodore and Archbishop Martin were from this church, "not far from the *ecclesia Gothorum*, near the house which is called Mariniana," outside the northeastern corner of the city.[105]	121, 167
Monasterium of St. John, which is called *ad Navicula*	bef. 700	Papyri from ca. 700 list donors as the *primicerius* of the *numerus Ravennas* John and his wife Stefania, witnessed by *Sergius domesticus numeri Armeniorum*.[106]	–
Monasterium of St. Andrew the Apostle, which is called *Ierichomium*	bef. 709	Given a lot of treasure by Iohannicis before 709; a γεροκομῖον is a hospice for the elderly.[107]	148
Monasterium of St. Donatus, which is called *in Monterione*	bef. 790s	A story about its abbot John; located "outside the gate of St. Lawrence next to Wandalaria," thus in Caesarea.[108]	162
Ecclesia of St. Euphemia *in Sancto Calinico*	bef. 790s	Agnellus reports the burial of a relative of his in this church at the time of John VI (778–785), outside the city; a document of 1047 mentions a "mon. S. Euphemiae foris portam S. Laurentii," which would be in Caesarea.[109]	163

None of these structures survives and so we know nothing about their relative size or decoration. Since we do not actually know when they were built, we cannot say anything about the rate of construction, except to note that if the dates derived from Agnellus are correct, the eighth century was a particularly low point, hardly a surprise given the political circumstances.

Church patronage took place in two other contexts also. One was restoration: We have already discussed the mosaic panels made by Archbishop Reparatus in Sant'Apollinare in Classe, and Archbishop Martin is said to have restored the church of St. Euphemia *ad Arietem* because it was underwater.[110] Some church furnishings were provided; Agnellus describes some examples, and the previously mentioned *ciborium* for the church of St. Eleuchadius, now in Sant'Apollinare in Classe, was made by a priest named Peter during the reign of Archbishop Valerius (ca. AD 789–810; Fig. 104). In the late seventh century, a bronze cross was placed at the summit of the Orthodox Baptistery, with an inscription commemorating its patrons Felix (the future archbishop?) and Stephen.[111] Finally, as already mentioned, Ravenna's cathedral and *episcopium* received additions in the eighth century, precisely the period in which the archbishops were emerging as the main authority figures in the city. Archbishop Felix added a *secretarium*, or entrance chamber in which the clergy assembled before processing into the cathedral, complete with a poetic inscription; in the *Ordo Romanus* I, which records the seventh-century liturgy of Rome, the *secretarium* plays an important role.[112] Felix also built a *domus*, some kind of residential building, on the northeast side of the cathedral, next to the baptistery, which still existed in the twelfth century, and was destroyed between 1207 and 1262.[113] Sometime in the eighth century, perhaps also at the time of Felix, a two-story set of arches and arcades was attached to the outside of the tower that contains the *capella arcivescovile*, and C. Ricci plausibly suggested that this was the *vivarium* mentioned by Agnellus, a structure for holding small animals, perhaps including a fishpond (Fig. 64).[114] And finally Archbishop Valerius (ca. 789–810) built a "New House," or a "Domus Valeriana," using building material taken from the Arian episcopal palaces; this stood next to the *Domus Felicis*, and remains survive within the current palace.[115]

By the ninth century, Ravenna's archbishops had taken control of the city both politically and topographically. The episcopal complex was the center of urban activity, and the trajectory begun by Maximian and continued by his successors had reached its ultimate expression. Ravenna was no longer a capital, but reminders of its secular rulers were everywhere, and would impress future generations of residents and visitors alike.

104. Sant'-
Apollinare in
Classe, *ciborium* of
St. Eleuchadius,
ninth century AD

Aftermath: Ravenna, Agnellus, and the Carolingians

A renewed sense of urban civic consciousness in Italy has been attributed
to the ninth century; in Verona and Milan, for example, texts were produced describing the cities and their major monuments.[116] Although it is
not usually considered in this context, Agnellus's *LPR* is also a text that
makes a major argument for civic consciousness. Writing a history of the
city through its bishops is a medieval, or at least a late antique, notion.
However, although Agnellus is certainly keen to trace the ecclesiastical
history of his see, he includes a surprisingly large amount of information
about the secular leaders and inhabitants of his city. We feel a clear sense
of local pride, which T. Brown has called *campanilismo*: civic consciousness,
awareness of a citizenry, and other aspects that would indicate that someone
was thinking about what city life meant in the early ninth century.[117] This

text, then, offers us valuable clues for concepts of the city and urban development in the early Middle Ages. How does Agnellus present Ravenna's history and does he periodize any break between late antiquity and the early Middle Ages?

Certainly in one sense Agnellus's text is designed to emphasize continuity, in particular the continuity of the archbishopric of Ravenna from the first century to the ninth. The archiepiscopal succession is presented as an almost seamless progression, occasionally marked by the intervention of an emperor or pope. The bishops regulate the church, build buildings, perform miracles, and are involved in the secular life of the city. The crowd of citizens of Ravenna also stands as a continuous presence within a city whose political affiliations change over time. It is clear that for Agnellus the city is not simply a collection of buildings, but a center of population in which the inhabitants are identified as Ravennate citizens (*cives Ravennates*).[118] The Ravennate crowd and its leaders feature prominently in many stories about Ravenna's history up to the ninth century, especially once Byzantine control of the city has fallen apart.[119] Justinian II kidnaps not just the archbishop, but also "all those noble by birth" in the city. With the loss of the leading citizens, a man named George (whom Agnellus claims as a relative) organizes the remainder, as well as the inhabitants of subject cities, into a militia to fight off the Byzantine army. "Noble Ravennate judges," including Agnellus's great-grandfather, are mentioned later in the eighth century, this time kidnapped by the pope. Although, as T. Brown has shown, the leadership of Ravennate society had changed from the sixth century to the eighth century, these *nobiles* still seem to represent urban secular authority, while the *cives* – "the great and the lowly and those in the middle," as Agnellus describes them – are an important component of the urban landscape.

Politically, the ancient Roman Empire barely exists for Agnellus. Aside from the fact that Apollinaris, the founder of Ravenna's see, is said to be a disciple of St. Peter and to have died in the time of Vespasian, there are no references to the empire before the early fifth century. After that, the city, with the aid of the bishops, moves fairly smoothly from imperial to Ostrogothic and then to Byzantine rule; rulers move in and out of the *palatium*. The exarch takes quite an active role in the life of the church and people, mediating in a dispute between archbishop and clergy, for example, or serving as a judge in a business case involving an abbot. Unfortunate incidents, such as the murder of various exarchs, are not mentioned by Agnellus. Contacts between Ravenna and Constantinople are portrayed as occurring regularly up to the eighth century and include private commercial ventures and appeals in court cases as well as official government business.

The break in this pattern occurs in the eighth century, and the unraveling of this imperial relationship is described by Agnellus in some detail, as we have seen. It is these ruptures, which occurred in the context of the end of Byzantine rule in Italy, that for Agnellus mark the end of the old order and the transition to the political situation that he knew, one in which the archbishop was the sole authority figure within the city, although the popes and the Carolingian emperors lurk offstage and make an occasional appearance.

As we have seen throughout this book, Agnellus's text is particularly important for what it tells us about the topography and structures of Ravenna. While he occasionally mentions Roman monuments (the amphitheater, the *stadium tabulae*) in the context of topographical references, he is uninterested in the *romanitas* of Ravenna, perhaps because, as the archaeology has shown, there really wasn't any. What most fascinate him about the physical structure of his city are the late antique monuments to be found there. Galla Placidia, the fifth-century empress-regent who built several churches, is one of his heroines. Theoderic too, who also constructed churches and palaces, and whose monumental statue had only recently been carried off by Charlemagne, is another focus of attention, while as for the churches built in the mid-sixth century, San Vitale is "like no other church in Italy." Although in the late antique period there was a shift in the focus of architectural patronage from secular to ecclesiastical buildings,[120] in the *LPR* we can see that walls, palaces, and other secular monuments were just as important a part of the antique fabric as the churches, and continued to be important into the ninth century.

Of the churches mentioned by Agnellus, most were still standing, and presumably in use, in the early ninth century. Only four are described as destroyed, although others are said to be in need of repair, and Agnellus describes some repairs sponsored by outsiders including the popes and Lombard kings. Likewise, although some palaces are in ruins or are being dismantled, the city walls and the main palace are described in the present tense, and Agnellus states that at least one bath was still operating in his day, which seems to indicate that the water supply still functioned at some level. Through the text, then, we get a sense of slightly crumbling glory.

If memories of the Ravenna's imperial past were apparent on all sides, by the ninth century they seem to have inspired the desire to remove pieces in order to appropriate some of that glory. One consequence of the decaying state of the city's fabric is that older buildings were often destroyed, or at least mined, for building and decorative materials. The best-known example of such spoliation is that done by Charlemagne, but several other instances of destruction or removal are also mentioned by Agnellus. He tells us that he himself dismantled a palace built outside the city by Theoderic, in order to use the building materials for his own house. Bishop Valerius apparently did the same thing to two *episcopia* built by the Arian Ostrogoths; according to Agnellus, the destruction took place around the year 816. A bishop of Bologna "carried off" a sarcophagus supposedly dating to the time of Apollinaris, and took it to his own church at Bologna, around 834.[121]

It is documented in two places other than the *LPR* that Charlemagne took *spolia*, that is, used building materials, from Ravenna.[122] In his *Vita Karoli Magni*, as part of the description of the Aachen Palatine Chapel, Einhard notes that "... since he could not get columns and marble from elsewhere, he took the trouble of having them brought from Rome and Ravenna."[123] This is confirmed by a letter from Pope Hadrian I to Charlemagne, dating to 787, authorizing him to take "mosaic and marble and other materials both from the floors and the walls" of an unnamed palace in Ravenna.[124] Since Ravenna was no longer the residence of a high-level ruler, it is often assumed that Charlemagne dismantled the main Ostrogothic/exarchal palace, but, as we have seen, there were several other palaces inside and near Ravenna that may have been meant. In the Aachen chapel, the so-called "throne of Charlemagne" is made of antique spolia, as are most of the columns, including some of green porphyry and red Egyptian granite. None of these pieces can be definitely linked to Ravenna, but the rarity and high quality of the stones would justify bringing them all the way from Italy.[125]

Agnellus does not mention the removal of these building materials by Charlemagne, but he does relate an event which took place some fourteen years later, just after Charlemagne's imperial coronation. Agnellus tells of an equestrian statue, whose rider was accepted as being Theoderic: Charlemagne took this statue back to Francia and set it up in his palace at Aachen.[126] The presence of the statue in Aachen is confirmed by a poem written in 829 by Walahfrid Strabo in which the poet describes a statue with many corresponding features in the palace complex at Aachen and interprets it allegorically as a symbol of pride and greed.[127] Charlemagne was not the last emperor to take *spolia* from Ravenna. Agnellus describes a large piece of polished porphyry in the church of San Severo, which was taken to Francia on the order of Emperor Lothar and used as a table in the church of St. Sebastian; Agnellus knows this because he himself was the one who supervised its packing, "but with my heart full of grief."[128]

Paul the Deacon, in his geography of Italy, names Ravenna as "noblest of cities" (*nobilissima urbium*). Saxo Poeta, who in the late ninth century wrote an epic poem about Charlemagne, describes Ravenna as "beautiful" (*pulcra*) and "famous" (*famosa*).[129] If Ravenna was noble and beautiful and famous, it was because of its glamorous late antique past that was still so evident in the city. The buildings and infrastructure constructed at the height of Ravenna's power were useable and used into the Middle Ages and could serve as inspiration both for new rulers with imperial ambitions and for new generations of Ravenna's own inhabitants. Ravenna in the ninth century was in one sense a relic of late antiquity, but it was a relic with a heartbeat, with a civic consciousness that did not need to be reinvented, but had maintained itself throughout the centuries in which darkness had overtaken the rest of the Roman world.

APPENDIX: TABLES

Table 1. Roman emperors

		Theodosius I	392–395
Honorius	395–423	Arcadius	395–408
[John	423–425]	Theodosius II	408–450
Valentinian III	425–455		
Maximian	455	Marcian	450–457
[Ricimer – various]	455–475	Leo I	457–474
Romulus Augustulus	476	Leo II	474
		Zeno	474–491
		Anastasius I	491–518
		Justin I	518–527
		Justinian I	527–565
		Justin II	565–578
		Tiberius II Constantine	578–582
		Maurice	582–602
		Phocas	602–610
		Heraclius	610–641
		Constans II	641–668
		Constantine IV	668–685
		Justinian II	685–695
		Leontios	695–698
		Tiberius III	698–705
		Justinian II	705–711
		Philippicus	711–713
		Anastasius II	713–716
		Theodosius III	716–717
		Leo III	717–741
		Constantine V	741–775

Table 2. Kings of Italy

Odoacer	476–493
Theoderic	493–526
Athalaric	526–534
Theodahad	534–536
Witigis	536–540
Hildebad	540–541
Eraric	541
Totila	541–552
Teia	552–553

Table 3. Exarchs (with attested titles)

Narses (v.g. patricius, praepositus sacri palatii)	551–566/8?
Longinus (praefectus praetorio)	ca. 567–572
Zacharias (patricius)	565 or 570
Baduarius (patricius, curopalates)	575–577
Decius (patricius v.g., exarchus)	584
Smaragdus (patricius et exarchus)	ca. 585–589
Julian (exarchus)	589?
Romanus (patricius et exarchus Italiae v.e. v.g.)	590–596
Gregory (praefectus praetorio v.g.)	595
John (praefectus praetorio Italiae v.e.)	598, 600
Callicinus (patricius et exarchus)	ca. 596–599 or 602
Smaragdus (patricius et exarchus)	ca. 602–608 or 613
John (exarchus)	608 or 613–616
Eleutherius (patricius et cubicularius)	616–619
Gregory (patricius Romanorum)	619–625
Isaac (patricius et exarchus Italiae)	625–643
Theodore Calliopas (patricius exarchus)	643–ca. 645
Plato (patricius v.g. v.c.)	645–?649
Olympius (cubicularius et exarchus)	649–652
Theodore Calliopas (patricius et exarchus)	653–666
Gregory (exarchus)	666–bef. 678
Theodore (patricius et exarchus v.e.)	ca. 678–687
John Platyn (exarchus v.g.)	687–692 or bef. 701
no exarch ?	692–701
Theophylact (cubicularius, patricius et exarchus Italiae)	701–705
no exarch?	705–710
John Rizocopus (patricius et exarchus)	710
Eutychius (patricius et exarchus)	710–713
Scholasticus (cubicularius, patricius et exarchus Italiae)	ca. 713–ca. 723??
Paul (patricius et exarchus)	ca. 723–726
Eutychius (patricius et exarchus)	727–751

Note: Derived from Brown, 1984, pp. 247–82; Ferluga, "L'esarcato," 1991; and Zanini, 1998, p. 377.

Table 4. Lombard kings

Alboin	565–572
Cleph	572–574
[Interregnum	574–584]
Authari	584–590
Agilulf	590–616
Adaloald	616–626
Arioald	626–636
Rothari	636–652
Rodoald	652–653
Aripert I	653–661
Godepert	661–662
Perctarit	661–662
Grimoald	662–671
Garibald	671
Perctarit	671–688
Cunipert	688–689
Alahis	689
Cunipert	689–700
Liutpert	700–702
Raginpert	702
Aripert II	702–712
Ansprand	712
Liutprand	712–744
Hildeprand	744
Ratchis	744–749
Aistulf	749–756
Desiderius	756–774

Table 5. Bishops of Ravenna

Apollinaris	?
Aderitus	?
Eleucadius	?
Marcian	?
Calocerus	?
Proculus	?
Probus I	?
Datus	?
Liberius I	?
Agapitus	?
Marcellinus	?
Severus	ca. 340s
Liberius II	?
Probus II	?
Florentius	?
Liberius III	?
Ursus	ca. 405–431?
Peter I	ca. 431–450
Neon	ca. 450–473
Exuperantius	ca. 473–477
John I	477–494
Peter II	494–520
Aurelian	521
Ecclesius	522–532
Ursicinus	533–536
Victor	538–545
Maximian	546–557
Agnellus	557–570
Peter III	570–578
John II	578–595
Marinian	595–606
John III	606–625
John IV	625–631
Bonus	631–642
Maurus	642–671
Reparatus	671–677
Theodore	677–691
Damian	692–708
Felix	709–725
John V	726–744
Sergius	744–769
Leo	ca. 770–778
John VI	ca. 778–785
Gratiosus	ca. 786–789
Valerius	ca. 789–810
Martin	ca. 810–818
Petronax	ca. 818–837
George	ca. 837–846

Table 6. Popes

Peter	–64/67
Linus	ca. 70
Cletus	ca. 85
Clement	ca. 95
Aneclitus	same
Evaristus	ca. 100
Alexander	ca. 110
Sixtus I	ca. 120
Telesphorus	ca. 130
Hyginus	ca. 140
Pius I	ca. 145
Anicetus	ca. 160
Soter	ca. 170
Eleutherus	ca. 180
Victor	ca. 195
Zephyrinus	198/9–217
Callistus	217–222
Urban I	222–230
Pontian	230–235
Anteros	235–236
Fabian	236–250
Cornelius	251–253
Lucius	253–254
Stephen I	254–257
Sixtus II	257–258
Dionysius	260–267
Felix I	268–273
Eutychian	274–282
Gaius	282–295
Marcellinus	295–303
Marcellus	305/6–306/7
Eusebius	308
Miltiades	310–314
Silvester	314–335
Mark	336
Julius I	337–352
Liberius I	352–366
Felix II	355–365
Damasus	366–384
Siricius	384–399
Anastasius I	399–401/2
Innocent I	401/2–417
Zosimus	417–418
Boniface I	418–422
Celestine I	422–432

(continued)

Table 6 (*continued*)

Sixtus III	432–440
Leo I the Great	440–461
Hilary	461–468
Simplicius	468–483
Felix III	483–492
Gelasius	492–496
Anastasius II	496–498
Symmachus	498–514
Hormisdas	514–523
John I	523–526
Felix IV	526–530
Boniface II	530–532
John II	533–535
Agapitus	535–536
Silverius	536–537
Vigilius	537–555
Pelagius I	556–561
John III	561–574
Benedict I	575–579
Pelagius II	579–790
Gregory I the Great	590–604
Sabinian	604–606
Boniface III	606–607
Boniface IV	608–615
Deusdedit	615–618
Boniface V	619–625
Honorius	625–638
Severinus	640
John IV	640–642
Theodore	642–649
Martin I	649–653
Eugene I	654–657
Vitalian	657–672
Adeodatus	672–676
Donus	676–678
Agatho	678–681
Leo II	682–683
Benedict II	684–685
John V	685–686
Conon	686–687
Sergius I	687–701
John VI	701–705
John VII	705–707
Sisinnius	708
Constantine	708–715

(*continued*)

Gregory II	715–731
Gregory III	731–741
Zacharias	741–752
Stephen II	752–757
Paul I	757–768
Stephen III	768–772
Hadrian I	772–797
Leo III	797–816
Stephen IV	816–817
Paschal I	817–824
Eugene II	824–827
Valentine	827
Gregory IV	827–844
Sergius II	844–847
Leo IV	847–855

Table 7. Dimensions of Ravenna's basilicas

Church	Date	Nave, aisles length	# of columns per row	Total width (ext.)	Nave width	Aisle width	Apse width	Apse depth
Ursiana Cathedral (Fig. 20)	ca. 400	60	14 (4 rows)	43	15	6	14	8
San Giovanni Evangelista, 1st phase (Fig. 10)	ca. 425	33	9	24.5	10.1	5.6	10.2	8.3
San Giovanni Evangelista, 2nd phase (Fig. 11)		42.6	12	24.5	10.1	5.6	10.2	8.3
St. Agnes	ca. 450s	29.3	9		8.9	?	?	?
Sant'Agata Maggiore (Fig. 27)	ca. 470s	37	10	23.5	10	5.2	8.9	7
Sant'Apollinare Nuovo (Fig. 46)	ca. 500	35.8	12	24	10.8	4.3	9.5	7.5
Santo Spirito (Arian cathedral, Fig. 59)	ca. 500	20.8	7	18.5	8.7	3.5	8	5.6
Ca'Bianca (Fig. 69)	6th c.	35.50	12		10.20	4.00	8.2	6.0
San Michele in Africisco (Fig. 88)	ca. 545	14.46	2 (piers)	14	6.04	2.7	4.93	3.72
Sant'Apollinare, Classe (Fig. 90)	530s–540s	47.25	12	32	14.5	7.17	12.4	8.4
San Severo, Classe (Fig. 99)	570s	44.65	12		12.35	5.6	12.6	8.15

Note: Only basilica churches with naves, aisles, and apses are included here; some data from churches that do not survive today (the Ursiana cathedral, the Ca·Bianca, St. Agnes) are speculative, and all measurements are approximate.

NOTES

One. Introduction

1 Chrysos, 2005, pp. 1061–2, who notes that *sedes imperii* is also common.
2 Duval, 1997, p. 129.
3 See Curran, 2000, pp. 43–7.
4 This is a question that many scholars have recently discussed; see most recently Marazzi, 2006; also Mazza, 2005, pp. 8–17; Pani Ermini, 2005; articles in the collection *Sedes Regiae*, 2000, ed. Ripoll/Gurt, esp. those by J. Arce and S. Gelichi; Duval, 1997; and Curcic, 1993.
5 There is an extensive bibliography on this topic; see most recently Curcic, 1993; and Baldini Lippolis, 2001, esp. pp. 29–46, and with a catalog of individual sites.
6 Joffe, 1998, p. 567. "Disembedded," according to the first proponent of this term, meant that the capital was removed from existing economic and social networks, but Joffe notes that in fact all such capitals were fully embedded in their socioeconomic matrices. A few examples from various historical periods include Akhenaten's capital at Tell el-Amarna in Egypt; Abbasid Baghdad; Washington, DC, USA; and Brasilia, Brazil.
7 Mazza, 2005, pp. 10–12, points out that if a city did not have a tradition that granted it legitimacy, one had to be created for it, as happened, most successfully, at Constantinople.
8 Chrysos, 2005, pp. 1061–2.
9 Of the vast scholarly literature on this subject, see especially for Italy La Rocca, 1992; Gelichi, 1994; Ward-Perkins, 1997; Brogiolo/Gelichi, 1998, esp. chs. 1 and 2 on the historiography of the debate; and Christie, 2006, pp. 183–280, with complete bibliography.
10 Gelichi, 2002, p. 181.
11 Brown/Christie, 1989, pp. 383–4.
12 Squatriti, 1992, p. 8.
13 See Bertelli, 1999.
14 See Deliyannis, ed., 2006, pp. 67–79.
15 See ibid., pp. 11–19.
16 See Deliyannis, "About the *Liber pontificalis*," 2008.
17 Vasina, "La fortuna," 1978, and idem, ed., 1991.
18 See Ropa, 1993; and Deliyannis, ed., 2006, pp. 68–71.

19 Vasina, "La fortuna," 1978, pp. 100–1.

20 Ibid., pp. 88–95.

21 Deliyannis, ed., 2006, pp. 53–67.

22 On Traversari, see Clarke, 1997, pp. 169–75; particularly interesting is that Traversari compared Ravenna's art and architecture favorably to that of Rome, showing that the rivalry continued into the Renaissance.

23 Vasina, "La fortuna," 1978, p. 113; Novara, 1998, pp. 15–16.

24 Benericetti, 1994, pp. 45–7, describes the historical writings of Ferretti in detail; the manuscripts are Vat. Lat. 3753, 4968, 5441, 5831; Vat. Urb. 408; Vat. Barb. 2479, 2746; and Firenze Bibl. Naz. II.IV.174.

25 Deliyannis, ed., 2006, pp. 78–9.

26 See esp. Vasina, "Benedetto Bacchini," 1978.

27 Novara, 1998.

28 See Maioli, 1990, esp. p. 376.

29 See esp. Bovini, "Principali restauri," 1966; and Iannucci, "Il mausoleo ritrovato," 1996.

30 Novara, 1998, pp. 23–5.

31 Iannucci, 1996, "Il Mausoleo," p. 184.

32 See a good summary at http://www.emiliaromagna.beniculturali.it/index.php?en/125/la-nascita-delle-soprintendenze-in-emilia-romagna.

33 Vols. 1–33 (1911–1929); n.s. vols 1–6=34–51 (1930–39); 3rd ser. vols. 1–49=52–100 (1950–69); 4th ser. vols. 1–8=101–108 (1970–74), vols. 109–156 (1975–2000).

34 The excavations were only partially published at the time; recently the notes, drawings, and photographs have been published in Savini, 1998; Novara, *Palatium*, 2001; and Augenti, ed., 2002.

35 See especially Cirelli, 2005.

36 For a detailed description, see Manzelli, *Ravenna*, 2000, pp. 33–8; Roncuzzi, 2005, p. 386; and Piancastelli, 2004. Roncuzzi notes, pp. 388–9, that recent industrial extraction of water and methane gas from beneath the surface has increased the rate of subsidence to 2 m per century, but Piancastelli points out that this high rate has decreased since the 1970s, and is now nearly back to the original rate.

37 See Roncuzzi, 2005, p. 389 and fig. 10; Bermond-Montanari, "Demografia," 1990, pp. 41–2; and Manzelli, *Ravenna*, 2000, pp. 39–41.

38 For example, *LPR* chs. 83, 168. Most comprehensively explained by Manzelli: *Ravenna*, 2000, pp. 39–41; see also Farioli Campanati, 1977, p. 9.

39 Manzelli, "La *forma urbis*," 2001, pp. 45–6.

40 Novara, 1998.

41 The excavations were only partially published at the time (Ghirardini, 1916); recently the notes, drawings, and photographs have been published in Savini, 1998; and Novara, *Palatium*, 2001.

42 Augenti, 2003, and idem, "Nuove indagini," 2005.

43 Cortesi, 1978 and 1980; Roncuzzi/Veggi, 1968. For criticisms of the test-pit sampling, see Maioli, 1990, p. 383; Manzelli, *Ravenna*, 2000, n. 219 and 220; and Cirelli, 2008, pp. 19 and 67.

44 Manzelli, *Ravenna*, 2000.

45 Cirelli, 2005, and idem, 2008; the latter was published too late to be fully consulted for this book.

46 Bowersock/Brown/Grabar, eds., 1999.

47 Strzygowski's book, *Orient oder Rom*, published in 1901, proposed that early Christian art drew its inspiration largely from eastern Mediterranean rather than classical Roman sources.

48 Galassi, 1930; essentially followed by many later scholars; for figurative art, see Rizzardi, "I mosaici parietali," 2005, pp. 233–5.

49 See Deichmann, 1989, pp. 243–6 and 353–7, for detailed summaries of the scholarly literature on the "Orient oder Rom" debate; Russo, "L'architettura," 2005.

50 Wharton, 1995, pp. 3–12; at pp. 153–9, she notes that in surveys of western/ Mediterranean art, Ravenna has always occupied an "ambivalent center" as a western outpost of Byzantine art: "the locus for the dangerous shift from clas- sical (natural, good, moral, skilled, masculine) to post classical (unnatural, bad, degenerate, unskilled, female). . . . Ravenna's art is good insofar as Ravenna's location is constructed as the West and problematic when it is constructed as the East, that is, the western outpost of Byzantium" (p. 158).

51 Elsner, 2002.

52 The fundamental study is Deichmann, 1954, pp. 41–55, who notes that impost blocks probably originated as a way of leveling spoliated columns and capitals of different heights. Deichmann offers a few fifth-century examples from the Aegean in order to show that the feature originated in the East; he rejects the examples from San Giorgio Maggiore in Naples by saying that the date (usually given at around 400) is undetermined, and likewise seems uninterested in the example of Ss. Giovanni e Paolo in Rome, of about the same date. Russo, "L'architettura," 2005, p. 91, suggests that the phenomenon began not in Constantinople and the East, but in North Africa. In light of archaeological and architectural investigations since 1954, by which several of Deichmann's exam- ples have been redated, another study of this question is warranted, although it is beyond the scope of the present book.

53 See De Angelis d'Ossat, 1962, pp. 137–55, for a detailed discussion, and more recently Whitehouse, 1988; for comparative material, see Russo, 1996, and idem, 2005, pp. 92–3.

54 On the fifth-century sculpture, see most recently Farioli, 2005.

55 See most recently Christie, 2006, pp. 130–3 and 208–13. The debate is summa- rized by Brenk, 1987, and Ward-Perkins, 1999; Deichmann, 1975, saw spolia as more pragmatic than symbolic, whereas others, including, e.g., Krautheimer, 1961, have seen aesthetic and ideological overtones, and Ward-Perkins, 1999, argues for both. See also Brenk, 1987; Pensabene, 1995; Kinney, 1997 and 2001; and Elsner, 2004. Most of these studies focus on Rome.

56 See Maguire, 1987, esp. pp. 8–15; see also Janes, 1998, pp. 6–9.

Two. Roman Ravenna

1 See esp. Patitucci Uggeri, 2005; Roncuzzi, 2005; Fabbri, 1990, 1991, and 2004; and Manzelli, *Ravenna*, 2000, pp. 31–8.

2 Patitucci Uggeri, 2005.

3 See Roncuzzi, 2005; and Fabbri, 1990, for surveys of the geology and geomor- phology of Ravenna in the prehistoric and Roman periods. See also Fabbri, 2004, pp. 17–18.

4 Pliny the Elder, *Historia naturalis*, 3.20; see Fabbri, 1990, pp. 24–5.

5 See Patitucci Uggeri, 2005, fig. 1. For a clear and concise description of the Po's course from the pre-Roman era to the mid-twelfth century, see idem, pp. 258–9. On attitudes to the river Po in the Roman period, see Fabbi, 2001, pp. 108–9.

6 Manzelli, *Ravenna*, 2000, p. 32, states that configurations of these watercourses cannot be really known.

7 On the prehistoric archaeology of the region around Ravenna, see Bermond Montanari, "Demografia," 1990; and Magnani, 2001, pp. 33–9.

8 Manzelli, *Ravenna*, 2000, pp. 98–102 and 222, esp. for the finds at the Via D'Azeglio and Via C. Morigia excavations; see also Bermond Montanari, "L'impianto," 1990; and Manzelli, "Ravenna, una città," 2000.

9 Magnani, 2001, p. 33 – but it seems to read too much into the much later statements of Strabo, Pliny et al., to assume that there were different ethnic groups in this area.

10 On the prehistoric Adriatic coast, see Malnati, 2005; on Italy generally, see, e.g., Pallottino, 1991.

11 On the textual sources for Roman Ravenna, see especially Vattuone, 1990; and Manzelli, *Ravenna*, 2000, pp. 20–30.

12 Strabo, *Geography*, 5.1.7 and 5.1.11; see Magnani, 2001, pp. 25–9, who notes that Zosimus in his *Historia Nova*, 5.27, also says that Thessalians founded it. See also Rebecchi, 1998, pp. 304–5.

13 Pliny the Elder, *Historia naturalis*, 3.46 (or 3.20); see Magnani, 2001, pp. 29–31, who proposes that Pliny should instead be read as referring to the Umbrian members of the tribe Sapinia.

14 Ptolemy, *Geography*, 3.1.20, discussed by Malnate/Violante, 1995, p. 102.

15 See Vattuone, 1990, pp. 52–7.

16 See Pellegrini, 1990, for a complete discussion of this issue; see also Bermond Montanari, "Demografia," 1990, p. 39.

17 Pellegrini, 1990, pp. 70–2.

18 Mansuelli, 1990, notes that this linking of Ravenna and Spina goes back to historians and antiquarians of the sixteenth century.

19 Fabbri, 1990, pp. 12–3; Malnati, 2005, p. 32. On Spina, see most recently Rebecchi, ed., 1998; and Bianchi, 2002.

20 Rebecchi, 1993 and 1998; see also P. Fabbri, 1990, p. 13.

21 Manzelli, *Ravenna*, 2000, p. 22.

22 Most influentially by Testi-Rasponi, ed., 1924, pp. 116–18; followed by Bovini, "Le origini," 1956; Mazzotti, 1967; Felletti Maj, 1969; Mazzotti, 1970; others, notably, Mansuelli, 1967 and 1971, place the origin under Claudius. See Manzelli, *Ravenna*, 2000, p. 205.

23 Manzelli, *Ravenna*, 2000, pp. 118–24; Magnani, 2001, pp. 34–5.

24 On the walls, see especially Fabbri, 2004; Manzelli, "Le mura," 2001; Manzelli, "Le fortificazioni," 2000, pp. 32–8. On the chemical makeup of the mortar, see Costa/Gotti/Tognon, 2001.

25 On the type of bricks, see Righini, 1990, pp. 263–81; Manzelli, "Le fortificazioni," 2000, pp. 34–5, and "Le mura," 2001, pp. 12–24.

26 Manzelli, "Le fortificazioni," 2000, p. 33. The date has been controversial. Deichmann, 1989, pp. 24–5, argues that the wall dates to the late second

century, on the basis of the letters stamped on the bricks, which he claims would not have been used in this part of Italy in the third century. Capellini, 1993, pp. 47ff., describes evidence from several sites excavated in 1983–8 that support the thesis of one late antique or early medieval foundation for the walls. He cites the section of wall excavated at Porta S. Vittore (p. 50) as cutting through an imperial-era house that was built in the first or second century and abandoned in the third.

27 Gelichi, 2005, p. 833–4. There has been some discussion about whether the wall that was discovered was parallel to, but not the same as, the eastern wall of the rectangular *oppidum* enshrined in the late antique wall (e.g., Maioli, "La Topografia," 2005, p. 46), but other scholars have concluded that they do fall on the same lines and that the late antique wall probably largely followed the path of the republican wall (Manzelli, *Ravenna*, 2000, pp. 204–5, and Gelichi, 2005, p. 832).

28 Fabbri, 2004, p. 20, esp. n. 12, thinks that there was a wall on the northeast that did not include the watercourses; Manzelli, "Le fortificazioni," 2000, p. 38, and p. 44 n. 52, also believes that there was a wall on this side, but leaves the question open; see also Manzelli, *Ravenna*, 2000, p. 205.

29 Manzelli, *Ravenna*, 2000, pp. 97–8.

30 Magnani, 2001, p. 36.

31 Malnate/Violante, 1995, pp. 116–17; Magnani, 2001, pp. 36–7; Manzelli, "Ravenna, una città," 2000, p. 62.

32 Tramonti, 1997; Manzelli, "Le fortificazioni," 2000, pp. 35–6; idem, "Ravenna, una città," 2000, p. 64.

33 Strabo, *Geography*, 5.1.11; Rebecchi, 1998, pp. 302–5; Manzelli, *Ravenna*, 2000, pp. 22–3 n. 33, notes that there is no concrete evidence for this.

34 See Patitucci Uggeri, 2005, pp. 288–95; Uggeri, 1997; Farioli Campanati, 1977, p. 11.

35 For the latter argument, see Cirelli, 2008, p. 67.

36 The sites of Via C. Morigia and Via D'Azeglio; see Manzelli; "La forma urbis," 2001, p. 48; and Manzelli, *Ravenna*, 2000, p. 66.

37 Manzelli, "Ravenna, una città," 2000, p. 64, and 2000, pp. 98–102.

38 Maioli, "La topografia," 2005. Manzelli; *Ravenna*, 2000, pp. 69–70.

39 Manzelli/Grassigli, 2001, p. 135.

40 Manzelli, "La forma urbis," 2001, p. 48; Christie, 1989, pp. 121–2. Capellini, 1993, p. 41, insists that the evidence is too scattered to definitively prove the location of the wall.

41 Manzelli, *Ravenna*, 2000, pp. 209 and 227. The location of the original settlement is controversial; for a description of the controversy, see Fabbri, 2004, p. 20. Mansuelli, 1971, proposed that the first habitations were along the east bank of the Padenna, and Roncuzzi, 1992 and 2005, insists on the existence of a well-developed town east of the *oppidum*, which he says dates to the fifth century BC. He states (2005, pp. 390–3) that the rectangular wall of the *oppidum* is simply part of the late antique wall and that the pre-imperial city center was located to the east of the Padenna. Roncuzzi argues (2005, pp. 400–1 n. 4) that the section of wall found in the Banca Popolare excavation, linked to the Torre Salustra and to other pieces of wall to the northeast, are all part of the aqueduct built by Trajan, not republican at all. Manzelli, *Ravenna*, 2000, p. 117 n. 378,

refutes Roncuzzi's 1992 arguments and notes that the unpublished remains on which Roncuzzi is basing his reconstruction for the eastern sector probably were sixth–fifth century BC, but it is impossible to know.

42 On the sources, see Mansuelli, 1971; and most comprehensively, Vattuone, 1990, pp. 57–9.

43 Plutarch, *Vita Marii*, 2.

44 Cicero, *Pro Balbo*, 50: "Ravennatem foederato ex populo."

45 See Susini, "La questione," 1968; and Vattuone, 1990, p. 58. Manzelli, *Ravenna*, 2000, p. 25, suggests instead that Ravenna had Roman municipal status already by 89 BC, citing Luzatto, 1968; and Tibiletti, 1973.

46 C. Julius Caesar, *Bellum civile*, 1.5; Suetonius, *Julius Caesar*, ch. 30; Appian, *De bello civili*, 2.32–5. Appian also tells us (1.89 and 1.92) that in 82 BC Metellus "sailed around toward Ravenna and took possession of the level wheat-growing country of Uritanus," but in the second c. AD, when he was writing, Ravenna was a major center and thus probably an important topographical referent. See Susini, "La questione," 1968.

47 Suetonius, *Julius Caesar*, ch. 30.

48 Suetonius, *Divus Augustus*, ch. 49; Tacitus, *Annales*, 4.5; Vegetius, *Epitoma rei militaris*, 4.31.

49 On the controversy, see Bollini, 1990, pp. 297–8 and p. 318 n. 1; and Tramonti, 1997.

50 Appian, *De bello civili*, 5.78 and 80; Manzelli, *Ravenna*, 2000, p. 26.

51 Tramonti, 1997, pp. 122–30.

52 Pliny the Elder, *Historia naturalis*, 3.20. See Roncuzzi/Veggi, 1968; Fabbri, 1990, pp. 24–5; Squatriti, 1992, pp. 3–5; and Cirelli, 2008, pp. 19–20.

53 Mansuelli, 1971, pp. 337–8, apparently accepted by Manzelli, *Ravenna*, 2000, p. 23, proposed that the large port thus mentioned was the port of Ravenna, and that the Vatrenus flowed into the harbor, but Pliny is clearly talking about Spina 25 km to the north.

54 Fabbri, 1990 and 2004, pp. 17–21; Cirelli, 2008, pp. 19–23. Patitucci Uggeri, 2005, pp. 280–1, who reports the excavation of a lighthouse at Baro Zavelea, presumably the point at which the river/canal joined the Po. Fabbri, 2004, p. 30, notes that it had always been presumed that a new canal of 25 km had been dug between the Po and Ravenna, but that this was not necessary since the Padusa/Padenna already covered most of this route.

55 See most recently Patitucci Uggeri, 2005; at p. 287 she notes that this network was particularly important because in parts of the year the Adriatic was not navigable because of weather. Cassiodorus, *Variae*, 12.24, writing in the mid–sixth century, notes that ships can always sail between Ravenna and Istria, "for when the sea is closed by the raging of the winds, a path through pleasant river country is opened to you.... From a distance, when their channel cannot be seen, it looks as if they [the ships] are moving through the fields. They were kept still by ropes, but they move drawn by cables..." (trans. Barnish, 1992, p. 176).

56 Fabbri, 2004, p. 30, notes that it had always been presumed that a canal of 25 kilometers had been dug between the main branch of the Po, the Eridanus to the north, and the port, but that this was hardly necessary since the Padenna already covered most of this route. Manzelli, *Ravenna*, 2000, pp. 219–20, on the

other hand, claims that if a river and canal, the Padenna and the *fossa Augusta*, flowed south into the harbor it would cause massive silting within the harbor, and that these watercourses instead flowed north from the harbor into the lagoons and the small port to the northeast of the city.

57 Cirelli, 2008, p. 20.
58 Roncuzzi/Veggi, 1968, pp. 193–201; see Manzelli, *Ravenna*, 2000, pp. 104–5, 132–3, and 161–2. Soundings in the northern section of Ravenna, near the Porta Cybo, have revealed a channel 50 meters wide flanked by strong cement and masonry embankments of unknown date; its bed was 3–4 meters below the top level of its embankments. Archaeological soundings at Via A. Guerrini, just to the east of the *oppidum*, revealed massive cement and masonry quays on either side of its course to a width of 65 meters, with pottery dating to the late republican and early imperial periods. At 2 kilometers to the north of the city wall it expanded to a width of over 200 meters.
59 Roncuzzi/Veggi, 1968, pp. 100–2; Manzelli, *Ravenna*, 2000, pp. 83–4; Maioli, "La topografia," 2005, p. 47. Fabbri, 2004, p. 29, proposes the hypothesis that this smaller port was for commercial use in contrast to the larger military port of Classe. Because the Rocca Brancaleone occupies the site, little can be known about it.
60 Pliny the Elder, *Historia naturalis* 36.18; *LPR* ch. 39.
61 Bermond Montanari, "L'impianto," 1990, p. 240.
62 Manzelli, 2005.
63 See esp. Maioli, 1990, for the detailed description on which the following is based.
64 Manzelli, "La forma urbis," 2001, p. 54, suggests that the second-century works were connected with the emperor Trajan's campaigns in Dacia; Maioli, "Vie d'acque," 2001, p. 220, proposes that they took place during the reign of Hadrian.
65 Jordanes, *Getica*, ed. Mommsen, 1882, 29.148–51: "classem ducentarum quinquaginta navium Dione referente tutissima dudum credebatur recipere statione." On the Roman imperial fleet, see esp. Bollini, 1990; and Frassineti, 2005.
66 See Fabbri, 2005.
67 Frassinetti, 2005, p. 68.
68 *Notitia Dignitatum*: "praefectus classis Ravennatium, cum curis eiusdem civitatis Ravennae." Susini, "Ravenna e il mondo," 1990, pp. 133–4; and Vattuone, 1990, p. 59.
69 Susini, 1988; see Deichmann, 1989, p. 131.
70 Frassinetti, 2005, p. 69.
71 Listed in Giacomini, "Anagrafe dei classiari," 1990, p. 321.
72 Frassinetti, 2005, p. 68; Donati, 2005; Bollini, 1990.
73 Published and discussed in Susini, "Un catalogo classiario," 1968.
74 This list is derived from Bollini, 1990, p. 312.
75 Bollini, 2005, p. 127.
76 Bollini, 1990, pp. 299 and 316.
77 Maioli, "Vie d'acqua," 2001, p. 220; see also Maioli, 1990; Manzelli, "La forma urbis," 2001, p. 54.
78 Maioli, 1992, pp. 502–11.

79 Maioli, 2002, pp. 41–2; idem, "La topografia," 2005, p. 49.

80 Maioli, "Approvvigionamenti," 2005, p. 174; see Mansuelli, 1962; and Maioli, *La villa romana*, 1989.

81 For a detailed summary, see Manzelli, *Ravenna*, 2000.

82 For example, Tacitus, *Annales*, 1.58; 2.63; many references to the fleet of Ravenna.

83 For example, Martial, *Epigrams*, 3.56 and 3.57 (bad water), 3.93 (frogs), and 13.21 (asparagus); Silius Italicus, *Punica*, 8.100 (swamps); Pliny the Elder, *Historia naturalis* 14.34 and 19.54 (vegetables). Interestingly, asparagus requires well-drained soil to grow, perhaps an indication that the terrain was not all marshy around the city.

84 See esp. Righini, 1990.

85 Strabo, *Geography*, 5.1.7.

86 Vitruvius, *De architectura* 1.4.11: "exemplar autem huius rei Gallicae paludes possunt esse, quae circum<cingunt> Altinum, Ravennam, Aquileiam, alia que quae in eiusmodi locis municipia sunt proxima paludibus, quod his rationibus habent incredibilem salubritatem."

87 Vitruvius, *De architectura* 2.9.11: "est autem maxime id considerare Ravennae, quod ibi omnia opera et publica et privata sub fundamentis eius generis habeant palos."

88 Manzelli, *Ravenna*, 2000, pp. 101 and 105.

89 Righini, 1990, pp. 259–61.

90 Fabbri, 1990, pp. 15–16; Manzelli, *Ravenna*, 2000, pp. 31–2.

91 Manzelli/Grassigli, 2001, p. 147.

92 Manzelli, "La forma urbis," 2001, p. 50; see also Johnson, 1983.

93 E. La Rocca, 1992, interprets the inscription to refer to 42 BC, although it had previously been read as referring to 43 BC.

94 Mansuelli, 1967; Capellini, 1987; Christie, 1989; Manzelli, "Le fortificazioni," 2000; also Manzelli, *Ravenna*, 2000, pp. 91–4. The inscription read, "Ti. Claudius Drusi F. Caesar Aug. Germanicus Pont. Max. Tr. Pot. II Cos. Desig. IIII Imp. III P.P. Dedit."

95 Mansuelli, 1967, p. 201; Fabbri, 2004, pp. 22 and 27, citing Manzelli, "Le fortificazioni," 2000; see also Manzelli, *Ravenna*, 2000, p. 206, and idem, 2005, p. 39.

96 Interestingly, this marble decoration does not seem to have been contemporary with the brick interior of the arch, implying that the decoration (presumably by Claudius) was applied to a preexisting structure. See Manzelli, "Le fortificazioni," 2000, p. 28, citing Mansuelli, 1967, p. 192.

97 Bermond Montanari, "L'impianto," 1990, p. 227. Mazzotti, 1967, p. 221, proposed that this road, the *decumanus*, also crossed the *fossa Lamisa*, intersecting with the *cardo*, and then leading to the Porta Asiana.

98 Bermond Montanari, "L'impianto," 1990, p. 227; Manzelli, *Ravenna*, 2000, pp. 66–71; Manzelli/Grassigli, 2001, p. 136.

99 Montevecchi, "La strada," 2004.

100 See Manzelli, *Ravenna*, 2000, pp. 206–7, and idem, "I monumenti perduti," 2001. The evidence is very scanty; several of the sixteenth- to nineteenth-century scholars who wrote histories of Ravenna identified the locations of such structures, but their information came from Agnellus or from topographical references in much later documents. For example, Agnellus (*LPR* ch. 2) tells

us that a Temple of Apollo, which stood by the Porta Aurea, was demolished
by the prayers of St. Apollinaris; he took this information from the sixth- or
seventh-century *Passio* of Apollinaris (see below, Chapter 6), but it is not clear
whether the information is accurate or merely a hagiographical *topos*. This
passage also says that the amphitheater was just outside the Porta Aurea, but
we do not know at what date such a structure would have been constructed,
and no trace of it survives; for comparative material, see Cirelli, 2008, pp. 38–9.

101 This location is on the present Via Guerrini; see Manzelli, "La forma urbis,"
2001, p. 52; Manzelli, *Ravenna*, 2000, pp. 104–5.

102 Susini, 1988.

103 Novara/Sarasini, 2001, p. 85.

104 Manzelli, "La forma urbis," 2001, p. 52.

105 The sixth-century *Anon. Vales.* 71, tells us, "He [Theoderic] restored the aqueduct of Ravenna, which the ruler Trajan had made, and after much time introduced water...."

106 Prati, 1988, pp. 32–4.

107 Idem, pp. 44–6. Manzelli, "La forma urbis," 2001, pp. 52 and 2000, pp. 214–16;
Manzelli, "Le fortificazioni," 2000, pp. 30–2.

108 Galetti, 2005, p. 891.

109 Idem, pp. 892–4; Manzelli/Grassigli, 2001, pp. 136–9; Manzelli, *Ravenna*, 2000,
pp. 65–71; Montevecchi, ed., "La strada," 2004. Both the Banca Popolare and
the Via D'Azeglio sites added hypocaust rooms.

110 Manzelli, "La forma urbis," 2001, pp. 51–2.

111 Manzelli, 2003, pp. 55–6.

112 Vitruvius, *De Architectura* 2.9.16: "haec autem per Padum Ravennam depor-
tatur, in colonia Fanestri, Pisauri, Anconae reliquis que, quae sunt in ea regione,
municipiis praebetur."

113 Mazza, 2005, p. 20, esp. n. 64.

114 Bermond Montanari, "L'impianto," 1990, pp. 241–8.

115 Maioli, "Vivere," 2001, pp. 179–80; Stoppioni, 2005, p. 228.

116 Maioli/Stoppioni, 1987, pp. 27–9.

117 Maioli, "Approvvigionamenti," 2005, pp. 174–5. Stoppioni, 2005, in a detailed
study of the ceramic evidence from Ravenna, concludes that olive oil was never
an important import, while the import of wine increased dramatically in the
first and second centuries AD. Fish sauce containers, which often make up an
important component of imported ceramics, were likewise relatively scarce,
although becoming a bit more frequent in the second and early third centuries.
Contacts with the Aegean were much more common than with the western
Mediterranean.

118 Rebecchi, "Grecità e Greci," 1998, pp. 306–15.

119 Idem, pp. 314–15; referring to Rebecchi, 1978.

120 Manzelli, *Ravenna*, 2000, pp. 140–1.

121 Idem, p. 210; Maioli, "Città dei morti," 2001, p. 243; Cirelli, 2008, p. 20, would
argue that the lack of bridges is evidence that there was no canal.

122 Giacomini, "Anagrafe dei cittadini ravennati," 1990.

123 Donati, 1990, p. 475.

124 Manzelli, "La forma urbis," 2001, p. 54.

125 Herodian, *History of the Roman Empire* 8.7.1, and *Historia Augusta, Duo Maxi-
mini* 24–5 and 33, and *Maximus et Balbinus* 11–12; see Neri, 1990, p. 543.

126 Eutropius, *Breviarium*, 9.7; Jerome, *Chronicon*, a. 2277: "Gallienus in omnen lasciviam dissoluto Germani Ravennam usque venerunt..." repeated in the sixth century by Jordanes, *Romana*, 287 (p. 37): "Germani et Alani Gallias depraedantes Ravennam usque venerunt, Greciam Gothi vastaverunt."

127 Lactantius, *De mortibus persecutorum* 17.2–3, cited by Neri, 1990, p. 542.

128 Neri, 1990, p. 542.

129 Christie, 1989, p. 117; citing Thomsen, 1947, pp. 217–30. See also Deichmann, 1989, pp. 130–1.

130 Cantarelli, 1901, pp. 161–4. Guadagnucci, 2007, p. 7, notes that at some point before 398 a new province, *Picenum*, was split off and made part of the diocese of *Italia Suburbicaria* under the *vicarius urbis Romae* in Rome, but by 402 *Flaminia et Picenum annonarium* were reunited as part of *Italia Annonaria*. See also Neri, 1990, pp. 540–1, who suggests that the change in territorial alliance may have something to do with rivalry between Rome and Milan in the later fourth century.

131 Neri, 1990, pp. 543–6 and 570–1.

132 For what follows, see Frassinetti, 2005, pp. 70–7.

133 *Historia Augusta, Didius Julianus* 6.

134 Bollini, 2005, p. 133, who notes that there are in any case fewer funerary monuments from the third century because these are the ones most likely to be reused in the massive building campaigns of the fifth century; but in any case there are still some inscriptions for civilians, just not for military personnel.

135 Frassinetti, 2005, p. 73, provides a summary of the arguments.

136 See MacGeorge, 2003, pp. 306–11.

137 Roncuzzi/Veggi, 1968, pp. 110–11; Fabbri, 1990, p. 25; Fabbri, 2004, p. 33.

138 Fabbri, 2004, p. 31; Cirelli, 2008, pp. 19–20.

139 Manzelli, "La forma urbis," 2001, p. 54.

140 Maioli/Stoppioni, 1987, pp. 56–63, date only the finds from the cemeteries at Cà delle Vigne and Cà Lunga to the fourth century. On late antique burial patterns around Ravenna, see Cirelli, 2008, pp. 114–30.

141 Manzelli, "La forma urbis," 2001, p. 54; Manzelli/Grassigli, 2001; Manzelli, *Ravenna*, 2000, pp. 66–71 and 236–8; Cirelli, 2008, p. 52. Chronologically, these houses are "Palace of Theoderic," abandoned after a fire in the second half of the second century; Ex orti Baccinetti, abandoned perhaps in the early third century; Porta Cybo, abandoned in the third century; Largo Firenze, Santa Croce, Sant'Andrea Maggiore, abandoned at the end of the third century (Santa Croce destroyed by fire); Banca Popolare, modified in third century, destroyed by fire in early fourth century.

142 Via D'Azeglio: Manzelli, *Ravenna*, 2000, pp. 66–8; UPIM: idem, pp. 112–13; and Gelichi, 2000, pp. 116–17. Russo, "Una nuova proposta," 2005, instead suggests that construction and modifications to the site called the "Palace of Theoderic" were continuous from the second to the sixth centuries, and included new rooms and pavements in the early to mid–fourth century. Russo follows Deichmann in identifying this area as the seat of the *praefectus classis*, but does not then explain who was modifying the structures in the fourth century.

143 This question is of fundamental importance for the choice of Ravenna as an imperial residence, as we will see in the following chapter. Manzelli, *Ravenna*, 2000, esp. pp. 209–11, following Berti, 1976, pp. 10–29, esp. pp. 26–7, claims

that this area was abandoned between the second and the fifth centuries, as a result of the development of cemeteries to the east of the *fossa Augusta*, and the consequent removal of the inhabitants to newly developed areas to the north, west, and south of the city. However, Deichmann, 1989, pp. 62 and 67, assumed that the building had been continually used in the third and fourth centuries as the *praetorium*, or military headquarters. Russo, "Una nuova proposta," 2005, pp. 174–6; and Augenti, "Archeologia e topografia," 2005, pp. 7–23, now place the second construction phase some time in the fourth century.

144 2000, pp. 238–41.
145 Manzelli, "La forma urbis," 2001, p. 54.
146 Fabbri, 2004, p. 33, citing Maioli, 1990.
147 Ortalli, 1991.
148 Manzelli, "La forma urbis," 2001, p. 54; and Manzelli, *Ravenna*, 2000, pp. 236–8.
149 Stoppioni, 2005, p. 230.
150 For discussion and bibliography, see Deliyannis, ed., 2006, pp. 39–41.
151 Mansi, ed., 1901–27, vol. 3, pp. 39 and 42.
152 For good summaries, see Mazzotti, 1986; and Picard, 1988, pp. 116–22.
153 St. Probus (*LPR* chs. 3 and 8) and St. Eleuchadius (*LPR* ch. 4).
154 *LPR* ch. 1; Lanzoni, 1910–11, pp. 330–46; and Testi-Rasponi, ed., 1924, pp. 36–7 n. 14, 63 n. 7, and 65 n. 7.
155 See especially Deichmann, 1989, pp. 165–7, who notes that neither the church of St. Probus nor the Ca'Bianca, both south of Classe, could have been the original church of the bishop. On St. Euphemia *ad Arietem*, see Baldini Lippolis, "La chiesa," 2004.
156 See Deliyannis, ed., 2006, pp. 94–7.
157 *LPR* ch. 22. Agnellus does say that various early bishops were buried in the basilicas of St. Probus (chs. 3, 6, 7, 8, 9, 10, 11, 12), St. Eleuchadius (chs. 4, 5, 7), or next to the Church of the Apostles (ch. 21), but he does not say that the churches were built at the time of their deaths, and indeed both the logic of the text and archaeological investigation have shown that some of these structures were built much later.
158 *LPR* ch. 1; Baldini Lippolis, "La chiesa," 2004.

Three. Ravenna and the Western Emperors, AD 400–489

1 Especially Olympiodorus of Thebes (preserved in the *Bibliotheca* of Photius written in the ninth century), Sozomen, Zosimus, and Orosius. For a fairly complete list of sources for Galla Placidia, see the entry in Martindale, ed., 1980, pp. 888–9.
2 Harlow, 2004. It is quite notable that even S. I. Oost, whose 1968 biography of the empress remains the most authoritative English treatment of her life, is not able to do much more than speculate about tantalizing references in these laconic sources. See also Connor, 2004.
3 On the date, see Rebenich, 1985.
4 Zosimus, *Historia Nova*, 5.38.1, who used the account of Olympiodorus of Thebes, implies that Galla had always secretly hated the woman who raised her (Oost, 1968, pp. 83–6).

5 Olympiodorus of Thebes, *Bibliotheca* fr. 33. Again, a tantalizing hint about imperial marriages and the role of women or does it just reflect the anti-Honorian politics of the author?

6 It is possible that Olympiodorus, whose chronicle is our main source for these events, accompanied the army that reinstated Galla and Valentinian; see Matthews, 1975, pp. 382–3, and idem, 1970.

7 See, e.g., Holum, 1982, pp. 1–2; and Thompson, 1996, pp. 145–6. Sources include the fifth-century Priscus (Fragment 15), and the sixth-century historians Marcellinus Comes (*Chronicon*, a. 434) and Jordanes (*Getica* 223–4; *Romana* 328).

8 Legend tells that the pope made an emotional appeal and convinced Attila not to sack Rome, and the same legend was repeated for various other cities in Attila's path, including Ravenna, which does seem to have been spared (*LPR* ch. 37). Either Attila really could be swayed by supplication from Christian bishops or this became a topos of episcopal hagiography; see Pizarro, 1995, pp. 104–11, and cf. also Josephus's story of Alexander the Great and Jerusalem, *Jewish Antiquities* 11.321–39.

9 There is an enormous bibliography now on the end of the Roman Empire in the west; two recent studies that focus specifically on the period from 455 to 493 are Henning, 1999, and MacGeorge, 2003.

10 Western senators and generals: Petronius Maximus (455), Avitus (455–6), Majorian (457–61), Libius Severus (461–5), Olybrius (472), and Glycerius (473–4). Eastern generals: Anthemius (467–72) and Julius Nepos (474/5–80).

11 *Codex Theodosianus* VII.13.15; see Gillett, 2001, for a complete list of imperial edicts and the places they were issued in the fifth century.

12 Gillett, 2001, pp. 139–41 and 157. Zosimus, *Historia Nova* V.27–31, mentions Honorius's change of residence to Ravenna as happening in 408.

13 Refugees fled from Rome to Ravenna before and after the Visigothic siege, for example, Pope Innocent I – *Epistola* 16 (*PL* 20.519); Orosius, *Adversus paganos* 7.39.

14 Socrates Scholasticus, *Historia Ecclesiastica* VII.23.

15 Squatriti, 1992, pp. 2–3, Fabbri, 2004, p. 35 n. 48, and idem, 1991, pp. 9–11, note that by the fifth century Ravenna's marshes and swamps were drying up which might be why the city had become more accessible.

16 Jordanes, *Getica*, 29 (148–50).

17 Procopius, *De bello Gothico* V.1.16–18, cited in Christie, 1989, pp. 114–15.

18 Squatriti, 1992, p. 2; Gillett, 2001, pp. 161–2.

19 Deichmann, "Costantinopoli e Ravenna," 1982; supported by Gillett, 2001, pp. 161–2.

20 Sotinel, 2004, p. 67.

21 Cosentino, 2005, p. 425.

22 Neri, 1990, and Mazza, 2005, pp. 8–10; Arslan, 2005, p. 195.

23 Manzelli, *Ravenna*, 2000, p. 241; see Gelichi, 2000, p. 118.

24 For example, Krautheimer, 1983.

25 *LPR* ch. 2.

26 Marazzi, 2006, pp. 48–50.

27 *LPR* ch. 40.

28 Claudian, *De VI Cons. Hon.*; see Gillett, 2001, p. 139.

29 Gelasius, *Epistolae* 26.10, ed. Andreas Thiel, *Romanorum pontificum genuinae et quae ad eos scriptae sunt*, vol. I (Braniewo: 1868), pp. 405–6, written in 495.

30 Gillett, 2001, p. 141, admits that after the death of Stilicho in 408, Honorius moved more or less permanently to Ravenna.

31 Cf. Wickham, 1981, p. 16. Gillett, 2001, pp. 133–4, summarizes scholarship on the history of the removal from Rome, going back to the third century.

32 This is a question that scholars have debated; see most recently Marazzi, 2006; also Mazza, 2005, pp. 8–17; Pani Ermini, 2005; articles in the collection *Sedes Regiae*, 2000, ed. Ripoll/Gurt, especially those by J. Arce and S. Gelichi; and Duval, 1997.

33 See most recently Kelly, 1998, p. 164; and Kulikowski, 2000.

34 Interestingly, the *Notitia Dignitatum* barely mentions either Milan or Ravenna. Both places are listed as locations of weaving factories, Milan has a government storehouse and Ravenna is a military and a naval base, but neither city is said to have a mint, although we know that both cities minted gold coins in the names of the emperors (see below). The *Notitia Dignitatum* lists mints in the west for Siscia, Aquileia, Rome, Lyons, Arles, and Trier. This omission is curious; Panvini Rosati, 1978, explains the mints of Milan and Ravenna as somehow special and outside of normal government channels, and notes that Ravenna and Milan did not mint bronze coins, as did the others. See also Arslan, 2005.

35 McCormick, 2000, p. 140, says 1,500, citing Deichmann, 1989, pp. 114–15 (who does not give this figure, but estimates a total population of Ravenna made up of nonmilitary officials and their families at about 5,000 persons). Deichmann in turn cites Jones, 1964, p. 366, who estimates 3,000 guards and an even larger number of civilian staff. Cosentino, 2005, p. 411, based on Justinian's *constitutio* for Vandal Africa, estimates 600 bureaucrats from the mid–fifth to the early sixth century.

36 Deichmann, 1989, pp. 108–15, follows Jones, 1964, p. 367: "When in transit the *comitatus* must have been packed for miles with thousands of troopers of the guard and clerks of the ministries. . . ."

37 See Jones, 1964, I, pp. 366–73; Gillett, 2001, pp. 133–4; and Kelly, 2004, esp. pp. 187–93. Kelly states, "To be sure, this concentration of power was to a great extent an inevitable result of the establishment of an institutionalized bureaucracy whose senior officials were resident in the imperial capital" (p. 193), which presumes the concept of a capital as residence of the government.

38 Liebeschuetz, 2000, pp. 10–12; McCormick, 2000, pp. 135–42; Deichmann, 1989, pp. 70 and 108–15.

39 See, for example, Pietri, 1983, p. 645: "Avec le déplacement de la cour, toute l'aristocratie du service impérial se transfère à Ravenne." Both Pietri, pp. 647–8, and Matthews, 1975, p. 359, cite the case of Petronius Maximus, who held many government positions between 416 and 443 (Martindale, 1980, *PLRE* vol. 2, *s.v.* Maximus 22), but only the rescripts specifically locate him in Ravenna, and Pietri notes, n. 6, that some of the praetorian prefects seem to have been based in Rome.

40 Pietri, 1983, pp. 654–6; on the sarcophagi, see esp. Lawrence, 1945; Kollwitz/Herdejürgen, 1979; and Dresken-Weiland, 1998, pp. 118–26; and on ivory carving, see Volbach, 1977; and Martini/Rizzardi, ed., 1990, although in fact for ivory-carving attributions to Ravenna are only hypothetical.

41 Marazzi, 2006, p. 53.

42 Deichmann, 1989, pp. 114–15, estimates a total population of about 5,000 persons, while Cosentino, 2005, pp. 411–12, estimates 9,000–10,000.

43 Sidonius Apollinaris, *Epistolae* I.8.2: "aegri deambulant medici iacent, algent balnea domicilia conflagrant, sitiunt vivi natant sepulti, vigilant fures dormiunt potestates, faenerantur clerici Syri psallunt, negotiatores militant milites negotiantur, student pilae senes, aleae iuvenes, armis eunuchi, litteris foederati."

44 See, for example, Pietri, 1991, pp. 288–9, based on the *Notitia dignitatum*.

45 There is an extensive bibliography on this topic; see most recently Curcic, 1993; and Baldini Lippolis, 2001, esp. pp. 29–46, and with a catalog of individual sites.

46 See Dagron, 1974; and Mango, 1985.

47 See *Milano Capitale*, 1990; Ausonius, *Ordo urbius nobilium*, vii "Mediolanum."

48 Farioli Campanati, "Ravenna, Constantinopoli," 1992, p. 150, and idem, 2005, p. 16.

49 *LPR* cc. 27, 34–5, 40–2.

50 Christie, 1989, pp. 117–18.

51 Farioli Campanati, "Ravenna, Constantinopoli," 1992, admits that her analysis is based on Agnellus's much later information.

52 On the walls, see most comprehensively Mauro/Novara, eds., 2000; Gelichi, 2005; Cirelli, 2008, pp. 55–67. The fundamental studies remain Christie/Gibson, 1988, and Christie, 1989.

53 See Christie, 1989, p. 118. Capellini, 1987, pp. 86–7, notes that the location of the walls, which presumably defined the city's *pomerium*, or sacred boundaries, may have had to be kept for juridical purposes.

54 Gelichi, 2005, esp. p. 830; Christie, 1989, p. 115. A detailed study of the remains was made in 1905 by Gaetano Savini, who included drawings and descriptions of sections that are now lost (Christie, 1989, p. 117). The most comprehensive history of the debate about the walls is Gelichi, 2005.

55 Gelichi, 2000, pp. 117–18.

56 *LPR* ch. 40.

57 Testi-Rasponi, ed., 1924, pp. 115–18 and table 3.

58 Christie, 1989, p. 128.

59 See esp. Cirelli, 2008, pp. 55–67. Although, as S. Gelichi elegantly describes (2005, p. 829), "one has the impression that the debate is coming round on itself again, like a uroburos" (a fantastic animal that eats its own tail). One still finds references in scholarly literature to later additions to this wall at the time of Odoacer or Theoderic, e.g., Maioli, "Le mura," 2000, and idem, "La topografia," 2005, pp. 50–1.

60 Christie, 1989, p. 130.

61 Cappellini, 1987; Manzelli, "Le fortificazioni," 2000, p. 28. Farioli Campanati, "Ravenna, Constantinopoli," 1992, pp. 140–1, notes that the name Porta Aurea is first attested by Agnellus, but argues that such a name would have no significance in the ninth century, and thus must have been applied earlier, most likely in the fifth century. For comparison, recent studies have proposed that the Golden Gate in Constantinople was originally built as a freestanding triumphal arch in honor of Theodosius I, around 388, and then incorporated into the walls built by Theodosius II after 413; see Bardill, "Golden Gate," 1999.

62 Gelichi, 2005, pp. 836–7, refuting Christie/Gibson, 1988, pp. 182–3, who stated that the walls were made mainly of new bricks, although of a type different from those used in the fifth-century churches of the city.

63 Gelichi, 2005, p. 837, notes that this need not mean that the walls were built in an emergency, but simply that bricks were reused for reasons of economy. A mysterious stretch of apparently defensive walls found just to the north of Santa Croce in 1989 and published in Capellini, 1993, would seem to predate the full circuit.

64 Gelichi, 2005, who supports the proposal of Christie, 1989, that the full circuit of these walls was built at one time.

65 Christie, 1989, pp. 135–6; the date is repeated in idem, 2006, pp. 332–3.

66 Fabbri, 2004, pp. 37–9. Bollini, 1990, p. 306, suggests that both Ravenna and Classe had walls built in the third century, like Rimini.

67 Gelichi, 2000, pp. 118–20; Fabbri, 2004, p. 34, notes that Manzelli, "La forma urbis," 2001, p. 56, states that when Ravenna became a capital, it already had the city walls. Several other scholars have stated in a speculative but unsubstantiated way that Ravenna's walls must have already existed in 402; see Bollini, 1990, p. 306; Maioli, 2004, p. 13; Maioli, "La topografia," 2005, pp. 50–1.

68 Claudian, *Panegyricus dictus Honorio Augusto sextum consuli*, *Carmina maiora* 28.494: "dixit et antiquae muros egressa Rauennae."

69 Zosimus, *Historia Nova* VI.7.4–9.3; Sozomen, *Historia Ecclesiastica* IX.12. See Gillett, 2001, p. 141 and n. 42.

70 One final, puzzling piece of evidence that has not been used in this discussion is the Peutinger Map, on which Ravenna is shown as a city with walls and towers. The Peutinger Map is a thirteenth-century copy of an earlier world map whose prototype is variously dated from the first to the ninth century (for the most recent discussions of the dating, see Salway, 2005; and Albu, 2005). Can the map be used to date Ravenna's walls, or vice versa? Early interpretations of the map and its information suggested a date for its prototype between 330 and 362. This argument, made without reference to the depiction of Ravenna, would imply that Ravenna's walls were already built in the fourth century (see Dilke, 1987). Others have argued that the prototype or a revision must have been made after the early fifth century because Ravenna's walls didn't exist earlier (argued by Levi/Levi, 1967; see also Arnaud, 1990; Weber, 1989, p. 116; and Salway, 2005, p. 125 and n. 37). Albu, 2005, finally, has recently argued that the map was based on Roman written itineraries and was made in the Carolingian period, when, of course, Ravenna's walls had long existed; but Albu does not really explain how the maker of the map, using textual itineraries, would know how to depict individual cities with walls or not.

71 Manzelli, *Ravenna*, 2000, pp. 238–41; Gelichi, 2005, p. 828 n. 23; see also Gelichi, 2000, pp. 116–17, who notes that only the Via D'Azeglio site has material from the fourth century.

72 Frassineti, 1995; Manzelli, *Ravenna*, 2000, p. 218. There has been a long debate about the relative legal status of Ravenna and Classe. Stemming from the identification in the early sixth-century mosaic in Sant'Apollinare Nuovo that identifies a *civitas Classe*, scholars have attempted to determine whether Classe was a distinct political entity in the sixth century, and, if so, how far back that status goes. Since the evidence consists of one fragmentary inscription that contains the word [c]*lasse*, a reference in the fifth-century *Notitia Dignitatum* has been used to identify *eiusdem civitas* as a separate city of Classe (Susini, "La questione," 1968), but others have disputed this (Frassinetti, 2005, p. 76).

73 Augenti, "Archeologia e topografia," 2005, p. 22.

74 Gelichi, 2005, pp. 838–9.

75 In addition to those mentioned above, also Zosimus, *Historia Nova* V.27: "Ravenna...is called Rhene because it is surrounded by water..."; see Magnani, 2001.

76 See Mazza, 2005; Sidonius Apollinaris, *Epistolae* I. 5 and I. 8; see also in VII.17.2, in an epitaph, "you despised the populous territory of swampy [*paludosae*] Ravenna...."

77 Fabbri, 1991.

78 Mazza, 2005, pp. 18ff.; Fabbri, 1991, p. 19.

79 Squatriti, 1992, p. 8; Manzelli, *Ravenna*, 2000, esp. pp. 210–11; Cirelli, 2008, p. 67; but Augenti, "Ravenna e Classe: il racconto," 2006, p. 30, on the contrary, says that the *fossa Augusta* probably still functioned in the time of Theoderic, without further explanation.

80 *Epist.* I. 5.5.

81 Fabbri, 1991, pp. 18–19, and 2004, pp. 45–6.

82 The first reference to a *palatium* in Ravenna comes from the *Anonymus Valesianus pars posterior*, 12, in reference to Theoderic.

83 Cf. Kelly, 1998, pp. 142–3.

84 Neri, 1990, p. 543, lists Valentinian I in 365 and Valentinian II in 378.

85 Flavius Merobaudes, *Carmina* I and II (MGH AA 14, pp. 3–4); see Oost, 1965, pp. 4–7; Clover, 1971, pp. 17–19; Barnes, 1974; and Baldini Lippolis, 1997. The poems list members of the imperial family at a banquet; it must be emphasized that the poems do *not* say that they are describing pictures rather than a living family scene, and that there is no evidence that the pictures were located in Ravenna – this is merely an assumption based on the idea that Valentinian III lived in Ravenna.

86 Marius of Avenches, *Chronica*, a. 493 (*MGH SS.* 11, p. 233): "...occisus est Odovacer rex a rege Theuderico in Laureto;" *Anon. Vales.* 55 (*MGH SS* 9, p. 320): "...manu sua Theodericus eum [Odoacrem] in Lauretum pervenientem gladio interemit." These chronicles are probably related to the chronicle by Archbishop Maximian that was Agnellus's source; see Deliyannis, ed., 2006, pp. 26–30.

87 Farioli Campanati, "Ravenna, Constantinopoli," 1992, pp. 141–4; on the Daphné palace in Constantinople, see Dagron, 1974, pp. 92–4; and Bardill, "Great Palace," 1999.

88 Baldini Lippolis, 1997, pp. 2–3.

89 C. Ricci had interpreted Agnellus's account of Galla Placidia going by night to Santa Croce (*LPR* ch. 41) to mean that there must have been an adjacent palace, and when Roman remains were discovered beneath Santa Croce in 1925–7, they were interpreted as the Honorian palace. But there is no need to interpret Agnellus in this way; see Berti, 1976, pp. 94–5; Novara, 1988; Deichmann, 1989, pp. 49–50; Porta, 1991, pp. 271–2; and Manzelli, *Ravenna*, 2000, p. 202.

90 Duval, "Comment reconnaître," 1978, and 1997, pp. 141–2; for a refutation see Gelichi, 2000, p. 110 n. 5.

91 For the clearest explanation of the building phases, see Augenti, "Archeologia e topografia," 2005, pp. 7–23, who argues, pp. 22–3, that what he identifies as Phase 2 dates to the fourth century, but says that it is possible to date it to the Honorian period, with Phase 3 dating to the mid–fifth century. See also Deichmann, 1989, pp. 58–70; Baldini Lippolis, 1997; Manzelli/Grassigli,

2001; Russo, "Una nuova proposta," 2005, pp. 174–6; and Cirelli, 2008, pp. 78–85.

92 *LPR* chs. 94 and 119; Farioli Campanati, "Ravenna, Constantinopoli," 1992, pp. 141–3.

93 The southern corridor around the courtyard was paved with mosaics depicting circus, mythological, and hunting scenes. Baldini Lippolis, 1997, dates the circus mosaics to the period of Theoderic, but Augenti, "Archeologia e topografia," 2005, dates them to the fourth century, thus before the arrival of the imperial court.

94 Ortalli, 1991, p. 171.

95 The mints of Rome and Milan continued to produce coins throughout the fifth century; Aquileia's mint continued until 425; see Arslan, 2005, pp. 195–6.

96 Arslan, 2005, pp. 197–201, who notes that the coins minted in Ravenna after 455 are less widely distributed in other areas of Europe, in favor of coins minted at Milan; this fits with Gillett's argument that Ravenna was not being used as a capital in this period.

97 *LPR* cc. 115 and 164.

98 For the clearest explication of these documents, see Augenti, "Archeologia e topografia," 2005, pp. 23–31.

99 Deichmann, 1989, pp. 54–6.

100 The identification as the mint is not without controversy; for all of the arguments and bibliography, see Augenti, "Archeologia e topografia," 2005, pp. 23–31. Deichmann (1989, pp. 54–6) had argued that the papyrus of 572, which identified a notary as "habens stationem ad monitam auri in porticum sacri palati" (Tjäder II, no. 35, p. 112), meant that the mint must have been in the portico of the palace, thus to the east of the *platea maior*, but Augenti shows that it is more logical to read this passage as meaning that the *notary* had his station in the part of the portico of the palace near the mint, which was across the street.

101 See esp. Vespignani, 2005; and Humphrey, 1986, pp. 578–638, who documents circuses for Nicomedia, Trier, Sirmium, Milan, Aquileia, Thessalonike, Antioch, and accepts a circus in Ravenna; but Duval, 1997, pp. 136–7 and 153, notes that the evidence for the linkage of circus and palace is not strong in other tetrarchal capitals, including Ravenna.

102 Sidonius Apollinaris, *Carmina* 23 *Ad Consentium*, lines 313ff. (*MGH AA* 8, pp. 257ff.). While Vespignani, 2005, p. 1135, repeats a common assertion that this circus must be in Ravenna, as that is where the emperor resided, Gillett, 2001, pp. 159–60 and esp. n. 133, refutes this assertion.

103 *Liber pontificalis*, *Vita Theodori* 2 (trans. Davis, *Book of Pontiffs*, p. 69). See Vespignani, 2005, pp. 1140–1, and also Johnson, 1988, p. 83 and n. 110, for post-ninth-century references to the circus. Despite several assertions, neither the *Anonymus Valesianus pars posterior* ch. 67 nor Cassiodorus's *Chronica* a. 519 (MGH *AA* XI, ed. Mommsen, p. 161) describes games or races held in honor of Eutharic at Ravenna, only at Rome; see Gillett, 2001, p. 160 n. 133.

104 *LPR* c. 22 and c. 153; Deichmann, 1989, p. 40.

105 The earliest such reference dates to 960 (Fantuzzi, 1801, I.150–1); see Johnson, 1988, p. 83 n. 110, for other references, including the thirteenth-century *Chronica de Civitate Ravennae*, which says that Theoderic "explevit murum civitatis, quo usque caput circo et therma" (ed. Muratori, *RIS* I. 2, p. 575).

106 *De gubernatione Dei* VI. 9: "... pars sunt Romanae plebis in circo, pars sunt populi Rauennatis in theatro."

107 Humphrey, 1986, pp. 580 and 636; the only exceptions to north–south orientation were in cities with preexisting racetracks. Humphrey notes, p. 306, that the smallest known imperial-period circus, at Gerasa, had an arena 244 meters long.

108 Johnson, 1988, p. 83.

109 Cirelli, 2008, pp. 90–2, who makes this suggestion because there is no archaeological evidence at all from this part of the city that might contradict it.

110 Mazza, 2005, p. 22; and Cosentino, 2005, pp. 413–15.

111 Sidonius Apollinaris, *Epist.* I.5.6: "nisi quod, cum sese hinc salsum portis pelagus impingeret, hinc cloacali pulte fossarum discursu lyntrium ventilata ipse lentati languidus lapsus umoris nauticis cuspidibus foraminato fundi glutino sordidaretur, in medio undarum sitiebamus, quia nusquam vel aquaeductuum liquor integer vel cisterna defaecabilis vel fons inriguus vel puteus inlimis."

112 Prati, 1988, p. 27; which is confirmed in the Anonymus Valesianus's description of Theoderic's restoration of the aqueduct, *Anon. Vales.* 71; see below, Chapter 4.

113 For bibliography, see Chapter 1.

114 About the cult of St. Lawrence, see, for example, Nordström, 1953, pp. 17–23; Lewis, 1973, pp. 214ff.; and Nauroy, 1989. Compare, for example, the basilica and poems by Pope Damasus (366–84), Ambrose's discussion of Lawrence in *De officiis* 1.41 and 2.28, and his Hymn 73, *De S. Laurentio* (*PL* 17, coll. 1216–17), the poem written in Spain around 405 by Prudentius, *Peristephanon* 2, the construction of another basilica in Rome by Pope Sixtus III (432–40), a sermon in his honor by Pope Leo I (440–61); another sermon falsely attributed to Ravenna's own Bishop Peter Chrysologus, *sermo* 135, had some sort of Ravenna connection, as it had become part of Felix's collection in the eighth century (see Olivar, 1962, p. 199).

115 See Deichmann, 1974, pp. 75–7. In Rome, Valentinian III and Pope Sixtus III built and endowed a basilica dedicated to St. Lawrence; see *Liber pontificalis*, *V. Sixti III*, 5–6.

116 Augustine, *Sermones* 322: "... ad gloriosi martyris laurentii memoriam, quae apud rauennam nuper collocata est, sicut audiuimus...." On the date, see Deichmann, 1976, p. 337, citing Kunzelmann, 1931, p. 508.

117 On Lauricius, see Martindale, *PLRE* 2, 1980, pp. 659–60.

118 Krautheimer/Curcic, 1986, pp. 51–4.

119 *LPR* chs. 34–6; see Deliyannis, trans., 2004, pp. 136–8 and notes. The relics of Stephen, considered to have been the first martyr, were discovered in 415 and enshrined in Constantinople, Jerusalem, and Rome in the fifth century (see esp. Clark, 1982), while Gervase and Protase were martyrs of Milan whose veneration had been promoted by St. Ambrose.

120 *LPR* ch. 36: "Lauricius huius dedicauit sub die tertio Kal. Octobris, Theodosio quinto decimo et Placido Valentiniano." IV augg. conss.

121 The *LPR* manuscript has Opilius; Deichmann, 1976, pp. 337–8, assumes that the name must have been Opilio. There are at least 4 men named Opilio known from the later fifth and sixth centuries who held the highest government positions under the emperors and Theoderic; see Martindale, 1980, *PLRE* 2, pp. 807–9.

122 Deichmann, 1976, p. 340.

123 See Oost, 1968, p. 265; Letters 56 and 58 in the Letters of Leo I the Great (*PL* 54, coll. 859–66).

124 See Oost, 1968, pp. 156–61; Galla's participation in Roman church affairs is reported in the *Liber pontificalis, V. Bonifatii I* and *V. Sixti III.*

125 *Liber pontificalis V. Martini* 2 and *V. Agathonis* 4, "in domo Placidiae"; *V. Constantini* 5, "a palatio in Placidias." Magdalino, 2001, p. 60, proposes that the house was inherited by Galla's granddaughter Placidia and perhaps then by her daughter Anicia Juliana.

126 On Galla's church patronage, see esp. Brubaker, 1997, pp. 53–61.

127 Constantius of Lyon, *Vita sancti Germani* (written in 475–80), chs. 35–44; Germanus's visit to Ravenna is probably dated to 436–7 (Thompson, 1984, pp. 57–66).

128 Holum, 1977, and idem, 1982, pp. 129–30; Rizzardi, "Il Mausoleo / The Mausoleum," 1996, p. 114.

129 *LPR* chs. 41–2, 27, and 41.

130 *LPR* ch. 51; see below.

131 *LPR* ch. 42. This storm probably happened, as Deichmann concludes (1974, p. 94), during Galla's return trip with the army in 425; while crossing the Adriatic from Salona to Ravenna, the army's fleet was hindered by a storm (Socrates Scholasticus, *Hist. Eccl.* 7.23).

132 The main publications on San Giovanni Evangelista are Grossmann, 1964; Deichmann, 1974, pp. 93–124; Farioli Campanati, 1995; Zangara, 2000; and Russo, "L'architettura," 2005, pp. 103–14.

133 Deichmann, 1974, pp. 101–2. In 1213 the church was given a lavish new set of floor mosaics that commemorated, among other things, the Fourth Crusade, including the sack of Constantinople; see Farioli Campanati, 1995.

134 Novara, "La Ravenna tardo-imperiale," 2001, pp. 267–71; Farioli Campanati, 1995.

135 See most comprehensively Deichmann, 1974, pp. 103–7, with a complete catalog of each piece, and also Novara, "L'edilizia di culto," 2001, pp. 288–9; and Zanotto, "Practica del reimpiego," 2005, pp. 1144–5, who notes that the columns came from at least two different buildings.

136 Russo, "L'architettura," 2005, pp. 111–12.

137 Deichmann, 1974, p. 102; for example, the narthex of St. John Stoudios in Constantinople, ca. 400, was subdivided with small chambers at the north and south ends that communicated with the aisles.

138 *LPR* ch. 147: "...in angulos ipsius introiti...." It should be pointed out that the site on which the church was built contained a cemetery that was used from the first–fifth centuries AD; see Manzelli, *Ravenna*, 2000, pp. 140–1.

139 Grossmann, 1964, p. 228.

140 Grossmann, 1964, p. 218, suggests that the spolia included twenty-four complete sets, which is why the church and narthex were built in this way.

141 Those who propose a date in the 430s include De Angelis d'Ossat, *Studi*, 1962, pp. 14–18; and Russo, "L'architettura," 2005, pp. 104–6, based on the fact that there is not much difference in the levels of the original nave floor and of the atrium, thus they must have been built close together in time (although if the church were in continuous use, this lack of difference in levels might not be so significant, Farioli Campanati, 1995, p. 25). A date at the time of Bishop Marinian ca. 600 (Deichmann, 1974, p. 10) is based on fragments of mosaic

apparently containing the name of Marinian (595–606); however, these were not found in the new western section of the nave. Grossmann, 1964, does not suggest a date for the modifications.

142 *LPR* ch. 147; Agnellus is here telling a story that took place in the eighth century. It is worth noting that according to Agnellus the notary Hilarus, who tells the story, was to be buried in the narthex; although Agnellus made up this story (see Deliyannis, trans., 2004, pp. 9–10), the features of San Giovanni Evangelista that he describes must correspond to ninth-century conditions. Farioli Campanati, 1995, pp. 25–6.

143 Interestingly, these columns were of different materials, the one on the north being granite and the one on the south cipollino marble; however, at least in the thirteenth century and possibly earlier their difference would not be noticed, as they were covered with silver (Deichmann, 1974, p. 107).

144 See most comprehensively Deichmann, 1974, pp. 98–100; and Russo, "L'architettura," 2005, pp. 111–13.

145 Deichmann, 1974, p. 99; Russo, "L'architettura," 2005, pp. 112–13; the comparative example is found on the exterior of the fourth-century chapel of San Aquilino in Milan, which has been attributed to the patronage of Galla Placidia; see Lewis, 1973.

146 Smith, "The Side Chambers," 1990; in "Form and Function," 1990, she discusses the side chambers at Santa Croce, San Vitale, Sant'Apollinare Nuovo, Sant'Apollinare in Classe, Sant'Agata Maggiore, and the Ca'Bianca basilica.

147 See Deichmann, 1974, pp. 95–7.

148 Deichmann, 1974, p. 97; followed by Farioli Campanati, "Ravenna, Constantinopoli," 1992, p. 143.

149 Zangara, 2000, pp. 278–9.

150 *LPR* ch. 42; *Tractatus edificationis et cunstructionis eclesie sancti Iohannis euangeliste de Rauenna* and *Item dedicatione eclesie sancti Iohannis euangeliste*, preserved in the fifteenth-century *Codex Estensis*, fol. 44v–47r, published in *RIS* I.2, pp. 567–72. Girolamo Rossi, *Historiarum Ravennatum Libri X* (Venice, 1572 and 2nd ed., Venice, 1589), pp. 101ff. The relevant passages from these sources are published in Deichmann, 1974, pp. 108–11; but a new edition of them, with discussion of their dates, appears in Zangara, 2000, p. 276.

151 Ricci, 1937, p. 36 and fig. 71; and Bovini, 1955, p. 59. See also Poilpré/Caillet, 2005, pp. 108–12, for further discussion.

152 Deichmann, 1974, pp. 112–13, notes that this depiction has no known iconographic parallels, although it is similar to scenes of Christ giving the Law and keys to Peter and Paul.

153 "Amore Christi nobilis et filius tonitrui Sanctus Johannes arcana vidit" is known only from the second sermon and is not quoted by Rossi; Deichmann, 1974, p. 114, argues that it was a separate horizontal band, as has been rendered here. Zangara, 2000, p. 282, discusses the fact that it is a close paraphrase of the first verse of the hymn composed by St. Ambrose in honor of St. John the Evangelist: "Amore Christi nobilis / Et filius Tonitrui / Arcana Iohannes Dei / Fatu revelavit sacro" (Hymn 6, ed. J. Fontaine, 1992). The phrase *filius tonitrui* comes from Mark 3:17.

154 "Galla Placidia Augusta pro se et his omnibus votum solvit"; Zangara, 2000, p. 284, proposes that *suis* is more plausible than *his*.

155 One of the sermons says, "sub quibus [the palms and ships] in junctura praefati arcus ita invenimus adsignatos versus, verum tantum super capita imperatorum divorum." Rossi, however, says, "Erant autem haec imagines in arcu testudinis. . . ." Bovini, 1955, p. 60, argues that the sermon must mean that the verses ran directly around the presumed medallions; he draws a parallel with the triumphal arch mosaics of Santa Sabina in Rome, also made in the 420s and now lost but drawn by Ciampini in his *Vetera Monimenta*. Although the Santa Sabina mosaics are presumed to be early fifth century, one of the main pieces of evidence for this is their similarity to the presumed arrangement at San Giovanni Evangelista! Deichmann, 1974, p. 117, suggested that the medallions were in a horizontal row beneath the inscription. Rossi's text, however, pretty clearly states that the medallions are in the soffit of the arch.

156 Rizzardi, "I mosaici parietali," 2005, pp. 237–8; Deichmann, 1974, pp. 115–16.

157 Rebenich, 1985, suggests that the Gratianus *nep.* was the full-blood brother of Galla Placidia; Mackie, "The Mausoleum," 1995, p. 401, citing Martindale, 1980, pp. 518, 594, and 1100, who also suggests that the Arcadius of the inscription was the son of Theodosius II (p. 130). Oost, 1968, pp. 56–7, suggests that they were Galla Placidia's deceased brothers, sons of Theodosius I by his second wife Galla (her mother); see Mackie, idem, p. 399. Valentinian III had been given the title *nobilissimus* at the age of one when his parents were named *augusti*; Olympiodorus of Thebes, fr. 34 in Photius, *Myrobiblion* 80.

158 Martindale, 1980, p. 1100; Mackie, "The Mausoleum," 1995, p. 401.

159 Deichmann, 1974, pp. 114–16.

160 Rossi cites the text as "Beati misericordes, quoniam miserebitur Deus." This seems to derive from the *Biblia Itala*, or the pre-Vulgate Latin Bible: "Beati misericordes, quoniam ipsis miserebitur Deus."

161 Zangara, 2000, pp. 281–2: "Sancto ac beatissimo apostolo Iohanni evangelistae Galla Placidia augusta cum filio suo Placido Valentiniano augusto et filia sua [Iusta] Grata Honoria augusta liberationis pericul(or)um maris votum solvunt." The inscription is also published as *CIL* XI. 267e.

162 *LPR* ch. 42: "Confirma hoc, Deus, quod operatus es in nobis; a templo tuo in Ierusalem tibi offerent reges munera." The inscription is repeated in the second sermon and by Rossi.

163 *LPR* ch. 27; Agnellus says this image shows the sanctity of this bishop. See Farioli Campanati, "Ravenna, Constantinopoli," 1992, p. 139; Deichmann, 1974, pp. 122–3; and earlier Grabar, 1936, pp. 28, 125–8, and 153–5. Zangara, 2000, pp. 289–92, suggests that the image depicted Melchisedek rather than Peter I, similar to the examples in San Vitale and Sant'Apollinare in Classe; but as we will see, there are specific reasons for the depiction of Melchisedek in those contexts, which in any case are not found in the same location behind the bishop's throne. Also, Agnellus notes that a depiction of Bishop John I was found in the same location in Sant'Agata (*LPR* ch. 44). Since Agnellus relates a story of John celebrating mass in the presence of an angel, it seems likely that Sant'Agata had a similar image to the one in San Giovanni Evangelista (although Nauerth, 1974, pp. 29–32, notes that Agnellus does not specifically describe such a liturgical image in Sant'Agata).

164 Deichmann, 1974, pp. 116–17; Grabar, 1936, p. 28, assumes that there must have been earlier examples, but offers no evidence for these. There are other

examples of pictures of imperial families in palaces, as we have seen for Ravenna, and as are known for the palace, especially the Chalke Gate, in Constantinople. In Rome, Galla Placidia apparently had pictures of herself and her children set up in the church of Santa Croce in Gerusalemme, which would parallel our example here (see Krautheimer, 1937, p. 168). The earliest such depiction in Constantinople was apparently set up by the emperor Leo I (457–73) in the apse of the chapel of the Theotokos of the Blachernae, depicting Leo, his wife, Verina, and their sons at the sides of the enthroned Virgin; see Farioli Campanati, "Ravenna, Constantinopoli," 1992, p. 147, and Mango, 1998.

165 Of all the beatitudes (Matt. 5), only the one on *misericordes* can unequivocally apply to those who are rich and powerful in society. In fifth-century exegesis, *misericordia* is usually interpreted as referring to charity and alms giving; see, for example, Leo the Great, *Sermons* 10, 16, 78, and 95; Peter Chrysologus, *Sermon* 8; Valerian of Cimiez's *Homilies* 7, 8, and 9 on *misericordia*, which are specifically addressed to the wealthy. John Chrysostom, in Homily 15.6 on Matthew, raises the question of what "ἐλεήμονες" means: "Here He seems to me to speak not of those only who show mercy in giving of money, but those likewise who are merciful in their actions." "Ἐνταῦθα οὐ τοὺς διὰ χρημάτων ἐλεοῦντας μόνον ἐμοὶ δοκεῖ λέγειν, ἀλλὰ καὶ τοὺς διὰ πραγμάτων."

166 Rizzardi, "Il Mausoleo / The Mausoleum," 1996, p. 112, and 1993, pp. 388–91.

167 *LPR* ch. 41. Zangara, 2000, p. 270, notes that Agnellus offers no evidence for attributing the church to Galla, and suggests that it was built by Honorius.

168 See Cortesi, 1978, pp. 48–52; Gelichi/Novara, 1995, pp. 365–6 n. 50; and Manzelli, *Ravenna*, 2000, p. 236.

169 For a detailed account of the history of the so-called "mausoleum of Galla Placidia," including information about Santa Croce, see Iannucci, "Il mausoleo ritrovato," 1996, pp. 198–9.

170 The main published descriptions of this building and its archaeology are Deichmann, 1974, pp. 51–9; Cortesi, 1978; and Gelichi/Novara, 1995. For the archaeological history of the church after the sixth century, see Gelichi, 1990; and Gelichi/Novara, 1995, pp. 364–77.

171 See Cortesi, 1978, pp. 61–2.

172 Lewis, 1969; Rizzardi, "L'architettura," 1996, pp. 131–3.

173 From the Lorsch Sylloge: "Forma crucis templum est, templum victoria Cristi/ sacra triumphalis signat imago locum." Lewis, 1969, discusses the meaning of this poem in the context of the newly developing use of cross-planned churches in both East and West.

174 Other churches from the fifth century that had a cross-ground plan were likewise dedicated to apostles and martyrs, such as the Apostoleion at Como, Santo Stefano at Verona, St. John at Ephesus, etc. It is interesting to note that in Ravenna, the church dedicated to the apostles (now San Francesco) was built as a regular basilica, not with a cruciform ground plan; Lewis, 1969, p. 213.

175 Cortesi, 1978, p. 66.

176 Gelichi/Novara, 1995, p. 352, report that this was seen in the excavations conducted by Di Pietro in the 1920s, and again by Cortesi in the 1970s.

177 Novara, "La Ravenna tardo-imperiale," 2001, p. 269. In the tenth or eleventh century, the walls of the church were rebuilt, the apse was redone as a semicircle, and a crypt was dug in the chancel: Cortesi, 1978, p. 66.

178 Smith, "Form and Function," 1990, pp. 191–5.

179 Rizzardi, "L'architettura," 1996, pp. 129–30.

180 Gelichi/Novara, 1995, pp. 358–9 n. 31; see Pavan, 1984–5.

181 Rizzardi, "L'architettura," 1996, p. 133.

182 Iannucci, "Il mausoleo ritrovato," 1996, p. 180.

183 Vernia, "L'analisi," 2005, p. 1119; see also Gelichi/Novara, 1995, p. 361.

184 Cortesi, 1978; originally Di Pietro, 1927. Its location is now covered by trees and a parking lot.

185 *LPR* ch. 41. Galla Placidia did not have a niece named Singledia, as far as we know; Testi-Rasponi, 1924, p. 118 n. 2, proposed that the tomb seen by Agnellus was that of Suinigilda, the wife of Odoacer.

186 Pavan, 1984–5, pp. 351–2.

187 Gelichi/Novara, 1995. Bovini, 1950, likewise does not include a northern chapel in his reconstructions of the narthex, but Cirelli, 2008, p. 235, does include it.

188 Novara, "La Ravenna tardo-imperiale," 2001, p. 269.

189 Gelichi/Novara, 1995, pp. 350–5. Proconnesian marble formed a large part of the gray-veined marble of this floor (p. 355).

190 See Deliyannis, trans., 2004, pp. 336–7.

191 On stucco, see below, with reference to the Orthodox Baptistery.

192 Christe, 1996, p. 91, notes that the reference to Christ having no beginning or end is a pointed statement of anti-Arian theology; for more on this, see the following chapter.

193 Nauerth, 1974, p. 92, notes that since this expression refers to the cross-shaped church of Santa Croce, any one of the arches at the crossing might be meant, not necessarily the arch of the apse.

194 Images of Christ over the doorway on the interior of churches are known from other structures in Ravenna, namely the "mausoleum of Galla Placidia," the *capella arcivescovile*, and the Petriana church in Classe; they exemplify John 10: 7: "I am the gateway of the sheep . . ."; see Deichmann, 1974, p. 57.

195 At least, this is how the poem has been interpreted; see Deichmann, 1974, p. 57; and Nauerth, 1974, pp. 91–4. For a discussion of the meaning of the mosaic, see Poilpré/Caillet, 2005, pp. 112–16; but their interpretation of the line "germanae morti crimina saeva" as referring to the "savage crimes of the Germans" is erroneous, as this cannot be the meaning of *germanae*.

196 Nauerth, 1974, pp. 93–4.

197 Farioli Campanati, "Ravenna, Constantinopoli," 1992, pp. 141–2; Rizzardi, "Il Mausoleo / The Mausoleum," 1996, p. 121. Ultimately, it is a Christian interpretation of Psalm 91:13; see Stamatiou, 1992, who notes that the image represents a triumphant emperor.

198 See esp. Post, 1982.

199 Most recently Rizzardi, "L'architettura," 1996, pp. 129–30; De Francovich, 1958–9; De Angelis d'Ossat, *Studi*, 1962.

200 For example, Bovini, "Note," 1952, followed by Gelichi/Novara, 1995, p. 357, who describe both the stylistic and other archaeological bases for proposed dates. Deichmann, 1974, p. 52, says that a more precise date cannot be identified.

201 Cortesi, 1978, p. 56. Novara, "La Ravenna tardo-imperiale," 2001, pp. 271–3, says that this seems unlikely, given that it stands inside the imperial walls of the city, and that under Roman law burial had to take place outside the walls of a

city; however, as we will see, many burials took place within the fifth-century walls from the beginning of the fifth century.

202 Gelichi/Novara, 1995, pp. 364–6.

203 Brubaker, 1997, p. 61; on Galla's work in the Roman church, see Krautheimer, 1937, p. 168.

204 See Holum, 1977, and below.

205 Deichmann, 1974, p. 55.

206 Johnson, 1991, pp. 336–8.

207 It was *not* Agnellus who identified this chapel as the burial place of Galla, as most people claim; see Deliyannis, 2000.

208 Major publications of this building are Bovini, 1950; Deichmann, 1974, pp. 63–90; and Rizzardi, ed., 1996. The narthex was demolished in 1602, at which point the original entrance was closed off and a new door was built in the west wall; the original form was restored in 1774. The building was in a fairly ruined state by the 1870s, when restoration efforts began, ending in 1901. The history of the restorations is described in detail by Iannucci, "Il mausoleo ritrovato," 1996; and Vernia, "L'analisi," 2005, pp. 1122–4.

209 For a detailed discussion of the various restorations of the exterior brick-work, and an analysis of the original masonry, see Vernia, "L'analisi," 2005, who notes, p. 1129, that the thickness of these bricks is a particularity of this building, but not a unique case, as similar bricks are found in the other build-ings of the period. Vernia also observes that some new bricks were used for the facing of the arches.

210 Vernia, "L'analisi," 2005, pp. 1130–31.

211 Deichmann, 1974, p. 69, calls this the first use of a blind arcade on a brick building in Italy, on the basis of comparisons with the Adriatic coast and Syria.

212 Rizzardi, "L'architettura," 1996, p. 136.

213 For a detailed description, see Franzoni, "Bracchio nord," 1996, who notes that many of the ornaments of pagan origin on this sculpture correspond to the Christian iconography of the mosaics inside the chapel. The architrave had been removed in 1754, but was then replaced around 1900; see Iannucci, "Il mausoleo ritrovato," 1996, pp. 173 and 185.

214 See Michelini, "Pigna marmorea," 1996, who notes that the pinecone has never been the subject of study; it is assumed by Deichmann that it dates to the period of construction of the chapel.

215 All of these window slits had been filled in at some point and were restored by Corrado Ricci around 1900; see Iannucci, "Il mausoleo ritrovato," 1996, p. 188.

216 Iannucci, 1996, p. 188.

217 Vernia, "L'analisi," 2005, p. 1120; Iannucci, "Il mausoleo ritrovato," 1996, pp. 185–6; Michelini, "Anfore," 1996.

218 Rizzardi, "L'architettura," 1996, p. 137.

219 For artists, Deichmann, 1974, pp. 89–90, who suggests that at least five dif-ferent workmen were responsible for the apostles in the tower.

220 Farioli Campanati, "Decorazioni," 1992.

221 Deichmann, 1974, pp. 80–1, assumes that they are prophets, because, he says, evangelists always hold codices, while prophets hold scrolls. Yet in the lunettes below the dome in this chapel, some of the presumed apostles hold scrolls.

222 Or a type long known in Mediterranean art; for example, in the impluvium of the House of the Trident, on Delos, made in the second century BC.

223 Angiolini Martinelli, 1996, p. 153, suggests that the naturalistic garland represents the world, whereas the geometric meander represents the heavenly Jerusalem promoted by St. Lawrence. This seems to be stretching iconographic interpretation a bit too far.

224 "Quemadmodum desiderat cervus ad fontes aquarum, ita desiderat anima mea ad te, Deus." Deer were often used in baptisteries, most famously, silver deer were placed in the Lateran Baptistery in Rome by Pope Hilarus I (461–8; *LP V. Hilari*, ed. Duchesne I.243). See Maguire, 1987, pp. 38–9.

225 Summarized by Mackie, 1990.

226 One other interpretation is that the entire chapel is filled with apocalyptic imagery, and thus the figure is Christ hastening to burn a heretical book (Rizzardi, "I mosaici parietali," 2005, pp. 239–40); see Deichmann, 1974, p. 75, for references.

227 See, for example, a fragment of gold glass depicting Lawrence bearing a processional cross, in the Metropolitan Museum of Art (Rogers Fund, 1918), described with other examples by Lewis, 1973, p. 216 n. 103.

228 Cf. Nordström, 1953, p. 15. There has also been disagreement over whether the grill is to be seen merely as a symbol for Lawrence's martyrdom, or whether the mosaic depicts the narrative act of his running toward it; see Courcelle, 1948; and Deichmann, 1974, pp. 75–6, for discussion.

229 Mackie, 1990, p. 55, notes that St. Vincent is depicted among the martyrs in Sant'Apollinare Nuovo, and that his relics, according to Agnellus (*LPR* ch. 72), were included by Bishop Maximian in his church of St. Stephen; both of these references date to the mid–sixth century.

230 Since the sixteenth century the chapel was mentioned as the *monasterium sancti Nazarii*; this title is based on a misinterpretation of Agnellus; see Deliyannis, 2000. Testi-Rasponi associated the chapel with a *monasterium S. Laurentii Formosi*, but it has been shown that this identification was erroneous; see Deichmann, 1974, p. 63.

231 Deichmann, 1974, pp. 70–2, discussed other biblical and patristic references to the Good Shepherd.

232 See esp. Deichmann, 1974, pp. 72–5, for an exhaustive list of types.

233 Imperial: Rizzardi, 1993, pp. 394–5, and idem, "Il Mausoleo/The Mausoleum," 1996, p. 121; divine: after Mathews, 1993, esp. pp. 101–3; Angiolini Martinelli, 1996, p. 159, compares the representation to Apollo and Dionysius.

234 Deichmann, 1974, pp. 74–5; see Mathews, 1993, pp. 68–9, who does not, however, discuss our image.

235 See Deichmann, 1974, p. 71; Rizzardi, 1993, p. 395; Pasi, "Lunetta del Buon Pastore," 1996, p. 215.

236 Deichmann, 1974, p. 82.

237 John 4:13–14: "Jesus said to her, 'Everyone who drinks of this water will be thirsty again, but those who drink of the water that I will give them will never be thirsty. The water that I will give will become in them a spring of water gushing up to eternal life." Rev. 21:6: "I am the Alpha and the Omega, the beginning and the end. To the thirsty I will give water as a gift from the spring of the water of life."

238 See Angiolini Martinelli, 1996, pp. 155–6.

239 Apocalypse: Rizzardi, "Il Mausoleo / The Mausoleum," 1996, p. 122, and 1993, p. 402. Planets: Nordström, 1953, pp. 26–7. Chance: Deichmann, 1974, p. 84.

240 For example, in the apse mosaic of Santa Pudenziana in Rome, ca. 390, and in the triumphal arch mosaics of Santa Maria Maggiore in Rome, created in the 430s and 440s. See Deichmann, 1974, pp. 86–7.

241 For example, Deichmann, 1974, p. 86; followed by Rizzardi, "Il Mausoleo," 1996, p. 128 n. 76.

242 Applying the correspondences defined by Jerome (*Preface to the Commentary on Matthew*, ll. 59–90 [SC 242, pp. 64–8]); Deichmann, 1974, p. 78, notes this parallel, but on p. 86 he claims that the living creatures did not represent the Gospels.

243 Nordström, 1953, pp. 27–8. Deichmann, 1974, pp. 84–5, explains the vision of the cross as a reference to the Second Coming of Christ, an interpretation, he says, that is so clear that other interpretations must be wrong, including those interpretations that might include more than one meaning.

244 See Mackie, "Symbolism," 1995, and idem, 2003, who discusses the chapel dedicated to St. Victor in Milan, originally a detached chapel built over the grave of St. Victor, which also contained the tomb of St. Ambrose's brother Satyrus. Most notable in Ravenna was the burial chapel of Lauricius at San Lorenzo, dedicated to Saints Stephen, Gervase, and Protase, that contained an image of these saints (*LPR* ch. 36).

245 Rizzardi, "L'architettura," 1996, pp. 134–5, who also identifies as funereal the pinecone on the roof, the dark colors of the mosaics, and the transcendental symbolism of the mosaics.

246 Deichmann, 1974, p. 65, who notes that these sarcophagi have been dated from the fourth to the sixth century, and that there is no real way of determining the dates absolutely; Rizzardi, "L'architettura," 1996, p. 135, says that they seem to have been planned from the start for the places they now occupy.

247 Deichmann, 1974, pp. 64–5, says that there is no reason that they should not have been there at the time of construction, despite the fact that Agnellus doesn't mention them, but as I have shown, Deliyannis, 2000, Agnellus did not describe this chapel at all. Currently they are known as the sarcophagi of Constantius III, Honorius, and Galla Placidia, but thirteenth-century traditions held that they contained either Galla, Valentinian III, and Honoria; or Theodosius (which?), his wife, two daughters, and the prophet Elisha; or Galla, Constantius III, and Valentinian III; see Deliyannis, 2000.

248 Pauselli, "Sarcofago detto di Costanzo III" and "Sarcofago detto di Onorio," 1996.

249 Deichmann, 1974, p. 64; see also Michelini, "Pigna marmorea," 1996, who provides a detailed history and bibliography of the motif of the pinecone as a funerary symbol.

250 Deichmann, 1974, p. 82. Cf. John 4:14: "Whoever drinks of the water that I shall give him will never thirst; the water that I shall give him will become in him a spring of water welling up to eternal life."

251 Cf. Psalm 23.

252 Cf. Deichmann's summary, pp. 86–7, in which he argues that the entire decorative program is funerary; adopted by Angiolini Martinelli, 1996, pp. 149–51.

253 Deichmann, 1974, p. 76, who specifically argues that Lawrence cannot be understood as an intercessor for the deceased before Christ because then he would have been found in a different pose.

254 Deichmann, 1974, p. 64 (followed by Rizzardi, 1993, p. 400), denies that there would have been such an altar, and interprets the eastern orientation as referring to the Second Coming of Christ from the east, as the Sun of the World.

255 Rizzardi, 1993, pp. 400–1.

256 See Holum, 1977, and idem, 1982, pp. 108–10 and 129–30.

257 Mackie, "The Mausoleum," 1995.

258 See Zangara, 2000, esp. pp. 298–304.

259 See Deliyannis, ed., 2006, pp. 102–3 and Benericetti, 1994, pp. 168–9. For a summary of other dates proposed for the Diploma, see Brown, 1979, p. 13 n. 2. Orioli, 1980, pp. 135–44, provides reasons that it should be dated to the end of the sixth century. The diploma of Valentinian is found in the *Codex Estensis*, fol. 44r, and is published in *Papiri diplomatici* – ed. Marini, no. 57 (p. 94); Agnellus used it as a source (*LPR* ch. 40). It lists the following sees as subordinate to Ravenna: Sarsina, Cesena, Forlimpopoli, Forli, Faenza, Imola, Bologna, Modena, Reggio, Parma, Piacenza, Brescello, Voghenza, and Adria.

260 See Zangara, 2000; and Palardy, 2004, pp. 10–11.

261 Two of Chrysologus's surviving sermons, nos. 165 and 175, were given on occasions when he was consecrating bishops for other cities. Some have claimed that Chrysologus was the first metropolitan of Ravenna, and point to his sermon 175 in which he seems to be saying that Marcellinus is the first bishop to be consecrated by a bishop of Ravenna. See Deliyannis, ed., 2006, pp. 102–3, for the controversy over whether these sermons mean that Chrysologus was the *first* metropolitan; see also Palardy, 2004, pp. 9–10.

262 See Benericetti, 1995, pp. 65–6; also Deliyannis, ed., 2006, pp. 102–3. Peter Chrysologus was not, as Agnellus makes him, the second bishop named Peter, but the first Peter, whom Agnellus calls Peter *antistes*; see Deliyannis, ed., 2006, p. 99.

263 See Benericetti, 1995, esp. pp. 53–76.

264 Agnellus, *LPR* c. 49, says that it was Pope Sixtus III (r. 432–40), but in light of what is known about the episcopal chronology of Ravenna in this period, it is more likely that he was ordained by Pope Celestine I (422–32); see Deliyannis, ed., 2006, p. 99.

265 Palardy, 2004, notes a letter from Theodoret of Cyrrhus to Domnus of Antioch, written in 431, which singles out Milan, Aquileia, and Ravenna as the three leading sees of Italy (*Epist.* 112, SC 111.46–57).

266 "Adest ipsa etiam mater christiani perennis et fidelis imperii, quae dum fide, opere misericordiae, sanctitate, in honore trinitatis beatam sectatur et imitatur ecclesiam, procreare, amplecti, possidere augustam meruit trinitatem." This "trinity" consists of Valentinian III, Constantius III, and herself, all *augusti* (see Oost, 1968, pp. 266–7). It should be noted that Eusebius, in his *Vita Constantini* IV.40, refers to Constantine's three sons as a "trinity of pious sons."

267 Sermon 85b; see Palardy, 2004, p. 8.

268 For a full discussion of the authenticity of this letter, see Olivar, 1962, pp. 89–94. The letter is published in *PL* 52, col. 71, and also among the correspondence of Pope Leo I, as *Epist.* 25, published in *PL* 54, cols. 739–44.

269 *LPR* ch. 39, but also Procopius, *De bello Gothico* V. 1. 24.

270 Major publications on the cathedral are Deichmann, 1974, pp. 3–13; and Novara, *La cattedrale*, 1997.

271 The choice of the Anastasis as a dedication is unusual in this period, and would repay further investigation; only a few early churches are known to have been

dedicated to the Anastasis or to St. Anastasia (a confusion of identity also found in Agnellus, *LPR* ch. 23), including one in Rome, one in Beirut (Hall, 2004, p. 172), and Gregory Nazianzus's church in Constantinople, built in the 380s as an anti-Arian foundation (Snee, 1998). Deichmann, 1976, pp. 301–2, contends that most of these were not dedicated to the Anastasis but to St. Anastasia. See also below, Chapter 5, about the dedication of the Arian cathedral.

272 See Ortalli, 1991.

273 Existence of such a porticoed street in Farioli Campanati, "Ravenna, Constantinopoli," 1992, p. 144; for the refutation of this thesis based on analysis of the tenth–century and later documents on which this interpretation is based, see Novara, *Un tempio nomato*, 2000, pp. 55 and 66–8. Excavations in 2004 revealed a row of pilasters along the present Via Mariani that are assumed to have formed part of such a *via porticata*; see Maioli, 2007, pp. 228–9, information as yet unpublished.

274 Marazzi, 2006, p. 51.

275 *LPR* ch. 23.

276 As explained most recently by Russo, "L'architettura," 2005, p. 89; see also Pasi, 2005, p. 48, and Deichmann, 1974, pp. 3–4.

277 See Orioli, 1997, who presents other arguments in favor of a post-400 date for Ursus. Novara, *La cattedrale*, 1997, pp. 48–9, suggests that since Zosimus, *Historia nova* 5.34, says that Stilicho took refuge in a church and was in the presence of the bishop in 408, this must mean that the cathedral was completed by that date; but Zosimus does not call it the cathedral and there was certainly a bishop's church in existence before Ursus built a new one.

278 For a complete discussion of this debate, see Deliyannis, ed., 2006, pp. 97–107. Novara, *La cattedrale*, 1997, p. 48, does not answer this question in either direction, although her work is often cited as though she proposes a date before 400.

279 The following is based on Novara, *La cattedrale*, 1997.

280 Idem, pp. 20–9.

281 Deichmann, 1974, pp. 8–9.

282 See Novara, *La cattedrale*, 1997, esp. pp. 68–70.

283 Idem, fig. 46, pp. 142–3 and pp. 70–2.

284 Furthermore, Novara admits that with each restructuring of the central nave colonnade materials were probably reused; while some new elements may have also been introduced, it does not make much sense that tenth-century architects would suddenly introduce impost blocks which were no longer part of the architectural vocabulary of Italy.

285 *LPR* ch. 23.

286 Testi-Rasponi, ed., 1924, p. 67 n. 4, countering Holder-Egger, ed., 1878, p. 289 n. 1; on commemoration of patronage in floor mosaics in northern Italy, see Caillet, 1993; see also Novara, *La cattedrale*, 1997, p. 56.

287 Novara, *La cattedrale*, 1997, pp. 53–7.

288 *LPR* ch. 44: "And in front of his image in a medallion in the Ursiana church, where it is fixed in the renovated church, a candle gleams with clear light the whole night long." This statement has led to the suggestion (Testi-Rasponi, ed., 1924, p. 132 n. 10) that portraits of Ravenna's bishops were depicted in medallions along the nave of the cathedral, but since Agnellus does not mention any other such portraits, this seems unlikely; see Deichmann, 1974, p. 9; and Novara, *La cattedrale*, 1997, pp. 57–8.

289 Saxer, 1988, esp. pp. 570–89 and 627–46.

290 Wharton, 1987, pp. 358 and 366; and esp. Wharton, 1995, pp. 122–31; in some cases baptism was performed at the feast of Pentecost.

291 The earliest case being the house-church at Dura Europos in Syria; see Wharton, 1999, and Cantino Wataghin et al., 2001, p. 236.

292 Cantino Wataghin et al., 2001, p. 233–8; Wharton, 1987, pp. 367–8, who notes that this is a development particularly in the western Mediterranean.

293 See Ristow, 1998, pp. 17–20 for a summary of the different forms.

294 Brandt, 1997–8.

295 See esp. Kostof, 1965, pp. 46–56, Deichmann, 1974, pp. 25–7, and, with a very complete bibliography, Ristow, 1998, esp. pp. 20–3.

296 "...octagonus fons est numere dignus eo / hoc numero decuit sacri baptismalis aulam / surgere, quo populis vera salus rediit...." The poem is preserved in a ninth-century manuscript, the *Sylloge Laureshamensis* (*Cod. Vat. Pal. 833*) III; see Deichmann, 1974, p. 25.

297 Krautheimer, 1942, pp. 21–33; Deichmann, 1974, pp. 26–7, argues without much evidence that there was no number symbolism of this sort in the use of eight-sided buildings as baptisteries.

298 Wharton, 1987, p. 368, and Cantino Wataghin et al., 2001, pp. 240–2.

299 For a comprehensive analysis, see Cantino Wataghin et al., 2001, pp. 234–42. Deichmann, 1974, p. 26, argues that Milan's and Ravenna's baptisteries were almost contemporary, and thus Ravenna's must have been modeled instead on Rome; another example in which the date of Ursus carries significant consequences for the history of architectural development. If, as I have argued above, Ursus's constructions date to the 420s, Milan becomes a possible model once more.

300 Ristow, 1998, pp. 35–8.

301 Kostof, 1965, p. 43.

302 Petriana: *LPR* ch. 26, 50, 67, and 91; Arian Baptistery: *LPR* ch. 86; Sant'Apollinare Nuovo: *LPR* ch. 89; for these, and the Ca'Bianca, see the following chapters. Compare the large numbers of baptisteries known for Rome in the fifth and sixth centuries; see Cantino Wataghin et al., 2001, pp. 242–50.

303 The main publications for the Orthodox (Neonian) Baptistery are Nordström, 1953, pp. 32–54; Mazzotti, 1961; Kostof, 1965 (with useful bibliographical notes at pp. 157–65); and Deichmann, 1974, pp. 17–47; for a good summary of more recent scholarship, see Pasquini, 2005.

304 The absidioles did not have a structural purpose, notes Kostof, 1965, p. 47, as can be seen by the fact that the ones on the northwest and southwest sides were removed at some unknown period, and then restored in the mid–nineteenth century (their existence was attested by excavations conducted by Filippo Lanciani at that time).

305 Kostof, 1965, p. 47; although Russo, "L'architettura," 2005, p. 98, seems to disagree. For the postmedieval history of the baptistery, see Kostof, 1965, pp. 18–30. In the seventeenth century a house for the rector of the cathedral was built abutting the south side of the baptistery and storehouses abutting the north side. Various other alternations were made to the structure in the eighteenth and nineteenth centuries, including the creation of new windows and doors and the alteration or filling in of old ones. The mosaics were restored in the 1790s, and again in the 1850s–70s, at the same time that

the two lost absidioles were also restored and the attached buildings were removed. In the 1890s the marble *opus sectile*, which had been removed, was remade.

306 Kostof, 1965, pp. 39–40 and 43–5, who notes an abrupt change of mortar and brick module beginning 0.42 meters above the cornice of the original Ursinian wooden roof.

307 Deichmann, 1974, pp. 23–4; Russo, "L'architettura," 2005, p. 102.

308 Identified by the remains of a stucco cornice found inside the exterior walls and just above the level of the springing of the dome; see Kostof, 1965, pp. 39–40, and Deichmann, 1974, p. 18.

309 Pasquini, 2005, pp. 328–9; Novara, "La Ravenna tardo-imperiale," 2001, p. 263; Russo, "L'architettura," 2005, p. 100. Kostof, 1965, pp. 40–2, argued that in the original form the baptistery had only one interior arcade and that the upper zone would not have been surmounted by the broad arches that now support the dome; others, especially Mazzotti, 1961, accepted by Deichmann, 1974, pp. 21–2, proposed that both zones were original; see most recently Pasquini, 2005, pp. 328–9.

310 Russo, "L'architettura," 2005, p. 101.

311 Kostof, 1965, pp. 35 and 42–3; Deichmann, 1974, p. 18.

312 De Angelis d'Ossat, *Studi*, 1962, pp. 148–9, followed by most later scholars.

313 Kostof, 1965, p. 31; Deichmann, 1974, p. 24.

314 Wharton, 1987 and 1995.

315 It is usually suggested that the absidiole on the southeast side, which now contains an altar, originally likewise housed an altar (Pasquini, 2005, p. 331) or a throne for the bishop (Wharton, 1987, p. 364).

316 Deichmann, 1974, pp. 21–2; Kostof, 1965, pp. 36–7; however, Kostof notes that some say that there was a door on each flat side, based on the presence of brick relieving arches on each wall, which Kostof says are not original; the idea of four doors is repeated by Pasquini, 2005, p. 330. From at least the fourteenth century and perhaps earlier, the baptistery was linked to the cathedral by a portico (Kostof, 1965, pp. 37–9).

317 Deichmann, 1974, p. 25.

318 Kostof, 1965, pp. 139–40. We do not know what provisions were made for water supply in Ravenna's baptistery, but given that the cathedral complex was next to a water distribution tower for the aqueduct, the baptistery was probably connected to the city's water and drainage systems.

319 *LPR* ch. 28.

320 Rizzardi, "I mosaici parietali," 2005, p. 241, notes that the alternation of colors in the depiction of the apostles creates a sense of rotation. See also Kostof, 1965, p. 121, and in general pp. 112–21, for a detailed analysis of the compositional scheme of the baptistery's architecture and decoration.

321 Nordhagen, 1983, p. 83 n. 30.

322 Theories that the lower levels of the baptistery decoration were carried out earlier or later than the mosaics of the dome have been refuted by Kostof, 1965, pp. 100–3; and Pasquini, 2005, pp. 340–4.

323 Wharton, 1987, pp. 364, 373–4.

324 Kostof, 1965, p. 54.

325 Novara, "La Ravenna tardo-imperiale," 2001, p. 265.

326 Pasquini, 2005, pp. 328–9.

327 Ambrose, *De sacramentis* 3.5. Kostof, 1965, pp. 59–61, provides a brief analysis of the verses and interpretations of them; see also Deichmann, 1974, pp. 28–30.

328 Kostof, 1965, pp. 61–2; Deichmann, 1974, p. 28, says the use of Bible verses as labels for images would go against what we know of early Christian usage.

329 Deichmann, 1974, pp. 30–1, notes various suggestions that, together with the stucco figures in the zone immediately above, there were a total of twenty-four prophets (8 + 16), or even that the twenty-four represent the twenty-four elders of the Apocalypse. If one wants to give these and other similar figures a feminist reading, one could say, as does Wharton, 1995, p. 116, that they "embody the patriarchal control of the Word."

330 Deichmann, 1974, pp. 22–3, discussed theories about such triple arcades in late antiquity.

331 The windows are currently enclosed with opaque glass panes made to look like alabaster; this was a restoration of the 1930s (Kostof, 1965, p. 30). We do not know what originally covered the windows, although it was quite likely glass that was not completely translucent. A document dating to 1573 orders that two of the windows be opened, implying that they had all been blocked up at some earlier point, while two more were opened in 1781; these were rectangular. In the 1850s all the windows were opened and restored with a semicircular upper part (Kostof, 1965, pp. 21–3).

332 Agnellus uses the term *gipsea metalla* for the Ursiana cathedral (*LPR* ch. 23), Santa Croce (ch. 41), and Sant'Apollinare Nuovo (ch. 86); see Deliyannis, trans., 2004, p. 325. Stucco survives in a few places in San Vitale, and in addition, fragments of probably sixth-century stucco were excavated at Sant'Agata; see Russo, 1989, pp. 2331–4.

333 Pasquini, 2005, p. 344; Kostof, 1965, pp. 71–6, suggests that the composition reflects facade compositions of buildings, especially *scaenae frontes* or theater backdrops.

334 Scholars have identified, based on formal differences between the figures, the hands of at least two artists (Deichmann, 1974, p. 45; Pasquini, 2005, pp. 339–44); Kostof, 1965, pp. 64–5 and 95–100, identifies four groups.

335 Kostof, 1965, pp. 65–6; Pasquini, 2005, pp. 334–40, refutes the idea proposed by Van Lohuizen-Mulder, 1990, that these stuccos were created by Coptic artists, although she notes that the motif of confronting animals is ultimately of Iranian derivation.

336 Pasquini, 2005, pp. 337–8, discusses specific comparisons.

337 Kostof, 1965, pp. 66–71; Deichmann, 1974, pp. 45–6; Wharton, 1987, p. 362.

338 Other similar faux-architectural zones in mosaic are known from the period; for example, at St. George, Thessalonike, whose mosaics date to the late fourth or early fifth century; see most recently Nasrallah, 2005.

339 See Janes, 1998, pp. 129–30.

340 Nordström, 1953, pp. 46–54.

341 Deichmann, 1974, pp. 41–3.

342 For discussion of various theories, see Kostof, 1965, pp. 79–82; and Deichmann, 1974, pp. 41–3; more recently, see Wharton, 1987, pp. 368–75; Wharton, 1995, pp. 126–7; and Pasquini, 2005, p. 333.

343 Matt. 28:19; see Deichmann, 1974, p. 38.

344 Kostof, 1965, p. 83: *Petrus, Andreas, Iacobus Zebedei, Iohannes, Filippus, Bartolomeus, Iudas Zelotes, Simon Cananeus, Iacobus Alfei, Mattheus, Thomas, Paulus.*

This is for the most part the list given in Matt. 10:2–5, with the substitution of Paul for Thaddaeus and of Judas Iscariot for Jude the Zealot.

345 Kostof, 1965, pp. 83–5; compare the slightly earlier apostles in the "mausoleum of Galla Placidia," and also the series in the *capella arcivescovile* and San Vitale.

346 Nordström, 1953, p. 36.

347 Kostof, 1965, pp. 89–93, reviews the theories before 1965; Engemann, 1989, and Rizzardi, "La decorazione musiva," 2001, pp. 922–6, include more recent ones.

348 Deichmann, 1974, pp. 39–40. Others have seen it more generally as a gesture of homage to Christ's baptism, e.g., Engemann, 1989; or to the cross at the center of the scene, Wisskirchen, 1993; and Rizzardi, "La decorazione musiva," 2001, but the latter explanation assumes that there was indeed a cross in the original mosaic. The alternative possibility, that they were offered to the empty throne(s) shown in the lower zone, is based on the fact that in the Arian Baptistery the apostles do offer their crowns to such a throne; see Chapter 5.

349 Nordström, 1953, pp. 41–6; Pasquini, 2005, p. 333.

350 Wharton, 1987, pp. 373–5.

351 Deichmann, 1974, p. 38, thinks that John the Baptist's halo, at least, is not original. Rizzardi, "La decorazione musiva," 2001, recently proposed, on the basis of a comparison with the Arian depiction of the same scene, that originally the Orthodox depiction had a beardless Christ and included the paten; she accepts that a drawing of the image made in 1690, showing the cross, the paten, and the beardless Christ, reflects the original depiction. However, Kostof (1965, p. 86) and Deichmann (1974, p. 33) note that no other early Christian depiction of the baptism includes a bearded Christ or a paten, and both are probably later additions by a preseventeenth-century restorer.

352 Kostof, 1965, pp. 105–6. Deichmann, 1974, pp. 33–4, also cites interpretations of the gold background as the great light that came on the water upon Jesus's baptism.

353 Cf. Wharton, 1995, pp. 121–2.

354 See Maguire, 1987, pp. 24, 44–8, who discusses sixth-century mosaics at Tegea and Qasr-el-Lebia with such portrayals. See also Spieser, 2001, pp. 8–9, reprint of 1995, regarding the depiction of the Jordan in the apse mosaic at Hosios David, of the mid–sixth century.

355 See Ristow, 1957, and Jensen, 2000, pp. 48 and 84; the personified Jordan became even more popular in sixth-century depictions of the baptism.

356 Peter Chrysologus, *Sermo* 160; Wharton, 1995, p. 120; Kostof, 1965, p. 87, citing Nordström, 1953, p. 33.

357 Kostof, 1965, pp. 122–3.

358 See especially Rizzardi, 2004, who notes comparisons between Ravenna's structures and those of other cities; also Miller, 2000, pp. 33–7. Rapp, 2005, pp. 208–11, states that in general episcopal complexes strove for functionality rather than ostentation, but this does not seem to have been the case in Ravenna.

359 See Müller-Wiener, 1989.

360 See Miller, 1991–2 and 2000.

361 Miller, 2000, pp. 52–3.

362 The major publications on the *episcopium* are Rizzardi, 2004; Miller, 1991–2, and idem, 2000, pp. 22–33; also Marano, 2007.

363 *LPR* ch. 23; Miller, 1991–2, p. 149, although I do not agree with her and with Deichmann, 1974, p. 194, that we can infer from Agnellus that the *episcopium* predated the cathedral, as his reference is too vague for specific meaning to be attached to it.

364 Rizzardi, 2004, pp. 162–7; for other interpretations of the iconography of these images, see Wickhoff, 1894; Weis, 1966; De Angelis d'Ossat, 1973; and Nauerth, 1974, pp. 81–91.

365 Rizzardi, 1989, p. 719; Miller, 1991–2, p. 150.

366 Cf. Rizzardi, 2004, p. 158; the examples most often compared to Ravenna are the Hall of Nineteen Couches in the Great Palace of Constantinople, a dining hall with seven apses excavated to the northwest of the Hippodrome in Constantinople and built in the fifth century (Bardill, 1997, pp. 86–9), and the Hall of Eleven Couches built in the late eighth century at the Lateran in Rome; see in general Krautheimer, 1966.

367 A second major construction, the *domus tricollis*, is said by Agnellus to have been begun by Bishop Exuperantius (473–7), although it was only completed under Archbishop Maximian in the 550s. Agnellus quotes the dedicatory inscription that lists Bishop Peter II (494–520) as the founder, (*LPR* ch. 75), so this building will be considered in the following chapter; see Deliyannis, trans., 2004, p. 134 n. 4.

368 See Deichmann, 1976, pp. 350–1; Novara, "La Ravenna tardo-imperiale," 2001, p. 265;

369 *LPR* chs. 151 and 155 (collapse and rebuilding attempt); *LPR* ch. 24: Fundator ecclesiae Petrianae, muros per circuitum aedificans, sed nondum omnia complens. Nulla ecclesia in aedificio maior fuit similis illa neque in longitudine nec in altitudine; et ualde exornata fuit de preciosis lapidibus et tessellis uariis decorata et ualde locupletata in auro et argento et uasculis sacris, quibus ipse fieri iussit. Ibi asserunt affuisse imaginem Saluatoris depictam quam numquam similem in picturis homo uidere potuisset, super regiam; tam speciosissima et assimilata fuit qualem ipse filius Dei in carne non fastidium, quando gentibus praedicauit.

370 The story that Agnellus tells has a specifically anti-Iconoclastic slant; see Deliyannis, 1996.

371 Deichmann, 1976, p. 350.

372 Cortesi, 1964; Novara, "La Ravenna tardo-imperiale," 2001, p. 265.

373 Augenti, "Nuove indagini," 2005, pp. 250–1. Augenti notes that although Agnellus says that the Petriana was "in civitate Classis," he uses the same phrase for the basilica of Probus, which was certainly outside Classe's walls.

374 *LPR* chs. 29, 83, and 98. See Cortesi, 1982; and Farioli Campanati, 1986.

375 *LPR* ch. 22; nothing more is known of this structure. St. Pullio/Pollio was from Cybalae near Sirmium, the birthplace of Valentinian I, and thus was associated with the imperial dynasty (Farioli Campanati, "Ravenna, Constantinopoli," 1992, p. 132).

376 Cortesi, 1982.

377 Deichmann, 1976, pp. 308–18.

378 *LPR* chs. 29–30 and 56, which tells also of the burial there of Bishop Aurelian in 521. Deichmann, 1976, pp. 309–10, speculates that the church was built during the reign of Honorius or Valentinian III, as in the 430s similar constructions were undertaken in Rome.

379 Deichmann, 1976, pp. 311–14, and idem, 1989, p. 279; also Farioli Campanati, "Ravenna e I suoi rapporti," 2005, p. 20.

380 Mazzotti, 1974; Deichmann, 1976, pp. 314–17.

381 *LPR* chs. 31 and 39.

382 See Deichmann, 1976, pp. 298–300, for a summary of the evidence.

383 *LPR* ch. 44; the apse vault was rebuilt in the sixth century, so we do not know whether this image, which from Agnellus's description was similar to a depiction of Peter Chrysologus in San Giovanni Evangelista, was made in the late fifth century or at the time of the rebuilding.

384 See Mazzotti, "La basilica ravennate," 1967; Deichmann, 1976, pp. 283–97; Picard, 1978; Torre, 1986; Russo, 1989, and idem, "L'architettura," 2005, pp. 170–6.

385 The dating of these chambers is controversial, summarized by Smith, "Form and Function," 1990, p. 183 n. 18 and p. 199. Mazzotti claimed that they were original to the building, while Deichmann dated them to the mid–sixth century; Smith likewise accepts them as later additions, largely because of the apse on the southern chamber, which is similar to other sixth-century side chambers. However, the doors at the east end of the aisles were part of the original building, implying that some sort of rooms existed there; perhaps the apse was added to the southern chamber as part of the sixth-century rebuilding of Sant'Agata.

386 Deichmann, 1976, pp. 286–91, says it is possible that originally the arcade was supported by piers rather than columns, as at the sixth-century San Michele *in Africisco*, but this is based on his assumption that the entire church dates to the sixth century, which is not accepted by most other scholars, e.g., Picard, 1978, p. 42, based on an analysis of the excavations of the atrium.

387 *LPR* ch. 51.

388 Deichmann, 1976, p. 332. Agnellus repeatedly confused the three bishops named Peter; see Deliyannis, 2006, p. 99.

389 See *BHL* 972. The eleventh-century manuscript in which the legend is found, Brussels, Bibliotheque Royale, Codex 64, also contains Lives of Peter Chrysologus, Severus of Ravenna, and many other saints to whom churches were dedicated in Ravenna, and must depend on a Ravennate source. Peter Damian, the eleventh-century monk and scholar of Ravenna, preached a sermon (*Sermo* 65) on Barbatian that included the same information. See Laqua, 1976, pp. 174–222.

390 See Deichmann, 1976, pp. 331–3.

391 Gillett, 2001, pp. 148–57 and 162–5.

392 Deichmann, 1982.

393 Even today scholars compare Ravenna unfavorably to Constantinople, e.g., McCormick, 2000, p. 136: "By about 425 the east's new capital of Constantinople had expanded into one of the empire's greatest cities, whereas Ravenna resembled rather a glorified military base."

394 Neri, 1990, p. 571; Mazza, 2005, pp. 10–11.

Four. Ravenna, the Capital of the Ostrogothic Kingdom

1 Jordanes, *Getica* 60 (316), explicitly tells his readers, "Do not think that I have added or taken away anything to make the Gothic race look good (as you might

expect of someone of my ancestry); I have written just what is in the sources. If I have written it all down as I have found it, you will see it redounds not so much to the credit of the Goths as to the credit of the man who conquered them" (trans. O'Donnell, 1982). While scholars disagree over Jordanes's precise motivations, most agree that he was not descended from the Goths who went to Italy, but rather from those who stayed in the Balkans, and that he was writing for a Roman/Byzantine audience; see, e.g., Croke, 1987, pp. 125–6, who notes that Jordanes is less pro-Gothic than Cassiodorus, and extremely anti-Arian; see also Heather, *Goths and Romans*, 1991, pp. 34–67; and Amory, 1997, esp. pp. 35–7 and 291–307.

2 See Wolfram, 1988, pp. 246–68; Heather, 1995, esp. p. 149; Heather, *Goths and Romans*, 1991, pp. 259–63.

3 The years of Theoderic's residence in Constantinople are somewhat conjectural, as is his age, since his birth date is not exactly clear (Wolfram, 1988, p. 262). We know that he was there for ten years, from age seven to age eighteen. Amory, 1997, suggests that he was there from 461–71; Rorh, 1995, pp. 203–4 n. 9, gives the dates as 459–70.

4 Theoderic's education has been the subject of some debate. Many scholars find it hard to imagine that a prince brought up in the palace at Constantinople would not have learned how to read (what else would he have been doing for ten years?), but the evidence in favor is very slim. Ennodius, in his panegyric on Theoderic, 11 (ed. and German transl. Rohr, 1995, pp. 202–3), states "Educavit te in gremio civilitatis Graecia praesaga venturi," which Moorhead, 1992, p. 14, interprets as meaning he was educated in Greek, although the text should actually be translated, "Greece, presaging things to come, brought you up in the bosom of *civilitas*..." (*educavit* could simply mean "raised," and does not necessarily connote literacy; on the meaning of *civilitas* see below). John Malalas, *Chronographia* 15.94, writing in Antioch in the late sixth century says "Θευδερί-χος... ἐν Κωνσταντινουπόλει ἀνατραφεὶς καὶ ἀναγνούς...," which means more explicitly, "Theoderic, brought up and taught to read in Constantinople...." On the opposing side, *Anon. Vales.* 61 says, "He [Theoderic], although he was illiterate [*inlitteratus*]..." and again, 79: "Therefore King Theoderic was illiterate [*inlitteratus*]... on account of which he ordered a gold plate to be made with the four letters 'legi' [I have read it] cut into it; with which, if he wanted to sign a document, the plate was placed on it and he led his pen through it, that his signature might appear." Procopius also, *De bello Gothico* I.2.16, says that the Gothic elders told Amalasuintha that Theoderic had conquered a vast territory "although he had not so much as heard of letters" (καίπερ γραμμάτων οὐδὲ ὅσον ἀκοὴν ἔχων); Procopius, *Secret History* 6, also tells that the emperor Justin I was illiterate and had to use a stencil to sign documents (Ensslin, 1940, suggests, rather plausibly, that the illiterate ruler of *Anon. Vales.* 79 was Justin I, later miscopied as Theoderic [earlier proposed by Hodgkin, vol. 3, 1885, p. 268 n. 1]; but this does not explain ch. 61). Grundmann, 1958, pp. 24–30, discusses the topos of the unlettered but wise king, and argues that warriors were not expected to be literate, thus the evidence against Theoderic's literacy is probably correct. More work should be done on the topos of the illiterate warrior. (See Rota, 2002, pp. 261–3.)

5 Ostrogothic Italy and Ostrogothic Ravenna have been extensively described and analyzed, especially in the past twenty years, and large numbers of articles,

books, and volumes of collected essays have exhaustively explored every angle of Gothic civilization. See esp. Barnish/Marazzi, eds., 2007; Carile, ed., 1995; CISAM volume, 1993; on Ostrogothic Ravenna, the fundamental article remains Johnson, 1988.

6 The *Anonymus Valesianus* 49 says that he was sent by Zeno to *praeregnare* for him in Italy (Claude, 1993, pp. 24–5); Jordanes, *Getica* 57, has Theoderic propose the expedition, but the same author in his *Romana*, 348–9, has the idea originate with Zeno. For a detailed analysis of the supposed pact with Zeno, see Neri, 1995, pp. 324–6, who concludes that such a pact probably did not exist, but Theoderic may have said that it did to gain legitimacy in Italy.

7 *De bello Gothico* V.1.12; *Anon. Vales.* 49 says that Theoderic entered Italy "cum gente Gothica." Heather, 1995, p. 153; Moorhead, 1992, pp. 67–8; and Wolfram, 1988, p. 279 (citing Ensslin, 1959), say 100,000 total people entered Italy (Wolfram has 20,000 warriors); Burns, 1978, argues for 40,000. Amory, 1997, p. 41, says the total number of Ostrogoths was 20,000 at most, and believes that most of them were soldiers; he doubts Procopius's claim that women and children came too.

8 At least according to Procopius, *De bello Gothico* V.1.15–23.

9 This is the story told by Procopius, *De bello Gothico* V.1.24–25, and *Anon. Vales.* 55, both of whom, along with Cassiodorus, *Chronica*, a. 493, say that Odoacer was plotting against Theoderic. For Theoderic's conquest of Italy, see Wolfram, 1988, pp. 282–3, and Moorhead, 1992, pp. 17–31, who provides a detailed analysis of the sources.

10 See Claude, 1993.

11 See Shanzer, 1998, p. 232.

12 This is noted by Jordanes, *Getica* 57.

13 See Claude, 1993, pp. 30–1; Wolfram, 1988, pp. 306–26.

14 For more on Theoderic's title and base of authority, see Jones, 1962; and Neri, 1995. See also Arnold, 2008, especially chapters 2 and 4, who argues that Theoderic did present himself as an emperor.

15 Johnson, 1988, p. 76. This coin is generally viewed as having been struck in 500 to commemorate Theoderic's thirty-year anniversary and his visit to Rome, but Grierson, 1985, repeated in Grierson/Blackburn, 1986, p. 35, argues that it was struck in commemoration of Theoderic's victory over the Franks and Burgundians in 509, while Arslan, 1989, pp. 22–6, and 1993, p. 520; and Metlich, 2004, p. 15, argue that it was struck between Theoderic's taking control in Italy in 493 and Anastasius's recognition of him in 497.

16 *Anon. Vales.* II.64: "et omnia ornamenta palatii, quae Odoacar Constantinopolim transmiserat, remittit." Odoacer's lack of insignia is also mentioned by Cassiodorus, *Chronica*, a. 476.

17 Cassiodorus, *Chronica* a. 500.

18 See Moorhead, 1992, p. 60.

19 *De bello gothico* II.1.26 and 29: "ἦν τε ὁ Θευδέριχος λόγῳ μὲν τύραννος, ἔργῳ δὲ βασιλεὺς ἀληθὴς τῶν ἐν ταύτῃ τῇ τιμῇ τὸ ἐξ ἀρχῆς ηὐδοκιμηκότων οὐδενὸς ἧσσον." Johnson, 1988, p. 74, notes that many epithets formerly used for emperors were used for him, such as *augustus* and *imperium*. See now Arnold, 2008.

20 The meaning of the ethnicity of the Ostrogoths has been the recent object of intense study; most scholars now agree that the "Ostrogoths" were really a collection of Gothic and other tribes who had only been united for the first time

by Theoderic before he invaded Italy. See especially Amory, 1997, who takes the extreme position that the main defining feature of Ostrogothic ethnicity was membership in Theoderic's army, rebutted most comprehensively by Heather, 2007.

21 Bierbrauer, 1975 and 1976, created a map that is subsequently much cited, e.g., by Heather, 1995, p. 156. Bierbrauer's map is based on finds of "Ostrogothic"-type jewelry in burials, but in fact the use of grave goods seems to have been restricted to a very small number of people in Ostrogothic society (on what basis we do not know), and recent scholars have questioned the attribution of ethnicity based on grave goods; see most recently Curta, 2007, who summarizes the debate.

22 On the question of whether the Ostrogoths were allotted land (which would involve a complex division of estates and farms) or tax revenues, see especially Goffart, 1980; Barnish, 1986; Durliat, 1997; Goffart again, 2006, pp. 119–86.

23 See Barnish, 1988.

24 Amory, 1997, pp. 50–78, traces a decline in the rhetoric of *civilitas* in Theoderic's later years.

25 See recently Saitta, 1993; Reydellet, 1995; and Stüven, 1995.

26 Saitta, 1993, notes that this tolerance was part of his concept of *civilitas*.

27 *De bello gothico* II.1.27–31; see Saitta, 1993, p. 148.

28 See Ruggini, 1961; Soraci, 1974; Marazzi, 1998; Cosentino, 2005.

29 Wolfram, 1988, pp. 288–9.

30 Letters adopt a patronizing tone to other "barbarian" rulers, emphasizing the superior Roman culture of Theoderic's court (I.46 and II.41); in another, addressed to citizens in newly conquered territories in Gaul, Theoderic urges them to "clothe yourselves in the morals of the toga, put aside barbarism…" (III.17). Other letters praise aspects of Roman life and culture: I.10 on arithmetic, I.20 on pantomimes, I.45 on philosophy and water clocks, II.40 on music, III.51 on chariot racing, III.52 on surveying, IV.51 on theater, V.42 (disapprovingly) on animal spectacles, VII.6 on aqueducts, and most eloquently, although written in the name of Theoderic's grandson Athalaric, VIII.28 on civic life.

31 See especially Momigliano, 1955; Deichmann, 1980; Everett, 2003, pp. 23–33; and Polara, 1995, who notes that most literary culture was based in Rome. Staab, 1976, identifies geographical works produced at the court of Theoderic as sources for the seventh- or eighth-century Ravenna cosmography.

32 See Courcelle, 1969, pp. 273–330; and Irgoin, 1995.

33 See Saitta, 1993, pp. 103–38; and La Rocca, 1993, p. 488.

34 Wolfram, 1988, p. 289; Saitta, 1993, pp. 104–10.

35 Cassiodorus, *Chronica*, a. 500.

36 For example, *Variae* I.25, 28, II.7, III.31, 44, IV.51, VII. 15; also *Chronica*, a. 500, which states that he surpassed ancient works. On Theoderic's building program, see esp. Saitta, 1993, pp. 103–38.

37 La Rocca, 1993, p. 466.

38 *Anon. Vales.* 2.70; Fredegar, *Chronica* 2.57: "Civitates universas quas regebat miri operis restaurare et munire sollertissime fecit. Palatia quoque splendedissime Ravennae urbis, Veronae et Papiae, quod Ticinum cognomentum est, fabricare iussit. Tantae prosperitatis post regnum tenuit, pacem cum gentibus vicinas habens, ut mirum fuisset." See La Rocca, 1993.

39 Brogiolo, "Ideas," 1999.

40 See La Rocca, 1993, pp. 480–4, who perhaps draws too sharp a distinction between Theoderic's ordering restorations at Rome and new buildings at Ravenna.

41 *Variae* III.30, trans. Barnish, p. 60.

42 *Variae* I.21, 25, III.29–31, IV.30, 51, V.9, VII.7, 15. For bibliography, see Johnson, 1988, p. 77 n. 44.

43 *Variae* III.21, trans. Barnish, p. 57.

44 Johnson, 1988, p. 77; *Variae* II.39 (Abano), III.44 (Arles), 49 (Catania), IV.24 (Spoleto), VIII.29–30 (Parma); *Anon. Vales.* 71 for Pavia and Verona.

45 Saitta, 1993, p. 105.

46 La Rocca, 1993, pp. 464–5 and 484–5, suggests that the omission of churches is because that kind of activity did not distinguish the king from his aristocratic subjects; secular patronage, however, by this time was viewed as the proper sphere of rulers.

47 Amory, 1997, pp. 43–78.

48 In *Variae* V.40.5, Theoderic commends Cyprian for knowing three languages; in VIII.21.6–7 and VIII.22.5, Athalaric praises Cyprian for raising his sons as soldiers and to speak Gothic ("Pueri stirpis Romanae nostra lingua loquuntur"); see Amory, 1997, pp. 154–5.

49 Amory, 1997, pp. 155–8.

50 Burns, 1984, p. 101. On the exact dates of the two executions, see Barnish, 1983.

51 This information is found in the Roman *Liber pontificalis, Vita Johannis I* 6, which says that John had been imprisoned by Theoderic, but the *Anonymus Valesianus* says only that Theoderic "declared him an enemy." See Noble, 1993.

52 Pietri, 1983, p. 664, referring to *Variae* XII.22, written in 537 from Cassiodorus himself.

53 Reydellet, 1992, p. 10.

54 Wolfram, 1988, p. 291, citing Ensslin, claims that Theoderic moved the court away from Ravenna only once, to Pavia in 508, in order to be closer to the war against the Franks; however, he is known to have been in Verona in 519, leaving Eutharic in charge in Ravenna (*Anon. Vales.* 81–2, "propter metum gentium"; see Moorhead, 1992, p. 70), and in Pavia when the initial charges were levied against Boethius (ibid., 87–88).

55 For example, Caesarius of Arles, as recounted in the mid–sixth-century *Vita Caesarii episcopi Arelatensis*, chs. 36–40.

56 Johnson, 1988.

57 For example, under Theoderic gold coins were minted only in Rome, whereas initially silver coins were minted in Ravenna, as well as in Milan; see Metlich, 2004, p. 38, and Arslan, 2005, p. 213.

58 *LPR* ch. 94. See below for more on the location of this image.

59 On city personifications, see Bühl, 1995. The image that is most similar to the one described by Agnellus is found on the *missorium* of Kerch (Hermitage Museum), in which an emperor, perhaps Constantius II, is depicted on horseback between a personification of *victoria* and a shield bearer; see Leader-Newby, 2004, pp. 36–8, who discusses iconographical similarities with mounted depictions of emperors on coins. Farioli Campanati, "Ravenna, Constantinopoli," 1992, p. 146, notes this similarity and suggests that Agnellus

misinterpreted such a depiction of Theoderic as indicating personifications of cities.

60 Bronze low-denomination coins were issued by the Roman Senate with, on the obverse, a helmeted female bust and the legend *Invicta Roma*, apparently a revival of a motif from republican Rome. After the death of Theoderic (Arslan, 2005, p. 213), or after the Byzantine capture of Rome in 536 (Grierson/Blackburn, 1986, pp. 32–3), the minting of Ostrogothic bronze coins moved to Ravenna, including a *decanummia* coin that contained a turretted female bust and the legend *Felix Ravenna* (however, Metlich, 2004, pp. 48–50, concludes that the *Felix Ravenna* coins were minted at Rome under Theoderic). For more on the origin of the *Invicta Roma* and *Felix Ravenna* legends, see Ercolani Cocchi, "Osservazioni," 1980, who proposes that the type defined Ravenna as a new Constantinople. After Ravenna was lost to the Ostrogoths in 540, there were some very rare pentanummia coins minted at Pavia with the bust and legend *Felix Ticinus*. Note also that bricks were made in Rome under Theoderic with the legend "Felix Roma"; see Righini, 1986.

61 *Anon. Vales.* II.80: "Ergo Theodericus dato consulatu Eutharico Romae et Ravennae triumphavit"; however, Cassiodorus, *Chronica*, ca. 519, mentions circus games only at Rome, with merely a ceremonial return to Ravenna afterward.

62 Cavallo, 1983; Pietri, 1983 pp. 661–2, and idem, 1991, p. 304.

63 Pietri, 1991, who notes, p. 294, that even up-and-coming members of new families, who made their careers in Ravenna, eventually turned to Rome. Ennodius, *Epistola* 5.18, written to the senator Faustus Niger, refers to the latter's departure from *inamabile Ravenna*, but he may mean that the city is now odious because Faustus has left. See also Pietri, 1983; and Barnish, 1988, pp. 131–3.

64 *Panegiricus* 11 mentions only Rome.

65 For example, compare the formulae in *Variae* VII: on the one hand, civic officials are named only for Ravenna and Rome, not for any other cities; but on the other hand, the appointments to Rome are praised in more extravagant terms than those for Ravenna; cf. VII.7 and 8 (the *praefectura vigilum*) and 13 and 14 (the *comitiva*), in which he charges the *comes* of Rome to protect the numerous beautiful public artworks of that city, but simply commends the *comes* of Ravenna to carry out royal orders. Certainly Ravenna is viewed as the *second* city in the kingdom; see, e.g., *Variae* X.28 and XII.22, in which the two cities are paired. Polara, 1995, p. 354, notes that although Ravenna houses scholars and schools, in *Variae* X.7, Cassiodorus gives highest praise to learning at Rome.

66 Cf. Barnish, 1988, pp. 127 and 151. La Rocca, 1993, pp. 481–4, implies that the rhetoric about construction at Rome was aimed at aristocratic Romans, while that at Ravenna was more aimed at the Constantinopolitan audience.

67 Wolfram, 1988, p. 298.

68 See, e.g., Budriesi, 1990, p. 109; Lazard, 1991, p. 122.

69 Deichmann, 1976, pp. 371–2, proposes that this was built by Odoacer.

70 Lazard, 1991, p. 116.

71 Cosentino, 2005, p. 411.

72 For example, *Variae* VII.31, which instructs the *principatus* of Rome to send key advisers to the court at Ravenna.

73 Pietri, 1991, pp. 300–1.

74 Lazard, 1991, p. 119.

75 See Maioli, "Il complesso archeologico," 1994; and Montevecchi, ed., 2004; the building to the north may have continued to be linked to the nearby church of St. Euphemia; see Baldini Lippolis, "La chiesa" and "Periodo byzantino," 2004.

76 *Getica* 29 (151); Jordanes is here quoting from someone he calls "Favius," whose identity is a mystery and rarely commented on; Kienast, 1966, states that he must have been a contemporary of Jordanes or Cassiodorus. An inscription that seems to confirm Jordanes's statement, attributing the land reclamation to Theoderic, was claimed by seventeenth-century and later scholars to have been reported in a manuscript: both inscription and manuscript are now lost, but the inscription is reported in *CIL* XI.2.1, Ravenna no. 10.

77 See Bermond Montanari/Maioli, 1983; Maioli, "Rapporti commerciali," 1995; Maioli, 2002; Augenti, "Nuove indagini," 2005; and idem, "Ravenna e Classe: archeologia," 2006.

78 Esp. Augenti, "Ravenna e Classe: archeologia," 2006, pp. 201–6. One striking amphora fragment found in the UPIM excavation contained an inscription in Hebrew, evidence, perhaps, of Jewish merchants in Ravenna, as may be attested on papyrus documents from 540 and 541; see Somekh, 1995.

79 Marazzi, 1998, pp. 136–41.

80 See Cosentino, 2005, pp. 415–19, for a detailed study of this issue.

81 *Variae* X.28 and XII.24, the latter concerning supplies from Istria; see Cosentino, 2005, p. 416. Thomas Hodgkin translates *mansio* as "royal residence at Ravenna," but since in many cases Cassiodorus uses the word *palatium* to refer to the government and/or the royal residence, *mansio* must instead have the meaning of "garrison" or "camp."

82 *Variae* XII.22 (trans. Barnish, 1992, p. 176 with some modification), as well as XII.24.

83 *Variae* II.20; Cosentino, 2005, pp. 416–17, notes the existence of *horrea* in various cities of Italy, and evidence of *horrearii*, or warehouse masters, in Ravennate documents and inscriptions.

84 *Variae* VI.6; see Cosentino, 2005, pp. 418–19, who assumes that Theoderic continued a tradition begun earlier.

85 *De bello Gothico* VI.28.25.

86 *Variae* V.16, also V.17–20. See Mauro, ed., 2005, for more on the fleet of Ravenna.

87 Farioli Campanati, "La scultura," 2005, esp. pp. 16–19.

88 Bayerische Staatsbibliothek, Munich, Clm. 6212, is an early ninth-century Gospel book that contains an inscription saying that a certain Patricius had emended the text at the request of Bishop Ecclesius; thus this Carolingian manuscript is assumed to be a copy of one produced in Ravenna in the early sixth century. The Orosius manuscript is Biblioteca Laurenziana, Florence, 65.1, on which see Tjäder, 1972; the document of 551 is quoted in full in the next chapter.

89 *Variae* III.19.

90 See Deichmann, 1989, pp. 204–8 (manuscripts) and 347–9 (ivory; further on ivory, see Volbach, 1977); also Cavallo, 1992. Deichmann cautions in both cases that there is no solid evidence linking most of the items attributed to

Ravenna. Volbach, 1977, pp. 10–12, notes that ivories attributed to Ravenna largely on the basis of iconographical or stylistic similarities with mosaics or stone sculpture share many characteristics with works made in Rome, Milan, and Constantinople.

91 *Variae* I.6 and VII.5, both cited by Ward-Perkins, 1984, p. 159.

92 *Chronica* a. 500; *Panegyricus* XI.56: "video insperatum decorem urbium cineribus evenisse et sub civilitatis plenitudine palatina ubique tecta rutilare." In seventh-century Francia, the historian pseudo-Fredegar, in his *Chronica* II.57 notes of Theoderic, "Palatia quoque splendedissime Ravennae urbis, Veronae et Papiae, quod Ticinum cognomentum est, fabricare iussit." See Ward-Perkins, 1984, p. 158 n. 7. As La Rocca, 1993, pp. 457–9, notes, such late notices show the efficacy of Theoderic's propaganda.

93 *Anon. Vales.* 2.71: "Palatium usque ad perfectum fecit, quem non dedicavit. Portica circa palatium perfecit."

94 Interestingly, the apses were polygonal on the exterior and semicircular on the interior, just like the apses of Ravenna's churches; Augenti, "Archeologia," 2005, p. 15.

95 Berti, 1976, pp. 77–81; see Johnson, 1988, p. 84.

96 Augenti, "Archeologia," 2005, esp. pp. 13–16; he dates what he calls Phase 4 to the Theoderican period.

97 Cassiodorus, *Orationum reliquiae* 2: "Renidet crusta marmorum concolor gemmis, sparsum aurum fulget in . . . s, rotatas saxorum venas musivi munera describunt; et totum metallicis coloribus comitur, ubi cerea pictura noscatur." Of course, this does not necessarily refer to the palace at Ravenna.

98 *LPR* ch. 94; Agnellus tells that the statue was made for the emperor Zeno, but Theoderic appropriated it for himself. There was certainly an equestrian statue of Justinian placed on the Augusteion during his reign, and he may have adapted it from an earlier statue of one of the Theodosius's. Furthermore, Jordanes, *Getica* 57 (290), tells us that Zeno set up an equestrian statue of Theoderic *ante regiam palatii* in Constantinople, this before Theoderic went to Italy. The statue in Ravenna seems to have stood in this place until the ninth century, when Charlemagne had it brought to his new palace at Aachen, as reported by Agnellus and in a poem by Wahlafrid Strabo (*De imagine tetricis* in *Versus in Aquisgrani Palatio*). For a complete discussion of the historiography of this statue and its eventual removal, see Deliyannis, trans., 2004, pp. 74–9, and idem, ed., 2006, pp. 75–7 and notes.

99 *LPR* ch. 94.

100 Deichmann, 1989, p. 51.

101 Duval, 1960, pp. 358–9; Deichmann, 1974, p. 140; Duval, "La mosaïque," 1978, pp. 95–6; and Porta, 1991.

102 Deliyannis, trans., 2004, pp. 72–6.

103 On the context of these buildings, see Ortalli, 1991, pp. 174–7; and Sfameni, 2004, pp. 356–9. On Meldola, see Prati, 1988, p. 27, and pp. 56–66; on Galeata, see most recently De Maria, ed., 2004. On Palazzolo, see Bermond Montanari, 1983.

104 *LPR* ch. 39. Agnellus tells us that he personally dismantled this palace and used the materials to build a house for himself in Ravenna! For an analysis of this passage from the *LPR*, see La Rocca, 1993, pp. 486–7.

105 *Anon. Vales.* 71; Cassiodorus, *Chronica*, a. 502: "In this consulship lord King Theoderic brought water to Ravenna, whose aqueduct he fittingly restored, which had been out of use for a long time before."

106 Prati, 1988, p. 27 and esp. pp. 46–50. Johnson, 1988, p. 78.

107 *Variae* V.38: "Tunc erit exhibitio decora thermarum, tunc piscinae uitreis fontibus fluctuabunt: tunc erit quae diluat aqua, non inquinet, post quam lauari continuo non sit necesse . . . si ad potandum unda suauis influxerit, omnia nostro uictui redduntur accepta, quando humanae uitae nullus cibus gratus efficitur, ubi aquarum dulcium perspicuitas non habetur."

108 See for Rome: Coates-Stephens, 1998, esp. pp. 171–3; for Constantinople: Mango, 1995, and Bono/Crow/Bayliss, 2001.

109 *Variae* III.9 and 10, and V.8.

110 I agree with Kennell, 1994, that it is marble workers rather than mosaicists who are here called *marmorarii*, since the letter goes on to talk about marble slabs split and rearranged so that their veins create pleasing patterns, "from art comes that which conquers nature: they weave the discolored slabs of marble in the most pleasing variety of depictions. . . ." This precise form of wall revetment is known from San Vitale in Ravenna, and from many sixth-century churches in Constantinople.

111 See Farioli Campanati, "La scultura," 2005, p. 15–16. Ideologically, late antique rulers liked to associate themselves with Hercules; see Kennell, 1994, although Nees, 1991, pp. 161–2, points out that this association ended with Diocletian, and Christian emperors did not associate themselves with the pagan hero.

112 Vitruvius, *De architectura* V.4.

113 This is the only use of the word *basilica* in the *Variae*; the word is used frequently in Cassiodorus's *Historia ecclesiastica tripartita*, usually with the meaning of "church," but sometimes referring to a secular building such as the Senate assembly building (10.17.8). Boethius never uses the word; Ennodius uses it only twice, referring to churches both times. More commonly in sixth-century usage generally are references to churches; but clearly a basilica named after Hercules could not be a church! On the other hand, *basilica* is never used to refer to a room in a palace; the word *aula* is universally used, and also by Cassiodorus, for this type of space.

114 *LPR* chs. 23, 76.

115 Johnson, 1988, p. 78.

116 Dyggve, 1957; Ward Perkins, 1984, p. 162; most recently Kennell, 1994, although her connection of the building to the circus whose existence, as we have seen, is based only on medieval topographical references, is dubious.

117 The first major study was Haupt, 1913; more recent comprehensive studies include Bovini, 1959; De Angelis d'Ossat, "Un enigma," 1960, pp. 93–111; Heidenreich/Johannes, 1971, and Krautheimer's review, 1973; and Deichmann, 1974, pp. 211–39. The later history of the monument is known only in fragments before the fifteenth century. Agnellus says (*LPR* ch. 39) that the mausoleum was built "where there is the *monasterium* of St. Mary which is called At the Tomb of King Theoderic." The implication of this statement is that at some point after the sixth century the building was converted into a chapel to the Virgin, presumably the lower chamber of the structure, around which a gallery with a wooden roof was erected sometime after its original construction (Heidenreich/Johannes, 1971, pp. 75–9; De Angelis d'Ossat, "Un enigma,"

1962, suggests a reconstruction of this chapel's furnishings). By the twelfth century, however, the lower level was probably already somewhat submerged in the surrounding ground, because in the middle of that century a nave was attached to the structure, with the upper chamber incorporated as the choir of the new church (Heidenreich/Johannes, 1971, pp. 70–106; Deichmann, 1974, pp. 212–14). In the sixteenth century, the earliest drawings made of the mausoleum show it half submerged in the ground and unused except as a cemetery, with a tower attached to the southwest side, probably a bell tower for the church. The mausoleum remained the subject of antiquarian interest and remarkably it appears in the backgrounds of various sixteenth- and seventeenth-century paintings (see Heidenreich/Johannes, 1971, pp. 90–4). In 1774 two staircases were built to access the upper floor; excavations were carried out in the early and mid–nineteenth century, and in 1879 the entire structure was released from the surrounding earth. The eighteenth-century staircases were demolished after World War I, and the current ramp and railings were set up in 1927.

118 *Anon. Vales.* II.96: "se autem vivo fecit sibi monumentum ex lapide quadrato mirae magnitudinis opus, et saxum ingentem quem superponeret inquisivit."

119 See Dinsmoor, 1908, p. 167 Jerome, *Adversus Iovinianum* I.44: "...et mirae magnitudinis exstruxit sepulcrum, in tantum ut usque hodie omnia sepulcra pretiosa ex nomine eius mausolaea nuncupentur." This description was widely known; cf. also Isidore of Seville, *Etymologiae* 15.11.3: "Nam eo defuncto uxor eius mirae magnitudinis et pulchritudinis extruxit sepulchrum in tantum ut usque hodie omnia monumenta pretiosa ex nomine eius Mausolea nuncupentur." On the fame of the eponymous mausoleum, cf. Vitruvius, *De Architectura* 2.8.10, and most notably for our purposes Cassiodorus, *Variae* VII.15: "Ferunt prisci saeculi narratores fabricarum septem tantum terris adtributa miracula: Ephesi Dianae templum: regis Mausoli pulcherrimum monumentum, a quo et mausolea dicta sunt...." He lists these in order to say that Rome surpasses them all.

120 Deichmann, 1974, p. 212.

121 *Historia Naturalis* 36.19. As Deichmann notes, 1974, p. 211–12, there is therefore no need to posit that the mausoleum or the tower built next to it sometime before the thirteenth century was used as a lighthouse.

122 Fiorin, 1993, discusses more precisely the exact origin of the stones which she says came from the Carso region around Trieste.

123 Deichmann, 1974, pp. 230–3, proposes more specifically that a wandering group of stonemasons from Isauria was employed.

124 See Bovini, 1959, pp. 13–17; the mausoleum was damaged by a bomb in World War II, at which time the interior of the walls was revealed.

125 Heidenreich/Johannes, 1971, pp. 8–14.

126 Heidenreich/Johannes, 1971, pp. 15–24 and 128–30. Krautheimer, 1973, notes that the decoration on the surviving piers is very similar to that found in sculpture from contemporary Constantinople, such as the church of St. Polyeuktos.

127 Johnson, 1988, pp. 93–5, citing earlier literature. On surviving imperial and royal mausolea in the west, see Mackie, 2003, pp. 144–211.

128 Johnson, 1988, p. 93.

129 Explored but not explained by De Angelis d'Ossat, "Un enigma," 1962, pp. 112–14. He gives the example of the supposed tomb of Ummidia Quadratilla at Casinum, (first c. BC–first c. AD), which contains a vaulted

cross-shaped space made out of ashlar masonry on the lower level, and had an upper story that is now lost.

130 Diocletian's mausoleum, built of ashlar masonry, has a crypt surmounted by a domed upper space, and the same was true for similar structures found at Sarkamen and Felix Romuliana (Gamzigrad), southeast of Sirmium and in a region well known to Theoderic; see Johnson, 2005; and Brandl/Vasic, 2007, pp. 46–9 and 85–6. In particular, Mausoleum 2 at Gamzigrad had a twelve-sided lower level with a cruciform vaulted chamber in the interior and an Ionic colonnade surrounding the upper level. The Serbian structures, moreover, were not built in or adjacent to the palace but some distance away, next to large tumuli. One wonders where and how Theoderic's father, Thiudimir, had been buried.

131 See Johnson, 1988, p. 94, esp. n. 198; *De institutione arithmetica* II.41 on 10 as a perfect number for the Pythagoreans; *Variae* I.10, a letter to Boethius, on 10 as symbolic of heaven.

132 De Angelis d'Ossat, "Un enigma," 1962, pp. 116 and 122, showed that the ratios of the width of the arms to their depth, the height of the vaulting to the width of the arms, and the height of the door to its width all equal the golden section, a numerical ratio that he thought was used also in other buildings from the era of Theoderic.

133 Bovini, 1959, p. 14–15, notes that Sangallo's drawing, from his *Libro romano degli schizzi*, contains many other inaccuracies, but accepts that an upper cornice makes decorative sense.

134 Bovini, 1959, pp. 45–6, presents the various opinions that the mausoleum was never completed, but he and De Angelis d'Ossat, "Un enigma," 1962, pp. 94–5, argue that this gallery was originally completed, and was later spoli-ated. Heidenreich/Johannes, 1971, pp. 107–27, on the other hand, argue that the decoration was never completed; this is supported by Deichmann, 1974, p. 222.

135 Heidenreich/Johannes, 1971, pp. 128–36, accepted by Deichmann, 1974, pp. 223–9; the wall articulation they propose is based largely on a late second-century AD mausoleum near Tripoli in North Africa. Krautheimer, 1973, rejects this reconstruction as a product of 1930s German architectural design.

136 Reconstructions of the loggia have been made by many scholars, most recently by De Angelis d'Ossat, "Un enigma," 1962. For a comprehensive analysis, with illustrations, of all the various proposals, see Heidenreich/Johannes, 1971, pp. 107–27. Differences between the various reconstructions of a loggia mostly center of issues such as whether the colonnettes had bases, how the corners were articulated, and whether statues originally stood under the arches.

137 Lewis, 1973, p. 220; Mackie, 2003, pp. 156–60.

138 Fifth- and sixth-century depictions of the Holy Sepulchre generally show the tomb as a single-storied, centrally planned building, although the Ascension plaque in Munich, Bayerisches Nationalmuseum, ca. 400, depicts a two-storied tomb of Christ featuring sculpted busts, an arcade, and a dome at the upper level. Another unusual object, known as the Buckle of St. Caesarius (Arles, Musée Departemental), dating to the early sixth century, also shows the tomb as a two-storied building, with doors on the lower level and whose upper level, capped by a dome, has a deeply carved colonnade, possibly set back from the lower level by a series of steps.

139 This niche may not have been part of the original plan, as the wall articulation on the exterior shows, although Heidenreich/Johannes, 1971, pp. 53–6, show that it is structurally bonded to the surrounding walls.

140 The larger windows on the diagonal are proposed by Heidenreich/Johannes, 1971, p. 87, to be later in date, although it is not clear whether smaller windows would have been there originally.

141 Deichmann, 1974, p. 217.

142 Bovini, 1959, pp. 26–30.

143 *LPR* ch. 39.

144 Bovini, 1959, p. 32, notes that St. Ambrose, *Epistolae* 34, recommends that Valentinian II be buried in a "porphyreticum labrum pulcherrimum et in usus huiusmodi aptissimum," just as the emperor Maximian had been. Bovini traces the history of the Ravenna bathtub back to 1564; the assertion of Heidenreich/ Johannes, 1971, p. 68, that it was identified at the mausoleum in 1346 is an error, as the fourteenth-century sources took their information from Agnellus; see Deliyannis, ed., 2006, pp. 73–7.

145 Bovini, 1959, p. 42; De Angelis d'Ossat, "Un enigma," 1962, pp. 112–14, Heidenreich/Johannes, 1971, pp. 166–7, accepted by most scholars, including Deichmann, 1974, pp. 221–2, who traces the various arguments. De Angelis d'Ossat interpreted slots in the walls of both chambers to support his contention that the lower chamber was originally fitted out as a chapel with an altar screen, while the upper had, according to his reconstruction, a complex series of twelve pilasters that upheld an architrave over the sarcophagus. The latter reconstruction is simply a fantasy (as Heidenreich/Johannes, 1971, p. 86, memorably say, it looks like "the grave-temple of a Wagnerian stage set"), but does not negate the idea that the upper chamber was the burial space.

146 Johnson, 1988, pp. 93–4. The problem of access to the upper level is not addressed; it should be noted that in the mausolea at Spalato, Sarkamen, and Gamzigrad, the lower levels are subterranean, with access to the upper level.

147 Six irregularly sized holes that surround this platform are of a later date; Heidenreich/Johannes, 1971, p. 81, propose that they were inserted in the twelfth century to support a bell tower on the dome.

148 Some scholars have questioned whether the inscriptions are original, since their epigraphy is completely different from anything known from sixth-century Ravenna (noted by Heidenreich/Johannes, 1971, p. 81, who nevertheless think that they were original, because it would have been too difficult to incise names once the monolith was in place). Deichmann, 1974, p. 219, claims that the abbreviation SCS was not used for apostles in the sixth century (but it was certainly used for various sorts of saints, as can be seen in the nave mosaics of Sant'Apollinare Nuovo); he also claims that the form *Iacopus* for *Iacobus* is a later name form. However, he does not offer any suggestion about when the inscriptions would have been made; as we will see, this list of apostles has connections to Constantinople, and it was surely only in the sixth century that such a connection would have been made (it does not make sense that the names of apostles would have been incised when the building became a chapel dedicated to the Virgin). As Johnson, 1988, p. 95, notes, the most convincing evidence that the names are original is the fact that there are twelve spurs.

149 Bovini, 1959, p. 54.

150 Baar, 1965, an engineer, provides a possible reconstruction of a technique; he argues that the monolith was rolled up a ramp to the top of the first level and then was raised by a system of levers as the upper story was built. Baar states that the spurs would have been strong enough to lift the monolith into place by such a mechanism and that the small openings beneath them show that they were intended to pass ropes through. Deichmann, 1974, p. 219, says they were nevertheless not used for this purpose.

151 Deichmann, 1974, pp. 219–20.

152 Bovini, 1959, pp. 55–8, cites the relevant theories, with illustrations.

153 Some scholars have proposed that the spurs were used as bases for statues of these saints, but this seems very far fetched; see Bovini, 1959, p. 55.

154 Johnson, 1988, p. 95; Schneider, 1941, pp. 404–5; the thirteenth-century author Nikolaos Mesarites lists these apostles for the Apostoleion in Constantinople; see Downey, ed., pp. 867–8. The fullest discussion of apostle lists is in Megaw/Hawkins, 1977, pp. 106–10. Deichmann, 1989, pp. 297–8, mentions the early sixth-century series of apostles in the church of Panagia Kanakaria at Lythrankomi on Cyprus, and that in St. Catherine's at Mt. Sinai, but then reasserts his belief that the inscriptions were made later.

155 De Angelis d'Ossat, 1962, "Un enigma," p. 109.

156 Deichmann, 1974, pp. 233–9. One example of such romanticism is the imitation of Theoderic's mausoleum, and even of the *Zangenfries* for the Bismarckturm in Jena, Germany, built in 1906–9.

157 Bovini, 1959, p. 59, cites J. Strzygowski and others, who proposed comparisons from Denmark, Armenia, and India! See also Deichmann, 1974, p. 218.

158 Deichmann, 1974, p. 219, reaches this conclusion.

159 Various examples are cited by Heidenreich/Johannes, 1971, pp. 152–60, from everywhere from Bulgaria to Norway; in a sense, they are so random that they are not convincing, and the authors conclude that the frieze represents motifs carved on wooden architecture, now lost. Deichmann, 1974, p. 221, states that the range of examples is not credible; Krautheimer, 1973, notes that Sassanian motifs were found in Constantinople at this period.

160 For example, the brooches from Kirchheim, Vedstrup, and Gummersmark; see Haseloff, 1981, vol. 2, pp. 302–18. It is also found on a buckle found at Sirmium, attributed to the Black Sea region (Brandl/Vasic, 2007, p. 31 Abb. 12). (A bracelet with a similar pattern, dated by Vickers, 1976, to the early sixth century is now dated to the second or third century; see MacGregor, 1997, p. 215). Salin, 1935, pp. 159–60, says that the motif on the mausoleum derives from the *kymation*, a classical architectural ornamental motif, but really the similarities with the metalwork borders are much more convincing.

161 See Halsall, 2002, pp. 106–8; and Cameron, 1985, pp. 199–200.

162 O'Donnell, 1979, ch. 3; in ch. 4, O'Donnell proposes that Cassiodorus was taken to Constantinople with other prisoners after the Byzantine capture of Ravenna in 540.

163 This arrangement is depicted on an ivory diptych first made in Constantinople and then adapted for Orestes, the western consul of 530, that depicts Amalasuintha and Athalaric at the top (now in the Victoria and Albert Museum); see Netzer, 1983; and McClanan, 2002, pp. 79–82.

164 *De bello gothico* 5.2.3: "τῆς δὲ φύσεως ἐς ἄγαν τὸ ἀρρενωπὸν ἐνδεικνυμένη." Cassiodorus praises her wisdom and education in *Variae* XI.1.6–8.

165 All of this from Procopius, *De bello gothico* 5.2–5.4.
166 At least, according to Procopius, *De bello gothico* 5.5.1.
167 On the date, see Deliyannis, trans., 2004, p. 179 n. 2.
168 *De bello gothico* 5.3.29.
169 *Variae* XI.1.9.
170 *LPR* ch. 62; Deichmann, 1976, p. 349.
171 *De bello gothico* 5.11.11, 18, and 26.
172 See, e.g., *De bello gothico* 6.10.8 and 6.22.9.
173 *De bello gothico* 6.23.1.

Five. Religion in Ostrogothic Ravenna

1 This Arian creed was rejected, for example, in the acts of the Third Council of Toledo of 589, at which the Visigoths converted from Arianism to Orthodoxy.
2 For a useful guide to the varieties of nonhomoousian belief, which are often (as here) grouped together as "Arian," see Heather/Matthews, 1991, pp. 137–9.
3 Meslin, 1967; and Amory, 1997, pp. 238–47.
4 See especially Snee, 1998.
5 See Sivan, 1996.
6 The copies of the Gothic Bible that survive, most completely the Codex Argenteus now in Uppsala, were produced in Ostrogothic Italy, perhaps in Ravenna; see Deichmann, 1989, pp. 204–6, and Tjäder, 1972, on the question of whether a "magister Villiaric antiquarius" at whose *statio* a manuscript of Orosius is said to have been produced (Firenze, Biblioteca Medicea Laurenziana, Plut. 65.1) may have been the same as the *Wiljarip bokareis*, a member of Ravenna's Arian clergy who signed the document cited below.
7 See Heather/Matthews, 1991, pp. 145–53, including a translation of the Letter of Auxentius.
8 See esp. Heather, 1986; and Russell, 1994, pp. 136–44.
9 Luiselli, 2005, pp. 735–9, notes that both Visigoths in Gaul and Vandals followed this radical Arianism, but other Goths who lived in Constantinople, according to Theodoret of Cyrene, seem to have believed in a more moderate version.
10 The best known possible example of a pagan Ostrogoth is Erelieva, the mother of Theoderic, as described in *Anon. Vales.* 58; see Moorhead, 1992, pp. 89–90, and Luiselli, 2005, pp. 749–50; but Amory, 1997, pp. 268–9 n. 138, interprets her Orthodox baptism as being from Arianism. Snee, 1998, pp. 177–9, describes interactions between Orthodox Christians and Goths in Constantinople in the fourth through sixth centuries.
11 Burns, 1984, p. 150; Rizzardi, "L'arte dei Goti," 1989, pp. 368–70, and idem, "Teoderico," 2001, p. 106.
12 Luiselli, 2005, pp. 750–2.
13 Burns, 1984, pp. 159–61; Wolfram, 1988, p. 85; Russell, 1994, esp. pp. 139–40.
14 Amory, 1997, pp. 195–276. Amory argues that the Arians who already existed in Italy adopted elements of Ulfilas's Gothic Bible and other literature, perhaps before the Ostrogoths arrived, and that while not all Goths were Arians, all Arians became associated with Gothic as a liturgical language and an identifying characteristic in this period (see esp. pp. 247–51 and 274–6).
15 See Mathisen, 1997, pp. 693–5.

16 Luiselli, 2005, pp. 752–3.

17 Amory's conclusion, as above.

18 Snee, 1998, pp. 183–4.

19 Amory, 1997, p. 197.

20 *Anon. Vales.* 48: "dum ipse esset bonae voluntatis et Arrianae sectae favorem praeberet...," and 60: "sic gubernavit duas gentes in uno, Romanorum et Gothorum, dum ipse quidem Arrianae sectae esset, tamen nihil contra religionem catholicam temptans...."

21 Cassiodorus, *Variae* II.27, trans. Barnish, p. 35. The letter specifies that the Jews may reroof their synagogue but not externally embellish it, according to imperial law. See also *Variae* IV.33 and 43 and V.37. See esp. Somekh, 1995.

22 Luiselli, 2005; see also Snee, 1998, pp. 180–1, who describes the Arianism of the generals Aspar and Ardabur in Constantinople in the 460s, at exactly the time Theoderic lived there, as being tolerant and semi-accepted by the Orthodox.

23 Amory, 1997, p. 261.

24 *Anon. Vales.* 80–82; Somekh, 1995, pp. 140–8, closely examines the meaning of this event in the context of Roman law and Christian attitudes toward Jews.

25 Boethius, *Opuscula sacra* 1 (often called *De trinitate*) and 2. On the date of these treatises, see Marenbon, 2003, p. 76. The anti-Arian letter "De ratione fidei," attributed to Archbishop Agnellus (*PL* 68, col. 381–6), is likewise concerned with the question of whether the Son was consubstantial with the Father and the role of the Holy Spirit in the Trinity. On its authenticity, see Huhn, 1954; and Montanari, 1971.

26 For example, Matthews, 1981, p. 24.

27 *Anon. Vales.* 94: "Igitur Symmachus scholasticus Iudaeus, iubente non rege, sed tyranno, dictavit praecepta die quarta feria, septimo kalend. Septembr., indictione quarta, Olybrio consule, ut die dominico adveniente Arriani basilicas catholicas invaderent."

28 Barnish, 1983, pp. 585–8.

29 Luiselli, 2005, pp. 755–7.

30 Budriesi, 1990.

31 Mathisen, 1997. Amory, 1997, p. 245, argues that in the fifth and sixth centuries, one of the features that defined Arians was their minority status, regardless of ethnic affiliation, and they thus saw themselves as like the pre-Constantinian church, without central leadership (citing Meslin, 1967, pp. 339–52).

32 See C. Cecchelli, 1960, pp. 757–3; but also M. Cecchelli/G. Bertelli, 1989, pp. 235ff.

33 *LPR* chs. 85–6; on the date, see Deliyannis, "Ravenna, St. Martin," 2009. Interestingly, to Archbishop Agnellus is attributed the only anti-Arian treatise composed in sixth-century Italy, "Ad Armenium epistola de ratione fidei"; see Brown, 2007, p. 423; *PL* 68, coll. 381–6.

34 *LPR* ch. 70.

35 *LPR* chs. 121 and 167. Deichmann, 1976, pp. 326–8; this church was demolished by the Venetians in 1457 and is documented simply as *ecclesia Gothorum* up to the fourteenth century, after which it was associated with St. Andrew. Agnellus himself uses it as a topographical reference to describe the location of a *monasterium* of St. Andrew. Eleven capitals, some of which include the monogram of Theoderic, survive in the Museo Nazionale or are incorporated into the Palazzo Veneziano in the Piazza del Popolo of Ravenna, which was built shortly after 1457. Another church, known from a tenth-century

document as S. Stefano "ad balneum Gothorum," stood just to the south of this church, providing another "Gothic" topographical reference in this area.

36 Cf. Amory, 1997, p. 246, who states without evidence that "some at least… pre-dated Theoderic."

37 Cartocci, 1993; von Simson, 1948, p. 70, mentions Archbishop Agnellus's military background, told by the historian Agnellus, *LPR* ch. 84.

38 Cf. Lucchesi, 1971, p. 74; and Deichmann, 1974, p. 244. Paul the Deacon, *HL* IV.42, reports that the Arian bishop of Pavia in the seventh century was seated at a basilica dedicated to a St. Eusebius.

39 Marini, no. 119, pp. 180–3; Tjäder, 1954, vol. 2, no. 34, pp. 91–104.

40 See also Cavarra et al., 1991, p. 403; Deichmann, 1976, p. 301.

41 Cf. Amory, 1997, pp. 252–74.

42 The date of the reconciliation of the Arian churches is often given as 561. Testi-Rasponi, ed., 1924, p. 216 n. 13, established this date on the basis of Agnellus's report (*LPR* ch. 86) that the church of St. Eusebius was rededicated on the Ides of November (Nov. 13), which was only a Sunday in the year 561 during Agnellus's reign, but in fact it also fell on a Sunday in 567. Agnellus does not mention a date, and the only piece of evidence we have is another papyrus document that lists properties being transferred from the Arian to the Orthodox church, written at the time of Emperor Justin II (565–78) and Archbishop Agnellus (d. 570), and hence between 565 and 570. Tjäder, 1954, I.2, pp. 178–83; idem, p. 407, notes that the document refers to imperial persons in the plural (*christianissimis ac tranquillissimis dominis nostris*), and since Justinian's wife, Theodora, had died in 548, before Agnellus became bishop, this must refer to Justin II and Sophia.

43 Brown, 2007, p. 422.

44 Amory, 1997, pp. 195–235 and 261.

45 Fanning, 1981; see Deliyannis, "Ravenna, St. Martin," 2009; we have seen in the previous chapter that the rededication of Theoderic's palace church to St. Martin of Tours displays the same militantly anti-Arian polemic in an anti-Lombard context.

46 The major publications include Deichmann, 1974, pp. 127–89; Novara, 1999; and Penni Iacco, 2004. After a Muslim attack that devastated the churches to the south of Classe, the relics of Saint Apollinaris were moved from his burial church to this location inside the city walls of Ravenna. Reported in the *Historia translationis beati Apollinaris*, RIS 1.2 (1723) pp. 533ff., written before 1137, which places the translation in the reign of Bishop John VII (ca. 850–78). This took place after the time of Agnellus the historian.

47 Fiaccadori, 1977, proposes that this inscription was set up when the church was restored after the early eighth-century earthquake, by the Lombard king Aistulf; however, although Agnellus says that Aistulf paid to repair the Petriana church that fell in the same earthquake (*LPR* ch. 155), he nowhere mentions any restoration in Sant'Apollinare Nuovo. Fiaccadori notes that it is surprising that such an inscription would have been allowed to survive the *damnatio memoriae* of Theoderic in this church, but Urbano, 2005, p. 97, argues that this was part of the program of "remembering to forget," and mentions that Ricimer's original dedication of Sant'Agata dei Goti in Rome also survived that church's rededication. On the appearance of the phrase "Theodericus rex" in other documents and inscriptions, see Deichmann, 1974, pp. 127–8.

48 Fiaccadori, 1977, pp. 164–5, points out that this inscription does not mean necessarily that the church was dedicated to Christ; however, most other contemporary dedicatory inscriptions mention the name of the saint to whom the church was dedicated. Deichmann, 1974, p. 128, sees the dedication to Christ as an imitation of the chapel built by Constantine in the imperial palace in Constantinople.

49 Wood, 2007, p. 252, questions whether the *fontes* mentioned by Agnellus were really a baptistery and suggests that they were fountains; however, every other time Agnellus uses this word he refers to baptisteries. As we have already seen, Ravenna in the sixth century had several baptisteries.

50 De Angelis d'Ossat, *Studi*, 1962, p. 60, notes that the term is mainly used for the Carolingian period and later.

51 Deichmann, 1974, p. 128, goes so far as to suggest that royal ceremonies such as crown wearing would have taken place here, but this is purely speculation.

52 On the history of the church and its renovations and archaeology, see comprehensively Deichmann, 1974, pp. 129–30; Novara, 1999; and Penni Iacco, 2004. In the ninth century, probably at the time that the relics of St. Apollinaris were translated into the church, an annular crypt was inserted beneath the apse, and in the tenth century a campanile was built on the right side of the facade. A Benedictine monastery was created at the church in 973, and by the fourteenth and fifteenth centuries included a large complex of buildings including a hospital. In 1513 the church was given to the Observant Friars Minor of St. Francis, and the sixteenth century saw major reconstruction works in all parts of the building: the atrium was eliminated and the porch rebuilt; two windows were opened in the upper wall of the west facade; seven small chapels were built along the external wall of the north aisle, five niches along the south wall; the apse was completely rebuilt, elongated, and flanked by two more chapels; the nave colonnade was raised by 1.20 meters; the marble furnishings in the nave were removed to one of the new chapels; and the present large cloister was built to the south of the church (using the columns of the former atrium). An elaborate wooden coffered ceiling was installed in 1611; at the end of the seventeenth century a new organ was attached to the south nave wall, destroying part of the mosaic of Christ and the angels on the west side (when this was moved to the west facade in the eighteenth century, the images were restored in paint).

53 Deichmann, 1974, p. 131, notes that the brickwork is very similar to that of the contemporary *capella arcivescovile* (see below); and also that wooden beams were inlaid in the upper nave walls, over the aisles.

54 Penni Iacco, 2004, pp. 30–1.

55 Russo, "L'architettura," 2005, p. 116.

56 For all this, see Penni Iacco, 2004, pp. 33–5. Fragments of the cornice were found in 1916; the cornice that appears now was made in the sixteenth century.

57 *LPR* ch. 87; Penni Iacco, 2004, pp. 36–7, and idem, 1993–4.

58 Penni Iacco, 2004, pp. 27–9; Deichmann, 1974, p. 130, says that no traces of an atrium or porticus have been found.

59 Penni Iacco, 2004, p. 29.

60 See the reconstruction in De Angelis d'Ossat, *Studi*, 1962, p. 26. The door at the western end of this wall is a later addition.

61 See Deichmann, 1974, pp. 131–6, and 1989, pp. 273–6; Harper, 1997; "Marble" in Bowersock/Brown/Grabar, eds, 1999; and Farioli Campanati, "Ravenna e i suoi rapporti," 2005.

62 See the complete catalog in Deichmann, 1974, pp. 131–6, and discussion in idem, 1989, pp. 273–6.

63 De Angelis d'Ossat, *Studi*, 1962, p. 26; Russo, "L'architettura," 2005, p. 116.

64 See esp. Deichmann, 1974, pp. 137–9, and Vernia, "L'arredo," 2005.

65 Vernia, "L'arredo," 2005, pp. 367–8, prefers this date accepted by Deichmann, 1974, p. 136, and Farioli Campanati, "Ravenna, Constantinopoli," 1992, pp. 167, 173, but notes that V. Martinelli prefers a date toward the middle of the sixth century, in which case the ambo would have been installed at the time of the rededication. The ambo was not originally supported by the columns that sustain it today, but probably with simple pilasters; in addition, a ramp would have led up to it on at least one side and probably both.

66 Deichmann, 1974, p. 139.

67 Vernia, "L'arredo," 2005, provides references to the various arguments.

68 See esp. Nordström, 1953, pp. 58–79; Bovini, *Mosaici*, 1958; and Deichmann, 1974, pp. 154–89, who provides a comprehensive analysis of each scene of the cycle.

69 Zanotto, 2000, p. 661.

70 Zanotto, 2000, reviews evidence for both interpretations and argues that this scene represents the Canaanite woman because Ambrose, in *De fide* 2.11, notes that the Arians make particular reference to this episode in their theology. Many scholars, including von Simson, 1948, p. 76; Nordström, 1953, p. 60; Bovini, *Mosaici*, 1958, pp. 30–1; and Deichmann, 1974, pp. 165–6, on the contrary accept it as the hemorrhaging woman (Mark 5:25–34); the debate usually concerns the identity of the three figures behind the woman and their relation to the Gospel passages. Sorriës, 1983, identifies the woman as the adultress of John 8:3–11.

71 Two-thirds of this scene is restored; Ciampini, 1690–99, published a drawing of it before the restoration that shows Christ performing the miracle with a wand and jars for water/wine rather than baskets for bread, as in the restoration; for a complete discussion see Bovini, *Mosaici*, 1958, pp. 17 and 21–4. Interpretation of the scene as originally showing the entry into Jerusalem is untenable; see Bovini, idem, pp. 23–4.

72 Elsner, 1995, pp. 236–7.

73 See von Simson, 1948, p. 76.

74 Both von Simson, 1948, p. 78, and Sörries, 1983, pp. 92–5, point out similarities and contrasts in the pairs of the cycle, but some are more convincing than others.

75 Deichmann, 1974, pp. 156–7. Peers, 2004, p. 16, attributes this to the monophysite tendency to downplay the human nature of Christ as seen in his suffering on the cross, but von Simson, 1948, p. 73, points out even the Passion scenes depicted here would have been jarring to monophysite sensibilities that may have surfaced in Justinianic Ravenna.

76 The Werden Casket, in the Victoria and Albert Museum, to which these scenes are often compared, is now dated to the ninth century; see Beckwith, "Werden Casket," 1958. The date of the Andrews Diptych in the same collection, which also has a Christological cycle, is controversial; Beckwith, *Andrews Diptych*,

1958 gives it a fifth-century date, but Volbach, 1976, no. 233, attributes it to the ninth century.

77 Summarized comprehensively by Deichmann, 1974, pp. 162–80.

78 See Deichmann, 1974, pp. 181–3, for an essay on this topic.

79 Deichmann, 1974, pp. 140 and 189; Nordhagen, 1983, pp. 75–9.

80 Nordhagen, 1983, esp. pp. 75–9.

81 Jensen, 2004, p. 159. Deichmann's analysis of the composition of all of the images (1974, pp. 182–8) led him to the conclusion that there were not major compositional differences between the two sides.

82 Mathews, 1993, p. 126, interprets the two general face types of Christ as indicating that Christ had triumphed over both young and old pagan gods; but that does not help to explain the appearance of both types here.

83 In the eighth- and ninth-century Iconoclasm controversy, Iconophiles equated Iconoclasts with Arians, who were equated with monophysites and theopaschites; see Gwynn, 2007, esp. p. 238. For a detailed discussion of fourth- and fifth-century Arian ideas of Christ's natures, see Hanson, 1988, pp. 108–22; Arians seem to have believed that Christ had two natures, but that the human nature was incomplete.

84 von Simson, 1948, pp. 73–5; refuted by Sorriës, 1983, pp. 57–60; and Jensen, 2002, p. 47, both of whom argue that a Nestorian position was not the same as an Arian position.

85 Jensen, 2002, p. 47, and idem, 2004, pp. 159–64.

86 Grabar, 1980, pp. 119–21; Urbano, 2005, pp. 99–107; and Jensen, 2004, pp. 159–64.

87 Sörries, 1983, pp. 77–97; Zanotto, "La chiesa," 2005, p. 356.

88 Sörries, 1983, pp. 77–97, followed by Rizzardi, "L'arte dei Goti," 1989, pp. 377–82.

89 For example, Bagatti, 1980, who suggests that the fish on the table at the Last Supper reflects an Arian practice of feasting on fish on Good Friday; however, fish are quite commonly found on the table of the Last Supper, e.g., on the Milan Ivory Bookcover and the St. Augustine Gospels, and become common in Byzantine and western art; see Deichmann, 1974, pp. 173–4.

90 Grabar, 1980, p. 121; also for the specific case of Sant'Apollinare Nuovo, Urbano, 2005, pp. 99–107.

91 Sörries, 1983, pp. 83–4, who cites Athanasius, *Contra Arianos* 3.

92 Baumstark, 1911; Nordström, 1953, pp. 63–78.

93 von Simson, 1948, pp. 79–81; Grabar, 1980, p. 121; Zanotto, 2000, p. 667. The relationship between late antique sermons and the art that decorated churches would repay further study.

94 See, e.g., Peers, 2004, pp. 16–17, who nevertheless provides several examples of sixth-century crucifixion depictions, most notably in a description (*ekphrasis*) by Choricius of Gaza, composed between 536 and 548, of the church of Saint Sergius at Gaza that describes images of the life cycle of Jesus, perhaps including a crucifixion (Choricius, *Laudatio Marciani* I.48–76, translated in Mango, *The Art of the Byzantine Empire*, 1986, pp. 60–8.)

95 I do not, however, agree with the conclusion of Wood, 1999, p. 36, that their primary function is therefore to mark out sacred space, as even if that were the case, someone nevertheless made a choice of scenes to include.

96 Deichmann, 1974, pp. 152–3, lists combinations proposed by various scholars (e.g., von Simson, 1948, p. 81: 4 patriarchs, 16 prophets, 12 apostles, and 2 nonapostolic evangelists), although such proposals seem simply to be manipulations of the numbers to fit the evidence. Lucchesi, 1971, p. 62 n. 2, identifies them as the authors of the books of the Old Testament. Sörries, 1983, p. 77, says that they symbolize the Arian insistence on the word of scripture, but this would not explain why similar figures are found in Orthodox churches. The scrolls, both open and closed, have black marks that suggest writing, but do not form actual letters in any language. They may be intended to be Hebrew or Greek, or, given how high the mosaics are, and the lack of specific identities for the individuals, they may simply be intended to represent "writing."

97 Roberts, 2002, p. 177; specifically Roberts refers to Venantius Fortunatus's poem *De Vita Martini*. On the connections between the poem and this church in Ravenna, see Deliyannis, "Ravenna, St. Martin," 2009.

98 Breckenridge, 1980, discusses the type of the throne. A similar throne was found in the apse mosaic of Sant'Agata Maggiore in Ravenna, whose date is not determined (Deichmann, 1974, p. 147).

99 Bovini, "Principali restauri," 1966, pp. 99–104, provides an exact image of what survived from the original mosaic and how it could be part of a book. The words in the book might have been original or might have been changed upon the church's rededication. Deichmann, 1974, p. 147, discusses the phrase "Rex gloriae," which comes from Ps. 24(23):7–10, is not used in the New Testament, but appears in the Gothic Missal, and thus may be a particularly Arian formulation. On the other hand, Ambrose, *De Fide* 2.13, uses the phrase "rex gloriae" with reference to Christ to indicate his equivalence with the Father, in an anti-Arian context. An alternative explanation is that it originally said, "Ego sum lux mundi" on the model of the figure of Christ in Hagia Sophia in Constantinople; for references, see Deichmann, 1974, pp. 146–7.

100 This thesis was laid out by Grabar, 1936, esp. pp. 189–234. Mathews, 1993, has argued that enthroned bearded figures are much more similar to images of Jupiter; he does not, however, discuss this image, but confines himself to other, less imperial-looking ones. It has also been noted that the Magi on the opposite wall were paying homage to Christ as *rex*; thus both sides emphasize the regal nature of Christ (see esp. Steigerwald, 1966). Clearly this theme would repay further study. If the book held here by Christ did contain the phrase reported in the sixteenth century, this would be strong evidence for the regal associations of the figure. Breckenridge, 1980, pp. 250–1, discusses the coin evidence for this type of throne.

101 Terry/Maguire, 2007, vol. 1, pp. 138–9, point to the sixth-century diptych in the Staatliche Museen, Berlin, and the bookcover of the Gospel Book of St. Lupicin, Bibliothèque Nationale, Paris, ms. lat. 9384.

102 Terry/Maguire, 2007, vol. 1, pp. 138–9, point to the sixth-century diptych in the Staatliche Museen, Berlin, and the bookcover of the Gospel Book of St. Lupicin, Bibliothèque Nationale, Paris, ms. lat. 9384.

103 Deichmann, 1974, p. 146, discusses at length the gestures, costumes, and offices.

104 These are often identified as the images described by Cassiodorus in his panegyric on Witigis and Matasuintha, *Orationum reliquae* 2; see Johnson, 1988, pp. 88–9.

105 Of the inscription over the gate of Classe, only "]SIS" is original, but Agnellus confirms that this city represented Classe. Deichmann, 1989, p. 42, correctly notes that the word *civitas* here is simply a hypothesis by Kibel.

106 For an analysis of the ships in this mosaic, see Bonino, 1991.

107 Cf. Swoboda, 1961, p. 82; Deichmann, 1974, p. 141.

108 For the criticisms of Dyggve's and Duval's theses, see Deichmann, 1974, pp. 141–3, and Porta, 1991, pp. 275–6, both of whom cite the comprehensive study by de Francovich, 1970. The latter, pp. 59–60, compares the *palatium* mosaic to the facade of the Great Mosque of Damascus, built in the early eighth century, and notes that it may also have been intended to resemble the Chalke gate of the palace in Constantinople (although whether the Chalke was on the west or the south side of the colonnaded Augusteion does not affect his argument).

109 Dyggve, 1941; proposed also by others; see de Francovich, 1970, pp. 7–9.

110 This concept was accepted by many scholars; see de Francovich, 1970, p. 8, and, e.g., Krautheimer, 1986, pp. 40, 77, 81, and 466 n. 24.

111 Duval, 1960; and in several subsequent articles, most recently "La mosaïque," 1978, in which he responds to de Francovich's criticisms.

112 Utrecht Psalter, 75v (Ps. 133), is very similar to the *palatium* mosaic. De Francovich, 1970, pp. 31–3 and 54–5, however, notes that the buildings in the Utrecht Psalter are used to frame figures rather than to be architecturally accurate, and that this tradition of imaginary architecture goes back to Roman art. Deichmann, 1974, pp. 141–5, and Johnson, 1988, pp. 89–91, present Dyggve's and Duval's arguments in detail and refute them.

113 See esp. de Francovich, 1970, with exhaustive bibliography.

114 Duval does not mention them in his articles, for example.

115 Even closer, perhaps, since it shows the roof of a building, is the Sarcophagus of Concordius in Arles (late fourth c.); here the left end has a pediment that might indicate the entrance, but Christ is seated in the middle of the colonnade, which does not look as though he is intended to be seen as in the apse of a basilica.

116 Johnson, 1988, p. 91.

117 Frugoni, 1991, p. 41.

118 De Francovich, 1970, p. 57, Deichmann, 1974, p. 141, and Johnson, 1988, p. 88, argue for an accurate depiction of the existing palace; Duval, esp. "La mosaïque," 1978, p. 118, prefers to see it as a generic "palace" depiction. Duval, idem, p. 96, argues that the label shows that the structure's function was not obvious, but surely one could also argue that the label indicates something about Theoderic's concept of power.

119 Duval, "La mosaïque," 1978, p. 102, dismisses these references to porticoes as too vague; this does not seem a good reason to summarily dismiss them.

120 Berti, 1976, p. 13 n. 4, cites Bovini, "La raffigurazione," 1968.

121 Johnson, 1988, p. 91, argues in favor of the main Chalke gate of the palace, and cites Cassiodorus's and Procopius's statements that the entrance to the palace symbolized its whole. Piccinini, 1992, pp. 42–3, argues that the intent of the image is to represent Theoderic's royal authority and not necessarily to depict a real building.

122 See Longhi, 2000, on which the following is based.

123 For example, Deichmann, 1974, p. 145.

124 Longhi, 2000, p. 650.

125 Frugoni, 1991, p. 46; supported by Johnson, 1988, p. 92.

126 Longhi, 2000, pp. 650–2. Longhi explains the other two figures as Sts. Gervase and Protase, who were also venerated at the church of St. Lawrence – he does not explain what would have happened to St. Stephen.

127 Frugoni, 1991, pp. 37–8.

128 Frugoni, 1991, pp. 41–2, based on comparison of this image with the apse mosaic of Santa Pudenziana in Rome.

129 Testi-Rasponi, ed., 1924, p. 220 n. 2; accepted by Bovini, *Mosaici*, 1958, p. 8. This proposal is then used to date Sant'Apollinare Nuovo to a later decade than the Arian episcopal complex.

130 Breschi, 1965, p. 10; then repeated by Rizzardi, "Teoderico," 2001, p. 108; Zanotto, "La chiesa," 2005, p. 352, among others.

131 Johnson, 1988, p. 88.

132 This depiction is often used as evidence that in the early sixth century, Classe was considered to be its own city (*civitas*); however, as we have seen, the "CIVITAS" of the mosaic today is a nineteenth-century restoration. While Classe in this period was walled and was developed by Theoderic, there is no evidence that it was considered a separate administrative unit from Ravenna, and much evidence that the port was a part of Ravenna. See, e.g., Piccinini, 1992, p. 45; Deichmann, 1989, pp. 42–3.

133 Frugoni, 1983, pp. 42–50.

134 Elsner, 1995, pp. 223–4. This sort of gradual mediation between the real and heavenly realms is something that we have already seen in the Orthodox Baptistery.

135 Deichmann, 1974, p. 142, says that the empty gold space of the central archway goes back to Theoderic's time; however, Frugoni, 1991, claims that something small was replaced there, not a full-scale figure but perhaps an empty throne. MacCormack, 1981, pp. 237–8, bases her interpretation on the mistaken assumption that an image of Theoderic was found in the central arch under the pediment.

136 Deichmann, 1974, p. 145, following Ricci, suggests that it was a seated female personfication or *tyche* of Ravenna, although there is no real reason to assume this.

137 Farioli Campanati, "Ravenna, Constantinopoli," 1992, pp. 145–6.

138 Urbano, 2005.

139 Note, however, that the phrase *malleus haereticorum*, almost universally used by scholars in the context of the choice of St. Martin, is a much later term that would never have been used in the sixth century.

140 See Deliyannis, "Ravenna, St. Martin," 2008.

141 *LPR* ch. 86.

142 *LPR* ch. 88.

143 Bovini, "Una prova," 1952; idem, "Antichi rifacimenti," 1966.

144 Bovini, "Principali restauri," 1966.

145 Penni Iacco, 2004, pp. 104, 110, and 119–20.

146 The most extensive study of these processions is von Simson, 1948, pp. 81–110.

147 von Simson, 1948, p. 87, and Lucchesi, 1971, p. 64, state that no martyr named Vincentia is known; yet the name turns up in various *martyrologia*, mostly dated to the eighth century or later. See, for example, Bede, *Martyrologium*, "VI kal. febr. . . . Et sanctorum Doti, Juliani, Vincentii et aliorum XXVII" but

"XIX KAL. SEPT. . . . In Aquileia natale SS. Felicis, Fortunatae, Vincentiae."
(PL 94, col. 826A) Hrabanus Maurus *Martyrologium*: "VI KAL. FEB. In Affrica
natale Dati, Iuliani, Vincentiae et aliorum XXXII"; in the *Martyrologium* in
the sacramentary of Gellone we find: "XVIIII kl. Sep. Fortunati, Vincentiae,
Tituli, Pauli, Parmi, Eracli, Demetri, Felicis" (CCSL 159A, ed, A. Dumas,
1981, dates 790–800). Given Vincentia's association here with other African
martyrs, it seems likely that this was her identity here. Furthermore, Lucchesi
notes that by the time of Agnellus, the wife of the saintly Bishop Severus is
called Vincentia, and perhaps Agnellus was influenced by this mysterious saint.

148 Interestingly, although Agnellus calls the female saints "virgins," they were not
all virgins, e.g., Perpetua and Felicitas, who were, however, martyrs like the
others.

149 See Brenk, 1999, pp. 164–7, who notes that the differences of pose, physiognomy, and ornament must nevertheless have been carefully planned.

150 He also holds a diadem rather than a wreath; however, so does Clemens.
Longhi, 2000, pp. 655–6, notes other examples in which Lawrence is shown in
a gold tunic or mantle, for example, at S. Senatore at Albano and S. Lorenzo
fuori le mura in Rome, and proposes that a similar depiction at Porec is also
Lawrence. Lucchesi, 1971, p. 66, says that Lawrence has a gold gown because
he was particularly venerated in Rome – this does not make much sense.

151 Lucchesi, 1971, p. 65.

152 In a liturgical entrance procession, the fourth place might be occupied by the
priest, after the thurifer, candle bearers, and Gospel bearer; in the Justinian
panel in San Vitale, the fourth place is occupied by Justinian himself, following
behind the priest. More study of this question is required. Agnes's lamb barely
figures in any analyses of this mosaic.

153 Terry/Maguire, 2007, vol. 1 p. 133, note that the Council of Chalcedon was
also a focal point in the Three Chapters Controversy, for which see the following chapter.

154 von Simson, 1948, pp. 84–5, with discussion after. The tables in von Simson
are somewhat misleading, as he combined saints from different sections of the
litany to create one list; moreover, the Canons of the Mass that he cites come
only from the seventh century and later.

155 Lucchesi, 1971, pp. 67–8 and 72–3. In this regard, as usual, much less attention
has been paid to the north side of Sant'Apollinare Nuovo; a study of female
martyrs in late antiquity would be very useful here. It is interesting to note that
the female saints depicted on the intrados of the triumphal arch at the Basilica
Eufrasiana at Porec include nine found here, but three (Tecla, Susanna, and
Basilissa) different ones.

156 Lucchesi, 1971, pp 66–7.

157 Such figures, for example, also appear in the mosaic of Theodora's procession
in San Vitale. The tenth-century *Book of Ceremonies* I.9 describes a ceremony
during the Pentecost liturgy in which the women of the court are presented
to the enthroned empress who is flanked by chamberlains and eunuchs; the
women are led in by male court officials, and the whole ceremony sounds very
like what we see on the north wall of Sant'Apollinare Nuovo; see Taft, 1998,
pp. 41–2.

158 Nordström, 1953, pp. 83–7; expanded by Steigerwald, 1966, pp. 275–7.

159 Grabar, 1980, p. 113.

160 *LPR* ch. 88. The current mosaic, above the legs, was restored by Felice Kibel in the 1850s based partly on this passage in the *LPR* and partly on the very similar image of the Magi found on the dress of the Empress Theodora in San Vitale, made at about the same time (although the latter are rendered monochromatically in gold). It is assumed that the colors Agnellus mentions were those that he saw in the mosaic; however, if Agnellus's entire passage is borrowed from a non-Ravennate source, the colors might also have been lifted wholesale from his source.

161 See Deliyannis, trans., 2004, pp. 36–45 and 201–2, notes. Pope Leo I wrote several sermons on the Trinity, as did Peter Chrysologus, noted by von Simson, 1948, p. 89.

162 Deichmann, 1974, p. 156.

163 Sörries, 1983, pp. 95–6, who argues, on very little evidence, that the Germanic Goths preferred their gods full grown.

164 *LPR* chs. 23, 36, 67, etc.; see Deliyannis, 2004, pp. 334–5.

165 von Simson, 1948, pp. 90–103.

166 Elsner, 1995, pp. 224–5.

167 Nordström, 1953, pp. 83–7; von Simson, 1948, pp. 99–101; Steigerwald, 1966, draws specific parallels between these images and those on the base of the Column of Arcadius in Constantinople. However, Deichmann, 1974, p. 149, reminds us that depictions of Rev. 4 often show the four-and-twenty elders holding the crowns, preparing to cast them down before Christ.

168 Piccinini, 1992, p. 44.

169 Steigerwald, 1966, pp. 275 and 280, who, however, goes too far in interpreting the male martyrs as senators, the female martyrs as personifications of provinces, and the Magi as barbarians. See especially the descriptions of Venantius's poems "De virginitate," *Carmina* 8.3, and "Ad virgines," *Carmina* 8.4, which list virgins and other saints by name, although not the same names as found in Sant'Apollinare Nuovo. See also his *Vita Sancti Martini*, 2.446–64; interpreted in Deliyannis, "Ravenna, St. Martin," 2009, and Roberts, 2002, p. 177.

170 Wharton, 1987; this theory seems borne out by the depiction of the apostles in the Arian Baptistery. Janes, 1998, p. 127, notes that Paulinus of Nola, *Carmina* 18.138–53, ed. G. de Hartel (CSEL 30, 1894), writes of Christ distributing robes and crowns to saints.

171 For example, Urbano, 2005; von Simson, 1948, p. 81; Johnson, 1988, p. 91; Deichmann, 1974, pp. 144–5; Steigerwald, 1966, pp. 283–4.

172 See Wood, 2007, pp. 255–9, who, however, does not come to any conclusion.

173 See Wood, 2007, pp. 257–8.

174 Some early Constantinopolitan churches (most notably St. John Studios) had galleries over the aisles, which would have eliminated the flat surface above the arcade as a location for continuous decoration (see Mathews, 1971, p. 38). Comparisons with secular monuments such as the obelisk bases of Theodosius I and Arcadius in Constantinople (e.g., Farioli Campanati, "Ravenna, Constantinopoli," 1992, p. 147) do not seem convincing, as their context was completely different.

175 See von Simson, 1948, p. 82.

176 On analogy with the images in San Vitale, another question would be the location of Theoderic. Given the depiction of the procession of martyrs, in

which the most important saints are found at the head of the procession, and the depictions in San Vitale, where the emperor is shown in the fourth place, it is most likely that if Theoderic and his court had been depicted on the walls, he himself would have been in the first or perhaps the fourth place, toward the east end of the church, and thus nowhere near the palace; the figures originally between the colonnades whose hands were raised in acclamation must have held this pose with respect to Christ at the far end, or perhaps in honor of the royal connotations of the *palatium*, rather than directly acclaiming Theoderic.

177 Choricius, *Laudatio Marciani* I.48–76, translated in Mango, *The Art of the Byzantine Empire*, 1986, pp. 60–8; Gregory of Tours, *Histories* II.17; Paulinus of Nola, *Carmina* 27, 512–95; St. Nilus of Sinai, *Letter to Prefect Olympiodorus*, PG 79: 577–80 (translated in Mango, idem, pp. 32–3; Nilus is responding to a question about whether the walls might be covered with depictions of animals). According to seventeenth-century drawings, the nave walls of St. Peter's and St. Paul's outside the walls at Rome also were decorated with narrative scenes. A comprehensive study of the decoration of nave walls would be most illuminating.

178 Procopius, *De Aedificiis* I.10, describes depictions of Justinian and Theodora standing among the Senate in the Chalke vestibule, but not in a church.

179 See Heather/Matthews, 1991, pp. 103–31; among the specifically Arian/Gothic saints the texts list Ulfilas, Saba, Sansalus, Gouthikas, Eutyches, Bathouses, Werkas, Arpulas, Abippas, Hagias, Ruias, Egethrax, Eskoes, Silas, Sigetzas, Swerilas, Swemblas, Therthas, Phigas, Frideric, Constantius II, Dorotheus, Innas, Remas, and Pinas (men); and Anna, Alas, Baren, Moiko, Kamika, Oneko, Anemais, and the old women at Beroea (women).

180 Urbano, 2005, pp. 96–8. It should also be noted that, according to Agnellus, images of Theoderic associated with the entrance to the palace were left in situ until the ninth century, showing perhaps that there was not a *damnatio memoriae* at all.

181 See most recently Baldini Lippolis, 2000.

182 *LPR* ch. 86.

183 For a summary of the scholarly discussion, see Deichmann, 1974, pp. 151–2; and Baldini Lippolis, 2000, pp. 467–9.

184 Baldini Lippolis, 2000, p. 473–4, who hypothesizes further that the third figure mentioned in the sixteenth-century sources may have been a captured barbarian, as are known for several late antique representations of emperors.

185 Breschi, 1965, p. 12, tells that in the fifteenth century the legend that bishops of Ravenna were selected by the dove of the Holy Spirit (written down by Agnellus for St. Severus, *LPR* ch. 17), led to the idea that this event happened at the site of the Arian Baptistery, and the church was subsequently dedicated to the Holy Spirit. Since these events had taken place in the third and fourth centuries, early historians like Rossi and Fabbri thought that these structures were older than the sixth century.

186 Mazzotti, 1957, p. 30. Breschi, 1965, p. 15, suggests that Theodore of Amasea was a notable anti-Arian saint, but perhaps she is confusing him with Basil or Asterius of Amasea.

187 See Snee, 1998 (referring to the sixth-century Life of St. Marcian, who oversaw the rebuilding), who says that the reason that the Arian generals made donations to a conspicuously anti-Arian church was that they had acquired the relics of

St. Anastasia from the Balkans, and that in the 460s they were trying to acquire public favor and to downplay their Arianism.

188 *Historia ecclesiastica tripartita*, 9.9.3; Cassiodorus specifically says, "Quam ob rem nimis inopinabilem Anastasiae nomen, id est resurrectionis, accepit." Thus for Cassiodorus, the word form *Anastasia* means *Anastasis*.

189 Deichmann, 1976, pp. 301–3, rejects this hypothesis, saying that Anastasis and Anastasia were not likely to be confused in the sixth century, and that cathedrals were never dedicated to saints. The latter statement, however, may not be true. It is also significant that on the papyrus the church is always called Anastasie, not Anastasiae, although other genitives are given in *-ae*. Since no other church dedicated to St. Anastasia is known in Ravenna, we must assume that this Gothic church became one of the ones listed by Agnellus.

190 See Breschi, 1965, pp. 15–26, for the later history of the complex and of its restorations.

191 Deichmann, 1974, p. 246, gives a different set of measurements: 18.50 meters wide including the wall thicknesses, 22.42 meters long not including the apse.

192 De Angelis D'Ossat, *Studi*, 1962, p. 25.

193 See Russo, "L'architettura," 2005, p. 117, citing Deichmann, 1974, p. 246: in Constantinople, the churches of St. John Stoudios and the Chalcoprateia; in Rome, also San Lorenzo fuori le mura; and in Ravenna, San Michele *in Africisco* and Sant'Agata Maggiore.

194 Breschi, 1965, pp. 37 and 28–9.

195 Mazzotti, 1957, pp. 44–5; Deichmann, 1974, p. 246; the new bricks were used for the apse and triumphal arch.

196 Russo, "L'architettura," 2005, p. 120, believes that this means that it was not built by Ravennate workmen.

197 Breschi, 1965, p. 31.

198 Cataloged in Deichmann, 1974, pp. 247–8.

199 Deichmann, 1974, pp. 249–50.

200 Deichmann, 1974, pp. 245–6, although he notes that Mazzotti, 1957, pp. 34–5, says that the excavations of 1954 did not reveal any mosaic tesserae.

201 *LPR* ch. 86.

202 *LPR* ch. 70.

203 Jones/Martindale/Morris, PLRE 3, 1971, p. 425–7; Paul the Deacon quotes his epitaph in full, *HL* III.19.

204 Cummins, 1994, pp. 97–9.

205 The most recent and comprehensive study of this building is Cummins, 1994; see also Rizzardi, "Teoderico," 2001; Deichmann, 1974, pp. 251–8; Breschi, 1965; and Mazzotti, 1957.

206 The theory that this baptistery was built on the site of a Roman bath, proposed by C. Ricci, is no longer believed credible; see Breschi, 1965, pp. 39–40. Santo Spirito's original floor level was .50 m higher than that of the Arian Baptistery, a fact that has not been explained; Cummins, 1994, p. 90.

207 The Arian Baptistery, like its cathedral, was modified radically at least since the sixteenth century, and the pavement was raised at least three times: in 1543; in the 1670s, at which time a new entrance porch was built in the northeast side; and an oratory was added after 1667 on the west side after the demolition of all of the apses, so that the baptistery became the apse of the new structure (see Breschi, 1965, pp. 41–7). Restorations of the surviving mosaics in the vault

began in the 1850s. From 1916 to 1919 G. Gerola oversaw the restoration of the building, excavation, restoration of the interior, and reconstruction of some of the apses; after the bomb damage of World War II, all of the surrounding buildings were removed, and in the 1950s the western apse was reconstructed. Enough fragments of the original apses survived, both at ground level and at the level of the vaults, for Gerola to estimate their dimensions; see Breschi, 1965, p. 53.

208 *LPR* chs. 86 and 157.

209 The conclusion of Meslin, 1967, pp. 386–90, esp. p. 387. Eunomian baptismal rituals attracted particular attention, for example, by Sozomen, *Historia Ecclesiastica* 6.26; Philostorgius, *Ecclesiastical History Epitome* (in Photius) 10.4; and in the canons of the Council of Constantinople of 381. Epiphanius of Salamis, *Panarion*, 6.76 (54.33), says that Eunomians baptize people upside down, "in the name of God the Uncreated, and in the name of the Created Son, and in the name of the Sanctifying Spirit created by the Created Son." C. Cechelli, 1960, p. 754, followed by Rizzardi, "L'arte dei Goti," 1989, pp. 368–9, proposed that even more moderate Arians may have used the Eunomian formula, but there is no evidence to support this, and on the contrary, as we have seen, there is more evidence that the Ostrogoths were of the more moderate Arian variety. Paul the Deacon, *Historia Romana* XVI.4, tells a story, in the same section in which he describes Theoderic, of an Arian bishop who baptized someone "in nomine Patris per Filium in Spiritu sancto."

210 Eusebius of Vercelli (dubium), *De Trinitate* 7.10: "Cur rite regulam baptismi celebratis et in confessione unito nomine trinitatis blasphematis?" (on the debate about the attribution of this text, see Williams, 1995, pp. 339–42). See Meslin, 1967, pp. 380–90.

211 Letter of Vigilius *ad Eutherium* (but assumed to be Profuturus of Braga, who must have consulted him on this question) in *PL* 69, coll. 15–18; the question was addressed more extensively by Bishop Martin of Braga, *De Trina Mersione*. In both cases, the question of immersion is related to belief about the Trinity. This debate is extensively discussed by McConnell, 2005, esp. pp. 40–4 and 194.

212 Martin of Braga, *De Trina Mersione* 4.

213 The poet Arator, initially a member of Theoderic's court, later wrote a lengthy work entitled *Historia Apostolica* with the meaning of baptism as one of its central themes (Hillier, 1993), but does not address Arian baptism directly.

214 Gerola only found evidence for the southern of these doors; the northern is only hypothesized (Breschi, 1965, p. 56).

215 An entrance was created in the northeast wall sometime after the building was first constructed, but while the original floor level was still in use; Mazzotti, "Scavi recenti," 1970, p. 120, suggests that this happened when the baptistery was converted from Arian use, but this is just speculation.

216 Cummins, 1994, pp. 82–4, based on Gerola's excavations.

217 Cummins, 1994, pp. 105–10. Rizzardi, "Teoderico," 2001, p. 110, claims that this sort of ambulatory must be an innovation of Theoderican Ravenna, connected to the Arian liturgy, but this does not explain its presence in the other examples cited by Cummins.

218 Deichmann, 1989, p. 263.

219 See Cummins, 1994, pp. 110–15.

220 Deichmann, 1974, p. 253.

221 Cummins, 1994, p. 70.

222 Dimensions from Cummins, 1994, p. 66–7.

223 Russo, "L'architettura," 2005, p. 120.

224 Cummins, 1994, p. 87.

225 Mazzotti, "Scavi recenti," 1970, pp. 121–3; *LPR* ch. 157.

226 Mazzotti, "Scavi recenti," 1970, p. 121.

227 Cummins, 1994, p. 104.

228 Mazzotti, "Scavi recenti," 1970, pp. 118–20 and 121–3.

229 Ibid., p. 122.

230 Cummins, 1994, pp. 70–2; see also Krautheimer, 1942, pp. 28–9. The Council of Auxerre of 578 issued a canon prohibiting burial in a baptistery.

231 Mazzotti, "Scavi recenti," 1970, p. 120–1.

232 Most obviously, the color of the halos and the shade of green used for the ground differs between Peter, Paul, and the apostle behind Paul and the rest. Cummins, 1994, p. 145, lists a preference for marble and checkerboard shading in the central medallion and Peter, while glass was primarily used for the other apostles; she provides a detailed analysis of the apostles and comparison with other mosaic figures in Ravenna. Nordhagen, 1966, p. 59, proposes that the marble in Peter's pallium was intended to represent wool, to distinguish him from the other apostles, but since this figure was made by a different workshop, it is also possible that it was just a question of technique.

233 Deichmann, 1974, p. 255; Gerola, 1923; also Bovini, "Note," 1957, who does not propose an amount of time between the phases.

234 Nordström, 1953, p. 34, citing Bovini and Ricci, among others, but not giving a reason for these attestations. The figures in this group, according to Nordström, display a solidity and monumentality that accords with the Theoderican figures in Sant'Apollinare Nuovo, while the others are more insubstantial; Cummins, however, 1994, p. 146, disagrees.

235 Wharton, 1995, p. 133.

236 See Deichmann, 1974, pp. 255–6, for analogies to this motif.

237 Terry/Maguire, 2007, I.62, note that Peter and the apostles behind him wear their mantles over both shoulders, while Paul and his followers wear mantles over only one shoulder; a similar arrangement is seen in the depiction of the apostles in the Basilica Eufrasiana in Porec. Quacquarelli, 1977, interprets the very prominent *gammadia* on these mantles as numerical symbols that had particular meaning for Arian theology, as revealed in an Arian theological work, the *Opus imperfectum in Matthaeum*, but this seems to be stretching interpretation too far; any number could have been applied and meaning found for it. The more generally accepted theory is that *gammadia* did not have any particular meaning; see Oakeshott, 1967, pp. 378–9.

238 While most scholars accept that the paten in the Orthodox Baptistery is a late restoration, and that the original scene there showed John with his hand on Christ's head, Rizzardi, "Teoderico," 2001, p. 116, and "Decorazione," 2001, pp. 917–22, proposes that the paten was original, and that the Arian depiction was deliberately different in order to make a theological point, although she does not say what that point would be. The argument seems rather circular.

239 See Deichmann, 1974, p. 254. Nordström, 1953, p. 35, calls it a courtly style.

240 Wharton, 1995, p. 134, although she does not say whether the ritual positioning would be different in an Orthodox church.
241 Cummins, 1994, p. 131.
242 Mathews, 1993, pp. 134–8.
243 Nordström, 1953, p. 49.
244 Wharton, 1995, p. 134. Rizzardi, "L'arte dei Goti," 1989, p. 376, claims that this Arian ritual must have been different from that of the Orthodox Baptistery, but there is no evidence other than the images for this.
245 Kostof, 1965, p. 92.
246 Sörries, 1983, pp. 99–100.
247 Ibid., pp. 77–97.
248 Deichmann, 1974, p. 254.
249 Sörries, 1983, pp. 99–100; repeated by Rizzardi, "L'arte dei Goti," 1989, p. 373. Nordström, 1953, pp. 50–4, says that Christ is the throne to whom things are offered,
250 Refuted by Nordström, 1953, pp. 50–4. Deichmann, 1974, p. 255, strongly opposes a connection of the dove with the throne, proposed by Nordström, and says that the two scenes are entirely separate.
251 Cummins, 1994, p. 140, following Deichmann, 1974, p. 254; Wharton, 1995, p. 135.
252 Rev. 4:10; Montanari, "I dodici Apostoli," 2002 (orig. 1969), pp. 207 and 218.
253 Wharton, 1995, p. 135.
254 See esp. Megaw/Hawkins, 1977, pp. 110–3.
255 For example, the Basilica Eufrasiana at Porec, St. Catherine's church at Sinai, and the church of the Panagia Kanakaria at Lythrankomi, Cyprus; see Megaw/Hawkins, 1977, pp. 100–9.
256 Cummins, 1994, p. 137.
257 Cf. Maguire, 2007, pp. 139–40, who suggests that images without labels may represent more than one thing at once.
258 See Deichmann, 1969, drawing no. 272, based on the drawing made by A. Azzaroni and G. Zampiga published in Ricci, 1932. The apostle behind him also appears to have a similar facial appearance, but his chin was restored in the nineteenth century. Note that my argument requires that these parts of the mosaics were made in the Ostrogothic period, and not later.
259 Grierson et al., 1986, p. 13; Metlich, 2004, p. 125; see Amory, 1997, pp. 338–41, who does not, nevertheless, comment on the significance of these mustaches. Ward-Perkins, 2005, p. 74, offers a very clear reproduction of the portrait on Theodahad's coin.
260 Dutton, 2004, pp. 24–42; and Ward-Perkins, 2005, pp. 72–5, both note that Latin does not have a word for "mustache." Dutton details the mustaches of Charlemagne and his successors, which he proposes were inspired by Theoderic's mustache.
261 Ennodius, 182 (*Carmina* 2.57); see Ward-Perkins, 2005, p. 79.
262 Cummins, 1994, p. 142.
263 *Variae* II.30, "hoc enim nos et Ravennati ecclesiae commemorant motos rationabili allegatione tribuisse…" X.15: "et ideo salutans clementiam vestram honorificentia competenti harum portitorem pro negotio Ravennatis ecclesiae venientem gratissima vobis petitione commendo…."
264 See Brown, 2007.

265 Lanzoni, 1927, pp. 755–6, citing especially the *Praeceptio regis III missa ad synhodum per germanum et carosum episcopos*, written in 501 (*MGH AA* 12, pp. 419–20).

266 *LPR* ch. 26, 50, 67, and 91.

267 *LPR* ch. 50.

268 *LPR* ch. 75.

269 See Deliyannis, trans., 2004, p. 319.

270 This is the least-studied of Ravenna's monuments; see Gerola, 1932; Ottolenghi, 1957; Deichmann, 1974, pp. 198–204; Miller, 2000, esp. pp. 29–31; Marzetti, 2002; and Mackie, 2003, pp. 104–15.

271 Gerola, 1932, p. 73; repeated by Deichmann, 1974, p. 199.

272 *LPR* ch. 40: "Fecitque … monasterium sancti Andreae apostoli; suaque effigies super ualuas eiusdem monasterii est inferius tessellis depicta."

273 *LPR* ch. 77; and see below, Chapter 6.

274 Manzelli, *Ravenna*, 2000, pp. 116–17. Why this should have been incorporated into the *episcopium* at the same time that Theoderic was restoring the aqueduct is not clear.

275 Gerola, 1932, pp. 121–2, based on Agnellus's story about such a hiding place for treasure, *LPR* ch. 158.

276 Deichmann, 1974, p. 199; Gerola, 1932, does not offer any suggestions; in his day the ground level was partially submerged.

277 On the reconstruction, see Gerola, 1932. In perhaps the eighth century the ground floor was extended into the garden; the surviving remains have been interpreted as a *vivarium* mentioned by Agnellus (see below, Chapter 7). A fourth story was added to the tower in the fourteenth century.

278 Gerola, 1932, pp. 98–101; Deichmann, 1974, pp. 201–2.

279 *LPR* ch. 50; Gerola, 1932, pp. 101–6; the upper levels of the revetment, including the cornice, are restored on the basis of the location of metal clamps found in the walls, and in comparison with what was known from the chapel.

280 Only the parts of this mosaic from Christ's waist up had survived in 1911 (Gerola, 1932, pp. 106–8); the lion and serpent were restored based on the iconography known from the Orthodox Baptistery and elsewhere.

281 *LPR* ch. 50: "… in ingressu ianuae extrinsecus super liminare…."

282 Gerola, 1932, pp. 107–8.

283 Cf. Janes, 1998, pp. 145–7, who does not, however, mention this poem. Similar poems praising the radiance of church decoration were put up in Santa Maria Maggiore in Ravenna (as reported in *LPR* ch. 57), and in the church of Sts. Cosmas and Damian in Rome (ca. 526).

284 Fragments of the *tubi* were found in the course of restoration; see Gerola, 1932, pp. 88 and 113–15.

285 Gerola, 1932, pp. 109–10, says that the form of this window is original, although it had been modified several times.

286 Gerola, 1932, p. 109.

287 See, most comprehensively, Megaw/Hawkins, 1977, pp. 100–19.

288 von Simson, 1948, pp. 84–5. All of these female martyrs are found in the procession in Sant'Apollinare Nuovo.

289 See most recently Cuscito, 2007; and Brenk, 2006; the latter's argument, p. 311, that Theoderic must have cosponsored this church because of the king's close connections with Felix IV, is unproved.

290 Deichmann, 1974, pp. 200–1, discusses similar contemporary chapels of S. Prosdocimo in Padua and S. Maria Mater Domini, to the south of the church of Sts. Felix and Fortunatus, in Vicenza, as well as in Asia Minor. See also Mackie, 2003, pp. 37–44.

291 Deichmann, 1974, p. 204.

292 Deichmann, 1974, p. 203, cites especially Athanasius, *Contra Arianos* 1.19 and 3.9, as well as works by Gregory of Nyssa, Hilary of Poitiers, and Leo the Great.

293 *LPR* chs. 50 and 67, respectively.

294 *LPR* ch. 26; probably the tomb of Bishop Peter III. Also *LPR* ch. 91.

295 See Lanzoni, 1927, pp. 735–6; comprehensively Susini, "La questione," 1968; and Deichmann, 1989, pp. 42–3, and most recently Pani Ermini, 2005, pp. 1027–8, based on the document of 551 cited above in connection with the Arian church (Tjäder, 1954, vol. 2 no. 34) that names a "Deusdedit for(ensis) civ(itatis) Classis Rav(ennae)."

296 Initially, the bishop was the only person who was authorized to baptize, but in the fifth century a distinction began to be drawn between baptism, which included some anointing with chrism (which had to be consecrated by the bishop), and the full anointing on the forehead and the laying on of hands to confer the Holy Spirit, which had to be performed by the bishop in all cases, but not necessarily at the same time as baptism; see Saxer, 1988, pp. 577–80.

297 Montanari, 1992, p. 245.

298 See Cortesi, 1968; De Angelis d'Ossat, 1968; Deichmann, 1976, pp. 318–21; Maioli/Stoppioni, 1987, pp. 90–3.

299 Gentili, 1972, p. 198;

300 Smith, "Form and Function," 1990, p. 198.

301 Gentili, 1972, p. 205, suggests instead that the two chambers at the eastern ends of the aisles belong to the first phase and the intervening spaces were added secondarily.

302 Cortesi, 1968, suggested that it was the church of St. Demetrius, mentioned by Agnellus (*LPR* ch. 2) as at the sixth milestone from Ravenna and destroyed by his day. On the various possibilities, see Gentili, 1972, pp. 200–2.

303 De Angelis d'Ossat, 1968, pp. 458–9.

304 *LPR* chs. 50, 67, 91.

305 *LPR* chs. 39 and 57, and also *Anon. Vales.* II.90.

306 *LPR* ch. 60. It would be interesting to compare the list of clergy given at the end of this document with the list from the Arian document of 551 cited above.

307 "Ex inuidia sacerdotes ecclesiae Rauennatis talia contigerunt quae omnium catholicorum animas contristasse noscuntur: altercationes, seditiones, praui-tates, quae omnem disciplinam ecclesiasticam disrumpere niterentur."

308 This document is in need of serious study to place it in the context of eccle-siastical dispute resolution and legislation in this period. Agnellus quotes this document in full because one of his main concerns was the distribution by the bishop of ecclesiastical property and income among the clergy; however, this does not mean that financial issues were the main concern of the sixth-century clergy.

309 *LPR* chs. 57, 59. See Barnish, 1985, who provides an explanation of the political and economic background of Julian's wealth.

310 *LPR* ch. 63. Deichmann, 1953 and 1976, pp. 10–11, notes emphatically that Agnellus says only that Santa Maria Maggiore was begun just after Ecclesius returned from Constantinople, and this cannot be used as a date for the founding of San Vitale also.

311 *LPR* ch. 77.

312 Expressed by Testi-Rasponi, ed., 1924, pp. 163–5, and then most extensively by von Simson, 1948, esp. pp. 5–9.

313 Deichmann, 1976, pp. 16 and 21–7; and Barnish, 1985, pp. 5–6. Deichmann, 1953, pp. 113–14, and 1976, pp. 22–3, notes that *argentarius* was not part of his name, since it does not appear on all the inscriptions, but instead an occupation; he was probably not a financial official of the Ravennate church, nor a government official, since his name is never given with any title such as *coactor* or honorific epithets such as *vir illustris*.

Six. Ravenna's Early Byzantine Period, AD 540–600

1 Young, 2000.

2 See Gunn, 2000, and Arjava, 2005.

3 Koder, 1996; Arjava, 2005, p. 78.

4 Gregory the Great, *Dialogues* III.19, cited and expanded upon by Paul the Deacon, *Historia Langobardorum* III.23–24; also reported by Gregory of Tours, *Historiae* X.1 and by various other biographers of Gregory; see Patitucci Uggeri, 2005, pp. 322–6. There are other river miracles in the *Dialogues*, see also III.9–10, and flood metaphors are common in his letters, implying that flooding was a serious problem in sixth-century Italy. However, Squatriti, 1998, pp. 72–5, suggests that after the sixth century, authors did not view flooding as such a problem, because economic and social conditions had become adapted to the new environmental situation.

5 See Giraudi, 2005; and Christie, 2006, pp. 486–8.

6 See Stathakopoulos, 2004, pp. 110–54 and 290–5; also Christie, 2006, pp. 500–4.

7 Bavant, 1989, gives a population estimate for Rome in the sixth–seventh centuries of 25,000–30,000 people, down from 100,000 in 500.

8 Guillou, 1991, p. 103, for example, accepts the sources as evidence of a crisis; Brogiolo, "Ideas," 1999, observes that the texts alternate between describing cities in crisis and cities being restored to their former splendor. See also Orselli, 2006.

9 Guillou, 1991, p. 105.

10 See Patitucci Uggeri, 2005, pp. 257–9. Procopius, *De bello Gothico* VI.28, reports a strange incident in 539 or 540 in which the water of the Po fell very low and then returned to its proper volume.

11 Squatriti, 1998, pp. 67–72, argues that with the breakdown of political order after the death of Theoderic, hydraulic conditions established during the imperial period were no longer being maintained by a central government, which led to increased problems with flooding; Christie, 2006, pp. 200–1 and 486–91.

12 CIL XI.11; see Prati, 1988, p. 29; and Gelichi, 1991, p. 159.

13 Amory, 1997, p. 12, notes, "After the 550's, no individual called a Goth ever appears again in Italy," although certainly individuals with Gothic names are still attested in Ravennate papyri until around 600, see Brown, 1984, pp. 75–6.

14 *LP Vita Johannis III* 2 and other chronicles; see Everett, 2003, p. 66.

15 An excellent summary of Lombard history can be found in Everett, 2003, pp. 54–79.

16 *HL* I.27.

17 *HL* II.26; the evidence is summarized by Everett, 2003, p. 68.

18 This is told in *HL* II.28–30, and then by Agnellus, based on Paul the Deacon's account, in *LPR* ch. 96.

19 *LPR* ch. 95: "palocopia in modum muri propter metum gentis"; see Deliyannis, ed., 2006, p. 369 n. 81, on the term *palocopia*; and Righini, 1991, p. 205.

20 *HL* III.13 and III.19.

21 Truces in 598 (*HL* IV.8), 605 (IV.28), 607 (IV.32), several more times before 619 (IV.40). See esp. Markus, 1997, pp. 99–100.

22 Published as Appendix VII to the *Novellae* of Justinian, ed. Schöll/Kroll, pp. 799–802.

23 *Pragmatic Sanction* 22.

24 *Pragmatic Sanction* 12 and 18; see Brown, 1984, pp. 6–8 and 114.

25 Brown, 1984, pp. 21–37; *LP Vita Vigilii* 7.

26 Brown, 1984.

27 First reported in *LP Vita Johannis III*, repeated by Paul the Deacon, *HL* II.5 and III.12, and *LPR* chs. 90 and 95–6. Narses was finally removed from office in 566 by Justin II, but refused to return to Constantinople, retiring instead to a villa near Naples. The *LP* accuses him of having invited the Lombards into Italy, and this story found its way into many chronicles such as the *Origo gentis Langobardorum* 5, and eventually *HL* II.1–2; for the complete list, see Everett, 2003, p. 66. It should be noted that this part of the *LP* was written in the 640s, thus many years after the fact.

28 Brown, 1984, pp. 10–12.

29 Brown, 1984, p. 49, notes that the term *exarchatus* to refer to the territory governed from Ravenna is only used in the sources after the collapse of Byzantine authority in 751. At the end of the century, Gregory the Great writes letters *romano exarcho per Italiam residenti Ravenna* (e.g., *Registrum epistolarum* 5.19).

30 Brown, 1984, p. 136, notes that the last record of a *praefectus* comes from the year 600.

31 For a summary, see Ferluga, "L'esarcato," 1991, pp. 356–8.

32 Brown, 1984, pp. 48–60.

33 See Pietri, 1983, pp. 664–6; and Brown, 1991, pp. 140–1.

34 Brown, 1984, p. 77, 85.

35 Brown, 1984, pp. 16–18.

36 The Agnellus who identifies himself as an *iatrosofista* and *archiatrus* (different from the author of the *LPR*) and who wrote Latin commentaries on works of the Greek physician Galen is thought to have worked between 550 and 700; see *Agnellus of Ravenna*, 1981, p. xiv.

37 See Pietri, 1983, pp. 664–7; Guillou, 1991, p. 102; and Brown, 1991.

38 Arslan, 2005, pp. 215–28. The building excavated at the Via di Roma in 1969 and identified as the mint (see above, Chapter 3) were modified in the mid–sixth century; see Manzelli, *Ravenna*, 2000, pp. 111–13.

39 Evidence for this is a story told by Agnellus, *LPR* 132, in which a petitioner goes to "...the [palace of] Theoderic, and he asked to be presented to the exarch."

40 Porta, 1991, p. 277, cites documents from 572 and 639.

41 Farioli Campanati, 1989, and "Ravenna, Constantinopoli," 1992.

42 Augenti, "Archeologia," 2005, pp. 22–3. Porta, 1991, notes that changes to the palace buildings after the mid–sixth century are not easy to date, so we cannot say how much redecoration belongs specifically to the later sixth century.

43 *LPR* chs. 66–7.

44 The dates of Victor's reign are given variously as 537–44 and 538–45. For a concise explanation of why the latter must be correct, see Andreescu-Treadgold/Treadgold, 1997, p. 712 n. 16.

45 Venantius Fortunatus's first two poems are titled in the earliest manuscript as addressed to a Bishop Vitalis of Ravenna, but George, 1992, p. 23, assumes that "ravennense" was added to the titles later, since the poems do not specifically say that Bishop Vitalis reigned in Ravenna; George suggests that Vitalis may have been the bishop of Altinum, which is where Venantius was raised.

46 Gregory, *Registrum Epistolarum* 5.21, 22, and especially 51, also 6.1, and 2; many subsequent letters concern controversies between the bishop and various clergy and monks. See Markus, 1997, pp. 148–56.

47 Markus, 1981, pp. 572–3, and idem, 1997, esp. pp. 100–7.

48 Gregory the Great, *Registrum Epistularum* 2.25; see Markus, 1981, pp. 572–3.

49 Deichmann, 1952; idem, 1976, pp. 13–15; Markus, 1979; idem, 1997, pp. 146–7; and T. Brown, 1979, p. 7. Deichmann makes the argument, subsequently repeated by everyone, that Maximian's title changes between the inscriptions for San Vitale (547) and Sant'Apollinare in Classe (549) from *vir reverendissimus* to *vir beatissimus*, and this marks the date of the change in title to *archiepiscopus* (*LPR* ch. 77). However, in these inscriptions both Ecclesius and Ursicinus are also called *beatissimus*. Deichmann says that they used this title, but that Maximian did not dare to use it for himself; this seems rather awkward. In both inscriptions, as well as the one in the church of St. Stephen dating to 550, Maximian is called *episcopus*. Of course, it is possible that Agnellus or his copyists got this information wrong, but in any case the titles cannot therefore be used for dating purposes; see Farioli Campanati, "Per la datazione," 2005, pp. 166–7. In a papyrus of 553 (Marini, n. 86; Tjäder I.13), Maximian is called *archiepiscopus*, the first definite date for the use of the title. In addition, in several inscriptions fom the second half of the sixth century, Ravenna's bishops are called *papa*, a title that, according to the Justinianic Code, was to be used only by the pope. Deichmann, 1976, pp. 13–15, partially revising his earlier arguments, says that these titles were in fact rather fluid and dependent on circumstances, but then insists that Maximian would have used the epithets according to Justinian's laws.

50 See, e.g., Abramowski, 2001, p. 296, who uses it to date the mosaics in San Vitale.

51 *LPR* ch. 70, then 40.

52 Markus, 1979, p. 296, argues that the *pallium* and the archiepiscopal title are not linked since he dates the title only to 548–9, but he accepts Agnellus's account that the *pallium* was given to Maximian upon his consecration. On the dating of the apse mosaics in San Vitale to the early 540s, see Andreescu-Treadgold/Treadgold, 1997, p. 721, and below.

53 See esp. Markus, 1981, pp. 574–6, and idem, 1997, pp. 143–56.

54 Gregory the Great, *Registrum Epistularum* 3.54, 5.11, and 5.15 (to John); 5.61, 6.31, 6.34, and 9.168 (to Marinian).

55 Gregory, *Registrum epistularum* 4.37. See Markus, 1997, pp. 143–56, on Gregory's relations with the bishops of Ravenna.

56 See esp. Markus, 1997, pp. 125–42, and Sotinel, 2007.

57 The story is told in the *Liber pontificalis*, *Vita Silverii*, and *Vita Vigilii*.

58 Markus, 1979. Sotinel, 2007, p. 92, notes that Pelagius I, *Ep.* 52, insisted that the new bishop of Milan be consecrated in Ravenna and not Aquileia in 553.

59 *LPR* ch. 85.

60 Markus, 1981, p. 573; on the Lombard position, see Everett, 2003, pp. 80–4.

61 *LPR* 81; see Deliyannis, trans., 2004, p. 195.

62 *LPR* chs. 42 and 78; see Deliyannis, ed., 2006, pp. 29–30.

63 Picard, 1988, pp. 489–90 and 560–9. It is also possible that the diploma of Valentinian III that conferred metropolitan status upon Ravenna's bishops, known as a forgery since the eighteenth century, was composed in this period or at the time of the *pallium* controversy; see Orioli, 1980, pp. 135–44 and below, Chapter 7.

64 *LPR* chs. 72–3, 75, 76–7, and 97.

65 *LPR* ch. 44.

66 *LPR* chs. 93 and 98.

67 See esp. Novara, *La cattedrale*, 1997, pp. 60–7.

68 *LPR* ch. 66; see Deichmann, 1974, p. 10.

69 Farioli Campanati, "Il pyrgus," 1994, p. 209.

70 Farioli Campanati, "Ravenna e i suoi rapporti," 2005, pp. 23–8, discusses ambos from Constantinople; there survive fragments of several others, from the churches of Sts. John and Paul, St. Agnes, and elsewhere, probably made locally in the later sixth–eighth centuries to imitate the one in the Orthodox cathedral.

71 See Farioli Campanati, "Il pyrgus," 1994, who argues that the term *pyrgos*, used in Constantinople for the ambo of Hagia Sophia, was deliberately imitated here by Agnellus. The fact that Agnellus is identified as *episcopus* and not *archiepiscopus* shows that the title *archiepiscopus* was not used on every inscription from the sixth century, and thus cannot be used for dating purposes.

72 *LPR* ch. 89; Mazzotti, "La croce argentea," 1960. The central roundels, as well as many of the smaller medallions, were remade in the sixteenth century or later.

73 On the throne, see esp. Cecchelli, 1936; Morath, 1940; Schapiro, 1952; Volbach, 1977, pp. 38–51; Montanari, 1984/5; Rizzardi, 2003; and Farioli Campanati, "Per la datazione," 2005. The throne is now in the Museo Arcivescovile.

74 In fact, depicted on the throne is a very similar one in which the Virgin sits in the Annunciation scene.

75 On the history of the throne, known damage, and restorations, see Volbach, 1977, pp. 38–40.

76 The seat and the interior of the arms were covered with blank panels.

77 See esp. Rizzardi, 2003, pp. 146–8, for a summary of the interpretations about the origin of the artists, and comes down on the side of Constantinople; Volbach, 1977, pp. 22 and 38–40, argues for Ravenna. Farioli Campanati, "Per la datazione," 2005, p. 167, argues correctly that the title *episcopus* that appears on the throne does not mean that it was made before 549.

78 Rizzardi, 2003.

79 Vikan, 1979, p. 105 n. 3, notes that Joseph was regarded as a local hero in Egypt, since that is where much of his story took place. In *LPR* ch. 78, Agnellus quotes a section of Maximian's chronicle in which Maximian says that he has visited Alexandria. For a summary of the arguments about the workshops that created the throne, see, e.g., Capp, 1942, who cites earlier literature.

80 Schapiro, 1952, p. 29, notes that Joseph, the husband of Mary, who is also compared to a bishop in patristic exegesis, is prominently treated in the scenes of the infancy of Christ; see Peter Chrysologus, *Sermons* 174 and 175.

81 Schapiro, 1952, pp. 29–30, cites Ambrose, *De Officiis*, esp. 2.11–16; Ambrose continues the analogy in a letter (*PL* 16, cols. 884–5) to the newly ordained Bishop Constantius of Imola. In addition, Cassiodorus (*Variae* 6.3, 8.20, and 12.28) holds Joseph up as a model for the Praetorian Prefect and other governing officials; see Shapiro, 1952, p. 32 and Montanari, 1984–5, pp. 308–10.

82 Schapiro, 1952, pp. 32–4; *LPR* chs. 70 and 80.

83 *LPR* ch. 66; on the excavation, see Bermond Montanari, 1984–5; and Manzelli, *Ravenna*, 2000, pp. 118–24. The bath had at least three building phases. Other bath complexes have also been identified among archaeological remains from this period; see Gelichi, 1991, p. 159. For comparable bath complexes near *episcopia*, see Deichmann, 1974, p. 205.

84 Art historians differ about the origins of the architects and workmen of these churches; Russo, "L'architettura," 2005, strongly argues in favor of masters from the east (Constantinople or Greece) working with local workmen in Ravenna between 540 and 590, while Deichmann, esp. 1976, p. 85 and 1989, pp. 243–6 and 256–63, argued instead for movement of materials and ideas but not actual master architects.

85 For a brief summary, see Harper, 1997, and Deliyannis, 2005, pp. 37–8.

86 See esp. Betsch, 1977, pp. 119–57; Terry, 1988, pp. 55–9.

87 Terry, 1988, p. 57.

88 See Deichmann, 1976, pp. 60–3; Righini, 1991, pp. 215–16; and Augenti, 2007, pp. 240. These bricks measure ca. 50 × 33 × 4.5 centimeters, a type that is called *sesquipedalis*; bricks of this type may have been used in Roman Ravenna, and were certainly common in sixth-century Constantinople. Another church built of this type of brick was that of San Michele in Acervoli at Sant'Arcangelo di Romagna, a dependent baptismal church in the diocese of Ravenna; see Russo, "L'architettura," 2005, pp. 149–54.

89 Lombardini, 2007, pp. 268–9.

90 See Angiolini Martinelli, 1968, no. 26. The central part of the ambo, with its inscription, survives: "De donis d(e)i et s(an)c(to)rum Iohanni et Pauli Adeodatus prim(us) strator inl(ustris) p(raefecturae) temp(ori)b(us) d(o)m(i)n(i) v(ene)r(a)b(ilis) Marinian(i) arc(hi)ep(i)s(copi) fec(it) ind(ictione) XV."

91 *LPR* ch. 57.

92 Mazzotti, "La basilica," 1960; Deichmann, 1976, pp. 343–8.

93 Deichmann, 1976, pp. 343–6.

94 Deichmann, 1976, p. 344.

95 The sanctuary of the Bethlehem church was an octagon; Deichmann, 1976, p. 345, also suggests similarities with the Church of the Holy Sepulchre in Jerusalem.

96 Krautheimer, 1953; as part of this trend, the Pantheon in Rome, also a rotunda, was rededicated to the Virgin and All the Saints in 610, and subsequently inspired many imitations.

97 *LPR* ch. 59. Deichmann's study of San Vitale, in 1976, pp. 34–205, is far more extensive than his coverage of any other building and offers a complete survey of the architecture and the mosaics. See also the recent studies in Angiolini Martinelli, ed., 1997, esp. the extremely detailed catalog on pp. 163–269, as well as the plates in vol. 2.

98 Ambrose, *Epistula* 77; Paulinus of Milan, *Vita Ambrosii* 14; for Rome, *Liber pontificalis*, *Vita Innocenti I.*

99 Paulinus of Milan, *Vita Ambrosii* 32 (Nazarius) and 39 (Vitalis and Agricola). The legend of Vitalis and Agricola was well-known in the fifth and sixth centuries, mentioned by, among others, Paulinus of Nola and Gregory of Tours.

100 Published as (Pseudo-)Ambrose, *Ep.* 2 (*PL* 17, coll. 742ff.); on the date, see von Simson, 1948, p. 15, and Deichmann, 1976, pp. 7–8. Agnellus knew this text well; he cites it in *LPR* ch. 32, and paraphrases it in ch. 15.

101 Pseudo-Ambrose, *Ep.* 2.10: "Sanctus autem Vitalis gloriosus martyr Christi, juxta civitatem Ravennensium praestat orationibus vel intercessionibus suis beneficia omnibus credentibus Jesum Christum usque in hodiernum diem." (PL 17, col. 745)

102 Deichmann, 1976, p. 47. By the early fourteenth century an altar is mentioned in the southwestern exedra of the core directly above this earlier chapel; it is not known whether there had always been something commemorating this spot here, although Deichmann, 1976, pp. 53–4, rejects the idea that the site of the earlier church had always had an altar above it, as some scholars had proposed.

103 *LPR* ch. 59. Julian also donated to the church a marble reliquary, which still survives, with the inscription "Julianus Argent(arius) servus vest(er) praecib(us) vest(ris) basi(licam) a funda(mentis) perfec(it)" (*CIL* xi.289, Deichmann, 1976, p. 4).

104 *LPR* ch. 61.

105 *LPR* chs. 59, 61, 65, and 68; Deichmann, 1976, p. 52. Other people also were buried around the church, perhaps in the atrium; inscriptions for a few clerical figures of unknown date, and the famous Sueve/Lombard warrior Droctulfus, who, according to Paul the Deacon (*HL* 3.19), was probably buried in the atrium; see Deichmann, 1976, p. 28.

106 *LPR* ch. 77.

107 Deichmann, 1976, pp. 7–33.

108 *LPR* ch. 57; see later in this chapter with reference to Santa Maria Maggiore.

109 Deichmann, 1953, and idem, 1976, pp. 10–11, 48–9, and 103. Deichmann argues that the monograms must have been carved at Proconnesus. I am not sure that anyone has ever questioned the attribution of these monograms to Victor, but it is worth pointing out that the same letters that spell VICTOR EPISCOPVS also are used in ECLESIVS EPISCOPVS, except for the letter *T*, which is only found as a small stem perpendicular and to the left of the leftmost vertical stem.

110 Agnellus even tells a story (*LPR* ch. 73) of the building-master of St. Stephen's, whose work came to a standstill because he could not obtain building materials while Maximian was away in Constantinople.

111 For the following, see Deichmann, 1976, pp. 49–60; and the articles by Foschi, Iannucci, and Lombardini in Angiolini Martinelli, 1997.

112 Other modifications made in the Middle Ages include the blocking of the exterior door of the southern chapel in the ninth century, the raising of the floors, perhaps in the late twelfth century, a new main entrance on the northeast face made after the mid–thirteenth century, and perhaps at the same time the atrium was rebuilt as a cloister.

113 Deichmann, 1976, pp. 69–72. The current cloister was built in the sixteenth century.

114 The narthex and stair towers were radically modified at various points in the building's history and were restored in 1929; Deichmann, 1976, pp. 72–6.

115 The large flying buttresses were added in the later Middle Ages when the ambulatory and gallery were vaulted.

116 Deichmann, 1976, p. 82.

117 In fact, the *tubi fittili* are used for the upper arches of the windows as well as for the dome proper; see Deichmann, 1976, p. 64, who argued that they form part of the dome, but for a contrary opinion see Russo, 1996, pp. 304–10.

118 For an extensive analysis of this see Deichmann, 1976, pp. 65–8, including an excursus by P. Grossmann. Before we express surprise at this, we should remember that all of Ravenna's basilicas were roofed with wood; a wooden ceiling could be quite elaborate.

119 Deichmann, 1976, pp. 139–41, who notes that depictions of buildings in Ravenna, for example the model of San Vitale carried by Ecclesius in the apse of this church, show windows filled with grilles for rectangular panes of glass. Some fragments of colored and painted glass, found in the church, probably do not belong to the original period but were installed later in the Middle Ages; see Dell'Aqua, 2005, pp. 205–7.

120 Deichmann, 1976, pp. 28–9, speculates that perhaps the northern chapel was intended for the burial of Julian the banker; it was dedicated to the Virgin at least by the seventeenth century. By the time of Agnellus, the south chapel was dedicated to Sts. Nazarius and Celsus, also Milanese saints. Deichmann, ibid., pp. 8–9, argues that the dedication to Nazarius and Celsus was later because they are not mentioned in the dedicatory inscription. Venantius Fortunatus (*Vita sancti Martini*, 4.680–5), writing after he left Ravenna in 565, says that there was a church dedicated to St. Ursicinus associated with San Vitale, and since we do not know of any other church with this dedication (Deichmann, 1976, p. 374), it is tempting to think that perhaps this was the original dedication of the northern chapel. Smith, "Form and Function," 1990, p. 197, suggests that they may have contained altars, although she does not cite *LPR* ch. 42, which mentions both altars and chancel screens.

121 Deichmann, 1976, p. 52; Smith, "Form and Function," 1990, p. 197.

122 Russo, "L'architettura," 2005, p. 128.

123 Deichmann, 1976, p. 83, argues that the construction of San Vitale only began during the reign of Victor, thus after 538, in order to explain that it was inspired by Sts. Sergius and Bacchus, but, as we have seen above, there is no evidence for this.

124 Grabar, 1946, and Mango, 1972.

125 Dynes, 1962–4, and, most extensively on the double-shell genre, Kleinbauer, 1987, pp. 287–91, who notes also that the church of St. John Prodromos at the

Hebdomon in Constantinople, built by Theodosius I and rebuilt by Justinian in the 550s, may also have been of this type (see Mathews, 1971, pp. 55–61, who concludes that it is the closest parallel to San Vitale). Deichmann, 1976, pp. 84–5, lists and dismisses most of the other examples. The Golden Octagon at Antioch collapsed in an earthquake in 526.

126 Lewis, 1973, argues that San Lorenzo was built for the imperial palace at Milan. On the date and function of Sts. Sergius and Bacchus, see most recently Mathews, 2005, who reviews earlier scholarship.

127 De Angelis D'Ossat, *Studi*, 1962, pp. 59–88; Dynes, 1962–4, repeated by Lewis, 1973, p. 208. But, arguing against the thesis in regard to Sts. Sergius and Bacchus, see Mango, 1972, and as regards San Vitale, Deichmann, 1953, p. 114.

128 Deichmann, 1989, pp. 49–50.

129 Deichmann, 1976, pp. 86–135 (part written by H. Raabe), and 206–30, provides an exhaustive survey of all of the marble elements in the building, as well as a detailed study of the workshop marks, many of which were in Greek, found on them.

130 Terry, 1988, p. 56.

131 On the procedures by which a church's marble was acquired, see most extensively Terry, 1988, pp. 55–9.

132 Russo, "L'architettura," 2005, pp. 121–8, argues that the architect of San Vitale was from the east, against Deichmann's claim (1976, pp. 84–5) that the architects must have been local. The arguments in each case have to do with construction techniques (the form of the bricks, which Russo argues are Constantinopolitan, the *tubi fittili*, which are characteristically Ravennate) and the effects of the architecture (Deichmann argued that the verticalism shows a western influence; Russo argues against this and says that the brilliance of the design must mean that the architect came from the eastern capital). Since, as we have noted many times, Ravenna was a meeting place for people and materials from around the Mediterranean, it seems likely that all influences were at play in the mind of whoever designed and built the church.

133 Harper, 1997, on the other hand, suggests that the quarries of Proconnesus had a permanent agent in Ravenna who transmitted orders back to the island.

134 Deichmann, 1976, p. 90.

135 Victor's monogram appears also on two imposts in the gallery; the monograms of Julian are found on the south side of the gallery, facing the gallery. Deichmann argues that Victor's monograms were made in Proconnesus, while Julian's were instead carved on blank medallions in situ in Ravenna. The very fact that the architects could send some of the imposts to Ravenna with blank space for carving is significant. Facing the central core, the imposts of the gallery arcade have a cross between acanthus leaves, while on the back side they have simply a cross. See Deichmann, 1976, pp. 100–4.

136 On the marks, see Deichmann, 1976, pp. 206–23.

137 Betsch, 1977, p. 216.

138 On the types of capital in this period, see Betsch, 1977, pp. 209–23; and Terry, 1988, p. 16.

139 Deichmann, 1976, pp. 108 and 111–12; then Betsch, 1977, pp. 149–50; responded to by Deichmann, 1989, pp. 273–6.

140 Krautheimer, 1986, pp. 233–4, who notes that the impost capitals have many similarities with those used in the church of St. Polyeuktos, built 524–7, while

composite capitals of this type were not used at all in Constantinople in this period; cf. also Deichmann, 1976, p. 110.

141 Terry, 1988, p. 57.

142 Marble from Iasos was used in many Justinianic buildings, including St. Andrew in Ravenna, and, most famously, in Hagia Sophia in Constantinople; see Deichmann, 1976, p. 117.

143 See the detailed study and reconstruction in Deichmann, 1976, pp. 118–35.

144 Deichmann, 1976, pp. 134–5; Iannucci, 1997, pp. 74–6.

145 Angiolini Martinelli, ed., 1997, pp. 171–6 and 201–3.

146 Deichmann, 1976, pp. 117 and 135–9.

147 Iannucci, 1997, pp. 77–9, and Angiolini Martinelli, ed., 1997, pp. 233–9.

148 Deichmann, 1940.

149 Angiolini Martinelli, 1997.

150 Andreescu-Treadgold/Treadgold, 1997, who note that much of what may seem to be portraiture is actually simply convention, applied by master artisans.

151 Deichmann, 1976, pp. 117 and 131.

152 Deichmann, 1976, pp. 117–8, who also notes, p. 106, in the context of noting that the sculptural details give no prominence to the dome, but only to the apse.

153 Deichmann, 1976, pp. 188–94, and Andreescu-Treadgold/Treadgold, 1997, pp. 715–16. The question of whether the workmen were local or came from Constantinople is discussed by Pasi, 2005, pp. 63–4, who concludes that the mosaicists were local.

154 Argued most recently by Rizzardi, 1988, pp. 59–60, and idem, "I mosaici parietali," 2005.

155 Andreescu-Treadgold, "The Mosaic Workshop," 1992, idem, 1994, and idem/Treadgold, 1997, pp. 714 and 719–20, who note, p. 721, that Deichmann was unable to date the two phases because he did not understand that the head and name of Maximian were inserted after the initial composition.

156 Muscolino, 1997.

157 The first to attempt to document which parts of the mosaics were not original was Ricci, in his *Monumenti: tavole storiche* of 1930–7. Deichmann, in the *plananhung* to his series, published diagrams of the mosaics that are largely based on Ricci's; for his specific analysis of the restorations in San Vitale, see 1976, pp. 141–2; see for the more modern era especially the very interesting article by Iannucci, "Appunti," 1992, and idem, 1997. The most recent work on these mosaics is being published by I. Andreescu-Treadgold, see esp. "Mosaic Workshop," 1992, 1994, and 1997.

158 Andreescu-Treadgold, 1994, shows that the new parts are typical of middle-Byzantine military costume and thus were made in the tenth or eleventh century.

159 Andreescu-Treadgold, 1994.

160 Cf. Caillet, 2003.

161 Maguire, 1987, pp. 77–9, interprets the cornucopia as a symbolic of the Earth, paired with Ocean as symbolized by the dolphins on the arch that leads west into the core of the church, and also, along with the eagles, as an imperial symbol of prosperity that is linked to the panels below.

162 Andreescu-Treadgold, 1994.

163 Deckers, 2002, esp. pp. 22–38, who discusses the difficulties inherent in presenting the supreme ruler of the empire in a subservient posture.

164 Andreescu-Treadgold/Treadgold, 1997, pp. 716–17.

165 MacCormack, 1981, p. 261; however, Andreescu-Treadgold/Treadgold, 1997, p. 711, see Justinian as leading the procession. In fact, the mosaic's ambiguous perspective allows the artists to express both that Maximian was first liturgically, but also that in terms of rank the emperor was first; cf. MacCormack, 1981, pp. 261–2.

166 Maguire, 1987, p. 80.

167 Pasi, 2006, p. 20.

168 von Simson, 1948, p. 27; and MacCormack, 1981, p. 263, expanded by Gulowsen, 1999, pp. 132–7, argue that the niche and doorway indicate that Theodora was already dead, but Andreescu-Treadgold's dating of the mosaic to before 544 negates this argument.

169 Barber, 1990, pp. 35–6, comments that the male costume worn by the empress creates for her an ambiguous gender identity, neither traditionally female nor male, and thus that Theodora here is a transgressor of gender expectations.

170 For a comparison of jewelry in the mosaics with surviving pieces from the sixth century, see K. Brown, 1979, who highlights the prominence of pearls, emeralds, and sapphires.

171 von Simson, 1953, p. 106; Deichmann, 1976, p. 183; cf. also Abramowski, 2001, p. 297.

172 McClanan, 2002, pp. 137–8.

173 McClanan, 2002, p. 128, who discusses various theories and provides a bibliography.

174 Most recently, I. Andreescu-Treadgold and W. Treadgold (1997) have argued that the aristocratic figures to the left of Justinian were Anastasius, the grandson of the empress Theodora (the younger man), and Belisarius, while the figure added between Justinian and Maximian represents John, the other Byzantine general who expected to take over from Belisarius after his recall to Constantinople in 544. They further suggest that the two women next to Theodora are Belisarius's wife Antonina and their daughter Joannina (following Manara, 1983), who was betrothed to Anastasius. The message would be that Belisarius and his family still had the support of the imperial couple and indeed were forming a marriage alliance with them. While the explanation is plausible enough, the scholars do not explain why Belisarius should have had the authority to decide on the content of these panels, in a church sponsored by the bishop and a private individual; and why the head of Belisarius was not simply changed to that of John, as was done with Maximian. Manara, 1983, had proposed also Narses, the praetorian prefect Anastasius; others have suggested Julian the banker among the figures.

175 McClanan, 1998, p. 12.

176 MacCormack, 1981, p. 260; Deckers, 2002.

177 Deichmann, 1976, p. 181; Deckers, 2002, p. 38; cf. also MacCormack, 1981, p. 260.

178 On earlier debates about the procession, see the summary in McClanan, 2002, pp. 124–7.

179 Mathews, 1971, pp. 138–47, and specifically about the San Vitale panels, pp. 146–7.

180 On the position of the women in Bzyantine churches, see Taft, 1998, esp. pp. 57–9; women were generally assigned locations in the galleries, although also in the aisles – and, of course, none of Ravenna's basilicas had galleries.

181 Another problem, that in this ceremony the emperor is not supposed to be wearing a crown when he processes with the bishop, is dismissed by Mathews, who says, "the crown, like the halo, is part of the ordinary identification of the Emperor..." (p. 147). A third problem is that the text says that the emperor is presenting a purse of gold, whereas here Justinian holds a paten.

182 For a description of the Roman *Ordo* of the mass, from the seventh century but thought to be based on earlier precedent, see Mathews, 1962, pp. 88–9; the *Ordo* specifically says that the men offer their gifts on the men's side and the women on the women's side.

183 MacCormack, 1981, p. 260; Andreescu-Treadgold/Treadgold, 1997, p. 708; Deckers, 2002, p. 30.

184 For a discussion of interpretations of whether Maximian or Justinian is more prominent in this image, see Andreescu-Treadgold/Treadgold, 1997, p. 711.

185 Gulowsen, 1999, pp. 143–4; see also McClanan, 2002, p. 123.

186 Andreescu-Treadgold, "The Mosaic Workshop," 1992, p. 31, who provides the most comprehensive discussion of the mosaics of the presbitery.

187 Rizzardi, 1988.

188 von Simson, 1948, p. 31, identifies Melchisedek's attire and halo as paralleling that of the emperor.

189 von Simson, 1948, pp. 32–3; Deichmann, 1976, pp. 159–61, says that Moses did not feature as a type of a Christian ruler in western iconography. See Rizzardi, 1995.

190 Brenk, 1982, traces this feature to Jerome's prologue to the Vulgate translation of the Gospels, in which he says that Matthew wrote in Hebrew.

191 See Deichmann, 1976, pp. 174–7, and Brenk, 1982.

192 Brenk, 1982, p. 22.

193 Ibid., p. 23. For the fullest discussion of this tradition, see Maguire, 1987, pp. 27–8 and 77.

194 For a complete description of the condition of these mosaics and their restoration, see the articles in Iannucci, ed., 1992.

195 Andreescu-Treadgold, "The Mosaic Workshop," 1992, p. 33.

196 Maguire, 1987, p. 76, identifies hare, antelope, fawn, ram, goat, panthers, lion, dove, parrot, owl, cock, quail, swallow, duck, stork, and peacock, and notes that the variety of creatures is similar to that found on the similar ornamental panels on Maximian's throne.

197 Lehmann, 1945, p. 15, pointed out that the light and dark areas on each globe are different and interpreted this as an attempt to represent the changing cycles of time; Maguire, 1987, p. 77, suggests that they represent the Four Seasons.

198 Noted by Maguire, 1987, p. 78.

199 Montanari, 1996, and von Simson, 1948, pp. 31–3, but denied by Deichmann, 1976, pp. 159–60. Sörries, 1983, pp. 159–60, saw these depictions of Moses speaking to God as another element of anti-Arian theology.

200 See most recently Sörries, 1983, and Rizzardi, 1988.

201 Abramowski, 2001, pp. 300–2.

202 Montanari, "Elementi," 2002 (orig. 1969).

203 Abramowitz, 2002, pp. 292–3.

204 Heb. 1:3: "qui cum sit splendor gloriae et figura substantiae eius"; on Melchisedek as a type of Christ, Heb. 5–8. The idea that this epistle was rejected by Arians is found in Epiphanius of Salamis, *Panarion* 69.37.2, and Theodoret

of Cyrrhus, *Commentary on Hebrews*, preface (PG 82, 673), although Hanson, 1988, p. 561, notes that Epiphanius also says that the Arians read Heb. 3:1 as proof of their views; see also Schäferdiek, 2002. More work is needed on this interpretation.

205 Proposed by many scholars; see Deichmann, 1976, pp. 143–6, for the bibliography.

206 Deichmann, 1976, p. 143; and Montanari, 1992, p. 255.

207 MacCormack, 1981, p. 265.

208 See Grossmann, 1973; Deichmann, 1976, pp. 35–45; Effenberger, 1989; and most recently the comprehensive set of articles in Spadoni/Kniffitz, ed., 2007.

209 *LPR* ch. 77. See most comprehensively Saxer, 1985, esp. pp. 382–95; the best-known shrine was at Colossae/Chonai. At nearby Germia (properly in Galatia, but associated closely with the Phrygian shrines) veneration associated with healing had existed since the 460s; see Mango, "The Pilgrimage Centre," 1986. For discussion of various other interpretations of *Ad Frigiselo*, see Effenberger, 1989, pp. 20–1: the epithet has been interpreted as referring to a cold bath (*frigisculum*), to a region of the city inhabited by Phrygians, or as a version of *Africus* referring to a location near a watercourse (the latter by Arcamone, 2007, who notes that toponyms of the form *Affrico* are common in Tuscany; but she does not address the term *Ad Frigiselo* in the *LPR*).

210 Maioli, 2007, p. 228.

211 Andreescu-Treadgold, 1990 and 2007, tells the story.

212 Grossmann, 1973.

213 Porta, 2007, explains that the two columns were transferred to the facade of the church of the Saviour *ad Calchi* in 1878, while the capitals, one of mid–sixth-century Constantinopolitan design and the other a Corinthian "a lira" capital perhaps originally from St. Agatha in Ravenna, were sold privately and are now in the Museo Nazionale in Ravenna.

214 Grossmann, 1973; note that the church of St. Michael at Germia in Phrygia had an arcade of piers; see Mango, "The Pilgrimage Centre," 1986.

215 Brenk, 2007, pp. 212–14.

216 Brenk, 2007, pp. 209–10.

217 See the articles by Augenti, Vernia, and Lombardini in Spadoni/Kniffitz, eds., 2007.

218 Farioli Campanati, 2007, and Fiorentini Roncuzzi, 2007.

219 Martindale, 1980, pp. 207–8.

220 Deichmann, 1976, pp. 17–20, notes a distinction between the *dedicatio*, referred to here, and the *consecratio*, which required a bishop, as noted on the dedication inscriptions of San Vitale and Sant'Apollinare in Classe. But what, then, would be the point of setting up an inscription to commemorate the *dedicatio*?

221 Deichmann, 1976, pp. 7 and 15–16, says that they must have been cured of an illness since Michael was a famous healing saint, but does not link this illness with the recent plague epidemic.

222 See Rohland, 1977, pp. 75–103, esp. pp. 94–9; and Mango, "The Pilgrimage Centre," 1986, who notes, p. 125, that the church at Germia may have been rebuilt at the time of Justinian.

223 Procopius, *Buildings* I.3.14–18 and I.8.1–19; it is interesting that Procopius says that the first of these was small, and built by a senator – similar to the church in Ravenna. See also Saxer, 1985, pp. 402–15, who notes, p. 416, that the church

of St. Michael built by Justinian in Antioch had an attached hospice for the sick (Procopius, *Buildings*, II.10.25).

224 See Petrucci, 1971. For Rome, see *Liber pontificalis*, *Vita Symmachi* 9.

225 The plague at the time of Pope Gregory the Great is related by Gregory of Tours, *Historiae* 10.1; the plague is caused by serpents and a dragon, and Gregory organizes intercessionary processions from various churches, including Sts. Cosmas and Damian, but St. Michael is not mentioned, nor in the ninth-century *Vita* of Gregory by John the Deacon. The chapel of St. Michael on the Castel Sant'Angelo is described by the tenth-century historian Liudprand of Cremona (*Antapodosis* III.45). It seems that the first literary reference to such an event is in the thirteenth-century *Legenda Aurea* of Jacobus de Voragine, described in his section on St. Michael in Book 5. More research is needed on this topic.

226 Note that another church dedicated to St. Michael, San Michele in Acerboli at Santarcangelo di Romagna near Rimini, was closely linked architecturally to mid–sixth-century Ravenna; see Russo, "L'architettura," 2005, pp. 149–54.

227 See esp. Effenberger, 1989, pp. 31–6; Andreescu-Treadgold, 1990, and idem, 2007. More modifications may have been made at the time of the installation in 1904, and after the reproduction suffered from bomb damage in World War II; see Gramentieri, 2007.

228 A standing angel in the Hermitage in St. Petersburg is also a reproduction by Moro; see Andreescu-Treadgold, 2007, p. 113.

229 Andreescu-Treadgold, 1990 and 2007.

230 Ciampini, 1690–9; for reproductions of all the various sketches, watercolors, and drawings, see Effenberger, 1989.

231 For examples, see Andreescu-Treadgold, 2007, pp. 131–5.

232 In both the Berlin reproduction and the head of Christ in London, the clothing of Christ was restored as a blue tunic and red mantle; Andreescu-Treadgold, 2007, pp. 120–2; the lack of a halo on the London head is likewise modern.

233 "Qui vidit me vidit et patrem: ego et pater unum sumus."

234 Effenberger, 1989, p. 4, notes that the Probus-sarcophagus in St. Peter's, Rome, and the "Passio-sarcophagus" in the Vatican Museum, both from the fourth century, display the same iconography as the San Michele image of Christ.

235 Rizzardi, 2007, pp. 85–6.

236 Rizzardi, 2007, pp. 90–1.

237 See esp. Christe, 1996, pp. 83–4.

238 Effenberger, 1989, pp. 43–8; Sörries, 1983, pp. 226–43.

239 Effenberger, 1989, pp. 48 and 60–4. Deichmann, 1976, pp. 40–3, interprets the scene in more general eschatological terms.

240 Deichmann, 1976, p. 43, suggests that relics of these saints were found in the church.

241 Horden, 1992; in Gregory of Tours, *Histories* 10.1, it is a dragon in the river Tiber that is said to have caused the plague at Rome in 590; this may be one of the origins of the linkage of St. Michael with this event, as was Gregory the Great's own interest in angels, seen in his *Hom. in Evang.* II.34.

242 They are the earliest surviving example of this particular part of the Book of Revelation; see Kinney, 1992, p. 208.

243 Deichmann, 1976, pp. 372–4.

244 *LPR* chs. 72–3.

245 Venantius Fortunatus, *Vita S. Martini* 4.680–98.

246 See Deichmann, 1976, pp. 333–4; parts of the church still survive, in smaller form, probably mostly medieval material, but a fragment of a nave arcade shows it was a basilica.

247 Marini no. 80 = Tjädcr no. 8; *LPR* ch. 70. See Deichmann, 1976, p. 374.

248 Mazzotti, 1959. The church, later attached to a monastery, was in use until 1798; by 1810 it was partially demolished and shortly afterward some excavations were done.

249 *LPR* ch. 76.

250 Manzelli, *Ravenna*, 2000, pp. 86–91; Deichmann, 1976, p. 306.

251 Deichmann, 1976, p. 305, however, rejects this interpretation.

252 Ibid., p. 306.

253 See Righini, 1991, p. 205, who suggests that wooden construction was more prevalent in Ravenna than surviving remains indicate. The reference to "nut trees" (*ligneae de nucibus*) may have come from an inscription.

254 *LPR* chs. 84 and 92. The stone slab with Agnellus's epitaph (reported in the *LPR*) was later used as a paving stone in the rebuilt Ursiana, with some damage to its right side (*CIL* 11, 1, 305); this is the only inscription that we can compare with the *LPR*'s text.

255 See Smith, "Form and Function," 1990, pp. 183–4; and Russo, "L'architettura," 2005, pp. 170–5, who claims that the use of filled *tubi fittili* indicates that the masters of the works did not understand the Ravennate tradition of hollow *tubi*, and thus filled them with mortar to make them more similar to their accustomed brick.

256 Russo, 1989, pp. 233–4.

257 The drawing by Cesare Ponti was published in Giovanni Ciampini, *Vetera monimenta* 1 (1690), pp. 184ff., as table 46; also published in Deichmann, 1976, ill. 167.

258 Deichmann, 1976, pp. 293–4.

259 *LPR* ch. 44; since the apse was rebuilt in the sixth century, the portrait of John I probably dates to this period.

260 *LPR* ch. 91.

261 *LPR* ch. 26.

262 Deichmann, 1976, pp. 318–21.

263 Greg. Mag. *Reg. epist.* 5.28 and 8.15; *LPR* 131.

264 In the tenth century all these remains were translated to the Ursiana; see Deichmann, 1976, p. 359.

265 *LPR* chs. 3, 6, 8, 9, 10, 12 (Probus), and chs. 4, 5, 7 (Eleuchadius); documents from 1037 and 1138, see Deichmann, 1976, p. 323.

266 Its dedicatory inscription reads, "Ad honorem D(omini) J(e)h(s)u XRI et s(an)c(t)i Eleuchadii sub temp(ore) Dom(ini) Valerii Archiep(iscopi) ego Petrus presb(yter) fecit"; thus it was made ca. 789–810.

267 Cortesi, 1982, p. 71.

268 *LPR* chs. 8 and 97. See Deichmann, 1976, pp. 355–9, who thought that the churches were built in the fourth century.

269 *LPR* chs. 97 and 77. Deichmann, 1976, p. 323.

270 Cortesi, 1970.

271 Cortesi, 1982, pp. 75–7.

272 Augenti, "Archeologia," 2005, pp. 246–7.

273 *LPR* ch. 8.

274 Testi-Rasponi, 1924, pp. 36–7 n. 14; Gerola, 1916.

275 Deichmann, 1976, pp. 357–9, who, however, suggests that the cemeterial basilica was built in the fourth century. This seems very unlikely, given Ravenna's relatively unimportant status at that time.

276 Mazzotti, 1954, is a beautifully written account of the history of the church; also idem, 1986; Deichmann, 1976, pp. 233–80; Michael, 2005.

277 Petrus Chrysologus, *Sermones* 128.

278 Deichmann, 1976, pp. 233–4, argues that the small chamber over the tomb was only built up in the mid–eighth century, based on a fragmentary reference in the *LPR* ch. 159, which says either that Bishop Sergius built a "*cella* on the men's side of St. Apollinaris" or a "*cella* of St. Apollinaris on the men's side" of a church whose name is missing; the latter, however, is more likely, see Deliyannis, trans., 2004, p. 285 n. 13. Moreover, Peter Chrysologus knew the location of the tomb, and it is hardly likely that it would not have been commemorated somehow, even if traces no longer survive.

279 For the date, see above, Chapter 2.

280 Deichmann, 1976, p. 234, argues that the body of the church was built after the dedication of San Vitale in 547, thus in under two years, because he feels that 15 years from the initiation of the work under Ursicinus is too long. Even more than in the case of San Vitale, when we consider the events of those 15 years (534–49), we can easily imagine that construction work frequently started and stopped.

281 *Sermo* 128.

282 Cf. Dinkler, 1964, pp. 15–16.

283 The debate over the date of the *Passio* is summarized in Deliyannis, 2006, pp. 39–40 n. 70. Some legends must have existed at the time of the construction of Sant'Apollinare in Classe, yet the early bishops of Ravenna listed in the *Passio* are different from those known to Maximian (see Deliyannis, ibid., pp. 41–2); therefore, the *Passio* must have been written at least after the mid–sixth century. Agnellus tells us (*LPR* ch. 114) that silver plates inscribed with Apollinaris's story (*historia*) were placed in his tomb by Archbishop Maurus in the mid–seventh century, and when Apollinaris's body was again translated in 1173, two silver plates were "discovered" with text written on them containing several phrases that correspond exactly to those used by Agnellus. (See Testi-Rasponi, 1909–10, pp. 257–9, for a detailed comparison between Agnellus's Life of Apollinaris and the supposed text of the tablets. The text is contained in the twelfth-century account entitled *De inventione corporis beati Apollinaris martyris* [*RIS* I.2, pp. 538–46] and reprinted in Deliyannis, 2006, p. 40 n. 72.) However, it is likely that whatever sheets Agnellus saw were lost in the ninth-century sack of the shrine, and thus the surviving silver tablets may have been replaced after this time, in the context of the twelfth-century argument over the relics, with a text based on Agnellus's account! (Mazzotti, 1954, p. 231).

284 See esp. Mazzotti, 1954, pp. 78–161.

285 *LPR* ch. 98; Deichmann, 1976, pp. 340–1. Mazzotti, 1954, pp. 78–81, notes that this was its location according to sixteenth-century sources (Rossi, 1572).

286 *LPR* ch. 114, 115.

287 On the date of the crypt, see Deichmann, 1976, p. 235, who believes that the crypt was built in imitation of, and soon after, the crypt in St. Peter's in Rome,

constructed by Pope Gregory I in the 590s. Others, however, have proposed that Maurus built the crypt when he moved the body or that it was built in the late ninth century (Mazzotti, 1954, pp. 142–53). The most recent excavations in the area suggest that it was built between the ninth and the twelfth centuries; Iannucci, 1982, pp. 202–3, accepts Mazzotti's date.

288 *LPR* ch. 168; *Liber pontificalis, Vita Leonis III* ch. 106. It has been suggested that the church was damaged in the earthquake that Agnellus reports as having taken place between 726–44 (*LPR* chs. 89, 151), which destroyed the Petriana and damaged Sant'Apollinare Nuovo; the latter was repaired fairly quickly, but the former never recovered, and thus it is possible that Sant'Apollinare in Classe, too, remained in poor condition until the early ninth century. Mazzotti, 1954, pp. 229–30, on the other hand, proposes that Classe was sacked by Muslim raiders early in the ninth century, which is what led to the restoration.

289 As Mazzotti, 1954, pp. 224–6, notes, this information comes only from the twelfth century, when both the monks of Sant'Apollinare Nuovo and those of Sant'Apollinare in Classe claimed that the relics were in their church (the date of 858 is first attested by Rossi, 1572); the dispute was finally mediated by a papal legate and the archbishop, who in 1173 "found" the relics under the altar in Classe, which is documented in a text known as the *Tractatus . . . de inventione corporis beatissimi Apolenaris* (*RIS* I.2, pp. 536–8), while the monks of the church in Ravenna composed their own text, *Historia translationis beati Apollinaris, quae celebratur XVII Kalendas Augusti* (*RIS* I.2, pp. 533–6). Mazzotti proposes that some of the relics were taken to Ravenna, while the remainder were buried beneath the altar.

290 Pavan, 1978; Iannucci, 1982; Iannucci, 1986.

291 Russo, "L'architettura," 2005, p. 144.

292 Deichmann, 1976, p. 238, remarks that the reconstruction of the narthex was entirely arbitrary and not based on any evidence about its form.

293 Mazzotti, 1986.

294 Only the contemporary San Vitale had so many doors directly to the outside.

295 Smith, "Form and Function," 1990, p. 199, who notes that the rooms were so secret that their existence was not rediscovered until 1877!

296 Deichmann, 1976, p. 240. Russo, however ("L'architettura," 2005, pp. 135–40), finds many similarities between this church and various examples in the eastern Mediterranean, which he says is evidence that, like San Vitale, this church was designed by an "eastern architect," whatever that might mean.

297 Mazzotti, 1954, p. 127–35, provides an extremely detailed study of the masonry.

298 Deichmann, 1976, pp. 238–9. Blocks of red marble, *rosso di Verona*, are placed under the Proconnesian marble bases of the columns, and different masonry in the upper levels of the window zone, originally led Mazzotti (1954, pp. 135–42) to suggest that at some point the entire nave arcade had been raised, as in Sant'Apollinare Nuovo. Mazzotti subsequently revised that opinion and decided that the nave colonnade had never been raised, and that the upper walls were original, see Deichmann, 1976, p. 238; and Mazzotti, 1986.

299 *LPR* ch. 114; Deichmann, 1976, p. 244.

300 *LPR* ch. 63.

301 Betsch, 1977, p. 223.

302 Mazzotti, 1954, pp. 189–215.

303 Mazzotti, 1954, pp. 108–9; Deichmann, 1976, pp. 239–40.

304 On the restorations, see Mazzotti, 1954, pp. 183–8: various modifications were made in the eighteenth century; the triumphal arch was restored in 1883 (by Pietro de Vecchis and then Carlo Novelli), and additional parts of the arch as well as large sections of the apse in 1906–11 (by Giuseppe Zampiga); in 1948–9 and 1970–2 sections of the mosaics were removed and reset under the supervision of Mazzotti, and further examinations were made in the 1980s; see Iannucci, 1986.

305 See Bovini, "Les 'Sinopie'" and "Qualche note," 1974; and Mazzotti, 1954, p. 173.

306 Mazzotti, 1954, pp. 176–83, esp. p. 178 (ninth century); and Deichmann, 1976, p. 246 (seventh century).

307 Isa. 6:3.

308 Much restored in 1906–7, but enough pieces survived from each to reconstruct both of them, assuming that they were identical (and that the text on their banners was the same).

309 The number 99 is assumed to have some significance, but it is subject to many interpretations; see Deichmann, 1976, pp. 256–7, who says that in Greek the letters of the word "amen" (ἀμήν) add up to 99, rejecting Dinkler's (1964, p. 64) thesis that 99 represents the number of angels, while Michael, 2005, pp. 177–8 and 187–9, is inclined to accept and expand on Dinkler's idea.

310 Mazzotti, 1954, p. 173, says that the head is original; however, Andreescu-Treadgold, 1994, reports that the tonsures of Ecclesius and the deacons in San Vitale date to the twelfth century, and one wonders here whether similar modifications have been undertaken. The lower edge of Apollinaris's chasuble was modified at some point (Mazzotti's diagram reports in the seventh century) and then restored; it is possible that a dalmatic was added to Apollinaris's costume.

311 von Simson, 1948, p. 54, points out that this pose is the same as the one reported by Agnellus for the mosaic of Peter Chrysologus in San Giovanni Evangelista (*LPR* ch. 27, "extensis manibus quasi missas canit"); he uses the same expressions for the images of Archbishop Agnellus in the Ursiana (*LPR* ch. 89, "in qua sua effigies manibus expansis orat"), and for other bishops in liturgical contexts (*LPR* chs. 37 and 52); see Michael, 2005, pp. 58–9.

312 Montanari, "L'abside," 1982 (reprint 2002), p. 219, suggests that the different patterns on these sheep's coats (those on the left are curly, those on the right are plain) correspond to the men's and women's sides of the church and that the number 12 can refer to the twelve tribes of Israel, thus the entire people of Ravenna.

313 Peter Chrysologus, *Sermones* 128; *LPR* chs. 121–2 (see Pizarro, 1995, pp. 52–60, on the metaphors of the shepherd in this story).

314 Mazzotti, 1954, p. 177.

315 See Bovini, "Les 'sinopie'" and "Qualche nota," 1974.

316 Bovini, "Qualche nota," 1974, pp. 100–6.

317 It is possible that originally Ursicinus and Apollinaris, perhaps presented by angels as in San Vitale, would have flanked the cross in the upper part of the apse; Abramowski, 2001, pp. 304–5, notes that the new program gave greater prominence to Apollinaris alone.

318 Another, installed also in the mid–sixth century, is reported for the apse of the cathedral at Naples.

319 Deichmann, 1976, pp. 248–51; and Michael, 2005, pp. 63–71; only a very few fragmentary images might possibly depict the Transfiguration in some other way.

320 See esp. Grabar, 1958.

321 As noted by Fox, 1995.

322 For example, Dinkler, 1964, p. 76.

323 See the excellent summary in Michael, 2005, pp. 13–22. Major studies include Grabar, 1946; von Simson, 1948, pp. 40–62; Nordström, 1953; Dinkler, 1964; Pincherle, 1966, and idem, 1976; Müller, 1980; Deichmann, 1969, pp. 261–77, and idem, 1976, pp. 246–80; Montanari, "L'abside," 2002 (orig. 1982); and Abramowski, 2001.

324 von Simson, 1948 (who, along with Grabar, 1946, links this to the supposed martyrdom of Apollinaris, which cannot be sustained given that Apollinaris was not thought to have been a martyr); Dinkler, 1964; Deichmann, 1976, p. 253; and Michael, 2005, who has recently pointed out that all the images are referred to in the liturgy, which thus links them together as a theophany made possible during the liturgy's enactment.

325 Rizzardi, 2007, p. 87.

326 Abramowski, 2001, pp. 309–13.

327 On these mosaics, see esp. Iannucci, 1986.

328 Caillet, 2003, pp. 27–8, citing Dinkler, 1964, p. 75.

329 Deichmann, 1976, p. 262, proposes that it was Ecclesius who "found" the tomb of Apollinaris, but this is purely hypothetical.

330 On the theories for the dates, see Iannucci, 1986, pp. 176–80.

331 Demus, 1969, suggests that an image of Abraham, as at San Vitale, was originally found in the left panel here, but when the Reparatus mosaic was inserted, Abraham and Isaac were moved to the right panel, which was remade with Melchisedek now in the center, larger than the others.

332 Iannucci, 1986, pp. 183–8.

333 *LPR* ch. 115: "Is igitur socius meritis Reparatus ut esset, / Aula nouos habitus fecit, flagrare per aeuum" and "Constantinus maior imperator, Eraclii et Tiberii imperator."

334 See Deliyannis, trans., 2004, pp. 54–6.

335 Deichmann, 1976, pp. 273–80. The bishop shown between the emperor and Reparatus would be Maurus, while the other three people to the left of Constans would be his three sons, Constantine IV, Heraclius, and Tiberius. Deichmann reconstructs the original inscription as reading, "Constantinus maior imperator, [pater Constantini, H]eraclii et Tiberii imperator[um]." This explains why, in the quotation by Agnellus, the names of Heraclius and Tiberius are in the genitive. Equally, as Deichmann also notes, the inscription could be reconstructed "Constantinus maior imperator, [frater H]eraclii et Tiberii imperator[um]."

336 See the diagram in Iannucci, 1986, p. 182; only parts of the altar, Melchisedec's upper face and right shoulder, the shoulders of Abel and Abraham, and the tops of the columns and curtains are original.

337 Demus, 1969, although he argues that major modifications were made; contradicted by Schrenk, 1995, pp. 63–9; and before him, Deichmann, 1976, p. 246, argues that the entire panel dates to the seventh century.

338 Ps. 110:4 and Heb. 5–7.

339 The major publications on this church and archaeological site are Bermond Montanari, 1968; Deichmann, 1976, pp. 361–71; Maioli, 1992; and Augenti, "Ravenna e Classe: il racconto," 2006, pp. 51–6. On the cult of Severus, see Lanzoni, 1910–11 and 1911–12; and Deliyannis, trans., 2004, p. 111 n. 4.

340 *LPR* chs. 93 and 98. Rossi, *Historiarum Ravennatium*, p. 178, reports a dedicatory poem not mentioned by Agnellus, which gives a dedication date of 575; see Deichmann, 1976, p. 361.

341 Maioli, 1992, p. 498.

342 See esp. Novara, 1990, and idem, "Materiali medievali," 1997.

343 Maioli, 1992, pp. 502–11.

344 *LPR* ch. 98. Rufillo was a bishop of Forlimpopoli who lived in the fourth century and attended the Council of Rimini in 359; we do not know why his cult should have come to Ravenna by the ninth century, although as a contemporary of Severus his cult here is understandable.

345 Originally Bovini, 1975; new data obtained from excavations conducted in 2007, as yet unpublished; information taken from *Ravenna e Dintorni*, 8 October 2007 (http://www.ravennaedintorni.it/leggi.php?leggi_articolo=1191833597).

346 Maioli, 1992, p. 511.

347 Bermond Montanari, 1968, pp. 19–20.

348 Bermond Montanari, 1968, notes that a *bema* of this size and shape is not known from any other Ravennate church, although similar examples are found in S. Tecla in Milan (fourth–fifth c.) and S. Eufemia in Grado (sixth c.).

349 See Bermond Montanari, 1968, pp. 35–61.

Seven. Ravenna Capital, AD 600–850

1 Cf. Augenti, "Ravenna e Classe: archeologia," 2006, p. 213.

2 Deliyannis, "About," 2008.

3 The fire in *LPR* ch. 134. For a list of documents, see Cavarra et al., 1991.

4 Staatsbibliothek, Munich, Clm 44; see Vasina, ed., 1985.

5 For a detailed summary of the politics of the exarchate in the eighth and ninth centuries, see Ferluga, "L'esarcato," 1991, pp. 361–73; for the papal point of view, see Noble, 1984.

6 *HL* IV.28.

7 Patitucci Uggeri, 2005, pp. 325–6.

8 McCormick, 2001, pp. 67–74, 108–14.

9 Ferluga, "L'esarcato," 1991, p. 362, sees it as a sign of regionalism.

10 *LP Vita Deusdedit* ch. 2.

11 *LPR* ch. 106 says Eleutherius "imperii iura suscepit," a phrase he copies from *HL* 4.34. The events are also recounted in *LP Vita Deusdedit* ch. 2 and *Vita Bonifatii V* ch. 2, where it says only that he "adsumpsit regnum." The chronicle known as the *Auctarii Havniensis Extrema* ch. 25 (MGH AA 9, p. 339) gives the most extended version, and says that one John (the archbishop of Ravenna?) told Eleutherius that he had to go to Rome to be crowned, since that was "Ubi imperii solium maneret." See T. Brown, 1979, pp. 15–16.

12 On the sarcophagus, see Deichmann, 1989, p. 335; and Angiolini Martinelli, ed., 1997, pp. 177–9.

13 *LP Vita Severini* chs. 1–5, and *Vita Theodori* chs. 1–2; the text puts the blame on Mauricius, and says that he induced Isaac to the crimes.
14 *LP Vita Martini*, chs. 4–8.
15 The story is told in *LP Vita Vitaliani*, chs. 2–4.
16 T. Brown, 1979, p. 25.
17 *LP Vita Sergii*, chs. 7–9, and *Vita Johannis VI* chs. 1–2; see Noble, 1984, pp. 17–18.
18 See Guillou, 1969; Wickberg, 1978; Noble, 1984; and Brown, 2005.
19 On Justinian II, see Head, 1972.
20 *LPR* chs. 137–43; Agnellus says that his great-great-grandfather Iohannicis was one of the victims. Brown, 2005, p. 323, proposes that the retribution was for Felix's snub of the pope, rather than, as Agnellus (and Guillou, 1969, pp. 211–18) suggests, for the Ravennate army's support of Pope Sergius or the leader's support of Justinian's deposition, but the punishment seems rather extreme.
21 *LP Vita Constantini* ch. 4. For all these events, see Noble, 1984, pp. 19–22; Brown, 2005, p. 323.
22 *LPR* ch. 142; Theophanes, *Chronographia*, A.M. 6203.
23 On Faroald, *HL* VI.44; Liutprand, *HL* VI.49: "Classem invasit atque destruxit"; *LP Vita Gregorii II* ch. 13; Noble, 1984, p. 25, conflates the second and third reports as describing the event of 717, and says that Liutprand took Classe from Faroald, although that is not what the text says.
24 *LP Vita Gregorii II* chs. 15–18, which accuses Paul of engineering several plots against the pope's life. Schreiner, 1988, proposed that the tax issue was more important, while Carile, 1986, pp. 387–8, argues that the rhetoric, at least, was based on theological issues. According to the *LP Vita Gregorii* ch. 17, some of the Italian rebels wanted to elect an emperor and take him to Constantinople, but Pope Gregory II rejected this idea; most scholars assume that such an emperor would have been based at Ravenna, and thus a threat to papal authority, although there is no evidence for this; see Noble, 1984, p. 32.
25 Noble, 1984, esp. p. 40.
26 *LP Vita Gregorii II* chs. 19–23, and Theophanes, *Chronographia*, A.M. 6224.
27 *HL* VI.54; John the Deacon, *Chronicon Venetum et Gradense* (*MGH SS* 7, p. 12), citing a letter written by Pope Gregory III to the patriarch of Grado. On the chronology, see Noble, 1984, pp. 41–2.
28 Both of these sieges took place during the episcopate of John V; Agnellus (*LPR* ch. 151) conflates the taking of Classe (based on an erroneous reading of *HL* VI.49, the event of 718) and the exile of the bishop, but does not mention the role of the Lombards. Agnellus also describes (ch. 153) a failed attack on Ravenna by a Byzantine army; this event is not known from other sources, but clearly there were many occasions in this period when such an attack was reasonable. At the least, the story displays Agnellus's hostility to the Byzantines. The more detailed version of the events of 743 is found in *LP Vita Zachariae* chs. 12–16.
29 These events are not mentioned in the Roman *LP*, only the aftermath, once Aistulf was ensconced in Ravenna (*Vita Stephani II* ch. 8). Brown, 1984, p. 151, mentions the possibility that the former exarch Eutychius may still have retained authority, or at least prestige, in 801.
30 The main studies are Simonini, 1969; Guillou, 1969; and T. Brown, 1979.

31 T. Brown, 1979, pp. 13–15, notes that an oratory in the atrium of St. Peter's in Rome was dedicated to St. Apollinaris in the 620s (*LP Vita Honorii* chs. 3–4), a sign of acceptance of Ravenna's claims at that time. As for the Diploma of Valentinian III, most scholars accept a date in the mid–seventh century (see Deliyannis, ed., 2006, pp. 102–3), although Orioli, 1980, pp. 135–44, provides reasons that it should be dated to the *pallium* controversy at the end of the sixth century, including the fact that the city of Brisillium (Brescello; Brintum in the *LPR*) listed as a suffragan church was destroyed in 603.

32 *LPR* ch. 110; Agnellus apparently did not know that Constans was in Italy at the time, as he refers to both Maurus and the pope sending messages to Constantinople. The privilege of Constans II regarding the autocephaly of the Ravennate church was given to Maurus on 1 March 666; it is published in *RIS* 2.1, p. 146.

33 This is how the account is described in *LPR* chs. 110 and 112; see also *LP Vita Leonis II*, ch. 4, in which the pope's action happened after autocephaly had been revoked; T. Brown, 1979, pp. 11–13.

34 *LPR* ch. 115. Deichmann, 1976, pp. 273–80, as we have seen in Chapter 6, suggested instead that the scene depicted the grant of autocephaly, but this is merely hypothetical. T. Brown, 1979, p. 23, notes that communication with Constantinople was particularly difficult during Reparatus's reign (673–8) because of Arab attacks on the capital, and thus it is more likely that he was sent as Maurus's envoy before 673.

35 *LP Vita Doni* ch. 2.

36 See Deliyannis, "About," 2008.

37 *LP Vita Agathonis* ch. 1 and *Vita Leonis II* ch. 4.

38 *LPR* chs. 137–45; *LP Vita Constantini* ch. 2. On the divergent points of view, see Deliyannis, "About," 2008.

39 *LP Vita Zachariae* chs. 9, 12–17.

40 Noble, 1984, pp. 53–5.

41 *LP Vita Gregorii III* ch. 3, and *Vita Stephani III* chs. 17 and 23; see Deliyannis, 1996, pp. 563–4.

42 On this period, see, in addition to Noble, 1984, also Savigni, 1992.

43 *LPR* ch. 159, which says that later in life, Sergius felt deceived by the Lombards and instead made an alliance with the Venetians; see also Brown, 2005, p. 327.

44 *LP Vita Stephani II*, ch. 47.

45 For a complete discussion, see Noble, 1984, pp. 104–6.

46 *LPR* ch. 159; one of them was Agnellus's great-grandfather; this may be a reference to the hostage taking mentioned in the *LP*. Agnellus gets his popes very mixed up here; see Deliyannis, "About," 2008.

47 *LP Vita Stephani III*, chs. 25–6; on Leo's subsequent relations with the popes, see *LP Vita Hadriani I*, chs. 7, 14–17.

48 Noble, 1984, pp. 171–2.

49 *Codex Carolinus* 49, 53, 54, and 55; see Noble, 1984, pp. 142 and 169–70.

50 *Codex Carolinus* 75; see Noble, 1984, pp. 170–1.

51 *Codex Carolinus* 85; see Savigni, 1992, p. 304; and Deliyannis, ed., 2006, pp. 113–14.

52 *LPR* chs. 167 and 169–70.

53 Cited by Brown, 1990, p. 304. The biography of Petronax is missing from the *LPR*, but there is reason to think that Agnellus did not approve of his actions; see Deliyannis, ed., 2006, p. 16.

54 *LPR* cc. 171–5. Agnellus might even have approved of these actions, had he not hated George for personal reasons. For a comprehensive account of Ravenna's relationship with Rome and the Frankish kings in the early ninth century, see Brown, 1990.

55 See esp. Diehl, 1959; Guillou, 1969; Brown, 1984; and Carile, 1992.

56 Miller, 2000, pp. 56–61.

57 Brown/Christie, 1989.

58 Brown, 1984, pp. 77–80.

59 Brown, 1984, pp. 16–18 and 93; Ausbüttel, 1987; Carile, 1992, p. 383; and Cecconi, 2006; cf. Wickham, 2005, pp. 596–602.

60 Carile, 1992, p. 382. After 751 Ravennate leaders mentioned in the Roman *Liber pontificalis* have the titles *consul* and *tribunus*; see Brown, 1984, pp. 126–43.

61 *LPR* ch. 140; see esp. Brown, 1984, pp. 89–90 and 97–8, who cautions, p. 84, that numbers of troops in Byzantine Italy or in Ravenna at this time cannot be established with certainty.

62 T. Brown, 1979, pp. 9–10; for an extended example, see *LPR* chs. 121–3 and 131–2.

63 T. Brown, 1979, pp. 199–200; the choice of 29 years was because of laws that said if a farmer farmed the same piece of land for 30 years, he could be considered bound to it.

64 Fasoli, "Sul Patrimonio" and "Il dominio," 1979, and idem, 1991.

65 *LPR* ch. 111.

66 T. Brown, 1979, pp. 17–19.

67 On Agnellus, see Deliyannis, trans., 2004, pp. 6–19.

68 Patitucci Uggeri, 2005, pp. 258–9.

69 Fabbri, 2004, pp. 47–8; since this part of the city is now under the Venetian fortress known as the Rocca Brancaleone, its development is not well understood.

70 Fabbri, 2004, p. 49.

71 Fabbri, 1991, p. 19.

72 Maioli/Stoppioni, 1987, say it was largely uninhabited, but Cirelli, 2008, p. 138, chooses instead the word "transformed"; for more recent excavation results from the Podere Chiavichetta site, see Augenti, "Nuove indagini," 2005, pp. 237–44.

73 *HL* 6.49; cf. *LPR* ch. 151.

74 *LPR* chs. 89, 151, and 155.

75 For example, Bavant, 1989; Gelichi, 1991; Ortalli, 1991; Maioli/Stoppioni, 1987. Cirelli, 2008, pp. 130–40 and 163–5, notes that trade with North Africa and the eastern Mediterranean continued until the late eighth century, but the volume declined and there was an increase in pottery made in the Adriatic region; after 700 the archaeological material is too scanty to say what was happening.

76 Ward-Perkins, 1996. On the causes of the decline, Wickham, 2005, pp. 609–92, 708–20, and 728–41, favors the invasions, while McCormick, 2001, pp. 38–41, also admits the impact of the plague.

77 Arslan, 2005, p. 227.

78 Augenti, "Nuove indagini," 2005.

79 Brown, 1984, pp. 214–15.

80 Antiolini Martinelli, 1992, pp. 162–3; on the ambo, see Deichmann, 1976, p. 307.

81 Agnellus of Ravenna, 1981; Cavarra, 1993.

82 *LPR* ch. 114; for the sources, see Deliyannis, ed., 2006, pp. 285 and 371 n. 94. Damian's poetic epitaph, *LPR* ch. 134, is a direct copy of that of Marinian, ch. 103.

83 *Ravennatis anonymi cosmographia*, ed. J. Schnetz, *Itineraria Romana* 2 (Leipzig, 1940); on this text, see Staab, 1976; and Dillemann/Janvier, 1997. The anonymous geographer quotes many Greek, Roman, and Gothic "philosophers," showing that he was well educated. This text certainly shows that there was still urban consciousness in the seventh century; does the fact that Ravenna is singled out in company with four of the patriarchal cities (replacing Jerusalem) indicate anything about the author's ecclesiastical ideas?

84 *LPR* ch. 150.

85 Guillou (1991, p. 104) argues that through the seventh century up to 50 percent of the population was Greek, and Carile (1992, p. 385) provides scattered information from throughout the Byzantine territories of individuals identified as of Eastern origin, including several popes, but Brown (1991, p. 141) notes that deducing ethnicity from names is hazardous, and that the number of documents is so small that it is not convincing to generalize from them. On officials from the East in exarchal government, see Brown, 1984, pp. 64–9. Sansterre (1992) likewise doubts that there were many, if any, Greek monks in Ravenna. Agnellus proudly tells the story of his great-great-grandfather Iohannicis, who in the late seventh century was noted for his unusual ability to speak both Greek and Latin (*LPR* ch. 120).

86 *LPR* chs. 126–9; see Brown, 1998.

87 Augenti, "Ravenna e Classe: archeologia," 2006, pp. 196–200.

88 Gelichi, 2000: "anche Ravenna si ruralizza"; see also Christie, 2006, pp. 249–52. Brown/Christie, 1989, argue that Ravenna and other cities in the Pentapolis always retained more of their urban character than those in the Lombard areas.

89 Cosentino, 2005, p. 411; this is based on an analysis of *LPR* ch. 140, which is hardly a reliable source for population figures.

90 See esp. Bavant, 1989; Ortalli, 1991; Gelichi, "L'edilizia," 1994; Gelichi, 1996; and Galetti, 2005.

91 Bavant, 1989.

92 Baldini Lippolis, "Periodo byzantino," 2004.

93 Bavant, 1989, identifies seven documents before 751; Gelichi, 1996, p. 70, cites papyri in Tjäder II. 38–41.

94 Gelichi, 2002.

95 Montevecchi, ed., 2004, esp. articles by Negrelli and Librenti; Augenti, "Ravenna e Classe: archeologia," 2006, pp. 194–5; Christie, 2006, pp. 233–5. Bavant, 1989, notes that burials appear within the walls of Rome in the seventh century, as in Ravenna, which, according to Brogiolo/Gelichi 1998, pp. 95–101, is a sign of continuing habitation with change in priorities, rather than abandonment.

96 Augenti, "Archeologia," 2005, p. 23.

97 Augenti, "Ravenna e Classe: archeologia," 2006, pp. 191–3.

98 Rusconi, 1971; Porta, 1991, pp. 278–80, discusses previous interpretations of this building as a secular structure attached to the palace.

99 Deichmann, 1976, p. 355, suggested that it was built in the late fifth century, but given F. Lifshitz's revised dating of the *Martyrologium* to the 620s in Luxeuil (Lifshitz, 2005), it seems more likely to have been a Byzantine-era construction (note that the legend of Polyeuktos was known to Gregory of Tours, *Liber in Gloria Martyrum* 102, in the 580s).

100 Deichmann, 1976, pp. 341–2, notes that the empress Pulcheria founded the original church in Constantinople in 450, Justinian rebuilt it, its icon saved the city from the Avar siege in 626, and the cult subsequently became very popular.

101 Deichmann, 1976, p. 318.

102 Ibid., p. 308.

103 Ibid., p. 349, notes that it stood until the thirteenth century.

104 Ibid., p. 374.

105 Ibid., p. 304; probably destroyed already in fourteenth century.

106 Ibid., p. 331; Tjäder, ed., 1954, no. 23.

107 Deichmann, 1976, p. 304.

108 Ibid., p. 323, notes that Donatus was the patron saint of Epirus across the Adriatic.

109 Ibid., p. 324.

110 The church dedicated to St. Euphemia in the eighteenth century was located in the west part of the *oppidum*; Baldini Lippolis, "La chiesa," 2004, suggests that it was just north of the excavation in Via D'Azeglio.

111 Kostof, 1965, pp. 19–20 and 142; now found in the southwestern absidiole, the cross has incised on it the following inscription: "De donis Dei et S(an)c(t)e Marie Felex et Stefanus optulerunt temporibus D(om)n(o) Theodoro Apostolicum," usually assumed as referring to Archbishop Theodore, r. 677–91.

112 Mathews, 1962, pp. 75–89.

113 Miller, 1991–2, p. 162, and idem, 2000, p. 57; Marzetti, 2002.

114 *LPR* ch. 164; Ricci, 1919; and Marzetti, 2002.

115 Miller, 2000, p. 57.

116 See Bertelli, 1999.

117 See Brown, "Romanitas," 1986.

118 *LPR* chs. 14, 37, 70, 101, 126–8, 151–3, 158, and 166.

119 Pizarro, 1998.

120 Ward-Perkins, 1984.

121 Respectively, *LPR* chs. 39, 70, and 1.

122 One other later source mentions marble columns from Ravenna being used at Ingelheim; the late ninth-century poet Saxo states, "To which he ordered marble columns from Rome, he gave noble ones from beautiful Ravenna." Saxo Poeta, *Annalium de gestis Caroli Magni*, 5.439–40.

123 Einhard, *Vita Karoli Magni*, ca. 26.

124 *Codex Carolinus* 81.

125 See Deliyannis, 2003.

126 *LPR* ch. 94.

127 Walahfrid Strabo, *Versus in Aquisgrani Palatio. . . . De imagine tetrici*. On the discussion about the statue, see Deliyannis, trans., 2004, pp. 78–9.

128 *LPR* ch. 113.

129 *HL* II.19; Saxo Poeta, *Annalium de gestis Caroli magni*, 5.439–40.

REFERENCES

Abramowski, Luise. 2001. "Die Mosaiken von S. Vitale und S. Apollinare in Classe und die Kirchenpolitik Kaiser Justinians." *Zeitschrift für Antikes Christentum* 5: 289–341.

Albu, Emily. 2005. "Imperial Geography and the Medieval Peutinger Map." *Imago Mundi* 57: 136–148.

Amory, Patrick. 1997. *People and Identity in Ostrogothic Italy, 489–554*. Cambridge: Cambridge University Press.

Andreescu-Treadgold, Irina. 1990. "The Wall Mosaics of San Michele in Africisco, Ravenna, Rediscovered." *CARB* 37: 13–57.

———. 1992. "The Mosaic Workshop at San Vitale." In *Mosaici a S. Vitale e altri restauri: il restauro in situ di mosaici parietali. Atti del Convegno nazionale sul restauro in situ di mosaici parietali, Ravenna 1–3 ottobre 1990*, ed. Anna Maria Iannucci: 31–41. Ravenna: Longo.

———. 1994. "The Emperor's New Crown and St. Vitalis' New Clothes." *CARB* 41: 149–186.

———. 2007. "I mosaici antichi e quelli ottocenteschi di San Michele in Africisco: lo studio filologico." In *San Michele in Africisco e l'età giustinianea a Ravenna: atti del Convegno "La diaspora dell'arcangelo, San Michele in Africisco e l'età giustinianea": Giornate di studio in memoria di Giuseppe Bovini, Ravenna, Sala dei mosaici, 21–22 aprile 2005*, ed. Claudio Spadoni: 113–150. Milan: Silvana.

Andreescu-Treadgold, Irina and Warren Treadgold. 1997. "Procopius and the Imperial Panels of S. Vitale." *Art Bulletin* 79: 708–723.

Angiolini Martinelli, Patrizia. 1968. *Altari, amboni, cibori, cornici, plutei con figure di animali e con intrecci, transenne e frammenti vari*. "Corpus" della scultura paleocristiana, bizantina ed altomedioevale di Ravenna, 1. Rome: De Luca.

———. 1976. "Aspetti della cultura figurativa paleobizantina nei mosaici di S Apollinare Nuovo di Ravenna: il ciclo cristologico." *CARB* 23: 7–20.

———. 1992. "La cultura artistica a Ravenna." In *Storia di Ravenna II.2*, ed. Antonio Carile: 159–176. Venice: Marsilio Editore.

———. 1996. "I mosaici: l'immagine da presenza scenica a suggestione simbolica/ The mosaics: the image from scenic presence to symbolic suggestion." In *Il mausoleo di Galla Placidia a Ravenna*, ed. Clementina Rizzardi: 147–170. Modena.

———. 1997. *La basilica di San Vitale a Ravenna*. Modena: F. C. Panini.

———. 1997. "La decorazione musiva: nel colore la via della salvezza." In *La basilica di San Vitale a Ravenna*, ed. Patrizia Angiolini Martinelli: 41–57. Modena: F. C. Panini.

Arcamone, Maria Giovanna. 2007. "Riflessioni linguistiche sull'agiotoponimo San Michele in Africisco." In *San Michele in Africisco e l'età giustinianea a Ravenna: atti del Convegno "La diaspora dell'arcangelo, San Michele in Africisco e l'età giustinianea": giornate di studio in memoria di Giuseppe Bovini, Ravenna, Sala dei mosaici, 21–22 aprile 2005*, ed. Claudio Spadoni: 389–397. Milan: Silvana.

Arjava, Antti. 2005. "The Mystery Cloud of 536 CE in the Mediterranean Sources." *Dumbarton Oaks Papers* 59: 73–94.

Arnaud, Pascal. 1990. "L'origine, la date de rédaction et la diffusion de l'archétype de la table de Peutinger." *Bulletin de la Société nationale des antiquaires de France*: 302–321.

Arnold, Jonathan J. 2008. Theoderic, the Goths, and the Restoration of the Roman Empire. Ann Arbor: PhD diss., University of Michigan.

Arslan, Ermanno A. 1989. "La monetazione dei Goti." *CARB* 36: 17–72.

———. 2005. "La zecca e la circolazione monetale." In *Ravenna: da capitale imperiale a capitale esarcale*, 1: 191–236. Spoleto: Fondazione Centro Italiano di Studi sull'Alto Medioevo.

Augenti, Andrea. 2003. "Ravenna: problemi di archeologia urbana." In L'archeologia dell'Adriatico dalla Preistoria al Medioevo: Atti del I Congresso Internazionale (Ravenna, 2001), ed. F. Lenzi: 537–551. Florence: All'insegna del giglio.

———. 2005. "Archeologia e topografia a Ravenna: il Palazzo di Teoderico e la Moneta Aurea." *Archeologia Medievale* 31: 7–34.

———. 2005. "Nuove indagini archeologiche a Classe." In *Ravenna: da capitale imperiale a capitale esarcale*, 1: 237–252. Spoleto: Fondazione Centro Italiano di Studi sull'Alto Medioevo.

———. 2006. "Ravenna e Classe: archeologia di due città tra la tarda Antichità e l'alto Medioevo." In *Le città italiane tra la tarda Antichità e l'alto Medioevo, Atti del Convegno (Ravenna, febbraio 2004)*, ed. Andrea Augenti: 185–217. Florence: All'insegna del giglio.

———. 2006. "Ravenna e Classe: il racconto di due città, tra storia e archeologia." In *Ravenna tra Oriente e Occidente: storia e archeologia*, ed. Andrea Augenti: 29–56. Ravenna: Longo.

———. 2007. "S. Michele in Africisco e l'edilizia ecclesiastica ravennate tra V e X secolo: archeologia e topografia." In *San Michele in Africisco e l'età giustinianea a Ravenna: atti del Convegno "La diaspora dell'arcangelo, San Michele in Africisco e l'età giustinianea": Giornate di studio in memoria di Giuseppe Bovini, Ravenna, Sala dei mosaici, 21–22 aprile 2005*, ed. Claudio Spadoni: 233–252. Milan: Silvana.

Augenti, Andrea and Carlo Bertelli, eds. 2006. *Ravenna tra Oriente e Occidente: storia e archeologia*. Ravenna: Longo.

Augenti, Andrea, Enrico Cirelli, Nicola Mancassola, and Valentina Manzelli. 2003. "Archeologia medievale a Ravenna: un progetto per la città ed il territorio." In *Atti del III Congresso Nazionale di Archeologia Medievale (Salerno, ottobre 2003)*, ed. P. Peduto: 271–278. Firenze.

Ausbüttel, F. M. 1987. "Die Curialen und Stadtmagistrate Ravennas im spätantiken Italien." *Zeitschrift für Papyrologie und Epigraphik* 67: 207–214.

Baar, P. 1965. "Propos d'un ingénieur sur le mausolée de Théodoric de Ravenne." *Felix Ravenna* ser. 3, 40: 77–97.

Bagatti, Bellarmino. 1980. "Il significato della cena nel mosaico di S. Apollinare Nuovo in Ravenna." *Felix Ravenna* 119–120: 89–94.

Baldini Lippolis, Isabella. 1997. "Articolazione e decorazione del palazzo imperiale di Ravenna." *CARB* 43: 1–31.

———. 2000. "Il ritratto musivo nella facciata interna di S. Apollinare Nuovo a Ravenna." In *Atti del VI colloquio dell'Associazione italiana per lo studio e la coservazione del mosaico*, ed. Federico Guidobaldi: 647–658. Ravenna: Girasole.

———. 2001. *La domus tardoantica. Forme e rappresentazioni dello spazio domestico nelle città del Mediterraneo*. Bologna: University Press Bologna.

———. 2004. "La chiesa di S. Eufemia ad Arietem." In *Archeologia urbana a Ravenna: la Domus dei tappeti di pietra, il complesso archeologico di via D'Azeglio*, ed. Giovanna Montevecchi: 71. Ravenna: Longo.

———. 2004. "Periodo byzantino." In *Archeologia urbana a Ravenna: la Domus dei tappeti di pietra, il complesso archeologico di via D'Azeglio*, ed. Giovanna Montevecchi: 76–78. Ravenna: Longo.

Barber, Charles. 1990. "The Imperial Panels at San Vitale: A Reconsideration." *Byzantine and Modern Greek Studies* 14: 19–42.

Bardill, Jonathan. 1997. "The Palace of Lausus and Nearby Monuments in Constantinople." *American Journal of Archaeology* 101: 67–95.

———. 1999. "The Golden Gate in Constantinople: A Triumphal Arch of Theodosius I." *American Journal of Archaeology* 103: 671–696.

———. 1999. "The Great Palace of the Byzantine Emperors and the Walker Trust Excavations." *Journal of Roman Archaeology* 12: 216–230.

Barnes, T. D. 1974. "Merobaudes on the Imperial Family." *Phoenix* 28: 314–319.

Barnish, S. J. B. 1983. "The *Anonymus Valesianus II* as a Source for the Last Years of Theoderic." *Latomus* 42: 472–96.

———. 1985. "The Wealth of Iulianus Argentarius: Late Antique Banking and the Mediterranean Economy." *Byzantion* 55: 5–38.

———. 1986. "Taxation, Land and Barbarian Settlement in the Western Empire." *Papers of the British School at Rome* 54: 170–195.

———. 1988. "Transformation and Survival in the Western Senatorial Aristocracy, c. AD 400–700." *Papers of the British School at Rome* 56: 120–155.

———, trans. 1992. *Cassiodorus: Selected Variae*. Liverpool: Liverpool University Press.

Barnish, S. J. B. and Federico Marazzi, eds. 2007. *The Ostrogoths from the Migration Period to the Sixth Century: An Ethnographic Perspective*. Woodbridge, Suffolk: Boydell Press.

Baumstark, Anton. 1911. "Frühchristlich-palästinensische Bildkompositionen in abendländischer Spiegelung." *Byzantinische Zeitschrift* 20: 177–96.

Bavant, Bernard. 1989. "Cadre de vie et habitat urbain en Italie centrale byzantine." *Mélanges de l'École française de Rome: Moyen âge – temps modernes* 101: 465–532.

Beckwith, John. 1958. *The Andrews Diptych*. London: H. M. Stationery Office.

———. 1958. "The Werden Casket Reconsidered." *Art Bulletin* 40, no. 1: 1–11.

Benericetti, Ruggero. 1994. *Il Pontificale di Ravenna: studio critico*. Faenza.

———. 1995. *Il Christo nei Sermoni di S. Pier Crisologo*. Studia Ravennatensia 6. Cesena: Centro Studi e Ricerche sulla Antica Provincia Ecclesiastica Ravennate.

Bermond Montanari, G. 1968. *La chiesa di S. Severo nel territorio di Classe. Risultati dei recenti scavi.* Bologna: R. Pàtron.

———. 1983. "La zona archeologica di Palazzolo." *CARB* 30: 17–21.

———. 1990. "Demografia del territorio nella pre-protostoria e la prima fase insediativa di Ravenna." In *Storia di Ravenna I*, ed. G. Susini: 31–48. Venice: Marsilio Editore.

———. 1990. "L'impianto urbano e i monumenti." In *Storia di Ravenna I*, ed. G. Susini: 223–256. Venice: Marsilio Editore.

Bermond Montanari, G. and M. G. Maioli, eds. 1983. *Ravenna e il porto di Classe. Venti anni di ricerche archeologiche tra Ravenna e Classe.* Imola.

Bertelli, Carlo. 1999. "Visual Images of the Town in Late Antiquity and the Early Middle Ages." In *The Idea and Ideal of the Town between Late Antiquity and the Early Middle Ages*, ed. Gian-Pietro Brogiolo: 127–146. Leiden: E. J. Brill.

Berti, Fede. 1976. *Mosaici antichi in Italia, 5. Regione ottava. Ravenna.* Rome: Istituto poligrafico e Zecca dello Stato, Libreria dello Stato.

Betsch, William E. 1977. The History, Production and Distribution of the Late Antique Capital in Constantinople. Philadelphia: PhD diss., University of Pennsylvania.

Bianchi, Cristina. 2002. *Spina entre le IVème et le IIIème siècle av. J.-C.* Villeneuve-d'Ascq: Presses universitaires du septentrion.

Bierbrauer, Volker. 1975. *Die ostgotischen Grab- und Schatzfunde in Italien.* Spoleto: Centro italiano di studi sull'alto Medioevo.

———. 1976. "Die Ansiedlung der Ostgoten in Italien." In *Les relations entre l'empire romain tardif, l'empire franc et ses voisins: colloque XXX: Nice, mercredi 15 septembre*, ed. Kurt Böhner: 42–70. Paris: Centre national de la recherche scientifique.

Bollini, Maria. 1990. "La fondazione di Classe e la comunità classiaria." In *Storia di Ravenna I*, ed. G. Susini: 297–320. Venice: Marsilio Editore.

———. 2005. "La flotta ravennate, la Grecia e l'Oriente." In *I porti antichi di Ravenna*, ed. Maurizio Mauro, *1: Il porto romano e le flotte*: 125–136. Ravenna: Adriapress.

Bonino, Marco. 1991. "Archeologia navale." In *Storia di Ravenna II.1*, ed. Antonio Carile: 27–53. Venice: Marsilio Editore.

Bono, P., J. Crow and R. Bayliss. 2001. "The Water Supply of Constantinople: Archaeology and Hydrogeology of an Early Medieval City." *Environmental Geology* 40: 1325–1333.

Bovini, Giuseppe. 1950. *Il cosidetto mausoleo di Galla Placidia in Ravenna.* Vatican: Società Amici delle Catacombe Presso Pontificio Istituto di Archeologia Cristiana.

———. 1952. "Note intorno alla chiesa ravennate di S. Croce." *Felix Ravenna* 60: 41–54.

———. 1952. "Una prova di carattere tecnico dell'appartenenza al ciclo iconografico teodoriciano della madonna in trono, figurata sui mosaici di S. Apollinare Nuovo e Ravenna." *Studi Romagnoli* 3: 17–29.

———. 1955. "Mosaici parietali scomparsi degli antichi edifici sacri di Ravenna." *Felix Ravenna* 68 and 69: 54–76, 3–20.

———. 1956. "Le origini di Ravenna e lo sviluppo della città in età romana." *Felix Ravenna* 72: 45–48.

———. 1957. *La cattedra eburnea del vescovo Massimiano di Ravenna.* Ravenna: Edizioni "Giorgio La Pira Soc. Coop. a.r.l."

————. 1957. "Note sulla successione delle antiche fasi di lavoro nella decorazione musiva del Battistero degli Ariani." *Felix Ravenna* ser. 3, 24: 5–24.

————. 1958. *Mosaici di S. Apollinare nuovo di Ravenna: il ciclo cristologico*. Firenze: Arnaud.

————. 1959. *Il Mausoleo di Teodorico*. Ravenna: Edizioni Dante.

————. 1966. "Antichi rifacimenti nei mosaici di S.Apollinare Nuovo a Ravenna." *CARB* 13: 51–81.

————. 1966. "Principali restauri compiuti nel secolo scorso da Felice Kibel nei mosaici di S. Apollinare Nuovo di Ravenna." *CARB* 13: 83–104.

————. 1968. "La raffigurazione del Palazzo di Teodorico nei mosaici di S. Apollinare Nuovo." *Bollettino Economico della Camera di Commercio di Ravenna* 8: 7–11.

————. 1968. *Saggio di bibliografia su Ravenna antica*. Bologna.

————. 1974. "Les 'Sinopie' récement découvertes sous les mosaïques de l'abside de Saint-Apollinaire-in-Classe, à Ravenne." *Académie des inscriptions et belles-lettres. Comptes-rendus des séances* 1: 97–110.

————. 1974. "Qualche nota sulle sinopie recentemente rinvenute sotto il mosaico absidale di S. Apollinare in Classe di Ravenna." *Atti dell'Accademia delle scienze dell'Istituto di Bologna – Classe di scienze morali* 62, no. 2: 95–107.

————. 1975. "Il recente rinvenimento del 'Monasterium Sancti Ruphilli.'" In *Studies in Memory of David Talbot Rice*, ed. G. Robertson: 164–170. Edinburgh.

Bowersock, Glen W., Peter Brown and Oleg Grabar, eds. 1999. *Late Antiquity: A Guide to the Postclassical World*. Cambridge, MA: Harvard University Press.

Brandl, Ulrich and Milohe Vasic, eds. 2007. *Roms Erbe auf dem Balkan Spätantike Kaiservillen und Stadtanlagen in Serbien*. Mainz: Philipp von Zabern.

Brandt, O. 1997–8. "Il battistero lateranense da Costantino a Ilaro: un riesame degli scavi." *Opuscula Romana* 22–23: 7–66.

Breckenridge, James. 1980. "Christ on the Lyre-Backed Throne." *Dumbarton Oaks Papers* 34: 247–260.

Brenk, Beat. 1982. "Welchen Text illustrieren die Evangelisten in den Mosaiken von S. Vitale in Ravenna." *Frühmittelalterliche Studien* 16: 19–24.

————. 1987. "Spolia from Constantine to Charlemagne: Aesthetics versus Ideology." *Dumbarton Oaks Papers* 41: 103–109.

————. 1999. "Mit was für Mitteln kann einem physisch Anonymen *Auctoritas* Verliehen werden?" In *East and West: Modes of Communication. Proceedings of the First Plenary Conference at Merida*, ed. Evangelos Chrysos: 143–172. Leiden: Brill.

————. 2006. "Zur Einführung des Kultes der heiligen Kosmas und Damian in Rom." *Theologische Zeitschrift* 62, no. 2: 303–320.

————. 2007. "San Michele in Africisco. Tendenze locali e internazionali nell'architettura ravennate del VI secolo." In *San Michele in Africisco e l'età giustinianea a Ravenna: atti del Convegno "La diaspora dell'arcangelo, San Michele in Africisco e l'età giustinianea": Giornate di studio in memoria di Giuseppe Bovini, Ravenna, Sala dei mosaici, 21–22 aprile 2005*, ed. Claudio Spadoni: 205–221. Milan: Silvana.

Breschi, Maria Grazia. 1965. *La cattedrale ed il battistero degli ariani a Ravenna*. Ravenna.

Brogiolo, Gian-Pietro and Sauro Gelichi. 1998. *La città nell' alto medioevo italiano: archeologia e storia*. Rome: Laterza.

————. 1999. "Ideas of the Town in Italy during the Transition from Antiquity to the Middle Ages." In *The Idea and Ideal of the Town between Late Antiquity and the Early Middle Ages*, ed. Gian-Pietro Brogiolo: 99–126. Leiden: E. J. Brill.

———. 2000. "Capitali e residenze regie nell'Italia Longobarda." In *Sedes regiae (ann. 400–800)*, ed. G. Ripoll and J. M. Gurt: 135–162. Barcelona: Memorias de la Real Academia de Buenas Letras de Barcelona.

Brown, Katharine R. 1979. "The Mosaics of San Vitale: Evidence for the Attribution of Some Early Byzantine Jewelry to Court Workshops." *Gesta* 18: 57–62.

Brown, Thomas S. 1979. "The Church of Ravenna and the Imperial Administration in the Seventh Century." *English Historical Review* 94: 1–28.

———. 1984. *Gentlemen and Officers. Imperial Administration and Aristocratic Power in Byzantine Italy A.D. 554–800*. Hertford: British School at Rome.

———. 1986. "The Aristocracy of Ravenna from Justinian to Charlemagne." *CARB* 33: 135–149.

———. 1986. "Romanitas and Campanilismo: Agnellus of Ravenna's View of the Past." In *The Inheritance of Historiography, 350–900*, ed. C. Holdsworth: 107–114. Exeter: University Publications.

———. 1990. "Louis the Pious and the Papacy, a Ravenna Perspective." In *Charlemagne's Heir, New Perspectives on the Reign of Louis the Pious (814–840)*, ed. Peter Godman: 297–308. Oxford.

———. 1991. "Ebrei e orientali a Ravenna." In *Storia di Ravenna, II.1*, ed. Antonio Carile: 135–149. Venice.

———. 1998. "Urban Violence in Early Medieval Italy: The Cases of Rome and Ravenna." In *Violence and Society in the Early Medieval West*, ed. Guy Halsall: 76–89. Woodbridge, Suffolk: Boydell and Brewer.

———. 2005. "Byzantine Italy, c. 680–c. 876." In *The New Cambridge Medieval History II, c. 700–c. 900*, ed. Rosamond McKitterick: 320–348. Cambridge: Cambridge University Press.

———. 2007. "The Role of Arianism in Ostrogothic Italy: The Evidence from Ravenna." In *The Ostrogoths from the Migration Period to the Sixth Century: An Ethnographic Perspective*, eds. S. J. B. Barnish and F. Marazzi: 417–426. Woodbridge, Suffolk: Boydell Press.

Brown, Thomas S. and Neil Christie. 1989. "Was There a Byzantine Model of Settlement in Italy?" *Mélanges de l'École française de Rome: Moyen âge – temps modernes* 101: 377–399.

Brubaker, Leslie. 1997. "Memories of Helena: Patterns of Imperial Female Matronage in the Fourth and Fifth Centuries." In *Women, Men, and Eunuchs: Gender in Byzantium*, ed. Liz James: 52–75. London: Routledge.

Budriesi, Roberta. 1990. "Ortodossi e ariani: questioni ravennati (riassunto)." *CARB* 37: 109–20.

Bühl, G. 1995. *Constantinopolis und Roma: Stadtpersonifikationen der Spätantike*. Zurich.

Burns, Thomas. 1978. "Calculating Ostrogothic Population." *Acta Antiqua* 26: 457–463.

———. 1984. *A History of the Ostrogoths*. Bloomington: Indiana University Press.

Caillet, J.-P. 1993. *L'évergétisme monumental chrétien en Italie et à ses marges, d'après l'épigraphie des pavements de mosaïque (IVe–VIIe s.)*. Collection de l'École Française de Rome 175. Rome: École française de Rome.

———. 2003. "Affirmation de l'autorité de l'évêque dans les sanctuaires paléochrétiens du Haut Adriatique: De l'inscription à l'image." *Deltion tes Christianikes Archaiologikes Hetaireias, s. 4* 24: 21–30.

Cameron, Averil. 1985. *Procopius and the Sixth Century*. London: Routledge.

Cantarelli, Luigi. 1901. *La diocesi italiciana da Diocleziano alla fine dell'Impero occidentale*. Roma: "L'Erma" di Bretschneider.

Cantino Wataghin, Gisella, Margherita Cecchelli, and Letizia Pani Ermini. 2001. "L'edificio battesimale nel tessuto della città tardoantica e altomedievale in Italia." In *L'edificio battesimale in Italia: aspetti e problemi: atti dell'VIII Congresso nazionale di archeologia cristiana: Genova, Sarzana, Albenga, Finale Ligure, Ventimiglia, 21–26 settembre 1998*, 1: 231–265. Bordighera: Istituto internazionale di studi liguri.

Capellini, Denis. 1987. "Considerazioni intorno al problema della cinta muraria di Ravenna tardoantica." *Felix Ravenna* 133–34: 81–120.

———. 1993. "Nuovi dati ed osservazioni sulla cinta muraria di Ravenna tardoantica." *Studi Romagnoli* 44: 31–60.

Carile, Antonio. 1986. "L'iconoclasmo fra Bisanzio e l'Italia." In *Culto delle immagini e crisi iconoclasta. Atti del Convegno di Studi, Catania 16–17 maggio, 1984*: 13–54. Palermo: EDI OFTES.

———, ed. 1991. *Storia di Ravenna II, 1: Dall' Età Bizantina all' Età Ottoniana: Territorio, Economia e Società*. Venice: Marsilio Editore.

———. 1992. "La Società Ravennate dall'Esarcato agli Ottoni." In *Storia di Ravenna, II.2: Dall'età bizantina all'età ottoniana, ecclesiologia, cultura e arte*, ed. Antonio Carile: 379–404. Venice: Marsilio Editore.

———, ed. 1992. *Storia di Ravenna II, 2: Dall' età Bizantina all' età Ottoniana: Ecclesiologia, cultura e arte*. Venezia. Marsilio Editore.

———, ed. 1995. *Teoderico e i Goti fra Oriente e Occidente*. Ravenna.

Cartocci, Maria Cecilia. 1993. "Alcune precisazioni sulla intitolazione a S. Agata della Ecclesia Gothorum alla Suburra." In *Teoderico il Grande e i Goti d'Italia: Atti del XIII Congresso Internazionale di Studi sull'Alto Medioevo, Milano, 2–6 novembre 1992*, 2: 611–620. Spoleto: Centro italiano di Studi sull'Alto Medioevo.

Cavallo, Guglielmo G. 1983. "La cultura a Ravenna tra Corte e Chiesa." In *Le sedi della cultura nell'Emilia Romagna: L'alto medioevo*, ed. Ovidio Capitani: 29–51. Milan: Silvana.

———. 1992. "La cultura scritta a Ravenna tra antichità tarda e alto medioevo." In *Storia di Ravenna II.2*, ed. Antonio Carile: 79–125. Venice: Marsilio Editore.

Cavarra, Berenice. 1993. "La cultura medica a Ravenna fra VI e VII secolo." *Medicina nei Secoli* n.s. 5: 345–360.

Cavarra, Berenice, Gabriella Gardini, Giovanni Battista Parente, and Giorgio Vespignani. 1991. "Gli archivi come fonti della storia di Ravenna: Regesto dei documenti." In *Storia di Ravenna II.1*, ed. Antonio Carile: 401–547. Venice: Marsilio Editore.

Cecchelli, Carlo. 1936. *La Cattedra di Massimiano*. Rome: La Libreria dello Stato.

———. 1960. "L'Arianesimo e le chiese ariane." In *Le chiese nei regni dell'Europa occidentale e i loro rapporti con Roma sino al'800*: 743–74. Spoleto: Centro Italiano di studi sull'alto medioevo.

Cecchelli, Margherita and Gioia Bertelli. 1989. "Edifici di culto ariano in Italia." In *Actes du XIe Congrès international d'archéologie chrétienne: Lyon, Vienne, Grenoble, Genève et Aoste (21–28 Septembre 1986)*, ed. Noel Duval, 1: 233–247. Roma: Ecole française de Rome.

Cecconi, G. A. 2006. "Crisi e trasformazioni del governo municipale in Occidente fra IV e VI secolo." In *Die Stadt in der Spätantike – Niedergang oder Wandel? Akten des internationalen Kolloquiums in München am 30. und 31. Mai 2003*, ed. Jens Uwe Krause: 285–318. Stuttgart: Franz Steiner Verlag.

Christe, Yves. 1996. *L'Apocalypse de Jean: sens et développements de ses visions synthétiques*. Paris: Picard.

Christie, Neil. 1989. "The City Walls of Ravenna: The Defence of a Capital, A.D. 402–750." *CARB* 36: 113–138.

———. 2006. *From Constantine to Charlemagne: An Archaeology of Italy, AD 300–800*. Aldershot: Ashgate.

Christie, Neil and Sheila Gibson. 1988. "The City Walls of Ravenna." *Papers of the British School at Rome* 56: 156–197.

Chrysos, Evangelos. 2005. "Conclusions." In *Ravenna: da capitale imperiale a capitale esarcale*, 2: 1059–1066. Spoleto: Fondazione Centro Italiano di Studi sull'Alto Medioevo.

Ciampini, Giovanni Giustino. 1690–9. *Vetera monimenta, in quibus praecipue musiva opera, sacrarum profanarumque aedium structura ac nonnulli antiqui ritus dissertationibus iconibusque illustrantur*. Rome: Ex typographia Joannis Jacobi Komarek.

Cirelli, Enrico. 2005. Archeologia urbana a Ravenna: piattaforma GIS delle evidenze archeologiche di età tardoantica e medievale. Siena: PhD diss., Università degli Studi di Siena.

———. 2008. *Ravenna: archeologia di una città*. Firenze: All'insegna del giglio.

Clark, Elizabeth A. 1982. "Claims on the Bones of St. Stephen: The Partisans of Melania and Eudocia." *Church History* 51: 141–156.

Clarke, Georgia. 1997. "Ambrogio Traversari: Artistic Adviser in Early Fifteenth-Century Florence?" *Renaissance Studies* 11, no. 3: 161–178.

Claude, Dietrich. 1993. "Theoderich d. Gr. und die europäischen Mächte." In *Teoderico il Grande e i Goti d'Italia: Atti del XIII Congresso Internazionale di Studi sull'Alto Medioevo, Milano, 2–6 novembre 1992*, 1: 21–44. Spoleto: Centro italiano di Studi sull'Alto Medioevo.

Clover, Frank M. 1971. *Flavius Merobaudes: A Translation and Historical Commentary*. Transactions of the American Philosophical Society, vol. 61, part 1. Philadelphia: American Philosophical Society.

Coates-Stephens, Robert. 1998. "The Walls and Aqueducts of Rome in the Early Middle Ages, A.D. 500–1000." *Journal of Roman Studies* 88: 166–178.

Connor, Carolyn L. 2004. "Female Imperial Authority: Empresses of the Theodosian House: Galla Placidia." In *Women of Byzantium*, ed. Carolyn L. Connor: 64–72. New Haven, CT: Yale University Press.

Cortesi, Giuseppe. 1964. "Recenti scoperte archeologiche nella zona di Classe. La basilica Petriana." *Bollettino della Camera di Commercio di Ravenna* 11: 842–847.

———. 1965. "La basilica della Casa Bianca." In *Atti del I Congresso nazionale di studi bizantini (archeologia-arte), Ravenna, 23–25 maggio 1965*: 43–64. Ravenna: A. Longo.

———. 1968. "Nuove indagini sulla topografia della zona della basilica recentemente rinvenuta a sud di S. Apollinare in Classe." In *Atti del Convegno Internazionale di Studi sulle Antichità di Classe, Ravenna, 14–17 ottobre 1967*: 441–453. Ravenna: Longo.

———. 1970. "Saggio di ricognizione sulla basilica classicana di san Probo." *Felix Ravenna* 101: 105–113.

———. 1978. "La chiesa di Santa Croce di Ravenna alla luce degli ultimi scavi e ricerche." *CARB* 25: 47–76.

———. 1980. *Classe paleocristiana e paleobizantina*. Ravenna: Libreria Sirri.

———. 1982. "I principali edifici sacri ravennati in funzione sepolcrale nei secoli V e VI." *CARB* 29: 63–107.

Cosentino, Salvatore. 2005. "L'approvvigionamento annonario di Ravenna dal V all'VIII secolo: l'organizzazione e i riflessi socio-economici." In *Ravenna: da capitale imperiale a capitale esarcale*, 1: 405–434. Spoleto: Fondazione Centro Italiano di Studi sull'Alto Medioevo.

Costa, U., E. Gotti, and G. P. Tognon. 2001. "Nota tecnica: malte prelevate da mura antiche dallo scavo della Banca Popolare di Ravenna." In *Fortificazioni antiche in Italia: Età repubblicana*, ed. Lorenzo Quilici: 23–28. Roma: L'Erma di Bretschneider.

Courcelle, Pierre. 1948. "Le Gril de Saint Laurent au Mausolee de Galla Placidia." *Cahiers Archeologiques* 3: 32 ff.

———. 1969. *Late Latin Writers and Their Greek Sources*. Translated by Harry E. Wedeck. Cambridge, MA: Harvard University Press.

Croke, Brian. 1987. "Cassiodorus and the *Getica* of Jordanes." *Classical Philology* 82: 117–134.

Cummins, Sheila. 1994. The Arian Baptistery of Ravenna. Bloomington: PhD diss., Indiana University.

Curcic, Slobodan. 1993. "Late-Antique Palaces: The Meaning of Urban Context." *Ars Orientalis* 23.

Curran, John. 2000. *Pagan City and Christian Capital: Rome in the Fourth Century*. Oxford: Oxford University Press.

Curta, Florin. 2007. "Some Remarks on Ethnicity in Medieval Archaeology." *Early Medieval Europe* 15, no. 2: 159–185.

Cuscito, Giuseppe. 2007. "Origine e sviluppo del culto dei santi Cosma e Damiano. Testimonianze nella *Venetia et Histria*." In *San Michele in Africisco e l'età giustinianea a Ravenna: atti del Convegno "La diaspora dell'arcangelo, San Michele in Africisco e l'età giustinianea": Giornate di studio in memoria di Giuseppe Bovini, Ravenna, Sala dei mosaici, 21–22 aprile 2005*, ed. Claudio Spadoni: 99–111. Milan: Silvana.

Dagron, Gilbert. 1974. *Naissance d'une capitale: Constantinople et ses institutions de 330 à 451*. Paris: Presses universitaires de France.

David, Jean-Michel. 1996. *The Roman Conquest of Italy*. Oxford: Blackwell.

De Angelis d'Ossat, Guglielmo. 1960. "Un enigma risolto: il completamento del Mausoleo Teodoriciano." *CARB* 7, no. 2: 77–83.

———. 1962. *Studi ravennati: problemi di architettura paleocristiana*. Ravenna: Edizioni Dante.

———. 1968. "Osservazioni sull'architettura delle basiliche scoperte a Classe." In *Atti del Convegno Internazionale di Studi sulle Antichità di Classe, Ravenna, 14–17 ottobre 1967*: 455–462. Ravenna: Longo.

———. 1973. "Sulla distrutta aula dei 'Quinque accubita' a Ravenna." *CARB* 20: 263–273.

de Francovich, Géza. 1958–9. "Studi sulla scultura Ravennate, I: I sarcofagi." *Felix Ravenna* 26–28: 5–172, 5–175.

———. 1970. *Il Palatium di Teodorico a Ravenna e la cosidetta 'architettura di Potenza.' Problemi d'interpretazione di raffigurazioni architettoniche nell'arte tardoantica e altomedioevale*. Rome: De Luca.

De Maria, Sandro, ed. 2004. *Nuove ricerche e scavi nell'area della Villa di Teodorico a Galeata: atti della Giornata di studi, Ravenna 26 marzo 2002*. Bologna: Ante quem.

Deckers, J. 2002. "Der erste Diener Christi. Die Proskynese der Kaiser als Schlüsselmotiv der Mosaiken in San Vitale (Ravenna) und in der Haghia Sophia (Istanbul)." In *Art, Cérémonial et Liturgie au Moyen Âge, Actes du Colloque de 3e Cycle Romand de Lettres, Lausanne-Fribourg, 24–25 mars, 14–15 avril, 12–13 mai 2000*, ed. Nicolas Bock: 11–57. Rome: Viella.

Deichmann, F. W. 1952. "I titoli dei vescovi ravennati da Ecclesio a Massimiano nelle epigrafi dedicatorie di S. Vitale e di S. Apollinare in Classe tramandate da Agnello." *Studi Romagnoli* 3: 63–67.

———. 1953. "Gründung und Datierung von San Vitale in Ravenna." In *Arte del primo millennio: atti del 2. Convegno per lo studio dell'arte dell'alto medio evo tenuto presso l'Università di Pavia nel settembre 1950*, ed. Edoardo Arslan: 111–117. Torino: Viglongo.

———. 1954. *Studien zur Architektur Konstantinopels, im 5. und 6. Jahrhundert nach Christus*. Baden Baden: B. Grimm.

———. 1969. *Ravenna, Hauptstadt des spätantiken Abendlandes*. Wiesbaden: F. Steiner.

———. 1974. *Ravenna, Hauptstadt des spätantiken Abendlandes*. Wiesbaden: F. Steiner.

———. 1975. *Die Spolien in der spatantiken Architektur*. Munich: Bayerische Akademie der Wissenschaften.

———. 1976. *Ravenna, Hauptstadt des spätantiken Abendlandes*. Wiesbaden: F. Steiner.

———. 1980. "La corte dei re goti a Ravenna." *CARB* 27: 41–53.

———. 1982. "Costantinopoli e Ravenna: un confronto." *CARB* 29: 143–158.

———. 1989. *Ravenna, Hauptstadt des spätantiken Abendlandes*. Wiesbaden: F. Steiner.

Deliyannis, Deborah M. 1996. "Agnellus of Ravenna and Iconoclasm: Theology and Politics in a Ninth Century Historical Text." *Speculum* 71: 559–576.

———. 2000. "Bury Me in Ravenna? Appropriating Galla Placidia's Body in the Middle Ages." *Studi medievali, n.s.* 42: 289–299.

———. 2003. "Charlemagne's Silver Tables: The Ideology of an Imperial Capital." *Early Medieval Europe* 12: 159–177.

———, trans. 2004. *The Book of Pontiffs of the Church of Ravenna*. Washington, DC: The Catholic University of America Press.

———. 2005. "Proconnesian Marble in Ninth-Century Ravenna." In *Archaeology in Architecture: Studies in Honor of Cecil L. Striker*, ed. Deborah M. Deliyannis: 37–41. Mainz: Verlag Philipp von Zabern.

———, ed. 2006. *Andreas Agnellus, Liber pontificalis ecclesiae Ravennatis*. CCCM. Turnhout: Brepols.

———. 2008. "About the *Liber pontificalis* of the Church of Ravenna: Its Relation with the Roman Model." In *Liber, Gesta, Histoire: Écrire l'histoire des évêques et des papes, de l'antiquité au XXIe siècle*, ed. François Bougard. Turnhout: Brepols.

———. 2009. "Ravenna, St. Martin and the Battle of Vouillé." *Illinois Classical Studies* 33: forthcoming.

Dell'Aqua, Francesca. 2005. "Enhancing Luxury through Stained Glass, from Asia Minor to Italy." *Dumbarton Oaks Papers* 59: 193–211.

Demus, Otto. 1969. "Zu den Apsismosaiken von sant'Apollinare in Classe." *Jahrbuch der österreichischen Byzantinistik* 18: 229–238.

Di Pietro, F. 1927. *Ravenna sepolta. Per la zona archeologica a Ravenna e a Classe.* Ravenna: Adriapress.

Diehl, Charles. 1959. *Études sur l'administration byzantine dans l'exarchat de Ravenna (568–751).* New York: B. Franklin.

Dilke, O. A. W. 1987. "Itineraries and Geographical Maps in the Early and Late Roman Empires." In *The History of Cartography*, vol. 1, *Cartography in Prehistoric, Ancient, and Medieval Europe and the Mediterranean*, ed. J. B. Harley: 234–257. Chicago: University of Chicago Press.

Dillemann, Louis and Yves Janvier. 1997. *La Cosmographie du Ravennate.* Brussels: Latomus.

Dinkler, Erich. 1964. *Das Apsismosaik von S. Apollinare in Classe.* Köln: Westdeutscher Verlag.

Donati, Angela. 1990. "Scrittura, società e cultura." In *Storia di Ravenna I*, ed. G. Susini: 469–480. Venice: Marsilio Editore.

———. 2005. "Il mondo dei Classiari." In *I porti antichi di Ravenna*, ed. Maurizio Mauro, 1: *Il porto romano e le flotte*: 117–124. Ravenna: Adriapress.

Dresken-Weiland, Jutta. 1998. *Repertorium der christlich-antiken Sarkophage, Vol. II: Italien, Dalmatien, Museen der Welt. Mit einem Nachtrag Rom und Ostia.* Repertorium der christlich-antiken Sarkophage. Mainz: P. von Zabern.

Durliat, Jean. 1997. "Cité, impôt et integration des barbares." In *Kingdoms of the Empire: The Integration of Barbarians in Late Antiquity*, ed. Walter Pohl. Leiden: E. J. Brill.

Dutton, Paul Edward. 2004. *Charlemagne's Mustache and Other Cultural Clusters of a Dark Age.* New York: Palgrave Macmillan.

Duval, Noel. 1960. "Que savons-nous du Palais de Théodoric à Ravenna?" *Mélanges d'Archéologie et d'Histoire* 72: 337–371.

———. 1978. "Comment reconnaître un palais impérial ou royal? Ravenna e Piazza Armerina." *Felix Ravenna* 115: 29–62.

———. 1978. "La mosaïque du 'Palatium' de Saint-Apollinaire-le-Neuf représente-t-elle une façade ou un édifice aplani?" *CARB* 25: 93–122.

———. 1997. "Les résidences impériales: leur rapport avec les problèmes de légitimité, les partages de l'Empire et la chronologie des combinaisons dynastiques." In *Usurpationen in der Spätantike: Akten des Kolloquiums "Staatsstreich und Staatlichkeit," 6.–10. März 1996, Solothurn/Bern: elf Beiträge*, ed. François Paschoud: 127–153. Stuttgart: F. Steiner.

Dyggve, Ejnar. 1941. *Ravennatum Palatium Sacrum. La basilica ipetrale per ceremonie.* Det Kgl. danske videnskabernes selskab. Archaeologisk-kunsthistoriske meddelelser. III, 2. Copenhaven: E. Munksgaard.

———. 1957. "Excursus sulla 'Basilica Herculis' ricordata da Cassiodoro." *CARB* 4: 75–78.

Dynes, Wayne. 1962–4. "The First Christian Palace-Church Type." *Marsyas* 11: 1–9.

Effenberger, Arne. 1989. *Das Mosaik aus der Kirche San Michele in Africisco zu Ravenna: ein Kunstwerk in der Frühchristlich-byzantinischen Sammlung.* Berlin: Staatliche Museen zu Berlin.

Elsner, Jas. 1995. *Art and the Roman Viewer: The Transformation of Art from the Pagan World to Christianity.* Cambridge Studies in New Art History and Criticism. Cambridge: Cambridge University Press.

_____. 2002. "The Birth of Late Antiquity: Riegl and Strzygowski in 1901." *Art History* 25: 358–379.

_____. 2004. "Late Antique Art: The Problem of the Concept and the Cumulative Aesthetic." In *Approaching Late Antiquity: The Transformation from Early to Late Empire*, ed. S. Swain and J. Edwards: 271–309. Oxford: Oxford University Press.

Engemann, J. 1989. "Die Huldigung der Apostel im Mosaik des ravennatischen Orthodoxenbaptisteriums." In *Beiträge zur Ikonographie und Hermeneutik. Festschrift für Nikolaus Himmelmann*, ed. Hans-Ulrich Cain: 481–489. Mainz: P. von Zabern.

Ensslin, Wilhelm. 1940. "Rex Theodericus Inlitteratus?" *Historisches Jahrbuch* 60: 391–396.

Ercolani Cocchi, Emanuela. 1980. "Osservazioni sull'origine del tipo monetale ostrogoto 'Felix Ravenna.'" *Studi Romagnoli* 31: 21–44.

Everett, Nicholas. 2003. *Literacy in Lombard Italy, c. 568–774*. Cambridge: Cambridge University Press.

Fabbi, Fulvia. 2001. "Ravenna romana nelle ricostruzioni storiche grafiche e cartografiche." In *Ravenna Romana*, ed. Maurizio Mauro: 107–132. Ravenna: Adriapress.

Fabbri, G. S. 2005. "La flotta militare orientale – Ravenna." In *I porti antichi di Ravenna*, ed. Maurizio Mauro, 1: *Il porto romano e le flotte*: 85–96. Ravenna: Adriapress.

Fabbri, Paolo. 1990. "Il paesaggio ravennate dell'evo antico." In *Storia di Ravenna, I: L'evo antico*, ed. Giancarlo Susini: 7–30. Venezia: Marsilio Editore.

_____. 1991. "Il controllo delle acque tra tecnica ed economia." In *Storia di Ravenna, II.1*, ed. Antonio Carile: 9–25. Venice.

_____. 2004. "L'età antica e medievale." In *Le mura nella storia urbana di Ravenna*, ed. Paolo Fabbri: 11–97. Ravenna: Società di studi ravennati.

Fanning, Steven. 1981. "Lombard Arianism Reconsidered." *Speculum* 56: 241–258.

Fantuzzi, Marco. 1801–1804. *Monumenti ravennati de' secoli di mezzo per la maggior parte inediti*. Venice: Francesco Andreola.

Farioli Campanati, Rafaella. 1977. *Ravenna romana e bizantina*. Ravenna: Longo.

_____. 1986. "Le tombe dei vescovi di Ravenna del tardoantico all'alto medioevo." In *L'inhumation privilegiée du IVe au VIIIe siècle en Occident*, ed. Y. Duval and J.-C. Picard: 165–172. Paris.

_____. 1989. "La topografia imperiale di Ravenna dal V al VI secolo." *CARB* 36: 139–147.

_____. 1992. "Decorazioni di origine tessile sul repertorio del mosaico pavimentale protobizantino del vicino Oriente e le corrispondenze decorative parietali di Ravenna, Salonicco, Costantinopoli e Qusayz Arura." *CARB* 39: 275–296.

_____. 1992. "Ravenna, Constantinopoli: Aspetti Topografico-Monumentali e Iconografici." In *Storia di Ravenna II.2*, ed. Antonio Carile: 127–157. Venice: Marsilio Editore.

_____. 1994. "Il pyrgus dell'arcivescovo Agnello e la sua datazione." *CARB* 41: 207–218.

_____. 1995. *I mosaici pavimentali della chiesa di S. Giovanni Evangelista in Ravenna*. Ravenna: Edizioni del Girasole.

_____. 2005. "Per la datazione della cattedra di Massimiano e dell'ambone di Agnello." In *Studi in memoria di Patrizia Angiolini Martinelli*, ed. Silvia Pasi: 165–168. Bologna: Ante quem.

————. 2005. "Ravenna e i suoi rapporti con Costantinopoli: la scultura (secoli V-VI)." In *Venezia e Bisanzio. Aspetti della cultura artistica bizantina da Ravenna a venezia (V-XIV secolo)*, ed. Clementina Rizzardi: 13–43. Venice: Istituto veneto di scienze, lettere ed arti.

————. 2007. "I mosaici pavimentali di Ravenna e di area adriatica in età guistinianea. Il tappeto musivo di San Michele in Africisco." In *San Michele in Africisco e l'età giustinianea a Ravenna: atti del Convegno "La diaspora dell'arcangelo, San Michele in Africisco e l'età giustinianea": Giornate di studio in memoria di Giuseppe Bovini, Ravenna, Sala dei mosaici, 21–22 aprile 2005*, ed. Claudio Spadoni: 179–192. Milan: Silvana.

Fasoli, Gina. 1979. "Il dominio territoriale degli arcivescovi di Ravenna fra l'VIII et l'XI secolo." In *I poteri temporali dei vescovi in Italia e in Germania nel medioevo*, ed. C.-G. Mor: 87–140. Bologna.

————. 1979. "Sul Patrimonio della chiesa di Ravenna in Sicilia." *Felix Ravenna* 118: 69–75.

————. 1991. "Il patrimonio della chiesa Ravennate." In *Storia di Ravenna II.1*, ed. Antonio Carile: 389–400. Venice: Marsilio Editore.

Felletti Maj, B. M. 1968–69. "Una carta di Ravenna romana e bizantina." *Rendiconti della Pontificia accademia romana di archeologia* 41: 85–120.

Ferluga, Jadran. 1991. "L'esarcato." In *Storia di Ravenna, II.1*, ed. Antonio Carile: 351–377. Venice.

Fiaccadori, Gianfranco. 1977. "Sulla memoria teodericiana di San Martino in Ciel d'Oro." *Felix Ravenna* 113–114: 161–179.

Fiorentini Roncuzzi, Isotta. 2007. "Degrado chimico-fisico nei mosaici pavimentali del VI secolo: interventi di restauro." In *San Michele in Africisco e l'età giustinianea a Ravenna: atti del Convegno "La diaspora dell'arcangelo, San Michele in Africisco e l'età giustinianea": Giornate di studio in memoria di Giuseppe Bovini, Ravenna, Sala dei mosaici, 21–22 aprile 2005*, ed. Claudio Spadoni: 311–315. Milan: Silvana.

Fiori, Cesare, Mariangela Vandini, and Valentina Mazzotti. 2005. "Tecnologia e colore del vetro dei mosaici di S. Vitale a Ravenna." In *Ravenna: da capitale imperiale a capitale esarcale*, 2: 915–942. Spoleto: Fondazione Centro Italiano di Studi sull'Alto Medioevo.

————. 2007. "Tecnologia del colore del vetro bizantino nei mosaici ravennati." In *San Michele in Africisco e l'età giustinianea a Ravenna: atti del Convegno "La diaspora dell'arcangelo, San Michele in Africisco e l'età giustinianea": Giornate di studio in memoria di Giuseppe Bovini, Ravenna, Sala dei mosaici, 21–22 aprile 2005*, ed. Claudio Spadoni: 317–324. Milan: Silvana.

Fiorin, Marisa Bianco. 1993. "Il monolite del mausoleo di Teodorico." In *Teoderico il Grande e i Goti d'Italia: Atti del XIII Congresso Internazionale di Studi sull'Alto Medioevo, Milano, 2–6 novembre 1992*, 2: 601–609. Spoleto: Centro italiano di Studi sull'Alto Medioevo.

Foschi, Silvia. 1997. "Appunti per una cronologia delle trasformazioni architettoniche di San Vitale." In *La basilica di San Vitale a Ravenna*, ed. Patrizia Angiolini Martinelli: 59–68. Modena: F. C. Panini.

Fox, Robin Lane. 1995. "Art and the Beholder: The Apse Mosaic of S. Apollinare in Classe." *Byzantinische Forschungen* 21: 247–251.

Franzoni, Claudio. 1996. "Braccio nord, portale d'ingresso. Architrave romano con fregio bacchico / North arm, entrance portal. Roman architrave with Bacchic frieze." In *Il mausoleo di Galla Placidia a Ravenna*, ed. Clementina Rizzardi: 209–210. Modena.

Frassineti, G. 1995. "L'antica Classe nel 'Liber pontificalis' di Andrea Agnello." *Ravenna, Studi e Ricerche* 2: 39–55.

Frassineti, Giancarlo. 2005. "La flotta imperiale romana dalla fine del sec. I a.C. alla tarda antichità." In *I porti antichi di Ravenna*, ed. Maurizio Mauro, 1: *Il porto romano e le flotte*: 67–84. Ravenna: Adriapress.

Frugoni, Chiara. 1991. *A Distant City: Images of Urban Experience in the Medieval World*. Translated by William McCuaig. Princeton, NJ: Princeton University Press.

Gaddoni, Wanda. 1989. *Il mausoleo di Teodorico*. Bologna: University Press.

Galassi, Giuseppe. 1930. *Roma o Bisanzio: i musaici di Ravenna e le origini dell'arte italiana*. Rome: La libreria dello stato.

Galetti, Paola. 2005. "Caratteri dell'edilizia privata in una città capitale." In *Ravenna: da capitale imperiale a capitale esarcale*, 2: 887–914. Spoleto: Fondazione Centro Italiano di Studi sull'Alto Medioevo.

Gelichi, Sauro. 1990. "Nuove ricerche archeologiche nella chiesa di Santa Croce a Ravenna." *CARB* 37: 195–208.

———. 1991. "Il Paesaggio Urbano tra V e X secolo." In *Storia di Ravenna II.1*, ed. Antonio Carile: 153–165. Venice: Marsilio Editore.

———. 1994. "L'edilizia residenziale in Romagna tra V e VIII secolo." In *Edilizia residenziale tra V e VIIII secolo, Atti del IV Seminario sul Tardoantico e l'Altomedioevo in Italia centrosettentrionale (Monte Barro-Galbiate-Lecco, 2–4 settembre 1993)*, ed. Gian-Pietro Brogiolo: 157–167. Mantova: Società Archeologica Padana.

———. 1996. "Note sulle città bizantine dell'Esarcato e della Pentapoli tra IV e IX secolo." In *Early Medieval Towns in the Western Mediterranean, Ravello, 22–24 September 1994*, ed. Gian-Pietro Brogiolo: 67–76. Mantua.

———. 2000. "Ravenna, ascesa e declino di una Capitale." In *Sedes regiae (ann. 400–800)*, ed. G. Ripoll and J. M. Gurt: 109–134. Barcelona.

———. 2002. "The Cities." In *Italy in the Early Middle Ages, 476–1000*, ed. Cristina La Rocca: 168–188. Oxford: Oxford University Press.

———. 2005. "Le mura di Ravenna." In *Ravenna: da capitale imperiale a capitale esarcale*, 2: 821–840. Spoleto: Fondazione Centro Italiano di Studi sull'Alto Medioevo.

Gelichi, Sauro and Paola Novara. 1995. "La chiesa di Santa Croce a Ravenna: la sequenza architettonica." *CARB* 42: 347–382.

Gentili, G. 1972. "Origini e fasi costruttive del complesso ecclesiale della Ca'Bianca presso Classe di Ravenna." *Arheoloski Vestnik* 23: 196–211.

George, Judith. 1992. *Venantius Fortunatus: A Latin Poet in Merovingian Gaul*. Oxford: Oxford University Press.

Gerola, Giuseppe. 1916. "Il valore della frase 'ante altare' nello storico Agnello." *Atti e memorie dell'accademia di Agricoltura, Scienze e Lettere di Verona, ser. 4* 19: 25.

———. 1923. "Il restauro del Battistero Ariano di Ravenna." In *Studien zur Kunst des Ostens: Josef Strzygowski zum sechzigsten Geburtstage von seinen Freunden und Schülern*, ed. Heinrich Glück: 112–129. Vienna: Avalun-Verlag.

———. 1932. "Il ripristino della capella di S. Andrea nel palazzo vescovile di Ravenna." *Felix Ravenna* 41: 71–132.

Ghirardini, Gherardo. 1916. "Gli scavi del palazzo di teodorico a Ravenna." *Monumenti Antichi, Reale Accademia dei Lincei* 24: 737–838.

Giacomini, Paola. 1990. "Anagrafe dei cittadini ravennati." In *Storia di Ravenna I*, ed. G. Susini: 137–222. Venice: Marsilio Editore.

———. 1990. "Anagrafe dei classiari." In *Storia di Ravenna I*, ed. G. Susini: 321–362. Venice: Marsilio Editore.

Gillett, Andrew. 2001. "Rome, Ravenna, and the Last Western Emperors." *Papers of the British School at Rome* 69: 131–167.

Giraudi, C. 2005. "Late-Holocene Alluvial Events in the Central Apennines, Italy." *The Holocene* 15: 768–773.

Goffart, Walter. 1980. *Barbarians and Romans, A.D. 418–584: The Techniques of Accommodation*. Princeton, NJ: Princeton University Press.

———. 2006. *Barbarian Tides: The Migration Age and the Later Roman Empire*. Philadelphia: University of Pennsylvania Press.

Grabar, André. 1936. *L'empereur dans l'art byzantine: recherches sur l'art officiel de l'empire d'Orient*. Paris: Les Belles Lettres.

———. 1946. *Martyrium: recherches sur le culte des reliques et l'art chrétien antique*. Paris: Collège de France.

———. 1958. *Ampoules de Terre Sainte (Monza, Bobbio)*. Paris: C. Klincksieck.

———. 1980. *Christian Iconography: A Study of Its Origins*. Princeton, NJ: Princeton University Press. Original edition, 1968.

Gramentieri, Claudia. 2007. "Il mosaico absidale di San Michele in Africisco attraverso le antiche riproduzioni iconografiche." In *San Michele in Africisco e l'età giustinianea a Ravenna: atti del Convegno "La diaspora dell'arcangelo, San Michele in Africisco e l'età giustinianea": Giornate di studio in memoria di Giuseppe Bovini, Ravenna, Sala dei mosaici, 21–22 aprile 2005*, ed. Claudio Spadoni: 337–348. Milan: Silvana.

Grierson, Philip. 1985. "The Date of the Gold Medallion of Theoderic the Great." *Hikuin* 11: 19–26.

Grierson, Philip and Mark A. S. Blackburn. 1986. *Medieval European Coinage: with a Catalogue of the Coins in the Fitzwilliam Museum, Cambridge*, vol. 1, *The Early Middle Ages*. Cambridge: Cambridge University Press.

Grossmann, Peter. 1964. "Zum Narthex von San Giovanni Evangelista in Ravenna." *Römische Mitteilungen* 71: 206–228.

———. 1973. *S. Michele in Africisco zu Ravenna: baugeschichtliche Untersuchungen*. Mainz am Rhein: P. von Zabern.

Grundmann, Herbert. 1958. "Litteratus-Illitteratus. Der Wandel einer Bildungsnorm vom Altertum zum Mittelalter." *Archiv für Kulturgeschichte* 40: 1–65.

Guadagnucci, Anna. 2007. Le città dell'Italia settentrionale nel IV secolo d.C. Laurea specialistica, Università di Pisa.

Guillou, André. 1969. *Régionalisme et indépendance dans l'empire byzantin au VIIe siècle. L'exemple de l'Exarchat et de la Pentapole d'Italie*. Studi Storici 75–76. Rome: Istituto storico italiano per il Medio Evo.

———. 1991. "Demografia e società a Ravenna nell'età esarcale." In *Storia di Ravenna II.1*, ed. Antonio Carile: 101–108. Venice: Marsilio Editore.

Gulowsen, K. 1999. "Liturgical Illustrations or Sacred Images? The Imperial Panels in S. Vitale, Ravenna." *Acta ad archaeologiam et artium historiam pertinentia. Serie altera in 80* 11: 115–146.

Gunn, Joel D. 2000. "A.D. 536 and Its 300-Year Aftermath." In *The Years without Summer: Tracing A.D. 536 and Its Aftermath*, ed. J. D. Gunn: 5–20. Oxford: Archaeopress.

Gwynn, David M. 2007. "From Iconoclasm to Arianism: The Construction of Christian Tradition in the Iconoclast Controversy." *Greek, Roman, and Byzantine Studies* 47: 225–251.

Hall, Linda Jones. 2004. *Roman Berytus: Beirut in Late Antiquity*. London: Routledge.

Halsall, Guy. 2002. *Humour, History and Politics in Late Antiquity and the Early Middle Ages*. Cambridge: Cambridge University Press.

Hanson, R. P. C. 1988. *The Search for the Christian Doctrine of God: The Arian Controversy, 318–381*. Edinburgh: T. & T. Clark.

Harlow, Mary. 2004. "Galla Placidia: Conduit of Culture?" In *Women's Influence on Classical Civilization*, ed. Fiona McHardy: 138–150. London: Routledge.

Harper, James G. 1997. "The Provisioning of Marble for the Sixth-Century Churches of Ravenna: A Reconstructive Analysis." In *Pratum Romanum: Richard Krautheimer zum 100. Geburtstag*, ed. Renate L. Colella: 131–148. Wiesbaden: Reichert.

Haseloff, Günther. 1981. *Die germanische Tierornamentik der Völkerwanderungszeit: Studien zu Salin's Stil I*. Berlin: W. de Gruyter.

Haupt, Albrecht. 1913. *Das Grabmal Theoderichs des Grossen zu Ravenna*. Monumenta Germaniae architectonica I. Leipzig.

Head, Constance. 1972. *Justinian II of Byzantium*. Madison: University of Wisconsin Press.

Heather, Peter J. 1986. "The Crossing of the Danube and the Gothic Conversion." *Greek, Roman, and Byzantine Studies* 27, no. 3: 289–318.

———. 1991. *Goths and Romans, 332–489*. Oxford Historical Monographs. Oxford: Clarendon Press.

———. 1995. "Theoderic, King of the Goths." *Early Medieval Europe* 4, no. 2: 145–173.

———. 2007. "Merely an Ideology? Gothic Identity in Ostrogothic Italy." In *The Ostrogoths from the Migration Period to the Sixth Century: An Ethnographic Perspective*, eds. S. J. B. Barnish and F. Marazzi: 31–80. Woodbridge, Suffolk: Boydell Press.

Heather, Peter J. and John Matthews, eds. 1991. *The Goths in the Fourth Century*. Translated Texts for Historians. Liverpool: Liverpool University Press.

Heidenreich, Robert and Heinz Johannes. 1971. *Das Grabmal Teoderich zu Ravenna*. Deutschen Archäolog. Instituts, no. 8. Wiesbaden.

Henning, Dirk. 1999. *Periclitans res publica: Kaisertum und Eliten in der Krise des Weströmischen Reiches 454/5–493 N. Chr*. Stuttgart: F. Steiner Verlag.

Hillier, Richard. 1993. *Arator on the Acts of the Apostles: A Baptismal Commentary*. Oxford: Oxford University Press.

Hodgkin, Thomas. 1885. *Italy and Her Invaders*, vol. 3, *The Ostrogothic Invasion, 476–535*. Oxford: Clarendon Press.

Holder-Egger, Oswald, ed. 1878. *Liber pontificalis ecclesiae Ravennatis*. MGH Scriptores rerum Langobardicarum et Italicarum saec. VI-IX. Hanover.

Holum, Kenneth. 1977. "Pulcheria's Crusade A.D. 421–22 and the Ideology of Imperial Victory." *Greek, Roman, and Byzantine Studies* 18: 153–172.

———. 1982. *Theodosian Empresses: Women and Imperial Dominion in Late Antiquity*. Berkeley: University of California Press.

Horden, Peregrine. 1992. "Disease, Dragons and Saints: The Management of Epidemics in the Dark Ages." In *Epidemics and Ideas: Essays on the Historical Perception of Pestilence*, ed. Terence Ranger: 45–76. Cambridge: Cambridge University Press.

Humphrey, John H. 1986. *Roman Circuses: Arenas for Chariot Racing*. Berkeley: University of California Press.

Iannucci, Anna Maria. 1982. "S. Apollinare in classe a Ravenna: contributi all'indagine dell'area presbiteriale." *CARB* 29: 181–211.

———. 1986. "I vescovi Ecclesius, Severus, Ursus, Ursicinus, le scene dei privilegi e dei sacrifici in S. Apollinare in Classe – Indagine sistematica." *CARB* 33: 165–193.

———. 1992. "Appunti per una storiografia del del restauro parietale musivo. Il caso di Ravenna." In *Mosaici a S.Vitale e altri restauri. Il restauro in situ di mosaici parietali. Atti del Congresso Nazionale sul restauro in situ di Mosaici parietali (Ravenna 1–3 ottobre 1990)*: 19–29. Ravenna.

———. 1996. "I mosaici di S. Apollinare Nuovo: rielaborazioni con Matlab e Image Processing di indagini diagnostiche multispettrali." *Pixel* 3/4: 5–14.

———. 1996. "Il Mausoleo ritrovato: dagli adattamentti settecenteschi ai progetti e restauri tra Ottocento e Novecento / The Mausoleum rediscovered: from eighteenth-century modifications to late-nineteenth- and twentieth-century projects and restorations." In *Il mausoleo di Galla Placidia a Ravenna*, ed. Clementina Rizzardi: 171–206. Modena.

———. 1997. "La lunga vicenda dei restauri in San Vitale fra cantiere e carteggio. Tre questioni particolari." In *La basilica di San Vitale a Ravenna*, ed. Patrizia Angiolini Martinelli: 69–89. Modena: F. C. Panini.

———. 1998. "The Importance of a Comprehensive Survey Project on Archaeological Structures: The Case of Neonian Baptistry at Ravenna." In *Atti del XIII Congresso UISPP (Forlì 8–14 sept. 1996)*, ed. Nicola et al. Santoupoli. Forlì.

———. 1998. "Integration of Multispectral Diagnostic Researches for Conservation and Restoration: An Application to the Parietal Mosaics in S. Apollinare Nuovo at Ravenna." In *Atti del XIII Congresso UISPP (Forlì 8–14 sept. 1996)*: 271–278. Forlì.

Iannucci, Anna Maria, Cesare Fiori and Cetty Muscolino, eds. 1992. *Mosaici a S. Vitale e altri restauri: il restauro in situ di mosaici parietali. Atti del Convegno nazionale sul restauro in situ di mosaici parietali, Ravenna 1–3 ottobre 1990*. Ravenna: Longo.

Janes, Dominic. 1998. *God and Gold in Late Antiquity*. Cambridge: Cambridge University Press.

Jensen, Robin. 2000. *Understanding Early Christian Art*. London: Routledge.

———. 2002. "The Two Faces of Jesus: How the Early Church Pictured the Divine." *Bible Review* 18, no. 5: 42–50.

———. 2004. *Face to Face: The Portrait of the Divine in Early Christianity*. Minneapolis: Fortress Press.

Joffe, Alexander H. 1998. "Disembedded Capitals in the Western Asian Perspective." *Comparative Studies in Society and History* 40: 549–580.

Johnson, Mark J. 1988. "Toward a History of Theoderic's Building Program." *Dumbarton Oaks Papers* 42: 73–96.

———. 1991. "On the Burial Places of the Theodosian Dynasty." *Byzantion* 61: 330–338.

———. 2005. "From Paganism to Christianity in the Imperial Mausolea of the Tetrarchs and Constantine." In *Niš i Vizantija: treci naućni skup, Niš, 3–5. jun*

2004: zbornik radova III, ed. Misa Rakocija, ed. Misa Rokocija: 115–123. Nis: grad Nis.

Johnson, Stephen. 1983. *Late Roman Fortifications*. Totowa, NJ: Barnes and Noble Books.

Jones, A. H. M. 1962. "The Constitutional Position of Odoacer and Theoderic." *Journal of Roman Studies* 52: 126–130.

———. 1964. *The Later Roman Empire, 284–602: A Social, Economic, and Administrative Survey*. Norman: University of Oklahoma Press.

Jones, Arnold Hugh Martin, John R. Martindale and John Morris. 1971. *The Prosopography of the Later Roman Empire*, vol. 3, *A.D. 527–641*. Cambridge: Cambridge University Press.

Kelly, Christopher. 1998. "Emperors, Government and Bureaucracy." In *The Cambridge Ancient History*, vol. 13, *The Late Empire, AD 337–425*, ed. Averil Cameron: 138–183. Cambridge: Cambridge University Press.

———. 2004. *Ruling the Later Roman Empire*. Cambridge, MA: Harvard University Press.

Kennell, Stefanie A. H. 1994. "Hercules' Invisible Basilica (Cassiodorus, Variae I, 6)." *Latomus* 53: 159–175.

Kinney, Dale. 1992. "The Apocalypse in Early Christian Monumental Decoration." In *The Apocalypse in the Middle Ages*, ed. Richard K. Emmerson: 200–216. Ithaca, NY: Cornell University Press.

———. 1997. " 'Spolia Damnatio' and 'Renovatio memoriae.' " *Memoirs of the American Academy in Rome* 42: 117–148.

———. 2001. "Roman Architectural Spolia." *Proceedings of the American Philosophical Society* 145: 138–161.

Kleinbauer, W. Eugene. 1987. "The Double-Shell Tetraconch Building at Perge in Pamphylia and the Origin of the Architectural Genus." *Dumbarton Oaks Papers* 41: 277–293.

Koder, Johannes. 1996. "Climatic Change in the Fifth and Sixth Centuries?" In *The Sixth Century: End or Beginning?* ed. Pauline Allen: 270–285. Brisbane: Australian Association for Byzantine Studies.

Kollwitz, Johannes and Helga Herdejürgen. 1979. *Die ravennatischen Sarkophage*. Berlin: Mann.

Kostof, Spiro. 1965. *The Orthodox Baptistery of Ravenna*. New Haven, CT: Yale University Press.

Krautheimer, Richard. 1937. *Corpus basilicarum Romae*, vol. 1. Monumenti di antichità cristiana, ser. 2 vol. 2. Città del Vaticano: Pontificio istituto di archeologia cristiana.

———. 1942. "Introduction to an 'Iconography of Mediaeval Architecture.' " *Journal of the Warburg and Courtauld Institutes* 5: 1–33.

———. 1953. "Sancta Maria Rotunda." In *Arte del primo millennio: atti del 2. Convegno per lo studio dell'arte dell'alto medio evo tenuto presso l'Università di Pavia nel settembre 1950*, ed. Edoardo Arslan: 21–27. Torino: Viglongo.

———. 1961. "The Architecture of Sixtus III: A Fifth-Century Renascence?" In *Essays in Honor of Erwin Panofsky*, vol. 1, ed. Millard Meiss: 291–302. New York: New York University Press.

———. 1966. "Die Decanneacubita in Konstantinopel. Ein kleiner Beitrag zur Frage Rom u. Byzanz." In *Tortulae: Studien zu altchristlichen und byzantinischen Monumenten*, ed. Walter Nikolaus Schumacher: 195–199. Rome: Herder.

————. 1973. "Review of Robert Heidenreich and Heinz Johannes, *Das Grabmal Theoderichs zu Ravenna* (Wiesbaden: Franz Steiner Verlag, 1971)." *Art Bulletin* 55: 299–289.

————. 1983. *Three Christian Capitals: Topography and Politics*. Berkeley: University of California Press.

Krautheimer, Richard and Slobodan Curcic. 1986. *Early Christian and Byzantine Architecture*. Harmondsworth: Penguin.

Kulikowski, Michael. 2000. "The Notitia Dignitatum as a Historical Source." *Historia* 49: 358–77.

Kunzelmann, A. 1931. "Die Chronologie der Sermones des hl. Augustinus." In *Miscellanea Agostiniana: testi e studi, pubblicati a cura del-l'Ordine eremitano di s. Agostino nel XV centenario dalla morte del santo dottore*, ed. Germain Morin, 2: 417–520. Rome: Tipografia poliglotta vaticana.

La Rocca, Cristina. 1992. "Public Buildings and Urban Change in Northern Italy in the Early Mediaeval Period." In *The City in Late Antiquity*, ed. John Rich: 161–180. London: CRC Press.

————. 1993. "Una prudente maschera 'Antiqua.' La politica edilizia di Teoderico." In *Teoderico il Grande e i Goti d'Italia: Atti del XIII Congresso Internazionale di Studi sull'Alto Medioevo, Milano, 2–6 novembre 1992*, 2: 451–515. Spoleto: Centro italiano di Studi sull'Alto Medioevo.

La Rocca, Eugenio. 1992. "Claudio a Ravenna." *La Parola del Passato* 47: 265–314.

Lanzoni, Francesco. 1910–11. "San Severo Vescovo di Ravenna (342–3) nella storia e nella leggenda." *Atti e Memorie della Deputazione di Storia Patria per le Provincie di Romagna, ser. 4*, 1: 325–396.

————. 1911–12. "San Severo Vescovo di Ravenna (342–3) nella storia e nella leggenda." *Atti e Memorie della Deputazione di Storia Patria per le Provincie di Romagna, ser. 4* 2: 350–396.

————. 1927. *Le diocesi d'Italia dalle origini al principio del secolo VII (604). Studio Critico*. Faenza: F. Lega.

Laqua, Hans Peter. 1976. *Traditionen und Leitbilder bei dem Ravennater Reformer Petrus Damiani, 1042–1052*. Munich: Fink.

Lawrence, Marion and Bruce Rogers. 1945. *The Sarcophagi of Ravenna*. New York: College Art Association of America.

Lazard, Sylviane. 1991. "Goti e Latini a Ravenna." In *Storia di Ravenna, II.1*, ed. Antonio Carile: 109–133. Venice.

Leader-Newby, Ruth E. 2004. *Silver and Society in Late Antiquity: Functions and Meanings of Silver Plate in the Fourth to the Seventh Centuries*. Aldershot: Ashgate.

Lehmann, Karl. 1945. "The Dome of Heaven." *Art Bulletin* 27: 1–27.

Levi, Annalina and Mario Levi. 1967. *Itineraria Picta: Contributo alla studio della Tabula Peutingeriana*. Rome: L'Erma di Bretschneider.

Lewis, Suzanne. 1969. "The Latin Iconography of the Single-Naved Cruciform Basilica Apostolorum in Milan." *Art Bulletin* 51: 205–219.

————. 1973. "San Lorenzo Revisited: A Theodosian Palace Church at Milan." *Journal of the Society of Architectural Historians* 32: 197–222.

Librenti, Mauro. 2004. "Ambiente a continuità d'uso (VII-VIII d.C.)." In *Archeologia urbana a Ravenna: la Domus dei tappeti di pietra, il complesso archeologico di via D'Azeglio*, ed. Giovanna Montevecchi: 126–127. Ravenna: Longo.

Liebeschuetz, J. H. W. G. 2000. "Ravenna to Aachen." In *Sedes Regiae (ann. 400–800)*, ed. Gisela Ripoll: 9–30. Barcelona: Reial Acadèmia de Bones Lletres.

_____. 2001. *Decline and Fall of the Roman City*. Oxford: Oxford University Press.

Lifshitz, Felice. 2005. *The Name of the Saint: The Martyrology of Jerome and Access to the Sacred in Francia, 627–827*. Notre Dame, IN: University of Notre Dame Press.

Lombardini, Nora. 1997. "Le vicende del monumento dal 1860 a oggi: l'eliminazione delle superfetazioni." In *La basilica di San Vitale a Ravenna*, ed. Patrizia Angiolini Martinelli: 91–110. Modena: F. C. Panini.

_____. 2007. "Sul comportamento strutturale di murature in laterizio in uso nel VI secolo. L'esempio di San Michele in Africisco." In *San Michele in Africisco e l'età giustinianea a Ravenna: atti del Convegno "La diaspora dell'arcangelo, San Michele in Africisco e l'età giustinianea": Giornate di studio in memoria di Giuseppe Bovini, Ravenna, Sala dei mosaici, 21–22 aprile 2005*, ed. Claudio Spadoni: 253–282. Milan: Silvana.

Longhi, D. 2000. "La porta urbica nella raffigurazione musiva della città di Ravenna in S. Apollinare Nuovo di Ravenna." In *Atti del VI colloquio dell'Associazione italiana per lo studio e la coservazione del mosaico*, ed. Federico Guidobaldi: 647–658. Ravenna: Girasole.

Lucchesi, Giovanni. 1971. "I santi celebrati dall'Arcivescovo Agnello." In *Agnello, arcivescovo di Ravenna. Studi per il XIV centenario della morte. (570–1970)*, ed. Paola Monti: 61–78. Faenza: Fratelli Lega.

Luiselli, Bruno. 2005. "Dall'arianesimo dei Visigoti di Costantinopoli all'arianesimo degli Ostrogoti d'Italia." In *Ravenna: da capitale imperiale a capitale esarcale*, 2: 729–760. Spoleto: Fondazione Centro Italiano di Studi sull'Alto Medioevo.

Luzzatto, Giuseppe I. 1968. "Sul problema dello statuto municipale di Ravenna." In *Atti del Convegno Internazionale di Studi sulle Antichità di Classe, Ravenna, 14–17 ottobre 1967*: 289–300. Ravenna: Longo.

MacCormack, Sabine. 1981. *Art and Ceremony in Late Antiquity*. Berkeley: University of California Press.

MacGeorge, Penny. 2003. *Late Roman Warlords*. Oxford: Oxford University Press.

MacGregor, Arthur et al. 1997. *Ashmolean Museum, Oxford: A Summary Catalogue of the Continental Archeological Collections (Roman Iron Age, Migration Period, Early Medieval)*. Oxford: Archaeopress.

Mackie, Gillian. 1990. "New Light on the So-called Saint Lawrence Panel at the Mausoleum of Galla Placidia, Ravenna." *Gesta* 29: 54–60.

_____. 1995. "The Mausoleum of Galla Placidia: A Possible Occupant." *Byzantion* 65: 396–404.

_____. 1995. "Symbolism and Purpose in an Early Christian Martyr Chapel: The Case of San Vittore in Ciel d'Oro, Milan." *Gesta* 34, no. 2: 91–101.

_____. 2003. *Early Christian Chapels in the West: Decoration, Function, and Patronage*. Toronto: University of Toronto Press.

Magdalino, Paul. 2001. "Aristocratic *oikoi* in the Tenth and Eleventh Regions of Constantinople." In *Byzantine Constantinople: Monuments, Topography, and Everyday Life*, ed. N. Necipoglu: 53–72. Leiden: Brill.

Magnani, Stefano. 2001. "La Ravenna preromana: Fonti e documenti." In *Ravenna Romana*, ed. Maurizio Mauro: 25–45. Ravenna: Adriapress.

Maguire, Henry. 1987. *Earth and Ocean: The Terrestrial World in Early Byzantine Art*. University Park: Pennsylvania State University Press.

————. 2007. "Eufrasius and Friends: On Names and Their Absence in Byzantine Art." In *Art and Text in Byzantine Culture*, ed. Liz James: 139–160. Cambridge: Cambridge University Press.

Maioli, M. G. 1995. "Edifici di età repubblicana e augustea nel complesso archeologico di via D'Azeglio a Ravenna." *CARB* 42: 507–521.

————. 2000. "Le mura di Ravenna in epoca imperiale: i dati di scavo." In *Mura, porte e torri di Ravenna*, ed. Maurizio Mauro: 47–52. Ravenna: Istituto italiano dei castelli, Adria press.

————. 2001. "La città dei morti: Ubicazione e caratteristiche delle necropoli ravennati; le tipologie funerarie, le persone e i corredi." In *Ravenna Romana*, ed. Maurizio Mauro: 243–250. Ravenna: Adriapress.

————. 2001. "Vie d'acqua e stutture portuali di Ravenna romana." In *Ravenna Romana*, ed. Maurizio Mauro: 219–224. Ravenna: Adriapress.

————. 2001. "Vivere a Ravenna." In *Ravenna Romana*, ed. Maurizio Mauro: 177–187. Ravenna: Adriapress.

————. 2005. "Gli approvvigionamenti." In *I porti antichi di Ravenna*, ed. Maurizio Mauro, 1: Il porto romano e le flotte: 173–178. Ravenna: Adriapress.

————. 2005. "La topografia di Ravenna e Classe in età romana." In *I porti antichi di Ravenna*, ed. Maurizio Mauro, 1: Il porto romano e le flotte: 45–56. Ravenna: Adriapress.

————. 2007. "San Michele in Africisco nella Ravenna del VI secolo." In *San Michele in Africisco e l'età giustinianea a Ravenna: atti del Convegno "La diaspora dell'arcangelo, San Michele in Africisco e l'età giustinianea": Giornate di studio in memoria di Giuseppe Bovini, Ravenna, Sala dei mosaici, 21–22 aprile 2005*, ed. Claudio Spadoni: 223–232. Milan: Silvana.

Maioli, Maria Grazia. 1989. "La villa romana di Russi." In *Russi, Un racconto sul territorio*, ed. Vittorio Pranzini: 183–202. Ravenna: Longo.

————. 1990. "La topografia della zona di Classe." In *Storia di Ravenna I*, ed. G. Susini: 375–414. Venice: Marsilio Editore.

————. 1992. "Nuovi dati sul complesso archeologico di S. Severo a Classe (RA): scavi 1981–1991." *CARB* 39: 497–520.

————. 1994. "Ravenna e la Romagna in epoca gota." In *I Goti*, ed. Ermanno A. Arslan: 232–251. Milan: Electra.

————. 1995. "Rapporti commerciali e materiali di Ravenna e Classe in epoca teodericiana." In *Teoderico e i Goti fra Oriente e Occidente*, ed. Antonio Carile: 227–236. Ravenna: Longo Editore.

————. 2002. "I porti antichi fino all'età moderna." In *Il porto di Ravenna*, ed. Maurizio Mauro: 37–45. Ravenna: Adriapress.

————. 2004. "Lo scavo archeologico di via D'Azeglio: inquadramento topografico." In *Archeologia urbana a Ravenna: la Domus dei tappeti di pietra, il complesso archeologico di via D'Azeglio*, ed. Giovanna Montevecchi: 13–14. Ravenna: Longo.

Maioli, Maria Grazia and Maria Luisa Stoppioni. 1987. *Classe e Ravenna fra terra e mare: Città-necropoli, monumenti*. Ravenna: Sirri.

Malnate, L. and A. Violante. 1995. "Il sistema urbano di VI e III secolo in Emilia Romagna tra Etruschi e Celti (Plut. *Vita Cam.* 16,3)." In *L'Europe celtique du Ve au IIIe siècle avant J.-C. Contacts, echanges et mouvements de populations. Actes du deuxième Symposium international d'Hautvillers, 8–10 octobre 1992*, ed. Jean-Jacques Charpy: 97–123. Sceaux: Kronos B.Y. éditions.

Malnati, L. 2005. "L'Adriatico prima dei Romani." In *I porti antichi di Ravenna*, ed. Maurizio Mauro, 1: Il porto romano e le flotte: 25–34. Ravenna: Adriapress.

Manara, Elena. 1983. "Di un'ipotesi per l'individuazione dei personaggi dei pannelli del S. Vitale a Ravenna e per la loro interpretazione." *Felix Ravenna* 125–126: 13–37.

Mango, Cyril A. 1972. "The Church of Saints Sergius and Bacchus at Constantinople and the Alleged Tradition of Octagonal Palatine Churches." *Jahrbuch der österreichischen Byzantinistik* 21: 189–193.

———. 1985. *Le développement urbain de Constantinople, IVe–VIIe siècles*. Paris: Diffusion de Boccard.

———. 1986. *The Art of the Byzantine Empire, 312–1453*. Toronto: University of Toronto Press. Original edition, Englewood Cliffs, NJ: Prentice-Hall, 1972.

———. 1986. "The Pilgrimage Centre of St. Michael at Germia." *Jahrbuch der österreichischen Byzantinistik* 36: 117–132.

———. 1995. "The Water Supply of Constantinople." In *Constantinople and Its Hinterland*, ed. Cyril A. Mango: 9–18. Aldershot, Hants.: Ashgate.

———. 1998. "The Origins of the Blachernae Shrine at Constantinople." In *Radovi XIII. medunarodnog kongresa za starokrscansku arheologiju: Split-Porec (25. 9.-1. 10. 1994.) [Acta XIII congressus internationalis archaeologiae christianae]*, ed. Nenad Cambi, 2: 61–76. Split and Vatican City: Arheoloski muzej and Pontificio Istituto di Archeologia Cristiana.

Mansi, Giovanni Domenico, ed. 1901–27 (repr.). *Sacrorum conciliorum nova et amplissima collectio*, 53 vols. Paris: H. Welter.

Mansuelli, Guido A. 1962. *La villa romana di Russi*. Faenze: Stabilimento Grafico Fratelli Lega.

———. 1967. "La Port'Aurea di Ravenna." *CARB* 14: 191–217.

———. 1971. "Le fonti su Ravenna antica." *CARB* 18: 333–347.

———. 1990. "Etnogenesi ravennati." In *Storia di Ravenna I*, ed. G. Susini: 103–112. Venice: Marsilio Editore.

Manzelli, Valentina. 2000. "Le fortificazioni romane e la Porta Aurea." In *Mura, porte e torri di Ravenna*, ed. Maurizio Mauro: 25–46. Ravenna: Istituto italiano dei castelli, Adria press.

———. 2000. *Ravenna*. Città Romane 2. Rome: "L'Erma" di Bretschneider.

———. 2000. "Ravenna, una città di frontiera: le antiche mura repubblicane." *Ravenna, Studi e Ricerche* 7, no. 1: 191–206.

———. 2001. "I monumenti perduti: Ipotesi ricostruttiva del foro della città." In *Ravenna Romana*, ed. Maurizio Mauro: 63–80. Ravenna: Adriapress.

———. 2001. "La forma urbis di Ravenna in età romana." In *Ravenna Romana*, ed. Maurizio Mauro: 45–62. Ravenna: Adriapress.

———. 2001. "Le mura di Ravenna repubblicana." In *Fortificazioni antiche in Italia: Età repubblicana*, ed. Lorenzo Quilici: 7–22. Roma: L'Erma di Bretschneider.

———. 2003. "La *domus del triclinio*: lo scavo della Banca Popolare." In *Domus del Triclinio. Alla scoperta di Ravenna romana. Mosaici e altri tesori mai visti*, ed. Monica Cardascia: 55–60. Ravenna: Fondazione RavennAntica, Parco archeologico di Classe.

———. 2005. "Fonti e documenti." In *I porti antichi di Ravenna*, ed. Maurizio Mauro, 1: Il porto romano e le flotte: 35–44. Ravenna: Adriapress.

Manzelli, Valentina and G. L. Grassigli. 2001. "Abitare a Ravenna: Edilizia privata e apparati decorativi nelle domus ravennati di età romana." In *Ravenna Romana*, ed. Maurizio Mauro: 133–176. Ravenna: Adriapress.

Marano, Yuri A. 2007. "Domus in Qua Manebat Episcopus: Episcopal Residences in Northern Italy during Late Antiquity (4th to 6th c. A.D.)." In *Housing in Late Antiquity: From Palaces to Shops*, ed. Luke Lavan: 97–168. Leiden: E. J. Brill.

Marazzi, Federico. 1998. "The Destinies of the Late Antique Italies: Politico-Economic Developments of the Sixth Century." In *The Sixth Century: Production, Distribution and Demand*, ed. Richard Hodges: 119–160. Leiden: Brill.

————. 2006. "Cadavera urbium, nuove capitali e Roma aeterna: l'identità urbana in Italia fra crisi, rinascita e propaganda (secoli III-V)." In *Die Stadt in der Spätantike– Niedergang oder Wandel? Akten des internationalen Kolloquiums in München am 30. und 31. Mai 2003*, ed. Jens Uwe Krause: 33–65. Stuttgart: Franz Steiner Verlag.

Marenbon, John. 2003. *Boethius*. Oxford: Oxford University Press.

Marini, Luigi Gaetano. 1805. *I papiri diplomatici raccolti ed illustrati*. Rome: Stamperia della Sac. congr. de prop. fide.

Markus, Robert A. 1979. "Carthage – Prima Justiniana – Ravenna. An Aspect of Justinian's *Kirchenpolitik*." *Byzantion* 49: 277–302.

————. 1981. "Ravenna and Rome, 554–604." *Byzantion* 51: 566–578.

————. 1997. *Gregory the Great and His World*. Cambridge: Cambridge University Press.

Martindale, J. R., ed. 1980. *The Prosopography of the Later Roman Empire*, vol. 2, *A.D. 395–527*. Cambridge: Cambridge University Press.

Martini, Luciana and Clementina Rizzardi, eds. 1990. *Avori bizantini e medievali nel Museo nazionale di Ravenna: catalogo*. Ravenna: Longo.

Marzetti, A. 2002. "L'Antico Episcopio di Ravenna e il moderno Palazzo Arcivescovile." *Ravenna, Studi e Ricerche* 9, no. 1: 99–135.

Mathews, Thomas F. 1962. "An Early Roman Chancel Arrangement and Its Liturgical Uses." *Rivista di archeologia cristiana* 38: 71–95.

————. 1971. *The Early Churches of Constantinople: Architecture and Liturgy*. University Park: Pennsylvania State University Press.

————. 1993. *The Clash of Gods: A Reinterpretation of Early Christian Art*. Princeton, NJ: Princeton University Press.

————. 2005. "The Palace Church of Sts. Sergius and Bacchus in Constantinople." In *Archaeology in Architecture: Studies in Honor of Cecil L. Striker*, ed. Deborah M. Deliyannis: 137–141. Mainz: Verlag Philipp von Zabern.

Mathisen, Ralph W. 1997. "Barbarian Bishops and the Churches 'in Barbaricis Gentibus' during Late Antiquity." *Speculum* 72: 664–697.

Matthews, John. 1970. "Olympiodorus of Thebes and the History of the West." *Journal of Roman Studies* 60: 79–97.

————. 1975. *Western Aristocracies and Imperial Court, A.D. 364–425*. Oxford: Oxford University Press.

————. 1981. "Anicius Manlius Severinus Boethius." In *Boethius: His Life, Thought and Influence*, ed. M. Gibson: 15–43. Oxford: Oxford University Press.

Mauro, Maurizio, ed. 2001. *Ravenna Romana*. Ravenna: Adriapress.

————, ed. 2002. *Il porto di Ravenna*. Ravenna: Adriapress.

————, ed. 2005. *I porti antichi di Ravenna*. Ravenna: Adriapress.

Mauro, Maurizio and Paola Novara, eds. 2000. *Mura, porte e torri di Ravenna*. Ravenna: Istituto italiano dei castelli, Adria press.

Mazza, Mario. 2005. "Ravenna: problemi di una capitale." In *Ravenna: da capitale imperiale a capitale esarcale*, 1: 3–40. Spoleto: Fondazione Centro Italiano di Studi sull'Alto Medioevo.

Mazzotti, Mario. 1954. *La basilica di S. Apollinare in Classe*. Vatican City: Pontificio Istituto di Archeologia Cristiana.

———. 1957. "La 'Anastasis Ghotorum' di Ravenna ed il suo battistero." *Felix Ravenna* 75: 25–62.

———. 1959. "La basilica di Sant'Andrea Maggiore." *CARB* 6: 157.

———. 1960. "La basilica di S. Maria Maggiore in Ravenna." *CARB* 7: 253–260.

———. 1960. "La croce argentea del vescovo Agnello del Museo Arcivescovile di Ravenna." *CARB* 7: 261–270.

———. 1961. "Il battistero della cattedrale di Ravenna." *CARB* 8: 255–278.

———. 1967. "La basilica ravennate di S. Agata Maggiore." *CARB* 14: 233–251.

———. 1970. "Scavi recenti al Battistero degli Ariani in Ravenna." *Felix Ravenna* Ser. 4, 1: 115–123.

———. 1974. "La cripta della chiesa ravennate di S. Francesco dopo le ultime esplorazioni." *CARB* 21: 217–230.

———. 1986. "S. Apollinare in Classe: indagini e studi degli ultimi trent'anni." *Rivista di archeologia cristiana* 62, no. 1–2: 199–219.

McClanan, Anne. 1998. "Ritual and Representation of the Byzantine Empress Court at San Vitale, Ravenna." In *Radovi XIII. medunarodnog kongresa za starokrscansku arheologiju, 1994*, ed. Nenad Cambi, 2: 11–20. Rome: Pontificio Istituto di Archeologia Cristiana.

———. 2002. *Representations of Early Byzantine Empresses: Image and Empire*. New York: Palgrave Macmillan.

McConnell, Christian David. 2005. Baptism in Visigothic Spain: Origins, Development and Interpretation. Notre Dame: PhD diss., University of Notre Dame.

McCormick, Michael. 2000. "Emperor and Court." In *The Cambridge Ancient History*, vol. 14, *Late Antiquity: Empire and Successors, AD 425–600*, ed. Averil Cameron: 135–163. Cambridge: Cambridge University Press.

———. 2001. *Origins of the European Economy: Communications and Commerce A.D. 300–900*. Cambridge: Cambridge University Press.

Megaw, A. H. S. and E. J. W. Hawkins. 1977. *The Church of the Panagia Kanakariá at Lythrankomi in Cyprus: Its Mosaics and Frescoes*. Washington, DC: Dumbarton Oaks.

Meslin, Michel. 1967. *Les Ariens d'Occident, 335–430*. Patristica Sorbonensia 8. Paris: Éditions du Seuil.

Metlich, Michael Andreas. 2004. *The Coinage of Ostrogothic Italy*. London: Spink.

Michael, Angelika. 2005. *Das Apsismosaik von S. Apollinare in Classe: seine Deutung im Kontext der Liturgie*. Frankfurt am Main: Peter Lang.

Michelini, Roberta. 1996. "Anfore degli estradossi della cupola e delle volte. Ravenna, Museo Nazionale / Vases in the dome extradox and in the vaults. Ravenna, Museo Nazionale." In *Il mausoleo di Galla Placidia a Ravenna*, ed. Clementina Rizzardi: 241–242. Modena.

———. 1996. "Pigna marmorea sulla sommità del tetto / Marble pinecone at the top of the roof." In *Il mausoleo di Galla Placidia a Ravenna*, ed. Clementina Rizzardi: 210–212. Modena.

Miller, Maureen C. 1991–92. "The Development of the Archiepiscopal Residence in Ravenna, 300–1300." *Felix Ravenna* 141–144: 145–173.

———. 2000. *The Bishop's Palace: Architecture and Authority in Medieval Italy*. Ithaca, NY: Cornell University Press.

Momigliano, Arnaldo. 1955. "Cassiodorus and Italian Culture of His Time." *Proceedings of the British Academy* 41: 207–245.

Montanari, Giovanni. 1971. "La lettera dell'Arcivescovo Agnello *De Ratione Fidei*: filologia, storia politica, religione." In *Agnello arcivescovo di Ravenna*, *Studi per il XIV centenario della morte (570–1970)*, ed. Paola Monti: 25–52. Faenze: Fratelli Lega.

———. 1982. "L'abside di S. Apollinare in Classe di Ravenna: Mistero Centrale, anamnesi ed eucaristia." In *Miscellanea di studi artistici e letterari in onore di Giovanni Fallani in occasione del XXV di presidente*, ed. Dante Balboni: 99–127. Napoli: A. De Dominicis.

———. 1984. "Giuseppe l'Ebreo della Cattedra di Massimiano: prototipo del buon governo?" *Felix Ravenna* 127/130: 305–322.

———. 1992. "Culto e liturgia a Ravenna dal IV al IX secolo." In *Storia di Ravenna* II.2, ed. Antonio Carile: 241–281. Venezia: Marsilio Editore.

———. 1996. "Iconologia nelle rappresentazioni di Mosè in S. Vitale di Ravenna." *CARB* 42: 627–647.

———. 2002. "Elementi per una ricerca storico-teologica sull 'arianesimo' nella città di Ravenna." In *Ravenna: l'iconologia. Saggi di interpretazione culturale e religiosa dei cicli musivi*: 189–204. Ravenna: Longo Editore. Original edition, Ravennatensia I (Cesena, 1969): 27–50.

———. 2002. "I dodici Apostoli nei monumenti ravennati. *Traditio legis* e collegialità." In *Ravenna: l'iconologia. Saggi di interpretazione culturale e religiosa dei cicli musivi*: 205–224. Ravenna: Longo Editore. Original edition, Ravennatensia I (Cesena, 1969): 337–369.

———. 2002. "Massimiano arcivescovo di Ravenna (546–556) come committente." In *Ravenna: l'iconologia. Saggi di interpretazione culturale e religiosa dei cicli musivi*: 11–54. Ravenna: Longo Editore. Original edition, Studi Romagnoli 42 (1991): 367–416.

Montevecchi, Giovanna. 2004. *Archeologia urbana a Ravenna: la Domus dei tappeti di pietra, il complesso archeologico di via D'Azeglio*. Ravenna: Longo.

———. 2004. "La strada e la struttura fognaria." In *Archeologia urbana a Ravenna: la Domus dei tappeti di pietra, il complesso archeologico di via D'Azeglio*, ed. Giovanna Montevecchi: 20–21. Ravenna: Longo.

Moorhead, John. 1992. *Theoderic in Italy*. Oxford: Clarendon Press.

Morath, Günther Wolfgang. 1940. *Die Maximianskathedra in Ravenna*. Freiburger Theologische Studien, 54. Freiburg: Herder.

Müller, Claudia. 1980. "Das Apsismosaik von S. Apollinare in Classe. Eine Strukturanalyse." *Römische Quartalschrift für christliche Altertumskunde und Kirchengeschichte* 75: 11–50.

Müller-Wiener, Wolfgang. 1989. "Bischofsresidenzen des 4.-7. Jhs. im östlichen Mittelmeer-Raum." In *Actes du XIe Congrès International d'Archéologie Chrétienne*, ed. Noel Duval, 1: 651–709. Rome: Ecole française de Rome, Pontificio Istituto di Archeologia cristiana.

Muscolino, Cetty. 1992. "I mosaici dell'arcone di S. Vitale a Ravenna. Osservazioni e scelte metodologiche per un restauro." In *Mosaici a S. Vitale e altri restauri: il restauro in situ di mosaici parietali. Atti del Convegno nazionale sul restauro in situ di mosaici parietali, Ravenna 1–3 ottobre 1990*, ed. Anna Maria Iannucci: 55–62. Ravenna: Longo.

————. 1997. "I restauri musivi." In *La basilica di San Vitale a Ravenna*, ed. Patrizia Angiolini Martinelli: 111–121. Modena: F. C. Panini.

————. 2007. "Il mosaico parietale bizantino fra tecnica e restauro." In *San Michele in Africisco e l'età giustinianea a Ravenna: atti del Convegno "La diaspora dell'arcangelo, San Michele in Africisco e l'età giustinianea": Giornàte di studio in memoria di Giuseppe Bovini, Ravenna, Sala dei mosaici, 21–22 aprile 2005*, ed. Claudio Spadoni: 297–310. Milan: Silvana.

Nasrallah, Laura. 2005. "Empire and Apocalypse in Thessaloniki: Interpreting the Early Christian Rotunda." *Journal of Early Christian Studies* 13, no. 4: 465–508.

Nauerth, Claudia. 1974. *Agnellus von Ravenna: Untersuchungen zur archäologischen Methode des ravennatischen Chroniste*. Munich: Arbeo-gesellschaft.

Nauroy, Gérard. 1989. "Le martyre de Laurent dans l'hymnodie et la prédication des IVe et Ve siècles et l'authenticité ambrosienne de l'hymne 'Apostolorum supparem.'" *Revue des Études Augustiniennes* 35: 44–82.

Nees, Lawrence. 1991. *A Tainted Mantle: Hercules and the Classical Tradition at the Carolingian Court*. Philadelphia: University of Pennsylvania Press.

Negrelli, Claudio. 2004. "Periodo altomedievale." In *Archeologia urbana a Ravenna: la Domus dei tappeti di pietra, il complesso archeologico di via D'Azeglio*, ed. Giovanna Montevecchi: 120–125. Ravenna: Longo.

Neri, V. 1990. "Verso Ravenna capitale: Roma, Ravenna e le residence imperiali tardoantiche." In *Storia di Ravenna I*, ed. G. Susini: 535–584. Venice: Marsilio Editore.

Neri, Valerio. 1995. "La legittimità politica del regno teodericiano nell' Anonymi Valesiani Pars Posterior." In *Teoderico e i Goti fra Oriente e Occidente*, ed. Antonio Carile: 313–340. Ravenna: Longo Editore.

Netzer, Nancy. 1983. "Redating the Consular Ivory of Orestes." *Burlington Magazine* 125: 265–271.

Noble, Thomas F. X. 1984. *The Republic of St. Peter, the Birth of the Papal State, 680–825*. Philadelphia: University of Pennsylvania Press.

————. 1993. "Theoderic and the Papacy." In *Teoderico il Grande e i Goti d'Italia: Atti del XIII Congresso Internazionale di Studi sull'Alto Medioevo, Milano, 2–6 novembre 1992*, 1: 395–424. Spoleto: Centro italiano di Studi sull'Alto Medioevo.

Nordhagen, Per Jonas and Hans Peter L'Orange. 1966. *Mosaics from Antiquity to the Early Middle Ages*. Translated by Ann E. Keep. London: Methuen.

Nordhagen, Per Jonas. 1983. "The Penetration of Byzantine Mosaic Technique into Italy in the Sixth Century." In *III Colloquio internazionale sul mosaico antico, Ravenna, 6–10 settembre, 1980*, ed. Rafaella Farioli Campanati: 73–84. Ravenna: Edizioni del Girasole.

Nordström, Carl Otto. 1953. *Ravennastudien: ideengeschichtliche und ikonographische Untersuchungen über die Mosaiken von Ravenna*. Stockholm: Almqvist & Wiksell.

Novara, Paola. 1988. "I Palazzi Imperiali di Ravenna. I. La traduzione del 'Palazzo di Galla Placidia.'" *L'Archidea* 2, no. 4: 10–13.

————. 1990. "Note sul 'palazzo degli Ottoni' in Ravenna e sulla cappella di San Paolo fuori Porta San Lorenzo. Le fonti." *Civiltà Padana* 3: 79–89.

————. 1997. *La cattedrale di Ravenna: storia e archeologia*. Ravenna.

————. 1997. "Materiali medievali dallo scavo della chiesa di S. Severo in Classe (RA)." In *I Congresso Nazionale di Archeologia Medievale*, ed. Sauro Gelichi: 328–331. Florence: Edizioni all'Insegna del Giglio.

————. 1998. *Storia delle scoperte archeologiche di Ravenna e Classe: i secoli XV–XIX.* Ravenna: D. Montanari.

————. 1999. *Ubi multi peccatores occurrunt. Storia e archeologia della chiesa di S. Apollinare Nuovo, del monastero benedittino, poi convento dei Frati Minori Osservanti, e del quartiere ritenuto l'area palaziale della Ravenna tardoantica.* Ravenna: D. Montanari.

————. 2000. *Un tempio nomato dai portici: le scoperte archeologiche effettuate nell'ambito della costruzione della sede centrale della Cassa di risparmio di Ravenna.* Ravenna: Fondazione Cassa di risparmio di Ravenna, Cassa di risparmio di Ravenna.

————. 2001. "L'edilizia di culto tardo-antica." In *Ravenna Romana*, ed. Maurizio Mauro: 281–308. Ravenna: Adriapress.

————. 2001. "La Ravenna tardo-imperiale." In *Ravenna Romana*, ed. Maurizio Mauro: 251–280. Ravenna: Adriapress.

————. 2001. *Palatium: le ricerche archeologiche nelle proprietà dei salesiani attraverso le relazioni di scavo di Gaetano Nave (1911–1915).* Ravenna: B. Montanari.

Novara, Paola and F. Sarasini. 2001. "Disiecta membra: la scultura decorativa e i capitelli antichi di Ravenna." In *Ravenna Romana*, ed. Maurizio Mauro: 81–106. Ravenna: Adriapress.

Oakeshott, Walter. 1967. *The Mosaics of Rome.* Greenwich, CT: New York Graphic Society.

O'Donnell, James J. 1979. *Cassiodorus.* Berkeley: University of California Press.

————. 1982. "The Aims of Jordanes." *Historia* 31: 223–240.

Olivar, Alexandre. 1962. *Los sermones de San Pedro Crisologo, estudio critico.* Abadía de Montserrat.

Oost, Steward Irvin. 1965. "Some Problems in the History of Galla Placidia." *Classical Philology* 60: 1–10.

————. 1968. *Galla Placidia Augusta: A Biographical Essay.* Chicago: University of Chicago Press.

Orioli, Giorgio. 1980. "Il catalogo episcopale Agnelliano e i vescovi di Ravenna nel V secolo." *Bollettino della Badia Greca di Grottaferrata* 34: 135–144.

————. 1997. "La data della dedicazione della basilica metropolitana dell'Anastasis di Ravenna." *Ravenna, Studi e Ricerche* 4, no. 2: 191–196.

Orselli, Alba Maria. 2006. "Epifanie e scomparse di città nelle fonti testuali tardoantiche." In *Le città italiane tra la tarda Antichità e l'alto Medioevo, Atti del Convegno (Ravenna, febbraio 2004)*, ed. Andrea Augenti: 17–25. Florence: All'insegna del giglio.

Ortalli, Jacopo. 1991. "L'Edilizia abitativa." In *Storia di Ravenna II.1*, ed. Antonio Carile: 167–192. Venice: Marsilio Editore.

Ottolenghi, Luisa. 1957. "La capella arcivescovile in Ravenna." *Felix Ravenna, 3rd ser.* 78: 5–32.

Palardy, William B. 2004. *Saint Peter Chrysologus, Selected Sermons*, vol. 2. The Fathers of the Church: A New Translation (Patristic Series) 109. Washington, DC: Catholic University of America Press.

Pallottino, Massimo. 1991. *A History of Earliest Italy.* Ann Arbor: University of Michigan Press.

Pani Ermini, Letizia. 2005. "Lo spazio urbano delle città capitali." In *Ravenna: da capitale imperiale a capitale esarcale*, 2: 1003–1058. Spoleto: Fondazione Centro Italiano di Studi sull'Alto Medioevo.

Panvini Rosati, F. 1978. "Tre zecche imperiali: Treviri, Mediolanum, Ravenna." *CARB* 25: 211–228.

Pasi, Silvia. 1996. "Braccio nord, lunetta del Buon Pastore / North arm, lunette of the Good Shepherd." In *Il mausoleo di Galla Placidia a Ravenna*, ed. Clementina Rizzardi: 215–216. Modena.

———. 2005. "Ravenna e Bisanzio." In *Venezia e Bisanzio. Aspetti della cultura artistica bizantina da Ravenna a venezia (V–XIV secolo)*, ed. Clementina Rizzardi: 45–70. Venice: Istituto veneto di scienze, lettere ed arti.

———. 2006. *Ravenna, San Vitale: il corteo di Giustiniano e Teodora e i mosaici del presbiterio e dell'abside*. Modena: Franco Cosimo Panini.

Pasquini, Laura. 2005. "Il battistero della cattedrale cattolica a Ravenna." In *Venezia e Bisanzio. Aspetti della cultura artistica bizantina da Ravenna a venezia (V–XIV secolo)*, ed. Clementina Rizzardi: 327–344. Venice: Istituto veneto di scienze, lettere ed arti.

Patitucci Uggeri, Stella. 2005. "Il sistema fluvio-lagunare, l'insediamento e le difese del territorio ravennate settentrionale (V–VIII secolo)." In *Ravenna: da capitale imperiale a capitale esarcale*, 1: 253–360. Spoleto: Fondazione Centro Italiano di Studi sull'Alto Medioevo.

Pauselli, Valentina. 1996. "Braccio est, sarcofago detto di Costanzo III / East arm, so-called sarcophagus of Constans III." In *Il mausoleo di Galla Placidia a Ravenna*, ed. Clementina Rizzardi: 219–220. Modena.

———. 1996. "Braccio ovest, sarcofago detto di Onorio / West arm, so-called sarcophagus of Honorius." In *Il mausoleo di Galla Placidia a Ravenna*, ed. Clementina Rizzardi: 229–230. Modena.

Pavan, G. 1978. "Restauri e ritrovamenti della Basilica di S. Apollinare in Classe." *CARB* 25: 233–264.

———. 1984–5. "I mosaici della chiesa di S. Croce a Ravenna. Vecchi e nuovi ritrovamenti." *Felix Ravenna* ser. 4, vol. 1/2: 341–380.

Peers, Glenn. 2004. *Sacred Shock: Framing Visual Experience in Byzantium*. University Park: Pennsylvania State University Press.

Pellegrini, Giovan Battista. 1990. "Toponomastica preromana e romana del ravennate." In *Storia di Ravenna I*, ed. G. Susini: 69–78. Venice: Marsilio Editore.

Penni Iacco, Emanuela. 2004. *La basilica di S. Apollinare Nuovo attraverso i secoli*. Studi e scavi, nuova serie 8. Bologna: Ante quem.

Pensabene, Patrizio. 1995. "Reimpiego e nuove mode architettoniche nel basiliche cristiane di Roma tra IV e VI secolo." In *Akten des XII. Internationalen Kongresses für christliche Archäologie, Bonn, 22–28 September 1991*, ed. Ernst Dassmann and Josef Engemann: 1076–1096. Vatican City: Pontificio istituto di archeologia cristiana.

Petrucci, Armando. 1971. "Origine e diffusione del culto di San Michele nell'Italia medievale." In *Millénaire monastique du Mont Saint-Michel*, ed. J. et al. Laporte, 3: 339–354. Paris: P. Lethielleux.

Piancastelli, Monica. 2004. "Note sulla velocità di subsidenza." In *Archeologia urbana a Ravenna: la Domus dei tappeti di pietra, il complesso archeologico di via D'Azeglio*, ed. Giovanna Montevecchi: 116–117. Ravenna: Longo.

Picard, Jean-Charles. 1978. "La quadriportique de Sant'Agata de Ravenne." *Felix Ravenna* 116: 31–43.

———. 1988. *Le souvenir des évêques: sépultures, listes épiscopales et culte des évêques en Italie du Nord des origines au Xe siècle*. Rome: École française de Rome.

Piccinini, Piero. 1992. "Immagini d'autorità a Ravenna." In *Storia di Ravenna II.2*, ed. Antonio Carile: 31–78. Venice: Marsilio Editore.

Pietri, Charles. 1983. "Les aristocraties de Ravenna (Ve–VIe siècles)." *Studi Romagnoli* 34: 643–673.

———. 1991. "Aristocrazia e clero al tempo di Odoacre e di Teoderico." In *Storia di Ravenna II.1*, ed. Antonio Carile: 287–310. Venice: Marsilio Editore.

Pincherle, Alberto. 1966. "Intorno a un celebre mosaico Ravennate." *Byzantion* 36: 491–534.

Pizarro, Joaquín Martínez. 1995. *Writing Ravenna: A Narrative Performance in the Ninth Century*. Ann Arbor: University of Michigan Press.

———. 1998. "Crowds and Power in the *Liber pontificalis ecclesiae Ravennatis*." In *The Community, the Family, and the Saint: Patterns of Power in Early Medieval Europe*, ed. J. Hill: 265–283. Turnhout: Brepols.

Poilpré, Anne-Orange and Jean-Pierre Caillet. 2005. *Maiestas Domini*. Paris: Editions du Cerf.

Polara, Giovanni. 1995. "Letteratura in Italia nell'età di Teoderico." In *Teoderico e i Goti fra Oriente e Occidente*, ed. Antonio Carile: 353–366. Ravenna: Longo Editore.

Porta, Paola. 1991. "Il centro del potere, il problema del palazzo dell'esarco." In *Storia di Ravenna II.1*, ed. Antonio Carile: 269–283. Venice: Marsilio Editore.

———. 2007. "San Michele in Africisco a Ravenna. La scultura architettonico-decorativa." In *San Michele in Africisco e l'età giustinianea a Ravenna: atti del Convegno "La diaspora dell'arcangelo, San Michele in Africisco e l'età giustinianea": Giornate di studio in memoria di Giuseppe Bovini, Ravenna, Sala dei mosaici, 21–22 aprile 2005*, ed. Claudio Spadoni: 205–222. Milan: Silvana.

Post, Paulus G. J. 1982. "Conculcabis leonem. Some Iconographic and Iconologic Notes on an Early-Christian Terracotta Lamp with an Anastasis Scene." *Rivista di archeologia cristiana* 58: 147–176.

Prati, Luciana and Alberto Antoniazzi, eds. 1988. *Flumen aquaeductus: nuove scoperte archeologiche dagli scavi per l'acquedotto della Romagna*. Bologna: Nuova Alfa Editoriale.

Quacquarelli, Antonio. 1977. "Le gammatiche del Battistero degli Ariani di Ravenna." *CARB* 24: 293–301.

Rapp, Claudia. 2005. *Holy Bishops in Late Antiquity: The Nature of Christian Leadership in an Age of Transition*. Berkeley: University of California Press.

Ravenna da capitale imperiale a capitale esarcale. Atti del XVII Congresso internazionale di studio sull'alto medioevo, Ravenna, 6–12 giugno 2004. 2005. Spoleto: Centro Italiano di Studi sull'Alto Medioevo.

Rebecchi, F. 1978. "Cronologia e fasi di fabbricazione dei sarcofagi pagani dell'officina di Ravenna." *Studi Romagnoli* 29: 247–275.

Rebecchi, Fernando. 1993. "Ravenna, ultima capitale d'Occidente." In *Storia di Roma, III: L'età tardoantica*, ed. Arnaldo Momigliano, 2: I luoghi e le culture: 121–130. Torino: Guilio Einaudi.

_____. 1998. "Grecità e Greci a Ravenna (e dintorni): notivà ed elementi di discussione." In *Spina e il delta padano: riflessioni sul catalogo e sulla mostra ferrarese: atti Convegno internazionale di studi "Spina: due civiltà a confronto" (1994: Università degli studi di Ferrara)*, ed. Fernando Rebecchi: 295–324. Rome: "L'Erma" di Bretschneider.

_____, ed. 1998. *Spina e il delta padano: riflessioni sul catalogo e sulla mostra ferrarese: atti Convegno internazionale di studi "Spina: due civiltà a confronto" (1994: Università degli studi di Ferrara)*. Rome: "L'Erma" di Bretschneider.

Rebenich, Stefan. 1985. "Gratian, a Son of Theodosius, and the Birth of Galla Placidia." *Historia: Zeitschrift für Alte Geschichte* 34: 372–385.

Reydellet, Marc. 1992. "La regalità teodericiana." In *Storia di Ravenna II.2*, ed. Antonio Carile: 9–30. Venice: Marsilio Editore.

_____. 1995. "Théoderic et la civilitas." In *Teoderico e i Goti fra Oriente e Occidente*, ed. Antonio Carile: 285–296. Ravenna: Longo Editore.

Ricci, Corrado. 1919. "Il Vivaio dell'arcivescovado di Ravenna." *Bollettino d'arte* 13: 33–36.

_____. 1930–7. *Monumenti: tavole storiche dei mosaici di Ravenna*. Roma: Istituto poligrafico dello stato.

_____. 1932. *Monumenti: tavole storiche dei mosaici di Ravenna, vol. 3, Il Battistero degli Ariani*. Roma: Istituto poligrafico dello stato.

_____. 1937. *Monumenti: tavole storiche dei mosaici di Ravenna, vol. 8, S. Giovanni Evangelista*. Roma: Istituto poligrafico dello stato.

Righini, Valeria. 1986. "*Felix Roma – Felix Ravenna*: i bolli laterizi di Teoderico e l'attività edilizia teodericiana in Ravenna." *CARB* 33: 371–398.

_____. 1990. "Materiali e tecniche da costruzione in età preromana e romana." In *Storia di Ravenna I*, ed. G. Susini: 257–296. Venice: Marsilio Editore.

_____. 1991. "Materiali e tecniche da costruzione in età tardoantica e altomedievale." In *Storia di Ravenna II.1*, ed. Antonio Carile: 193–221. Venice: Marsilio Editore.

Ristow, Günter. 1957. "Sulla personificazione del Giordano nelle rappresentazioni battesimali nell'arte del primo Cristianesimo." In *Aus der byzantinischen Arbeit der deutschen demokratischen Republik*, ed. Johannes Irmscher, 2: 120–126. Berlin: Berlin Akademie-Verlag.

Ristow, Sebastian. 1998. *Frühchristliche Baptisterien*. Jahrbuch für Antike und Christentum, Ergängunsband 27. Münster: Aschendorff.

Rizzardi, Clementina. 1988. "Paradigmi ideologici ed estetici nei mosaici ravennati di età giustinianea." *Felix Ravenna* 135–136: 37–61.

_____. 1989. "L'arte dei Goti a Ravenna: motivi ideologici, aspetti iconografici e formali nella decorazione musiva." *CARB* 36: 365–388.

_____. 1989. "Note sull'antico episcopio di Ravenna, formazione e sviluppo." In *Actes du XIe Congrès International d'Archéologie Chretienne*, 1: 711–731. Vatican City.

_____. 1993. "Mosaici parietali esistenti e scomparsi di età placidiana a Ravenna: iconografie imperiali e apocalittiche." *CARB* 40: 385–407.

_____. 1995. "Considerazioni sui mosaici di San Vitale di Ravenna: il ciclo di Mosè." In *Fifth International Colloquium on Ancient Mosaics, Bath 1987*, ed. Peter Johnson: 219–230. Ann Arbor, MI: Journal of Roman Archaeology.

_____. 1996. "Il Mausoleo nel mondo culturale e artistico di Galla Placidia / The Mausoleum in the cultural-artistic world of Galla Placidia." In *Il mausoleo di Galla*

Placidia a Ravenna, eds. Clementina Rizzardi and Patrizia Angiolini Martinelli: 109–128. Modena.

———. 1996. "I mosaici del triclinio del *Palatium* di Teodorico a Ravenna." In *Atti del III Colloquio dell'Associazione italiana per lo studio e la conservazione del mosaico, Bordighera, 6–10 dicembre 1995*, ed. Federico Guidobaldi: 353–362. Bordighera: Istituto internazionale di studi liguri.

———. 1996. "L'architettura del Mausoleo tra Oriente e Occidente: cosmopolitismo e autonomia / The Mausoleum's architecture between East and West: cosmopolitanism and autonomy." In *Il mausoleo di Galla Placidia a Ravenna*, eds. Clementina Rizzardi and Patrizia Angiolini Martinelli: 129–146. Modena.

———. 2001. "La decorazione musiva del battistero degli ortodossi e degli ariani a Ravenna: Alcune considerazioni." In *L'Edificio Battesimale in Italia, aspetti e problemi. Atti del'VII Congresso Nazionale di Archeologia Cristiana Genova, Sarzana, Albegna, Rinale Ligure, Vetimiglia, 21–28 Settembre 1998*, 2: 915–930. Bordighera: Istituto internazionale di studi liguri.

———. 2001. "Teoderico a Ravenna: il Battistero degli Ariani alla luce dell'ideologia politico-religiosa del tempo." In *Wentilseo. I Germani sulle sponde del mare Nostrum – Atti del Convegno Internazionale di Studi, Padova, 13–15 ottobre 1999*, ed. Alessandro Zironi: 101–118. Padova: Unipress.

———. 2003. "La cattedra eburnea di Massimiano a Ravenna: relettura stilistica." In *Hadriatica: attorno a Venezia e al medioevo tra arti, storia e storiogafia: scritti in onore di Wladimiro Dorigo*, ed. Ennio Concina: 145–150. Padova: Il Poligrafo.

———. 2004. "L'Episcopio di Ravenna nell'ambito dell'edilizia religiosa occidentale ed orientale dal Tardoantico nell'Alto Medioevo: gli ambienti di rappresentanza." *Atti e Memorie della Deputazione di Storia Patria per le Provincie di Romagna, n.s.* 55: 147–175.

———. 2005. "I mosaici parietali di Ravenna da Galla Placidia a Giustiniano." In *Venezia e Bisanzio. Aspetti della cultura artistica bizantina da Ravenna a venezia (V–XIV secolo)*, ed. Clementina Rizzardi: 231–273. Venice: Istituto veneto di scienze, lettere ed arti.

———. 2007. "I mosaici parietali di Ravenna di età guistinianea e la coeva pittura occidentale e orientale." In *San Michele in Africisco e l'età giustinianea a Ravenna: atti del Convegno "La diaspora dell'arcangelo, San Michele in Africisco e l'età giustinianea": Giornate di studio in memoria di Giuseppe Bovini, Ravenna, Sala dei mosaici, 21–22 aprile 2005*, ed. Claudio Spadoni: 83–98. Milan: Silvana.

Rizzardi, Clementina and Patrizia Angiolini Martinelli, eds. 1996. *Il mausoleo di Galla Placidia a Ravenna*. Modena.

Roberts, Michael J. 2002. "Venantius Fortunatus's Life of Saint Martin." *Traditio* 57, no. 129–187.

Rohland, Johannes Peter. 1977. *Der Erzengel Michael Arzt und Feldherr: Zwei Aspekts des Vor- und Frühbyzantinischen Michaelskultes*. Leiden: Brill.

Rohr, Christian. 1995. *Der Theoderich-Penegyricus des Ennodius*. Monumenta Germaniae historica Studien und Texte 12. Hannover: Hahnsche Buchhandlung.

Roncuzzi, Arnaldo. 1992. "Topografia di Ravenna antica: le mura." *CARB* 39: 691–742.

———. 2005. "Il territorio di Ravenna nell'antichità." In *Ravenna: da capitale imperiale a capitale esarcale*, 1: 383–404. Spoleto: Fondazione Centro Italiano di Studi sull'Alto Medioevo.

Roncuzzi, Arnaldo and Lelio Veggi. 1968. "Contributo allo studio dell'evoluzione topografica nel territorio ravennate in rapporto agli antichi insediamenti umani." In *Atti del Convegno internazionale di studi sull'antichità di Classe, Ravenna, 14–17 ottobre 1967*: 91–114. Ravenna: Longo.

Ropa, Giampaolo. 1993. "Agiografia e liturgia a Ravenna tra alto e basso medioevo." In *Storia di Ravenna, 3: Dal mille alla fine della signoria Polentana*, ed. Augusto Vasina: 341–393. Venice: Marsilio Editore.

Rossi (Rubeus), Gerolamo. 1572. *Historiarium Ravennatum – Libri Decem*. Venice.

Rota, Simona. 2002. *Panegirico del clementissimo re Teodorico*. Rome: Herder.

Ruggini, Lellia. 1961. *Economia e società nell' "Italia annonaria": rapporti fra agricoltura e commercio dal IV al VI secolo d. C.* Milan: A. Giuffrè.

Rusconi, Antonio. 1971. " Una nuova ipotesi sul cosiddetto 'Palazzo di Teodorico' a Ravenna." *CARB* 18: 475–506.

Russell, James C. 1994. *The Germanization of Early Medieval Christianity: A Sociohistorical Approach to Religious Transformation*. Oxford: Oxford University Press.

Russo, Eugenio. 1989. "Scavi e scoperte nella chiesa di S. Agata di Ravenna. Notizie Preliminari." In *Actes du XIe Congrès International d'Archéologie Chretienne*, 3: 2317–2341. Vatican City.

———. 1996. "Sulla cupola in tubi fittili della chiesa di S. Vitale di Ravenna." *Rivista di archeologia cristiana* 72: 285–329.

———. 2005. "L'architettura di Ravenna paleocristiana." In *Venezia e Bisanzio. Aspetti della cultura artistica bizantina da Ravenna a venezia (V–XIV secolo)*, ed. Clementina Rizzardi: 89–229. Venice: Istituto veneto di scienze, lettere ed arti.

———. 2005. "Una nuova proposta per al sequenze cronologica del Palazzo imperiale di Ravenna." In *Ravenna: da capitale imperiale a capitale esarcale*, 1: 155–190. Spoleto: Fondazione Centro Italiano di Studi sull'Alto Medioevo.

Saitta, Biagio. 1993. *La civilitas di Teoderico. Rigore amministrativo, "tolleranza" religiosa e recupero dell'antico nell'Italia ostrogota*. Rome: "L'Erma" di Bretschneider.

Salin, Bernhard. 1935. *Die altgermanische Thierornamentik, typologische Studie über germanische Metallgegenstände aus dem IV. bis IX. Jahrhundert, nebst einer Studie über irische Ornamentik*. Stockholm: Wahlström & Widstrand.

Salway, Benet. 2005. "The Nature and Genesis of the Peutinger Map." *Imago Mundi* 57: 119–135.

Sansterre, Jean-Marie. 1992. "Monaci e Monasteri Greci a Ravenna." In *Storia di Ravenna II.2*, ed. Antonio Carile: 323–329. Venice: Marsilio Editore.

Savigni, Raffaele. 1992. "I Papi e Ravenna. Dalla Caduta dell'Esarcato alla Fine del Secolo X." In *Storia di Ravenna II.2*, ed. Antonio Carile: 331–368. Venice: Marsilio Editore.

Savini, Gaetano. 1905. *Le mura di Ravenna*. Ravenna.

Saxer, Victor. 1985. "Jalons pour servir à l'histoire du culte de l'archange Saint Michel en Orient jusqu'à l'iconoclasme." In *Noscere sancta: Miscellanea in memoria di A. Amore O. F. M.*, 1. *Storia della chiesa, archeologia, arte*, ed. Isaac Vázquez Janeiro: 357–426. Rome: Pontificio Ateneo Antoniano.

———. 1988. *Les rites de l'initiation chrétienne du IIe au VIe siècle. Esquisse historique et signification d'après leurs principaux témoins*. Spoleto: Centro italiano di studi sull'alto Medioevo.

Schäferdiek, Knut. 2002. "Der vermeintliche Arianismus der Ulfila-Bibel. Zum Umgang mit einem Stereotyp." *Zeitschrift für Antikes Christentum* 6: 320–329.

Schapiro, Meyer. 1952. "The Joseph Scenes on the Maximianus Throne in Ravenna." *Gazette des Beaux-Arts* 40: 27–38.

Schneider, Alfons Maria. 1941. "Die Symbolik des Theodorichsgrabes in Ravenna." *Byzantinische Zeitschrift* 41: 404 ff.

Schöll, Rudolf and Kroll, Wilhelm. 1895. *Corpus Iuris Civilis*, vol. 3, *Novellae*. Berlin: Weidmann.

Schreiner, Peter. 1988. "Der byzantinische Bilderstreit: kritische Analyse der zeitgenössischen meinungen und das Urteil der Nachwelt bis heute." In *Bisanzio, Roma e l'Italia nell'alto Medioevo, 3–9 aprile 1986*: 319–407. Spoleto: CISAM.

Schrenk, Sabine. 1995. *Typos und Antitypos in der frühchristlichen Kunst*. Jarhbuch für Antike und Christentum, Ergänzungsband 21. Münster: Aschendorffsche Verlagsbuchhandlung.

Sfameni, Carla. 2004. "Residential Villas in Late Antique Italy: Continuity and Change." In *Recent Research on the Late Antique Countryside*, ed. William Bowden: 335–376. Leiden: Brill.

Shanzer, Danuta. 1998. "Two Clocks and a Wedding: Theoderic's Diplomatic Relations with the Burgundians." *Romanobarbarica* 14: 225–258.

Simonini, Augusto. 1969. *Autocefalia ed Esarcato in Italia*. Ravenna: A. Longo.

Sivan, Hagith. 1996. "Ulfila's Own Conversion." *The Harvard Theological Review* 89, no. 4: 373–386.

Smith, Janet C. 1990. "Form and Function of the Side Chambers of Fifth- and Sixth-Century Churches in Ravenna." *Journal of the Society of Architectural Historians* 49, no. 2: 181–204.

———. 1990. "The Side Chambers of San Giovanni Evangelista in Ravenna: Church Libraries of the Fifth Century." *Gesta* 29: 86–97.

Snee, Rochelle. 1998. "Gregory Nazianzen's Anastasia Church: Arianism, the Goths, and Hagiography." *Dumbarton Oaks Papers* 52: 157–186.

Somekh, Alberto. 1995. "Teoderico e gli Ebrei di Ravenna." In *Teoderico e i Goti fra Oriente e Occidente*, ed. Antonio Carile: 137–149. Ravenna: Longo Editore.

Soraci, Rosario. 1974. *Aspetti di storia economica italiana nell'età di Cassiodoro*. Catania: Nova.

Sörries, Reiner. 1983. *Die Bilder der Orthodoxen im Kampf gegen den Arianismus. eine Apologie der orthodoxen Christologie und Trinitätslehre gegenüber der arianischen Häresie, dargestellt an den ravennatischen Mosaiken und Bildern des 6. Jahrhunderts; zugleich ein Beitrag zum Verständnis des germanischen Homöertums*. Europaische Hochschulschriften 23, Theologie 186. Frankfurt: Peter Lang.

Sotinel, Claire. 2004. "How Were Bishops Informed? Information Transmission across the Adriatic Sea in Late Antiquity." In *Travel, Communication and Geography in Late Antiquity: Sacred and Profane*, ed. Linda Ellis: 63–72. Aldershot: Ashgate.

———. 2007. "The Three Chapters and the Transformations of Italy." In *The Crisis of the Oikoumene: The Three Chapters and the Failed Quest for Unity in the Sixth-Century Mediterranean*, ed. Celia Chazelle: 85–120. Turnhout: Brepols.

Spadoni, Claudio and Linda Kniffitz, eds. 2007. *San Michele in Africisco e l'età giustinianea a Ravenna. Atti del convegno "La diaspora dell'arcangelo. San Michele in Africisco e l'età giustinianea," Giornata di studio in memoria di Giuseppe Bovini, Ravenna, Sala dei Mosaici, 21–22 aprile 2005*. Milano: Silvana.

Spieser, J.-M. 1998. "The Representation of Christ in the Apses of Early Christian Churches." *Gesta* 37: 63–73.

_____. 2001. "Further Remarks on the Mosaic of Hosios David." In *Urban and Religious Spaces in Late Antiquity and Early Byzantium*: 1–12. Aldershot: Ashgate.

Squatriti, Paolo. 1992. "Marshes and Mentalities in Early Medieval Ravenna." *Viator: Medieval and Renaissance Studies* 23: 1–16.

_____. 1998. *Water and Society in Early Medieval Italy: AD 400–1000*. Cambridge: Cambridge University Press.

Staab, Franz. 1976. "Ostrogothic Geographers at the Court of Theoderic the Great: A Study of Some Sources of the Anonymous Cosmographer of Ravenna." *Viator: Medieval and Renaissance Studies* 7: 27–58.

Stamatiou, Aristides. 1992. "The Mosaic of Christ in the Episcopium of Ravenna." *CARB* 39: 743–775.

Stathakopoulos, Dionysios. 2004. *Famine and Pestilence in the Late Roman and Early Byzantine Empire: A Systematic Survey of Subsistence Crises and Epidemics*. Aldershot: Ashgate.

Steigerwald, Gerhard. 1966. "Christus als Pantokrator in der untersten Zone der Langhausmosaik von S. Apollinare Nuovo zu Ravenna." In *Tortulae, Studien zu altchristlichen und byzantinischen Monumenten*, ed. Walter Nikolaus Schumacher: 272–284. Rome.

Stoppioni, M. L. 2005. "Le produzioni e le merci: i contenitori da trasporto." In *I porti antichi di Ravenna*, ed. Maurizio Mauro, 1: Il porto romano e le flotte: 215–231. Ravenna: Adriapress.

Stricevic, G. 1959. "Iconografia dei mosaici imperiali a S. Vitale." *Felix Ravenna*: 5–27.

Stüven, Aarne. 1995. *Rechtliche Ausprägungen der "civilitas" in Ostgotenreich. Mit vergleichender Berücksichtigung des westgotischen und des burgundischen Rechts*. Frankfurt am Main: P. Lang.

Susini, Giancarlo. 1968. "La questione della 'civitas Classis.'" In *Atti del Convegno Internazionale di Studi sulle Antichità di Classe, Ravenna, 14–17 ottobre 1967*: 331–345. Ravenna: Longo.

_____. 1968. "Un catalogo classiario ravennate." *Studi Romagnoli* 19: 291–307.

_____. 1988. "Un fragment épigraphique pour l'histoire de Ravenna." *Compterendus des séances de l'Academie des Inscriptions et belles-lettres* 132: 636–642.

_____. 1990. "Ravenna e il mondo dei Romani." In *Storia di Ravenna I*, ed. G. Susini: 125–136. Venice: Marsilio Editore.

_____, ed. 1990. *Storia di Ravenna, vol. 1, L'evo antico*. Venezia: Marsilio Editore.

Swoboda, Karl M. 1961. "The Problem of the Iconography of Late Antique and Early Mediaeval Palaces." *Journal of the Society of Architectural Historians* 20: 78–89.

Taft, Robert F. S. J. 1998. "Women at Church in Byzantium: Where, When – And Why?" *Dumbarton Oaks Papers* 52: 27–87.

Tagliaferri, Maurizio. 2005. *La Chiesa metropolitana ravennate e i suoi rapporti con la Costa adriatica orientale: atti del XXVII Convegno del Centro studi e ricerche antica provincia ecclesiastica ravennate, Ravenna 29–31 maggio 2003*. Imola: University Press Bologna.

Terry, Ann. 1988. "The Sculpture at the Cathedral of Eufrasius in Porec." *Dumbarton Oaks Papers* 42: 13–64.

Terry, Ann and Henry Maguire. 2007. *Dynamic Splendor: The Wall Mosaics in the Cathedral of Eufrasius at Porec*. University Park: Pennsylvania State University Press.

Testi-Rasponi, Alessandro, ed. 1924. *Codex pontificalis ecclesiae Ravennatis*. RIS n.s. 2.3. Bologna: Zanichelli.

Thompson, E. A. 1984. *Saint Germanus of Auxerre and the End of Roman Britain*. Woodbridge, Suffolk: Boydell Press.

Thompson, E. A. and Peter Heather. 1996. *The Huns*. Cambridge, MA: Blackwell Publishing.

Thomsen, Rudi. 1947. *The Italic Regions from Augustus to the Lombard Invasion*. Copenhagen: Gyldendal.

Tibiletti, G. 1973. "Ravenna *populus foederatus* e le zone della Cisalpina rese *latine* nell'89 a.C." *Studi Romagnoli* 24: 25–29.

Tjäder, Jan Olof. 1954–82. Die nichtliterarischen lateinischen papyri Italiens aus der zeit 445–700. 3 vols. Lund: C. W. K. Gleerup.

———. 1971. "Ravenna ai tempi dell'arcivescovo Agnello." In *Agnello arcivescovo di Ravenna. Studi per il XIV centenario della morte. (570–1970)*, ed. Paola Monti: 1–23. Faenza: Fratelli Lega.

———. 1972. "Der Codex argenteus in Uppsala und der Buchmeister Viliaric in Ravenna." In *Studia Gotica: Die eisenzeitlichen Verbindungen zwischen Schweden und Südosteuropa, Vorträge beim Gotensymposion im Statens Historiska Museum Stockholm, 1970*, ed. Ulf Erik Hagberg: 144–164. Stockholm: Almqvist & Wiksell.

Torre, Franco. 1986. *La Basilica di Sant'Agata Maggiore in Ravenna*. Ravenna: Cassa di risparmio di Ravenna.

Tramonti, S. 1997. "La pirateria adriatica e la politica navale augustea (36–31 a.c.). Una proposta di esegesi delle fonti sulla scelta augustea del porto di Ravenna." *Ravenna, Studi e Ricerche* 4, no. 1: 89–130.

Uggeri, Giovanni. 1997. "Il nodo itinerario di Ravenna in età Romana." *CARB* 43: 887–910.

Urbano, Arthur. 2005. "Donation, Dedication, and Damnatio Memoriae: The Catholic Reconciliation of Ravenna and the Church of Sant'Apollinare Nuovo." *Journal of Early Christian Studies* 13, no. 1: 71–110.

Van Lohuizen-Mulder, Mab. 1990. "Stuccoes in Ravenna, Poreč and Cividale of Coptic Manufacture." *Bulletin Antieke Beschaving* 65: 139–156.

Vasina, Augusto. 1978. "Benedetto Bacchini e l'Edizione del 'Liber Pontificalis' di Agnello Ravennate." In *Lineamenti culturali dell'Emilia-Romagna, antiquariato, erudizione, storiografia dal XIV al XVIII secolo*, ed. Augusto Vasina: 130–148. Ravenna: Longo.

———. 1978. "La fortuna di Agnello ravennate fino al XVI secolo." In *Lineamenti culturali dell'Emilia-Romagna, antiquariato, erudizione, storiografia dal XIV al XVIII secolo*, ed. Augusto Vasina: 79–129. Ravenna: Longo.

———, ed. 1991. *Repertorio della Cronachistica Emiliano-Romagnola (secc. IX–XV)*. Nuovo studi storici 11. Rome: Istituto storico italiano per il Medio Evo.

Vasina, Augusto, Sylviane Lazard, G. Gorini et al., eds. 1985. *Ricerche e studi sul Breviarium ecclesiae Ravennatis (Codice Bavaro)*. Studi Storici 148–149. Rome: Istituto Storico Italiano per il Medio Evo.

Vattuone, Riccardo. 1990. "Ravenna nella letteratura antica." In *Storia di Ravenna I*, ed. G. Susini: 49–68. Venice: Marsilio Editore.

Vernia, Barbara. 2005. "L'analisi delle strutture murarie degli edifici di culto di Ravenna: il caso del mausoleo di Galla Placidia." In *Ravenna: da capitale imperiale a capitale esarcale*, 2: 1107–1132. Spoleto: Fondazione Centro Italiano di Studi sull'Alto Medioevo.

———. 2005. "L'arredo liturgico della basilica di Sant'Apollinare Nuovo a Ravenna." In *Venezia e Bisanzio. Aspetti della cultura artistica bizantina da Ravenna a venezia (V–XIV secolo)*, ed. Clementina Rizzardi: 363–376. Venice: Istituto veneto di scienze, lettere ed arti.

Vespignani, Giorgio. 2005. "Il circo di Ravenna *regia civitas* (secc. V–X)." In *Ravenna: da capitale imperiale a capitale esarcale*, 2: 1133–1142. Spoleto: Fondazione Centro Italiano di Studi sull'Alto Medioevo.

Vickers, Michael. 1976. "An Ostrogothic Bracelet with 'Zangelornament' in Oxford." *Archäologischer Anzeiger* 11: 278–80.

Vikan, Gary. 1979. "Joseph Iconography on Coptic Textiles." *Gesta* 18: 99–108.

Volbach, Wolfgang Fritz. 1976. *Elfenbeinarbeiten der Spätantike und des frühen Mittelalters*. Mainz: Von Zabern.

———. 1977. *Avori di scuola ravennate nel V e VI secolo*. Ravenna: Longo.

von Simson, Otto. 1948. *Sacred Fortress: Byzantine Art and Statecraft in Ravenna*. Princeton, NJ: Princeton University Press.

———. 1953. "Zu den Mosaiken von S. Vitale in Ravenna." *Byzantinische Zeitschrift* 46, no. 1: 104–109.

Ward-Perkins, Bryan. 1984. *From Classical Antiquity to the Middle Ages: Urban Public Building in Northern and Central Italy, A.D. 300–850*. Oxford: Oxford University Press.

———. 1996. "Urban Survival and Urban Transformation in the Eastern Mediterranean." In *Early Medieval Towns in the Western Mediterranean, Ravello, 22–24 September 1994*, ed. Gian-Pietro Brogiolo: 143–153. Mantua.

———. 1997. "Continuitists, Catastrophists, and the Towns of Post-Roman Northern Italy." *Papers of the British School at Rome* 67: 157–176.

———. 1999. "Re-using the Architectural Legacy of the Past, entre idéologie et pragmatisme." In *The Idea and Ideal of the Town between Late Antiquity and the Early Middle Ages*, ed. Gian-Pietro Brogiolo: 225–244. Leiden: Brill.

———. 2005. *The Fall of Rome and the End of Civilization*. Oxford: Oxford University Press.

Weber, Ekkehard. 1989. "Zur Datierung der Tabula Peutingeriana." In *Labor omnibus unus: Gerold Walser zum 70. Geburtstag dargebracht von Freunden, Kollegen und Schülern*, ed. Heinz E. Herzig: 113–117. Stuttgart: F. Steiner Verlag.

Weis, A. 1966. "Der römische Schöpfungszyklus des 5. Jh. im Triklinium Neons zu Ravenna." In *Tortulae, Studien zu altchristlichen und byzantinischen Monumenten*, ed. Walter Nikolaus Schumacher: 300–316. Rome.

Wharton, Annabel Jane. 1987. "Ritual and Reconstructed Meaning: The Neonian Baptistery in Ravenna." *Art Bulletin* 69: 358–375.

———. 1995. *Refiguring the Post Classical City: Dura Europos, Jerash, Jerusalem and Ravenna*. Cambridge: Cambridge University Press.

———. 1999. "Baptisteries." In *Late Antiquity: A Guide to the Postclassical World*, ed. Glen W. Bowersock: 332–334. Cambridge, MA: Harvard University Press.

Whitehouse, David. 1988. "Comment on '*Tubi fittili* (Vaulting Tubes) from the Sea – the Roman Wreck at Punta del Fenaio, Island of Giglio' (IJNA, 16: 187–200)." *International Journal of Nautical Archaeology* 17, no. 2: 182.

Wickberg, Paul Gordon. 1978. "The Eighth-Century Archbishops of Ravenna: An Ineffective Alternative to Papalism." *Studies in Medieval Culture* 12: 25–33.

Wickham, Chris. 1981. *Early Medieval Italy, Central Power and Local Society, 400–1000*. London.

————. 2005. *Framing the Middle Ages: Europe and the Mediterranean, 400–800*. Oxford: Oxford University Press.

Wickhoff, F. 1894. "Das Speisezimmer des Bischofs Neon von Ravenna." *Repertorium für Kunstwissenschaft* 17: 10–17.

Williams, Daniel H. 1995. *Ambrose of Milan and the End of the Arian-Nicene Conflicts*. Oxford: Oxford University Press.

Wisskirchen, Rotraut. 1993. "Zum Medaillon im Kuppelmosaik des Orthodoxenbaptisteriums." *Jahrbuch für Antike und Christentum* 36: 164–170.

Wolfram, Herwig. 1988. *History of the Goths*. Translated by Thomas J. Dunlap. Berkeley: University of California Press.

Wood, Ian. 1999. "Images as a Substitute for Writing: A Reply." In *East and West: Modes of Communication. Proceedings of the First Plenary Conference at Merida*, ed. Evangelos Chrysos: 35–60. Leiden: Brill.

————. 2007. "Theodoric's Monuments in Ravenna." In *The Ostrogoths from the Migration Period to the Sixth Century: An Ethnographic Perspective*, eds. S. J. B. Barnish and F. Marazzi: 249–278. Woodbridge, Suffolk: Boydell Press.

Young, Bailey. 2000. "Climate and Crisis in Sixth-Century Italy and Gaul." In *The Years without Summer: Tracing A.D. 536 and Its Aftermath*, ed. J. D. Gunn: 35–42. Oxford: Archaeopress.

Zangara, Vincenza. 2000. "Una predicazione alla presenza dei principi: la chiesa di Ravenna nella prima metà del sec. V." *Antiquité Tardive* 8: 265–304.

Zanini, E. 1998. *Le Italie bizantine: Territorio, insediamenti ed economia nella provincia bizantina d'Italia (VI–VIII secolo)*. Bari: Edipuglia.

Zanotto, Rita. 1995. "Reimpieghi di scultura architettonica e rapporti con l'Antico: il caso di Ravenna." *CARB* 42: 949–975.

————. 2000. "Riesame iconografico di un pannello del ciclo cristologico in S. Apollinare Nuovo di Ravenna." In *Atti del VI colloquio dell'Associazione italiana per lo studio e la coservazione del mosaico*, ed. Federico Guidobaldi: 659–668. Ravenna: Girasole.

————. 2005. "La chiesa di Sant'Apollinare Nuovo a Ravenna." In *Venezia e Bisanzio. Aspetti della cultura artistica bizantina da Ravenna a venezia (V–XIV secolo)*, ed. Clementina Rizzardi: 351–357. Venice: Istituto veneto di scienze, lettere ed arti.

————. 2005. "Practica del reimpiego architettonico in una capitale tardoantica: il caso di Ravenna." In *Ravenna: da capitale imperiale a capitale esarcale*, 2: 1143–1150. Spoleto: Fondazione Centro Italiano di Studi sull'Alto Medioevo.

Zirardini, Antonio. 1762. *Degli antichi edifizii profani di Ravenna*. Faenza: Presso l'Archi Impressor Carnerale e del S. Ufizio.

————. 1908–9. *De antiquis sacris Ravennae aedificiis liber postumus Antonii Zirardini – Degli antichi edifici sacri di Ravenna libro postumo di A. Zirardini*. Ravenna.

INDEX